LOUIS XIV

'This was a king, wise in his councils, valiant in his armies and magnanimous in his victories.'
FLÉCHIER

'Not only were great things done in his reign but he did them himself.'
VOLTAIRE

LOUIS XIV

FRANÇOIS BLUCHE

Translated by
Mark Greengrass

Franklin Watts
New York
1990

Copyright © François Bluche 1984; English translation
© Basil Blackwell 1990

First published 1990 by Basil Blackwell Ltd
108 Cowley Road, Oxford, OX4 1JF, UK

First published in the United States of America in 1990 by Franklin Watts,
387 Park Avenue South, New York, NY 10016

Library of Congress Cataloging in Publication Data
Bluche, François.
[Louis XIV. English]
Louis XIV/François Bluche; translated by Mark Greengrass.
p.   cm.
'English translation first published 1990 by Basil Blackwell' —
T.p. verso.
Includes bibliographical references.
ISBN 0–531–15112–3
1. Louis XIV, King of France, 1638–1715.   2. France—History—
Louis XIV, 1643–1715.   3. France—Kings and rulers—Biography.
4. France—Court and courtiers—History—17th century.   I. Title.
DC129.B5513   1990
944'.033'092—dc20
[B]   90–33022   CIP

Printed in Great Britain by
T.J. Press Ltd, Padstow, Cornwall

Contents

List of Plates

Between pages 238 and 239 and pages 462 and 463

Acknowledgements

The publishers are grateful to the following for permission to use, and for their help in supplying, photographs: Ets J E Bulloz, Paris (Plates 1, 2, 5, 8, 9, 11, 12, 15, 17, 18, 19, 21, 26, 29, 30, 31, 32, 33, 34, 43); Mansell Collection, London (Plate 38); Roger-Viollet, Paris (Plates 3, 4, 6, 7, 10, 13, 14, 16, 20, 22, 23, 24, 25, 27, 28, 35, 36, 37, 39, 40, 41, 42).

Prologue

VOLTAIRE, a great man, had no difficulty in identifying the greatness in Louis XIV. 'It must be acknowledged', he tells us, 'that Louis always had a sense of exaltation in his soul which drove him to great things.' (112) This sense of greatness has been much denigrated in these times of ours, obsessed as they are by an illusion of equality and indulgent of instincts for levelling.

The denigrators of Louis XIV are legion – writers, teachers, intellectuals and the wider public – all of them the posthumous, unintentional allies of Marlborough and William of Orange. They are ignorant of, or choose to ignore, the latest and most sophisticated historiography, which has tended to rehabilitate their *bête noire*. From the historians of institutions to those of climatic change, from art historians to historical demographers, from literary as well as social historians there are emerging studies which present the reign in a favourable light, or exonerate the king. They reflect things as they were. Yet how difficult it is to abandon the old clichés! Voltaire, a contemporary, or near contemporary, to events as well as the inventor of 'total history', devoted his intelligence and conviction in vain to the writing of *The Century of Louis XIV* (112). This masterpiece is now largely unread; or, rather, it is explained away by assertions made with apparent conviction that the book was written with the intention of denigrating Louis XV. It seems of no importance that learned articles, Sorbonne theses and plenty of recent studies support, in a modern and scientific fashion, many of Voltaire's assertions. Frenchmen prefer the simple verities of their school textbooks and popular novels: 'L'état, c'est moi', said the king; Fouquet had done nothing wrong; the Iron Mask is a symbol of the

'appalling arbitrariness' of the regime; Louis XIV made war
to satisfy his own whims; the court was only interested in festivities whilst peasants survived on nothing more than 'root vegetables' . . .

Eventually, everything which is to be deplored has been
attributed to the king, even the poisonings, Black Masses and
witchcraft. He has even been held implicitly to blame for the bad
weather. Nobody has actually accused Louis XIV of being
responsible for the appalling winters of 1693, 1694, 1709 and
1710, but how often we hear: 'Louis XIV? Ah! The Great Winter
of 1709!' Some of his detractors have associated him with a
clutch of malign associates whom he let into his confidence and
whose bad advice he listened to: Colbert for the arrest of
Fouquet, Louvois for the Dutch War and the devastation of the
Palatinate, père de la Chaize and Madame de Maintenon for the
Revocation of the Edict of Nantes and père Le Tellier for the
destruction of Port-Royal and the bull *Unigenitus*. Underlying
these assessments is the assumption that, since the king was
taking advice, allowing himself time for consultation and reflection, his personal responsibility for what happened must be the
greater.

Moreover, if Louis is the incarnation of all that is bad, he can
therefore do nothing right. At the beginning of the reign, he was
too fond of the theatre; by the end of the reign, he did not like it
enough. At the beginning, he was faithless towards the queen,
Maria Theresa; by the end of his life, he showed too much
devotion towards his second wife, Madame de Maintenon. The
court of his earlier years was as frivolous as that baroque *Satiricon*
the *Amorous History of the Gauls* (19) suggests; that of Versailles
was a world of tedious routines. Sometimes the king is held to
account for having delegated too much authority to his 'viziers';
at others, he is accused of having reduced his ministers to the
rank of simple servants.

The Protestants' greatest enemies have criticized Louis XIV
for the Revocation of the Edict of Nantes (inexplicable and unex-
plained unless it is placed within a broad and secular historical
context); the most ardent anti-Catholics have failed to accept
that the king made the most of his disputes with Rome. The most
inveterate opponents of peasant revolts and of Vendée-style
insurrections – those who find it hard to justify a civilian uprising in the midst of a foreign war – condemn the repression of the

Camisard revolt. Those whose origins lie in French Flanders, Hainaut, Alsace, Franche Comté, Ubaye and Roussillon – happy now, and proud, to be French – will sometimes tell one, nonetheless, that Louis XIV should not have undertaken and pressed ahead with his wars of conquest. And there are patriotic Strasbourgeois who nevertheless criticize the politics of the Reunions.

If so many (who cannot all be ignorant) still retain elements of these hostile prejudices, it is because those prejudices are based on antagonisms which themselves have a long history. Even the cultivated section of the public is still under the influence of a 'black legend' (162), whose progenitors were far from united. One distinct strand, not of great literary interest but very tenacious in the longer term, was assembled, above all in the Netherlands, by the French Huguenots in exile, willing accomplices, directly or indirectly, of William of Orange. In France, some attacks and false rumours and much misrepresentation of the king and his reign originated with the abbé de Saint-Pierre, Robert Challes (22), and the Princess Palatine (Elizabeth-Charlotte of Bavaria). Nobody now reads a line of the first; the other two mix acute observations with gross misrepresentations. But it was the pens of the best writers that did the gravest damage: Fénelon, the court's spoilt child, and Saint-Simon, that frustrator of military talent greater than his own. Fénelon no longer has much direct effect; perhaps he tried to mix too much sugar and holy water into his vitriol. But the duc de Saint-Simon has never enjoyed a larger audience.

Some consider the *Mémoires* as an historical document and the duke as an historian and a man of honour. Others recognize that what he wrote did not appear until the nineteenth century because the author rightly feared the recriminations of the survivors of the reign and their offspring. Should one find oneself being told with a benign smile (as though it were the ultimate justification) 'Never mind, he writes so well!' how should one reply? The biased Tacitus also wrote well, the scandalmongering Suetonius too. Tallemant des Réaux and Bussy-Rabutin also could write well, but one would hardly dream of trusting their opinions. We should unhesitatingly give more credence to *The Century of Louis XIV* (1739–51) (112) than to the *Mémoires* of Saint-Simon (1743–52) (94).

It is not astonishing that Voltaire, the supporter of

enlightened despots, should have admired Louis XIV, the promoter of enlightened despotism. Nor is it remarkable that the
'black legend' should have reappeared, and the credence given it
have grown, in the course of the nineteenth century, when the
complete edition of Saint-Simon was published as well as
Michelet's *History of France* and the textbooks of Ernest Lavisse.
Jules Michelet was inspired by his love of the Middle Ages to
write affectingly of that period, his narrative skills reinforced by
his magnificent powers of evocation. But he exacted his revenge
on the *ancien régime* monarchy. 'For the sixteenth and seventeenth
centuries', he wrote (1869), 'I paint a terrible picture. Rabelais
and Voltaire turn in their graves. Overturned altars and the
rotten carcasses of kings appear in the cold light of day. Gone is
the insipid backcloth, the self-satisfied and shameful prudery.
From the Médicis to Louis XIV a rigorous autopsy is conducted
on this government of corpses.' Carried away by the strength of
his passion, Michelet followed his convictions; the *dragonnades*,
forced conversions, Huguenot refugees, galleys, miseries of war,
and dearth all appeared to satisfy him, as did French military
defeats. More scientifically, albeit much less systematically,
Ernest Lavisse, forty years later, placed himself on the judgement seat of the historian. In the *Illustrated History of France*,
written for an adult audience, he treated Louis XIV with consideration (216). But, in the primary school textbooks which
appeared under his name, Louis XIV was depicted as a despot
who was both cruel and flippant (162).

We have all to some degree felt the influence of this legend. As
a result, the author of this book is sure to be assailed for having
written this prologue. He will be accused of being an aggressive
and hypercritical polemicist. Yet the author's purpose is quite
simply to say, 'Cease the recriminations', rather as the general of
an army might say, 'Cease fire!' And it is not merely because
Saint-Simon, Michelet and Lavisse have acted as lawyers for the
prosecution that one must try to approach Louis XIV with the
sympathetic attention incumbent on a defence lawyer. When the
author began to collect together the documentation for this book,
he was less than sympathetic towards the king, seemingly a cold,
distant, insensitive figure, very much the prisoner of *raison d'état*.
But, as months and years passed, this image began to change its
shape and gain more colour. It became clearer that the king
should not be regarded as an autocrat, that the Sun King did not

imagine that he was Apollo, that the most powerful and most famous sovereign in Christendom at that time was nevertheless a human being, sometimes transparently so, in what he said, in his silences and in his treatment of people, and not just in his weaker moments of passion.

This is not to suggest that it was a reign without difficulties or that he was a king without defects. His anti-Protestant policy, albeit explicable in its context, remains inexcusable in retrospect. The persecution of the Augustinians, or so-called Jansenists, had moral consequences far graver than the physical destruction of the Convent of Port-Royal des Champs. The Eure canal and the devastation of the Palatinate did little to enhance the king's glory. This book offers no new light on these subjects. But the author believes that it is possible to reach a positive assessment of the seventy-two years of this reign (1643–1715), of which fifty-four were under Louis' personal rule (1661–1715). The recent works of Ragnhild Hatton (197), André Corvisier (165) and Jean Meyer (240), and the articles of Professors Mousnier (249), Frostin (183–7) and Taillemite (273–7), offer assurance as to this assessment. And assurance may also be had by returning to the primary sources in which one can have some confidence. The best writers, as we have seen, are not necessarily the most trustworthy. The best primary sources for the reign are Dangeau (26), Sourches (97), Madame de la Fayette (49), Madame de Sévigné (96), and often Jean Racine (90). We need to examine various aspects too. An elementary examination of chronology allows us, for example, to explain the changes in naval strategy of 1693 in terms of the need to combat the dearth of that year. The account of the religious development of the king indicates the extent to which his anti-Protestantism and anti-Jansenism emerged from his childhood religious education and centred around his sense of devotion, the workings of which always took first place over political themes and arguments, even the most dramatic.

On seventeenth-century France, there is probably not much of genuine novelty in the way of documentation to add to the common stock. There remains, however, much to 'discover' in the elementary sense of *uncovering*. It is easy to ignore the simple verities and take things for granted. This is why the author has concentrated on recovering some things, simple truths, which have tended to be forgotten. The historian should not always be trying to distribute praise and blame. Whilst it is impossible to avoid judgements of value, one should not imagine oneself as a Minos or a Rhadamanthys. A reign of the stature (if only in terms of its length) of Louis XIV's is, in the nature of things, inseparable from the biography of its king. The number of provinces by which France was enlarged is more interesting than the number of the royal mistresses. If, after 300 years, Louis XIV is held to account for the negative part of the balance sheet, the positive side should also appear in the accounts, as a matter of honesty. Since the king rather than Louvois is held responsible for the destruction in the Palatinate – and there is justice in this since an absolute king should shoulder his responsibilities absolutely – and since the king rather than Colbert is held to account for the persecution of Fouquet, then, by the same token, it should not be Colbert who is given the credit to the detriment of the king for having protected the arts and literature. Le Vau, Le Nôtre and Mansart should not be awarded the accolade of Versailles at the expense of Louis XIV.

Absolute authority has, often more than other articulations of power, its sense of duty: it would be a curious paradox to deprive an absolute monarch of the positive share of his responsibilities.

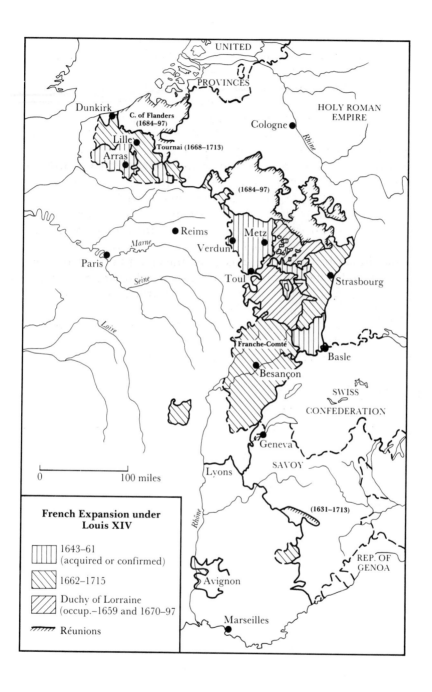

UNITED
PROVINCES

HOLY ROMAN
EMPIRE

Dunkirk

C. of Flanders
(1684–97)

Cologne

Rhine

Lille
Arras

Tournai (1668–1713)

(1684–97)

Reims

Marne

Metz

Verdun

Paris

Seine

Toul

Strasbourg

Loire

Franche-Comté

Basle

Besançon

SWISS
CONFEDERATION

Geneva

SAVOY

Lyons

0   100 miles

Rhône

(1631–1713)

**French Expansion under
Louis XIV**

REP. OF
GENOA

1643–61
(acquired or confirmed)

Avignon

1662–1715

Duchy of Lorraine
(occup.–1659 and 1670–97)

Marseilles

Réunions

1

The Consecration of Louis the 'Dieudonné'

THERE ARE some rituals which haunt one's imagination: the baptism of Clovis, the consecration of Charles VII, perhaps that of Henry IV. Without a consecration, Henry of Navarre would never have conquered his kingdom, or the hearts of so many. Others, on the other hand, have not passed into the collective memory. Who can remember anything of the consecration of Louis the Great? Yet, on 7 June 1654 at Reims – eighteen months after the Fronde – that unwritten contract which united the French monarch with God, and with the country's aristocracy and its people, was sealed, in pomp and ceremony, with a king who was yet to be seen as an Apollo or the Sun King. The most ordinary of spectators on this auspicious day would have appreciated, through what they saw and heard, the religious character of the monarchy. A young prince, imbued with a sense of religious devotion, read into each symbol of the 'eighth sacrament' of consecration the sacred roots, the constituent elements and the limits of his authority.

CLAMOROUS EXPECTANCY

On Wednesday, 3 June 1654, Reims was in great excitement. Louis the 'Dieudonné' was within the city walls. After receiving the keys of the town in the presence of its notables, 2,000 mounted guards and 5,000 soldiers, he travelled by carriage to the cathedral. There, dressed 'pontifically' and awaiting his arrival, were the Bishops of Soissons, Beauvais and Noyon, as well as the cathedral canons dressed in their golden capes. Simon Le Gras,

Bishop of Soissons, greeted His Majesty with lavish compliments and references to Clovis and St Rémy. Everyone, nobles and commoners, would soon kneel in submission:

> Before you, Sire, the Lord's Anointed, son of the Most High, shepherd of the flock, protector of the Church, the first of all kings on earth, chosen and appointed by Heaven to carry the sceptre of the French, to extend far and wide the honour and renown of the Lily, whose glory outshines by far that of Solomon from pole to pole and sun to sun, making France a universe and the universe one France. (55)

During the *Te Deum*, and to the sound of cannon and muskets, Louis had time to reflect on the meaning of his consecration. The bishop had called him the Lord's anointed' because all power came from God. On this point, Catholics and Protestants were in agreement, for the testimony of St Paul (Romans 13:1) was incontrovertible. The French king was not just king by divine right: he was a Messiah in the tradition of King David. The clergy, the jurists and the people regarded the French monarchy as predestined. Only the French called their sovereign 'Eldest Son of the Church' – the result of the date of and the circumstances surrounding the baptism of Clovis – and 'Most Christian King'. When the Bishop of Soissons recited the attributes of royalty, he was merely anticipating by a few years the theses of Bishop Bossuet, the 'Eagle of Meaux'. The Church already knew how to put together divine right and absolute monarchy, divine delegation and privileged sovereignty.

The church service completed, the monarch left for the archiepiscopal palace, furnished specially for the king. The following day, escorted by his mother Anne of Austria, by his brother the duc d'Anjou, by Cardinal Mazarin and by the court, he devotedly took part in an interminable procession amidst vivats and benedictions. On 5 June, the royal party visited the tomb of St Rémy; then, in a session of the Council, Louis decided on the final details of the consecration. On Saturday the 6th, the king went to Mass at Saint-Niçaise and was present at Vespers in the cathedral. When he left, the captain of the guards then took charge in order to watch over the royal vestments brought from Saint-Denis: camisole, sandals, ankle-boots, spurs, sword, tunic, Dalmatic, mantle, and above all the sceptre, which symbolized absolute authority, the hand of justice, which represented divinely delegated power, and 'the diadem of honour, glory and majesty' (55).

THE 'EIGHTH SACRAMENT'

At daybreak on Sunday, 7 June, the prelates and canons took their places in the cathedral stalls. The walls of the vast church were covered with royal tapestries and the floor with Turkish carpets. On the altar stood the reliquaries of St Rémy and St Louis. Following the king's orders, a prayer-stool and a chair were in the choir and there was a throne aloft on the rood-screen. At about half past five, the Bishop of Soissons sent the Bishops of Beauvais and Châlons to wait on His Majesty. Preceded by his musicians, who were dressed in white, and by the gentlemen of the chamber with their halberds, Louis XIV was escorted by his 100 Swiss guards, the officers of the Crown and the court dignitaries up to the cathedral choir. After reciting the *Veni Creator*, the prelates and canons went to the cathedral steps to welcome the sacred phial, 'this precious treasure sent from Heaven to the great St Rémy for the consecration of Clovis', brought by the prior of Saint-Denis.

When it had been placed on the altar, the king was invited to proclaim his consecration oaths. Like his predecessors, Louis XIV promised to preserve the liberties and immunities of the Church. Then he took the solemn 'oath of the kingdom'. With one hand on the Bible, he proclaimed his promise to give peace, justice and mercy to his people,* in other words to declare law in conformity with the commandments of God and natural law. Since the thirteenth century, the oath of the kingdom had concluded with the phrase: 'Also do I undertake in good conscience and according to my powers to eliminate totally from my dominions the heresies condemned by the Church.' The oath had been drafted with the Cathar heresy in mind, but, with the advent of the Reformation, it had acquired a new meaning. The young king knew enough Latin to understand the implications of the oath. It required the monarch to 'extirpate heresy'. The Revocation of the Edict of Nantes (1598) in 1685 would be the late and inexpedient (albeit strictly logical) consequence of this

---

* Psalm 85.

promise. As if to put a seal on this last promise, the king then kissed the scriptures.

The rituals which followed were punctuated with prayers. The comte de Vivonne, first gentleman of the chamber, removed from the king his silver robe. Then his grand chamberlain, the duc de Joyeuse, placed velvet ankle-boots on his feet, followed by the duc d'Anjou, who gave him his gold spurs. The royal sword, reputed to have been Charlemagne's, was then blessed. The Bishop of Soissons took the holy chrism and dispensed seven unctions whilst the clergy recited: 'May the King bring down the proud, be an example for the rich and the powerful to follow, be good towards the humble, charitable towards the poor, just to all his subjects and work for peace among the nations.' (149) Divine right carried responsibilities with it. The grand chamberlain next helped the king into the tunic and the Dalmatic and covered his shoulders with a violet mantle covered with fleurs-de-lis, and the king was then anointed with a fresh unction on each hand before the prelate presented him in turn with the ring, the sceptre, the hand of justice and, finally, the crown of Charlemagne. Louis then went up the staircase of the rood-screen and sat on the throne where, before all those present, he received the homage of each peer of the realm in turn. At length the bishop proclaimed in a loud voice 'Vivat rex in aeternum' and the doors of the cathedral were opened for the crowd to echo the reply, 'Vive le Roi!' A deafening noise of spontaneous acclaims, martial music, cannon-fire from the French guards and harquebus-volleys from the militia gradually built up, halting the ceremony until, as the din subsided, it could continue, with a *Te Deum* and a Mass. Once this was over, the king descended from the throne, recited the *Confiteor* and received absolution, and communion in both kinds. Now that His Majesty had been blessed, the bishop removed the Charlemagne crown from his head and replaced it with a lighter one and then accompanied the king to the banqueting hall 'amidst acclamations and joyful shouts from everyone, crying "Vive le Roi"' (55).

The next day, the king crossed the city to the Church of Saint-Rémy to hear Mass, everyone being impressed by his devotion. After the ceremony, the Bishop of Montauban, Pierre de Bertier, did not hesitate to remind the king of the Protestant problem in the south of France, asking him for action 'with regard to those of the so-called Reformed religion (*religion prétendue réformée*)' (149).

The royal entourage was disconcerted but the king, in the context of his oaths taken the day before, sensed that the request was not as inappropriate as it seemed. Events would show how every detail of his trip to Reims remained engraved on his memory.

His stay in Reims was notable in other ways too. On Monday afternoon, the king received the blue riband of the famous order of chivalry the Order of the Holy Spirit, of which he was the grand master and which he would turn into an instrument of his rule. On Tuesday, he laid his hands on 2,000 victims of scrofula. In the great traditions of thaumaturgic kingship, he said to them in turn, 'The king touches thee: may the Lord heal thee', before they received a silver coin. This exhausting ceremony, which Louis XIV would repeat throughout his life several times each year, drew admiration from spectators, such was his spontaneity, mildness and self-composure: 'although there was such a large crowd of sufferers, the king only stopped twice for a drink of water' (149). Two days after his consecration, Louis had not forgotten that royalty was a kind of priesthood.

INCARNATE KINGSHIP

Louis undoubtedly saw the ceremony of consecration at Reims as one of the turning-points in his life. But consecration, however important an event in itself, was only one rite of passage in the life of the Most Christian King, a confirmation to his contemporaries of a self-evident incarnate kingship. For, if the monarchical ideal can tend to be somewhat abstract, the fact and greatness of monarchy rest in its incarnation. 'The originality of monarchy lies precisely in the way in which the man is regarded.' Royalty 'begins where the man begins: in the loins of a man and the belly of a woman' (296). Kings have to be born and accept their mortality. Yet the king's body must appear sacred, must remain venerated, even if, as in the case of Charles VI, he has lost his wits. The king's body was a 'focus of identity'; for his subjects, a pledge of love.

And if the physical embodiment of the prince was divine, in a quotidian, almost banal sense of the word, that divinity was infinitely more real when consecration linked him to Heaven, 'when the head received the crown, and when his stomach, feet, hands, nostrils and eyelids were anointed with the holy unction'.

When this took place in adolescence, consecration took on all the mighty and magnificent force of a rite of passage. The royal pledge, offered to God and to his people at the moment when the allure of a young king was most likely to sustain and enhance the love of his subjects, became, transcendentally, the means to perpetuate that love. It should be remembered that, according to Arthur Young in 1788, the average Frenchman 'loves his king ... almost to madness', which makes it easier to imagine the reactions of his predecessors in 1654. What is now (anachronistically) called public opinion was then an emotional and passionate response.

But love takes pleasure in contemplating the object of its affections. French monarchs knew that, in encouraging the emotional loyalties of their subjects, they were also demonstrating their own devotion to them. Coins, even of the smallest denomination, provided everyone with a portrait of the king which grew, matured, became more majestic, aged gently, with each successive minting. The size of the image remained the same, but its form changed, and the engravers would not try to make the young sovereign older than his years or hide the age of the old king. The king's body was never thought of as immortal. 'An immortal king would be a god or an automaton; never a monarch.' (296)

In June 1654, Louis had no conception of the degree to which, later on, he would exploit the resources of Mount Olympus to compel the attention of his people. But he was already aware that classical images were purely decorative. The reality of royalty, as presented in Reims, was Frankish, Christian, human and incarnate, without any illusions of immortality. Louis would experience physical discomforts and the infirmities of age. Throughout his life, he would be dependent upon the willing services of surgeons and apothecaries, strangers to Mount Olympus. He would have headaches, toothache, stomach pains and sciatica. He would suffer from haemorrhoids, and, in 1686, everyone would know that he had a fistula. At the same time, all his subjects, even those in the Midi or the North, knew something of his physical pleasures. Because royalty became flesh, there were royal mistresses and royal bastards. For the holy unction of the consecration did not transform the king into a saint in stained-glass. It called upon and transmitted God's benediction, but the king remained human, and, thus, a sinner.

At Reims, however, sin and adultery were far from Louis' thoughts, since everything, at that moment, led him towards higher things. Christian prayer is based upon the mystery of the Incarnation. 'The promise of God's love rests in His Son and, specifically, upon Christ's body.' Thus, in meditation, the Lord's anointed worked his way transcendentally towards the heart of that immanence in which lies divine revelation. Louis knew that he was not called upon to be an angel but to follow Christ's example. The preachers compared the king to a Messiah (such as David) and Holy Scripture saw in Christ a God who was prophet, priest and also king. Terrestrial and celestial kingship were at one in a common sense of incarnation. 'In royalty, nothing smacks of the abstract, the premeditated. Monarchy rests in the spark of life which dies but which is rekindled, the sons who follow in their father's footsteps, man as created in the image of God. There is life in it.' (296) The holy unction, a divine promise, was a symbol of this life-force and imprinted a spiritual and ineradicable mark of it upon the king.

2

The Miracle Child

L OUIS XIV reigned for seventy-two years, from 1643 to 1715. This was something of a record; but the time spent awaiting his birth would have spanned a normal reign. Everyone therefore interpreted the coming of the Dauphin as a sign from Heaven. Fléchier would speak of the king's '*miraculous birth* which promised the world a life of miracles' (39). To immortalize the 'miracle', Anne of Austria would build a commemorative chapel at Val-de-Grâce whose symbolism has often not been sufficiently appreciated.

Louis XIII's marriage had taken place in 1615. Twenty-two years later, Anne of Austria was still childless. The hopes of an heir had proved several times to be false (158). Louis XIII, like Henry III, hoped to become a father without always doing what would have contributed to the required result. There was then the additional obstacle of a royal estrangement, which Cardinal Richelieu appeased but which was not wholly dissipated. In 1637, Louis XIII had proof, by means of Mme de Chevreuse and his valet La Porte, of his wife's correspondence with the Spanish court. In the midst of the Franco-Spanish war, Anne was calmly committing treason against her country by adoption. On 10 August, the queen was assigned a separate residence, at Chantilly.

These details were not widely known and, in the popular mind, hopes for an heir lived on. Then, on 10 February 1638, the king signed letters-patent at Saint-Germain-en-Laye placing the realm under the protection of the 'most holy and glorious' Virgin Mary. When, almost at once, it was learnt that the queen was expecting a child, the two events were seen as cause and effect and there was great public rejoicing. The declaration of February 1638, imbued with the spirit of the Council of Trent (1545–63) and a distinctive French Counter-Reformed spirituality, is a remarkable document. Its political coherence and the logic of its timing are less apparent. The Protestant jurist Grotius wrote: 'If the Blessed Virgin is now to have, as one hears, the Cardinal de Richelieu as her vicar-general, the king has no choice but to behave himself.' (169) The preamble included among its justifications the uprising of Protestants in the south of France which had been defeated; but no revocation of the Edict of Nantes, which had granted Huguenots liberty of conscience and of public worship, was envisaged in it. However, when Louis XIII took his vow to the Virgin Mary on behalf of France ('Our person, our state, our Crown, and all our subjects'), he made no exception for the one million or so Protestants in France. But, although the Marian vow of the king must have appeared to them a provocative gesture, they were too anxious to maintain their recently found loyalism and too committed to public service (notably in the army) not to wish for the birth of a successor to the throne.

Catholic France conspired with the Almighty to bring the event to pass. Jean-Jacques Olier, founder of Saint-Sulpice, 'scourged himself regularly' (47). Jeanne de Matel (1596–1670), founder and mother superior of the Institute of the Incarnate Word, prophesied the birth of the Dauphin (145). A more detailed prophecy had already been forthcoming from a friar called Fiacre of the discalced Augustinians: whilst Anne of Austria had been in disgrace, he publicized his 'official revelation of the future birth of the king and of that of Monsieur' (97). One of the strangest predictions came from a Carmelite at Beaune, Marguerite of the Blessed Sacrament. From the age of thirteen, this devout young girl claimed to have seen the infant Jesus and received an order to pray that Louis XIII should have an heir: 'her prayer would be answered by the Holy Child'; 'it would be the work of the infant Jesus' (145). On 25 December 1635, the infant Jesus promised her that the queen would have a son. Two years later, on 15 December 1637, she learnt from

God that Anne of Austria was pregnant – something that no one could yet know. In stories, good fairies attend the birth of princes; but, in baroque France, holy men and women said their prayers at the moment of the child's conception.

The event had, in fact, taken place at the Louvre on 5 December 1637. Louis XIII, returning from Versailles, had gone to the Monastery of the Visitation, rue Saint-Antoine, to speak to Louise de la Fayette, formerly his chaste companion and now a novice who used prayers and good advice to obtain the royal couple's reconciliation. Caught in a storm and following the persuasions of M. de Guitaut, captain of the guards, the king gave up the idea of going to Saint-Maur and went instead to dine at the Louvre and spent the night in the queen's apartment. Nine months after this encounter Anne of Austria gave birth to her son, on Sunday, 5 September 1638, at the new château of Saint-Germain. He was immediately dipped (*ondoyé*) by the king's chaplain, Dominique Séguier, Bishop of Meaux.

Up to the birth of the infant, the Almighty had been besieged with supplications: prayers in Paris were said from 28 August; the Blessed Sacrament had been on display (158). When Louis XIII unveiled the cot of the little Dauphin to the ambassador of Venice, he said: 'Here is the miraculous result of the grace of Almighty God, for what else may describe such a beautiful child after twenty-two years of marriage and my wife's four unfortunate miscarriages.' (158) To Mademoiselle de la Fayette, the king despatched a letter of unrestrained enthusiasm. In France, the Dauphin, who had existed in the prayers of so many, was thus soon known as the 'gift from God' (*Dieudonné*). The *Te Deum*, that ancient canticle of praise and thanksgiving for God's grace which would punctuate each success of this long reign, celebrated its beginning. The priority accorded to religious expressions of joy did nothing to diminish displays of public delight. On Sunday evening in Paris, the cannon were sounded, the tapers lighted and there were bonfires. The *échevins* led the way with a great bonfire in the forecourt of the city hall. Full peals of bells rang out and, on the Monday, the shops remained closed. Everywhere there were processions, public prayers and exhibitions of the Blessed Sacrament; cannons and firecrackers sounded alternately and, in the evening, the city presented a firework display. The festivities lasted through the following day and into Wednesday when, although the supplies of wine began to dry up, the general rejoicing seemed unquenchable (73). 'Never had a population, upon any occasion whatsoever, demonstrated such delight', wrote Grotius from the Dutch Republic (169).

The public life of a prince begins at birth. From as early as 6 September, Louis gave audiences. A delegation from the Parlement of Paris and the other sovereign courts came at four o'clock to Saint-Germain to present their compliments to the king. M. de Brienne, the secretary of state, then led the magistrates into the Dauphin's bedchamber. The *procureur général*, Mathieu Molé, recorded this first encounter between the future Louis XIV and the gentlemen of the 'long robe':

> He was under a grand canopy of white floral damask which stretched across the breadth of the room and with screens at either side. A large balustrade stood in front of it so that he was about ten or twelve feet away ... Madame de Lansac, his governess, sat at the back on a chair and held the Dauphin asleep on a pillow of white satin. His face was uncovered and she showed him to us and said that 'he would open his eyes to see his faithful servants'. (73)

The governess could not, of course, have foreseen, ten years before it happened, the *parlementaire* Fronde and the civil war which ensued.

THE ANCESTRAL GALLERY

Some learned men attempted to find out the infant's destiny. Anne of Austria invited the astronomer Jean-Baptiste Morin to draw up his horoscope. The Dominican Campanella, and the jurist Grotius, also set to work. Racine had a particular reason for being interested in the matter since he would be both historiographer royal and himself born a year later in 1639. He recorded the results of these speculations thus:

> Predictions of CAMPANELLA upon the future greatness of the Dauphin ... Prognostications on the same, GROTIUS. The constellation of the Dauphin was composed of nine stars, the nine Muses, as the astrologers call them: he lies in Aquila, signifying great genius; Pegasus, the puissant horserider; Sagittarius, the

infantry; Aquarius, naval power; the Swan, meaning that poets, historians and orators would sing his praises. The Dauphin's constellation touches the Equator, a sign of justice, and he was born on a Sunday, the day of the Sun. *Ad solis instar, beaturus suo calore ac lumine Galliam Galliaeque amicos. Jam nonan nutricem sugit; aufugiunt omnes quod mammas earum male tractet* [The Dauphin, like the rays and light of the sun, will bring radiance to France and her allies. Already he was at the breast of his ninth wet-nurse; they all left him in haste because he maltreated their breasts]. 1 January 1639. (90)

In the past, historians pored over the genealogies of princes hoping to find there the key to their great fortune. Following their example, we might venture the thought that, from one grandfather, Henry IV, Louis had inherited his bravery, his secrecy and his taste for fine women, and that, from his other grandfather, Philip II, he had inherited an obsession to perfect his craft of kingship. This kind of analysis is not wholly worthless: in great families, the fascination with one's ancestry often weighed more heavily than the mysterious workings of heredity.

But this particular family vault teemed with a multitude of contrasting figures from the past. In it were Charles V, Rurik (the descendant of a Russian noble), Frederick Barbarossa, Charles the Bold, the *condottiere* Jean de Médicis and the poet Charles d'Orléans. Some faces kept recurring and are worth noting: from Charles the Bold, Louis was descended through 6 different lineages; from the murdered queen Inés de Castro, 22 times; and 368 times from St Louis, whose sanctity he did not inherit. There is something rather touching in the knowledge that Louis, a great devotee of Corneille's style of heroism, was descended 1,575 times from El Cid Campeador.*

The grand dynasties, with their dynastic ties spreading across political frontiers, were always cosmopolitan in their families. However, the dominant national identity in all famous monarchs has been a matter for concern. Barrès wrote: 'Louis XIV was a Médicis. Bonaparte was Tuscan, quintessentially Tuscan.' More methodical research has examined the genealogical quarterings of Louis' ancestry (the four quarters of an individual being his four grandparents, the eight quarters his great-grandparents, and so on). Some have claimed to have found a

---

* The Grand Dauphin was, genealogically, 3,150 times removed from El Cid.

Germanic predominance and to have thus explained the King of France's disposition to become a candidate for the empire in 1658 (263). Others found dominant Spanish ancestry, and used this finding to explain why the creator of Versailles elaborated its court etiquette. But nobody had the patience to go sufficiently far back until a recent genealogist reconstituted 510 of the 512 quarters of Louis XIV, tracing his ancestry back nine generations (150). The Germanic element (43 German quarters and a further 14 Austrian) constituted 11 per cent in total. The Slavic component (36 quarters) and the English (35) were each 7 per cent. Latin countries made up the remaining 75 per cent: 145 French quarters, 8 from Lorraine and 5 from Savoy, 133 Spanish, 50 Portuguese, 41 Italian. The King of France was, it turns out, of strongly French ancestry.

In any case, such considerations did not strictly matter. Not only was the king essentially French but his lineage was indefeasible. By the public law of France, a prince of the lineage of Hugh Capet and of legitimate birth could not juridically lose his Frenchness. In 1589, what stood against Henry IV was not his title of King of Navarre but his Protestantism; and no one held it against the Valois Henry III that he had been king in Poland. This was why, when it came to the question of the French candidature to the throne of Spain at the end of Louis XIV's reign, the duc d'Anjou, by then Philip V, knew that he would retain all his rights in any future succession to the throne of France. It inevitably followed from the fundamental law, the irreducible basis of the unwritten constitution, that no international agreement could stand in the way of the customary rights of the kingdom (120).

Besides, it is wholly inadequate to itemize the quarterings of a king with arbitrary labels upon the 'nationality' of this or that ancestor. The 'realm of Catherine de Médicis', Henry II's widow, was far removed from her native Tuscany. Anne of Austria, although she sometimes indulged in dealings with Spain whilst Louis XIII was alive, abandoned them all after his death. From 1643 onwards, she was more wedded to the interests of her adopted country than were many French princes (176). Such was the force of the fundamental laws. They not only channelled public law over a long period of time, but also moulded attitudes and structured the best traditions of the French court. After the death of her husband, Anne of Austria became queen mother and all that was left which could be called Spanish was her pride, her sense of honour and her devotions.

THE INHERITOR OF THE CROWN

When the childhood of the future Sun King is mentioned, there is a tendency to paint a rather sombre picture, to stress the interest of some of the anecdotes left by history and legend to posterity. The legend of an unhappy childhood originates both in the reality of the Fronde and in the insinuations of the royal valet Pierre de la Porte. The underlying notion that small princes were born into and grew up in perpetual bliss has no foundation, not even in fairy stories. In the *Universal Dictionary* (*Dictionnaire universel*) there appears this dictum: 'Great princes were never raised in the lap of luxury.' (42)

Some anecdotes concerning the young king's life from 1643 to 1658 are often quoted but they are unreliable concerning the Dauphin. Such evidence as we have presents Louis XIII as proud of his first-born, jealous when the child seemed to go more spontaneously to his mother, but loved by the small boy and responsive to his least attention. Louis XIV would hardly know his father; yet the memory of him would haunt him as an adolescent, as an adult and even as an old man. His loyalty to Mazarin from the Fronde until the death of the cardinal was, first and foremost, a mark of respect to Louis XIII, who had chosen Mazarin as the godparent to the Dauphin and principal minister. The consistency with which the king would set aside the objections of his architects and require them to respect the little hunting-château constructed by the late king at the heart of the palace of Versailles is also a significant pointer to the con-sistency of his filial devotion. Even on his death-bed, Louis would ordain that his heart be buried beside that of Louis XIII at the Jesuit house in the rue Saint-Antoine (26). This continuity argues against any idea of an unhappy childhood.

The births of Louis XIV and of the duc d'Anjou (21 Septem-ber 1640)* did not permanently restore harmony between Louis XIII and his wife. The rashness of Cinq-Mars, who negotiated with Spain in the midst of declared hostilities, would have done

* 'Le petit Monsieur' became the duc d'Orléans in 1660 on the death of his uncle, Monsieur, i.e. Gaston d'Orléans, the brother of Louis XIII.

infinite harm to the queen had it not been for the ability and tact of Cardinal Richelieu. The misunderstanding between the royal couple began to diminish in the summer of 1642: Cinq-Mars was in prison and Marie de Médicis was dead (soon to be followed by the cardinal himself, on 4 December).

The months which separated the cardinal's death from that of the king himself were for Louis XIII a period of great strain culminating in six weeks of physical suffering. The atmosphere at court was equally tense; but it seems clear that Louis was kept ignorant of the difficulties between his parents. Besides, it would have penetrated the consciousness of the child that there were many points in common between his mother and father: an exalted sense of the rights and prerogatives of princes, a weakness for heroism, an active and personal Catholic faith, and even a common devotion for the Virgin Mary. These qualities – and many of their defects as well – Louis would inherit, particularly their notion of the state. Louis XIII and Anne of Austria were probably reconciled to each other in 1642 by Richelieu; but also, in a longer perspective, and posthumously, by Louis XIV himself.

The influence of Anne on her son would be felt beyond the declaration of his majority and, in some ways, continued until her death in 1666. 'A son never honoured his mother more throughout his life than Louis XIV did', said Charles Perrault (85). Before the death of Louis XIII, the affection of Anne of Austria for her two sons was already remarked on at court. After Louis XIII's death, she lavished affection on the princes. 'She brought them up close to her', Mme de la Fayette wrote, 'with such tenderness that she became jealous of those with whom they chose to play.' (49) La Porte accused the queen mother of spoiling her eldest son. This does not appear to have been the case save that aristocrats in France prided themselves on their sturdy independence and apparent lack of warmth whilst a Spanish princess could more naturally display the demonstrative tendency often attributed to Mediterranean peoples. Besides, it was not the romantic age which invented maternal love. Furetière wrote in his *Dictionary*: 'It is a maternal fault to mollycoddle the young, to pamper and humour them.' (42) In any case, for Anne, Louis was the miracle child. How could she not lavish affections on her Dieudonné?

But loving children also meant bringing them up well. The

children of the Counter-Reformation – even those of the royal house – were no angels. Good parents, even those of royal blood, knew it was their duty to correct their offspring. Thus, when one day the young nine-year-old king crossed the line between playfulness and impertinence in his mother's presence, the valet Marie Dubois recalls how Anne of Austria grew pink with rage and told Louis XIV: 'I will make you realize that your authority is as nothing compared with mine. It is a long time since you have been whipped; you shall find out that they spank in Amiens like they do in Paris.' (75) A few minutes later, Louis was at his mother's feet declaring: 'Maman, I am sorry: I promise you that my wish is to obey your will.' The queen forgave him and kissed him gently. This anecdote, which has all the signs of being true and in which the loyal Dubois re-creates the scene so vividly for us, has the nice touch of the king using the familiar 'Maman' like a modest bourgeois or young peasant.

Charles V's granddaughter had nothing of the bourgeois about her. 'Beautiful as the day is long' (6), elegant, sociable, adoring 'sweet-smelling gloves, carefully laundered linen – she had a sense of cleanliness surprising for the period – mirrors, flowers with strong scents' (291), she enforced decorum, refinement and display upon her retinue. From his earliest years, Louis took to his mother's tastes, fell under her influence and was delighted to hold pride of place amidst her affections. Le Boux, Bishop of Dax, recalled, in unctuous terms, the loving relationship between Anne and Louis: 'God wanted to make two hearts incomparable, one a mother's and the other a son's. Of Anne of Austria's it might well be said that, for her tenderness, *tam mater nulla*, and of Louis's, for his respect and love, *tam filius nemo*. This was Tertullian's way of expressing God's relationship to the hearts of men: *tam pater nemo*.' The queen's influence upon her son was always dominated by her devotion, which, in turn, affected the king's religiosity.

On his death-bed, Louis XIII's preoccupations were with his son. On his orders, the Dauphin was publicly baptized at Saint-Germain on 21 April 1643. He chose the princesse de Condé as godmother and Mazarin as godfather. The choice of Mazarin had immense consequences. This prelate, Italian still in outlook and new to the kingdom, would become the incarnation of Cardinal Richelieu's political will and diplomatic skill. Despite the paradox, a new man was called on to symbolize continuities and rally traditional loyalties. These were qualities without price on the eve of a regency.

On 14 May 1643, Louis XIII died. Turenne wrote to his sister, Mlle de Bouillon, 'Truly no one has died better or more steadfastly. But as to the court mourning, it has been very modest.' (107) On the same day, in conformity with monarchical continuity ('The king is dead, long live the king!'), began the reign of Louis XIV, FRANCORUM SPES MAGNA ('Great Hope of the French'), as the legend on the official commemorative medal ran (71). He was four years, eight months and nine days old.

On 19 May – the day when the body of the late king was taken to Saint-Denis – the duc d'Enghien attacked the (stronger) Spanish army and won the Battle of Rocroi. French losses were 2,000 dead; Dom Francisco de Mello lost half his army (8,000 dead, 6,000 taken prisoner, 200 flags and 60 standards captured). As Mazarin said, it was 'the most signal victory for many years' (157). Its champion – later prince de Condé* – was not yet twenty-two years old. It is easy to imagine how this success was immediately seen as symbolic. By the victory over the Spanish forces, the duc d'Enghien had cemented the regency and prevented invasion. In such a climate, the youth of the king and his servants could be taken as a sign of hope.

In Louis' case, 'youth' is something of a fiction since, from his earliest years, the elaborate mechanisms of royal obligations required Louis' presence. He had to appear to command everything, whilst he nurtured a taste for and evident consciousness of his dignity which enabled him, little by little, to move from the illusion of power to its reality. It was as a little boy that he held the *lit de justice* of 18 May 1643. Before his death, Louis XIII had signed a declaration restricting the powers of the queen as regent. Whilst ordering that she 'be Regent in France' and 'that she have charge of the education and instruction' of Louis and Philippe 'and the administration and government of the realm' until the thirteenth birthday of his eldest son, Louis XIII also enveloped these powers by the creation of a council. Composed

* He only gained the title of prince de Condé following his father's death in December 1646. At the same time he became first prince of the blood.

of Gaston d'Orléans, named *lieutenant général* of the kingdom, the prince de Condé – the father of the victor of Rocroi –, Mazarin, the chancellor Séguier, the *surintendant* Bouthillier and the secretary of state Chavigny, the council took charge of all the regent's powers. The declaration was registered in the Parlement on 21 April. But on 18 May, reassured as to Anne of Austria's intentions towards the magistrates (she promised them the granting of the privilege of automatic ennoblement to the *noblesse de race* within eighteen months), the same Parlement registered without demur the quashing of the last wishes of the late king. It happened in the ancient ceremonial of a *lit de justice*. Louis, 'dressed in violet, was *carried* by the grand chamberlain, the duc de Joyeuse, and the comte de Charost, captain of his guards, to his *lit de justice*' (105). The princes de Condé and de Conti, the dukes, many prelates and marshals and others invited to attend completed the gathering. They each took their places and then the regent and Madame de Lansac lifted the royal infant onto his throne (176). He then stammered out a few incomprehensible words, which the record of the occasion translated as: 'The said king said that he had come to demonstrate his good will towards the Parlement and that M. the chancellor would tell them the rest.' (105)

Louis was too young to appreciate the significance of the events of 18 May. Who had a clearer idea of them? Certainly not the *avocat général*, Omer Talon, who was carried away by his own empty oratory. Séguier? Mazarin? Anne of Austria had persuaded Gaston d'Orléans and Condé to let her compose the council as she wished (and herein lay Mazarin's great opportunity), and to turn it into a purely consultative body whose opinions she need not follow. Royal sovereignty remained intact; the absolute monarchy was reinforced. By contrast, the aristocrats were right to be concerned and the magistrates who had allowed themselves to become the willing tools of high politics would pay a heavy price for their compliance.

A king's childhood is never one of complete spontaneity. We sometimes imagine that a five-year-old prince would have passed the time in playing being king, like an actor in a farce. But this is to forget that he is never a representative; he is an *incarnation* and, as such, he cannot play the double to his own persona. He is always the king. He is child *and* king and never only one or the other. Because he was so small, M. de Joyeuse lifted him onto the *lit de justice*; but, because he was king, his words, even his mumblings, would have the force of law and the will of Louis XIII would have no effect.

Besides, who knows when or to what extent each formal act, each royal edict, was understood by its signatory? It would be wrong to imagine that at that age he had no comprehension, that he did not collaborate in any way, since Louis XIV had a lively and alert intelligence. 'From his earliest years', according to La Porte, 'he made one aware that he was intelligent, seeing and understanding all sorts of things.' (51) At five, he did not act like a king aged thirty-five; but he 'has the potential of being a great king' (149), as Contarini, the Venetian ambassador, said when, in 1643, Louis received the congratulations of all the ambassadors upon his accession. The ceremony was a tiring one, a test of the little king's concentration. When the ambassadors addressed their speeches to the regent, he fidgeted; but, when they turned to address him, he was attentive.

The audiences which he granted and the acts of state which he made the semblance of signing were foretastes of his existence as an absolute ruler. Each word he said was of importance to him, to France, and to those attending the audience; each act 'signed' was a commitment by the king and the kingdom. Of course, there were distinctions made between routine and regulatory ordinances and major political acts of state. Mazarin doubtless did not bother Louis with the edict of March 1644 confirming the privileges of the Paris butchers (201), but it is inconceivable that he did not seek his accord to the declaration of the same date granting an amnesty to some gentlemen from Rouergue who had been compromised in a popular uprising (149).

There were other *lits de justice* to follow. In that of 7 September 1645, the king displayed a mature self-assurance (149). Royal duties grew more burdensome, involving inevitably a widening pattern of political and religious obligations and prestigious and humanitarian duties. On 16 September 1643, Louis had expressed his satisfaction to the duc d'Enghien on his successful military campaign. The *Gazette* wrote: 'Everyone takes great pleasure in seeing how the encouragements offered by this young king were more like what might be expected from one much older than he.' (73) In the following spring, Louis reviewed his regiment of Swiss guards in the Bois de Boulogne; military parades already gave him great pleasure. On Maundy Thursday,

1645, he washed the feet of twelve poor people of his parish (Saint-Eustache) and served them at table. During the summer of 1647, at Mazarin's instigation, Louis went to visit the frontier. He was there to mobilize the nobility and to make the realm aware of the dangers of a Spanish attack; for the Spanish had besieged and taken Armentières. The king, already a soldier, was only eight years old.

On 15 January 1648, he held his third *lit de justice*. Having listened to Omer Talon sketch out his critical and gloomy picture of the state of the realm, Louis had no second thoughts about insisting on the registration of the unpopular taxation measures proposed by Mazarin. This was the reason why, having been forced to listen to further jeremiads from Talon during the fourth *lit de justice*, on 31 July, he would be overjoyed to learn the news of the victory over the Spaniards by Condé at Lens; this was to be for him the monarchy's response to the *frondeur* magistrates. Before the civil war, and without a clear idea of the future, Louis knew who his current enemies were: the aristocrats of the kingdom who, from 1643, had grouped themselves together into the *cabale des Importants*, and had tried to bend the will of the regent to satisfy their own sectional interests; and the grandees among the magistrates, 'proud of their new-found glory', who attempted, above all in 1648, to bring the monarchy under their control.

A BAROQUE EDUCATION

Until September 1645, the king was under female guardianship. At that date, he had attained what the Church, and the state, determined to be the 'age of reason' (the age at which one acquired a sense of moral conscience as well as an intellectual consciousness) and his education was entrusted to men. In March 1646, the queen mother named 'Monsieur le cardinal Mazarini as entrusted with the superintendence of the government and of the conduct of the king' and the marquis de Villeroy 'as the governor, responsible to him, of the person of His Majesty' (70). Villeroy would be deluged with unmerited rewards, made a marshal (1646) and a duke (1648). It is not clear whether or not he had a great effect on the development of his young charge, save to instil a measure of good sense or discipline from time to time in some subordinate or other, for example, the valet La Porte (51). The king's director of studies was Hardouin de Péréfixe, abbé de Beaumont, who taught him history and the liberal arts and was rewarded with the episcopal see of Rodez. Péréfixe had at his command a college of tutors: Jean Le Bê (for writing), Le Camus (for arithmetic), Antoine Oudin (for Italian and Spanish), H. Davire (for drawing) and Bernard (for reading) (149). But it was neither Villeroy, nor Péréfixe, a prelate more devout than intelligent, who was in charge of 'the king's conduct'. That responsibility was Mazarin's.

Mazarin enjoyed the confidence of the queen – for whose political development he was also responsible. Against him lay the animosity of La Porte. This extraordinary individual, having suffered on behalf of the queen under Cardinal Richelieu, had by 1643 become more royalist than his mistress. He attempted to guide her, to enlighten her on the rumours which tarnished her public reputation, to separate her from Mazarin. Anne of Austria was more faithful than she has been portrayed, and, in recognition of his former services, did her best to support the valet, until the close of 1653. But La Porte showed himself to be as intolerable as he was indispensable to her. His vanity had perhaps been inflated by receiving in 1643 the title of *premier valet de chambre* to His Majesty and by letters of nobility, and he often took it upon himself to replace the tutor (reading the king the *History of France* by Mézeray during the evenings), the governor (making his own judgements about the degree of severity necessary for the king's well-being), and even the superintendent himself.

Even before Mazarin had been granted this title, one day at Compiègne in 1645, the six-year-old king saw the cardinal 'passing along the terrace of the château with his large retinue and could not resist shouting out: "There goes the Great Turk" '. His Eminence the cardinal was informed by a gentleman of the king's bedchamber of the incident, and he told the queen mother, but the king refused to reveal the identity of the person from whom he must have learnt the expression (51). Thus the young king grew up, knowing how to keep quiet and be faithful to those who served and loved him. He did not yet understand the value of Mazarin to his kingdom; but he knew that he was wholeheartedly loved by M. de la Porte. It would take until the

Fronde for Louis to replace the prejudices and antagonism towards Cardinal Mazarin which La Porte had imbued in him with an admiration for his worth.

It is usual to deplore the lack of provision of a formal education for the future Sun King. Louis himself is responsible for this since these were his own sentiments expressed in conversations with Madame de Maintenon. His failure to master Latin still irritated him (but Péréfixe was often replaced by La Mothe le Vayer, one of the best humanists of his generation). He seems to have been resentful of the excessive liberalism of those concerned with his education. His governesses let him play as he wanted; Villeroy and Péréfixe were similarly inclined. Voltaire would be closer to the truth when he wrote: 'Mazarin had tried to prolong the childhood of the king for as long as possible.' (112) For, despite his undistinguished background, Mazarin was an aristocrat, a *caballero*. He had fought duels in his youth and demonstrated his chivalry by his respect for the queen.

That same branch of liberalism which led Mazarin to approve of La Mothe le Vayer ('His Pyrrhonism', according to Voltaire, 'did not exclude him from being provided with such an important educational task') prevented him from becoming too involved in the details of his godson's educational programme. At the most, he altered the king's catechism. He did not press Péréfixe to begin early on with instruction in Latin, but the texts and speeches attributed to Louis XIV are such that they prove the quality of the lessons received by the king. In a period dominated still by Renaissance humanism, lessons in French from a humanist could only inculcate an admiration for Antiquity. To this should be added an important stock of historical knowledge (Péréfixe would print his lessons in his *History of Henry the Great* in 1661) (119); a basic grasp of public law (fundamental laws and regalian rights); a solid grounding in a catechism founded on the decrees of the Council of Trent; and sacred history, with the figure of King David at the very heart of it, the Messiah-King whose praises Louis XIV would have sung for him right up to his death, and who, even in his sins, was an epitome of all kings. Mathematics, drawing and modern languages were added to this elementary course of study.

In any case, the education of kings is more a matter of continual apprenticeship. In the autumn of 1648, Péréfixe would take the opportunity provided by the Peace of Westphalia to give the king a lesson in the history of the Holy Roman Empire, with the accompanying geography and politics (149). Mazarin was almost certainly behind the initiative. Louis XIV would make use of Latin throughout his life, notably in putting together, admiring, expanding and annotating his collection of medals, the most important in the kingdom and the core of the present French medal collection in the Bibliothèque Nationale (the Cabinet des Médailles). At the same time, although Antoine Oudin had not been too insistent in his teaching of the Romance languages, the king persisted with his education in them until the cardinal's death. From 1658 to 1661, the 'chevalier Amalteo, counsellor and interpreter of the Italian language' would give him exercises to do. These were proper exercises since they included a *Résumé of the Description of the World* in both French and Italian.

At all events, the distinction between a gentleman and a pedant was that a gentleman's education was not limited to the subjects of a school curriculum. The king not only learnt arithmetic, modern languages and how to express himself on paper; he also had a master of horsemanship, the *écuyer* Arnolfini, a dancing-master and a fencing-master. Florent Indret taught him to play the lute. Later, the Spaniard Bernard Jourdan de la Salle would show him how to play the guitar. If he was not the equal in these matters of Louis XIII, it is clear that he 'enjoyed a tolerably good musical education' (115). After the lute and guitar, he tried to master the spinet, choosing 'Estienne Richard to show him the way' (122).

Mazarin knew that broad programmes of study must inevitably be incomplete. He believed the most important thing was to initiate a head of state into its affairs. He tried, progressively, to do just that, thinking it best to invite the king to a short Council meeting or to participate in a small part of the business of a longer one. He was soon pleased with the progress of his young charge. Péréfixe 'told His Eminence one day that the king was not putting his mind to his studies and that he [Péréfixe] would have to make use of his authority and reprimand him lest there came the day when he behaved in the same way in matters of state. "Rely on my judgement and do not be too concerned", replied the cardinal. "He can know too much; as it is, when he is present at the Council he asks me a hundred questions about the subject in question" ' (51).

The cardinal perhaps made too much of the economies he undertook in the king's household. But he gave his godson an initiation in artistic judgement, in the kind of discernment which made him a true *amateur* collector of fine art. To Mazarin, fine art consisted of the durable – illuminated manuscripts, antiques brought from Rome at great expense, pictures by the great masters – but he also appreciated the more ephemeral delights which gave shape to distractions and formed the taste of the courtier and the *honnête homme*. Sumptuous ballets, firework displays, garden designs and triumphal arches were indispensable to the court. From Italy, His Eminence imported 'singers . . ., instrumentalists . . ., composers . . . and inventors. . . . The minister attempted to introduce Italian opera in the form of the scores of Cavalli' (122). Although Louis XIV quickly broke away from facets of these traditions – he would prefer Perrault to Bernini and Lully to Cavalli – the essential features of his artistic taste and judgement remained based on Mazarin's initiation.

And yet the superintendent 'of the government and conduct of the king' never ignored the fact that the king was a child. In 1649, Louis XIV, confronted with the Parisian uprising, had the sense to act and appear the king; yet, at the same time, he was playing with toy soldiers: 'The king having had a fort made in the Palais-Royal gardens became so involved in his attack upon it', said La Porte, 'that he worked up a considerable sweat.' (51) From the real war to war-games and then back again, the young king made the transition with ease and self-assurance.

THE KING'S HEALTH: THE FIRST ILLNESS

When he was nine, Louis was the victim of smallpox, a frequent, serious, and often mortal, illness. Antoine Vallot, future chief physician (*archiatre*) kept a diary of the king's health, by means of which we can reconstruct the distress at court and the vicissitudes of this anxious period.

According to Vallot, the tranquillity of the court and the queen was 'troubled by a sudden and violent pain in the king's bowel and the lower part of His Majesty's spine felt at five o'clock in the evening on Monday, 11 November 1647', in the Palais-Royal (108). The queen immediately sent for the *premier médecin du roi*, François Vaultier. On Tuesday, the king was running a high temperature and he was bled. The same thing happened on the following day at midday. 'The efficacy of this second blood-letting appeared that same day', noted Vallot, 'with the appearance of spots on his face and other parts of his body.' Smallpox had been diagnosed. On Thursday, 'the sieurs Guénault and Vallot, the most renowned and sought-after doctors in Paris, were called for'. Vaultier presided over the case-conference and, following the custom, the new consultants approved the measures already taken and then 'restricted themselves to proposing the continuation of minor treatment'. But that same day, from 4 to 10 p.m. the patient went into a delirious fever. On Friday, Vallot (supported by Guénault) was strongly of the opinion that a third blood-letting should be attempted (the Parisian Faculty of Medicine was very keen on the practice), but ran into a veto from the other physicians.

'Confronted by this contradiction, the *premier médecin*, taking into account the gravity of the illness and the necessity for a remedy, confirmed the views of those who proposed a blood-letting, and this was straightway carried out without further delay.' The king learnt, if only in a state of semi-conscious fever, that he had to submit to the tyranny of the Faculty of Medicine – just as, in 1649, he would have to submit to his confessors when preparing for his First Communion. These were two permanent limits to the authority of the absolute monarchy which should not be forgotten; the king, who is often presented as all-powerful, always accepted them as inevitable.

Although the third blood-letting upset the queen's doctors, its effects on the king 'were admirable and, by the evening, the king's paroxysms had ceased along with his high fever'. On 21 November, however, the king's fever increased 'along with all the other symptoms, and with such violence that the spots appeared dry and badly discoloured'. On the 22nd, all the doctors were in agreement that a fourth 'phlebotomy' should be undertaken. Once this was achieved, the king's temperature subsided. He was more comfortable, albeit very thirsty. But, by this time, the blissful harmony between the doctors was wearing thin and Doctor Vallot now wanted to prescribe the application of a purgative. A glass of calomel and senna was administered and, two hours later, the king's thirst had vanished: the purge 'had cleared the humour which was fermenting in the lower bowel and particularly in the stomach'.

One might be forgiven for imagining that, twenty-six years before *Le Malade Imaginaire*, one had heard the famous triplet:

Clysterium donare,
Postea seignare,
Ensuita purgare.

[Administer a clyster, then a blood-letting, and afterwards a purge.]

'The king proved, during this great and dangerous illness, that one is right to have great hopes of his considerable courage, since, at the age of ten [*sic*], he showed great self-assurance and fortitude during the greatest pain, and, despite the many, oppressive symptoms of his illness, he never refused either a blood-letting or an incision, nor any other remedies proposed to him.' This stoicism would remain with him until the end of his life, giving the lie to the legend that he had been molly-coddled. Anne of Austria, too, had displayed courage. 'The constancy of the queen has been admirable in this affair.'

To complete the trio, the cardinal also received his share of the compliments. 'His Eminence has been strangely perturbed to see his master in so serious a condition and to be in danger of his life; and yet, whilst he laboured under this enormous burden, he never left off ordering the most important affairs of state.' (108) Within these ordinances lay the origins of the Fronde.

3

A Civil War

'**F**ROM MY youth', wrote Louis XIV for the benefit of his
son,

> even the names of pretender kings and mayors of the palace
> irritated me whenever I heard them mentioned. But one must
> present things as they really were. There were dreadful agitations
> throughout the realm both during and after my majority.* There
> was a foreign war in which domestic discord had lost France all
> kinds of advantages. There was a prince of my own family and of
> great renown at the head of my enemies and a host of plots in the
> state. The *parlements* were in the habit of (and enjoyed) usurping
> authority, and in my court fidelity was hardly to be seen without
> some accompanying self-interest. Thus, my superficially most
> submissive subjects were as much a burden and a fear to me as
> the most mutinous. (63)

These 'dreadful agitations' appeared after five years of the
regency when Louis XIV was not yet ten years old and when his
majority could not traditionally be proclaimed before 1651. Can
one imagine the strain of such a crisis upon someone as young as
that?

Until the end of 1647, according to the maréchal d'Estrées:

> it seemed as if the spirit of Cardinal Richelieu, who had governed
> things with such authority, had continued both in the conduct of
> the war and at court. But, in 1648, things changed; the transform-
> ations were so great that, for those who had experienced the first
> five years of the queen's regency, the swiftness of the change and

* His majority was declared in the Parlement of Paris on 7 September 1651.

the confusion and unruliness which lasted from then until 1652 could only be regarded with considerable astonishment. (34)

It is no accident that the marshal should mention Richelieu and nor was he wrong to stress the underlying continuities between the two ministries, the histories of which, when studied together, explain the Fronde.

FROM ONE CARDINAL TO ANOTHER

Richelieu's discovery of Mazarin would remain one of French history's more intriguing mysteries if we were to retain the picture of a brutal, obstinate and headstrong Richelieu. In fact, he showed imaginative flair (political, economic, maritime and colonial), wrote poetry (although his tragedies lacked inspiration) and was more Mazarinist than appearances would suggest. Upon this reading, the combination of his complementary and contrasting qualities with his intuition explains his discovery in Louis XIII's ministry of the presiding genius who succeeded him. Conversely, the stereotype of Mazarin conceals how much there was of Richelieu in him. When one takes into account the similarity between their policies, their loyalty and their patriotism, this becomes clearer.

A satirical poem of 1643, entitled *Richelieu Reincarnate*, began with the couplet:

> He is not dead, he's merely changed his age,
> This cardinal, the object of men's rage. (157)

It is not difficult to imagine the sentiments of those of similar disposition after five years' observation of this strange kind of mimicry. We should not distinguish between a 'bellicose' Richelieu and a 'diplomatic' Mazarin. Both had experienced warfare. If the eighteen years of Richelieu's dominance (1624–42) were marked by twelve years of war, the eighteen years of Mazarin's ministry (1643–61) included no less than sixteen at war. Both Richelieu and Mazarin were obsessed by the struggle against the House of Austria. When this became more intense, Mazarin was obliged to devote more effort to it than his predecessor. The same underlying purposes had resulted in policies very different in shape but similar in aims.

To supply the needs of this interminable war, Richelieu – and then Mazarin – had been forced to enrol, arm and equip large armies, and also to ensure their supply, organize their transportation and garrison strongholds with food and munitions. They had thus to create and develop an administrative infrastructure, in which the army commissioners (*commissaires des guerres*) were the linchpins. Between a judicial state (such as that in France in the sixteenth century) and the more modern French state with its administrative monarchy (1661–1789), there lay a state which one is forced to call a military one. It gradually supplanted its predecessor – as the dictator in ancient Rome, in times of peril, supplanted the consulate – and served as a transition to the more modern state, having, in common with it, a dominance of the 'men of the pen'. In order to co-ordinate the military administration, oversee matters of recruitment, fortifications and defence, and keep an eye on the local military governors, whom the war had rendered too powerful and independent, Richelieu and Mazarin were obliged to breathe new life and power into the institution of the intendants, the *missi dominici* invented in the reign of Henry II who would become Louis XIV's active and docile agents.

The war-effort was immensely costly. Now that war no longer always paid for itself (at least not in France), the maintenance of so many troops, their equipment and transportation, became very burdensome and transformed the budget in a revolutionary way. The royal fiscal regime, less burdensome than that of the seigneurs up until this point, became much more onerous. In the five years preceding the war with Spain (1635), taxation tripled in France (7). In some areas, the weight of the *tailles* was almost quadrupled; in others, Richelieu attempted to introduce the unpopular *gabelle*. It constituted the 'greatest fiscal offensive in French history' (7). It is not surprising that it provoked an equally vigorous popular reaction. As early as 1624, the *croquants* rose in revolt in Quercy in protest at the introduction of royal 'élections' (a fiscal regime in which royal officeholders replaced officials responsible directly to provincial representative assemblies or Estates). In the years from 1635 to 1637, other *croquants* set ablaze the provinces of Guyenne, Saintonge, Angoumois and the Périgord. In 1639, lower Normandy experienced the general uprising known as the revolt of the *nu-pieds*. The ministry of Richelieu took place amidst 'the irruption of peasant revolts' (7). These uprisings are a reliable measure of the pressure of royal taxation. 'The fruits of the politics of the harsh and hard-won victories of France against the Habsburgs were the centralizing institutions of great long-term importance that they created; but they had been paid for at the price of the sacrifice of up to two generations of peasantry' (7) – at least in the provinces of western France.

Mazarin and the regent inherited the foreign policy of Louis XIII's reign and the institutional framework which had pro-voked such popular anger – anger which had created turmoil so endemic as to be almost a civil war. In the summer and autumn of 1643, Cardinal Mazarin had to confront a sustained uprising of *croquants* in Rouergue. He had – like Richelieu before him – to choose between concessions and repression. Like his predecessor he combined both. The estimates for the *taille* in the disturbed areas of Rouergue were at first reduced; and then, in December, when calm had returned, some fifty of the mutinous peasants were led off to the galleys.

The genesis of the Fronde was therefore far from being spon-taneous. In many cases, it was apparently the final spasms of these *croquant* revolts begun a quarter of a century earlier. Although the Fronde began as an urban movement in Paris, this did not prevent it from perpetuating peasant insurrections. It is also the case, though, that the Fronde was not just a popular insurrection, since every class of society was represented in it. While the *croquants* and *nu-pieds* enjoyed the support of only a few indigent petty nobles, the great rebellion of 1648 included princes of the blood, dukes, senior magistrates and rich bourgeois, *privilégiés* and notables; yet without the ability and 'good fortune' of the cardinal, the explosion might have occurred five years earlier.

EXPLAINING THE ILLOGICAL

From 1639, the popular insurrections had shown how much the peasantry were suffering under the unprecedented fiscal pres-sures. However, the Fronde did not begin in the countryside but in the capital. Paris had its share of the poor but the barricades would be the work of the bourgeoisie. It might have been pos-sible to imagine a kind of municipal insurrection manipulated by the Parisian bourgeoisie – whether in commerce or from 'the robe'. But the Fronde was directed by the greatest among the notables: princes of the robe, princes of the Church and princes *tout court*.

The princes who took part in this dangerous game were Monsieur, the brother of Louis XIII; the prince de Condé, 'first prince of the blood' and believed to be the greatest military figure of his generation; and the prince de Conti, Condé's younger brother. There were also the illegitimate scions of the royal house who had been legitimized: the duc de Longueville and the duc de Beaufort. None of them wanted a revolution. They were all royalists, wanting for themselves either places on the Council, or governorships, pensions or gratifications. The triumvirate of the king, the queen mother and Mazarin was not at all to their liking. Monsieur and Condé had not lightly surrendered the role of protector of the queen provided for them in the will of Louis XIII and which the *lit de justice* of 18 May 1643 had blown away like chaff in the wind (105). Five years later, the princes were ready to contest for the prize once again.

Jean-François Paul de Gondi, coadjutor of his uncle the Archbishop of Paris, was a princely prelate who was socially on a par with the princes themselves. He was endowed with more political skill but he shared their sense of ambition. A prelate without an ecclesiastical vocation who was imbued with nostalgia for military command and judged himself more capable than Mazarin of governing France, he would be a member of all the plots, a party to all their treasonable engagements. His position in Paris was of great strategic importance. Indispensable to the princes, a friend to the aristocrats, a master of public opinion through the deployment of his *curés* and the city's bourgeois, it only remained for him to play on the self-esteem of the magistrates in the sovereign courts.

Some of the senior judges – such as Broussel, dean of the Parlement, and the *président* Blancmesnil – played the bourgeois and became party leaders in 1648. But the high Parisian magistrature had insinuated itself into the richest, most influential and enlightened segment of the French nobility. The *parlementaire* magistrates despised the gentry and, although they sometimes married into the families of financiers, they kept their distance from them. The most respected amongst them were already allied to the royal court. Blancmesnil, the *président*, who attracted Mazarin's attention in July 1648, was a Potier by birth and his cousin René Potier was a captain in the royal guards and

was created duc de Tresmes and a peer of the realm by letters-
patent of November 1648. It all helped to elevate the *noblesse de
robe* to the *noblesse d'épée*. The edict on the *tailles* of March 1600
had confirmed in law the customary gradual ennoblement over
three generations in offices in the sovereign courts. The edict of
Paulet (or *paulette*) in 1604 had encouraged the succession of
offices within families. With Mazarin's blessing, the magistrates
in Paris had benefited from notable concessions, particularly
during the regency. *Noblesse de race* status was granted by the
regent to the *maîtres des requêtes* on 10 August 1644, to the magistrates of the Parlement in July 1644, to the Chambre des Comptes in January 1645 and to the Cour des Aides in the following
September (137). Failure to understand the significance of this
torrent of privileges results in a misunderstanding of, first, why
the Parisian robe provoked the Fronde, secondly, why the
aristocrats could ally with them – in an alliance of princes,
coadjutor and magistrates – without demeaning their status,
thirdly, why the Parlement tried to redirect the monarchy itself
and, lastly, why an apparently revolutionary movement would
turn out to be an attempt at a counter-revolution. Every time the
judges called themselves protectors of the people, they revealed
the collective self-interest of the corporation on behalf of which
they spoke and acted.

This pride, coupled with this ambiguous paternalism, created
great temptations. The Parlement of Paris was a court of law, the
world's oldest and most famous judicial tribunal, holding its
sessions in the *palais* on the Ile de la Cité. Its jurisdiction covered
almost a third of the realm. It was also remarkable for being a
court of peers. Princes of the blood and dukes had to come and
take their places, according to their rank, on the seats of the
Great Chamber, and there was not a duke who had not had his
title registered in the Parlement. However, the principal power
of the Parlement lay in its right to register all manner of acts of
sovereign power. With this right went that of 'remonstrance', or
even 'repeated remonstrances'. In cases of prolonged conflict,
the king had the last word, either by the publication of letters of
imperative royal command (*lettres de jussion*) or by the holding of
a *lit de justice* to force the assembly to register the edicts. This
mechanism made the Parlement the guardian of the law, something akin to a constitutional senate.

Herein lay a twofold temptation. On the one hand, there was

an inevitable and traditional tendency to magnify the semi-legislative role of the Parlement, encouraging it either to take on various areas of competence normally within the remit of the Council or to profit from the decline in the provincial Estates and become a more active overseer of royal finances. The moderate *parlementaires* were thus partisans of a monarchy which they 'advised, surrounded and counterbalanced' (233). The other temptation was to transform the Parlement of Paris into a kind of English Parliament, which would change the constitution in France and its *modus operandi*. Both tendencies were present in the Palais de Justice in 1648. The English House of Commons was at this date just appearing as a sovereign body; Charles I was a prisoner and the English Parliament would decide, on 23 December 1648, to put him on trial.

From 1643 to 1648, the financial pressure which began to be felt under Richelieu was sustained by the controller-general (*contrôleur général*), Particelli d'Emery (*surintendant des finances* in 1647). At Mazarin's behest (and to provide the resources for war), Particelli looked to 'extraordinary' means – the legal term for a variety of expedients. Those most affected were the ordinarily exempt, the royal officeholders and the Parisian bourgeois. But, when the rich suffered, the costs were borne by others (merchants, servants, tenants); just as, when the *tailles* increased, the nobility found that the returns from seigneurial dues declined. But it was less the weight of the fiscal regime that aggravated the Parlement than the unprecedented ways of collecting tax. These patrimonial *officiers* detested intendants as *commissaires* of the king. Towards those on the fringes of state power, their hatred was even greater – especially for the tax-farmers (*traitants*), *partisans* and other agents for the collection of the new taxes. Behind a social conflict lay one between a judicial state and a financial state born from wartime expediency.

The *toisé*, an edict of January 1644 which imposed a tax on the houses built outside the ramparts of Paris, was an occasion for the magistrates to appear to sustain the lesser privileged. The tax was, however, registered. The edict of September 1646 increasing the tariffs on goods imported into Paris was only registered after a year's delay. The opposition in the Parlement was more exercised by the unprecedented decline in the value of the *rentes* on the Hôtel de Ville and the non-payment of interest on them. Towards the end of 1647 and at the beginning of 1648, the anger of the *rentiers* provoked public disorders, especially in the rue Saint-Denis. There was a similar outcry against the reduction in the salaries (*gages*) of judicial officers. In these last two cases, the members of the robe felt themselves directly affected. Moreover, the battle for the maintenance of salaries became closely intertwined with the crusade on behalf of the *rentiers*. As there were large numbers of lesser *rentiers* affected by the measures of d'Emery, the actions of the Parlement appeared on the surface to be purely public-spirited.

It would have required a considerable degree of indulgence to have discerned the same disinterest in the *parlementaire* campaign against the creation of offices and for the maintenance of the *droit annuel*. Yet the queen mother found it impossible to impose an edict creating twelve new offices of *maître des requêtes*: she held a *lit de justice* on 15 January 1648 only to find the Parlement boldly annulling the forced registration on the following day. For three months, from February to April 1648, Paris witnessed a war of official declarations, edicts, ordinances of the Council and decisions of the sovereign courts. For the Chambre des Comptes, the Cour des Aides and the Cour des Monnaies joined their opposition to that of the Parlement. The question of the salaries of officials was again raised, along with that of whether their purchased right to the inheritance of their offices, the *paulette*, was to be maintained or whether it was to be re-established and if so on what terms. But these were sectional matters and they were contrary to, rather than supportive of, the common weal. (The circumstances of 1648 seem to foreshadow those of 1788.) For, if the realm was invited to make sacrifices to replenish the state's coffers, why should the poorest be those who made the most sacrifices? Why should Richelieu and Mazarin have increased the *tailles* on the peasantry and refused to levy a tax upon the bourgeois of Paris or make the senior judges contribute to the common effort? In what way did the cuts in the salaries of a judge on behalf of the war-effort differ, if at all, from the sacrifices demanded of the common people?

And yet the Parisian magistrates clung to the pretext of fiscal 'persecution' and went one step further and created the outline of a constituent assembly. On 13 May, the sovereign courts of the capital decided formally to unite in an *arrêt d'union*. Their deputies would henceforth sit together in a novel assembly, known as the 'Chambre Saint-Louis', a 'kind of republic within the monarchy' (233). The queen was more worried than Mazarin by their move and she declared the *arrêt d'union* and, with it, the sessions of the Chambre illegal. Despite this, it proceeded to hold its meetings.

Mazarin then took charge of events and the regent accepted, against her will, the need for a period of concessions (whilst awaiting the successes abroad which would enable the queen and her minister to restore their authority). The Chambre Saint-Louis was in session from 30 June until 9 July and it put together a kind of charter of twenty-seven articles. There were all sorts of issues touched on in it: the defence of subjects, the supposed tyranny of the fisc, the defence of the authority of the courts against that of the Council and against the power of the intendants. They demanded the suppression of the intendants, the dismissal of the *traitants* and the introduction of a kind of habeas corpus (long enshrined in English law, and given an additional legislative basis in 1679). The creation of new offices was to be stopped and a judicial tribunal (*chambre de justice*) set up to prosecute the financiers. They demanded freedom of commerce and a diminution in the *tailles*. The latter demand cost them nothing and was designed for popular appeal. But the sovereign judges had not forgotten their own interests: condensed into the third article, this formed a potentially explosive clause. In it, the Parlement and the courts declared their right to oversee the application of the fiscal decisions of the Crown. They thus, potentially, would become the main instrument of power in the state. If the Parlement succeeded in exercising the 'right of consenting to the levy of taxation', it would be transformed into a House of Commons.

On 9 July 1648, Mazarin sacrificed Particelli d'Emery. On the 18th, a royal edict confirmed many of the Chambre Saint-Louis' terms, notably the abolition of the intendants and the diminution of the *tailles*. But the Parlement, far from being appeased, grew more insistent, particularly after the speeches of Broussel and Blancmesnil. The queen and her minister pretended to give further ground. By a declaration of 31 July virtually all the terms of the Chambre Saint-Louis were given the force of law (233). But it is dangerous to make concessions from a position of weakness. Broussel knew that and increased his demands, while Anne of Austria awaited the moment to take her revenge. It would cost her dearly.

THE CONFLICTS UNFOLD: THE OLD FRONDE

The events of the Fronde are not easily presented. Its inner logic is hidden beneath the surface texture of intrigues, plots and *coups de théâtre*. Its history has still to be written and it is not necessarily the case that the means to do so will be found in the analysis of the thousands of *mazarinades*, the pamphlets which attacked the cardinal. This was the Fronde which the young king experienced at first hand, painfully learning from it, reading Machiavelli and Tacitus instead of, as normal at his age, Aesop's fables. The first, or 'Old', Fronde was political madness. Neither the victory at Lens (20 August 1648) nor the great treaty at Münster (24 October 1648) prevented the magistrates of the sovereign courts, the grandees of the royal court and M. de Gondi, coadjutor of Paris, from rebelling against the authority of the queen under the pretext of defending the interests of the young king and the realm against Mazarin. The Parlement, jealous guardian of the fundamental laws of the country, infringed them with impunity, forgetting that sovereignty in France was never divisible and that Anne of Austria exercised it in the name of her son. To attack the powers of the regent was thus inevitably to attack the prerogatives of the king.

The king knew that the Peace of Westphalia, which had humiliated the emperor and diminished the authority of the Holy Roman Empire, was an event of the first importance. He understood, also, that the revolt of his subjects, on their chosen pretext, was laughable. The name of the Fronde was well chosen, based as it was on that of a children's game. Louis XIV had no reason to dissociate himself from his mother or his godfather (even if his daily life was disrupted as he changed endlessly from one residence to another sleeping in undarned linen). This was something that irritated the *frondeurs*, whose politics consisted in pretending that they were attempting to snatch the king from the hands of his errant servants. Without the loyalty of the young prince to his mother, everything would have shifted and this revolt, which never succeeded in becoming a revolution, would have offered the extraordinary spectacle of its becoming an anti-monarchical insurrection, sanctioned by a king. These facts should not be overlooked; nor should the paradoxes or the principles of French public law. We view them at a distance, but it is from within an encircled Palais-Royal that we must comprehend Louis XIV's reaction to the complex events of these civil disturbances.

Whilst the coadjutor Gondi presided over the *Te Deum* sung at Notre-Dame on 26 August 1648 for the victory at Lens, the queen mother ordered the arrest of the *parlementaire* ringleaders, Blancmesnil and Broussel. The result was 1,260 barricades on the streets of Paris. During the night of 26–27 August, Gondi and the duc de Longueville agreed the terms of their coup. Once Broussel had been liberated, the barricades disappeared, but the royal court left the capital on 13 September on the pretext of the health of the king. Anne gained little by this manœuvre and Mazarin even less. Having left Gaston d'Orléans and Condé behind to discuss the details of an accord with the delegates from the Parlement, the queen mother signed, on 22 October, not without misgivings, the declaration of Saint-Germain. All the demands of the *parlementaires* were accepted, both those presented in the Chambre Saint-Louis, and later ones such as the abandonment of *lettres de cachet*. By one of those curious coincidences, the Parlement verified this capitulation on the same day as the signing of the Peace of Westphalia. It is easy to understand Mazarin's passing comment, made on 30 October: 'You must admit that it requires a commitment to the very limit and a quite extraordinary zeal to redouble one's efforts in public service – as I do – when one is treated so badly and at a time when it would seem possible to say without vanity that my efforts are beginning to bear fruit.' (70)

After this interval and the declaration of 22 October, the royal court returned to Paris. The queen was preparing her revenge but she had to retain the support of Monsieur and Condé. Under the cover of Twelfth Night celebrations, she fled from Paris with her son during the night of 5–6 January 1649. Mazarin wrote: 'We must give thanks to God for Her Majesty's resolution to leave Paris. The resulting events clearly prove that we would all have been quickly caught up in a plot to seize the person of the king; and that once this had happened, all hopes for the minority would have been lost, all attempts to moderate the authority of the Parlement, or do anything but what it wanted, would have failed.' Three days later, the Parlement declared the cardinal a 'disturber of public tranquillity' whilst the leaders of the Fronde – d'Elbeuf, Bouillon, the coadjutor, Beaufort, Conti and the rest – swore to sustain the Parlement until the hated first

minister was expelled from the country. In this Fronde, Conti
was the most important grandee, Beaufort the most popular, and
Bouillon the most conspiratorial. But none was more busy and
effective than the coadjutor.

Of Gondi, Mazarin painted an amusing and satirical portrait:
'He is pious, understanding, moderate, good, humble, true, loving the tranquillity of the state for which he works with ease and
success, knowing how necessary it is to negotiate with the
Spanish. He is an enemy to all intrigue and burns with ardour
for the greatness of the state and the re-establishment of royal
authority.' (70) Whilst awaiting his succession to the see of Paris
(his uncle was still alive), Gondi was Archbishop of Corinth *in
partibus*. Before he added a temporal authority to his spiritual
title, he showed himself as an agitator by equipping a regiment
of *chevau-légers*, the so-called Corinthian regiment, the first rebel
troops of the Fronde. But, although placed under the command
of Beaufort, the coadjutor's troops lost the skirmish at Juvisy (28
January 1649). Condé called this, in a joking reference to the
New Testament Epistle, 'Corinthians I'. It was no better at
Bourg-la-Reine at the beginning of February; 'Corinthians II',
calculated Condé.

The king, the queen mother and the cardinal became the
masters of the situation thanks to the victor of Rocroi. Paris was
in awe of Condé. The royal court gave support, albeit without
enthusiasm, to his overbearing arrogance; for there was no one
to replace him. On 8 February, he took Charenton and from 12
to 28 February, his troops tightened their grip around Paris. The
Parisian reaction knew almost no bounds. The physician Guy
Patin, later a dean of the Faculty of Medicine in Paris, wrote on
6 March: 'The printing of new libels against Mazarin and all
those associated with his unfortunate party continues apace . . .
and nothing pleases so much as those which claim to be "against
this wretched tyrant, cheat, imposter, clown, buffoon, Italian
thief, here held in common odium by everybody."' The insults
became daily more bitter. In July, a pathetic pamphlet entitled
'The Custodian of the Queen's Bed' appeared which, in crude
alexandrine couplets, elaborated an old libel (dating from 1643)
claiming that Mazarin was Anne of Austria's lover: 'Doubt no
more, good people, he kisses her, it's true.' (84) Louis XIV did
not read these calumnies, but his valet La Porte was so opposed
to the cardinal that the young king no doubt received a milder

version of the *mazarinades*. These libels pretended to a great loyalty towards the king. But what was the value of such loyalty if, at the same time, the king's godfather and the queen were publicly vilified? One of their effects was surely to reinforce the affection that Louis felt towards the cardinal.

Whilst the *premier président* Mathieu Molé opened up negotiations with Anne of Austria, the generals of the Fronde contacted Spain through the mediation of M. de Turenne. On 4 March, the *parlementaire* Fronde sent diplomats to the royal court and, on 11 March, were signed the articles of Reuil which the Parlement decided to validate on 1 April. Molé had succeeded in isolating, firstly, his colleagues and, then, a large group of Parisians from the blundering cohort of the Fronde generals. The peace was inevitably a compromise. The royal court confirmed the concessions already obtained by the magistrates in July and October 1648, whilst the Parlement withdrew its anti-Mazarin declaration of January 1649. Paris accepted it quickly and with warmth but the Archbishop of Corinth took two months to make his mind up before he went to Compiègne and invited the royal court to return to Paris.

On 18 August 1649, Louis XIV entered the capital to considerable acclaim, unlike Mazarin, a lesson in the fickleness of popular emotions. The king's return 'evoked cheers, shouts of joy; and every heart sent forth these lovely words, inspired by every faculty of their souls: "Vive le Roi. Vive Louis" ' (70). Even Guy Patin, who hated large crowds, came to cheer the royal procession: 'I was there too, and saw a greater crowd than I had ever seen before. The queen said over supper that evening in the Palais Cardinal that she would never have believed that the people of Paris so loved their king ... the following day, Thursday, 19 August, all the corporations and guilds of the city came to offer him their obedience and compliment the queen on her return and for having brought the king back to Paris.' (84) The coadjutor would not be among the most reluctant to pay his respects.

THE CONDÉAN FRONDE

Hardly had the *parlementaire* Fronde been pacified than the noble Fronde began. The origins of this new conflict lay in the demands of Condé, who wanted a high price for his services to the queen. He even obtained a promise that he would lead the government, and on 2 October the cardinal signed a declaration to the effect that he would guarantee to seek the advice of M. le Prince before making any important appointment. Meanwhile, Monsieur had been reconciled with his sister-in-law, whilst Gondi tried once more to raise Paris.

For his part, Mazarin continued the war against Spain, repressed the troubles in the south of France, saw to the frontiers of the northern provinces and fomented dissension among the former *frondeurs* to the queen's advantage. His political skills were never better demonstrated than during the autumn of 1649. Even if Louis XIV was not in a position to appreciate all his various initiatives, the cardinal's godson witnessed the most astonishing demonstration of political acumen that could possibly be provided for a young king. For example, Mazarin profited from the quarrel between Gondi and his secretary, Guy Joly (on 11 December), to stir dissension between Gondi and the prince de Condé. He then won the allegiance of the duchesse de Chevreuse and Gaston d'Orléans to the royal court, thus dividing the rebels. Condé, Conti and Longueville were arrested on 19 January 1650 and incarcerated at Vincennes. Monsieur took refuge in his contingent loyalism and declared: 'Here is a good catch; they have taken a lion, a monkey and a fox!' (70) Unfortunately, the lion, the monkey and the fox had supporters, and the arrest of the princes restarted the civil war.

The queen had to pacify Normandy and Burgundy and she left Paris in the hands of Monsieur (Gaston d'Orléans) whilst she went to Guyenne to restore loyalty there. But Gaston's loyalty was insecure, and Gondi, still waiting for his cardinal's hat, tried to bring him into his orbit. Mazarin, on the other hand, made great efforts to detach the duc de Bouillon and his brother, Turenne, from the Fronde; but this able manœuvring was still somewhat premature. In August 1650, Turenne had some successes in Champagne, and so alarmed the court that the queen transferred Condé, Conti and Longueville to Le Havre in order not to lose the hostages. In November, Gondi joined the princes' grouping, and the two Frondes – that of Gondi and Paris on the one hand, and that of the princes on the other – were united. They might possibly have succeeded towards the end of 1650, had Turenne not been beaten at Rethel by the small force under the maréchal du Plessis-Praslin (Choiseul).

They were again out in force in February 1651. On 30 January, a formal treaty uniting the two Frondes was signed, the handiwork of Anne of Gonzaga, the Princess Palatine. Alongside this ambitious young lady were the princes' representatives: the duc de Nemours, the maréchal de la Mothe-Houdancourt and others. They all accepted Gaston d'Orléans as their leader and swore to obey him, whilst he undertook to liberate his cousins. The exile of Mazarin was to be the first step. On 4 February, after being addressed by Gondi, the Parlement demanded the cardinal's exile. Mazarin could not turn a blind eye and, menaced with threats to his own life, he left Paris two days later. It was the beginning of his first exile.

Had the twelve-year-old king thought that the exile of his godfather would act as a sop to make France governable again, the provocative actions of the *frondeurs* would have made him think again. Charles de l'Aubespine, marquis de Châteauneuf, the *garde des sceaux* from 2 March 1650, strove to obtain the now vacant post of first minister. On 9 February 1651, Gondi had the audacity to surround the Palais-Royal. Châteauneuf had revealed to him the plan that the king and queen were to take flight. During the night of the 9th to the 10th, the regent was obliged to watch helplessly while a crowd filed through the royal bedchamber so that they could be assured as to the king's presence there, as though he were a precious hostage. Louis feigned sleep, and these few minutes must have passed more slowly than any others in his long life.

The following day, the king placed his signature – as the queen directed – on the order for the liberation of the princes, whilst, on 17 February, the Parlement registered a royal declaration to the effect that 'no foreigner, even if a naturalized subject', should henceforth be promoted a minister. Mazarin – who had undertaken to release the princes at Le Havre – retired first to Bouillon, and then to the electorate of Cologne, where he remained in contact with Anne of Austria, while the queen remained in Paris almost a prisoner and the Parlement began (on 12 March) a lengthy trial against him. From there, he surveyed events in France and made plans for the future. On the one hand, he ordered his intendant, Colbert, to prepare an inventory of his wealth and, on the other, he used a large part of it to recruit reliable soldiers to his service. The King of Spain's offers to the cardinal, made in April 1651, were in vain: 'With all politeness, I replied that I would do my duty', said Mazarin, 'and end my life as a servant of France both in my thoughts and in my desires; for I could not act otherwise.' (70) He corresponded with Michel Le Tellier from exile, stressing three points: the divergence of interests between the princes and Paris, the lack of common ground among the aristocrats, and the imminent declaration of the king's majority.

The queen, for her part, fully understood the importance of the king's coming of age, for, as soon as he was proclaimed a major, it would be difficult for anyone to claim to represent the interests of His Majesty against a wronged regent or a wrongful minister. Whilst she awaited this moment, she weaved so tortuous a path that even Mazarin trembled – both for himself and for the state. On 2 April, she recalled the chancellor, Pierre Séguier (disgraced thirteen months previously), removed the seals from Châteauneuf (and gave them to the *premier président* Molé) and named Léon Bouthillier, comte de Chavigny, who held the confidence of Condé, as her first minister. Gaston d'Orléans was outraged, and Gondi found himself isolated as the princes seemed to have recovered royal favour. But in May everything was reversed. 'Mazarin governs France from Brühl through the regent and her ministers by secret correspondence.' (233) The influence of Condé decreased and the regent had several meetings with the coadjutor, who was appeased by the renewed promise of a cardinal's hat. With this degree of ambiguity in the relations with the political factions, it is possible to discern the distinctive patterns of Mazarinian diplomacy.

In July 1651, there were further dramatic political moves. Anne of Austria appeared to sacrifice everything to the ambitions of Condé and temporarily dismissed three overtly pro-Mazarin ministers (Servien, Lionne and Le Tellier) in order to satisfy the prince. But July was also a month full of surprises, because, on the 31st, Condé quarrelled with the queen. August provided the most baroque melodrama and an elaborate sequence of events recalling the famous Day of Dupes in 1630. On the 17th, Anne presented a new declaration before the Parlement: whilst confirming the exile of Mazarin, she also denounced the shadowy intrigues of Condé. But the day after, Condé came to explain his actions, and avoided a skirmish with Gondi. The regent quickly assigned troops to the coadjutor. On

the 21st, the prince and Gondi met once more in the Palais de
Justice, and Mathieu Molé intervened to appease the two sides.
'The next day one of the moments of pure comedy in the Fronde
took place: the retinue of Condé, returning from the Parlement,
came upon a religious procession led by the coadjutor. The
prince descended from his carriage and came to kneel before
Retz [Gondi], who gravely blessed him and then knelt in
reverence before him.' (233)

The history of these intrigues and conflicts – even in this
simplified form – appears immensely complex. Louis XIV,
however, although immersed in the events, did not cut a bad
figure. It is possible that he was at that time more devoted to
Mazarin than was his mother, despite the colourful language in
her letters to the cardinal. At all events, Colbert wrote to
Mazarin on 2 September 1651: 'I am charged to make you
acquainted with the fact that the behaviour of Châteauneuf and
the coadjutor seems more and more to be insincere as regards
both the queen and yourself . . . they are installing themselves in
the queen's mind through flattery' (70), pretending to sustain
the cause of the former first minister but in reality prolonging his
exile. M. Colbert was well informed. Under pressure from the
anti-Mazarin cabal, Anne of Austria had demanded that the
exiled cardinal should go to Italy to prepare for the forthcoming
conclave. The cardinal was wild with anger: Colbert was
instructed to tell the queen 'that such treatment was unheard of,
and that she had taken advantage of his good nature by instruct-
ing someone to write to him, telling him to go to Rome like a
knave' (70). Within days of the king's majority, therefore, no
political move was without an ulterior motive.

LOUIS' MAJORITY

The time had come to proclaim the king's majority, the only way
to be rid of Gaston d'Orléans and the prince de Condé and the
only means of preventing equivocal 'loyalism'. It took place in
the Parlement of Paris on 7 September 1651 with all the pomp of
a *lit de justice*. 'On the upper tiers to the right' were seated the
queen mother, the duc d'Anjou, Gaston d'Orléans, the prince de
Conti, the dukes and peers, the marshals of France, the Archbishop of Paris and the Bishops of Senlis and Tarbes. 'On the

upper tiers to the left' were the ecclesiastical peers, the *conseillers de grand-chambre*, the *présidents* and *conseillers* of the Parlement, the papal nuncio and 'the ambassadors of Portugal, Venice, Malta and Holland, and many other people of rank' (105). The latter, accommodated on seats on the courtroom floor, included councillors of state, *maîtres des requêtes*, the princesse de Carignan and her daughter Louise, 'the queen's daughters' and provincial governors. At the centre sat the king 'in his *lit de justice*'. At his feet were the duc de Joyeuse, who was the grand chamberlain, and the comte d'Harcourt. Then came the provost of Paris M. de Saint-Brisson, 'the guards of the chamber kneeling with hats doffed and bearing a chased silver mace', the chancellor Séguier 'wearing a mantle of crimson velvet and a satin gown of the same colour', the *grand maître* of France, who was the master of ceremonies, the *présidents à mortier*, with Molé at their head, the secretaries of state, the *avocats généraux* Talon and Bignon, and the *procureur général* Fouquet. In a wing to one side sat Henrietta-Maria of France, the widow of Charles I, and the Duke of York, his son, Mademoiselle, the duc d'Orléans' daughter, 'and many other duchesses and ladies of quality'.

The august assembly having taken their places, Louis made a short speech: 'Messieurs, I have come to my Parlement to tell you that, following the law of my state, I wish henceforth to take upon myself its government and administration. I trust that, with God's grace, this will be with piety and justice. Monsieur the chancellor will explain my intentions in greater detail.' There then followed the chancellor's speech. The queen then turned to her son and declared: 'We are now in the ninth year since, according to the wishes of the late king, my dread lord, I took charge of your education and the government of your state. God has, by his goodness, blessed my work and kept you safe, you who are so dear and precious to me and to all your subjects. As the law of the kingdom presently calls you to govern this kingdom, I remit to you with great pleasure the power which was given to me for its government. I trust that God will give you grace and help you with the spirit of vigour and prudence and give you a happy reign.' (105) Anne of Austria then knelt before her son, who went forward to kiss her. Returning to his place, he paid her this compliment: 'Madame, I thank you for the pains you have taken with my education and the administration of my kingdom. I beg you to continue to give me the benefits of your good counsel and desire that, after me, you should be the head of my Council.' Everyone then came to offer reverence to the king, and Molé made a speech on behalf of the Parlement before several royal decisions were presented for registration. One concerned blasphemers; another renewed the edict against duelling; and a third declared the prince de Condé innocent.

But the king soon learnt that his cousin had been negotiating with Spain since the previous May (he would sign a treaty on 6 November). This was why, on 8 October 1651, Louis issued a declaration against the princes de Condé and de Conti, the duchesse de Longueville, the duc de Nemours and the duc de la Rochefoucauld. A few days later (on 31 October), Louis XIV and the queen mother wrote to Mazarin from Poitiers inviting him to return. The cardinal was much relieved and, in the course of his journey back across Champagne, became aware that provincial opinion either was in the course of changing, or had already shifted behind the royal court. In a pointless and malicious gesture, the Parlement put a price on Mazarin's head on 29 December and began the sale of his library. On 28 January 1652, Louis saw his godfather arrive in Poitiers at the head of 1,500 horse and 2,000 foot soldiers. Mazarin quickly re-established his former authority. He dismissed Châteauneuf and recalled the duc de Bouillon and Bouillon's brother Turenne to lead the royal army, and established a plan of campaign. Like Richelieu, Mazarin never drew a line between military strategy and diplomacy; like his predecessor he excelled in both. Louis' first significant line of action as a major, and one of great merit too, was to check his own self-esteem and until 1661 to accept (now voluntarily), as he would accept all good advice, nearly all the decisions of his godfather.

Nothing had been settled, even if the Fronde was tiring. 'Hydra-headed rebellion' – as one would have said then – was still capable of extraordinary convulsions. Monsieur was so hostile to the cardinal that he signed an alliance, on 24 January 1652, with Condé. The latter had devastated Guyenne whilst the duc de Rohan had raised an insurrection in Angers and the duchesse de Montpensier, La Grande Mademoiselle, tried to do the same in Orléans. But the king's troops retook Angers on 28 February, and Mazarin set up plans to bring the king back to Paris. The project was not ideal. The provinces were exhausted and Paris, although it was still active and able to be rallied, also displayed signs of weariness. One document asserted that the capital had more than 60,000 poor within its walls on 20 June 1652, one in seven of the population (70). Five days later, a nicely phrased 'counter-*mazarinade*' was distributed in Paris:

> I am for neither prince nor Mazarin, I am for no party or faction ... I want peace and hate war. I am a loyal Frenchman and I only take part when the interests of the country of my birth are concerned ...
>
> Go in force to the Palais d'Orléans to His Highness [Gaston d'Orléans] and tell him that you are weary of such misery and that you want your king and peace and that he should be allowed to come without preconditions to his noble city (*bonne ville*) of Paris and receive the obedience and love of his people. (70)

On 29 June, the royal court took up residence at Saint-Denis. Three forces were close by: the royal army under Turenne, newly recruited and keen to acquire the king's goodwill; Paris itself, where the duc d'Orléans never succeeded in establishing his authority; and finally M. le Prince (Condé), the ally of Spain, commanding a small army encamped at Saint-Cloud. In principle, the two Frondes could have united once more and made things difficult for the royal court. In fact, the Parisians detested the victor of Rocroi and the capital was weary; loyalism had spread widely since the declaration of the king's majority. It would be sufficient, therefore, to prevent Condé joining forces with the duc d'Orléans, to defeat him in open battle and then enter Paris, whose gates would be opened automatically to the king. The Fronde could be mastered in two days.

As with all good plans, circumstances sent this one astray, notably on the night of 2 July. The prince de Condé circled the walls of the city, intending to enter Paris via Charenton. Turenne harried him close by the porte Saint-Antoine and the maréchal de la Ferté, with artillery, delivered a rude awakening to the enemy's forces. Condé was about to be overwhelmed when Mademoiselle ordered the cannon of the Bastille to fire on the royal forces whilst, at the same time, she opened the gates of the city to her cousin. The solidarity of the princes was reinforced by their common peril.

Paris then witnessed a summer of extraordinary developments. Condé encircled the Hôtel de Ville on 4 July and damaged the surrounding areas of the city. The Parlement briskly usurped legislative authority on 20 July, and declared Gaston d'Orléans *lieutenant général* of the kingdom and Condé as its generalissimo. But August brought something of a pause in these upheavals. Against the rebels in the capital, Mazarin delivered a double blow. On 7 August, a group of moderate judges in the Parlement, led by Mathieu Molé and Fouquet, arrived in Pontoise, obeying a royal declaration of 31 July which had ordered the transfer there from Paris of that sovereign court. Henceforth, if hot-headed judges decided on declarations, ordinances and regulations, they would be acting with the most manifest illegality. The transferred court in Pontoise, on the other hand, progressively increased its numbers with the rallying of the more pacific elements. Secondly, it was informed on 18 August that His Majesty had consented to the voluntary departure of Cardinal Mazarin. The wily politician knew that if he retired from events for a period then the princes, the more stubborn *parlementaires*, and even all those Parisians claiming that they only opposed the king because he had Mazarin as his minister would be disarmed. The cardinal's hat handed to Gondi on 11 September, with nice timing, helped to change people's minds in Paris.

Then everything came into place. The king made an unforgettable royal entry into Paris on 21 October. 'Nearly everybody from the city came to greet him outside at Saint-Cloud', claimed Michel Le Tellier (70). On the 22nd, the Parlement was reestablished in Paris. On the 25th, the duc d'Orléans put his signature to a declaration of submission. The day after, Louis XIV wrote to Mazarin: 'My cousin, it is time to bring an end to the afflictions you have willingly suffered through love of me.' On 12 November, the monarch signed a new declaration against the last of the rebels (Condé, Conti, Madame de Longueville, La Rochefoucauld, the prince de Talmond and the rest). On 19 December, he arranged the arrest of Cardinal Retz – Gondi, from whom, if not all, at least a good measure of the trouble had flowed. Finally, on 3 February 1653, Mazarin – who had made good use of the latter period of his exile in bringing back to the king the obedience of the stronghold fortresses of the duchy of Bar – made a triumphal return to Paris. Amidst such damage to the body politic, it only remained to begin the reconstruction.

4

The Lessons of the Fronde

FROM THE age of nine to the age of fourteen – during the years when his noble or bourgeois contemporaries were mastering a good Latin education at the hands of the Jesuits, the King of France witnessed appalling divisions in the country and endured considerable tribulations. An individual with a less well-adjusted equilibrium would have been scarred for life; all are agreed on that point. But the Fronde did not merely leave an impression on the king's senses; it formed his mental outlook and forged his character. Mazarin had been an excellent mentor, always preferring practical instruction in the affairs of the realm over a more scholastic education. He had not, of course, deliberately provoked a civil war; a tactic which might have been fatal both for himself and for France. But as he returned from exile at the height of his authority, he knew that the times of troubles had, better than any other experience could have done, developed Louis' intelligence, political appreciation, memory and determination. The brutal train of events which shook the nation between 1648 and 1653 made him grow up from an adolescent prince into a great king. From the complex and embattled inheritance of Louis XIII would emerge a more modern realm, in some respects a model for others to follow. 'The Fronde, which might have ruined the monarchy, emancipated it.'*

* The apposite expression of Alexandre Dumas.

THE BANNERS OF REBELLION

One of the inventors of the *honnête homme* of the generation of Louis XIV aptly wrote: 'I believe that, to form the common sense and opinions of young princes . . . it would not be pointless to accustom them at an early age to see things as they are, clearly and lucidly.' (72) But, unless Louis XIV had been short-sighted, he could scarcely have failed to see 'clearly and lucidly' the part played in the rebellion by the aristocrats, as manifest as during the worst days of the Catholic League at the end of the sixteenth century.

The *parlementaires* who took up a stand in Paris in 1648 were not the victims of a crisis. If they befriended Port-Royal this was not because their mental outlook drove them to some form of collective pessimism. They had just obtained, in 1644, nobility of the first degree and they took their new status very seriously. Among the most senior ranks of the *noblesse de robe* – the ministers – there were those who had shown divided loyalties. The chancellor Séguier took part in the Fronde. Michel Le Tellier, secretary of state for war, was often on the brink of doing the same. The clergy was divided. Gondi, the coadjutor, who wanted a cardinalcy and was granted it on 19 February 1652, was not the only bishop in the Fronde's ranks.* Moreover, the House of Gondi was almost princely in the extent of its influence and clientele. St Vincent de Paul was one of his *fidèles*. The Fronde would have its saint, as well as its cardinal.

Such reflections might have led the king to meditate on the ingratitude of men and the extraordinary ingratitude of grandees. At any one moment in the Fronde, a number of peers supported it. The escutcheons of the *frondeurs* included those of the duc de la Rochefoucauld (who joined the rebellion in December 1650), and of the ducs de Luynes, de Brissac, de Noirmoutier and de Vitry (who all joined as early as 1649). According to Madame de Nemours, Luynes committed himself 'through devotion to a somewhat misunderstood Jansenism'. The king also noticed among the rebels François-Henri de Montmorency-Bouteville (1628–95), posthumous son of a *frondeur* before the Fronde who had been condemned and beheaded in 1627 for duelling illegally.

---

* The pope promoted Retz to the cardinalcy on 19 February 1652, and the king provided him with his biretta on 11 September.

In addition to the ducal contingent, the Fronde also enjoyed the support of the 'foreign princes': the duc de Bouillon and his brother, the vicomte de Turenne. The latter rallied to the king at an opportune moment but the head of the house hesitated. It appeared as though 'Monsieur de Bouillon had fallen in with the *parlementaire* interests [in 1649], upon the pretext that the court had not compensated him for his loss of the sovereignty of Sedan, which he claimed had been seized from him by the late king'. But, as the duchesse de Nemours suspected, 'it is much more likely that M. de Bouillon took the part of the Parisians on the assumption that he would be the leading figure there'. Turenne and Bouillon were in addition allied to the royal house, distant cousins of the king.

At another level, this revolutionary pantheon included the legitimized princes. The duc de Longueville was a descendant, like Louis XIV, of Charles V de Valois in the paternal line. He had been a member of the council of the regency and he was governor of Normandy. He was accepted as a prince not merely because of his own pedigree but also because he had married Anne-Geneviève de Bourbon, the prince de Condé's sister. Her influence over her husband was great. 'Madame de Longueville understood little of political affairs' (80) but she was by instinct a *frondeur*, like the rest of her family. The Vendômes were the same. No one was ignorant of the fact that the duc de Beaufort, the 'king of Les Halles [the Parisian market-place]', was a cousin to Louis himself or that he had already played a leading part in the 'cabale des Importants', a *fronde* before the Fronde.

The overall paradox in the Fronde was the involvement of almost all the royal house in an anti-French movement. To the fore were Condé and Conti, arrested as rebels, released, and then rebellious again. Condé was the victor of Rocroi, of Freiburg, of Nördlingen and of Lens and, like Conti, a prince of the blood. His reputation as a successful military leader further underlines the foolhardiness and criminal negligence of his political and military standpoint. It was in full knowledge of the facts that Louis XIV signed the declaration of 12 November 1652 condemning Condé and Conti, the duchesse de Longueville and other nobles in the rebellion as guilty of treason (70).

But there was still worse to come. Beyond the princes of the blood, the heirs to the royal house were also engaged in the Fronde. Gaston d'Orléans, called 'Monsieur', brother to Louis

XIII and the king's uncle, took part in the rebellion along with his daughter, La Grande Mademoiselle, under cover of their hatred for Mazarin. Mademoiselle opened the gates of Paris to Condé and commanded the Bastille cannon against the royal army. Posterity has accorded her a kind of half-baroque, half-chivalric image which has inclined historians towards indulgence on her behalf, but Louis XIV knew that cannon and muskets were lethal weapons. He knew too that Mademoiselle was his cousin. The interests of the state would not allow him to forget the criminal folly of the battle of the faubourg Saint-Antoine. The duc d'Orléans could offer neither his youth nor a romantic image by way of excuse. He consorted with the adversaries of the king, the queen mother and the cardinal, repeatedly trying to run with the hare and hunt with the hounds. 'M. the duc d'Orléans was always on the *frondeurs*' side when he was with them; but when he talked to the queen, this all disappeared. And he changed his mind so often that it was almost impossible for any of the factions to build anything solid on him.' (80) Not even Retz manœuvred in such an unscrupulous fashion; but, then, the cardinal was not Louis XIII's brother.

We need to make a considerable effort to separate the history of the Fronde from the romance which has surrounded it. Louis XIV, however, had been directly involved and (despite the fact that the worst *frondeurs* declared themselves to be royalists) he had no need to embellish a sad and often bloody reality. That his peers, his cousins, his uncle, his heirs and his commanders had been caught up in this spider's web would leave a permanent impression on him. He often pardoned them, but he never forgot the conspiracies of the aristocrats, who had been so richly rewarded by the monarchy, and especially the treason of the closer members of his family. The troubles were by no means over before Louis XIV pardoned some and made his displeasure known to others. The twelve-year-old king who signed the letter offering pardon to the vicomte de Turenne on 6 March 1651 overcame his antipathy and, like a hero from a Corneille play, declared in the letter: 'I excuse all that you have done and wish to forget it.' (107) Louis thus gained a precious ally and the best military chief of his first two wars. Against this, when Cardinal Retz was arrested on 19 December 1652 (Mazarin would return on 3 February of the following year), it was a sign to everyone that this was a treason the king would never forgive.

The Protestants took no part in the Fronde; but that did not prevent the demolition of their churches from 1661 onwards. Port-Royal remained loyal; but that did not prevent an accumulation of political and theological grievances against it. Fouquet did not participate in the Fronde; but his fidelity counted for nothing during his trial. On the other hand, those who later became the king's most competent generals fought at various times for the Fronde. This was true of Condé and his cousin and rival, Turenne, of the maréchal de Luxembourg, of Beaufort (who was victorious at Candie before his death, in the true style of a grandson of Henry IV), and even of good old Vauban. Saint-Aignan's loyalty earned him a dubious reward (224); and La Rochefoucauld, for his defection, would deserve his disgrace. For Saint-Simon, the author of the *Maxims* was an example of a *frondeur* 'to whom the king never gave a pardon' (94). It would be better to say that he was a rebel whom the king had perhaps pardoned, privately in the daily recitation of his *Pater Noster*, but whose felony he never succeeded in forgetting.

In his capacious memory, the king stored up the names of those who had revolted, accompanied with their titles and honours and a summary of their errors. He knew, thanks to Péréfixe and Mazarin, the details of previous rebellions (from the death of Henry IV to the conspiracy of Cinq-Mars); his tutors had outlined for him the civil wars in France in the sixteenth century. He understood that the Fronde was based on a peculiar set of circumstances, but that the political lightheadedness of the grandees was a structural fact. To punish or pardon? The choice remained specific to each case but each decision was to be seen as an example to others; such was his concern for over sixty years.

If this process involved analysing the past, Louis XIV was also concerned to construct the future. This presupposed an overall political purpose, one which matured in the king's mind over the eight years from 1653 to 1661. In France, it was impossible to do without the grandees. A wise king could not, however, continue to distribute favours to them without returns nor expose the state and the country to their capricious disturbances. One solution alone would overcome these problems: to structure the court in such a way that the grandees were constantly watched over, and were encouraged to participate either in the entourage of His Majesty or in his armies, with the hope of rewards, but of rewards which would no longer be excessive or freely distributed. Above all, the king alone would be the one to reward merits, notable service or fidelity to his person or to the state.

But the court which Louis had in mind could only be perfectly regulated, in an efficient way, if the sovereign's entourage lived with him, remained night and day within the court, at least during their quarterly period of service. This was why, first Saint-Germain, and then Versailles, whose buildings were the size of a whole town, would be chosen as its venue rather than Paris. It was not the fear of rebellion which would drive Louis from the capital but the overwhelming necessity of ruling over the aristocracy.

THE INCONVENIENCE OF PARIS

Paris had often demonstrated its unruliness in the past – as in the days of Etienne Marcel or the Massacre of Saint Bartholomew – and it would often do so again in the centuries after the day of the barricades in the summer of 1648. The young king's bedchamber had been invaded, he had fled the capital twice by night; it is not surprising that the turbulent events in Paris created in him a kind of fear of large crowds which would remain with him until his death. But, in the end, it was less Paris than the Palais-Royal which was the important consideration. This building in the heart of the capital was easily surrounded and, as had been proved, easily invaded. The queen mother and Mazarin spent a lot of money on it. This was why, when calm was re-established, Anne of Austria resided in the Louvre, where Louis XIV spent the next eight years. If Paris had been unbearable, would he have patiently accepted – and enjoyed – staying there? If Paris had seemed intolerable, would he have remained there after the cardinal's death, from 1662 to 1666? It has been suggested that this was in deference to the queen mother, who was very attached to the old palace. But if he held his capital in low esteem would he have waited for the death of Anne of Austria before moving to Saint-Germain?

Certainly, as has just been noted, Louis disliked large crowds – the disciplined reviews of his household troops apart – and hated being closeted and confined. He was a man for the open spaces who slept with his windows wide open (the delicate Mme de Maintenon would suffer in consequence). Although the Louvre was less restrictive than the Palais-Royal, it had something of the same inconveniences. This was why Louis moved his apartments to the Tuileries. There he would face the sunset, almost as if in the countryside. The excellent Le Nôtre took tremendous pains to redesign and improve the palace garden, and the king's passion for parks and, above all, flowers would never desert him. After the Louvre and the Tuileries, the king opted for Saint-Germain-en-Laye, where there were more trees and flowers than in the Tuileries and where there was the atmosphere of the forest. As for Versailles, it would be constructed where there was always fresh air.

The Parisian effect of the Fronde upon the king has thus been exaggerated. In the quest for fresh air, a breeze, light, trees, flowers and fruit, in the search for walks and hunting grounds, distractions and ordered tranquillity, for nature as it was then regarded, the departure from the Palais-Royal, decided upon by Anne of Austria rather than the king, was only a preliminary step. But it remains the case that the longer and more frequent became the king's absences from Paris after 1666, the less he was tempted to return. There must be another explanation for the lack of attractiveness of Paris to the king. Perhaps his aversion to large gatherings of people lay at the root of it, his last great public engagement being the day of triumph in 1687 when the Hôtel de Ville celebrated the king's recovery from illness. And, if the Parisian Fronde held no obsessions for the king, it must be remembered that, though Versailles became the royal city, Paris remained the capital, with much to offer. Within this vast metropolis the regime sponsored new projects: the Hôpital Général, the Hôtel Royal des Invalides, the Gobelins manufactory, the academies, the Observatory, the Botanical Garden (refounded by Louis XIV). There it left its monuments: the Cour Carrée and east colonnade of the Louvre, the porte Saint-Denis, the porte Saint-Martin, the Pont Royal and the place Vendôme. An extraordinary effort went into urbanization and urban cleanliness and security. Such diligent efforts would never have been made had Louis XIV been vindictive towards, or afraid of, the Fronde.

THE DISCOVERY OF FRANCE

Historians often criticize the Sun King for remaining closeted in his ivory tower, never leaving Versailles save to conquer a few towns in Flanders. Textbooks present him as cut off from the concerns of his people, oblivious of all save that which arose from his overweening pride and egotism. This is to forget the essential fact that the experience of a few years, even a few months, can stay with an individual for the rest of his life. The Fronde gave Louis XIV the occasion to take the measure of his great kingdom.

When a king in the plenitude of power thought it useful to visit his provinces, this was not to inform himself about them, but for political purposes. The sovereign was presented with a contrived and colourful world. The height of absurdity would be reached when Catherine the Great visited Tauridia in 1787. Prince Potemkin ordered the construction of new villages of wood along her route, inhabited by well-nourished peasants who proclaimed their loyalty with enthusiasm. The same brigade of *moujiks* were used over and over again to greet Catherine in the streets of the same prefabricated and prosperous village. But, when Louis XIV travelled round France in 1650 to 1652, no such mirages were created for him; no one 'potemkinized' the countryside for him.

The first trip was not an arduous one. It was a matter of reassuring loyalties against the activity of the duchesse de Longueville in Normandy. The expedition had its risks; a handful of men, rather than an army, escorted Anne of Austria and Louis. But the presence of the king was worth a whole regiment. The entry into Rouen passed off without incident, the town having disposed of Mme de Longueville before greeting their sovereign. From 5 to 20 February 1650, the king's role was to be seen in the capital of Normandy. 'It is a mark of favour to see the king. In France, it is the most precious, the most treasured of favours. For such is the majesty of our prince, his generosity and good humour, his elegance and his gentle demeanour, that, despite his being only twelve years old, I know of no potion more powerful', wrote the king's confessor, Père Paulin, 'to stimulate affection. The whole of Normandy cannot see enough of him.'(156)

In the spring of 1650, Louis crossed Champagne, a devastated province (17), and went to stay in Burgundy, which was still in rebellion. He visited Joigny, Auxerre, Montbard, Saint-Seine, Dijon and Cîteaux. In April, he rejoined the small army which was laying siege to Bellegarde (Seurre). Mazarin had asked him to come, and the royal presence had the desired effect. The besieged let it be known that, out of respect for His Majesty, they would respect a day's truce. The cardinal recalled that the soldiers in the royal army repeatedly threw their caps in the air and cried 'Vive le Roi!' with the result that, despite their officers, the soldiers on the ramparts of the town opposing them also 'started to cry out "Vive le Roi!"' and with no less enthusiasm. The stronghold shortly afterwards negotiated a surrender. The young prince went among the officers and soldiers, talked to them, and gained an idea of their way of life. They were badly paid and ill-fed, and risked their lives for a small pittance by way of reward, but mainly for the honour and *esprit de corps* they enjoyed. Louis found the right level when talking to them, inspiring the kind of confidence that comes to great leaders. For his part, the cardinal was delighted. Around 800 men from Bellegarde reinforced the royal army. Presently, it was the rest of Burgundy which appeared content to abandon the Fronde. 'The pleasure throughout this province is inexplicable. The king returned this evening [to Dijon] where he was met by the queen and all the town outside the walls with such rejoicing as can scarcely be conveyed fully. Without flattery, the king has conducted himself extremely well throughout this trip. The soldiers are entirely content.' (73)

Towards the end of April, the royal party took the road to the Ile de France. Then, on 4 July, the court headed south, the queen having found it more urgent to go and appease Guyenne than attack the Spanish in Champagne. These were not rich provinces through which they passed. The preparations for each stage of the trip were improvised, so that the king and queen mother were in contact with Frenchmen of all conditions. Louis perhaps knew Grotius's definition of France as the most beautiful realm after Paradise. Now he traversed it, and witnessed the fragility of certain elements of the rural economy, the hazards of craft production, the ravages produced by dearth and economic crisis. In the midst of civil war, the head of state was (in such appalling circumstances) well placed to feel the pulse of the country.

But this trip did not go as well as that to Normandy. Their Majesties encountered a degree of malaise and a level of malnutrition worse than those encountered in Burgundy. And the southern French were stubborn. Bordeaux was not like Rouen or Bellegarde. Its inhabitants refused to open their doors to the king throughout August and September, complying eventually on 1 October because their grape harvest was more important than rebellion against the king. Then the return journey to Paris via Poitou revealed to Louis other regions and different kinds of hardships.

After the *lit de justice* of the king's majority (7 September 1651) and during the voluntary exile of Mazarin, Anne of Austria's small court again took to the road. They spent October in Berry, and from November 1651 to February 1652 they were in Poitiers, which was where Mazarin rejoined them. In February, they went to Saumur; in March to Tours, Blois and then Sully-sur-Loire; in April to Gien and then on to Corbeil. Until the king's return to Paris on 21 October 1652, we should imagine him more in the company of postmasters and innkeepers, bourgeois and postilions, townsmen and soldiers, than of courtiers and flatterers. The years of the Fronde were for him those of a relentless and exhausting apprenticeship. The true lesson of the Fronde for Louis was an unvarnished knowledge of the wider France.

THE CONSCIENCE OF A CHILD; THE RESPONSIBILITIES OF AN ADULT

Père Paulin, Jesuit and confessor to the young monarch, accompanied him throughout these travels and he transmitted regular reports of his impressions both to his superiors in Rome and to the cardinal. The reverend father never forgot his duty to indoctrinate his charge. He exploited every opportunity to accentuate Louis' dislike of Calvinism and to increase his suspicions of the activities of Port-Royal and its supporters. His correspondence with Mazarin betrays him as an ultra-Molinist. But, although often displaying his sectarian and intolerant tendencies, Paulin also occasionally reveals the other side of his nature, that of the good catechist, intensely concerned for the well-being of his pupil. His letters present a likable and plausible picture of Louis XIV as an adolescent painted by someone not without love and affection for him. This kind of account, with its evident sincerity, is so rare that it is worth looking at more closely.

The king had great presence, which was enhanced by the good looks of youth. When he went to Rouen in February 1650, he provoked spontaneous 'vivats' because (according to Paulin) 'he seemed made to command and to please'. He knew what he wanted, prepared for it in secret and acted to obtain it with rapidity and surefootedness. At the beginning of January 1653, Mazarin had not yet returned to Paris and it was for the young sovereign to confront the small group of hotheads still left in the Parlement. Paulin wrote: 'The king is tough and resolute in everything.' The arrest of Retz on the preceding 19 December provides a further illustration. His confessor wrote:

> I was present when the king gave the command, in the presence of the cardinal [de Retz] himself, to have him arrested, which he did with such wisdom that it is difficult to describe. I would only add that such a difficult political manœuvre could scarcely have been better handled. I was standing close to the cardinal and engaging him in conversation about the king's benevolence and greatness and we were agreeing on how well he handled his court when the king approached both of us and mentioned that he had in mind some theatricals. He then called M. de Villequier to him and, with a smile, whispered something in his ear (which was the moment when the arrest was ordered) and, with the words 'Leave the stage, everyone', withdrew immediately as though he had played his part in the drama. I asked the king to attend Mass, as it was then midday, and this he did directly. During the service, M. de Villequier came to whisper to him that his order had been carried out and, as I was alone with the king on that day, he turned to me and said: 'I have just arrested Cardinal de Retz.' (156)

Mazarin had, of course, overseen the execution of the arrest from Bar-le-Duc, but the carrying out of this delicate matter was, nevertheless, effectively handled. It 'surprised and astonished everyone' except, perhaps, Mazarin, the king's mentor.

It was something of a paradox that the prince who exercised his sovereignty with such firmness was still a student. Péréfixe, abbé de Beaumont and Bishop of Rodez, was often absent, so that the king was frequently assigned temporary tutors. After the Fronde, this temporary tutoring was generally undertaken by La

Mothe le Vayer. At Rouen, in February 1650, the task was accomplished by Paulin: 'In accordance with the queen's wishes. Everything went, God be thanked, smoothly and for the best.' Louis had, in fact, the same cast of mind as his mother. He hated books and, throughout his life, preferred conversation. His confessor rather disingenuously made use of this fact and, rather than boring him with a formal statement on Jansenism, fed him stories and gossip designed to make him detest the associates of Port-Royal. The king's religion was much less concerned with theology and based more on a warmhearted piety. This did not mean that he followed Italianate devotions in the fashion of his predecessor Henry III or the Spanish mysticism which attracted his mother, Mazarin and many Parisians. Nor did it prevent him from joining the queen mother in the celebration of papal jubilees or in innumerable processions of the Blessed Sacrament, or from taking communion beside her on feast-days. 'There they both are', said Paulin in 1650, 'with such piety towards God and for their people that nothing more could be added.' Within the orthodoxy of the Council of Trent, Louis attached great importance to the Marian cult. He signed the declaration of 25 March 1650 renewing the Marian vow of Louis XIII. Each morning and evening he devoted some time to prayers (in the summer and autumn of 1652, Louis prayed for the soul of Paul Mancini 'loving him as though he were still a living soul'). He attended Mass daily until his death-bed.

This religiosity did not change the king (any more than the demands of *raison d'état* had done); he did not become a sad recluse or a bigot. He was inordinately fond of dancing; and the same prince who, at thirteen, was attending Lenten preachings and processing round the stations of the cross with his mother 'swims across the Marne and conducts a mock-battle at his fort in the palace at Brion'. After the Fronde, with all its upheavals, risks and humiliations, Louis was still, beneath a stoic exterior, an adolescent. Père Paulin constantly reminded Mazarin that Louis XIV was still of tender years. 'I assure Your Excellency that his is the most open and sincere soul to be found in the state ... He is truly the Dieudonné; respectful towards the queen as ever; judicious and self-aware; gallant and genuine. All this is God's handiwork' (14 October 1652). 'Never has there been the like in wholesome innocence' (17 November). 'The king is always happy and good company, knowledgeable and devout, holding his mother, the queen our sovereign, and his brother, Petit Monsieur, in the highest esteem. He never shows his temper now; Your Excellency will hardly recognize him' (25 November). Père Paulin, whose words of praise these were, was extremely fond of his student. As a result, he reinforced Louis' affection towards his mother and Mazarin. (It may even have been the case that it was through the posthumous influence of Paulin that the young king accepted Mazarin's political tutelage until 1661 (156).) In return, Louis had a high regard for Paulin. When, in the spring of 1653, the Jesuit fell ill, the king incessantly sent for news of his condition, 'often sending little gifts'. Upon Paulin's death (on 12 April), Louis gave twenty gold *pistoles* for requiem Masses for his soul.

THE QUEST FOR STABILITY

One part of the French character relishes tumult, aggression and attack (military or political). This is the *furia francese*, the love of outright victories which treats stubborn endurance with contempt. This pattern is as applicable in politics as in warfare. Why had France emerged from five years of turbulence? The return of the king to Paris on 21 October 1652 was a triumph because everybody wanted the long-awaited pacification. Besides, both sides recognized and accepted the same king, so the popular enthusiasm on that day is hardly surprising. The duchesse de Nemours tells us: 'Since the day after the king's arrival in Paris, everything has been at peace, as though there had never been a Fronde and as if royal authority were as well established as it had been before the troubles began.' (80) And when, on 3 February, the cardinal returned to the capital which had slandered, attacked and abused him, the king went to greet him and it was then that the popularity of the king appeared. From the porte Saint-Denis, the crowd cheered 'Vive le Roi!' whilst the royal carriage escorted Mazarin to the Louvre, where all was ready to welcome his return. On the same day, the cardinal received deputies from the city and the Parlement, 'which recognized the debt which France owed to his great and illustrious efforts, and came to assure him of their joy at his happy return'. A supper and fireworks followed that same night. The cursed cardinal had returned in triumph. The following day, the courtiers came to bury their differences with him and pay their respects. This was the sign that Paris (representing the realm) desired peace, security and order. The realm had witnessed a *croquant* revolt in 1624 and again between 1635 and 1637; in 1639, that of the *nu-pieds*; in 1643, a rising of the *croquants* of Rouergue; and now the Fronde. There had also been the Protestant uprising of the Midi from 1621 to 1629, the troubles of the regency of Marie de Médicis and the conspiracies and plots against Richelieu and Louis XIII, not to mention the *cabale des Importants*. On top of this had been the Thirty Years' War, followed by the struggle against the House of Austria. It was not just the end of the Fronde for which there was widespread yearning but the end of forty years of upheaval.

Among those who wanted stability at all costs, the grandees were least conspicuous. As always, they knew how to extract the best advantage from things. Despite a few arrests, imprisonments, banishments and confiscations, they had not suffered greatly from the rebellion which they had sponsored. The letters of pardon already indicated how much it was believed necessary to compromise with them. But stability was of greater concern to the merchant, the manufacturer, the artisan and the peasant. And stability was of even more vital importance to the humble: the journeymen apprentices, fishermen and day-labourers. Stability was the demand of each and every subject, not just the king. In France under the absolute monarchy, overwhelming popular wishes orientated overall political attitudes.

Louis was devoted to stability. He was concerned above all to satisfy this expression of popular will, since he had experienced it uncamouflaged and at close quarters. Louis had played a leading part in events whose turbulence could have destroyed him and the monarchy as well. He was shrewd and, henceforth, experienced. He knew that politics cannot be summed up in the simple dichotomy of order at the expense of justice as opposed to disorder, but justice maintained. He would not have accepted Goethe's sentiment that 'One injustice is better than popular disorder.' He would have preferred the formulation: 'An injustice which forestalls popular disorder (for example, the trial and sentencing of Fouquet) is preferable to the manifold injustices which always accompany that disorder.'

5

From Westphalia to the Pyrenees

I N S O M E operas, the musical themes which lie scattered through the whole work are brought together in the overture. The years which separate the Fronde from the death of Mazarin form this kind of overture, preparing us for the major themes which would be developed in the course of the personal rule. This prelude gives us a glimpse of the companionability of the king, his liveliness, his taste for glory, his interest in politics and his diligence in getting to know his kingdom. It demonstrates his maturing artistic, dancing and musical tastes, not to mention his amorous encounters. Religion was not excluded; the king did not turn his back on the piety of his infancy nor on the powerfully inculcated sense of family. Anne influenced her son and drew upon herself a large part of his need for affection. For this prince, whose dignity and maturity astonished many contemporaries, retained his capacity to respond spontaneously in such matters and with individuality. His initiation in the affairs of state, which the cardinal continued to supervise, did not occupy him to the exclusion of other things, but he was nevertheless always intelligent and effective when it came to strategic or diplomatic decisions relating to war and peace.

THE HOLY ROMAN EMPIRE ECLIPSED

From the autumn of 1648 onwards, France became predominant in Europe, even though the civil war enfeebled the realm and obscured the full measure of its successes. When the young king had cause to reflect upon the duel between France and Spain, he knew how much he depended upon the cardinal. For, in the wake of the deaths of Richelieu (1642) and his adversary Olivares, Mazarin took charge of the wartime strategy and politics of France. Like Richelieu, and Louis XIV at a later date, Mazarin never separated military and political decisions. Well before Frederick of Prussia and Clausewitz, these men pursued a global strategy with which to overwhelm their enemies.

Up to 1648, the trend was evident: France was obliged to fight on several fronts, but it was opposed by a disunited coalition. The striking contrast between the unity of decision and action imposed by Mazarin and the lack of cohesion among the allies was not lost on Louis XIV. For the second cardinal, freer to act than Richelieu had been, had full command of the armed forces. He was the inspiration behind the 'Instructions' which Le Tellier drew up for the military commanders (70). The results testify to their efficacy. In 1643 came the victory at Rocroi, the capture of Trino by Turenne, and the capture of Stura by Du Plessis-Praslin. In 1644, thirty towns or fortresses were seized and Condé had the better of Mercy in the bitter conflict at Freiburg (3–9 August). In 1645, Rosas was taken by Du Plessis-Praslin, whilst Condé and Turenne were victorious at Nördlingen (3 August) against the same Mercy, who died there. Meanwhile, the comte de Harcourt was successful at Llorens (23 June) and Balaguer was seized (20 October). In 1646, the fruitful collaboration between the forces of Wrangel and Turenne resulted in the capture of Aschaffenburg (21 August), whilst Courtrai, Bergues, Mardyck and Dunkirk in Flanders as well as Piombino in Italy and Porto-Longone on the island of Elba fell to the French. In 1647 came the siege of Worms. In 1648, the capture of Ypres (28 May) was followed by the victory of the Franco-Swedish forces under the Duke of Bavaria beyond the Inn, the seizing of Tortosa (13 July) and the Battle of Lens (20 August).

On the diplomatic front, the successes were equally decisive. French arbitration put an end to the war between Pope Urban VIII and Odoard Farnese, Duke of Parma (31 March 1644). The marriage between Władysław IV, King of Poland, and Maria Louise of Gonzaga, Princess of Mantua (6 November 1645), was also of the cardinal's making. Nine days later, the Danish plenipotentiaries ratified the Franco-Danish alliance which had been signed on 13 August. Shortly afterwards, on 19

November, Turenne took possession of Trier and the elector was reinstalled on the following day. The event demonstrated the 'faithfulness of France in the protection of its allies' ('TUTELAE GALLICAE FIDELITAS'). Negotiations for peace opened in the autumn of 1646. The result was the Peace of Ulm (14 March 1647), between France, Maximilian of Bavaria and the Elector of Cologne – an ephemeral affair, however, because of Bavarian duplicity. In revenge, the Franco-Swedish alliance was renewed on 25 April 1647. For most of the German princes, the desire to end the war was deep-seated and frustrated only by the emperor and, in 1648, he could no longer hold out. The success of Condé at Lens had been a telling one and, even more importantly, the victory of Turenne and Wrangel at Zusmarshausen (17 May 1648) had opened up the way to Vienna. The negotiations which had been continuing since 1644 at Münster between France and the Catholic states, and at Osnabrück between Sweden and the Protestant coalition, began to change pace. Mazarin profited from the agile diplomacy of Hugues de Lionne. The Peace of Westphalia was signed on 24 October 1648.

This pacification was, as has been noted, used as a pretext by Péréfixe to give the young king a lesson in geography and political history. He learnt that the empire was in no sense a unified country. Whilst the Most Christian Kingdom had long ceased to be a feudal entity, the emperor had to live with the existence of nearly 350 little states whose differences in attitude the interminable war had accentuated.

Sometimes their disagreements were dynastic ones. In the midst of the conflict, the emperor had deposed the Palatine Elector Frederick V and deprived him of his electoral dignity. Bavaria had become the seventh electorate of the empire and its duke would have his new title confirmed in the Treaty of Münster as well as his possession of the upper Palatinate. On the other hand, Frederick V's son, Charles-Louis, was reinstated as elector with sovereignty over the lower Palatinate. The remodelled Holy Roman Empire would henceforth enjoy eight electorates: the archbishoprics of Mainz, Cologne and Trier, the realm of Bohemia (Habsburg), the duchy of Bavaria, Brandenburg, the duchy of Saxony and the Palatine County of the Rhine. The first five were Catholic, Saxony and Brandenburg were Lutheran, and the Palatine County of the Rhine was Calvinist.

Herein lay the novelty imposed upon Emperor Ferdinand III

by the pacification: not only was the Peace of Augsburg of 1555 confirmed but all the Reformed confessions were henceforth officially tolerated. The complex divisions which separated the Germany of the Reformation from the Germany of the Counter-Reformation became the great scar left by the wars which the pacification ended in 1648. Louis XIV could think himself more fortunate than the emperor; for France had towards eighteen million Catholics as against fewer than a million Protestants. (Neither Henry IV nor Richelieu nor Mazarin had wished to achieve unity on the basis of the application of *Cujus regio, ejus religio* – 'The religion of a country is that of its prince' –, the famous phrase which summarized the religious peace of Germany at Augsburg in 1555. This was why, in the end, an illusory French unity would create more fuss than the reality of German diversity.)

And here were the difficulties the Peace posed for the House of Austria. The states of the Holy Roman Empire were granted 'the free exercise of territorial superiority in both ecclesiastical and political matters' (216), the 'LIBERTAS GERMANIAE' (71). The German princes had every reason to be grateful to France. The Duke of Bavaria had not been dispossessed, the Archbishop of Trier had been restored to his estates, Brandenburg had gained the rich secularized bishoprics of Halberstadt and Minden and the archbishopric of Magdeburg. They were all grateful to be released from the tutelage of Vienna and took up a more independent political stance, whose orientation would be swayed by subsidies from France.

Sweden became a German power. Having acquired the duchy of Bremen, Verden and western Pomerania, it controlled the Baltic outlets of the Elbe, Weser and Oder rivers. France, satisfied with having made the emperor the august head of an anarchy, limited its own further demands. This was a wise prudence, born of essentially Mazarinist principles. The cardinal had possibly drawn the king's attention to the need for such restraint in 1648; he had surely done so by 1661. Through Hugues de Lionne, Mazarin left Louis XIV a legacy which would channel the external affairs of France into a diplomacy more subtle and adaptable than commonly imagined.

France's territorial advances were twofold. Louis XIV saw himself reconfirmed in his possession of the Three Bishoprics, Metz, Toul and Verdun, which had protected the realm so efficiently and whose garrisons paralysed the Duke of Lorraine. Above all, though, the emperor ceded to the victor 'the rights, properties, possessions and jurisdictions which had hitherto belonged to him, the empire and the House of Austria in the town of Breisach, the landgravate of upper and lower Alsace, the Sundgau, the provincial administration of the Ten Imperial Towns of Alsace ... and all the territories and other rights whatsoever which depend upon this administration' (216).

With regard to Alsace, the articles of the treaty were, however, ambiguous. The rights it ceded were only superficially all-embracing. There was, for example, clause 89, which excluded the bishopric and town of Strasbourg from its terms (but the bishop was landgrave of lower Alsace!) Besides, the imperial towns (Landau, Wissembourg, Haguenau, Rosheim, Obernai, Sélestat, Colmar, Münster, Turckheim and Kaysersberg) were so dispersed and the overlordship of this 'decapolis' so vague that everything was left up to the two powers involved. Territorially, the immediate acquisitions did not even amount to the whole of upper Alsace; but, on the other hand, whilst the rights to lower Alsace consisted only of vague overlordship in five or six towns, the pacification and the feudal organization of Alsace allowed between them for the possibility of future piecemeal encroachment. The trial of strength would begin within the lifetime of the cardinal. Profiting from the civil war, the emperor began encroaching. Those who condemn the later Reunions of Louis XIV should remember that the incursions of the Habsburgs between 1649 and 1657 provided an object lesson in how to interpret the Westphalian peace in a hostile way. Mazarin only re-established the position, during an imperial interregnum, thanks to the efforts of the maréchal de Gramont and Lionne in the period from October 1657 to March 1658 and to the constitution of the League of the Rhine (14 August 1658). Mazarin thus consolidated a difficult frontier. With garrisons at Metz, Toul, Verdun, Landau, Philippsburg and Breisach and troops stationed in upper Alsace, the regime strengthened its position on the Rhine. The military 'iron curtain' was taking shape on the frontiers.

SPANISH INTRANSIGENCE

The Treaties of Münster and Osnabrück were made without Spain and the Netherlands. The United Provinces, for its part, feared France and preferred to see the southern Netherlands controlled by Spain. And Philip IV never forgave France for its intervention in 1640 in the revolt of Catalonia and the uprising of Portugal. This explains why, by the treaty of 30 January 1648, Spain recognized the independence of the United Provinces and withdrew from the Congress of Westphalia.

Between Spain and France, nothing had been decided. Mazarin had not followed Richelieu's policies through to a conclusion. Despite Rocroi (1643) and Lens (1648), Philip IV remained confident. The Fronde worked to his advantage by diminishing French forces, financial strength and morale, and by leading to the exiles of Mazarin, the temporary defection of Turenne and the more prolonged exile (1651–59) of Condé. Events seemed to be leading towards another Hundred Years' War.

Even when the Fronde was at an end, military operations remained indecisive, despite the fact that the loyalist Turenne was always the victor and the rebellious Condé beaten nearly every time. In 1653, the French took Mouzon and Sainte-Ménéhould but abandoned Rocroi. In 1654, Conti campaigned in Catalonia and Fabert took possession of Stenay (one of the engineers of the siege was Vauban). In July, Turenne met Condé's forces in Artois and, the following month, overwhelmed them, assisted by Hocquincourt and La Ferté. In 1655, the armies of Louis XIV took Landrecies, Condé and Saint-Ghislain, but Charles de Monchy, marquis d'Hocquincourt, a marshal from 1651 and governor of Péronne, Montdidier and Roye, seemed on the point of deserting to the prince de Condé. Mazarin had to forestall his treason with a gift of 600,000 *livres* (70). The campaign of 1656 lost the initiative in Picardy and left Turenne perplexed. The Spanish had military commanders whose abilities could not be underestimated (107). In July, the prince de Condé liberated the town of Condé, besieged Valenciennes and crushed the army of the maréchal de la Ferté-Senneterre. Fortunately, for Lionne had left for Madrid to negotiate a peace, Turenne took La Capelle on 27 September. Lionne had two trump cards up his sleeve: an English alliance and the increasing popularity of the French king.

The origins of the plan for an alliance between England and France were to be laid in London in July 1654. Mazarin was not unaware of the hatred for Cromwell in France, but he could envisage no other means except a coalition to seize, or recover, the towns along the northern French seaboard. In November 1655, the two countries signed a commercial treaty which outlawed piracy and privateering. Then, on 3 March 1657, the Treaty of Paris was concluded. The two countries would unite in opposition to Spain in maritime Flanders; Gravelines would become French and Dunkirk English. It only remained to capture these seaports. Dunkirk only held out for a month, thanks to the victory of Turenne over Condé at the Dunes on 14 June. Gravelines would fall on 30 August.

Mazarin closely associated the king's personal reputation with this siege of Dunkirk. With Turenne as his mentor, Louis' mission was to acquire military experience and renown. Everyone believed that his presence stimulated local loyalties, motivated the soldiers, encouraged their leaders and underlined Condé's crime. The king faced dangers, and his stamina was strengthened by physical exercise. He adapted to life in bivouacs and was introduced to military command. He had already taken part, in the autumn of 1653, in the siege of Sainte-Ménéhould and, in 1655, in the Flanders campaign. He took so many risks that it worried his mother as well as the cardinal and the generals. This was the reason why, in 1656, Mazarin cautioned him, and Turenne insisted that His Majesty was not sent to the fiercest military engagements. From Enghien to Rocroi, officers, soldiers, and the inhabitants of frontier provinces caught sight of their prince, a fitting grandson of Henry IV, dressed informally. On his return to the Louvre, courtiers wondered if he was really the same king.

A DAY IN THE LIFE OF A SIXTEEN-YEAR-OLD KING

Dubois, the king's valet, returned to Paris towards the end of March 1655 delighted to find his 'dear master' greatly altered, 'so accomplished'. He noted down how this sixteen-year-old prince 'spent the day' (75). The king's childhood piety still shone through, although neither austerity nor sentimentality was in his nature. His political education continued without excess or pedantry under the intelligent and indulgent direction of the cardinal, whilst entertainment in body and spirit (hunting, fencing, dancing, conversation, the theatre, music) provided a balanced timetable for the sovereign. The Fronde, with its hastily prepared departures and the discomforts of makeshift lodgings, appeared forgotten. The king was at the Louvre, the palace which was preferred to the Palais-Royal and where Le Vau was beginning the building of the queen mother's summer apartments (199). He was no prisoner there: the Tuileries and the Cours la Reine (Queen's Walk) were no distance away and he felt himself almost in the countryside.

'As soon as he woke', Dubois reported, 'he recited the office of the Holy Spirit and his rosary.' Then M. de la Mothe le Vayer entered the private apartments to take him through some biblical history or French history, lessons whose sparkling presentation kept the king attentive. Once he was out of bed, the king's daytime valets appeared and a servant of the chamber, and the king sat in his 'cut-away chair' or commode, sometimes for up to twenty minutes. 'Then he entered his grand chamber, where the princes and *grands seigneurs* normally awaited to attend his *lever*.' Still in his dressing-gown, the king met the courtiers and 'spoke to them on familiar terms, one after the other, winning their respect'. In their presence, having washed his hands, face and mouth, he 'offered prayers to God alongside his chaplains in his antechamber whilst all present knelt with him'. His devotions completed, the king combed his hair and then dressed modestly (short coat, Dutch waistcoat, serge breeches) before withdrawing to undertake his 'exercises', such as horseriding, fencing and dancing. His physical exertions completed, Louis returned to his chamber to change and take lunch. After lunch, he went up to the rooms of Mazarin, 'who lodged above him and who received an individual report from one of the secretaries of state each day on the substance of which, along with other closely guarded matters of state, the king was instructed for about an hour or an hour and an half'.

Louis then went to greet his mother and, after a horseride, rejoined her at Mass and escorted her back to her apartment. From there, the king returned to his own chamber. On hunting days, the king wore his 'ordinary' clothes. Otherwise, he wore his 'simple' attire. The monarch generally sat down to dinner with the queen mother, and the time after dinner was often devoted to the reception of ambassadors. Politeness, but also political interest, determined that Louis listen intently to what they had to say, and he 'would talk to them in a relaxed fashion for a quarter of an hour' about their rulers and countries, 'the alliances and friendships they had long had in their dynasties and realms'.

'Towards the end of the period after dinner,' Dubois continued, 'the king goes along the Cours [la Reine] meeting and talking to men and women of quality on the way.' Then His Majesty rejoined the cardinal in the Council. At other times, he attended a comedy, never forgetting the elaborate display of courtesy to the author. Then 'Their Majesties go to supper, after which the king dances, accompanied by the queen's ladies and others, to the music of violins'. 'Various distractions' followed up to midnight. 'They play at parlour games (*petits jeux*) and storytelling. They sit in a circle, and then someone begins a story and continues until he can go no further and the one sitting next to him has to take it up and thus it goes on from one to another, often with very amusing results.' When the games were over, Louis XIV took his leave of his mother and went back to his chamber. As with the *lever*, his preparing for bed was a public event. The monarch said his prayers and undressed whilst entertaining the princes and courtiers 'in a delightful way' before wishing them goodnight and retiring to his alcove bedchamber. There he sat on his 'cut-away chair', 'where his most intimate servants attended to him such as the first gentlemen [of the chamber] and others with authority to enter there' (75). These fortunate few were the recipients of a *brevet d'affaires*, the *chaise d'affaires* being the proper name for the commode.

The baroque exuberance has been eliminated from this description of the royal day: at times the prince is a Solomon, at others he has within him the piety of a St Louis and the benevolence (*sic*) of a Caesar. This is, nevertheless, a remarkable document. The piety of Louis was never mere conformism. The king's affection for his mother appears throughout the day. The way in which the cardinal associated the younger man with affairs of state was an excellently judged mixture of good sense and efficiency. Louis' life was remarkably well balanced. Physical and mental exercises were mutually complementary. The king's sociability appears directly and by implication in Dubois' account. From the moment he awoke until bedtime, at the audiences and in his individual conversations with courtiers, it was developed almost to perfection. There is no hint of that hatred of Paris, that sense of fear of crowds, that so many authors have attributed to Louis XIV as an indelible consequence of the troubles.

But Versailles was already in gestation in these moments in the Louvre. Between the court and the sovereign, a sense of solidarity is visible, born of what is known as *l'honnêteté* and contributing to the perfection of the image of the court. Père Bouhours believes that these years were the moment when France attained its apogee of civilization ('We were never more refined than during the years of that tough war between France and Spain' (15)). The court rounded out the king's education. In a few years' time, the king would complete the evolution of the court.

THE MALADY AT MARDYCK

After the fall of Dunkirk (25 June 1658) and up to that of Ninove (28 October), Turenne pressed on with a remarkable Flemish campaign, which put all the territory between the Yser, the Scheldt and the Lys in French hands. Unfortunately, the king was unable to follow it, because he had fallen ill at Mardyck on 29 June. Brought back to Calais, he seems to have been at death's door between 1 and 13 July. The attentive physician Vallot, ever proud of his own abilities, kept the journal of the king's illness. According to this doctor, His Majesty, having been exposed to the corruption of the air and infection in the water, had fallen prey to a chill which had been badly treated, since he had refused the proposed blood-letting. The result was that the king had 'little by little contracted an unidentified poison, which, having infected his humours, gave him a temperature and then a fever' causing his physician some concern. The illness began on the 29th with 'a high temperature, a weakness in all the limbs, a dreadful headache, limpness and no appetite'. The king put a brave face on things, but he had contracted a fever.

At Calais, on 1 July, he finally consented to be nursed, injected and then leeched. During the night, he was massaged and given cordial medicine. On Tuesday the 2nd, His Majesty was again leeched and submitted himself to a clyster. On the 3rd, as his fever increased, more blood was let and several injections were administered. On Thursday the 4th, Louis was leeched twice more and given some medicine. On Friday the 5th, Vallot prescribed an emetic followed by hot plasters. His remarks in the journal display his remarkable vanity: 'These two remedies . . . deserve to be glorified by the king's recovery.' But at the time few shared his confidence. On the 7th, His Majesty was subjected to a phlebotomy, a clyster and some medicines. On the 8th, after a leeching, the king suffered an inspection by six consultants. Vallot's wishes prevailed; a further emetic was required. Not cinnamon this time but antimony. Vallot wrote that he 'had already ordered the preparation, that morning, of three large doses of laxative and three ounces of emetic wine . . . the king *twenty-two times* cleared his system of a greenish serum, tinged with yellow, without too much pain since he only vomited twice, about four or five hours after taking the medicine'.

Vallot thought that he had played his ace on the Monday and 'that the advantage which the king would feel in his own person would be communicated to everyone, not only in his realm, but also throughout Europe, who had thought that the king was at death's door'. On 9 July, His Majesty was only given a clyster, on the 10th purged, and on the 11th leeched. On the 12th syrups and a further clyster were prescribed and, on the following day, the last purge was administered. The fever was at an end. From the 14th to the 17th, Vallot persuaded his colleagues to stop prescribing laxatives. In the preceding nine days of his treatment, the patient had passed large quantities of water but had scarcely drunk a drop. On Thursday the 18th, the Faculty took the view that the king was recovering; the cure 'seemed miraculous'. The young monarch began his convalescence.

No one could predict the outcome of these tribulations and this was not just a time of trial for the physicians. There were political and psychological aspects too. Louis believed himself at death's door. On the 7th, he said to the cardinal: 'You are a man of resolution and my best friend. This is why I beg of you to tell me when I am at my last extremity.' (70) The king's illness reinforced Mazarin's sincere affection towards his godson. It provided another occasion for Anne of Austria to demonstrate hers; the queen mother 'denied herself . . . sleep' to care for her son (70). And it afforded another instructive revelation. As soon as the court thought that the king was about to die, 'the courtiers turned their attentions towards his brother, Monsieur' (112). In his less feverish moments, the sovereign could not have helped hearing about it. One more cruel experience after those of the Fronde!

The Mardyck illness also revealed the mutual affections of the king and Marie Mancini, the cardinal's niece. For over two years, this 'Mazarinette' had hoped to succeed her sister Olympe in the king's good graces. Olympe was pretty, but without much intelligence; despite her efforts, her suitor grew bored with her and left her to marry the comte de Soissons in 1657. Marie, on the other hand, though she lacked grace, was both clever and ambitious. Having caught the king's attention, she knew how to sustain it by her mental agility. She annotated several novels in the chivalric tradition for him, encouraging him to live out a chivalric romance with her.

'Some ways of speaking', according to Furetière, 'are better capable of certain delicate and pretty effects than are others.' Marie Mancini's way began to have its impact on the king. He saw in her the freshness of youth. He admired her culture, her intelligence, her coyness: shrewdly, she only permitted the most furtive physical advances. Now Marie thought the king might die, and that her stratagems might have been in vain. Mocked for her 'barmaid' looks, and knowing the sad fate of her sister, the comtesse de Soissons, she had gambled everything on the king's affections. How sweet the revenge, had she become queen, upon her sisters, her late mother and the cardinal, that meddlesome uncle who mistrusted her, not to mention the courtiers who had treated her as a joke! This was why, throughout the 'malady of Mardyck', Marie was 'drowned in tears' (125).

A SECOND TOUR OF FRANCE

War taught the king a lot about his kingdom. What he had not found out from the Fronde, he learnt in the years immediately afterwards. During the troubles, he had come to know the Parisian basin and had once gone in the direction of the southwest. Beyond the Ile de France, he had already come to know Picardy (1647, 1649), Rouen and Normandy (1650), Champagne (1650), Burgundy (1650), Poitou (1650, 1651), Guyenne (1650), Berry (1651) and Anjou (especially Saumur, intellectual heart of French Protestantism) and the regions of the Loire (1652). A dozen provinces in six years!

Thereafter, between the Fronde and the death of Mazarin (1661), Louis XIV discovered a further eight provinces in the course of an itinerary determined for him by political and military affairs, by the lure of a Savoyard marriage and by the reality of a Spanish match. Some of these regions had long been part of France; others were in the process of being annexed. He visited Lorraine (1653, 1656), Flanders (1658), the Lyonnais (1658), where the escapade with his Mazarinette became a serious love-match, Saintonge (1659) (he would not forget visits to Saint-Jean-d'Angély and Brouage . . .), both upper and lower Languedoc (1659) and Provence, and Avignon and the Basque country (1660).

The king was observant and gained an overall view, taking in, thanks to a good memory, the fundamental details of France. For he had other affections besides those for Marie Mancini. The young monarch observed that his realm was a country of contrasts; that the North was richer, more industrious, more easily taxed and more readily mobilized. He understood the diversity within regions, comparing upper and lower Picardy, upper and lower Languedoc. He realized that there was not one single nobility in France but half a dozen different nobilities, not one bourgeoisie but dozens of differing urban social elites. These diversities, held in place with 'liberties', went to make up the forceful originality of the country.

To this multi-dimensional comparison of provinces, towns, regions and *estates* (social groups), the king was in a position to add a historical perspective and see the differences between France during the Fronde and France during its reconstruction. The celebrated remark in Louis XIV's *Memoirs for the year 1661* – 'Disorder ruled everywhere' – was an obvious exaggeration for political and pedagogical purposes. It may have misled the Dauphin, for whom it was written, but Colbert and the king knew the reality. Writers of the twentieth century who choose to write about Louis XIV, taking 1661 as their starting-point, neglect this period in the making of the king. On the question of his knowledge of the kingdom, they forget that Anne of Austria's son visited twenty provinces before his personal reign began, with the result that they often present Louis XIV as shut up in his palace, even accusing him of being ignorant of his people. It

is, of course, the case that Louis only visited five provinces after
1661 – Brittany (1661), Artois (1662), Franche Comté (1668),
Hainaut (1677) and Alsace (1681) –, four of which were not part
of the old domain. But he already had a good knowledge of over
four times that number. Mazarin had ensured that his godson
was spared the greatest vice of all statesmen – abstraction.

SOME PRACTICAL LESSONS

Louis XIV absorbed the cardinal's political perspectives. It was
time to exploit the universal weariness of political disorders. The
strengthening of the monarchy, so difficult under Richelieu,
could begin again without too much trouble. Of course, Mazarin
was too involved with matters of peace and war to be concerned
with the details of internal affairs. But he had several trump
cards in his hand, notably the king himself. Nothing would
contribute more to the restoration of moral and political unity
than the consecration at Reims in June 1654, where no one was
in a position to take the king's place. Nothing, not even the
intendants, would bring the subjects of politically troubled provinces back to submission better than the presence of the king in
those provinces. This was the great benefit of his tour of France.
But from 1653, Mazarin had, in the king's name, sent commissioners (*missi dominici*) into the provinces. At first, for fear of
arousing the *frondeurs*, it was not a matter of putting intendants
back into their previous posts but of sending *maîtres des requêtes* on
perambulating commissions (*chevauchées*). Their task was to re-
establish order and collect taxes. This innovation was a success.
The *maîtres des requêtes* were sent simply under letters of the privy
seal (*lettres de cachet*). However, nobody was despatched either to
Navarre or to Brittany (179).

The resurrection of the intendants might have meant a return
to the spirit of 1648. In fact, however, the royal officers, especially the magistrates of the Parlement of Paris, realized that the
bourgeoisie and the people would have given them little support
in a further Fronde. A compromise was reached in the spring of
1655, a compromise which legend has transformed into a kind of
coup d'état. At the beginning of the year, the exchequer was bare
and Fouquet, joint superintendent of finances (*surintendant des
finances*), persuaded the cardinal to have recourse to financial

'expedients'. The king was to sign seventeen 'fiscal edicts'. He accepted that he would need to present them before the Parlement in a *lit de justice*. The session took place on 20 March in the habitual fashion. Louis called on the chancellor to present the case. Séguier emphasized Spanish obstinacy, the necessity for an advantageous peace and the costs which this entailed. He ended by expressing the hope 'that the Parlement would provide a new mark of its affection for the service of the king and of the state, and an example to his subjects of perfect obedience and fidelity' (149). The *avocat général* Bignon replied by referring to the sufferings of the people, but then, albeit without enthusiasm, recommended the registration of the edicts, which took place later that same day. The following day, however, some young *conseillers* from the Chambres des Enquêtes demanded another assembly, saying that the king's presence had denied them their 'freedom to decide'. At the beginning of April, the issue widened and Mazarin feared a new Fronde. He acted in concert with Louis to teach the *parlementaires* a lesson. This was the background to the session of 13 April. If the magistrates felt themselves cajoled, they had only themselves to blame.

According to Lavisse:

> The events of that day are legendary. The king learnt at Vincennes that the Parlement was about to debate the edicts which had been registered in his presence and he made his way to the Palais directly, in his hunting-clothes, riding crop in his hand, fuming angrily and when the *premier président* Pomponne de Bellièvre referred to the interest of the state, he replied: 'L'état, c'est moi!' (216)

Unfortunately, neither the setting nor the sentiment is likely in this age of civility and decorum. As we shall demonstrate later, it would have been impossible for Louis XIV to have said 'L'état, c'est moi', for the simple reason that he never thought in these terms. But something still needs to be said about the affair of 13 April and about the king's attitude.

> The novelty of his visit was that he had appeared 'in informal attire' and had forbidden their debates without following the usual precedents. Also, the Parlement sent a delegation to Vincennes to complain that His Majesty had proceeded 'in a strange fashion far removed from that of his predecessors'. The deputation was politely received, but the Parlement continued its

examination of the edicts, and Mazarin, after threatening the judges with 'the most terrible uproar', gave some concessions. (216)

Over the next few days, pensions began to shower upon various members of the Palais de Justice. Bellièvre alone received 300,000 *livres*. The *président* Le Coigneux contented himself with 2,000 *écus* (216). Such rewards must have given Fouquet much pleasure. As *surintendant*, he had provoked the crisis; as *procureur général* he worked to appease it. He talked with Pellisson philosophically about winning over the magistrates to these *affaires extraordinaires*, without which there would have been no pensions. But there was some substance behind this affair, so neatly brought to a conclusion (save in an ill-informed legend): Mazarin and Fouquet were lining their own pockets from almost every tax receipt. But Louis XIV understood little of financial affairs and the cardinal was not the man to enlighten him. From this one abuse, however, something positive emerged. The Parlement was put in its place – still a privileged one – and would no longer restrict the initiatives of the Great King.

On the other hand, during these years when Mazarin and Louis appeared to rule conjointly, two thorns – Jansenist and Protestant – were pricking the nation's conscience, and they would create abscesses during Louis' personal rule. We shall have cause to return to the Augustinianism which profoundly influenced the whole of the century. It was a Christianity of the elite, a doctrine of which Port-Royal was the transmitter, the abbé de Saint-Cyran the propagandist and Antoine Arnauld the theologian. Amongst the elite which came together at Port-Royal, they then discovered in Pascal the ideal herald of their cause. His first *Provincial Letter* appeared on 23 January 1656, the eighteenth on 24 March 1657. This strand of Augustinianism had its part to play in the intellectual and spiritual hot-house environment of the French Counter-Reformation; but, unfortunately, it attempted to dominate it.

Richelieu had detected political opposition from amongst them. He had ordered the imprisonment of Saint-Cyran, not realizing that every religious movement needs its martyrs. Mazarin inherited his prejudices, and the king, as we have seen, had been alerted to its danger. For, under the name of Jansenism, five theses of the *Augustinus* (written by Jansen, Bishop of Ypres, and published posthumously in 1640) had been condemned on 31 May 1653 by Pope Innocent X. The 'Jansenists' were no longer just the 'Messieurs', the 'Solitaires' of Port-Royal, the revered school-teachers of the 'primary schools' with their admired teaching techniques, the enthusiastic devotees of the efficacy of God's grace. They were now to be treated as heretics, both in Rome and in the Sorbonne. Mazarin, it appears, was 'inclined to be tolerant' (70), unlike the Jesuits; but it is also clear that he regarded the Jansenists as a reflection of the Fronde. The liaisons between Gondi and the Augustinians irritated him, and the cardinal did not need to use much eloquence to gain the king's approval for his views.

The elderly Archbishop of Paris died on 21 March 1654, and Mazarin thought it prudent to transfer the prelate's nephew and successor, the imprisoned Cardinal Retz, to safe-keeping in Nantes. But Retz escaped on 8 August. Since Louis XIV refused to answer his repeated letters to him, the new archbishop took refuge in Rome under the protection of Innocent X and, later, Alexander VII. Louis and Mazarin pursued him in Rome in various ways, sowing discord between him and Alexander VII. From 1656 onwards, Retz was condemned to a wandering life, never assured of his liberty; in 1657, Mazarin's spies tried to kidnap him in Cologne. In April, he sued for grace before Louis XIV but was granted nothing, because he refused to resign his see. The archbishopric thus, in effect, remained vacant from 1654 until 1662, the date when Louis XIV finally granted him a pardon.

In his attitude towards the Protestants, the king ignored Mazarin, the intricacies of whose mind and actions in this area were arcane, and followed the prejudices of père Paulin and père Annat. As with Port-Royal, Louis XIV's hostility was, at root, religious, even if psychological and political elements were grafted onto it. After his consecration at Reims, the king had been warned against the Protestants, and the incident was never forgotten. It would have been in Louis' mind in December 1659, during his visit to Toulouse. Following precedents, the deputies from the Protestant synod at Loudun requested an audience with the king. Entrusted with the task of addressing His Majesty, the Protestant minister Daniel Eustache found out the details of the forthcoming ceremony. He was told that he would have to speak kneeling down. He asked if he might present his address standing up, 'making it understood that he would rather be excused the honour of doing reverence to His Majesty than endure this disgrace'. His request was refused, and he delivered his speech on his knees. Louis XIV, informed of this earlier difficulty, listened politely. He then humiliated the deputies with this peremptory reply: 'I will serve you, I will maintain you in my edicts and you shall receive your expenses', a reference to a 16,000 *livres* subvention, similar to that paid to the preceding synod. On 19 December, the deputies returned to Loudun, 'highly satisfied with the welcome which had been accorded them' (147). They were mistaken. Behind the cool formality of their prince, they should, with greater intuition, have discerned the tribulations which would befall the poor Protestants of France.

MARRIAGE IS IN THE AIR

Louis was at Compiègne on 31 July 1658, in Paris for the second fortnight of August, in Fontainebleau for September and back in the Louvre in October. It was there, on the 24th, that the company of Molière presented Corneille's *Nicomède* before the king (190). The king's twentieth birthday was on 5 September and, for this event, 'prose encomia' were all the rage in Paris. The daughter of Gaston d'Orléans, Mademoiselle, took part in these amusements, and not without shrewdness. Fond of her cousin, she sketched a verbal picture of him on 7 October. Like many of her contemporaries, the princess equated dignity with stature; she sought a harmony between the physical characteristics of the sovereign and his moral qualities. 'The stature of this monarch is grander than that of others, as are his birth and demeanour. He has a lofty air, dignified, proud, courageous and pleasing, something very majestic and moderate in his expression, the most beautiful hair imaginable both in colour and in curls. He has fine legs and good deportment. All in all, he is the finest and best-endowed man in the realm.' (75) As is well known, he danced to perfection. He enjoyed physical exercise, especially hunting. We know that he was adept in the ways of the battlefield, and Mademoiselle did not hesitate to compare him with Gustavus Adolphus. She admired her cousin's courage, his ability to take command, his understanding of detail and his willingness to risk his own skin in order to lead 'officers and soldiers by his own example'. As long as Louis XIV went to the front with his armies (until 1693), testimonies of his personality in this regard continued; it had already taken shape by the age of twenty.

The rest of her pen-portrait remained as true for 1688, even 1708, as for 1658: 'His is a reserved manner, he speaks little; but to people with whom he feels at home he is a good conversationalist, never saying anything not absolutely to the point. He has good taste, discernment and a natural good temper. He is charitable and generous, and plays the part of a king without ever demeaning himself.' It might seem strange, but Louis was timid and remained so. It showed in the way he hid his emotions, something which the king never overcame; it helped him to cultivate his taste for secrecy, a political virtue. This goes beyond the princess's analysis. But her encomium left nothing important out. She outlined his talents as a statesman: 'He has a good sense of business, expresses his opinions clearly in council and in public too, when it is necessary.' Mademoiselle did not ignore, either, his attraction to good-looking women ('Gallantry is entirely proper'). His discriminating taste would, however, prevent her from ever becoming queen of France. Finally, shrewder than other commentators, she recognized the degree to which Anne of Austria had influenced indelibly the religiosity of her son: 'He has great piety and devotion.' (75) Thus, far from being a 'laborious exercise', this portrait was baroque and naïve, but lively and basically true.

In the text, and reading between the lines, the king's earnest, even sometimes passionate, desire to be married is apparent. Mazarin, in accordance with the queen mother, had given Philip IV to understand that a marriage of the king to the Infanta could form the firm basis of a proper peace. But, although Spain did not exclude women from the succession to the throne, Philip had a son the following year, in 1657, Felipe-Prosper. However, he was so sickly that the possibility of a French succession was not excluded. Then came Louis' illness in 1658, which some members of the court interpreted in symbolic and prophetic fashion. Here was what the Venetian ambassador had to say:

> The queen mother was so overcome and the cardinal so perturbed that it was firmly believed that she took a secret vow to do all that she could to bring about peace. It is certain that, by reminding Cardinal Mazarin how, at the time of the barricades and civil war, she had risked herself and the monarchy at personal cost in order to defend him, so she demanded, in return, that he do all in

his power to make her niece her daughter-in-law with peace as her dowry, promising to maintain him in overall charge of affairs in such a way that he would have no less authority in the state in peace than he had done in the time of troubles and war. (216)

The cardinal thus intensified his pressure upon Madrid. In order to force Philip IV to a decision or, failing that, to find another match, he appeared to put his weight behind an alternative bride, Marguerite of Savoy, another of Louis' cousins. This was why the court left Paris in November for Dijon and Lyon.

It was agreed that the King of France would decide for himself, following a meeting at Lyon, where the court arrived on the 24th. Marguerite, although dark-skinned, was pleasing to the eye, appearing to everyone 'the most demure and reserved person in the world', 'softly-spoken and cultured' (70). She was the ideal match for Louis XIV, attractive enough to the eye to awaken his emotions, yet with spirit of mind to keep him engaged. The king and his mother went out of their way to welcome the princesses from Savoy. He appeared well pleased with the encounter, but there was more than one arrow in Eros' sheaf and, whilst smiling sweetly in the direction of Savoy, Louis flirted openly with his 'Mancinette'. One might have been forgiven for imagining that Marie was already betrothed to him. 'No gallantry was spared on her behalf, with offers of music, receptions and outings on horse-back.' (70)

Did Mazarin perhaps, in December 1658, have more than one iron in the fire? It would seem improbable, given that he was so committed to the peace negotiations. If the Spanish marriage had proved an impossibility, Savoy would have been widely regarded as an acceptable second-choice. But no one would have approved of the *mésalliance* of a Mancini match. Besides, the cardinal was better placed than anyone to gauge the temperament of his niece, who was so independent and stubborn that she had always rejected the authority of her uncle. Furthermore, Spanish pride was engaged in the affair, once Madrid knew of the king's presence in Lyon. Philip IV observed of the Savoy match that 'Esto no puede ser, y no sera' ('It cannot and shall not take place') (216), and he despatched to Lyon the marquis de Pimentel with instructions to offer the hand of the Infanta, Maria Theresa. Mazarin accepted at once and Anne of Austria was plainly delighted. The Savoyard princesses were showered with gifts and Louis appeared not to have any objection to the match. This was the most spectacular triumph of the cardinal's career. From that moment, no alternative to the Spanish marriage appeared acceptable.

From January to May 1659, the court, by then back in Paris, set in train the negotiations for the pacification and marriage. Mazarin and Dom Luis de Haro signed the draft treaty on 4 June, although discussions continued throughout the summer on an island in the River Bidassoa. The King of Spain and his councillors, although they had accepted the French terms, seemed to want to postpone the inevitable outcome; and the French king also acted as though the Spanish marriage was only a distant prospect. Did he dream of putting his Mancini passion before the interests of state? Or did he want to gain a little time before becoming engaged in a match to which he had no emotional commitment? With Marguerite of Savoy he would have enjoyed a happy marriage. In marrying Maria Theresa, he was submitting himself to a worthy, but joyless, matrimony. Thus he allowed himself to be flattered by his Marie, to the alarm and irritation of Mazarin and the queen mother.

Between them, the cardinal and Anne of Austria organized a painful separation of the two lovers, which took place on 21 June. But Louis XIV continued to correspond with her, and the cardinal, fully engaged in the Spanish negotiations, was obliged to intervene on several occasions. On 16 July, he begged the king not to let himself be ruled by emotion: 'The *Confidente* [Anne of Austria] wrote to me to tell me the state in which she found you and I am in despair about it, for it is vital that you put this matter straight, if you care for your own well-being and do not want to worry to death all your good servants . . . And should you decide not to change your conduct for the better, things will go from bad to worse. I beseech you to think of your glory, your honour, the service of God and the good of your realm.' (70) Learning that Louis had seen Marie Mancini again, at Saint-Jean-d'Angély on the 13th, he pressed the king one last time (on 28 August) to put aside this impossible love affair. Only then did Louis accept, leaving Marie at Brouage to brood, with the aid of the works of Seneca, on his cruel deception. She was married in 1661 to Lorenzo Onofrio Colonna, Duke of Tagliacoli, Prince of Paliano and Constable of Naples, with the accord of, and to the satisfaction of, Maria Theresa, Queen of France, her 'fortunate' rival.

THE PEACE OF THE PYRENEES

It took a long time to draft the peace treaty. Mazarin tried to be too cunning and Dom Luis de Haro too languid. This was why the court did not await the outcome before beginning the journey to the south-west. In August, it was in Saintonge; by September it had reached Bordeaux. On the military front, a suspension of hostilities had been agreed in May, and the truce was revived in June. Many of the problems were already resolved; 'but, because there were still numerous obstacles to a pacification, Cardinal Mazarin and Dom Luis de Haro, first ministers of the two Crowns, personally took charge of the negotiations'. The conferences were held on the island of Faisans, equidistant from Hendaye and Fuentarabia, in the River Bidassoa. 'Their first encounter took place on 13 August; they continued to meet there for the following three months and only broke off when all the articles of accord had been agreed.' (71) Faisans became known henceforth as 'l'île de la Conférence'.

Nothing was easily arrived at, since the treaty underlined the decline of Spain and the more recent French preponderance, which the Peace of Westphalia had imposed upon Europe. The esteem of the two nations was intermingled with that of the two monarchs. Philip IV was pleased to secure the marriage of the Infanta, but irritated because the match had been forced on him and disturbed by its potential consequences. Mazarin and Louis XIV were willing to make numerous concessions to have the marriage, but that of pardoning the prince de Condé for his treachery was understandably difficult to accommodate. The result was a series of carefully matched clauses, each heavily fought over. Thus, Spain obtained for Condé his return to the French court, and his reinstatement to his offices and governorships; but, in return, Philip IV ceded Jülich to the Duke of Neuberg (a French ally) and surrendered Avesnes, Philippeville and Marienburg. Spain abandoned Roussillon, part of Cerdagne, Gravelines, Saint-Venant, Bourbourg, Artois (save for Aire and Saint-Omer), Le Quesnoy and Landrecies in Hainaut, and parts of Luxembourg. But France gave up all its other conquests and undertook not to support either Cromwell or the King of Portugal. It is true, however, that, in return for these last concessions, France was given compensation on its north-east frontier. Spain, although not a signatory to the Treaty of Münster, now accepted its clauses. With scant regard for Duke Charles IV of Lorraine, it was agreed that Lorraine would cede the duchy of Bar, Clermont en Argonne, Stenay, Moyenvic, Dun and Jametz to Louis XIV. The citadel at Nancy was to be dismantled and France would enjoy rights of passage for its troops through the duchy. If Charles IV refused to accept these clauses, France would occupy the duchy militarily.

These clauses 'gave the two states frontiers which were more carefully delineated' (71) – from Flanders to the Sundgau and from Mont Louis to Port Vendres. They extended the realm of France and increased its strategic opportunities. Mazarin had not, of course, gained all the concessions which he had hoped for, especially in the Low Countries. But he no doubt thought it more worthwhile to count on the hopes contained in the Infanta's wedding-gifts. The Spanish succession was already an issue on the horizon in the chancelleries of Europe. Philip IV, a victim of the abuse of consanguinity, appeared only to be able to sire sickly children from his second marriage. The King of Spain was sufficiently alarmed to demand that the treaty contain a clause renouncing Maria Theresa's rights to the succession. Mazarin accepted this, but required an exception in the case of the Low Countries. With the inevitability of a *quid pro quo*, this was agreed. But the cunning cardinal had another card up his sleeve. The clauses concerning the dowry also mentioned the rights of the Infanta, and therefore of Louis XIV. The value of the dowry was vast: 500,000 *écus d'or*, to be paid in three instalments. But Spain, despite its American treasure, was invariably short of funds. As a result of M. de Lionne's subtlety, one word, a preposition of apparent inconsequence, was slipped into article 4 of the marriage contract, a word which reasserted the possibility of rights of succession apparently ceded away elsewhere. 'That, *on condition* (*moyennant*) that the sums are made over to His Most Christian Majesty[,] . . . the said most serene Infanta will rest content with the said dowry and not thereafter sue for any other of her rights.' (216) If the dowry was unpaid, the renunciation clause would be rendered void.

The first instalment was due to be paid over to France 'at the time of the consummation of the marriage'. This occurred in June 1660, but not a single *écu* crossed the Pyrenees. Mazarin and Louis XIV held back from making an issue of it; but, only seven months after the Peace of the Pyrenees, Philip IV's safeguard was already compromised. Eight years later, Lille and Walloon Flanders would be in French hands as 'the rights of the queen'.

Such an outcome could have been foreseen by no one on 7 November 1659, when the king's glory was undoubtedly shared by the cardinal. An engraving pictured 'Cardinal Mazarin opening the door to the temple of peace and Dom Luis de Haro, closing the door to the temple of war'. An eighty-page quarto brochure celebrated the cardinal, the queen mother and Louis XIV in Latin and French anagrams. And, to add to the stature of the cardinal, the 'Baltic pacification', the two treaties of Oliva and Copenhagen, which were signed in the spring of 1660, should not be ignored. Neither would have come about so quickly without French mediation and the skills of Mazarin. Mme de la Fayette wrote: 'No minister has governed with such an absolute authority as Mazarin and none has used his power more effectively to establish his greatness.' (49)

THE SPANISH MARRIAGE

Whilst the duc de Gramont was in Madrid requesting the hand of the Infanta in matrimony officially, Louis and his mother were visiting the south of France, in the provinces of Languedoc, Armagnac and Provence. On 18 January 1660, they arrived in Aix, which was where the prince de Condé came to do Louis homage. Setting aside his resentment, Louis was courteous towards the former rebel, even going so far as to invite him to the wedding, an invitation which Condé politely declined. It was whilst he was in Aix also that the king learnt of the death of his uncle Gaston, who had left him his collections of books and medals. The death of one *frondeur* prince of the blood and the formal capitulation of another looked like the end of a whole baroque generation.

The festivities for the Spanish marriage were nothing if not baroque. The court of Philip IV set off in the direction of Saint-Jean-de-Luz 'with majestic slowness, following the Spanish custom. The royal cortège was no less than six *lieues* [fifteen miles] long' (190). It was agreed that the sovereigns should converge 'simultaneously at the frontier. Their encounter took place on 6 and 7 June upon the same island where, seven months previously, Cardinal Mazarin and Dom Luis de Haro had signed the treaty. The magnificence of the apartments, the impressive retinues of the two kings and the crowds of spectators made this spectacle as renowned as it was extraordinary; what made it still more unusual and interesting were the displays of friendship and mutual trust with which the monarchs greeted each other' (71).

The marriage had been celebrated by proxy on the 2nd at Fuentarabia in 'the great church, which was draped with rich tapestries'. The King of Spain and his daughter took their seats 'in a kind of chapel decorated with cloth of gold'.

> The chaplains began straightway to say a Mass, at the end of which the king and the Infanta stood up and, after Dom Luis de Haro had read his procuration from the French king ..., the Bishop of Pamplona conducted the marriage service. Before giving her consent, she went down on her knees before her father the king, and he, giving his permission to reply 'yes', was so affected that tears came to his eyes ... As soon as she was pronounced queen, he took her by the hand. (6)

French onlookers thought that Maria Theresa resembled Anne of Austria – 'a pious demeanour', the 'picture of good health', 'a good complexion' – albeit that she was less tall. Throughout the ceremony, she had seemed 'modest but very pleased'. Everyone saw her future that day, it seems, through rose-tinted spectacles; even the Spaniards were enthusiastic.

The marriage was celebrated again on the 9th, at Saint-Jean-de-Luz. 'It was a fairy-tale wedding!' (190) 'The queens, each under a high canopy, were the most beauteous in the world.' (6) Louis was dressed in a suit of golden cloth. Maria Theresa 'wore the great royal cape [in deep-red velvet embossed in gold with fleurs-de-lis], which would be remembered for the rest of her life and which can sometimes be seen in pictures of her, with the golden crown on her head'. The Mass was long and very solemn, and, 'at the end, the king and queen were seated under a canopy, called the pall. All the court was present in the church, as you might imagine, with everybody ceremonially dressed for the occasion. Without distortion, this was an entirely different kind of ceremony from that which we experienced in Fuentarabia' (6). The cortège processed out of the church as it had arrived. At its head came the king and queen. Maria Theresa's train was carried by the princesses. Then came the queen mother, 'Mme the countess of Flex carrying her train. Mademoiselle followed her, M. Mancini carrying her train'. The streets were 'draped with tapestries, decorated with garlands attached to pillars painted white and gold' (190). The marriage was speedily consummated. That evening, 'the queen mother drew the bed-curtains on the new couple and then retired. The next day, the two young spouses seemed very happy with each other' (190).

It only remained to return (with celebrations *en route*) to the capital, where the triumphal entry of the sovereigns was being prepared. The king could scarcely bring himself to make the detour to Brouage to bring to a sad conclusion the episode of his love affair. In Paris, all 'was ready for one of the most splendid entries which had ever been seen. The streets were decorated with foliage, tapestries and pictures; and there were triumphal arches in various places with devices and inscriptions' (71). Paris had forgotten the Fronde; the king had forgotten certain events of his childhood. Many came from the provinces to celebrate the royal marriage and the great pacification. From eight o'clock to midday, the young monarchs, seated on a throne 'prepared for them at the entrance to the faubourg Saint-Antoine, received the homage and submission of all the senior corporations'. Then came the clergy, marching behind crosses and banners, the University, the Six Guilds and other fraternities, and then the sovereign courts, with the Parlement at the rear as the most prestigious. The solemn procession began at two o'clock in the afternoon. 'The king was on horseback, preceded by the troops of his household, and accompanied by the princes and the gentlemen in his service. The queen came immediately behind him in an open carriage, followed by the princesses and other aristocratic ladies.' In this elaborate procession, the sovereigns crossed the capital from the porte Saint-Antoine to the Louvre, 'and at every point along the route they met with great jubilation at such a happy day' (71).

After such a triumph and at almost twenty-two years of age, one might wonder, what routes lay open to the king. Would he suffer the cardinal's tutelage for another twenty years and become another of those *rois fainéants* that he had despised as a child? Or would he dispense with the services of a minister who had rendered France such services that his prevarications paled into insignificance? For his part, Mazarin had to look to the future, and this was one reason behind his desire to take holy orders and be elected pope. But Providence put an end to such delicate considerations. Giulio Mazarini died on the night of 8–9 March 1661, thus gently withdrawing from the scene at the right moment, as all good servants should.

6

The Restoration of the State

ON 1 AUGUST 1664, the tragedy written by 'the worthy Corneille' entitled *Othon* was performed before the court at Fontainebleau. The plot was a political one: Who was to succeed the Emperor Galba, Othon (candidate of the consul Vinius) or Pison (proposed by the prefect Lacus)? Behind it lay an obvious political message. In Othon, the courtiers recognized their young king, the enemy of disorder and conspiracies; a prince determined to rule. In fact, Louis XIV had already been 'at the helm' (99) for three years. In the trappings of a Roman play, Corneille eulogized the king.

LOUIS, THE PERSONAL RULER

The personal rule had begun several hours after Mazarin's death on 9 March 1661. On his death-bed, this Mentor had whispered to his Telemachus his last words of advice. He told Louis to 'maintain the rights of the Church', to nominate 'capable, pious and well-disposed' men to Church benefices, to treat the nobility 'with respect and liberality', to keep the judges within the remit of their offices and to 'relieve the people not only from the *taille*, but also from all their other fiscal burdens'; finally, he should choose ministers 'according to their talents' (171). The cardinal left the king with three ministers: Fouquet, expert in locating credit, Le Tellier, the reformer of the army, and Lionne, a diplomat of the highest calibre.

Mazarin did not tell the king to dismiss Fouquet. The latter had been loyal to the cardinal during the Fronde; his financial wizardry had been of use to him. Contrary to a belief popular among historians, Mazarin was not so maladroit as to advise the king against appointing a first minister. But, as he reflected on what Mazarin had said, how could the king not have deduced that he should take these responsibilities upon himself? The cardinal breathed his last at two o'clock in the morning. The following day, the 10th, the young king, having summoned his ministers, told them his intentions. The courtiers either could scarcely believe their ears or thought that this was perhaps just a passing whim. For, in reality, Mazarin's predominance and the king's discretion had obscured from many the direction that events were likely to take. The king lost no time in replacing the rule of the ministers with a personal rule because he wanted to create a strong impression. Some historians have spoken of it as a *coup d'état*, but nothing could be further from the reality. Others have spoken of it as a unique event, but this is to ignore the personal rules of Francis I, Henry II, Henry IV and even Louis XIII when he chose so to act. But there was a further reason for the king's haste. He was dissatisfied with the overall state of France, and particularly with its administration and with the court. At the beginning of the *Mémoires*, Louis XIV wrote of 1661: 'I began to look around me at the various organs of the state, and not with the eyes of a spectator but those of a ruler, and I became very much aware of the fact that there was not one which did not require urgently that I take matters in hand ... Disorder ruled everywhere.' (63)

For these two reasons, Louis was determined to act quickly, albeit prudently. From this moment, pragmatism predominated. Louis XIV sensed that the time was right: 'In fact, everywhere was calm; there was neither unrest nor fear nor even a semblance of unrest in the kingdom which might have interrupted or opposed my proposals. Peace was established with neighbouring countries, apparently for as long as I chose, given the circumstances in which they were placed.' (63) Internal peace was a guarantee of loyalty. As to the external peace, it coincided with a tendency in Europe at large towards absolutist monarchy. In 1660, the great elector inaugurated a series of reforms in Berlin. On 29 May 1660, Charles II entered Whitehall, putting an end to the long Cromwellian interregnum; and, on 8 May 1661, the extraordinary Cavalier Parliament began its sittings. In October 1660 in Copenhagen, the court, clergy and bourgeoisie proclaimed the heredity of the Danish Crown, before affirming the absolute power of the sovereign in the following January. These coincidences deserve careful consideration. Too often, historians today are obsessed by 'conjuncture', conceived of only in terms of a price curve. The turning-point of 1660–1 cannot be explained purely in terms of economic circumstances. Politics came first.

Brienne, the secretary of state for foreign affairs until the office passed to his son, left an account of the surprise move of 10 March 1661:

> The king asked . . . the princes, dukes and ministers of state . . . to assemble in the queen mother's chamber so that he could explain to them himself that 'he had decided to take charge of the state in person and to rely on no one else' (these were his own words) and courteously discharged them from their duties, saying that 'when he had need of their good advice, he would call for it' . . . I was ordered to write to all the foreign secretaries to explain the decision that His Majesty had taken to govern his state in person so that they could advise their princes accordingly. (43)

The 'royal entry', as Pierre Gaxotte called it, was perfectly handled. Its brusqueness was designed to make the aristocracy sit up and take notice.

INDIVIDUAL AND CORPORATE POWER

The royal entry was only the beginning. Before taking the court to Fontainebleau (20 April to 4 December), even before the end of March, Louis had established the essential features of his governmental reform. The system was new only in degree and presentation. He remained faithful to the old tradition which saw an equilibrium between corporate and individual power. Without a balance of that kind, any regime would tend to become arbitrary. The Turkish sultan depended solely upon his viziers, and the result was despotic. Corporative states like Poland, where councils had predominance, were paralysed. Countries where the constitution had not sufficiently laid down the responsibilities as between corporations and their leaders were doomed to instability, as the events in the United Provinces in 1672 would illustrate. France, however, was better provided

for. Since the reign of Charles VII, the absolute monarchy had
taken shape. But, from the central Middle Ages, the realm had
been protected by its customary constitution and by a strong
juridical tradition. This did not resolve every problem; Louis
XIV had much to do in 1661. The difficulties stemmed from
former kings who had relied on favourites or who had proved
incapable of setting down the rules for ministerial office. The
institution of secretaries of state was, in fact, of recent origin,
their powers having grown up gradually (in 1547, 1559, 1560,
1588) (227). The monarchy proceeded cautiously in regard to
the Council. No one knew for sure where its boundaries of
responsibility lay, since, for so long, it had been a flexible instrument of government. Some of its sections changed their name
and functions, and the overall body was governed by contradictory ordinances. Under Louis XIII, from 1611 to 1630, the
Council was the object of twenty-six regulatory edicts (250).
This was why Louis XIV's contemporaries were so impressed by
the arrangements of 1661; subsequent historians have been
impressed by the fact that they lasted for 128 years.

As regards individuals, Louis XIV confirmed the division of
duties as between the various departments such as the chancellery, the superintendency of finances and the four offices of secretary of state. Judicial matters, such as the presidency of the
conseil des parties and the guard of the seals of state, were the
responsibility of the chancellor, who remained the leading officer
of the Crown, the premier judge and president of the councils of
state. But Louis did not want the chancellor's responsibilities to
be overwhelming: he kept him out of the innermost council
(*conseil d'en haut*) where the essential principles of policy were
debated.

The leading office of secretary of state, the individual who had
jurisdiction over 'war, military impositions (*taillons*), artillery
and the Mediterranean navy' as well as eight provinces in
France, was held by Le Tellier. The king would pay him this
compliment after his death: 'He had never had a better councillor, and in all sorts of matters.' (39) The second office was held
by Guénégaud, who had, like Le Tellier, been in his post since
1643. He looked after Paris, the king's household, the clergy, and
five provinces in France. The third secretaryship was held in
tandem by Henri-Auguste de Loménie de Brienne, who had long
held the post, and his son Henri-Louis. Louis XIV only retained

them temporarily. From September 1661, Colbert had taken control *de facto* of the Atlantic fleet from the Briennes, as well as that of the Mediterranean from Le Tellier (273). In April 1663, the Briennes offered their resignations, surrendering their pensions and the administration of four provinces. But it was already the case that nobody at court knew to what extent, if any, they were responsible for foreign affairs, since the king and M. de Lionne had taken charge of them over their heads. There remained the final secretaryship, then held by the elderly Louis Phelypeaux, sieur de la Vrillière, who had served in office since 1629. He was in charge of matters concerning the *religion prétendue réformée* as well as thirteen provinces or fifty-seven per cent of France. However, the division of responsibilities scarcely changed, although, from time to time, Louis XIV altered the assignment of provinces as between the secretaries in order to link frontier provinces or conquered ones to the department of war.

The sixth area of administration, that of the superintendency of finances, lay in the hands of Nicolas Fouquet, marquis de Belle-Isle. He held this office concurrently with that of *procureur général* in the Parlement of Paris, the holding of which was of importance since this gave him judicial immunity. Fouquet was appointed as superintendent in the aftermath of the Fronde on 7 February 1653 at the same time as Abel Servien, but he remained in sole charge after the death of his colleague in February 1659. He was brilliant and approachable, and generated in others both enthusiasm and loyalty, but also hatred. He befriended poets, pretty women and painters; he was imaginative; but he was held in suspicion by many. He was a great patron who forgot that Maecenas himself would not have become a legend without Augustus. He was wholly ambitious, but too short-sighted to follow any more deeply laid plan, and quickly exhausted the stock of renown that he had cultivated. His methods of raising funds were nothing if not orthodox, but they had been successful. The balance of his vices and virtues made him the scapegoat of a glorious Louis XIV and an envious Colbert. Fouquet had unfortunately treated the latter as a bankrupt and the former as an adolescent.

As for the Council, its organization depended upon the king himself. Its lower tier was made up of the privy council or *conseil des parties*. The king left the presidency of this council to the chancellor. It dealt with important matters of administration, disputed cases and judicial business 'reserved' from the law-courts for the king's council. It was composed of the secretaries of state, councillors of state and *maîtres des requêtes*, was open to many expert talents, and was a training-ground for administrators. In addition, there were particular departments of the privy council to manage such matters as appeals, lawsuits and the postal services, and various matters commissioned to it, such as the oversight of the royal finances and military supplies. These all provided around 100 senior administrators with posts of the highest importance.

Above the privy council lay the penultimate tier of government. Here Louis XIV presided over meetings of what was known as the 'council of despatches' (*conseil des dépêches*). It began life in the Fronde, and its uniqueness lay in the fact that the king presided over it personally. It dealt with home affairs when they concerned several secretaries of state, particularly handling the correspondence between the government and the governors and intendants. In the reorganization of 1661, this council was an important one, meeting twice a week, but its significance gradually waned: between 1691 and 1715, it only met every second Monday. The chancellor, the secretaries of state and their successors, the superintendent of finances, several councillors of state (depending upon their responsibilities) and the ministers all served on it.

The title 'minister of state' became, as the king hoped, something of a rarity; only those fortunate enough to be chosen by His Majesty to attend the most senior organ of government, known as the 'upper council' (*conseil d'en haut*) because it sat on the first floor in the royal residences, would use it. In the course of the reign, it would more often be called the 'council of ministers', a more accurate description since only those who sat on it had the right to the title. This kind of council had been in existence for a long time, and the regency council envisaged by Louis XIII was of this type. Members of the royal family, princes of the blood, dukes and peers, the great officers of the Crown, and the chancellor had generally sat on it. But Louis XIV now restricted its composition by not summoning the queen mother, Séguier or Henri-Louis de Loménie de Brienne to its meetings, and never even dreamt of inviting Condé, Conti, Longueville or Beaufort to attend. Not a single duke was summoned there; even Turenne, who taught the king the art of war, was too grand a seigneur to serve Louis XIV in this capacity. Instead, a triad of ministers, Le Tellier, Fouquet and Lionne, sufficed. For the king, 'in the most important and secret affairs of state', 'the smallest number of advisers' was to be preferred (63). As soon as his choice was known, the aristocrats, forever malcontent, criticized the absence of the high nobility in this council, the council responsible for all the most important political decisions. The ministers were even criticized for being 'bourgeois', members of the *noblesse de robe*. In his *Mémoires*, the king defended his decision like this: 'Doubtless, I could have found men of a higher social station, but they would not have matched the capacity of these three.' (63)

To be there, one needed the king's blessing. He had chosen Fouquet but excluded Séguier. He had elevated the secretary of state Le Tellier but ignored his colleagues – even Loménie de Brienne the younger, who had held ministerial rank for over a year. He had chosen Lionne, who, until 1663, was not even a secretary of state. But Lionne had been a member of Mazarin's remarkable team, the successful negotiator of the Peace of the Pyrenees, outstanding in his diplomatic skills, his taste, intelligence and tact. Saint-Evremond wrote of him:

> The most divergent skills were brought together in him. He enjoyed both the keenest awareness of men's abilities and a profound understanding of issues. In truth, I never cease to be amazed that a minister who was more than a match for the politicking of the Italians and the inveterate prudence of the Spanish, who turned so many of the German princes in our favour and even put those to work for our interests who had difficulty working for their own, to be astounded I say that someone so consummate in diplomacy nevertheless can display all the sensibility of the most polished courtiers in conversation and distractions. (92)

Bearing in mind also that Le Tellier was not only a talented administrator but also an able courtier, and that Fouquet, despite his defects, acted and thought like a gentleman, it is evident that the royal triad was no bourgeois club but a group of competent and civilized statesmen.

The division of responsibilities between departments and councils, and between the various organs of the Council, and the fact that the king, the ministers and the chancellor linked together the various sections of the administration and the privy council, ensured that the machinery of government worked well. Without the decisions of Louis XIV and his presence in the councils, the successes would have been less evident. In addition, the king had inserted his most loyal servant in a modest, but strategically important, post. This was the man whom the inveterately suspicious Mazarin had most trusted, the most precious gift from the cardinal to the king, Jean-Baptiste Colbert.

On 8 March, the day before the cardinal's death, Colbert was named intendant of finances. Louis XIV had 'the greatest confidence in him', recognizing his 'energy, intelligence and scrupulousness' (63). The task of this former client of Mazarin's was to oversee royal income and expenditure. But his master knew that he did not just do that: he also kept an eye, for the king, on the superintendent of finances.

THE SNAKE AND THE SQUIRREL

The heraldic crest of the Fouquets was a crimson squirrel (a *foucquet*) on a silver background; that of the Colberts was an azure snake upon gold. The heraldry evokes the characters of a fable. Fouquet's ambition has never been denied and it was reinforced by the proud boast of the family motto: *Quo non ascendam?* (Whither shall I not ascend?) The agile squirrel seems, symbolically, a prey to the snake, who, with cunning, disguises his enmity.

To explain Fouquet's fall, we must return to the period immediately after the Fronde (170). In 1653, the king was ignorant in all matters of finance. Mazarin had neither the competence to initiate him in this area, nor the desire to see his godson become involved in its details. This left three individuals: Mazarin, Fouquet and Colbert. The latter, as the cardinal's intendant, occupied himself in administering Mazarin's immense fortune, which had been put together on his return from exile. Having come back almost penniless, Mazarin left on his death thirty-five million *livres*, plus his account at the Bank of Amsterdam (170). Colbert knew that the cardinal minister had grown too rich too quickly, despite the great services which he had rendered. (Indeed, part of his huge fortune lay in five million *livres* of unpaid Treasury bills (*assignations*).) But there were several reasons for his discretion. The cardinal was his protector and the scions of Mazarin were also making their fortunes, and Colbert was the best placed amongst them to do so. And he was biding his time, preparing the way by accumulating the facts and figures on which to base the future denunciation of the superintendent Fouquet. In 1659, when Fouquet alone held that post, Colbert began to incriminate him. Mazarin, who was playing more than one game at the same time, appeared not to listen. The cardinal's health, of course, was deteriorating and he hoped to be able to maintain his own fortune intact, so it was difficult for him to accuse Fouquet of self-enrichment and he chose to maintain the status quo.

Fouquet had inherited a bankruptcy in the Treasury which had existed since 1648. It was the combined effect of the Fronde (which had eliminated the 'extraordinary revenues' (*affaires extraordinaires*), which were vital expedients since they were more important than the *tailles*) and of the pronounced scarcity of money (from 1641, precious metals in Europe were in short supply). Mazarin gave Fouquet the principal role in the superintendency of finances: he was told to find resources fast, because the state was in desperate need, and in large quantities, since the war was cripplingly expensive. In these circumstances, the superintendent undertook no innovations. He kept the existing arrangements, which meant that almost every asset was farmed out, not only the indirect taxes and 'extraordinary revenues', but even the direct taxes, since the treasurers and receivers of the *pays d'états* farmed-out receipts. Fouquet thus preserved a system which no one had ever asked him to change, which had hitherto justified its existence, and which suited his character. He had a talent for persuading revenue-farmers (*traitants*) and other financiers to sustain the flow of credit to the regime. And, to persuade them to advance their funds, he increased their percentage profit.

Such a policy did not seem absurd. It assured the monarchy its resources. And, although, perhaps, it made the government the prisoner of its creditors, it preserved the king from unpopularity. Nothing proved, in fact, simpler than to denounce the avariciousness of the financiers; nothing was more usual than, having trapped them, to persuade them to disgorge. In 1661, however, it was a double trap. Not only were the financiers to be forced to pay up, but there would also be an unusual victim, the superintendent of finances himself. All that was needed was to persuade the king of the unscrupulousness of his minister. Colbert knew how to do it, and succeeded in getting the king to play his game. On 4 May 1661, more than three months after the famous festivities at Vaux-le-Vicomte, the king decided the fate of his superintendent.

Colbert's role appears clear in retrospect (170). From 1659 onwards, it was evident to the ever-faithful intendant that, in the event of Mazarin's departure, it would be difficult to prevent a financial investigation from taking place. The cardinal knew this as well, which was why he tried to arrange things so that Louis XIV would refuse to be his inheritor, and why he did all in his power to prevent a probate inventory being conducted in the event of his death, an inventory which would reveal all his prevarications. For Colbert, it was a matter of staying on good terms with Mazarin, gaining the favour of the king, and finding a way of ousting Fouquet without disgracing Mazarin himself, for Mazarin was even more compromised than Fouquet. Hence the Colbertian tactics of March and April 1661. The new intendant of finances could rely on the king's support. He had persuaded the king of his own integrity, thus masking an ambition even more deeply entrenched than that of his rival. He flattered Louis, stressing his own concern for the well-being of the state. It was not a difficult hand to play. Louis XIV scarcely understood anything about financial matters, and he was irritated by the superintendent. The latter had not taken into account the royal declaration of 10 March. He acted and spoke as though this was merely a moment of transition between two periods of ministerial dominance, as though he, Fouquet, was going to become first minister.

The subtle part of the Colbertian plot concerned the late cardinal. Louis XIV had set aside the express wishes of the prudent Mazarin and had ordered an inventory of his fabulous fortune. There was a contrast of scandalous proportions between the cardinal's legacy and the emptiness of the state's coffers. But Mazarin had enjoyed the confidence of the queen mother and of Louis himself. He was the king's godfather and he had left his fortune to grandees. How could the will be overturned? How could it be revealed that the first minister had fleeced the tax-payer? At this point, Colbert insinuated, and the king was happy to accept this reassuring picture of things, that it was all the fault of Fouquet. Colbert attacked the superintendent in order to take attention away from Mazarin. He even cleared the cardinal of blame by assuring the king that Mazarin himself had dreamt of orchestrating Fouquet's dismissal. In the name of financial rectitude in general, and the good of the state in particular, Colbert persuaded the king that Fouquet had been, and remained, a dishonest extortioner, enriching himself at the expense of the state, and hiding his own malversations and those of his entourage behind the unbelievable disorder in the accounts. He was the prisoner of the financiers. And, for good measure, the azure snake pretended that the crimson squirrel was undermining public office by fortifying the island marquisate of Belle-Isle, and that he was even hoping, in the event of his dismissal, to make alliance with the English or, worse still, the Spanish.

Louis XIV was persuaded of the necessity of his arrest; it only remained to arrange the trap. This involved showering Fouquet with expectations, flattering him with audiences, encouraging him to give up his office of *procureur général*, and then getting him away from Paris so that his papers could be seized and his accomplices arrested. Fouquet, although aware of Colbert's machinations, accepted each of these lures. Even worse, by his conception of the huge festivities at Vaux-le-Vicomte,* where Molière's play *Les Fâcheux* was performed, and by inviting the king there, he sealed his fate. He put himself in the position of a king who had invited a poor relative to attend, thus showing, if not an innocence, at least a straightforwardness which never deserted him. He has sometimes been presented as a monster and a schemer, but he demonstrated that he possessed neither the hypocrisy nor the singlemindedness of a man of intrigue, nor, above all, the avarice of a financier.

The king and Colbert were not the only ones to want Fouquet out of the way. The superintendent had made, 'with the riches of iniquity', as many enemies as friends. His ambition had frustrated others besides M. Colbert. It is interesting, at this juncture, to gain a sense of the more general reactions. Here are those of a poet of some repute, a man capable of rising above the prejudices of the moment. Writing to the marquise de Sévigné, Chapelain set aside his formal academic style and penned an emotional letter:

Why all this fuss, my dear friend? Was it not enough [for this

* On 17 August 1661.

man] to ruin the state and make the king hateful to his people by
the enormous taxes with which they are overwhelmed, and by
deflecting all his revenues into imprudent expenses and impudent
acquisitions, he who had no regard for either the king's honour or
his service but, instead, reinforced himself against the king by
corrupting his subjects and servants? Should we not also, as the
crowning crime to his profligacy, put up a monument to the
favours, real or supposed, that he had from women of quality and
keep a horrifying list of his liaisons with them so that his downfall
might also take with it their reputations? (96)

This obliging individual summarized the formal accusations
levied against the superintendent. Note that Vaux-le-Vicomte is
contained under the brief mention of 'imprudent expenses',
whilst the handling of the finances, the weight of taxation and its
ill-justified diversion, and the Belle-Isle 'plot' play a much
greater part in the list of accusations.

The ostentation of the superintendent had so irritated the king
that he had hoped to order his arrest on 17 August in the midst
of the festivities at Vaux. Fortunately, the queen mother made
him realize that a king had no right to violate the laws of
hospitality, and thus followed the scenario at Nantes. Under the
pretext of opening the Estates of Brittany, the king left Fontainebleau on 29 August, accompanied by Condé, the duc
d'Enghien, the comte d'Armagnac, the duc de Bouillon,
Turenne and Saint-Aignan. Louis entered Nantes on 1 September. He stayed at the château, whilst the superintendent, perturbed at last, lodged in a house at the other side of the town. On
Monday the 5th, Louis ordered the arrest of Fouquet. The man
charged with this delicate task was Charles de Batz-Castelmore,
sieur d'Artagnan, a sub-lieutenant of the musketeers.

PERFECTING THE COUNCIL

The arrest of Fouquet had two immediate consequences. Firstly,
the vacancy on the council of ministers was filled by Colbert. In
place of the trio of Fouquet, Lionne and Le Tellier, there was
that of Colbert, Lionne and Le Tellier. Secondly, the king
deprived him of a successor as superintendent of finances. He
wrote: 'What I believe I did which was more worth following,
and of greater advantage for my people, was to have suppressed

the post of superintendent, or rather, to have taken that responsibility myself.' (63) Louis became his own superintendent.

Financial affairs were henceforth to be handled, at least in principle, by a council. A regulation of 15 September, which Colbert drafted (252), created a new branch of government, the 'royal council of finances' (called the 'royal council' (*conseil royal*)). The king would preside over it, and, besides, reserved to himself 'the signing of all ordinances concerning expenditures and accounts (*comptants*)' as well as all budgets for the repartition of tax, Treasury accounts and demands for taxation. For those who think that these might have been merely dispositions on paper, Pontchartrain gives us the answer, saying that 'a paid scribe would not write as much as this king does' (116). For those who imagined that the disgrace of Fouquet changed nothing, Louis XIV would reply by accepting these 'enormous secretarial duties' (116). Under the direction of the king, the royal council brought together the chief of the council of finances and three councillors, Colbert, d'Aligre and Alexandre de Sève. But, from its inception, it was understood by everyone that M. Colbert, despite his modest title of intendant, was the driving force. He had drawn up the clause specifying its duties: 'The intendant of finances will have the honour of being a member of the royal council, will have responsibility for the Treasury, and, consequently, will keep the register of all receipts and dispenses which are made; he will give it to no one else save upon the express orders of His Majesty.' (252) The king had wanted the council of finances to meet three times every week, but, in 1665, this was reduced to twice a week. From this date onwards, Colbert, enjoying the title of controller-general, undertook the lion's share of the financial work with Louis XIV, leaving the royal council to accept the *fait accompli*.

In September 1664, Colbert persuaded the king to create a fourth council of government, the royal council of commerce (*conseil royal de commerce*). It was to have been concerned with all matters of the economy, an instrument in the hands of the powerful minister. But, in fact, it overlapped so much with the council of finances that Colbert grew tired of it. Its effective life was of only four years, and it was finally disbanded in 1676.

These examples show how power under Louis XIV was far from being an abstract formality. The council of commerce was ephemeral because the king did not want conciliar government for its own sake, but for the sake of efficient government. The royal council, on the other hand, grew in importance and eclipsed the council of despatches. Empirical change did not end there. In June 1700, Louis XIV created without hesitation a bureau of commerce, which would last through to 1722. It was this new council which would prepare the celebrated edict of 1701 declaring commercial activities non-demeaning to nobles, save those currently serving as judges. This council would include three councillors of state, the secretary of state for the navy (Pontchartrain), the controller-general, six intendants of commerce, two tax-farmers general and, finally, thirteen deputies from the chambers of commerce. The addition of representatives from the commercial world as well as of the relevant royal servants to this council is one of those fruitful innovations which were customary under the Louis XIV regime.

Another important novelty was the development of the 'royal working sessions' (*travail du roi*), meetings which sometimes prepared Council business and sometimes saw to the implementation of its decisions. Thanks to these, His Majesty could, keeping ministers in the background, reflect on issues whilst increasing, *de facto*, the credit of the most effective of his chief administrators. This way of proceeding introduced and sustained a rapport between Louis and his collaborators which was rarely to be found anywhere, certainly outside France, under the *ancien régime*. Such methods preserved the realm for a long time from the double danger of, on the one hand, the arbitrariness of its master and, on the other, a ministerial despotism. Thus an absolute monarchy gradually adapted itself to the rhythms of an administrative monarchy.

MINISTERS AND THEIR ACOLYTES

Superficially, Louis XIV governed with a very small group of six collaborators. In fact, he used other heads of department, in addition to other individuals associated with government bodies. Every seigneur had to have his honour satisfied. The council of ministers, which, the king not included, was composed of between three (in 1661) and seven individuals (in 1709 it included Monseigneur, the Duke of Burgundy, the duc de

Beauvillier, the marquis de Torcy, the chancellor Pontchartrain, Desmarets and Voysin), was not always strictly limited to his six advisers. From 1691 to 1714, M. de Beauvillier, minister without portfolio, was on it, and it was open to the Dauphin and, then, to the Duke of Burgundy to attend. Below this rank lay the post of the senior figure of the royal council of finances. The king entrusted this to a trusted aristocrat: the marquis de Villeroy or Beauvillier.

There were then those whom Saint-Simon neatly described as the 'ministerial acolytes (*tiercelets*)'. Like the secretaries of state, they were admitted as a group to the king's working sessions. The most important among them had some departmental responsibilities, such as the superintendent of the king's buildings (*surintendant des bâtiments du roi*) (in 1661 Antoine de Ratabon, in 1699 Mansart) or the superintendent of the postal services (in 1661 Nouveau de Fromont, in 1668 Louvois). This group would be strengthened later on by the addition of the director-general of fortifications. To the annoyance of Saint-Simon, the titular holder of this office, Le Peletier de Souzy, was allowed into the king's working sessions and, as though he were a proper minister, was entitled to be present 'with his cane in his hand and without his cloak' (94).

Working directly with the king were also three other important individuals. His confessor, who was always a Jesuit (in 1661 this was François Annat), spent Friday morning with him. This meeting was known as the 'council of conscience'. It was used, above all, to choose candidates for benefices. The Archbishop of Paris would sometimes be present at this council, and would sometimes be consulted separately. These two men can be considered as acolytes of an invisible ministry for Church affairs, the third being the secretary of state whose responsibilities included Paris, the household of the king and Church matters, Guénégaud in 1661, Colbert after 1669.

In 1667, when Gabriel-Nicolas de la Reynie was created lieutenant of police of Paris, he would escape, at least partially, the tutelage of the minister with responsibility for Paris and work directly with the king. Finally, since financial matters bulked so large because the former portfolio of M. Fouquet had involved finance, administration, industry and commerce, the royal council and the *contrôle général* employed dozens of senior administrators. Some of them had powers equivalent to those of a secretary of state. Others carried out their responsibilities almost invisibly, so that we can no longer gauge the extent of their powers with precision. Among those with influence in 1661 were the two councillors in the royal council of finances (d'Aligre and Sève), the two intendants of finances (Colbert and Marin), the great officers of accounts (the *trésorier général de l'extraordinaire des guerres* and the *gardes du trésor royal*, among others) and, finally, the tax-farmers general, who might be compared to a conjoined ministry of taxation.

The development of the administrative monarchy increased the numbers of these posts of key administrative importance. The state never became huge (its top-heaviness was a legacy of the past: there were in excess of 40,000 venal offices); but its superstructures were refined. From 1701 to 1708, to prop up the *Contrôle* and relieve M. de Chamillart, the king instituted two overall directors of finance, thanks to which the able Desmarets was able to restore himself to favour. Two intendants of finances gradually became seven (there were that number between 1708 and 1715). Bureaucratic routine was confronted with empiricism and adaptability, the hallmarks of Louis XIV's government.

Thanks to the king's pragmatism, there was a world of difference between the official administrative formalities and the real functioning of power. There is still much research to be undertaken in this area: many *éminences grises* remain unknown; their history has still to be written. But Saint-Simon records that, towards the end of the reign, the comte de Bergeyck was given an audience almost as a minister. Seignelay's navy, the most powerful in the world, only achieved this strength thanks to M. Jacques de Bonrepaux. The military administration of Louvois's armies would have been less successful had it not been for the collaboration of Vauban on fortifications and sieges, and of Chamlay on logistics. Vauban, who cut through all the red-tape and spoke to the king without reserve, and who was one of the creators of the science of statistics, would be more influential, more listened to, than the three Phelypeaux de la Vrillières, holders of the fourth office of secretary of state. This was the paradox but also the strength of the *ancien régime*. It was not a rigid, tentacular state which Louis XIV shaped and directed. The state was not a machine; and Louis was never a *roi-machine*.

The Most Christian King's power was immense, and many other princes had reason to envy him. Louis XIV could tax at will, unlike the monarch in England. He could dispense with parliaments, unlike the King of Sweden. He was king and sovereign lord in all his provinces, unlike the Habsburgs in Vienna. But, although he was not subjected to control by an elective body and enjoyed a plenitude of power, there were certain areas where he was more constrained in his actions and dispositions than many modern heads of government.

It is often assumed that he chose to do something when he accepted that he could no longer refuse to do it. The weight of tradition was enormous. Richelieu discovered Mazarin and trained him. Louis XIII imposed Mazarin upon the regent and upon Louis XIV. Mazarin trained Colbert and left his godson the great ministers of the personal rule: Colbert, Le Tellier and Lionne. The dismissals of Brienne in 1663 and Guénégaud in 1669 were achieved tactfully. The only serious fracture following the death of Mazarin was Fouquet's disgrace, and this had been unavoidable, although it might have been handled more sensitively.

The ministers often handed their posts on to their sons. Le Tellier, Louvois and Barbézieux, for example, held the department of war from 1643 to 1701, and Seignelay continued the good work of his father, Colbert. Louis XIV maintained his vigilance over such successions. He discouraged the marquis de Cany, the mediocre offspring of the indifferent Chamillart. He dismissed Courtanvaux, Louvois' eldest son in preference to Barbézieux. He had no qualms about encouraging ministerial dynasties, so long as competence and morality were not in doubt. Following in Colbert's footsteps were his brother Croissy, at the foreign ministry, as well as his son Seignelay and his nephew Torcy, whilst another nephew, Desmarets, served in the finance department. However, the family which was most solidly installed in the corridors of power was that of Phelypeaux; it had been there since 1610 and would remain until 1780. Under Louis XIV, it provided up to five secretaries of state. It was no coincidence that so many royal acts were signed: LOUIS and, lower down, PHELYPEAUX.

The king had entirely to lose his patience with a minister or senior official before he was dismissed. It was with a heavy heart that Louis removed Chamillart (a close friend) from his financial responsibilities in 1708, and from those in the war ministry in the following year, but the conduct of affairs was in the worst possible state. The only severe disgrace which befell a minister (apart from that of Fouquet) was that of Arnauld de Pomponne on 18 November 1679. There had been nothing of the mediocre about Pomponne. Like his predecessor Lionne, he was a diplomat of the highest calibre, well informed, likeable and able. The pretext for his dismissal was a charge of negligence; the real reasons lay elsewhere. During the Dutch War, his advice had been contrary to that of Louvois. Pomponne was an Arnauld, a friend of Port-Royal. And Colbert de Croissy, who was after his post, did his best to injure his ministerial reputation. Croissy was rewarded with the post, for the king had decided upon the policy of the 'Reunions' and he needed a minister who was both a good jurist and a bruiser: Croissy was the man for the job. But Louis XIV could not have been very happy with his dismissal of Pomponne. He wrote about it in his *Reflections on the Craft of Kingship*, sensing the need to justify his action and provide a plausible explanation for it, even if it did not fit the facts of the case very well: 'Kings are often obliged to do things which are against their will and which go against their better nature', but 'the interests of the state should come first ... Nothing is more dangerous than weakness, wherever it is found ... The craft of kingship is a great, noble and delightful one, especially when one feels that one has acquitted oneself well in all one's endeavours; but it has its difficulties and its tiresome problems'. Louis pretended to believe that Pomponne had not been cut out to be a minister: 'The responsibilities I gave him were too great for him. I endured several years of his indecisiveness, his stubbornness and his negligence ... In the end I had to demand his resignation, because everything which he was deputed to execute dragged on and lost the momentum which is required for the orders of a king of France who is not going to be a failure.' (63) In other words, Pomponne's moral scruples and developed sense of diplomatic relations had ceased to be compatible with the armed aggression of 1679. That this was the case is proven by the king's recall of Pomponne to the council of ministers (alongside Croissy) in 1691, after Louvois' death, and his giving him the superintendency of the postal services in 1697.

Louis XIV's patience with the feeble Chamillart and the mediocre La Vrillière, his unwillingness to undertake ministerial reshuffles and his scruples towards Pomponne are indicative of the degree to which the exercise of royal authority in France was far from being 'arbitrary'. Royal authority was not arbitrary, save in the sense of acting as an 'arbitrator'. The king would even persuade the hostile Saint-Simon of this. Historians have repeated Saint-Simon's claim that Louis XIV only went against the advice of the majority of his council of ministers six times in the course of fifty-four years. In fact, Saint-Simon was not in a position to know the truth of the matter; the council of ministers kept no minutes. If, however, the remark is considered in the light of the memorialist's antipathy to Louis XIV, it becomes more significant. The duke was acknowledging that the king respected the advice of his councillors. If Louis only tapped the council table once every nine years, even though there was a meeting twice or three times a week, this was because he accepted the rules of reasoned collegiality, rules far removed from the practices of the Turkish sultan or even many of the monarchs of Christian Europe.

The area where the king was most the prisoner of prejudice and the cumulative weight of institutional traditions lay in the sphere of officeholding. Forty-five thousand venal officeholders could be nominated, remunerated and promoted without any intervention from the supposedly all-powerful monarch. At best, French kings had the right to nominate to the posts of *premier président* in the sovereign courts and the possibility of rewarding the best amongst them with letters-patent to promote them to the status of councillor of state (*conseiller d'état*) or *maître des requêtes*. The king also maintained his right to choose, the functions of intendant being merely extensions of the royal will, the thirty administrators from the eighty *maîtres des requêtes* whom he would send to the financial districts (*généralités*). As against 45,000 officeholders, proprietors of their posts, independent and irremovable, there were fewer than 150 great 'functionaries' who were directly chosen by the Crown. In the judiciary and the administration, the king's margin for manœuvre was much reduced.

By contrast, Louis XIV retained his freedom of action towards the old nobility. Not only did he appoint the commanders-in-chief of his armies and naval forces, distributing the marshal's baton to whomsoever he pleased and nominating vice-admirals, lieutenant-generals, squadron chiefs and brigadier-generals (*maréchaux de camp*), he also chose all the ranking officers of the navy, and the army chiefs down to the rank of colonel. Despite Louvois' apparent power, no regimental commander was appointed without the king's explicit approval. Most of the regimental offices were venal, but the acquiring of one was not just a matter of having the money or currying favour with the secretary of state for war. It was the king alone who decided the matter, and he did so because his intention was always actually to command his own armies, and because he wanted to use nominations and promotions to inculcate a sense of service more widely in France, and particularly among the nobles. He believed such decisions to be of great importance. Perhaps, too, he was keen to undertake the task because he found in the military environment an effective individual authority which the hierarchy of robe officialdom denied to him.

Despite the imbalance in his authority, the king remodelled the top ranks of French society during the fifty-four years of his personal rule, taking care to preserve the delicate relationship between the nobility and the administrative elite. In order to do this, one of his first tasks was to bridle the headstrong French nobility.

MAKING THE NOBILITY CONFORM

On Monday, 28 September 1665, at Clermont, M. Denis Talon, *avocat général* in the Parlement of Paris, opened the assize courts (*grands jours*) of Auvergne with a speech of 'amazing eloquence'. Beginning with praises for His Majesty, 'he presented a brief account of the king's life, showing that the only great task left for him to undertake was to repress the felonies committed in his realm and "deliver the people from their oppression by the powerful"' (38). A number of exemplary sentences would persuade France of his intentions. On 23 January 1666, the court at Clermont condemned to the gallows one Gaspard, comte de Espinchal, of whom the clerk to the court, Dongois, declared: 'A book could be written of the crimes of this man, as wicked as any ever seen on this earth.' Two days later, the magistrates decided the same fate for Jacques-Timoléon, marquis de Canillac. The

Espinchals and Canillacs were among the most important noble families of central France. Of the 692 sentences handed out by the assize court at Clermont, 87 were against gentlemen. Even though these decisions were often only carried out in effigy, only twenty-three of the men being finally executed, the effect of these show-trials was immense. A medal proclaimed: 'The king's concern for the repression of the injustice and oppression of the grandees in 1665 and 1666 has been for the well-being of the provinces.' (71)

The effect of the assize courts, in Clermont in 1665 and in Le Puy in 1666, was psychological, in both a political and a judicial sense. The mountainous Auvergne seemed like the last place on earth to Parisians. The centrality of the Auvergne within the realm meant that the judges did not need to travel from province to province. To the king, Séguier and Colbert, the holding of the *grands jours* signalled the end of the disorders of the past, not just those of the Fronde, but the uprisings which had torn the provinces apart since 1639 as the burden of the state on the peasantry had been increased. Now the state, profiting from its increased prestige and from the desire for peace and quiet, was more firmly in place. Its role was not entirely accepted but at least taxation had ceased to go up. Henceforth, the judges, under the watchful eye of the intendants, were told to stop favouring the nobility and being brutal towards the poor. The financial administrators were told to desist from the arbitrary levying of taxation. The religious orders were warned that their privileges were not limitless. Thus, at the moment when the government began to work towards more-codified laws, the holding of the *grands jours* was a contribution to the harmonization of laws and their more impartial execution.

The assizes at Clermont thus represented an important element in Louis XIV's policy towards the nobility. In the middle of that decisive year, 1664, the king wanted to make his nobility march in step with him. Having already begun, following Mazarin's death, with the senior judges, he now turned his attentions to the whole of the 'second estate'. During the winter of 1664, the idea of reviving the assize courts was conceived; in December, judgement was given on Fouquet; and, in June, the decision was taken to conduct an investigation into titles of nobility (the *recherche de la noblesse*). The latter neatly complemented the assize courts and took place in their wake. The *grands jours* of the Auvergne finished on 30 January 1666; the investigation began on 22 March. The assizes were Séguier's responsibility; the investigation was Colbert's. There were two reasons for this shift. Firstly, the investigation was mainly fiscal and therefore was the principal concern of the controller-general. But, secondly, Séguier's influence was on the wane from the beginning of 1666, and Colbert took advantage of this to increase his own. In this, he was assisted by his uncle Pussort, who was the linchpin of the Council, and much concerned with the drafting of the great ordinances of state.

The intendants were required by the investigation to track down false titles of nobility. Those who claimed the status of gentleman were required to present legal documents proving that their entitlement went back, generally speaking, a century. The king would not be satisfied with vague certificates from English or German heralds at arms, France being a country of jurists. The nobility had to produce authentic letters of entitlement. Notaries or the clerks of judicial courts were required to submit their registers to the intendant's employees or provide copies of them when asked. Nobles who presented false letters of entitlement would be dealt with by the court of requests in the king's household (*tribunal des requêtes de l'Hôtel*). In addition, the king's instructions required the intendants to establish whether the noble lived the 'life of a gentleman', in other words, whether he or his ancestors had ever demeaned themselves by dabbling in 'manual crafts', retail trades or other activities unbecoming to the 'second estate'.

Failure to satisfy the intendants on these counts meant that the name of the individual concerned was inscribed on the tax-rolls and he was condemned to pay a fine as a usurper of the title. He had six months in which to lodge an appeal with the special commission of the Council. The number of false nobles was, and would remain, very high. Some of those who were found guilty in 1667 would still be trying to attach themselves to the nobility in 1669 or 1670, not just for reasons of fiscal self-interest, but for their own self-esteem. A Council decision (*arrêt*) of 19 July 1672 renewed the penalties against these individuals. The Dutch War brought the investigation to an end by 1674, but it would be taken up again in 1696 and this time it would continue through to 1727.

These dates delineate a vast operation. But Louis XIV, despite his power, did not transform the nobility into a caste nor was this his aim. Throughout his personal rule, the creation of new nobles was a political weapon. Colbert aimed to suppress the abuse of privilege and to lessen the prejudice of noble derogation. The controller-general wanted to eliminate those who hid behind the pretext of living the life of a noble to avoid paying the *taille*, and the king supported him in this objective. If all those who lived the life of a gentleman had seen service in arms or exercised some office in the state, Louis XIV's attitude might have been different. As it was, in most cases, it was merely a false pretext. However, this investigation was feared by the minor nobility, whose titles had, perhaps, been mislaid in the course of time and whose nobility was, sometimes, in doubt, and it certainly made entry to the second estate more difficult.

Whatever Saint-Simon may have thought, there was no fundamental hostility towards the nobility in all this. The king was the first gentleman of the realm and needed a nobility, even though his sense of an elite was less circumscribed by his sense of nobility than that of other monarchs. But he wanted a nobility which would *serve* in the army or navy or in the judicature. The investigation of noble titles brought a long-delayed benefit to the gentlemen in the king's army and navy. Service alone justified the granting of privilege. The nobility had to do more than just cultivate its own patch: it must become, once more, a military service. Living the life of a nobleman recovered some of its meaning. The grand assizes had not been open longer than a month when the intendant of the Auvergne wrote: 'When the men of quality are somewhat surer of themselves, I do not doubt but that I shall enrol many of their children in the musketeers.' (38) The lesson was not learnt by everyone: of the feudal levy (*ban et arrière-ban*) raised in 1674, the maréchal de Créqui said that it was 'a body incapable of action' (136). We shall see, when discussing the king's servants and his court, how Louis XIV did not taunt the higher nobility any further, and merely restrained them slightly. It was, after all, the official aristocracy, despite its faults, and the natural supporter and pillar of the Crown. The memory of the Fronde, a baroque interregnum between two regimes of fidelity, had to be erased.

7

The Monarchy Unfettered

FROM I NOVEMBER 1661, the personal rule, so brilliantly inaugurated by Louis XIV, was given additional assurance; to universal relief, the royal succession seemed secure. The successor to the throne, Louis, was accorded scrupulous attention. He was provided with a remarkable governess by the name of Julie d'Angennes, the marquise de Montausier. He was not to be known as 'M. le Dauphin' or even 'Monseigneur le Dauphin', as his predecessors had been, but purely by the title, formerly forbidden, of 'Monseigneur' on its own. An exceptional monarch required a unique progeny. From his birth onwards, he was accorded a remarkable degree of attention. There is nothing to the legend that the Dauphin was reduced to a minor role: the king never attempted to turn his heir into a 'winter sun'.* Until the Dauphin entered the royal council of finances and the council of despatches in July 1688 and was assigned an army in September 1688, entering the council of ministers in July 1691, his father saw to it that he had an exemplary education. 'No prince could have had better teachers', claimed Voltaire. One of them was the king himself, whose *Mémoires*, summarizing his political notions, were drawn up for Monseigneur's education. Another was the Bishop of Condom, Bishop Bossuet, whose lessons appeared in print in his *Discourse on Universal History* (1681) and in his *Politics Taken from the Words of Holy Scripture* (1709). He became the theoretician of the absolute monarchy, explaining to his pupil the greatness of his future inheritance.

---

* According to Furetière's *Dictionary*: 'The January sun, whose sunlight has such little warming-power, is used to describe an individual with little authority.'

THE EDUCATION OF THE DAUPHIN

Louis XIV had been brought up by a courtier, the maréchal de Villeroy, and as governor to his son he chose a grizzily old courtier, the duc de Montausier, a former Protestant who still retained his Huguenot rigour. Montausier is thought to be the model for Molière's Alceste. His stoic virtues were widely acknowledged, his integrity respected and his religion beyond doubt. The king appreciated his capacity to speak his mind honestly. Montausier was in charge of the succession of tutors to the Dauphin and directed his education. He drew up the *Christian and Political Reflections for the Education of a Prince* (39) and commissioned a *History of France from Gallic Times* from Cordemoy and a *History of Theodosius the Great* from Fléchier, as well as a famous collection of expurgated classical texts, *Ad usum Delphini*, from Huet.

The *président* Périgny, His Majesty's reader and the Dauphin's tutor from 1668 to 1670, established a curriculum which Bossuet would then follow from 1670 to 1679. Périgny wanted to provide the Dauphin with two groups of acquirements, those of a gentleman and those of a statesman. He wanted the prince to learn jurisprudence, French public and canon law, and the science of politics and government. As a gentleman, the Dauphin should have a decent awareness of Holy Scripture and the catechism, a good deal of Latin, some Greek, and Italian and Spanish. To this should be added ancient and modern history, philosophy, the main elements of rhetoric and, finally, sufficient mathematics to come to grips with the military arts, especially fortification (39). Under the guise of providing the Dauphin with all this enlightenment, he was presented with a thorough educational programme of mammoth proportions. The little prince, whose baby talk was collected by the court, was surrounded by a pleiad of distinguished figures: the humanist Danet, who wrote Latin dictionaries for him, the Jesuit père de la Rue, who adapted Virgil to suit him, the abbé Huet, a man of 'encyclopaedic intellect' (112). The sturdy good sense of Monseigneur was vital if he was to endure this onslaught of educationalists, not to mention the cane of M. de Montausier. He listened to Bossuet politely, sometimes with a frown, not always devoting his whole attention to what he was saying. The prelate complained about that, but the little prince knew his catechism off by heart and large parts of biblical history. Bossuet and his companions spared nothing as regards his religious education. 'By constant repetition', Bossuet wrote to Pope Innocent XI, 'we ensured that three words, *piety, benevolence, justice*, remained imprinted in his memory.' (106)

The Dauphin also excelled in horsemanship, dancing, and military exercises, hoping to become the best huntsman in France. Monseigneur took after his father. Like him, he was not a reader although he had good taste. The Princess Palatine would say of him: 'He knew a great deal but he never talked about it and concentrated all his energies on unlearning it all, for such was his "good pleasure".' (87) He shared Louis XIV's love of the arts, of collections of art, and of the theatre, and his penchant for grandeur, his physical prowess and his political judgement. It is hard to distinguish what he inherited from his father and what he learnt during his education.

'THE SECRETS OF KINGSHIP'

In a speech to the Académie française on 3 February 1671, Pellisson recalled the *Instructions* or *Mémoires* which had been drawn up for the Dauphin's education, containing, as he put it, 'the secrets of kingship and the eternal verities as to the paths to avoid and those to follow' (63). For several years, the king had kept a 'scrapbook' and a 'diary', with the aid of which Périgny had been able to write the memoirs for 1666 to 1668. In 1671, Louis XIV, with the assistance of Pellisson, gathered together the texts concerning the first years of the personal rule, 1661 and 1662. He made use of the memoranda of the Council, preserved by his former personal secretary, *président* Rose, as well as various summaries by Colbert. The *Memoirs for the year 1661*, thus corroborated ten years after the events, are well known. They are not the reflections of a Marcus Aurelius or a Frederick the Great, but they present, in an excellent prose style, the essence of the king's political message: the theory and practice of the French absolute monarchy.

The Dauphin was given no lessons in modesty. He would discover in his father's writings an undeniable self-esteem. Louis XIV was proud of being an absolute sovereign. For him, to reign without the power to rule was nonsensical; he would employ no first minister. Ministerial power permitted ministers to govern but not to reign. The king did both. The verb 'to reign' carries an enormous significance here. There were probably politicians more adept than Louis; but they did not have the unique privilege of reigning. Louis alone reigned in France. Other pre-occupations flowed from this: glory, honour, reputation, the motifs and temptations of a young sovereign. Intoxicating concepts, these, and this obsession with honour, glory and reputation linked warfare and internal matters. Glory and honour were the two axles upon which the royal carriage rolled.

The concern for reputation did not stifle initiative. The king did not need a 100 per cent chance of success before he decided to act. He led from the front, for the good of the state and his glory, seizing the advantages which providentially came his way. He accounted to no one for his actions; posterity would be his judge. In the meantime, he was the first ruler on earth. The German emperor was, by comparison, merely a subordinate sovereign: 'Thus I do not see by what logic the kings of France, hereditary monarchs, who may claim without contradiction that there is not a dynasty in the world better than theirs, not a monarchy that is older nor a power which is greater nor an authority which is more absolute, should be inferior to elective princes.'

The temptation of pride was held in check by Christian principles. Divine right demanded that the sovereign undertake duties. 'Heaven', Louis wrote, 'has *entrusted* us with people and states', a trust which brought with it its own limitation upon princely power. A monarch had a graver responsibility than his subjects to obey the commandments of God and His Church. Modesty, too, was required of him: 'If there is a legitimate pride attached to our station, there is a modesty and humility which are also praiseworthy.' The king must examine his own conscience, the antidote to flattery. Finally, even more than others, sovereigns must 'instruct their children by their example and their advice'.

So far, the principles laid down are traditional ones. Francis I, Henry II and Henry IV would have written in a similar vein. But the *Memoirs for the year 1661* also have a modern feel to them. They foreshadow enlightened despotism. The twin aims of the reforming monarchs of the Enlightenment, reason (the dominant theme of Frederick the Great) and the welfare of the people

(Joseph II's obsession), may be found in Louis XIV's *Instructions*. The king wrote, concerning reason: 'the course of my actions shows that, giving reasons to no one, I nonetheless governed myself in accordance with reason'. On the subject of happiness, or the general good, he wrote: 'To reward merit, in short to do good, should not just be the greatest preoccupation of a prince, but also his greatest pleasure.' Elsewhere, Louis wrote:

> We must consider the good of our subjects much more than our own. It should even seem to be a part of us since 'we are the head of a body of which they are the members'. It is only for their own good that we should make laws; the power that we have over them should only serve to make us work more effectively for their well-being.

Frederick II of Prussia would rediscover this pronouncement and he would be given the credit for its originality.

Having defined monarchy, Louis XIV taught his son that a prince had two resources: his personal endeavour and the efficient co-ordination of his *équipe*. From 1661, the king was obliged to shoulder 'a huge work-load'. 'That is how, and for what, one reigns.' Without this personal application, there was no craft of kingship; it was the hallmark of a monarch. 'However able and enlightened his ministers are, it always shows when a king takes things in hand himself.' After the death of Mazarin, Louis XIV yoked himself to the task. Ten years later, he had not changed his mind or his pattern of work:

> Now, ten years on, I am still ploughing, as it were, the same furrow; receiving my most humble subjects; knowing at any hour of the day the number and quality of my troops and the state of my fortifications; forever issuing orders to satisfy their every need; negotiating directly with foreign ministers; receiving and reading despatches; drafting responses to some myself and giving my secretaries the gist of the replies to others; administering the receipts and expenses of my state; receiving reports directly from those whom I have placed in positions of importance; keeping my affairs as secret as any who have gone before me; distributing favours according to my own personal choice, and retaining, unless I am mistaken, those who serve me in a modesty far removed, despite the benefits showered upon them, from the power and eminence of first ministers.

Such tasks required a strict timetable: two sessions a day, of two or three hours each, with a variety of individuals: sometimes a Council meeting; sometimes a personal meeting (*liasse*) with an individual minister.

Ministers signed nothing without the king's permission. Yet, although they were controlled by the king, they retained an important role. Over and above the king's endeavours lay the other resource, the 'great choice of individuals to act in place of' the monarch. This choice had to be made without a favourite or even a chief minister; hence the necessity and concomitant benefits of working with a group. 'It was necessary', said Louis, 'to trust many with the execution of my orders, and not rely on one individual alone, delegating these various individuals to separate domains, according to their various talents, as is perhaps the first and greatest talent in princes.'

Personal rule did not entail solitary rule. However useful 'silent and individual contemplation' was, it was never sufficient on its own and had its dangers. The mind needed 'company to excite and challenge it'. The king must therefore choose his ministers with care, a branch of the difficult 'art of judging men'. Their abilities and limitations would be of vital importance. They are closer to the people and generally can call upon the advantages of mature years, experience and knowledge. These were essential ingredients for the exercise of supreme power. But ministers did not determine policy; that was for the king to decide upon. 'No one is in a better position than ourselves to do so; for decision-making needs the mind of a master, and it is incomparably easier to do when one is the master than imitating it when one is not.' (63)

ONE EXAMPLE: 1661

With Louis XIV, practice was never divorced from theory. The year 1661 began the king's *Mémoires*. Without keeping to a strict chronology, Louis noted seventeen personal decisions, decisions which, taken together, made up a programme of government.

The first concerned the *noblesse de robe*: it involved the clipping of the wings of the senior magistrates by the exile of the judges in the Cour des Aides of Paris. The king repeated that it was not a matter of reaping vengeance after the Fronde. This 'reminder of their duty' was, nevertheless, linked to the troubles of 1648. 'The overweening position of the *parlements* had become dangerous to the whole realm during my minority. They had to be curbed, not merely because of the harm they did, but even more for what they might do in the future.' The closure of the session of the Assembly of the Clergy, which had become prolonged, was also indispensable. The king was the protector of Gallican liberties, but the Church should not dictate his decisions.

The *Mémoires* then mentioned the suppression of the office of colonel-in-chief of the infantry (*colonel général de l'infanterie*). The death of the duc d'Epernon provided the opportunity to quash a post whose incumbent was, within the army, almost the equal of the king; it was all a modern monarchy could do with these old feudalities. In the same vein, the king launched into the powers of provincial governors, military officers of high standing who acted as though they were some kind of viceroy. They were deprived of their financial autonomy, and their prerogative powers over appointments and troop movements were restricted.

Newly acquired provinces were allowed some latitude, although it was impossible not to treat them 'as conquered provinces'. The same political objective – to reconcile the irreconcilable, by respecting local liberties whilst strengthening national unity, and by imposing French rule whilst winning people's loyalty – would be practised in Flanders in 1667 and in Franche Comté in 1674. In 1661, it was the turn of Artois to be wooed. The next issue was the strengthening of the frontiers. Vauban was still only a captain, but the king was closely involved in what would become the military 'iron curtain'.

The *Mémoires* then turned to the enforcement of the laws against oaths, blasphemy and duelling. The comte de Soissons, convicted of duelling, would be sent into exile as an example. The upper nobility had to learn how to keep its old-fashioned independence in check.

At the same time, the king began the battle against a Jansenism which was believed to be successful and to be attracting adherents of great calibre. And he agreed to a bequest to the population of Dunkirk to stop them from becoming Protestant and English. As to those of the 'religion prétendue réformée' in France, Louis XIV was careful to avoid any changes, not wanting to push them into a revolt but not offering them his favour either.

Under the heading of the reform of the royal finances, the king then moved on to the disgracing of the superintendent and its results. The king no longer held that Fouquet had attempted to become 'the sovereign arbiter in the state'. In any case, the king had become his own superintendent. The creation of the royal council was the consequence, as was the nationalization and control of all the *key* elements of the budget, which involved the revaluation of the tax-farms, and the establishment of a judicial inquiry (*chambre de justice*) into the activities of the financiers. The final matters concerned patronage, particularly the choice of eight prelates and of sixty-three chevaliers of the Holy Spirit, the first to be appointed since 1633.

Five of these measures indicated a willingness to undertake social reform, five concerned financial matters and three concerned military affairs. But the details of the measures of 1661 must be seen in the light of the Fronde. Royal authority was strengthened against various pressure groups, and to the profit of the people and the state itself. In his comments on the first few months of his personal rule, Louis XIV drew on simple rules which were reflected in effective action. We should not be surprised at his audience. The King of France was providing instructions not only for the heir to his throne, but also for the great elector and Peter the Great, Maria Theresa of Austria and Joseph II, Gustavus III of Sweden and Catherine the Great, as well as many other so-called 'enlightened' rulers.

ABSOLUTE MONARCHY

From 1661 onwards, Louis XIV imbued the French *ancien régime* with a certain style and coherence. The result was that absolute monarchy which the French admired and which was copied by other European monarchs. The concept of absolute monarchy has been obscured by over-simplification. In the nineteenth century, it was replaced by the dreadful word 'absolutism', which turned the *ancien régime* into an arbitrary system of government, even into a tyranny or a despotism. The monarchy of Louis XIV became the rule of personal whim. All legends have some basis in fact. From Charles VII onwards, letters-patent of kings in France concluded with the phrase: 'For thus is our pleasure.' (285) This was a reading of the Latin phrase: *Placet nobis et volumus* ('It is our considered wish'). The formula was regarded as reflecting royal deliberation, not royal capriciousness. In a similar way, they would have translated *monarchia absoluta* as 'perfect monarchy'.

From the enthusiasm of 1661 to the underlying sourness of 1715, lay fifty-four often difficult years, but the admiration of the French for this system of government was not diminished. Even those who criticized the king found it natural to sing the praises of the absolute monarchy. In the eyes of Pasquier Quesnel, an exiled Jansenist, the French constitution was perfect, 'royalty having something eternal' in it (100). Bayle (1647–1706), an exiled Calvinist, followed Hobbes and exalted 'the authority of kings', declaring that 'the only sure way for France to avoid civil wars is the absolute power of the sovereign, sustained with vigour, and equipped with all the necessary power to instil fear' (133).

But the word *absolutus* comes from the verb *absolvere* (to loose or unbind), and it was understood in France in the seventeenth century that *monarchia absoluta* signified a monarchy without shackles, and not one without limits. The legal theoreticians of sovereignty (Duchesne, Loyseau, Bignon) had developed their theories by 1610, in the years immediately after the great anarchy of the wars of religion and the realm's reconstruction by the Béarnais. In 1610, there was no question of confusing absolute monarchy with despotism.

In any case, power, though absolute, was circumscribed. The monarchy had to respect the fundamental laws of the kingdom. The most important of these was the law of succession, the 'Salic law'. Unique, entirely logical, the product of history and the guarantor of continuity and unity, this law indicated that 'the state had precedence over the king'. This was the next best thing to a constitution for France. The second law affirmed the inalienability of the royal demesne. This was based on the principle that 'the sovereign ruler was only a tenant' of his realm. The third law has been called the 'law of independence': the Parlement of Paris created the 'system of liberties in the French Church', a safeguard against encroachments from Rome. From these great principles of French public law, the sense of the monarchy as more absolute than the monarch was articulated.

THE SUPPORT OF DIVINE RIGHT

Kings in France 'draw their power from God and their sword alone' (37); from the latter through their conquest of Gaul, and from the former through the Holy Scripture. St Paul assured them that 'There is no authority but by act of God' (Romans 13:1). Endless arabesques were elaborated on this favourite theme: 'Every good Christian must submit himself to the *authority* of the Church,' wrote Furetière, 'and all good subjects to royal *authority*'; 'The commandments of God and His Church are to be obeyed. So are those of the king.' These parallels instilled into even the most recalcitrant skulls the religious character of monarchical power. 'Kings are the *ministers of God* on earth', and thus one could speak without blasphemy of 'the sacred person of His Majesty'. He was sacred in the direct sense of having received, as King of France, an unction 'with an oil ... sent expressly from Heaven in a holy ampulla'. And if every ruler of a Christian state governed by divine right, the French monarchy claimed precedence over the rest. It enjoyed a kind of predestination since 'the King of France is uniquely given the title of the *Most Christian King* and the *Eldest Son of the Church*' (42).

Absolute monarchy should not, of course, be confused with divine right. Although they would refuse the divine right of kings, Voltaire and Frederick the Great would be partisans of the absolute monarchy. But, under Louis XIV, divine right provided the foundations for absolute monarchy so neatly that he tended to mix the one with the other. The churchmen took up the baton of the jurists, their loyalty legitimizing and consecrating royal power. We should think ourselves fortunate, thought Bourdeloue, that a Christian king had absolute power. This was the concluding theme of a Christmas Day sermon before the court in 1697. But no one contributed more than Bossuet to the magnification of the sovereign's power. 'God establishes kings as his ministers and reigns through them over his people.' Thus, 'the person of the king is sacred'. Such was divine right, deduced directly from the prescriptions of biblical teaching, and upon this authority rested the rules of the absolute authority of the monarch:

> First proposition. The prince need render account to no one for what he ordains. Second proposition. When the prince has pronounced a decision, no other decision may stand. Third proposi-

tion. No other power may challenge that of the prince. Fourth proposition. Kings are not thereby emancipated from the laws. (106)

These propositions are in no way original. They are similar to what Cardin Le Bret had written in *Of the Sovereignty of Kings* in 1632. But, whilst the lawyers combined Roman law and divine right to justify the absolute monarchy, Bossuet founded it on divine right alone. To his eyes, there was a congruence between divine right and absolute monarchy, an indissoluble link between altar and throne. As a theologian, he had an advantage over the legists, and he had the additional advantage of being a contemporary of Louis XIV. His learning, eloquence and reputation gave the political statements of the Eagle of Meaux a European dimension, although this did not prevent him having a popular appeal. He had not wanted to make the king holy, but he virtually succeeded in making the monarchy divine.

SOVEREIGNTY AND ITS LIMITS

Law, for the jurists of the seventeenth century, was a general prescription requiring obedience from subjects because it emanated from a sovereign authority. Law thus implied sovereignty; and sovereignty was defined as the power to make laws. However, in *ancien régime* France, sovereignty belonged to the king and to him alone. The monarch alone could legislate, according to Le Bret, to make, change and interpret laws. 'The will of the king is the rule of law' was the basis of French law. It owed its indefeasible character to its Roman and Christian origins. That is to say, the law was believed to be inspired by God and to act upon subjects through their consciences; only the prince remained not subject to 'positive' laws.

From this legal sovereignty, precise powers may be deduced. These are the rights of the king, or 'regalian rights', inseparable from the sceptre and supreme power, fifteen or twenty cases of royal authority and its legislative, executive and judicial power. These regalian rights included those to make laws, to be called sovereign 'by the grace of God', 'to strike coins', to name officials and magistrates, to decide upon matters of war and peace, to convoke the Estates General or the provincial Estates, to assemble councils, to judge cases upon final appeal, to issue privileges and to impose, or exempt from, taxation upon individuals, to modify or withdraw rights of individual status (to naturalize, legitimate or ennoble), and to found universities, fairs, and postal services. One of the most important prerogatives was called the *régale*. This was the somewhat redundant terminology for the king's right to collect the revenues from vacant episcopal and other ecclesiastical benefices until a successor had been appointed. It is clear that royal sovereignty was already an established fact and that the absolute monarchy enjoyed immense power. In reality, though, there is another important, and simple, fact to remember: if the jurists had spent a great deal of time delineating and refining regalian rights, this was because the king did not enjoy a monopoly of rights.

Absolute power was confronted with several theoretical limitations. The sovereign had to respect divine laws and obey God's commandments. The Decalogue is, however, an awesome catalogue of burdensome duties. If the king became, for example, idolatrous, sacrilegious or polygamous, then he risked the full weight of divine vengeance. In the most serious circumstances, subjects would be entitled to rebel since they would, *ipso facto*, be released from their duty of obedience. The king was also bound to respect natural law, that mysterious and immutable force which makes man capable of rationality, equity and justice. Natural law represented what was implicitly held in common by all humanity, Christian and non-Christian alike. When the king made laws, he had to legislate in conformity with reason and justice. Inequitable laws did not command obedience from the consciences of subjects (this is what the Protestants would argue in 1685).

The third limit upon sovereign authority lay in the respect for subjects. In the area of public law, this implied that the French king could not legally countermand or infringe the fundamental maxims or laws of the kingdom, considered as prior and superior to the laws of the king. In the realm of private law, constitutional lawyers considered that the monarch was required to respect the property and person of the individual. Although there was no writ of habeas corpus, some protection was retained: torture outside normal criminal proceedings was classified as personal assault. The right to property was apparently more secure: 'The king could not appropriate to himself the inheritance of a subject and nor could he dispose of it at will.' On the matter of the royal demesne, the king (in the person of the farmers of the demesne) was often condemned before his own lawcourts.

PRACTICAL LIMITS TO ABSOLUTE POWER

The practical limits to the exercise of absolute power were also considerable. The Estates were the first rampart against arbitrary government. Louis XIV, of course, did not summon the Estates General, but it would be wrong to write off the provincial Estates. A third of the realm was subject to them. They were of considerable significance in Brittany and Languedoc, where they enjoyed unchallenged fiscal and administrative privileges. The extreme case lay in Brittany, a province which royal administration had scarcely penetrated. Colbert, who had wanted to use the intendants as the instrument of overall monarchical control, was in his grave before an indendant was sent to Rennes. Pomereu, the first intendant in Brittany, only received his commission in 1689, and he was especially picked out from the *maîtres des requêtes* for his tact, charm and ability (182). It would be easier for Louis XIV to revoke the Edict of Nantes than to send an intendant to Rennes.

The *parlements* and the other sovereign courts, relying on their right to register royal enactments, were another practical limitation. Certainly, Louis XIV had clipped their wings following the experience of the Fronde. In 1655, he emphasized the authoritarian nature of the *lit de justice* and, in 1665, he instituted a *lit de justice* in the king's absence. In 1673, he forced the courts to register edicts *before* they prepared remonstrances, thus denying them any remaining powers of delay. At the same time, he withdrew their right to call themselves 'sovereign'. These facts are well known; but perhaps they have been misinterpreted. For, in reality, the *parlements*, though weakened, continued to be a limitation upon monarchical power. The king's death in September 1715 would be a sufficient precipitant for the Parlement of Paris to rediscover its energy, nullify the king's will, recover its full right of remonstrance and begin a steady resistance which would last seventy-five years. If it rediscovered this energy in 1715, this was because it had never completely lost it during the preceding period of relative quiescence. Louis XIV had pressed the *parlements* almost to breaking-point and, had he pushed any harder, the result would have been open revolt.

The Parlement of Paris remained a court of peers. It retained its right to register royal enactments; the king could not just make what laws he chose. The registration of laws maintained the legal traditions of the French state. The constitutional lawyers were in agreement that 'laws have no validity unless made public', that is, registered. Besides, even if the Parlement did not exercise its full right of remonstrance, registration entailed an examination of the law by men who knew the principles of French jurisprudence (principles such as, for example, the one that states that 'laws should not act retrospectively'). Inequitable legislation would not pass their scrutiny. 'It was through the laws that kings reign'; by the registration of laws, the Parlement restrained the monarchy and regularized it.

The authority of the king also had to work with what Montesquieu would term the 'intermediary bodies' (*corps intermédiaires*). Dear to Montesquieu's heart, these were institutions similar in kind to the *parlements*, official bodies restraining the monarchy and transforming it into a composite regime. In 1715, as in 1661, such institutions had not the power to gain the upper hand, but the whole range of municipal and provincial, royal and professional bodies remained in place, and the monarchy had to work with them. Everything in France was corporative (260). There were scholarly bodies (universities, colleges), merchant guilds, craft fraternities, companies of finance and chambers of commerce, even colleges of royal officials.

The French were more involved in the privileges of such groups than they were in the great matters of politics. But, on the other hand, it was easier for the king to restrain the Parlement of Paris than to attack the corporative aristocracy, the six merchant guilds, in his capital. The challenge to one privilege ruffled the feathers of other privileged groups. The slightest threat to one body provoked the resistance of them all in remarkable mutual support. The monarchy sensed all this. These seventeenth-century corporations were intermediary bodies, embracing individuals, protecting them from superior authority and able to resist royal power. And, even though the moment for such resistance never arose, their existence was, nevertheless, a flywheel acting as a regulator to the monarchy. For such bodies were the staging-posts for public opinion.

Through them, it spread to numerous levels of public awareness.

The importance of public consciousness to Louis XIV may best be measured in the newly acquired provinces. The war was hardly won, the campaign scarcely over, before the political process began in the occupied regions. The articles for the capitulation of Besançon in 1674 illustrate its character. The town had resisted the attack for twenty-seven days, and the citadel still held out, but the Bisontins were already being offered the retention of their privileges. No inhabitant would be required to fight against the citadel. There would be no salt tax. All the corporative privileges of the town were renewed, including those of the archbishop, the clergy, the town administration, the gentry and the people (102). Louis did not wait until the conquest had been completed to begin the manipulation of popular opinion.

The French absolute monarch was thus neither a tyrant nor a despot. This is why some historians have suggested replacing the term 'absolute monarchy' with 'administrative monarchy'. During the reign of Louis XIV, the abbé de Véri suggested a more apposite expression, speaking of it as a 'moderate monarchy' (290).

8

Time of Reform

THE KING'S collaborators were responsible for helping to transform the absolute monarchy into an administrative (and thereby moderate) monarchy. Relying upon the king's confidence, endlessly encouraged by him, they gave the first years of the personal rule that nervous energy which so astonished the rulers of Europe. At the time of the Dutch War, when one asked for the names of the more renowned members of the king's entourage, the reply was: Messieurs Colbert and Louvois. However, ten years earlier, no one would have doubted the primacy of Colbert. Close companion to the king, enjoying lodgings close to his, Colbert was a compendium of talents. Consulted regularly, his advice was indispensable upon matters of the economy, and of the navy, police and fine arts. He was the inheritor of the secrets of Mazarin and an admirer and imitator of Richelieu.

From the moment of his death in 1683, two contradictory images of him have formed, as such images do of all great individuals. 'Such was the fury of the people unleashed against him', according to the queen, 'that they wanted to tear his poor dead body limb from limb' (87), proof that the deceased had not only restored the royal finances but also preserved the popularity of his master. On the other hand, the *New Abridged Chronology* noted that 'the prosperity and brilliance of this regime, the grandeur of the monarch, the well-being of the people will forever mourn the death of the greatest minister that France has ever had' (258).

During his lifetime, once Fouquet was imprisoned, Colbert's only open enemy was his rival Louvois. Those who hated him

did so in silence. The king appreciated his singleminded dedication, his precision and his remonstrations, accepting him in the
same way that Louis XIII accepted his cardinal minister. The
court, the capital and the realm trembled before Colbert. His
lack of warmth was renowned: Madame de Sévigné christened
him 'the North'. His patronage was vital; everyone wanted to
benefit from the enormous influence his circle enjoyed. The
aristocracy seemed the most intimidated. To this minister, born
a commoner, the duc de Beaufort, the king's cousin, wrote: 'The
honour of being in your good graces is more desirable to me in
this difficult matter than anything else.' (111) The duc de la
Rochefoucauld, an arrogant *frondeur*, terminated his letters to
Colbert with an almost incredible formula:

> I am much ashamed, Monsieur, that I am not able to offer you
> proof of my gratitude other than by means of worthless compli-
> ments; I shall endeavour, in so far as lies within me, to offer you
> further proofs of my gratitude, and not a single opportunity of
> acting as your servant shall pass but that you shall be aware of
> the degree to which I desire to merit the honour of your friend-
> ship and of the extent to which I am, Monsieur, your most
> humble and most obedient servant. (52)

COLBERT, THE ALL-PURPOSE MINISTER

This exceptional individual enjoyed an outstanding career.
Whilst the title and functions of minister of state were generally
the summit of a career, Colbert's followed a different pattern,
one without logic; his functions increased in accordance with the
needs of government and the king's will. He was intendant of
finances when Fouquet's removal made him a minister in 1661.
The further reform of the Council transformed his post of
intendant into one of overall direction. From 15 September,
Colbert became the principal figure in the royal council. At
about the same date, Louis entrusted the navy to him, although
without any official departmental status. In 1663, he gave him
the post of superintendent of the king's buildings, a title which
he assumed on 2 January 1664. In December 1665, Colbert
received a commission as controller-general of finances. In
February 1669, he took up his duties at the desk of the second

secretary of state, which included responsibilities for Paris, the king's household and the affairs of the clergy. Finally, an ordinance of 7 March released him from his accountability to M. de Lionne and attached the navy, commerce and the consulates and the companies of the Indies to his secretaryship (227). 'He administered everything except for foreign affairs and war.'

Was the king not taking a grave risk in placing such responsibilities upon one individual? Was there not some inconsistency in diminishing the prerogatives of the chancellor, suppressing the superintendency of finances and declaring his wish to be his own first minister, whilst investing Colbert with so many tasks and duties, rendering him as untouchable as Richelieu, as influential as Mazarin? Louis XIV took a risk, but it was a limited one. Despite his own powerful personality, Colbert never imposed himself upon the king in the way that Richelieu had been able to do with Louis XIII. And he had not the twin advantages of being the king's guardian and godfather which Mazarin had enjoyed. The king could have dismissed Colbert without creating a Day of Dupes, and without provoking a Fronde. Besides, in 1669, when Colbert was at the height of his influence, that of Louvois was in the ascendant. These were the reasons why the relationship between Louis XIV and Colbert, which lasted twenty-two years, although of curiosity to some contemporaries, was not at all surprising.

Colbert was nineteen years older than his master; but this discrepancy was made up for by an enormous difference in their backgrounds. Mesmerized by Richelieu and trained by Mazarin, Colbert represented a vital tradition in the modernizing forces of the reformed state, a state based upon the absolute monarchy. Louis respected the past, but was convinced of the need to reform the state. If Colbert had not been provided by Mazarin, Louis XIV would have found his like.

Despite the king's confidence in him, Colbert had his irritating side. His ideas became set in tablets of stone and were sometimes little more than prejudices. His requirement for properly presented accounts forced him to employ petty arguments in opposition to the king. However, this was of no great importance to Louis XIV, who appreciated efficiency and recognized the qualities of his colleague. They shared the same obsession for the state, for its continuity and its glory. They were both stubborn, patriotic taskmasters, both mediocre Latinists who had only mastered the language in adulthood (112). They had both been introduced at an early age to the realities of life and had thrived on the experience. They were both pragmatists, comprehending each other instinctively. Their collaboration was so close and over so long a period that historians will never disentangle the secrets of how it worked in individual instances.

The king had the broader vision. In the area of royal buildings, he was the one who formulated the projects and made the decisions. He required Colbert to carry nothing out without his validation. If the minister appeared only to be keeping him informed in the most general way of the work in hand, he received by return the brisk order: 'All the details!' (291) From then on, Colbert was to concern himself exclusively with the minutiae. In other areas, they complemented each other. The *code Louis* rightly carries the name of its instigator, but, had Colbert not been there, would it still be remembered? The shipping ordinances of 1681 and the naval ordinances of 1669 and 1689 were finalized by the king but prepared by Colbert and Seignelay. Their relationship was collaborative; the king signed and the minister countersigned: L O U I S and, below it, C O L B E R T.

Collaborative decisions were never a handicap. Louis did not hide behind Colbert. His protection of his associates was the more natural since he was committed to the policies they were carrying out. Royal power, measured in terms of the enormous standing of its greatest minister, appeared to shed itself of its absolute character, finding itself remarkably free of legal restraints, yet, in reality, limited by its own volition. Grandeur of conception and minute attention to detail, freedom and service were conjoined in Louis XIV and Colbert. There was no great project without a corresponding budgetary estimate.

ORDINANCES AND REGULATIONS

'The irresistible impetus towards reform and centralization, the quest for order and stability which swept over the generation of the younger Louis XIV',* twelve years after the Fronde produced an extraordinary crop of ordinances and regulations. It would provide a model for the enlightened despots of the next

* This is Professor Y.-M. Bercé's conclusion.

century. Historians generally give all the credit to Colbert and his collaborators, but 'for this body of French law, put together for the first time, contemporaries naturally praised the king' (251). This was not mere flattery but rather a recognition of his intentions and plans. Without Louis XIV's overall conception, Colbert's achievements would have been limited. Without Colbert's rigorous and effective investigation of the old laws, the king's dream would never have been so fully accomplished. The imagination of the king and the practical genius of the minister were mutually supportive. Their aims coalesced since the 'great corpus of French law promulgated by Louis XIV was the legislative foundation for Colbert's administration' (251).

Three examples will help to prove the point. The ordinances on water and forest resources (1669), on commercial life (1673) and on shipping (1681) provided the kind of regulation which the minister wanted as a backdrop to the bureaucratic activities of a part of his department, and laid down ground-rules of national and enduring significance. Three hundred years after the shipping ordinance of 1681, thirty or so of its clauses are still in common use, notably the one concerned with the 'definition of the sea-shore and its legal status' (chapter IV, article 7) (251). The ordinance on water and forest resources represented a kind of 'nationalization' of the forests, and was concerned with the conservation and development of the patrimony as well as the provision of timber for the king's naval arsenals. There was nothing abstract or utopian about it; this is why it was a model for this kind of legislation. The ordinance on commercial activity was prepared in the years from 1669 to 1673. That on shipping took longer still to prepare. Based upon a commission for harbours, which reported at the end of 1670, the ordinance took eleven years of Colbert's time to prepare – hence its comprehensiveness. This famous edict provided 'a co-ordinated series of initiatives to improve the port facilities of the kingdom and to increase the shipping as well as to establish a good maritime law' (251). Louis XIV and his minister together drew up legislation of an exemplary kind which also had practical, administrative utility. In providing a model for the administrative modernity of Europe, Louis and Colbert adapted and refined French law.

Such reforms were not revolutionary. Where modifications to existing laws could take place, they were preferred to starting from scratch. Old structures were adapted. The codes and prestigious ordinances were prepared by three dozen commissioners, and it was to such intendants that the ordinances assigned the most substantial power. Colbert had no difficulty in persuading the king, who never forgot the years of the Fronde, that these commissioners were well-organized, adaptable functionaries, keen and capable, far removed from their relatives amongst the *noblesse de robe*, the proud, stubborn judges with their narrowly legalistic prejudices. On the contrary, although from a *parlement-aire* background, the intendants had turned their backs on the old institutional structures and had chosen to serve a modern state. A few dozen intendants became the mainsprings of the realm, and the king put his confidence in them. Would they take advantage of the king's impetus towards reform to achieve a complete administrative revolution? France was, in reality, not rich enough to reimburse all the proprietors of royal offices at a stroke. More importantly, there was the political objection that the realm was an organism, which it was better to treat with gentle remedies rather than by inflicting a series of amputations. This was why Louis XIV and Colbert tolerated the existence of 45,000 for the most part highly cultivated, patrimonial office-holders, who hankered at times for a further Fronde and who rarely supported change. This burden of the surviving judicial state explains the origins, the extent and also the limitations of the *code Louis*.

Neither Justinian nor Louis XIV nor Colbert, let alone Napoleon Bonaparte, was a trained lawyer. But they shared the common objective of integrating scattered laws into a logical and coherent whole. This is why edicts worthy of the name of legal codes were prepared. France was not entirely backward in this respect. The sixteenth century had seen the publication of engrossed customary laws relating to particular regions. But France, the 'mother of laws', had been more concerned with enacting new laws than with codifying what already existed. That the realm was divided into two different legal systems, the North being a region of customary law and the South being the home of Roman law, was a positive hindrance. The independence of the judges, strengthened by patrimonial office-holding, as well as the autonomy of the various jurisdictions, complicated the system. An army of judicial clerks were on hand to exploit the differences in the customs and practices of each tribunal. At the higher levels, the clear and well-ordered ordinances which might help the suitor through this maze were mostly ignored: the 461 articles of the *code Michau* of 1629 were only irregularly followed. And besides, who knew in 1660 which laws still remained in force? This was why, from 1661 onwards, Louis XIV and Colbert hoped to codify, if not the whole of French private law, then at least its procedures. Even before the arrest of Fouquet, Colbert had discussed the matter with his uncle, the councillor of state Pussort. Later, the minister established a 'detailed table of royal ordinances'. In the spring of 1665, the project for the reform of justice was pushed one stage further by the obtaining of royal assent and direction. In the autumn, Colbert envisaged something rather more radical. He wanted statutes which would enable him to say: if the king codifies the laws, it is because he wants 'all his realm to live under the same law with the same penalties' (251). But too many difficulties prevented this kind of unification. The king did not go as far as his minister – he had to consider the chancellor Séguier, even though Colbert often acted in the chancellor's stead. And also, since the reforms were based on the sovereignty of the king and not on an Estates General, prudence demanded that a number of senior magistrates be associated with the plan. From all their efforts, Colbert and Pussort presented the results to the king in March 1667. Signed by the king, they became the ordinance upon the procedures in civil law of April 1667 (201).

This enactment consisted of 'thirty-five chapters, each enunciated with perfect clarity and brevity' (259), regulating the format of judicial cases and decisions, laying down rules for the judges, limiting chicanery and protecting the suitor. The ordinance on criminal law, pronounced in August 1670, constituted the second stage of reform. Today, it might seem repressive, given that the death penalty, despatch to the galleys and other harsh punishments are writ large in it. But this was not a matter of comment for contemporaries, mindful of past troubles. Furetière wrote: 'The severity of the law and its penalties is what keeps states in peace.' (42) Before its publication, only the *premier président* of the Parlement of Paris, Lamoignon, had called for the abolition of judicial torture. Two perspectives should prevent us from regarding this code in too harsh a light. Firstly, there was a contrast in France between the rigour of the law and the leniency of its application. Secondly, shortly after its promulgation, and especially during the two or three years when Colbert replaced Séguier, the legal prosecution of witches was eliminated from the penal code.

INVESTIGATION BEFORE ACTION

Some call Colbertianism the rigid application of economic rules known as mercantilism. This is, quite simply, an error. Others call Colbertianism the dominance of the state over finance, industry and manufacture, that is, *dirigisme*, but they ignore the fact that Colbert practised something much more open-minded and pragmatic. 'Colbertianism' should stand for what was original in Louis XIV's collaborator, and this was the practice of investigating a subject thoroughly before making a decision. This was a cast of mind he shared with the king.

In September 1663, Colbert put the finishing touches to his remarkable *Instruction for Maîtres des Requêtes and Commissioners in the Provinces*. Intendants sent out on commission should look at each matter following a set of common guidelines designed to reveal the distinctive character of the communes, their aptitude for war, cultivation, industry and trade. The fertility of all cultivatable land should be estimated as well as, among other things, the agricultural capacity of the peasantry, the forest resources, the importance of commerce and its nature, industry, maritime activities. 'One might call it a blueprint for a voyage of discovery into a *terra incognita*.' (216) Colbert always felt the need for general and detailed inquiries. This particular one would advance Louis XIV's knowledge of his realm. And, given the nature of the questions in the *Instruction*, the intendants would have interpreted it as being mainly a demographic survey. Indeed, Colbert revealed here a remarkably prescient concern for demography besides demonstrating his efforts to organize and stimulate the economy.

At the same time, the minister multiplied his demands for information. In 1664 at his request, the directors of the West Indies Company (*compagnie des Indes occidentales*) provided him with an estimate of the number of Europeans in Martinique (178). In 1665 and 1666, the intendant in Canada, Talon, presented Colbert with 'an exact roll of all the inhabitants of the colony', the first census of 'New France' (178). One of the most precise statistical inquiries remained, however, that of May 1665 into the number of venal offices in the kingdom. This revealed 45,780 officeholders, representing a capital value of 419,630,000 *livres* (179). In 1666, Colbert organized a census of Dunkirk. In 1670, he ordered the preparation of year by year statistics upon the population of Paris (there were, for example, 16,810 baptisms and 21,461 burials in the capital that year). Colbert's curiosity, mingled with obstinacy, resulted in a government better accustomed to basing its decisions upon statistics. The censuses conducted by Vauban from 1678 onwards, and those of Pontchartrain in 1693 and Beauvillier in 1697, were but continuations of Colbertian political practices.

These were 'populationist'. To ensure the defence of the country, to populate the colonies and to increase French production, Colbert stimulated population resources ('la peuplade') and employment. Emigration was controlled and the immigration of technical specialists was systematically encouraged. The king, the court and the aristocrats needed glassmakers, sculptors and cabinet-makers. The arsenals required carpenters, sailmakers and caulkers. Industry was short of manufacturers, inventors and high-calibre craftsmen. At home, Colbert granted exemptions from the *taille* to young people willing to marry before their twenty-first birthday. He tried, without provoking religious antipathies, to reduce the number of clerics. The intendants and police officers were asked to arrest and punish those undertaking pilgrimages under false pretences. Monks were invited to give less by way of food in charity and more in the form of knitting wool. The *rentiers* were requested to reinvest part of their capital in manufacture, and the governors of *hôpitaux* to set the indigent to work (216). In short, Colbert's aim was to gain a thorough knowledge of France, to help increase its population resources, and to put those people to work.

THE NEW FINANCIAL SYSTEM

Louis XIV and Colbert grasped that all economic policies required a sound basis in the public finances. The king recalled the sorry state of the Treasury on the death of Mazarin in a passage at the beginning of his *Mémoires* for the education of the Dauphin: 'The finances, the mainspring for the activities of this great monarchy, were wasted away to such an extent that its resources were scarcely visible.' After the fall of Fouquet, he expressed his dissatisfactions more precisely: 'The way in which receipts and expenditures were handled was almost unbelievable. My revenues were no longer handled by my treasurers but by the lackeys of the superintendent . . . and money was spent at a time, in a manner, and for the purposes which he decreed.' (63) From the death of Fouquet until the end of the reign, Louis and his treasurers relied on a new system of financial management.

It has been recently suggested that nothing had changed in the system's fundamentals, since behind the financial officials and the tax-farmers general (*fermiers généraux*) swarmed taxfarmers (*traitants*), *partisans* and financiers, behind whom lay their backers, great figures at court and in Paris who were often close to the king.* From this perspective, the Colbertian reforms were only a kind of smoke-screen behind which the system of Fouquet would be perpetuated, more hypocritically and less efficiently even than before. If Desmarets, Colbert's nephew, held the confidence of the financiers, Colbert lost their goodwill by bullying them in the *chambre de justice*, and because he had compromised them in the eyes of the king by informing him of their shady practices (170).

This historical revision cuts both ways, demonstrating that it was wrong to imagine Fouquet as guilty of all the faults of the financiers and Colbert as the sole promoter of the virtues of a proper system of public finances. But, with the truth somewhere in between, Colbert emerges with an enhanced stature. The reform of the visible parts of the financial system – the rationalizing of public funding required by Louis XIV and undertaken by Colbert – was important in three ways. It cleared up part of the system. It was a promise of future improvement. And it reassured taxpayers.

The suppression of the superintendency of finance was an improvement in that the royal council of finances, presided over by the king and managed by Colbert, replaced it (in 1661). In place of a strict control upon expenditure, this collegial neosuperintendence introduced a welcome openness into affairs, what Colbert called 'the rule of order'. Its application was not

---

* Contrary to current views, these royal servants were not cynical profiteers who gained from the people's distress, but, rather, individuals who sought the best investment for their capital.

perfect, but it was a useful beginning. Colbert demonstrated its importance in the establishing of three books of accounts. A 'register of funds' identified the budgetary receipts and a 'register of expenditures' did the same with budgetary expenditures, whilst a 'diary' (*journal*), presented before the Council monthly, itemized the ordinances of contingent expenditure, which the king then signed. To simplify matters, the controller-general combined these documents in 1667 into two registers, one of budgeted receipts and expenditures and the 'diary'. After each year, the accounts were audited and a definitive statement (*état au vrai*) was passed to the chamber of accounts (*chambre des comptes*) (216). The concept of a state budget was born, a patrimonial budget hardly less artificial or less to be trusted than those which we are familiar with today.

To retain the king's confidence, Colbert made full accounts of the direct taxes, constituted mainly by the *tailles*, and attempted to increase indirect revenues as much as possible (those from taxes on non-necessities, paid for by the rich), by establishing a series of targets. Henceforth, he did not flinch from demanding stricter conditions in the terms on which tax-collectors undertook their duties. From 1661 to 1666, the minister pursued the policy, begun by Fouquet, of giving relief from the *taille personnelle* – the tax paid by the non-nobles in northern France and the directly administered provinces – but he used intendants to see that its burden was more equitably distributed and that poorer taxpayers were protected. Thus, the tax-receivers, the office-holders in the *élections*, all the royal officeholders, found themselves, along with the *communautés d'habitants*, the collectors of the *taille*.

With revenues which were farmed out, it was a matter of not becoming too craven towards the tax-farmers and their agents. Strengthened by the king's authority, the controller-general attempted to arrange more-precise contracts with them: both sides should expect to profit, but not at the expense of the activity being taxed. From 1661 until the Dutch war of 1672, the royal demesne, hitherto substantially alienated, was largely put back together. The overall contract for the farming of the royal demesne was worth 1,160,000 *livres* in 1666, 4,100,000 in 1676 and 5,540,000 in 1681 (251). It is true, however, that in 1674 a return to the era of expedients took place and the demesne was once again alienated. The tax on salt (the *gabelle*), the various customs dues (*aides, traites*) and taxes upon consumption (*octrois*) were already collected by means of tax-farmers and their clients, but this did not stop the state having recourse to 'extraordinary means of taxation'. Sales of offices, a doubling-up of existing officers in some posts, a devaluation of the *rentes* issued on the Hôtel de Ville in Paris and a reduction in the precious-metal content of the coinage were a few of these expedient measures. For Colbert, a good accountant to the king, one not hostile to his construction or military expenditures, never pretended that he could work miracles or that financial rectitude should always take first place before imperative need. To the end, he remained pragmatic. When he created the 'loan fund' (*caisse des emprunts*) in 1674, requiring the tax-farmers general to lend money to it at five per cent, he was only adding one more expedient to an already long list (251). The financiers still retained their influence. But Colbert had nevertheless given the king and the state a measure of independence.

ENDS AND MEANS

The reforms of justice and finance were only a kind of ground-clearing exercise in the eyes of the controller-general and king's minister. Although always portrayed as a man attentive to detail, Colbert had a 'grand design', a broad political vision which was not so very different from Richelieu's. The minister whom historians have dismissed as too 'Cartesian' can be sometimes found engaging in broader speculation. He was much less 'bourgeois' than he seems, capable of a wider vision, which explains why he could work so closely with his sovereign. It was in 1664 that Colbert expressed himself with greatest clarity, and established what was almost the essence of his doctrine. But his writings, alongside his actions, helped to refine and orchestrate the plans he presented to the king. His doctrine therefore appears in them in an applied and deductive fashion. To articulate it completely one must work backwards from its applications to its first principles.

Like the king, not to mention other statesmen, Colbert took as axiomatic the importance of national political goals: 'The glory of the king and the furtherance of the state' (236). These were to be achieved above all by success in arms. Nothing, however, was more expensive than a permanent, modern army. Such expenditure required a strong fiscal basis. A highly productive tax-system which did not cripple the nation presupposed increased prosperity for the largest possible number of the population, and it was this development of general prosperity which was the preoccupation of the minister. He invented nothing new in all this. The distinctive hand of Colbert can be seen more in the transparent nationalism running alongside his economic notions and the great energy which he put into their application.

Louis XIV's councillor measured the richness of the country by the volume of precious metals it possessed. But France had no silver or gold mines of its own and had to draw what it could from the arrivals of precious metals from America. It had to watch carefully what happened to its specie and increase its volume. This meant having a favourable balance of trade. To sustain this favourable balance, it was essential to prevent the export of silver and gold, by limiting or preventing the purchase of foreign manufactured goods, especially luxury goods from Italy and Flanders. Imports had to be limited to essential primary products. Certain purchases might even be made by means of the exchange of products. On the other hand, all had to be done to develop sales of French goods abroad, something which required an overall economic policy enjoying a degree of conscious collaboration from the king's subjects.

The king and Colbert did their best, developing the road network, tackling regressive tolls, encouraging water-borne transportation; but it was still necessary to have a wider degree of co-operation. Colbert reproached his compatriots for their laziness: the clerics without a sense of vocation, the merchants who retired early, the *rentiers* who set no example. The national obsession with offices turned away thousands from the world of commerce. And then there was the prejudice provoked by noble derogation (*dérogeance*). A Colbertian ordinance of 1669 announced, and an edict of 1701 repeated, but to no avail, that merchant endeavour did not demean noble status; the French aristocracy would never imitate the English gentry in this respect.

Although the nobility baulked at trade, Colbert did not abandon his aspiration to develop trade and industry in France. He saw these as 'the two means by which alone we may draw riches to our realm and ensure that an infinite number of our subjects may live with comfort and an ease growing ever greater as the years go by, providing God maintains peace' (236). This policy had its polemical aspects. To Colbert, to enrich oneself in reality meant beggaring one's competitors. Some had lost the means of resisting a large country which had now become versed in the arts of industrial espionage: such was the case with Venice, which found the secrets of its glass manufacture and luxury textiles pillaged. Spain also lost much of its mercantile greatness. England more than held its own, basing its maritime growth upon the Navigation Acts and the capture of Dutch assets in the course of three Dutch wars (1652–3, 1665–7, 1672–3), during which New Amsterdam became its colony of New York. England was not, however, the greatest competitor in commercial matters faced by France. To Colbert's eyes, the most worrying nation was the United Provinces. As a competitor to its East India Company, he devised the French counterpart, the *Compagnie française des Indes orientales.* To its 16,000 merchant ships of substantial tonnage, he hoped to oppose 2,000 French vessels.* Against its intrusive commerce, its irritating habit of selling abroad at a loss, His Majesty's government had only one mechanism of defence: the 'skirmish' of protective tariffs. They were put in place in 1664 and reinforced in 1667. When it became clear that this combative protectionism was met with tit-for-tat reprisals even the pacific royal treasurer became bellicose. In 1670, 'Colbert was pushing for the Dutch war, even more than Louvois'. In 1672, when the bourgeois of Amsterdam were looking forward to a further period of peace, Colbert was the one 'hoping to make Holland simply disappear' (236) by means of a French annexation.

GREAT HOPES . . .

A hundred years before Adam Smith's *Wealth of Nations* (1776), an economist wrote: 'Liberty is the lifeblood of commerce' (1671) and 'Anything which restricts this liberty . . . can be nothing but worthless' (1673) (251). These liberal-sounding maxims come straight from the correspondence of Colbert. The mention of them serves as a reminder that the Colbertian

---

* In fact, France possessed only about 300 large merchant ships.

initiatives, creations and reforms were never systematically *étatiste*, not even during the period between 1664 and 1670. If the state lay at their heart, it nevertheless remained only one means by which to achieve his ambitions.

The creation of privileged manufactories and the organization of arterial trade were primary components in the Colbertian programme. Throughout a period of six years, letters-patent and Council decrees proved the government's persistent desire to redress the balance of trade in France's favour. In May 1664, an edict called for the 'establishment of a West Indies Company to carry out all the trade with the islands and continent of America and other countries' (201). In August came the creation of the highly ambitious East India Company. Louis XIV granted it the base at Lorient in 1666 as its trading headquarters. Another edict of August 1664 saw to the 'establishment of royal tapestry manufactories in the town of Beauvais and other places in Picardy'. The manufactory in Beauvais received privileges lasting thirty years, and the state would support the construction of the buildings up to the maximum of 30,000 *livres*: 'The remaining subsidies were proportionate to the number of workers at the rate of twenty *livres* per individual, with an obligation upon the manufactory to recruit 100 craftsmen in the first year and a similar number in the following five years.' (161)

On 18 September of the same year, 1664, a decision of the Council established the custom tariffs for France. An edict of February 1665 was published 'for the establishment of royal manufactories of tin-plate and all other sorts of metalwork'. In July, letters-patent were issued re-establishing the tapestry works of Aubusson. In August came a declaration 'for the establishment of the manufacture of gold-braid (*points*) in France'. In October, other royal patents created the 'manufactory for glass, crystal and glassware' at Reuilly (Louis XIV visited the works on 29 April 1666). This became the Saint-Gobain Company, which is still in profitable existence. Similarly, in October 1665, the king granted privileges, on Colbert's suggestion, 'to M. Van Robais the elder' to establish a manufactory for fine cloth in the Spanish and Dutch style at Abbeville (201). Then came a declaration on 11 March 1666 'for the privileged establishment of soap manufactories' (201). On 16 September, a patent established 'statutes and regulations for the fabrication and manufacture of cloth' in favour of Nicolas

Cadeau, a merchant from Sedan (161). In October, at the same time as the edict for the construction of the Midi canal was issued, the 'statutes and regulations for cloth manufacture in Carcassonne' were published.

On 18 April 1667, a further declaration, replacing that of September 1664, appeared 'in the form of a new increased tariff for customs duties upon itemized imported and exported goods' (201). In November, an edict confirmed the establishment of the Gobelins as a 'manufactory of furnishings for the Crown'. In March 1669, an edict created the free port at Marseille. In June, a declaration instigated the Northern Company (*Compagnie du Nord*), with instructions to trade in Holland, Zealand, the German littoral, the Baltic, Denmark, Norway, Sweden, Russia and 'the other lands and islands to the north' (139). A royal instrument of 6 August adjusted industrial law by clarifying the jurisdiction of the 'guardian magistrates of the privileges of the Lyon fairs' (201).

These measures are but a small fragment of the political actions of Colbert and the king. Other letters-patent encouraged more-specific inventions or industrial innovations. Thus, a declaration of 18 December 1664 stimulated the 'manufacture and sale of artificial wax candles . . . in four different sizes and prices', and a privilege was granted to sieur Elie Bonnet on 1 March 1665 'for a new method of preparing leather' (201). The craft guilds were the subject of a great deal of legislation, generally affecting those crafts which were already subject to regulation. This proliferation of regulations, statutes and privileges has often given rise to the view that Colbert wasted a great deal of time trying to control and regulate craft skills. In fact, he exercised a supervisory role without giving excessive privileges to the guilds. The letters-patent of May 1661 'for the freedom of craftsmen in Lyon from guild regulation' (201) were by no means an isolated measure. In Paris, the turnover of the unregulated artisans was higher than that of the incorporated craftsmen, and the Mercers' Guild was a kind of Trojan horse for unregulated craft skills functioning within the Six Guilds (*Six Corps*), the prestigious craft guilds of the capital (251). The king's concerns lay (thanks to Colbert's insistence) with regulations designed to ensure the quality of industrial production vital to exports, rather than with the guilds as such. Colbert's policy aimed to 'restore the quality of manufacture' in order to stimulate new ventures. How would France match up to Venetian, Flemish or Dutch competition with a poor quality of cloth? How could one prevent the rich in France buying abroad if there were not competitive products available to them at home? This is how one should seek to understand the edicts which erected a rigid framework to which national manufacture had to comply. The edict of August 1669 with its 'regulations and general statutes for the length, breadth, quality and dye of cloths, serges and other woollen and woven fabrics' was not the expression of a cumbersome state intervention but an appeal to professional conscience. It was not a matter of overturning structures so much as changing mentalities to win the war for trade.

. . . PARTIAL RESULTS

So much effort deserved to see results. But too many things intervened to deflect or debase Colbertianism. In public finance, the prolonged Dutch War required the French government to return to expedients. Although Colbert attempted to put things right after the Peace of Nymwegen in 1679, he did so without the same enthusiasm or the same success. The king's subjects, easily mobilized for wartime defence, were not great partisans in a trade war, preferring to wage it after their own fashion rather than in Colbert's cohorts. The merchants of Marseille showed little interest in Colbert's trading companies, and the merchants of Nantes, Saint-Malo and La Rochelle were hardly better disposed towards them. Many preferred privateering enterprises to chartered-company endeavours. The edict of 1669 did not create a commercial aristocracy: at best, it allowed merchants ennobled by the king to continue their trading activities. Private capital failed to materialize to support state endeavours: a specific royal command (*lettre de cachet*) was required in 1669 to release the second third of the engaged capital to the coffers of the East India Company (201). In colonial companies, as in manufactories, the minister's intention was that private venture capital should replace that of the state so that a regime of free trade should prevail. The reluctance of merchants undermined this 'state disengagement' and also rendered many of these enterprises vulnerable.

The Levant Company of 1670 had a particular fatal flaw.

Instead of being mercantile, maritime and based in Provence, it was based in the capital and involved sixteen Parisians with financier connections, friends of the minister, and only two merchants from Marseille (129). The West Indies Company, incapable of nourishing its Caribbean colonists and providing them with sufficient African labour, lost its monopoly in 1666. The Northern Company was, like the others, shunned by the merchants and under the influence of the financiers. It made no profits and did not survive beyond 1684. It ensured the presence of the French merchant marine in the Baltic and provided the naval arsenals with essential supplies, but, even here, it was a matter of royal capital subsidizing merchant shipping to increase the king's military capability. Without the engagement of private capital, profitability lay in doubt; without profitability, private investment withdrew the more speedily. *Etatisme*, or state control, is the only way to describe the method of economic management of a state thus left to its own devices by its own people.

The French East India Company, although established so long after its English and Dutch rivals, which had been founded in 1601 and 1602, had all that was needed to establish it as a major plank in the French economic and colonial organization. The Dutch had, with remarkable energy, established themselves in the Near East, the Cape, Ceylon and the Indies. With 80,000 sailors or agents, and 15,000 soldiers, they had the power of a major European state, but deployed in the Indian Ocean (129). And the English had Bombay, Madras and the coast of Bengal. But, in this distant world where undreamt-of riches became a reality, there was still room for a nation with intrepid seamen, mercantile experience, and colonizing energies. The distance, the cost of expeditions, made individual initiatives almost impossible. If the existence of a chartered company was to be justified, it was surely in these distant waters. Unfortunately, France was never able to draw on as much private capital and as many good administrators, seamen, colonizers and merchants as its rivals. Even with this company, the king had to provide almost everything. And the difficulties experienced in the attempted colonization of Madagascar (1665–74) tested even the patience of Louis XIV and Colbert. The establishment of a colony on the 'Ile Bourbon' (Réunion) in 1665, and the foundation of commercial manufactories at Surat (1667) and Pondicherry

(1670) in south-east India, although very promising, were not adequate rewards for the hopes raised and the effort expended. What had been a political success was an economic flop.

Maritime France may have failed to play the part projected for it by the king, but craftsmen, merchants and artisans showed hardly any greater enthusiasm to obey the directives of M. Colbert. If private funds had materialized, Louis XIV would not have been obliged to invest between 500,000 and 2,000,000 *livres* a year in manufactories between 1660 and 1690 (251). The state manufactories functioned well (the arsenals, their suppliers, the Gobelins) and so did some of the others (the *Compagnie des glaces*, Van Robais, the textile firms of Languedoc), but the remainder were neither profitable nor enduring. The established view has, though, over-played these failures, for the successes are striking enough to eclipse them. It is also often said that, without the necessities of war and the demand for luxury goods, nothing would have survived of Colbert's initiatives. If this were the case, it would still mean that what he did was a success. For all had to contribute to the glory of the state, and the provisioning of fortresses, garrisons and arsenals was the *sine qua non* of that glory. War was the premier industry of France in this period, and one should not overlook the importance of the technological input it demanded. And everything had to be done to stop the haemorrhage of specie, that is, to prevent the rich from purchasing finished products from abroad. Thus, if the expenses of the court and urban living, and the enrichment of innumerable centres of bourgeois ways of life in the provinces, went to encourage the production of luxury products in France, one part of the battle for a favourable trade balance had been won.

It is difficult to be so charitable towards the Colbertian campaign for high quality manufactures. The famous edict of August 1669 regulating textile production overturned too many established patterns of work and was shown to be needlessly severe. The following year, Colbert drew up the general instruction, of 30 April 1670, which established agents for the inspection of manufactured goods, and charged them with the task of enforcing the regulations throughout the realm. This formidable instruction gave them powers of control and enforcement, the latter including the confiscation and destruction of merchandise. Twelve years later, Colbert's correspondence, still harping on the same theme, indicates that these regulations were not being

enforced, even in industrial locations only 150 miles away from
Paris. But was that really so important? To talk of Colbert's
failure and to emphasize the inertia, resistance and reluctance
which were inevitable and whose existence is easily compre-
hended is to judge him by the false dawn of Utopia rather than
the difficulties of the real world.

POLICING PARIS

One of Colbert's fruitful and lasting initiatives was his
reorganization of the policing of Paris, a city of more than half-a-
million inhabitants. For thirty years, it had been the 'capital of
the world of letters' (254), taking over from Rome, Antwerp and
Oxford. But the huge city suffered an insecurity and a filthiness
in the post-Fronde period quite beneath this reputation. The
Hôpital Général could not cope with all the vagabonds and
beggars. Entire *quartiers* remained without effective law enforcement, open to pickpockets, street-walkers, cut-purses and cloak-
snatchers, not to mention that alarming underworld, the *cour des
miracles*. Against them stood an overwhelmed city-watch and
several police officers responsible to a lawcourt known as the
'Châtelet'. The administration of Paris was a many-headed
monster. The city provost (*prévôt des marchands*), a kind of mayor,
had jurisdiction over the quays of the Seine, and the port,
rampart and boulevard areas. The remainder of the policing
functions were split between the Parlement of Paris and the
Châtelet. The latter was the most senior lawcourt in the kingdom after the Paris Parlement. The position of its titular head,
the *prévôt de Paris*, was purely honorary, the real power lying with
its *premier président*, an important member of the robe nobility
who was called the 'civil lieutenant'. The latter, assisted by a
criminal lieutenant (*lieutenant criminel*), presided over the activities of the Châtelet, and exercised policing powers, aided by
commissioners and agents, wherever he was allowed to by the
Parlement and the city provost. It was not his fault that these
tasks were not well carried out.

In 1665, however, Colbert involved the king in a reform of the
municipality. He told the king that 'the political magistrates',
the city provost and co-opted aldermen (*échevins*), were only
interested in making sure that the city was not policed. In the

autumn of 1666, Colbert instigated a police council, which he presided over every week until the following February. The creation of the Parisian lieutenancy of police in March 1667 was the result. It was of enormous consequence since the new institution not only lasted through to 1789 but also would be resurrected, with some modifications, in Year VIII after the French Revolution (1797) as the prefecture of police.

Louis XIV's contemporaries did not see it from this perspective; many did not understand the significance of the lieutenancy, but it did not pass completely unobserved. The preamble of the edict of March 1667 said that it was often impossible to combine the functions of dispensing justice and of policing; the men of the pen thus took over where the men of the robe had left off. The judicial state was becoming an administrative state. In addition, the king chose a remarkable individual to inaugurate the institution, Nicolas de la Reynie. From 1667 to 1674 (the date when the powers of the lieutenant of police were confirmed), he waged war not only against petty crime but also against the civil lieutenant and his wounded *amour propre*. La Reynie's achievement was magnificent, in terms both of the security and of the quality of life in Paris. He was encouraged in his efforts by the privileged access he enjoyed to the king's working sessions (*liasses*). His reputation increased with the length of time he occupied the post – the king left him there for thirty years. He made himself indispensable in political investigations and general matters of policing.

La Reynie was more faithful than shrewd, as the *affaire des Poisons* demonstrated.* Nor was he as powerful as we like to think; for he was dependent upon the minister for Paris, Colbert. He had to pretend to take orders from the *premier président* and *procureur général* of the Parlement. His jurisdiction was challenged by the city council, and, in matters of the environment and highways, he had to manipulate things past the bureau of finances. The existence of many seigneurial jurisdictions within Paris further restricted his activities. Within these limits, the lieutenant of police enjoyed great powers. His jurisdiction included the control of printing, bookshops and the sale of the printed word. He supervised security, and held judgement over 'illegal meetings, riotous, seditious and disorderly assemblies'. He summoned the police tribunal twice a week at the Châtelet to

* See ch. 14.

hear cases involving trade disputes, giving judgement upon the most serious offences. He policed the provisioning of the city, controlled the guilds, surveyed troops on the march through the city, and supervised quarrying, road-maintenance, a large part of the urban fabric, foreigners in the city, public morals and the prisons. All the industrial activity of Paris and a good deal of its commerce lay within his remit. Like the intendants, only with greater frequency, he indicated to the king which individuals should be detained, by specific royal command (*lettre de cachet*), in royal châteaux or convents.

To itemize the powers of the lieutenant of police, even in this cursory and simplified way, indicates that he did not have just the threefold responsibility implied in the engaging phrase 'muck, street-lights, and whores'. La Reynie (1667–97) and his successor, Argenson (1697–1718), were superb administrators.* La Reynie saw off the *cour des miracles* of organized crime. Under his aegis, security after dark improved and the cleanliness of the city increased somewhat. Under Argenson, the lieutenancy of police benefited from the exalted social station of his family, since the Voyer d'Argensons were of ancient lineage. A royal declaration superimposed upon the sixteen *quartiers* of the city the twenty *quartiers* of the Châtelet. Forty-eight commissioners of police and twelve inspectors kept an eye on the city and its suburbs. In 1715, the capital and its 22,000 houses had 5,522 street-lights.

MONSIEUR COLBERT'S MAUSOLEUM

Like many great statesmen, Colbert died amidst indifference and popular rejoicing. Even the king displayed no regrets proportionate to the services which had been rendered to him, a phenomenon replicated in 1691 with the death of Louvois. Not to be seen to depend upon irreplaceable collaborators was part of the royal illusion; it would be a fine judgement which determined how much of this lay in the king's egotism and how much in *raison d'état*. What should be remembered is that Louis XIV and Colbert enjoyed a long and close collaboration of a quarter of a century. Such faithful service abraded friendship, its

---

* See ch. 17.

shared complicities undermining the more-personal emotions. Posterity has hardly been more generous. Voltaire's *Century of Louis XIV* did, however, praise Colbert the administrator, the legislator and, above all, the Maecenas to the new Augustus. 'It does not matter to me', wrote Voltaire, 'whether Colbert had thick-set eyebrows, an uncouth and low-born face, a glacial expression . . . I look to what he did which was memorable, what succeeding centuries will owe to him.' Voltaire elevated Colbert without diminishing Louis XIV. But, in the eyes of historians, criticism followed appreciation. The nineteenth and early twentieth centuries elaborated a myth about Colbert, trying to prove that, while Louis XIV amused himself with his warfare and wasteful expenditure, Colbert was at work, restraining his prodigalities and desirous of peace. Then came the demolition of that myth. For a number of years, it came to be said that the economic achievement of the controller-general was illusory. Colbert, a slave to the excessive mercantilism of his age, a man of the system, imprisoned the industries and commerce of the realm in a *dirigiste* state- and guild-dominated straitjacket. Working within a period of deflation, Colbert was building on sand. Colbertian patronage is either ignored or misjudged. Critics have now, however, changed tack. In the most recent perspective, Colbert came from a financier background and, like Fouquet, depended upon financiers; there was no revolution in public finances, where he showed himself less astute than his predecessor (170).

It is now over 300 years since the death of the great minister. The tricentenary of his death was not forgotten. It brought together, paradoxically, those who lessen his achievement as well as those who, in their recent works (236), have rehabilitated him (251). The promoters of the tricentenary celebrations envisaged the celebration of Colbert as a kind of minister for state socialism and nationalization. But, at the same time, a 'Colbert Committee' was seen to present the underlying qualities of diversity, competition and economic liberalism. Such a striking contrast warns us against making any simple-minded generalizations.

But, by the standards of an absolute monarchy – and taking account of Louis XIV's own activity –, what appears to Colbert's credit should also appear to the credit of his master; and the same applies to his demerits. We should also avoid being bound by the affections or antipathies of sentiment. Voltaire was right: Colbert should not be judged by his grey exterior but 'by what he did which was memorable', following the king's orders, and by the fact that he enjoyed the confidence of the latter for twenty-two years. Colbert did not try hard to please people. He was no courtier. But his ability was demonstrated during his career. Becoming indispensable to Mazarin, and imposing his ideas on a king who rarely had anything forced upon him, required more than one talent; it demanded a certain combination of talents, a combination which the sieur de Vandières' son amply possessed. It made him rich, richer than Fouquet – like Mazarin this was with the king's approval –, and allowed him to fulfil every ambition his family could have desired of him. Although Louis XIV did not raise his estates at Seignelay into a dukedom, he encouraged his minister to marry his three daughters to dukes.* The same qualities allowed Colbert to rule over four departments of state – the equivalent of ten modern ministries – and he became renowned both for his keen sense of synthesis, and for his prodigious capacity to absorb detail. The latter capacity is often imputed to him as a crime. But this is to forget that the ability to move from the general to the particular is a distinguishing feature of the statesman. One cannot hold against Louis XIV, Colbert and Louvois those qualities which one exalts in Caesar, Louis XI, Frederick of Prussia or Napoleon Bonaparte. Although the rationalization of the state finances, the industrial initiatives and the stimulus to commerce were less positive and durable than Voltaire thought, there still remain the merits of his legislative achievement, his success with the navy, the beginning of a considerable colonial empire and his unique role as an artistic patron.†

---

* The eldest married the duc de Chevreuse in 1667, the second the duc de Beauvillier in 1671 and the youngest the duc de Mortemart in 1679.
† See ch. 9.

9

The Sun King

WHEN THE king, at twenty-three years of age, took the sun as his emblem twenty years before his court was installed at Versailles, he obviously did not dream that the ambiguous title of Sun King would be for ever attached to his memory, held against him in reproach, stuck to him like Nessus' tunic. We must begin with that entertainment in the Tuileries in 1662.

THE TRUE KING IS ALWAYS A SUN

The symbol of the sun was not the product of the flattery which surrounded a monarch. Louis XIV did not associate himself with the symbol by chance. 'His sense of history is profound', recorded La Grande Mademoiselle. 'He talks about it with authority, praises the virtues of his predecessors and remembers things of use to him on future occasions.' (75) Over several centuries, the royal myth had become more precise. Sometimes the sovereign was seen as the helmsman steering the ship of state; at other times as the healing physician. The image of the star which gives out light and heat was also frequently invoked. It was often to be found in the pamphlets of the regency of Marie de Médicis (175). It reappeared during the Fronde. In *The Royal Triumph*, a piece celebrating the return of the king and court to Paris on 18 August 1649, Louis was 'this shining star, this radiant sun, this day without night, this centre, visible from all points of the circumference' (70).

Far from being a pagan image, the royal sun was the image of divine right kingship. This was how Bérulle put it when, in his work *The State and Majesty of Jesus* (1623), he told the Huguenots:

> Since the king is in your part of the world, he who, in his person, represents the image of God, the light of His rays imprinted upon his countenance, should you not sink your differences and bury your bitternesses? The king is a sun [Louis XIII!] which you should look up to . . . a sun which rises in his *Midi* and which you should hold in awe. Do not be blinded by that light for more than a moment from the fact that his heat and influence are necessary to you. He is the guiding star of France. He is the Lord's Anointed, spoken of in the Scriptures. He is the true image of God, bearing the authority and majesty of God, visible in his person. Render him homage and obedience. Open your hearts to him as well as your cities. (9)

Rooted in Counter-Reformed Catholic orthodoxy, the solar theme for the monarchy, like the *Mémoires* of Louis XIV, looked forward to what would be called a century later 'enlightened despotism'. The sun illuminates, just as reason does. The sun's rays have a warming effect, symbolizing an attention to the well-being, the good of the people, 'giving life, joy and happiness to all without ceasing', as the Sun King neatly put it, with Pellisson's help. It is thus too easy to say that Louis XIV was intelligent enough to exploit and modify the old metaphors for his personal ends. In the particular case of the sun image, the monarch, imbued with an acute sense of propaganda, articulated the symbolism of a more modern state.

WORSHIP, PROPAGANDA AND PATRIOTISM

This adulation should not surprise us. Our own century has seen greater excesses for leaders who were not of Louis XIV's calibre. Besides, posterity has too often taken this praise of the monarch as evidence for his inordinate vanity. The Princess Palatine, who made her own enquiries, confirms what shrewd analysts have always understood to be the case, namely, that there was more than a whiff of propaganda around, propaganda intended to engender loyalty and encourage enthusiasm.

> I asked a thoughtful person one day why everything that was published praised the king. The reply came back that the printers had been specifically ordered 'not to print any book which did not

contain praises of the king', and that 'this was for the sake of his subjects'. The ordinary Frenchman reads a great deal and in the provinces they read everything which comes from Paris so that praises of the king inspire respect and indulgence towards him. This was why it was done, and not for the sake of the king, who never saw or heard any of it since he no longer even went near the opera. (87)

The results contributed to *national* propaganda. To praise Louis XIV and his government was to praise the state. To sing of the victories of Mars was to celebrate the army and its bravery. To applaud the legislator was to heap praises on the law. To shower praise upon Apollo was to congratulate Huygens and Cassini, Perrault and Mansart, Le Nôtre and Racine. This was why new members of the Académie française had no second thoughts about offering flattering remarks about the king in their inaugural speeches after 1672.

Louis XIV was a connoisseur of rhetoric and, as with the closely related art of sacred eloquence, he spurred others on. A good speech in honour of the king remained within certain limits, limits dictated by good taste and intelligence. In the seventeenth century, rhetoric was not the baroque showpiece which we sometimes imagine. It had its own rules of decorum, albeit forgotten by most of the authors in 1686 who tried to outshine each other in praise of the operation on the king's fistula. This was why Racine's couplets mentioned the abject flatterers who struck such false notes:

Upon the Compliments that the King Received on the Subject of His Convalescence

God on High! Preserve for us this our victorious king . . .
    Don't let him stray close by
  Dark griefs, a dread ally,
  Save him from pain, a mortal enemy,
    And the couplets of the Academy. (90)

Even gentle praise seemed somewhat excessive to Louis. The court learnt as much in 1685 when, on the day after New Year's Day, Racine, the author of *Phèdre*, welcomed Thomas Corneille to the Académie française, a splendid moment for him to pay homage to Pierre Corneille. But, as his son Louis Racine tells us, 'he not only succeeded in honouring the person he admired, he also praised Louis XIV' by showing that diplomacy had become an easy matter, now that the king's ministers had only 'the embarrassment of telling foreign courts politely what his wisdom dictated'. Racine depicted the prince, a few hours distant from his armies, dictating six lines of protocol so tightly drafted that foreign countries 'could not step out of the narrow circle drawn out for them by these few instructions' so that they were like Antiochus trapped in a vicious circle of the Roman ambassador's making. The speech was so widely praised that Louis XIV asked Racine to read it to him. The king heard the honours heaped upon Corneille the elder as well as those lavished upon his own diplomacy and then said to his historiographer: 'I am very happy with that; but I would praise you more if you had praised me less.' (90)

REWARDS TO MEN OF LETTERS

On 1 January 1664, Jean-Baptiste Colbert, newly appointed superintendent of the king's buildings, confirmed, by order of the king and to the astonishment of Europe (as was intended), the arrangements for pensions and rewards to 'men of letters' – poets, prosewriters and intellectuals. Charles Perrault, the minister's right-hand man, and Chapelain, 'the regent of Parnassus', and one or two others, helped him draw up a list of beneficiaries. In 1664, there were already fifty-eight of them (of whom eleven were foreigners) and the annual budget ran to 77,500 *livres*. The following year, the amount rose to 82,000 *livres*, disbursed to sixty-five people, and in 1666 this had increased to seventy-two receiving 95,000 *livres* (45).

It is common these days to denigrate Louis XIV's patronage to writers and men of science. True, no ministry ever created a masterpiece, but it was a political step which deserves admiration. He made the superintendency of buildings into the first department of culture, changing what already existed rather than starting from scratch. A medal was soon struck to commemorate these gratifications. 'The king's liberality is to be seen in the form of a lady holding a cornucopia. Four young children represent the spirits of the four different art-forms.' (71)

It was not the first time that writers and intellectuals had received pensions, but no head of state had distributed so much, so regularly or for such a long period. Up to the end of 1690, over forty men of letters and scientists had been in receipt of annual pensions. To popular acclaim and despite the irritation of Europe's crowned heads, the names of distinguished foreigners (about ten a year on average) figured among those of the humanists, scholars, grammarians, rhetoricians, poets, historiographers, mathematicians, geographers, astronomers and physicists at the king's service. Some of them were Protestants, such as Heinsius and Vossius, citizens of the Low Countries, although the Dutch War put an end to the pensions of such Dutchmen. Those for the native-born Protestants on the list continued to be paid until the War of the League of Augsburg.

In return for a few flattering odes or complimentary prefaces the beneficiaries of royal largesse were otherwise free to pursue their subjects. What we now interpret as servility contemporaries saw as freedom: what harm came from a small dose of sycophancy in exchange for daily independence? We find Louis XIV very quickly being congratulated for his protection of poets and researchers. But, even as late as 1666, Boileau-Despréaux tried to ignore the active role that Colbert played in this process. His *First Satire* ran:

> From the king, it is true, the gentle light
> Of bounty looks upon the Muses' plight,
> And saving Phoebus from his fatal fall
> Will save him also from the hospital.
> This, we hope, a just monarch may offer us,
> But sans Maecenas, what use Augustus? (11)

However, the arrangements for pensions lasted and soon the poet found himself mentioning the king's minister. In the *Ninth Epistle* (1675), the superintendent of buildings was compared with Augustus' famous companion:

> And he is just the equal to Maecenas
> ... portrayed in him are noble actions,
> Solid virtues, wide intelligence,
> Zeal for his king, ardour, vigilance,
> Constant fairmindedness, a love for the arts ...

Flattery brought rewards. From 1676, Despréaux was rewarded with a pension of 2,000 *livres* 'in consideration of his literary pursuits' (45). Putting the flattery to one side, a comparison between Maecenas and Colbert is not difficult to make. One was a Roman soldier, the other humbly born. One was descended from a 'royal' house of Etruria, the other claimed descendance from the kings of Scotland. Both were counsellors of their prince in artistic affairs as well as his friend. Both protected poets, created academies and patronized writers to laud the state. But Maecenas sustained the Muses from his own purse whilst Colbert used the public purse. Maecenas was an officious benefactor, Colbert an official patron.

The most lavish pensions went to foreigners to attract them to Paris – 6,000 *livres* to the Dutch physicist Huygens, 9,000 to the great Italian astronomer Cassini. Among the native Frenchmen, the best rewarded was Mézeray, whose monumental *History of France* earned universal praise. The scholars Baluze and Du Cange received pensions of 2,000 *livres* and Chapelain received 3,000 *livres*. Some received amounts which never changed: Boileau and Corneille the elder were granted 2,000 *livres*, Molière 1,000, Fléchier 800. For others, the accounts of the superintendency of buildings reveal their increasing favour. Quinault steadily progressed from 800 *livres* to 1,200 in 1672, and then to 1,500 in 1674. In 1667, the pensions of Charles Perrault and the mathematician Carcavy moved from 1,500 to 2,000 *livres*. Racine's pension changed the most often, an example of how the personal influence of Louis XIV could count, and of how his administration adjusted to personal relationships. In 1664 and 1665, the fledgeling author of *La Thébaïde* was granted a pension of 600 *livres*. From 1679 onwards, the author of the forthcoming *Esther* and *Athalie*, the future gentlemen in ordinary to His Majesty's privy chamber, received, like his rival Corneille the elder, a pension of 2,000 *livres*.

No other country enjoyed such an Augustan patronage. Louis XIV, guided by a respect for human values and a breadth of taste which made his artistic judgements almost flawless, took a risk in protecting a republic – the republic of letters – and sustained the patronage of his collaborator, Colbert, which itself patronized his Augustan age. This is why Charles Perrault's flattering couplet

> One may compare without any fear of injustice
> The age of Louis to the great age of Augustus

understates the reality of the reign (132).

THE GREAT ESTABLISHMENTS

However remarkable the pensions to individuals in Louis XIV's Augustan age, they were overshadowed by its artistic and scientific institutions. Over a twelve-year period, the king and Colbert invented or brought to maturity many of the cultural institutions which are still part of the French heritage in the twentieth century. These dozen years on their own justify the expression 'the century of Louis XIV'.

The Royal Manufactory of the Gobelins took shape in 1662; the Academy of Inscriptions in 1663. The *Journal des savants* dates from 1665. The Academy of Sciences goes back to 1666. The Villa Médicis, the French Academy in Rome, was also created, by Colbert, in 1666. The Observatory was begun in 1667. As for the Museum, it continued to amass its collections, and the Royal Botanical Garden for Rare Plants was provided with its modern organization by letters-patent of 20 January 1673. Louis XIV and Colbert put institutions in place which lasted over three centuries, surviving both revolutions and changes in artistic fashion. It is difficult to know which to admire most, the intelligence which went into these establishments, the empiricism which was the distinguishing feature of their development or the harmony of vision of their twin instigators.

Shortly after the cardinal's demise, Louis inaugurated his personal rule with the 'establishment of a royal academy of dance in the city of Paris'. Letters-patent of March 1661 granted thirteen dancing-masters the right to teach individuals 'to perfect their dance' (201). This royal (though not state-dominated) initiative reflected the king's taste for this particular art-form. 'In his dancing, he surpassed himself. Even his most stringent critics were of one mind on the matter. He played the leading roles in ballets and *divertissements* until he was about thirty, a tribute to his famous dancing-master Pierre Beauchamp.' (122)

In the following year, Colbert, 'having foreseen', so Perrault wrote, 'or already knowing that the king would appoint him to the superintendency of buildings, began to prepare for the post' (251). For 40,000 *livres* he bought a 'large house situated on the faubourg Saint-Marcel les Paris ... commonly known as the Gobelins' (161). There he brought together several tapestry workshops. On 8 March 1663, Charles Le Brun – a former Fouquet protégé – became director of the Royal Manufactory of the Gobelins. Le Brun not only prepared, with the help of a team of specialist artists, a series of tapestries depicting the life of the king, but also quickly became the director of 'over 800 tapestry workers, sculptors, artists, goldsmiths, embroiderers and, in general, workers in all that made for splendour and magnificence' (18). Many were foreigners, lured there by Colbert. The Gobelins gathered together the essential elements of those who would be employed on the royal residences and the king's works. Le Brun worked in close co-operation with Berbier du Metz, intendant of the royal furnishings from 1663. Beyond the Faubourg Saint-Marcel, he supervised the royal 'Persian and Indian-style' carpets manufactory called La Savonnerie. At the Gobelins he directed the largest manufactory in the world for tapestry, jewellery, cabinet-making, painting and sculpture, the greatest fine- and applied-art school. On 15 October 1667, the king came on a visit from Saint-Germain to admire the range of delicate work of those who manufactured his glory.

One of the fourteen embroidered hangings of the *History of the King*, sketched out by Le Brun himself and painted by Pierre de Sève the younger, presented 'King Louis XIV Visiting the Gobelins Manufactory'. Louis was accompanied by Monsieur, the duc d'Enghien and Colbert. Le Brun presented the artists and their products – tapestries, pedestals, vases, silver ornaments, 'vast cabinets inlaid with pewter and decorated with scrollwork' (161). Until his death in 1690, Le Brun, the *premier peintre du roi* from 1664, directed the fortunes of this manufactory. His all-embracing talents, his genius as a designer and Colbert's protection explain why he held the king's confidence. Upon Colbert's death, the scrutiny of the accounts of the Gobelins revealed some serious irregularities. But the king was sufficiently confident in the trustworthiness of his *premier peintre* to retain him in the post (251). This is a sketch of one institution which played more than a small part in the wider picture of Louis XIV's patronage. Neither Augustus nor Maecenas had gone beyond his own individual patronage to envisage such a great artistic arsenal.

In the one month alone of February 1663, Colbert laid down the final structure of the Academy of Painting and Sculpture and created the embryo of the Academy of Inscriptions. The former, founded in 1648 and enjoying royal incorporation under Mazarin from 1655, was the protégé of the elderly Séguier. Colbert was its deputy protector from 1661 and attempted, with the assistance of Le Brun, to increase its significance. A Council decision of 8 February 1663 signalled approval for new charters for this academy of painting and sculpture (53b). Le Brun would be its permanent chancellor. Its members alone would have the right to be the artists and sculptors to His Majesty by appointment. The academy would organize exhibitions of its members' work (the first took place in 1667). The academicians would hold meetings on artistic matters. Thus Le Brun read a paper before Colbert on physiognomy (53b). From 1661 onwards, the Academy of Painting held its meetings in the Palais-Royal. Within a few years, it had become the greatest fine-art centre of Paris, the most energetic in Europe.

As against the ninety members of the Academy of Painting and Sculpture, Colbert chose four literary figures to become the intellectual centre of the superintendency of buildings. Their first meeting was on 3 February 1663 in Colbert's house under the chairmanship of Chapelain. The minister chose members of the Académie française to become members of his own *petite académie*. In 1664, this smaller group studied 'the use of allegory in the pictures and tapestries' commissioned by Colbert (161). From 1663 onwards, it composed the legends on the commemorative medals of the reign. In 1694, it conducted a revision of all royal heraldic devices. All this resulted in *The Metallic History of the Reign*, Félibien's *Conversations* as well as his *Principles of Architecture, Sculpture and Painting* (1676) and his *Memoir on the History of the Royal Buildings* (1681) (231). In July 1701, under the inspiration of the Pontchartrains and the abbé Bignon, a new disposition appeared under the king's seal providing for a 'royal academy of inscriptions and medals' (forty members, of whom ten were honorary, ten in receipt of pensions, ten associates and ten apprentices) (231). All that was left was to change the title in 1716 to that of the 'Academy of Inscriptions and Belles-Lettres'.

In 1665, a year before the *Philosophical Transactions* of the Royal Society of London, the *Journal des savants* made its appearance. This national periodical, a scientific and literary review sponsored by the superintendent of buildings, provided an effective complement to the political and official-sounding *Gazette de France*.

The following year was much more significant. The king and Colbert inaugurated the French Academy in Rome and, back in Paris, the Academy of Sciences. The former, like so many of the reign's successes, was not created from scratch. It regularized the traditional practice of sending artists to Italy to complete their training. From 1660 onwards, Colbert had issued a pension to Charles de la Fosse in Rome. In 1666, he found no difficulty in gaining Louis XIV's approval for the new foundation, and acquired a staunch ally in the great painter Errard (251). Since Poussin was now dead, the king offered the directorship of the 'Royal French Academy in Rome' to Errard. Twelve artists, all under twenty-five years of age and of the Catholic religion, went at His Majesty's expense to stay in the capital of Pope Leo X for three years to deepen their artistic awareness and also to copy paintings and antiques, sketch 'the beautiful palaces and buildings' and augment the realm's artistic collections.

The Academy of Sciences, like the Académie française, had begun as a private institution, priding itself on its connections with the Mersenne circle in the years before 1648, and, later, with that associated with Habert de Montmor. As early as 1662, Colbert, assisted by Chapelain, Charles Perrault and the mathematician Carcavy, formulated various plans for institutes of science. In 1666, the plan which was finally decided upon envisaged a group under monarchical protection, sponsored by the superintendent of buildings, and bringing together some twenty eminent mathematicians and physicists (of whom Huygens would be one). Louis XIV provided pensions and paid for the expenses of the new 'Royal Academy of Sciences' to be installed in the King's Library on the rue Vivienne. Among the twenty-one founder-members of the academy were Carcavy, Huygens and Roberval, classed as mathematicians, and Mariotte and Claude Perrault, among the physicists. On 5 December 1681, Louis XIV visited the academy's collections, before attending one of its sessions. On 26 January 1699, he laid down a formal constitution for the learned body in fifty articles (229).

From 1667, the Academy of Sciences became a great centre of scientific research. It experimented, for example, with the transfusion of blood from one dog into another (161). At the same time, the Observatory in the faubourg Saint-Jacques was begun (completed 1672), following the designs of Claude Perrault. This TURRIS SIDERUM SPECULATORIA (71) would be directed by the astronomer Jean-Dominique Cassini, an academician, a royal protégé and the first of a formidable dynasty of astronomers. On 20 August 1690, the exiled King James II spent a morning at the

Observatory. He was shown round by Cassini, who was impressed by his knowledge (229).

In these matters, the king provided the initiative and approbation, Colbert their overall shape. The Royal Academy of Music, established in letters-patent of 28 June 1669 and handed over to Lully in 1672, put together *Cadmus and Hermione*, the first French opera, and was primarily Louis XIV's creation. With the remarkable emergence, in December 1671, of the Academy of Architecture, the pattern resembled once again the close collaboration of master and servant. 'The king chooses its members upon Colbert's nomination and wants to have a specialist council on all matters of architecture.' (161) It was the establishment of a council on royal buildings.

The Royal Botanical Garden for Rare Plants, outlined by Henry IV and set up by Louis XIII, found its definitive shape as a research institute through the dispositions of Louis XIV and his collaborators. A declaration of 20 January 1673 saw the modernization of this collection. The text stated that 'the demonstrators of the Royal Botanical Garden will continue to provide lessons and demonstrations of the benefits of medicinal plants in both the old and new pharmacopoeia. The surgical operations and anatomical dissections will also continue and, to this effect, they will have first refusal upon the bodies of executed criminals' (201). M. de Tournefort went on expeditions worldwide 'in search of rare species' (45). D'Aquin and Fagon, as well as being physicians by appointment to the king, also enjoyed the title of superintendents 'of the botanical dissections and medicinal operations' in the Botanical Garden (45).

From 1661 onwards, Louis XIV and Colbert had thus established in Paris a dozen institutions of scientific, literary, artistic, musical and theatrical significance. And this is not to mention those institutions whose establishment cannot be precisely dated, such as the Cabinet du Roi, to which we shall return, the royal collections and the King's Library. The 'enlightened interest' of Colbert in the arts (251) complemented the king's own tastes and this was no fortuitous occurrence but a deliberate association of taste and political will, an association which determined the extraordinary enrichment of the patrimony under the king. With His Majesty's assent and on his behalf, Colbert bought the art collection of the banker Jabach in 1662 for 330,000 *livres*. Among its 'numerous beautiful Italian canvases' were two remarkable Titians. Three years later, it was the turn of the duc de Richelieu's collection, which included no less than thirteen Poussins. In 1671, new purchases were made from Jabach, which comprised over 5,000 drawings, the heart of the Louvre collection (161). Up to 1680, these treasures lay in the capital. The improvements at Versailles temporarily broke up the collection. But the Louvre, in spite of appearances, was never the loser in an astonishing game of musical chairs of which Paris, and eventually the nation, would be the beneficiaries.

THE LOUVRE: PALACE OF CULTURE

On 28 January 1672, on the eve of war, chancellor Séguier breathed his last. He was the final political representative of the era from Louis XIII through the Fronde to the Fouquet trial, an era which had included the active phase of the Counter-Reformation. His death was not a turning-point in political terms, but it did signal a change in terms of patronage and the established institutions for cultural activities.

The Académie française had, up to that date, preserved its autonomy. Richelieu had been its first protector, followed by Séguier. What would happen after his death? The Academicians had a simple choice, either to ask the king to choose M. Colbert to replace the chancellor as patron or to solicit the king to become the institution's patron himself. Given the known dispositions of Louis XIV's personality, the latter alone was a realistic proposition. In the long term, it resulted in the dependence of the institution upon the state. In the more immediate term, the forty Academicians enjoyed great benefits, particularly that of being accommodated in the Louvre.

The whole matter was handled by Charles Perrault and Colbert. The king did not have a great hand in it. In 1672, the Louvre had been the site for building-works for fourteen years, the colonnade was still under construction and Louis XIV only made use of one apartment, which had been completed in 1654. After having preferred the Tuileries to the inconveniences of the Louvre, the king began to neglect Saint-Germain for Versailles. It was therefore no great sacrifice to give the Académie française a 'magnificent apartment, with everything needful for the comfort of its meetings' (18). At first, it was given the right to meet in the antechamber separating the winter apartments from the queen mother's summer apartments; 'later, it occupied the Lemercier Wing rooms, formerly restored for the king's council, between the Clock Pavilion and the Beauvais Pavilion. These were magnificently furnished for it' (199). It was the sign of a continuing process. There was a time when French kings, installed in the Louvre, had given over their palace on the Ile de la Cité to the institutions of state. Now Louis XIV lent out part of the Louvre, 'the most beautiful building in the world' (42), to the nation's elite. A medal was struck for the occasion. It celebrated *'Apollo in the Palace of Augustus . . . 1672'* (71). The famous academy continued its work, notably the dictionary (which was begun in 1638 and which would be completed in 1694), in these prestigious surroundings.

Soon it was joined by its sister institution, the Academy of Inscriptions, whose room was decorated by Coypel and Rigaud. As for the Academy of Painting, it was moved several times before a suitable home was found for it, in 1692, in the wing constructed by Le Vau in 1661–3 around the Cour de la Reine. Ten years later, the king granted it the use of the Salon Carré and the Old Library for its own collection of pictures, whilst, in the adjacent Great Gallery, *salons*, or exhibitions, of paintings and sculptures by the academicians, were held, by permission of His Majesty, in 1699, 1704 and 1706. Also in 1692, the Academy of Architecture was transferred from the Palais-Royal to the former apartments of Maria Theresa. The Academy of Sciences, with its bulky collections, was also given a home in the Louvre, in 1699, and was granted the king's former apartments. Its meetings would take place in the Henry II chamber, whilst its stuffed camel and the elephant dissected by Claude Perrault were the crowning features of His Majesty's former presence-chamber. The anatomy collections littered the Louis XIII bedchamber and its adjoining study, decorated by Le Brun, where the *Palatine Apollo* reclined complacently in this abode of king's.

Whilst Louis XIV granted the academies a substantial part of the Louvre, the smaller rooms in the old palace were thrown open to all sorts of people. Louis XIV's wishes prevailed over those of Colbert, who judged the Louvre more regal than Versailles. He gave the Louvre to the nation, and not in one capricious gesture, but by signing, over forty-five years, permits to lodge there. Some were granted to courtiers, such as M. de

Saint-Aignan and Mme de Thianges; others to royal servants, such as M. Seguin, captain of the Louvre, who kept the sub-tenants, and the prostitutes, squatters, crooks and swindlers at bay. But the majority of the rooms on the ground floor and the mezzanine floor above the Great Gallery were generously put at the disposal of artists and scholars. Living there in around 1680, were Israël Silvestre, the engraver, the painter Jean Bérain, the geographer Guillaume Sanson, the architect for the Auditorium of Mechanical Devices M. Vigarani, the sculptor Girardon, comfortably installed, Renaudot the younger the editor of the *Gazette de France*, the engraver Châtillon, and the cabinet-maker André-Charles Boulle (199). These lucky ones, often of humble origins, were by no means intimidated by their surroundings. They installed themselves by grace and favour of the king, but then settled down to take possession of what they had no rights to. Girardon set out his own rarities and arranged his studios in a part of the Gallery of Antiquities, even finding room for a mummy.

The palace still housed part of the royal treasures, the kernel of the future Louvre collections, including the majority of the king's antiquities, brought from Italy originally, on Mazarin's orders. There was also a royal printing-press, whose noise disturbed those living alongside it. It provoked considerable comment that, in defiance of the danger of fire, the king had granted pères Aignan and Rousseau, known as the 'Capuchins of the Louvre', the labora-tory facilities of an apothecary. The king invited, or tolerated, people of all different walks of life there, and they made themselves at home. When festivals were organized in Paris, notably in August 1682 when the Duke of Burgundy was christened, the artists in residence constructed staging the length of the Great Gallery and hired out seats to the public. In return, they agreed to assist in making the ceremony a success, and Berain organized the illumi-nations which lit up the immense façade of the Louvre.

After 1672, a tacit agreement had been arrived at. The king became the owner in name alone of the structure of the Louvre. The artists in residence had possession and the area occupied by their studios and apartments had doubled. Strangers asked to see inside. In 1698, the English naturalist Martin Lister went to see François Girardon's mummy. Parisians found no difficulty in gaining entry in order to view the dispensary of the Capuchin chemists, to visit the royal apartments or to attend a party held by M. Vigarani and M. Boulle.

In 1682, Europe was in raptures over the perfection of Versailles. But Versailles was nothing more than Vaux-le-Vicomte on a much grander scale. Louis XIV's greatest success was the new Louvre, royal but popular, a success as perfect as it seemed natural. While Versailles had endless ways of fascinating people, the nationalized Louvre was more celebrated. By the steady will of the French king, the greatest palace in Europe, open to the wider public, had become an artistic city.

BAROQUE AND CLASSICAL

Some years before this generous bequest, Louis had formulated some important artistic preferences. For Colbert, there was no doubt that the completion of the Louvre palace would result in the enhanced reputation of an already famous monarch and bring the king into a closer relationship with his capital. 'The construction of the Louvre appeared to him to be in the national interest, even, one might say, an integral part of his monarchical system.' (279) In a letter of September 1663 (291), the minister regretted that in two years 1,500,000 *livres* had been spent at Versailles, a house which 'looked to satisfy the king's pleasure and distraction more than his glory', whilst the king 'has neglected the Louvre' (291). These 'words of reflection' were not lost on the king and, although he was happy to be in Versailles, in Le Vau's little château and Le Nôtre's beautiful park, he had not yet decided to leave Paris, even though Colbert had persuaded him to move from the Louvre to the Tuileries until the Louvre had become a building worthy of being the king's permanent residence. Besides, as a born architect, Louis XIV found nothing wrong in commissioning two building-programmes, both worthy of him and the realm, one particularly concerned with distractions and the other with his glory. Up to 1670, the Parisian palaces enjoyed a rate of investment which was double that of Versailles, as the royal building accounts make clear (45):

	Paris	Versailles
	(in *livres tournois*)	
1664	855,000	781,000
1666	1,036,000	291,000
1668	909,000	339,000
1669	1,108,000	676,000

The real change came in 1670, when Versailles cost 1,633,000 *livres* as against Paris's 1,150,000, and the change became more marked in the following year, when Versailles soaked up 2,621,000 *livres* whilst the Louvre only cost 789,000, with the contrast becoming more striking in 1672 (2,144,000 *livres* as against 117,000), 1678 (2,179,000 as compared with 52,000) and above all in 1680 (5,641,000 and 29,000) (45). One must accept that the expenditures on the Louvre and the Tuileries throughout the six-year period from 1664 to 1669 were more than just a way of satisfying the wishes of a determined minister of state. Until Anne of Austria's death, Louis XIV himself was committed to the idea of a grand Louvre.

This was why the sovereign and his superintendent of buildings created a competition in 1664 for the east façade of the palace, which was intended as its principal point of access. The moment seemed to have arrived when native French architects like Houdin, François Mansart, Marot and Cottard would put their talents to the test, but it was also an opportunity for the Italians. Thus, in under two months, Bernini, 'the cavalier Bernin', had put aside the necessary time and imagination to provide a ground plan and elevation for this great structure. At the centre of it, 'a great oval pavilion decorated with two sweeping convex arcades [was] superposed between classical pilasters' while 'two concave wings stretched out to two further, rectangular pavilions of the same height. A top storey with a balustrade decorated with statues completed the edifice' (279). Colbert saw that the plans were 'immense and magnificent', but was dismissive of their practicability. He therefore asked 'M. the cavalier Bernin ... to consider once again his designs and modify them'. Although easily offended, the great architect drew up a second scheme of work. The new plans were less baroque and more adapted 'to practical necessity'. Pope Alexander VII granted him leave of absence from Rome, and he was given a warm reception at Saint-Germain by Louis XIV on 4 June 1665.

'Sire, I have seen the palaces of emperors, popes and princes *en route* from Rome to Paris, but for the King of France we must construct something greater and more magnificent than all these.' (279) To which he might have added: 'Let no one ask me for a scheme on a small scale!' The king was too polite to disillusion the megalomaniac and replied that he had 'some inclination to preserve what his predecessors had built, but that, if nothing could be done on a grand scale without knocking down their efforts, then he would not object; and, as for money, that would not be a constraint' (279). However, Colbert told Bernini that expense had to be taken into consideration – a wasted effort since the new scheme continued to give pride of place to décor and took little account of practicalities. True, the old church of Saint-Germain l'Auxerrois was retained, but it envisaged the destruction of a whole *quartier* of the city. Although Bernini no longer planned to reconstruct the whole palace, he still planned to refashion the Grande Cour, whilst Le Vau's Cour Carrée would lose its symmetrical proportions. The minister's objections began to multiply, although this did not prevent Colbert from asking the architect to design various urban improvements; getting such plans from a great architect was one way of gaining value for money from the overall costs of the original commission. As to the French architects, they swamped the superintendent with competing schemes for the Louvre, knowing that Bernini was becoming intolerable. He had criticized the work of Le Vau at the Tuileries, talked of the 'awful distortions' of Parisian roof-profiles, put the king to considerable inconvenience during sittings for his bust, and then sulked during the consultations overseeing the detailed internal arrangements of the palace.

Nevertheless, in the presence of the king, the first stone was laid on 17 October and, although the project was now less disconcerting than that of 1664, nothing was more baroque than this inaugural occasion. Bernini's plans had been presented at the end of September to Jean Marot, who had transferred them rapidly into engravings. But, by the time the first stone was being laid, these plans were already the subject of modification. On 17 October, Paris was given to believe that the works would follow Bernini's plans exactly, but, on the 20th, it was learnt that the cavalier was about to leave for Rome, 30,000 *livres* the richer thanks to a gift and with a pension of 6,000. Rumour had it that he would return, but everything turned out as if Colbert and the king had already decided how things would be done in future, a future in which the principal architect for the east colonnade would be Claude Perrault (1667–78). In 1667, it is widely held, the War of Devolution required the king to turn, in his plans for the Louvre, to a less costly architectural project (278). But this does not explain why, from as early as October 1665 until the end of 1667, the construction on the east façade of the Louvre came to a halt. Parisian architects capable of stepping into Bernini's shoes – Le Vau, Perrault or Dorbay – were all well known in 1665. The changes were thus, above all, dominated by matters of style. But 1665 was not so much a turning-point as a moment for reflection and meditation.

Too often, Bernini's visit to France is depicted as a Herculean struggle for Louis XIV. In fact, the truth was closer to Apollo than Hercules, for Louis XIV had already decided upon the way forward, politely putting to one side the projects of the great Roman urban designer. Even though the later designs of Bernini were more measured, they remained too baroque. Although tightly disciplined, they kept to the excessive primacy that the baroque accorded to form. All those involved from the king downwards understood the problem. Bernini's mannerism merely accelerated an already emerging consensus against Italianization and Hispanicization and towards the French taste of the elite and its best artistic talents. Neither the superintendents of buildings, nor the great painters of the century nor its architects, nor the writers around the king, nor his musical director, Lully, nor the shaper of his rural landscapes, Le Nôtre, had problems about the choice, which was why the spread of the famous French style, the *classical* style, was universal throughout the realm after the Fronde, a particular example of that passion for order which possessed the kingdom in the years around 1660. The classical style was regular but not monotonous, grand but not dessicated, logical but not abstract, royal without giving offence to humanity and domestic without vulgarity; Versailles would be its most spectacular example.

But, although this was to be the preferred style, the baroque had not been eliminated. Even at court, the baroque enjoyed its adherents, to Boileau's indignation:

> Every day at the court, a foolish man of quality
> Takes a different line from others with impunity,
> Instead of Malherbe or Racan, he takes Theophilus' part,
> Preferring Tasso's glitter to the gold of Virgil's art.

However, the attacks of the intolerant M. Despréaux did not influence Chapelain, Benserade or Quinault. Marc-Antoine Charpentier found he could compete with the powerful Lully without too much difficulty. Jean de la Fontaine was, if the terms have any meaning, at least as baroque as he was classical. The Catholic religion, with its ceremonies, magnificent altarpieces and processions, its panegyrics and triumphalism, also remained baroque, as did its counterparts in popular superstition and witchcraft. The *grotesques* were as baroque as the *précieuses*. Styles of internal décor often came close to the baroque with Berain working at Meudon for Monseigneur and at Marly for the king. The great artistry of Charles Perrault in the *Tales of Mother Goose* (1697) reconciled and drew upon the most varied stylistic elements: without its classical stylistic purity, this masterpiece would have been limited by its baroque form; but without this form, Perrault would never have enjoyed more than an ephemeral success.

Thus classicism dominated, not because the king willed it, but with the blessing of a man with a sense of order and common sense whose tastes were also those of his people. But classical and baroque could coexist, sometimes in competition with one another, at other times in alliance. It was a very French phenomenon, typical of the century of Louis XIV. Just as silver often needs to be mixed with an alloy to gain strength, so the classicism of the decade of the 1660s was never a pure classicism. It was strengthened by an alloy which gave it staying-power, turning it into a regulated, self-disciplined baroque.

A MIRROR FOR THE PRINCE

From 1660 to 1715, baroque vitality and classical decorum discovered a constructive *modus vivendi* in the arts and in society at large, and even in the image that the French constructed of their monarchy. The Middle Ages had a taste for the political and ethical treatises sometimes known as *A Mirror for the Prince*. They laid down the virtues and obligations of the ideal prince, sometimes depicting the antithesis of the current reality, and sometimes being a means to flatter a contemporary, reigning monarch. In the seventeenth century, this kind of literature no longer existed, but the histories of France still provided a sketch of the 'image of the king' (289), laying down what was to be expected of Louis XIV, what a king's admirable qualities were.

The Sun King, for all his distinctiveness, was only the latest in a long line of kings. To the readers of Mézeray and the devotees of Bossuet, and to the young students using the textbooks written by Le Ragois or père Daniel, the monarch was always to the fore, the history of France being seen as, above all, the history of its kings. Kings were the object of historical inquiry, the subject of its narrative flow. 'Their presence ordered all forms of historical reality.' (289) But the prince was only one link in the chain. It was not as an individual that Louis, Charles, Jean or Philippe was placed at the centre of events. It was as the King of France, as the man who incarnated the royal function. Kingship was the 'sacred focal point of a religious universe', a point which marked amidst the shifting sands of events a more lasting and deeper tradition.

Up to 1660, traditional historiographers celebrated Pharamond. But this mythical 'founding-father figure' unfortunately symbolized the popular and elective character of the monarchy. From the beginning of the personal rule of Louis XIV, Pharamond fell from favour. The development of historical criticism explains, in part, this change, but more important was the aim of presenting the 'immemorial' character of the monarchy. By elevating Clovis over Pharamond, someone like père Daniel Christianized and also sanctified the monarchy. Passing from one dynasty to the other, avoiding sharp breaks and usurpations, contemporary historians became genealogical sleuths trying to demonstrate that the three royal lineages of France were, in fact, only one. To avoid even the suspicion of anything else, they abandoned the explanation of Hugues Capet's elevation by popular acclamation and replaced it by the acclamation of God.

In the course of the seventeenth century, the model monarch had been Charlemagne, who was still popular in the baroque textbooks. But Louis XIV never dreamt of making himself an emperor, and Charlemagne was too distant and too barbarian. The new hero to appear was Philippe Augustus, and it is easy to see why. He was a Capetian, and a valiant king, determined to unify his states and increase their power. He was a defender of the faith and, like Louis, was the long-awaited, the Dieudonné (289). But then, with the help of the Counter-Reformation, St Louis dethroned Philippe Augustus. Louis XIV certainly did not possess, especially before 1683, all the qualifications of this ancestor, but he had the same Christian name and had chosen him as his protector. It was on the feast of St Louis (25 August) that France enjoyed a public holiday. After the Revocation of the Edict of Nantes in 1685, nobody, save for the *nouveaux convertis* (Protestants newly converted to Catholicism) and other independent thinkers, found the comparison between Louis XIV and Louis IX extraordinary. If, as historians of the time said, devotion was the first virtue of the ideal prince, then the Sun King in the 1660s was far from that ideal's full realization. He was more interested in meeting the other conditions of the perfect ruler: grandeur, good looks, presence, valiance, wisdom, a sense of justice, prudence, and a love of letters, the sciences and the arts (289). This is why one always returns to the image of the Augustan age.

10

The Pleasures of the Enchanted Isle

FOR SOME, the most agreeable aspects of the reign of Louis XIV are symbolized by the fête at Versailles in May 1664, a week of court spectacles, extravagant decorations, masques, games, receptions, gallantries, theatrical devices, ballets and firework shows. It was a fairy-tale, dreamt by the king and brought into being with the assistance of MM de Saint-Aignan, Périgny, Benserade and Molière, Vigarani and others. All the promise of the reign was encapsulated at this moment, the king in command but stepping to one side to let the genius and talents of his friends and collaborators have a free hand. This is why this fête, full of youth yet impeccably ordered, ephemeral yet leaving lasting memories, still lingers on in people's minds after more than three centuries, a baroque extravaganza, disciplined by a new classicism.

THE PALACE OF ALCINA (6–13 MAY 1664)

Every couple of years, it seemed, it was necessary to put before the court, the capital, and the nobility and people, both at home and abroad, a public spectacle, in order to encourage their admiration for the king, the wealth of his kingdom, the glory of his reign and the talents of his artists. The sequence of events had begun in August 1660 with the entry of Louis XIV and Maria Theresa. In 1664, it was to be something unforgettably splendid, the fête of the *Pleasures of the Enchanted Isle*, inspired by Ariosto's *Orlando Furioso*. It took place in the gardens at Versailles (beautifully laid out by Le Nôtre), signalling

Louis' attachment to this still rather modest royal residence.

In February, the king entrusted his friend François de Beauvillier, whom he had created duc de Saint-Aignan the previous December, with the organization of the festivities. Saint-Aignan had already sketched out the ballet and he now needed to envisage its sequel. 'He took as the subject the palace of Alcina, which provided him with the title of the *Pleasures of the Enchanted Isle*. It was there that, according to Ariosto, the brave Roger and other knights were kept captive by the beauty and enchantments of Alcina, only to be released, when they had sampled the pleasures of the island, by the wave of a wand which broke her magical powers.' (74) Dancing, music, comedy, tournaments, receptions and concerts, all were woven into the magic which captivated Roger and his knightly companions. The mechanical devices were of such importance that Vigarani had to set about constructing them as early as 1 March. Madrigals were commissioned from Benserade and Périgny. Lully was in overall charge of the music. By the king's command, all the theatrical events were under Molière's direction (191). Over 600 guests were invited to watch what 'seemed like a small army' (74) of players, clowns and stage-hands. The court was ready on 5 May and the proceedings began on the 7th.

At nightfall on the first day, a cavalcade was opened by a king's herald, three pages, four trumpeteers and two percussionists, all richly costumed, who were followed by Guidon the Savage (M. de Saint-Aignan). Then came the king, dressed like a Greek warrior, personating Roger, 'mounted on one of the finest horses' and preceded by eight heralds with trumpets and two drummers. Roger was followed by Olger the Dane (the duc de Noailles), Aquilant the Black (the duc de Guise), Griffon the White (the comte d'Armagnac), Renaud (the duc de Foix), Dudon (the duc de Coislin), Astolphe (the comte de Lude), Brandimart (Marsillac), Richardet (Villequier). . . The rich caparison of their horses, and the costumes, arms and liveries, were much admired. Roland, played by M. le Duc (Condé's son), closed the procession. Then came Apollo's golden chariot, eighteen feet high, transporting the four Centuries, Python the serpent, Atlas, Time and 'other figures'. Four horses pulled this assortment of allegories, escorted by the Hours of the Day and the Signs of the Zodiac.

Once the cavalcade had passed, the Age of Bronze (Mlle

Debrie) presented a speech to Apollo (La Grange) and a tournament began, in which the king distinguished himself along with La Vallière. Night had fallen but, by candlelight, thirty-four musicians played 'the most satisfying concert of music imaginable', arranged by Lully. A 'magnificent reception' then followed, punctuated by ballets. By way of consolation to Maria Theresa for the presence of Louise de la Vallière at the festivities, Spring presented her with his compliments. The meal was a sumptuous affair, the illuminations so lavish that it could have been by daylight. 'All the knights, with their helmets covered in plumes of different colours and their tournament cloaks, gathered round the tournament barriers making an enchanting scene.' (74)

The following evening, under a makeshift dome 'to protect the vast numbers of candles and tapers which illuminated the stage', which was set in front of the decorations for the palace of Alcina on the enchanted island, Molière and Lully set out to amuse the assembled company. *The Princess of Elida* was the main show, a romantic and baroque piece which kept to the conventions of *Astraea*. The king had only given Molière a few days to write and rehearse it, and only the first act was in verse. The last scene, bringing the second day's events to a close, was danced and sung by a small shepherd choir, accompanied by keyboard, woodwind and thirty violins. The song's simple refrain struck Louise de la Vallière's heart as well as Louis':

> There's nothing which surrenders not
> Before the gentle charms of love. (74)

On the 9th, on the same stage, the scene was set for something majestic. The pastoral was transformed into the chivalric romance. Alcina, realizing that the liberation of her captive prey would not be long delayed, sought to fortify the island. Vigarani had arranged for a rock to rise from the waves to form a central island on the stage, flanked by two others. Three monsters of the deep rose up, one carrying the princess Alcina, the others two nymphs. Once ashore, Alcina, Celia and Dircé came to present greetings in alexandrine couplets to the queen mother. Then Alcina returned to fortify the bastion whilst violins played and 'the façade of the palace opened to reveal four enormous giants'. This was the signal for the ballet of Alcina's palace: firstly four giants and four dwarfs, then eight Moors, and finally the unequal combat of six knights with four frightening monsters. The fourth scene involved the dance of two sprites in Alcina's command, the fifth four demon jugglers who calmed Alcina's fears. The climax came in the sixth when Melissa handed Roger the wand which would break the magic spell, the signal for thunder and lightning, whereat Alcina's palace, stormed with a tremendous hullabaloo, was reduced to cinders in a firework display. 'The number of exploding rockets high in the sky, not to mention the fireworks on the banks and those which rose up from the water itself, provided such a magnificent and glorious spectacle that nothing could have completed to greater perfection the enchanting moments.' (74)

The theme of the *Pleasures of the Enchanted Isle* was somewhat lost in the ensuing entertainments. A tournament of mounted heads followed on 10 May. A series of heads were mounted on spikes at the end of the tilt-yard and each of them (a Turk's, a Moor's, and a Medusa's) had to be either stabbed with or carried off on the point of a javelin. The king won the competition, with the marquis de Coislin and marquis de Soyecourt in second and third places. After lunch on 11 May, the king invited the court to view his menagerie, 'where one admired the particularly beautiful specimens and the incredible number of birds of all species, some of them very rare'. In the evening, after a splendid reception, the king invited everyone to the château to see Molière's play *Les Fâcheux*. The play had been 'conceived, written, learnt and rehearsed in a fortnight', not, in fact, for the king, but for M. Fouquet for the fête of 17 August 1661. On Monday, 12 May, the king organized a lottery after dinner. The prizes were the opposite of small trinkets, consisting of 'precious stones, beautiful pieces of furniture and silverware'. Louis had gallantly arranged for the largest prize to go to the queen; but, in the romantic spirit of *The Princess of Elida*, the marquise de la Vallière and her sister-in-law, Louise, also won prizes (213). Immediately afterwards there followed a tournament. Saint-Aignan, whose office had prevented him from taking part in the Saturday tournament, took on M. de Soyecourt. In the evening, Louis XIV offered the courtiers *Tartuffe*, a play which he had found 'richly amusing' (191), but which did not please either the queen mother or the *dévots*; the king had to ban it for three years shortly afterwards.

Then came the last day of the festivities. A new mounted-heads tournament confirmed the prowess of the king and Saint-Aignan in the game and a further play of Molière's, a comedy-ballet called *The Forced Marriage*, in which the king had already once danced a part, sealed his reputation. On the 14th, the king and his court took their leave for Fontainebleau, everyone in raptures over 'the variety and charm of the entertainments' (191). Seven months later, Colbert made no demur at the expenses.

As for the king, he had shown himself to be respectful towards his mother, solicitous towards the queen, in love with his mistress, a good horseman, an able jouster, an attentive host, a notable impresario and a strikingly good producer of plays. He had given his court a style to follow in beauty, youth, taste, intelligence, and knightly and sporting pursuits. He had enticed the principal figures of the realm into a wonderful world of Ariosto knights, and thereby shaped, formed and moulded his court. And yet there would eventually be some sad figures who would accuse him of 'domesticating' and debasing the French nobility.

THE *HONNÊTE HOMME*

Louis XIV's entertainments not only provoked amazement abroad, they also formulated taste, encouraged the chivalric spirit and contributed to public education. The court and the capital were, in reality, closely associated with one another. When the king was at the Louvre (1662–6), or passed the winter months in the Tuileries (1666–71), a ditch here, a street or a garden there, were all that separated the two worlds. Although Louis XIV took up residence in Saint-Germain (1666–73, 1676, 1678–81) or in Versailles (1674 and 1675, 1677, 1682–1715), the courtiers never left Paris, each having his own individual Paris *hôtel*. They gave the capital the benefit of their ideas and tastes and the prejudices of a court which was never far away. After the queen mother's death in 1666, Monsieur inherited the Palais-Royal, and he was a great lover of Parisian life. Nor was the court cut off from France – as the king knew and informed opinion welcomed. Furetière's *Universal Dictionary* cited numerous proverbs upon this theme: 'The court gives a touch of class to the provinces'; it 'is a good school in which to learn how to live'; 'those from the provinces will soon be stretching their legs in Paris, at the court and in the army' (42). Père Bouhours dated the peak of gracious living in France to the period immediately after the Fronde, and the codes of conduct of *honnêteté* were refined well before Gracian's translation of *The Man of the Court* appeared in 1684 (44). The court was by no means the creation of 1682. Its ceremonial dated from the reign of Henry III. Its style and spirit owed much to the court ballets of Mazarin's time. From 1643, the court shaped (42) the country. 'Good manners, good-breeding, politeness, the air of decorum, the knowledge of how to behave in public . . . came from the court either directly or by imitation, albeit sometimes by the more distant route of the Hôtel de Rambouillet or the backstreet world of the *précieuses*.' (135) Thus, if Paris was indispensable to the background of an *honnête homme* ('honest man'), he was nevertheless a product of the court. Some handbooks laid down the rules to follow. Méré published three catechisms of good conduct in 1677: *On Compliments, On the Mind, On Conversation* (72). There was much which was owed to the Italian Mazarini and to the Spaniard Anne of Austria in the formation of both Louis XIV and the style of the French *honnête homme*. From the beginning of the personal rule, the *honnête homme* became a widely dispersed model, but it did not lose in the process any of its allure or its distinctive national quality. This was what marked him out – and never to his disadvantage – from the *cavaliere*, the *caballero*, the English gentleman and the *Kavalier*.

The *honnête homme* of Louis XIV's period was refined and sociable, well mannered and good company. He cultivated civil proprieties and shunned ill-becoming behaviour. The art of good manners was a code of obligations binding upon the *honnête homme*, almost an asceticism. And, because good breeding was the close ally to good conduct, the same concerns for logic, moderation and taste governed it. The rude behaviour of Henry IV's court was henceforth banished, whilst some of the proprieties of the court of Henry III were restored. Ignorance was no longer acceptable. 'An enquiring mind was no longer the preserve of the men of letters; it was also required in the men of the sword and even in personages of the highest quality, who seemed to enjoy a monopoly upon ignorance in recent times.' (15) In 1671, père Bouhours welcomed this cultural revolution with the words: 'There are once again dukes, counts and marquises, both of great piety and of great learning, who wield the pen as well as they do the sword and who are no less at ease in writing the score of a ballet or a history than in drawing up an army encampment or a battlefield.' (15)

The *honnête homme* saw himself as worthy, gallant, well spoken and courageous, in short, guided by a sense of honour. In France, it did not require a Montesquieu to understand that the monarchy was founded on honour. It was not a coincidence or an economical use of language which made 'honesty' a social and civilizing, as well as a moral, virtue.

The final constituent element of the *honnête homme* was birth. But Fléchier, Colbert, Racine, Boileau and others from bourgeois origins may also be taken as providing examples of the *honnête homme*. They earned it by their merits and by the king's will. Louis spent his whole reign in establishing this ideal of the 'man of quality', distinguished in his talents and his achievements, without necessarily being 'nobly born'. It was an innovation which ensured widespread acceptance of the ideals of the *honnête homme*.

ROYAL FAMILIARITY

In the twenty years of the personal rule before the completion of the reconstruction of Versailles, Louis XIV was not an inaccessible monarch, and he kept open to his subjects a number of means of access to him. It was possible to prevent the aristocrats enjoying too close a relationship with him and, at the same time, not be cut off from the people. Beginning in 1661, Louis XIV regulated and encouraged the use of petitions (*placets*), which were an admirable feature of good government. Every Monday at Versailles, a large table was laid out in the guardroom for petitions to be presented. Up to 1683, the marquis de Louvois, and after that date Courtanvaux, his son, received the submissions. At the close of each week, Louvois presented them before the Council and they were then despatched to the various secretaries of state concerned. A week later, each individual concerned would present a report on the matter and Louis XIV would make his decisions, using three customary replies:

'Nothing', 'Agreed' and 'The king will give the matter further thought'. The ambiguity of the third did not necessarily imply a negative response.

When the king did make himself accessible, he did not stand upon ceremony. He elevated Louvois into 'the court idol', whilst Condé seemed 'more ignored than if he were dead' (265). Vardes and Rabutin remained in exile, whilst Lully was given every freedom. 'Nothing approached the friendship, the meeting of minds, between Louis XIV and Jean-Baptiste Lully, the jester and buffoon of his youth, the power in the land and superintendent of the finest years of the reign.' (122) Boileau would call him 'the shady dealer' and La Fontaine denounced him as 'a rake', but this champion of the *cabarets* who went on the town with the young chevalier de Lorraine was always protected by the king, who excused his insolent display of wealth, overlooked his immorality and accepted his moodiness.

Louis XIV's fidelity towards Molière, Lully's exact contemporary, was also a matter for comment both at court and in the capital. He not only invited the author of *Le Bourgeois gentilhomme* to court to save him from bankruptcy and restore his credit, but also championed him against his critics. What Pierre Gaxotte has called 'the *Tartuffe* war' lasted no less than five years, from 1664 to 1669 (191). Molière had the queen mother, the *premier président* of the Parlement of Paris, the Sorbonne, the Company of the Blessed Sacrament, the Archbishop of Paris and the *dévots* against him and only Monsieur, La Première Madame and the prince de Condé on his side; without the king's support, he would not have survived. But Louis XIV went against the tide of opinion. He saw in Molière an author of profundity and invention who politely pointed the way to a reformed morality without moralizing about it and who was always ready to obey the orders of the prince. Jean-Baptiste Poquelin was, in the king's eyes, a particular example of the *honnête homme*. Molière's plays poked fun at the ridiculousness of some courtiers, but never criticized the court itself. Indeed, they contributed to its ideals, and thus became the allies of royal policy.

It is not difficult to imagine why the king was taken with the Acknowledgement with which Molière prefaced his *Versailles Impromptu* of October 1663. The poet imagines himself amidst the king's *lever* at the Louvre, and he lampoons the predictable courtiers he meets (74):

This morning we must go without delay
And be present at the king's *lever.*

. . .

You know best how to appear the marquis,
Ignoring nothing of his airs and graces;
Flourish a hat festooned with thirty plumes
    Upon a periwig of fantastic price;
The cloak should be as wide as folio volumes,
    The doublet of the smallest size.

. . .

Take a tour about the guardroom.
    And, with make-up giving you a gallant mein,
Look about you with a stern expression;
    And those that you recognize,
        Do not fail, in ringing tones,
        To greet by name,
Of whatsoever rank they chance to be.

. . .

    Tap with your comb upon the door
    That leads to the apartments of the king

. . .

    And without a doubt or hesitation say,
    In your natural tone of voice and pose:
    Open, guard, for the marquis de so and so! (74)

'The prince under whom we live abhors all deceit' is a line from
the fifth act of the revised, corrected and completed *Tartuffe.* He
was also a prince who hated the social climbers without solid
worth (he could not sit through *Le Bourgeois gentilhomme* without
bursting out with laughter), the false *dévots* (this was why he put
himself out over the *Tartuffe* affair), the petty, precious, and lazy
marquises. It has too often been said that Molière exalted an
idealized picture of bourgeois values; he was too much the friend
of and too often associated with the king for that. He was more
an *honnête homme* who made the *honnête homme* his model.

FÊTES AND PLEASURES

The first court of Louis XIV, from 1661 to 1682, appeared to
posterity as an endless and brilliant sequence of spontaneous
and captivating events. Behind its makeshift stages, its ballets,

its dancing, its hunting and its fireworks, one may detect the amorous escapades of the king, and one might even call this a lover's court. But the royal sense of purpose was never absent. An amorous distraction was also a political and educational experience. The best way, according to Louis, of keeping the aristocracy at court was to make it an attractive place to be. Ceremonial played its part, and here the first Bourbons had let the experiences of the Valois go to waste. Louis XIV exploited everything learnt by the 'inventor' of this delicate courtly machine, Henry III, who had issued regulatory edicts for the court in 1574, 1578 and 1582 before bringing them all together in 1585.* Louis XIV knew that, if he returned to this kind of regulation, he would not be able to enforce it immediately and that he would only succeed if his brother, a great expert in matters of etiquette, assisted him. The king also recognized that this small world of ceremonial was only worthwhile if its regulations were adjustable. Until the end of his reign, Louis XIV therefore kept a firm hand upon court protocol, knowing its finer points of detail, keeping himself well informed and arbitrating upon conflicts of precedence. The law in such matters became a way of ruling, the quarrels between grandees being diverted from major plots into minor intrigues and cabals. Thus the court became a showcase, where each component provided, on its own, a separate spectacle.

One of the privileges of the senior household staff and the regular courtier was a front seat in some of the theatrical events. On 14 February 1662, the 'Auditorium of Mechanical Devices', a new type of theatre, invented by the Vigaranis, was inaugurated at the Tuileries (199). From 24 June to 11 August, Molière was at the palace of Saint-Germain-en-Laye to amuse the court (191). On 29 January 1664, he presented *The Forced Marriage* at the Louvre in the apartments of Anne of Austria. On 13 October, his group was invited to Versailles, and remained there until the 24th. This continued for over ten years. When Louis XIV so wished, he was capable of the most astonishing fidelities. The court followed the king's judgement in the normal way, but there was probably a preference among courtiers for ballet rather than comedy. On 26 July 1661, Louise de la Val-

* Information kindly provided by Jean-François Solnon, whose work on the French court (272b) appeared after the publication of the French edition of this book.

lière danced the ballet *Les Saisons* (213). In February 1662, the Auditorium of Mechanical Devices at the Tuileries was inaugurated with the ballet *The Amorous Hercules*, which evoked Louis XIV's marriage, two years earlier. The Vigaranis excelled themselves and no expense was spared. The king and queen danced together (242), the expert Louis XIV leading Maria Theresa across the floor. Seven years later, in February 1669, in the same room, Louis made his last appearance on stage (242). In fact, the court ballet was beginning to be replaced by French opera, and the king did not let himself take a part in the last dying act of this courtly, chivalric and stately art-form, the *Ballet des ballets*, which was staged at Saint-Germain in December 1671 (242).

Although the distractions at court changed and the king's increasing preference for the permanence of stone to the ephemeral decorations of a day's festivities reduced the expenses incurred, the tradition of festivities continued until 1682, as though the *Pleasures of the Enchanted Isle* continued to haunt people's memories and imaginations. The 'great royal entertainment' at Versailles, presented to the court on 18 July 1668, attempted to rival in one day the whole week of the *Enchanted Isle*. The king spent over 150,000 *livres* on it. It was in celebration of the Peace of Aix-la-Chapelle, in which France gained Walloon Flanders. In fact, this fête at Versailles celebrated both the conquest of Flanders a couple of months earlier and the wooing of Madame de Montespan, a year previously. The duc de Créqui, first gentleman of the chamber, was in charge of the theatrical events, whilst the maréchal de Bellefonds saw to the reception and the supper. Colbert was director of constructions and ornamental fittings and presided over the firework display. From midday until six o'clock, the château was open and refreshment- and retiring-rooms were made available. At six o'clock, the gardens were opened and the king showed his court 'the pleasures of a walk' there, pointing out the new parterres, pools and groves. A splendid reception awaited them in the grove of the Star. Then, upon the 'King's Avenue', in a theatre which had been constructed by Vigarani, 1,500 spectators were presented with Molière's comedy *George Dandin ou Le Mari confondu*, punctuated with ballets and intermezzi from *Les Fêtes de l'Amour et de Bacchus*, for which Molière wrote the words and Lully the music, and therein discovered, as Félibien put it, 'the secret of satisfying and charming the whole world'.

What had never been seen before was this harmony of pleasing voices, this symphony of instruments, this beautiful blend of different harmonies, these soft canzonets, these tender and romantic speeches, these echoes and, above all, this admirable orchestration of all the ensemble, where, beginning with one solo part, the music developed until, by its close, there were more than a hundred musicians all performing on one stage, playing their instruments in concert and unison so that, as the final notes died away, the sounds left in everyone an inexpressible admiration. (74)

Then supper was served in an octagonal tent fifty feet high and constructed in the form of an antique temple. Forty-eight ladies joined the king's table, amongst whom were duchesses and the wives of marshals and notables of the robe such as Le Reynie's wife, 'Mme la lieutenante civile', and the wife of Tubeuf, the *président* of the Parlement. In neighbouring tents, other ladies, and ambassadors, shared the queen's table. For the rest of the spectators, buffets were organized in the park. A stunning ball then took place in another octagonal room, presided over by the mythological figures of Orpheus and Arion. The festivities continued with illuminations and a firework display which filled 'the air with a thousand twinkles brighter than the stars', the fireworks launched from seventy-two points along the Grand Avenue, from the Grand Pool, which became like 'a sea of flame and light', from three pools to the left of the Iron Horse and from the grand avenues around the parterres. The last to be let off delineated the monogram of the king in the night-time sky, 'double "L"s in a pure and brilliant light' (74). The court left Versailles by night so as not to break the enchantment of a fête which 'surpassed whatever had been done, in whatever way, in its memorability' (74).

If he could not surpass this effort, it certainly seemed that the king was going to try to rival it. The fête of 1668 had celebrated the annexation of Flanders; the new 'entertainments at Versailles', of July to August 1674, came amidst the conquest of Franche Comté. Molière had died the previous year, but Lully was at the peak of his favour, having become 'the veritable master of ceremonies at the court' (242). On 4 July, the opening of the 1668 entertainments was evoked with a walk followed by drinks; then, in the Cour de Marbre in front of the old château, His Majesty's guests were treated to *Alceste* by Quinault and Lully, before 'midnight came'. On the 11th, before the Trianon, a beautiful and much-admired piece by the master of the king's music was presented called *L'Eglogue de Versailles*, followed by a concert and reception in a glade. On the 19th, the court sampled a further reception, offered at the Menagerie, a voyage across the Grand Canal and a performance of *Le Malade imaginaire*, presented just in front of the Grotto of Thetis. The reception of 28 July eclipsed all the others. With the hour of dusk, in a specially constructed theatre, Lully directed his opera *Les Fêtes de l'Amour et de Bacchus*, the ballets from which had been presented in 1668. A banquet, set up by Vigarani, followed in the Cour de Marbre. The fifth day of the entertainments opened on 18 August. After light refreshments laid out on a table with sixteen pyramids of fruits and confectionary, the tragedy of *Iphigénie* was presented in the Orangery. At night, there was a vast illumination of the Grand Canal and a great unleashing of 5,000 fireworks, which created a vast dome in the sky. Finally, on the 31st, a new night-time celebration tried to rival the previous one in splendour. Late into the evening, 650 'illuminated statues' marked the banks of the Grand Canal, whilst the court took to gondolas and, passing between the illuminations and to the sound of violins, they sailed towards Neptune's palace, shimmering with precious stones, which had been set up by Vigarani at the end of the canal. The illuminations would be repeated at Versailles in July and August 1676 at a cost to the king of 71,000 *livres*, but they never obliterated the memory of their predecessors in 1674.

Although the gardens at Versailles and, latterly, the Grand Canal, were the settings preferred by Louis XIV for the putting on of special festivities, his other royal residences – Chambord in October 1668 and October 1670, Saint-Germain-en-Laye in February 1670, Fontainebleau in August 1671 – also played a part, albeit to a lesser extent (242). One might say that the king was playing off four sumptuously decorated rivals, one against the other, delaying the moment when he would make his final choice between them.

FROM ONE CHÂTEAU TO ANOTHER

The court remained at the beginning of the reign an itinerant one, as in the time of the Valois, a fact which did not suit M. Colbert's affairs. These frequent movements fractured

administrative routines, increased the numbers of couriers and
held up orders and the carrying out of them. But they also
provided moments for the prince to meet his subjects, maintained the aristocracy in a state of readiness and satisfied the
king's restlessness.

Some journeys were necessary ones. Louis XIV did not like
staying in places where someone he had been close to had died.
In April 1661, after Mazarin's death, he left the Louvre for
Fontainebleau. In 1666, after the death of Anne of Austria, he
left the Louvre for Versailles, then Saint-Germain, then Fontainebleau and then Vincennes. He only returned to his capital
in November 1667 (167). The death of his beloved mother was
an important reason for the king's disenchantment with Paris.
This king, the least romantic of sovereigns, abandoned his
reserve when he recorded the circumstances of his departure:
'Not being able afterwards to bear the sight of the place where
this sadness happened to me, I left Paris immediately and retired
firstly to Versailles (as the place where I could be more to
myself) and then, some days afterwards, to Saint-Germain.' (63)

It is often said that Fontainebleau was associated in the king's
mind with autumn, the hunting season, and it was the case that
Louis XIV often spent a month or two there in the autumn, to
the sound of hunting-horns. But, exceptions proving the rule, he
did not visit in 1662, 1663, 1665, 1667–70, 1672–3, 1676, 1706 or
1709–10. There were moments, too, when the court went to
Fontainebleau in the spring (in 1680) or early summer (in 1664).
Despite their being further away, his passion for hunting sent the
king to Villers-Cotterêts and even to Chambord. This latter
residence often enchanted him. It was there where he always
went to hunt in September and October – the only exceptions
being in 1670, when the château dear to Francis I's heart was
instead the scene of a 'royal entertainment', and in six further
years – until 1686, 'the year of the king's fistula', which marked a
turning-point.

The smaller moves did not involve great disturbance. When
the court was at Saint-Germain, the king would often go on to
Versailles, which was in the process of being enlarged and
beautified. He did so in 1671 and 1672, for example, and it is
evident that these shifts were more than routine ones, and that
there was almost a direct competition between the two palaces,
no one knowing which would predominate in the king's affec-

tions. When the king, the queen, the royal family and the best part of the court went for a long stay in a more remote residence, the disturbances became much more elaborate and the court relived its old Valois past. But the royal household was a relatively efficient administrative machine, even though there was no guarantee against delays and difficulties. Three services shared the burden between them. The preparations of the palaces, parks and forests were undertaken by the superintendent of buildings. The removal of furnishings in heavy carts was the responsibility of the *garde-meuble*, whilst those in charge of the *menus-plaisirs du Roi* looked after the court *en route*. Together these services ensured, 'under the overall command of the first gentleman of the chamber currently in post, the smooth running of the court fêtes' (143).

Despite the inconveniences *en route*, Louis XIV never abandoned his more distant residences. Fontainebleau, which Francis I, Henry IV and Louis XIII had adorned and beautified, remained an especially magnificent abode, even though the Primaticcio frescos were showing 'the march of time a little'. The king recognized it as a fitting place for his command performances. On 26 July 1661, the ballet *Les Saisons* was given its première. On the following 1 November, Monseigneur was born there. In 1664, the papal legate Chigi was treated to 'a grandiose reception which made him forget, in part, the disagreeable purpose of his mission'. It was there, too, that the king 'learnt, on 24 August [1678], of the ratification of the [first two] treaties of Nymwegen'. And there he celebrated the engagement of his niece Marie Louise d'Orléans to the King of Spain, Charles II (31 August 1679) (143). Mme de Maintenon did not care for Fontainebleau, but the Princess Palatine was delighted with it and, as for the king, he was 'strongly attached' to it (143). But Versailles soon occupied, in both his life and his heart, an ever more dominant place.

THE FIRST VERSAILLES

At the time of the king's marriage, Versailles was only a hunting-lodge. On 25 October 1660, however, the young king took Maria Theresa there, and 'it was like a thunder-bolt' (291) – not unlike the striking emotion which attracted him to Louise de la Vallière. The inconvenience of its site, the surrounding marshes, its unfavourable climate, the lack of water close at hand and the distance from Paris made Versailles a kind of Thebes. For Louis XIV 'it was a place of refuge for his love-affairs; he could find a retreat there as he could in none of the other great châteaux. He went in private from Saint-Germain, accompanied by a few privileged courtiers, just as, at a later stage, he would go for little retreats from Versailles to the Trianon or to Marly' (291). Louis improved the château to act as a setting for his amorous encounters. If he made the gardens such a magnificent feature, it was in order to seduce his mistress – although also to give him the opportunity for inviting a larger court there. Before Colbert became superintendent of buildings, in the period from 1661 to 1663, Versailles had already cost Louis 1,500,000 *livres*, thus absorbing in those years what Fontainebleau would take in seventeen. Nearly all this, to Colbert's alarm, had gone on the gardens. The king expanded his domain, dreaming of pools here, new parterres there, an orangery, groves of trees. The west-facing parterre, as conceived of by Louis XIV and Le Nôtre, 'was given an axis onto an unlimited vista'. The northern parterre 'was made up of lawns and led up to a canal, whilst the southerly one was given over to flowers and its focus was a parterre of orange trees. Louis XIV seems to have already had a glimpse of his future Versailles' (291). Such was the touch of genius in the king and Le Nôtre, to accept what had been pragmatically arrived at as a sketch for the later masterpiece.

The team which had already created Vaux-le-Vicomte, and which the king had transferred to Saint-Germain, was already at work. Le Vau constructed the Orangery and Le Brun awaited his orders, whilst Le Nôtre was at his busiest. The fête of the *Pleasures of the Enchanted Isle* could never have taken place without Le Nôtre, and, without the captivating gardens, Bernini would not have spoken of Versailles, as he did in 1665, as 'such an agreeable place' (291). In 1664, Versailles cost 781,000 *livres*; in the following year 586,000 (45). The east façade of the palace was renovated, the interior was redesigned with collections of curios and, in the great courtyard, some pavilions were put up for the domestic services. But these were small matters in comparison with the gardens.

The low-lying parts were drained and the water retained in enlarged or re-positioned pools. The Grand Canal was dug out in 1668. Stone sculptures, bronze statues, vases, flowers and greenery were progressively introduced to increase the decorative features. The Grotto of Thetis (1665–6) graced one side of the palace. The well-to-do saw for themselves the changes which had been wrought, while progressing round the park during the 'royal *divertissement*' of 1668. These festivities 'proved to Europe at large Louis XIV's commitment to his property at Versailles. The king's passion was no longer in doubt' (291), though Colbert still entertained hopes for the Louvre. In 1668, Versailles took up 339,000 *livres*, which became 676,000 in 1669, 1,633,000 in 1670 and 2,621,000 in 1671 (45). Only the outbreak of war would reduce this spending to a more reasonable amount.

Reason lay, however, in the king's will, and his elementary whim had become shaped into a vast enterprise. It was by no means an idle dream. Louis XIV told his architects to maintain the Louis XIII portion of the building, the east façade, the 'old château'. He was only interested in enlargements, and it was on the west side that the king commissioned his new château to be built. This would not be a modest brick edifice in the Louis XIII style but a palace in the Louis XIV style, stone-built, imposing, harmonizing with its surroundings, decorated with columns, sculptures, trophies, its roof-line hidden, its classical proportions fully displayed. Le Vau was instructed to quadruple the size of the old Louis XIII building by extending it on three sides, 'following the lines of the old château and meeting it at the four points where its former corner wings had been' (291). By the early summer of 1669, the ground-floor reconstruction had been completed.

The interior reconstruction took a number of years to complete. Le Vau died in 1670 having hardly begun the 'Grand Staircase' (or *escalier des Ambassadeurs*), for which Le Brun would undertake the decorations. The work was taken up again in 1671 and achieved in 1678, in Mansart's time. The Grand Apartment, conceived around the theme of Apollo, was begun in 1670, but was not inhabitable until November 1673. From this date onwards, the silver furnishings in the palace began to be assembled, whilst His Majesty's Grand Chamber, or Salon d'Apollon, was 'lined with a gorgeous gold brocade touched with silver, called the Lovers' Brocade' (291). The slow progress, the endless construction work and the contrast between the discomfort of the temporary visits and the projected luxury of the apartments are something of a symbol of the private history of Louis XIV. Before ruling over these splendid palaces, he reigned over construction sites; ruler and compasses had to make way for the builders.

But, though the king was creative, guiding his artists and working for his own glory, Versailles was not conceived for himself alone. Le Brun provided him with a perpetual torment; for the king's *grands salons* were designed to glorify the reign and symbolize the grandeur of the kingdom, to stupefy ambassadors, to seduce princes and to receive a court. From 1671 onwards, the king's premier painter also took charge of the apartments for Maria Theresa. 'The queen's apartments were, to all appearances, almost the equal of the king's.' With a southerly aspect, they comprised a guardroom, where the décor invoked Mars, the god of war, the queen's antechamber, the Grand Chamber and a large corner-studio. Rumour had it, though, that the true queen of Versailles was not the king's wife but his mistress and favourite, Françoise-Athénaïs de Rochechouart, marquise de Montespan. For her, Louis XIV instructed Le Vau to erect (or it was constructed in 1670–2 from his drawings) a miniature palace decorated with faience tiles in Chinese style: the porcelain Trianon. He also instructed Mansart to build Clagny for her, a 'folly' which astonished Mme de Sévigné. Above all, the delectable Athénaïs was assigned, entirely for her own use, one of the finest apartments in the palace, one which was indistinguishable in splendour from that of the king himself.

The rooms of her apartment were to be found at the top of the Grand Staircase. Five windows looked out onto the Cour Royale, and she enjoyed access to the king's apartments. From 1671 onwards, the gallery and rooms of Mme de Montespan were provided with their own paintings and gilded decorations. For sixteen years, and despite her disgrace in 1680, the king's mistress went on enjoying her privileged place of residence. But her realm possessed an annexe, on the ground floor beneath the king's apartments. This was the famous 'Bathroom Suite' (*appartement des Bains*), completed in the years 1671 to 1680. It became the temporary place of exile for the marquise de Montespan from 1685 to 1691. Before the latter date, this was where Louis XIV's private life really took place. The king retired there to find Athénaïs amidst a décor of 'unimaginable magnificence' (291). Paintings by Le Brun, sculptures by Le Hongre, Tuby,

Girardon, Desjardins and others, bronzes by Caffiéri and embossed work by Cucci, made these rooms exquisite rivals of the royal rooms above. A 'Doric hall', with a painted ceiling by Le Moyne, was entered either from the south by the Cour Royale or from the garden to the north side. Then there was an 'Ionic room' or Salle de Diane, decorated with twelve marble columns, statues of Pallas and Flora and two couches. Then came the 'Studio of the Months of the Year', the twelve months being represented there in statues made following Le Brun's designs. To the left, the room led on into the still more sumptuous Chambre des Bains, where an alcove and bed were ornamented with one of the most beautiful brocades made in the seventeenth century, 'in a pattern of shepherds and shepherdesses'. From there one finally entered the bathroom, the Cabinet des Bains, which contained 'a great octagonal tub, cut from a single piece of marble from Rancé' and costing 15,000 *livres*. In 1678, Louis XIV installed two further white marble baths. Many of these treasures no longer survive, but inventories give us a glimpse of their splendour.

11

'The Sun Has its Spots'

SINCE THE baroque term 'Sun King' possibly gives the reign
of Louis XIV a false image, it is all the more important to
offset this effect with a corrective chapter indicating that the
king was not infallible, that 'the sun has its spots' and that
the realm was not transformed with the wave of a magic wand.
Once Mazarin was in his grave, difficulties and mistakes did
occur. The Fouquet affair did nothing for the king's reputation.

A SHABBY AFFAIR

We left the unfortunate Fouquet on 5 September 1661 in the
hands of a musketeer, the sieur d'Artagnan. Louis XIV had
made a good choice. For three years, this officer looked after
his prisoner humanely (83). But this did not stop the king's
obstinate pursuit of his quarry. On reflection, this pursuit had a
political motive, for, in the downfall of Fouquet, he saw the
enhancement of monarchical power. He would not need to spur
Colbert on so long as the latter was concerned to ruin his
predecessor.

The king established an edict in November 1661 'for the creation and establishment of a special judicial tribunal (*chambre de
justice*) to search out the abuses and corruption which have
occurred in the royal finances since the year 1635'; he then
signed a commission on 15 November 'containing the names of
the judges and officers who would make up the tribunal' (201),
which did sit for seven years and eight months. This became a
'hunt for the wicked tax-gatherers (*maltôtiers*)' (170). It would

have the result of increasing the revenues of the Treasury, thanks to the fines it exacted, of imposing on the financiers the sense that the king and Colbert expected a new style in such matters and, in the condemnation of Fouquet, of providing the public with a sacrificial lamb to atone for past extortions.

By means of Séguier, who refused the king nothing, Colbert appointed judges whom he believed to be compliant. The *premier président* Lamoignon, who was suspected of being too lenient, was replaced in the midst of the trial by Séguier himself. As for Colbert's uncle, Pussort, he led the onslaught upon the former superintendent. It was not the principle of holding a special tribunal upon such matters which was in doubt, but rather 'the overt and intentional irregularities of procedure' (170). For three years, the judges tried to establish the evidence for Fouquet's wrongdoing without judging the cardinal or involving Colbert or his clients. The skilfully selective investigation which resulted can readily be imagined.

Those in a position to know feared that the trial would rebound against the accusers and expose too much about a financial system which enmeshed a host of prominent individuals who had profited greatly from the state's financial embarrassment. Once under way, would not the tribunal accuse M. de Turenne, the dowager duchesse d'Orléans, the *président* Maupeou, the comte d'Estrées, and other seigneurs of illicit profiteering? (170) The judges knew that one of the two main charges, that of high treason, was not really sustainable, being based on the plan for the defence of Belle-Isle en Mer, found at Saint-Mandé. They also knew that the other charge, of peculation, was not as clear-cut as Colbert imagined. The accounts discovered among the papers of the former superintendent were in considerable disorder. Was this really unique to him or was it the normal pattern for a financier in a period of impecunity and in a system where, without financiers, the public treasury would have been forced to declare a bankruptcy? 'The affair demonstrated that the finances were not the sole preserve of the infamous tax-farmers, but were equally the domain of ministers and great aristocrats.' (170) In his defence, Fouquet was not afraid to compromise former colleagues, such as, for example, his friend Hugues de Lionne. All these deals had to be kept out of the public domain, in order to please the king and satisfy Colbert's thirst for vengeance.

So Séguier and the *avocat général* Talon bombarded the accused with leading questions, and used against him every legal means of pressure. Fouquet was intelligent enough to counter-attack. The more he implicated Colbert and his clients, the more he embarrassed the tribunal. He was a good enough lawyer to sense the weakness of the accusations against him. It was said that he had set up fictitious loans to the state, that he had agreed to private advances of money to the king, that he had utilized the revenues of the state for his own purposes and that he had used false identities to speculate in tax-farming. But these were all mere accusations. The charge of illegal profiteering rested on the presumed sources of his apparently prodigious wealth, encapsulated in Vaux-le-Vicomte. His defence was that his debts were greater than his assets, although no one listened to him. He demanded an inventory of his wealth, but the tribunal ignored his request.

It was fortunate for the former superintendent that venality of office allowed judges a certain freedom – which is not the case now in such special tribunals – one to which their way of life as well as their Gallican and Jansenist leanings contributed. There were still true judges in the realm and amongst the most honest was Olivier d'Ormesson. He was responsible for the summing-up (*rapporteur*), and he earned an 'everlasting reputation for probity' (97) because he championed the case for a life-sentence against those who pressed for Fouquet's execution. On 19 December 1664, Mme de Sévigné, who backed Fouquet, counted seven votes with Ormesson and only six for the death penalty. On the following day, a Saturday, the verdict was pronounced: the former superintendent was given a life-sentence by thirteen votes to nine.

At the close of this interminable trial, the sentence was well received because public opinion had changed. The news was greeted, according to Ormesson, 'with considerable joy, even by the ordinary shopkeepers', because Fouquet had 'become the object of public guilt and public pity' (97). Colbert was beside himself with anger. Olivier d'Ormesson ruined his own career and never became a councillor of state. The king was aghast and 'altered the punishment of banishment to one of prison' (96). Mme Fouquet and various other members of his family were exiled. The former superintendent was escorted to the fortress at Pinerolo by a new musketeer, d'Auvergne de Saint-Mars.

Mme de Sévigné was sure that Louis XIV was not to blame in the matter. Those who clamoured for vengeance were the ministers and their subordinates. She forgot, however, that the regalian power of pardon existed. The king's alteration to the sentence of his former minister was not against the law, but it did offend against equity. The only clemency Fouquet received was in 1679, when, still imprisoned, he was permitted to talk with his companion in captivity, Lauzun. A year later, in 1680, after nineteen years of incarceration in this savage fortress, the former superintendent died ('His soul went from Pinerolo to Heaven', wrote Mme de Sévigné). By a particular act of clemency from Louvois, and thus from the king, 'the body of M. Fouquet' was carried back to Paris in 1681 and buried in the Monastery of the Visitation in the faubourg Saint-Antoine (96).

PEASANT FURIES

The Fouquet affair seems like the final release from a vanishing past. As much may also be said of the rural revolts which marked the first few years of the personal rule. We may again mention the disdain with which they were greeted by the Parisian Furetière: 'The peasants who attempt revolt are but poor *croquants.*' This was the word given to the peasants who rose in revolt in south-west France under Richelieu and at the beginning of the king's minority: in 1624, and again in 1635 to 1637, Quercy, Guyenne, Angoumois, Saintonge and the Périgord witnessed the bloodshed of 'croquant' revolts. In 1643, there were renewed 'croquant' risings in Rouergue. And, in addition to these events, two great popular insurrections also stood out: that of the *nu-pieds* in Normandy in 1639 and that of the *sabotiers* of the Sologne in 1658.

One would search in vain in these often bloody insurrections for signs of a conflict between peasants and gentlemen. For the *croquants* of the Périgord and the *nu-pieds* of Normandy were largely sustained by, and recruited from amongst, the lesser nobility, rather than by and from amongst the poorest inhabitants of the countryside. All these revolts were against the fiscal demands of the state, sometimes against the *tailles*, sometimes against the replacement of the local representative institutions by tribunals of royal officials (*bureaux d'élections*), and sometimes against the introduction of or increase in the tariff of the *gabelle*, the hated salt tax. The revolts were serious, causing deaths by the hundreds, and they worried the state. Chancellor Séguier was sent to judge the *nu-pieds*. They were repressed, but only after a delay and haphazardly. The soldiers seized the *révoltés* whom they found still armed, and a few poor individuals were hanged, not always because they were guilty of much (7). But there then followed general letters of clemency and an amnesty. It was a pattern which emphasized the king's clemency; it also underlined the weakness of the state.

With the personal rule of Louis XIV, much began to change. Peasant revolts did not disappear, but there were only four of them – in the Boulonnais in 1662, the Audijos revolt of 1663 to 1665, the Roure revolt of 1670 and the Breton *bonnets rouges* revolt of 1675. With the Fronde out of the way, the peasants were not the 'wild animals' which La Bruyère, the inveterate townsman, wrote about, 'swarthy, ghastly and shrivelled by the sun', living 'in dens' and sustained by only 'black bread, water and roots' ('roots', in the seventeenth century, meant vegetables). They enjoyed a standard of living better than that of the majority of the rural world in Europe. They would derive some benefit from Colbert's policies, since he stopped increasing the *taille* (a tax which was borne disproportionately by the poor) in favour of indirect taxes (which were paid by the rich especially). They found that the administration of the intendants had its advantages. A more-modern state acted to protect them. It was a paradox that they had been presented with the demands of a more-modern state before they had been given time to appreciate its benefits.

In his *Mémoires*, Louis XIV recalled the first revolt of the personal rule, that of the Boulonnais, which is known, no one knows quite why, as the *guerre du Lustucru*. In statistical terms, the text implies that about 400 *révoltés* had been sent to the galleys and 'a dozen more hanged or broken on the wheel' (43) to leave no one in any doubt that civil war was a thing of the past and that the state had to be obeyed. The following year, however, the Chalosse rose up under a lesser noble called Audijos. It was about an increase in the salt tax and looked back to the days of the *croquants* and *nu-pieds*. The intendant Pellot reacted vigorously: several *révoltés* were executed, and dozens more sent to the galleys. In 1670, the Vivarais revolted upon the rumour that royal officials (*élections*) were to be introduced to levy the *taille*. It found a local leader in a rural notable called Antoine du Roure. Several judicial officials were killed and Aubenas was subjected to some looting. The troubles lasted for three months, before a defeat in pitched battle at Lavilledieu on 25 July. Du Roure was broken on the wheel in Montpellier (7).

A fourth revolt began, in the Breton towns, in April 1675 as a protest against the edict of 1674 which had introduced a stamp duty upon all legal documents. However, the violence took a hold in rural lower Brittany and in the county of Cornouaille. Around 2,000 peasants, led by 'parochial captains', who often wore red bonnets (hence the name given to the revolt), went round the countryside terrorizing villages, attacking châteaux and burning the offices of tax-farmers or clerks of the courts. In the *croquant* and *nu-pieds* tradition, they stood against the demands of the state, although it was also the case that this revolt was against seigneurial rights, which many estate officials were forcibly constrained to sign away in acts of renunciation. However, as soon as the governor of the province, the duc de Chaulnes, had the reinforcements he had asked for, he began to advance upon the *révoltés* with 6,000 troops. The mere arrival of royal troops re-established order (247). The poor Bretons 'threw themselves on their knees and said *mea culpa*; this was the only expression in French they knew' (96). Near Quimper, fourteen who had refused to surrender were hanged. Other *révoltés* who were still armed when they were seized were executed. The amnesty was signed by Louis XIV on 5 February 1676 and, except for about 100 ringleaders, the rest of Brittany was pardoned. The king had found the best way of handling revolts, unequivocally and without prolonged repression. The *pax gallicana* was imposed without too high a price.

THE KING AND THE 'JANSENISTS'

Louis XIV hoped to establish the same kind of peace in the Church, but he could not treat churchmen and magistrates in the way he could his peasants. And there was the complication of the inheritance of Richelieu's arrest of Saint-Cyran, confessor to the Cistercian nuns of Port-Royal in the faubourg Saint-Jacques (they had abandoned their nunnery at Les Champs in the

Chevreuse valley) and his disbanding of the 'Solitaires', the name given to a group of eminent laymen, Le Maître, Singlin, de Séricourt and Lancelot, among others, who had created the 'little schools', elitist educational institutions of a kind attended by Racine.

The publication of the *Augustinus* by Jansen, Bishop of Ypres, which was first seen in Paris in 1641, seemed to justify the cardinal's fears. The Jesuits and a number of Sorbonne doctors saw in the book an undue emphasis upon the doctrine of the efficacy of grace, a close ally of Calvinist predestination, the abnegation of Christian liberty. Port-Royal (under the direction of Jacqueline Arnauld, mère Angélique) found itself compromised, along with its educational efforts, not to mention the clerics and laymen from solid families and of intellectual prowess who had been attracted to Augustinian theology. Scholasticism was stifling and Augustinianism seemed a breath of fresh air.

Mazarin's regime coincided with the reactions amongst Augustinians. In January 1643, Saint-Cyran's *Familiar Theology* appeared, and he was released from prison in February and died the following October. The same year marked a critical juncture in *dévot* publications, for in it Antoine Arnauld, the Sorbonne theologian, produced his treatise *On Frequent Communion*. Thirty-one-years old, the brother of mère Angélique and a convert to Cartesian philosophy, he became the leading theologian of Augustinianism. Thirty-four years after François de Sales' *Introduction to the Devout Life*, which had presented religion as a friendly comfort, *On Frequent Communion* offered a very different basis for devotion, grounded in the fear of God (145). Arnauld criticized the Jesuits and their casuists for their worldiness and Pelagianism, their exaggeration of free will at the expense of God's divine grace. This was why the Jesuits were roused to become 'Molinists', supporters of the theses of their fellow-Jesuit, Molina, against whom Jansen had written his book in the first place.

Other theologians joined in the fray. The Sorbonne denounced many of the theses of the *Augustinus*. Their principal opponent was the syndic of the Sorbonne, Nicolas Cornet (d. 1663), who applied for the papal bull *Cum occasione*, which condemned five propositions supposedly to be found in Jansen's work. Mazarin was not guilty of any part in these proceedings, but, once they had occurred, he supported Rome. The bull appeared in May 1653; in August, the Port-Royal schools found themselves the object of police investigations. When, two years later, the conflict in the French Church erupted, the cardinal did nothing to ease the tensions.

In January 1655, one of the great seigneurs of France, the duc de Liancourt, was refused absolution until he took his young daughter away from Port-Royal and dismissed two supposedly Jansenist clerics from his household. On 24 February, Arnauld published a *Letter to a Person of Quality* and followed it on 10 July with his *Letter to a Duke and Peer*. In the interim, the Assembly of the Clergy had drawn up a declaration or *formulaire* requiring clerics to assent to their condemnation of the Five Propositions; the formulary itself would be clarified and broadened by Assemblies of the Clergy in 1657 and 1661. Arnauld remained indomitable, however, and exploited the distinction between the 'law' and the 'facts' of the matter. He assured everyone that he was ready to accept that the Five Propositions were contrary to the law of the Church, but he denied the fact that they appeared in Jansen's work. But of this fact he failed to persuade the faculty of theology, before which he was condemned on 14 January 1656. The views of the Sorbonne and the learned theologians counted for little, however, when the public was offered a defence of the efficacy of grace in matchless prose and the dismissal of attendant grace and the other tiresome formulae of the casuists. On 23 January, just after Arnauld's defeat, appeared the *First Provincial Letter from one of his Friends, on the Subject of the Current Disputes in the Sorbonne*. Louis de Montalte, alias Blaise Pascal, thus began his brilliant *Provincial Letters*, which won over educated opinion to the Augustinian cause. On 26 January, Arnauld became a semi-recluse. 'On 6 March', a contemporary recorded, 'Port-Royal was the subject of much conversation at the Louvre, and it was decided to withdraw those children who were being educated there in the tenets of Jansenism, as they falsely asserted, and put an end to the large numbers who were joining Port-Royal, amongst whom, it was alleged, again falsely, there were many clerics.' (160) This 'decision' was Mazarin's and the king's. But Anne of Austria, the friend of M. Arnauld d'Andilly, told him of it, and on 20 March, the little schools decamped before the arrival of the civil lieutenant at the gates of 'Port-Royal des Champs'.

Alexander VII, however, issued a new bull, *Ad sacram beati*

Petri sedem, on 16 October, which declared the Five Propositions to be contained in Jansen's work. The Assembly of the Clergy modified the formulary, but certain prelates – such as the Bishop of Alet, Nicolas Pavillon – refused to sign it. A *lit de justice* was required to register it. Such opposition continued to give Port-Royal a breathing-space, and Mazarin, preoccupied with the negotiations for peace with Spain and impressed with the kind of support which Arnauld enjoyed, did not urge the government into fresh initiatives.

Up to 1660, the public impression was that, if there was a danger, it lay more in the laxism among the Molinists than in the heresy contained in the *Augustinus*. As for the friends of Port-Royal, they were divided over tactics. But, in 1660, the issue of the formulary surfaced once more following the initiative of Harlay de Champvallon, Archbishop of Rouen, who enjoyed Louis XIV's support. In the Assembly of the Clergy in 1661, the decisions of 1657 were confirmed. The council of state, by an order of 13 April, 'required everyone to sign the formulary, and a *lettre de cachet* made it clear to the bishops that it applied not only to all ecclesiastics, but also to nuns and schoolmasters. To Port-Royal, this was a bitter blow' (160). And it was one delivered upon a royal initiative, now that the cardinal was dead. 'From 23 April, the civil lieutenant . . . issued orders requiring scholars and novices to leave Port-Royal de Paris and Port-Royal des Champs.' (160) Louis XIV was already treating it as a revolt.

Arnauld's friends counter-attacked. Since Cardinal Retz was in flight but had not resigned from the archbishopric of Paris, it was administered by two vicars-general, both Augustinians. They issued on 8 June their *Summons to Sign the Formulary*, which admitted the distinction between law and fact in the matter, a formula which the nuns would, despite the strong objections of Jacqueline Pascal, agree to sign.* The king's council then demanded in August that all those who had signed this *Summons* should retract. As Retz was in the process of negotiating his

---

* Jacqueline Pascal was Blaise Pascal's sister. The day the formulary was signed, she wrote this formidable indictment: 'I fully comprehend that it is sometimes said that it is not for women to defend the cause of truth. Whether this be the case or no, following the sorry upturned state of affairs in which we find ourselves, since bishops display no more than a girl's resolve, it is left to the ladies to show the courage which the bishops should be demonstrating. And, if we cannot defend the cause of truth, we can nonetheless die for it.' She would die, in the house at Les Champs, on 4 October 1661, not a martyr but certainly having suffered indirectly from persecution.

pardon, contingent upon his resignation of his see, the vicars-general of the diocese were obliged themselves to back down (31 October–20 November). It was thus with a heavy heart that the nuns of Paris signed the formulary on 28 November (those in Port-Royal des Champs did so the following day), although they added 'a restrictive clause which explicitly made the distinction between law and fact'. This new revolt incurred the king's displeasure and, in January 1662, he imposed an additional formulary upon them requiring their signature to the facts of the case. The death of M. de Marca (29 June), who had been nominated archbishop following Retz's resignation (26 February), gave them a breathing-space. At the close of July, the Port-Royal nuns lodged an appeal on technical grounds (*appel comme d'abus*). The great epoch of persecution only began to take effect in 1664.

THE KING AND 'JANSENISM'

Port-Royal symbolized the zeal and spirituality of the Counter-Reformation, albeit perhaps to excess and with the warping effects of controversy. In order to render 'Jansenism' odious, its enemies sought to link it with its opponent, Protestantism. In 1643, the Jesuits published a Latin litany in which, with more than a touch of malice, Port-Royal was accused of holding to John Calvin's doctrine upon grace: *Paulus genuit Augustinum, Augustinus Calvinum, Calvinus Jansenium, Jansenius Sancyranum, Sancyranus Arnaldum et fratres ejus* ('St Paul begat St Augustine, Augustine begat Calvin, Calvin begat Jansen, Jansen begat Saint-Cyran, Saint-Cyran begat [Antoine] Arnauld and his brethren') (99).

In reality, Port-Royal and Calvinism had nothing in common beyond their shared orthodoxy on the recognition of God's omniscience and man's degeneracy, on the vital importance of divine grace, on the inward spiritual life, and on the outward demands of the moral life. Jansen and Saint-Cyran, director of Port-Royal, both detested Calvinism and venerated the Virgin Mary (269). Arnauld's assault upon the Huguenots did not cease, despite his sharing in their experience of persecution and exile (89). What could have been more foreign to Protestantism than the adoration of the host as practised at Port-Royal? In a century in which most clerics found St Thomas rather wearisome after a thorough exposure to St Augustine (269), the 'supposed heresy of the Jansenists' (42) was in fact an Augustinianism taken straight from the Church Father himself rather than indirectly via Luther or Calvin. In the Middle Ages, salvation, the Christian obsession, centred around the communion of saints, was always a collective salvation. Jansen, Saint-Cyran and Port-Royal found that Augustine preached the way of individual salvation, the sinful man powerless to gain salvation without the miracle of grace. 'St Augustine and St Paul', Mme de Sévigné wrote, 'were the great labourers for the sovereign will of God.' (96) These awesome mysteries did not worry her. When the Jesuits of the seventeenth century spoke of the pessimism in 'Jansenism', they failed to appreciate that a lack of confidence in the power of human endeavour was not pessimistic; rather, it was a recognition of what Blaise Pascal termed 'the misery of man without God'. This was the beginning of a belief in the doctrine of grace, of a respect for God's almighty power and His infinite mercy. Those who feel God's saving mercy become the most optimistic of believers, predestined by the Creator, strengthened in the knowledge of their having been created by Him.

The predestination which Augustinians supported appeared to the Jesuits as the heresy of despair. Although they rarely adhered to the worldly latitudinarianism that their casuists sometimes presented to the world, or championed the bitter sectarianism of someone like père Brisacier, author of *Jansenism Confounded* (1651), the counsellors of the young king, members or supporters of the Jesuit Order, were Port-Royal's enemies. They encouraged his hostility. In his *Memoirs for the year 1661*, Louis wrote this dismissive paragraph on Port-Royal: 'I applied myself to the destruction of Jansenism and the dissipation of the communities which fomented this novelty, [communities] which, though perhaps well intentioned, were ignorant of or chose to ignore the dangerous consequences which might ensue from it.' (63)

Louis' animosity towards Port-Royal would last throughout the reign, nourished by the Jesuits' hatreds for the Arnauld tribe. The Jesuits defended their apologists, and supported the philosophy of Aristotle and Aquinas against Port-Royal's acceptance of Cartesianism. Despite the huge success of the Jesuit colleges at popularizing Christian Renaissance Humanism, they resented Port-Royal's little schools, whose reputation was greater than the number or spread of these institutions merited. In 1661,

Louis XIV had not forgotten Pascal's insolence towards père Annat, the royal confessor, in the seventeenth and eighteenth *Provincial Letters* (1657). But it would be too restrictive to attribute Louis XIV's anti-Jansenist stance wholly to the influence of his confessors. Even at the times when their influence had clearly become considerable, such as in 1709 when père Le Tellier directed the king's conscience, the king always remained the master of his own decisions.

It is sometimes said that the moral austerity of Port-Royal was a standing reproach to a king who had engaged in adultery. The proposition is hardly a convincing one, for, in reality, the 'Peace of the Church', which lasted from 1668 to 1679 and which gave 'Jansenism' a chance to regroup, coincided with the most flagrant of royal indiscretions. When the persecution recommenced in 1679, it was at a time when the king was about to return to the uprightness of conjugal life. In fact, the king lay mid-way between the extremes of moral austerity and laxity, the 'middle way' defined by Bossuet in his funeral oration for Cornet: 'We must follow the middle path.' (14)

Furthermore, political considerations supported the religious convictions. Richelieu and Mazarin were hostile towards Port-Royal because its fundamentalism denied any civil compromise. 'Jansenist' utopianism was far removed from what has been termed 'politique Jansenism' and it blocked the pragmatism of the cardinals and the appreciation of reality by their disciple, Louis XIV. In any case, 'Jansenism' appeared inseparable in Louis XIV's mind from the *parlementaire* Fronde, in which the friends of Port-Royal had been evidently engaged, and from the princely Fronde too, through Mmes de Chevreuse and de Longueville. Port-Royal, as an institution, had not taken sides, but too many *frondeurs* in 1649, and even after 1652, were attached to the famous convent for it not to fall under suspicion.

The king was no less exasperated by the disciples of Saint-Cyran amongst the clergy. He forgave the 'Jansenist' bishops for their portrayal of a pattern of religion less triumphalist than that of their colleagues, but he could never accept their lack of Gallican conviction, as the regalian-rights issue demonstrated. The friends of Port-Royal alarmed Louis XIV above all because of their sense of community. They had 'secret habits', which persecution intensified. In the letters from M. de Sacy to Arnauld, mère Agnes was 'the Little One' (*la Petite*), M. Lancelot was known as 'd'Olib.', Arnauld d'Andilly was '900', Henri Arnauld, '905' (28). They seemed to be a sect, provocatively half-visible, with a disturbing effect upon society at large. Their influence was even felt at the court and in government through Arnauld de Pomponne. Their influence upon judges seemed to threaten the whole of public service. In the judicature alone, 40,000 office-holders were exposed to their influence, and it was from amongst this group that senior members of the administration were recruited. To have allowed Port-Royal to have a great say would have meant irritating the Jesuits and abandoning public service to a group whose interests did not coincide with the state's. Louis refused to take that risk. His sense of the state and his desire for uniformity directed him in around 1661 towards a policy of fundamental hostility towards Port-Royal, a policy for which the issue of the formulary was but a pretext.

ROYAL IMPATIENCE

Marca died not long before a crisis placed Louis XIV in opposi-tion to Pope Alexander VII. His death created a further vacancy in the see of Paris, and Hardouin de Péréfixe, the king's former tutor, received in April 1664 papal letters confirming him in the see. Following the Peace of the Pyrenees, the Roman Curia had refused any extension of the terms of the Concordat of Bologna (the agreement signed with the Papacy in 1516 which governed most of the important regalian rights in the French Church) to France's new provinces in Artois, Roussillon and the Three Bishoprics. The Holy See considered that, short of pontifical *indults*, Louis XIV could not nominate to the consistorial benefi-ces in those areas, that is, choose the incumbents to bishoprics and abbacies. But, just when Louis seemed about to accept the pope's stand, his ambassador to Rome, Créqui, upon his arrival there on 20 August 1662, found himself imbroiled in a diplo-matic incident arising from a brawl between French guards and the pope's Corsican guards which led to a siege of the Farnese palace with the duke and duchess inside taking cover from the gun-fire. The king was incensed and ordered the return of Créqui from Rome, the removal of the papal nuncio from Paris and the publication before the Parlement of Aix of the integra-tion of Avignon into the realm. There then followed eighteen months of negotiations until finally, on 12 February 1664, agreement was reached. Various concessions were made by Rome: the governor of the pontifical city would provide France with an explanation of events, the chief of police would be dismissed, the Corsican guard would be disbanded, Cardinal Chigi would present His Holiness's apologies in person and, finally, a pyramidal monument would be erected upon the spot where the outrage had taken place which would itemize the compensations exacted. In return, the king would surrender Avignon (130). Almost all these terms were adhered to. The legate was received at Fontainebleau and delivered the apology on 29 July. But the rights to patronage (or *indult*) for the bishopric of Metz were only signed on 11 December, and Alexander VII died three years later without having given any assurances over Artois and Roussillon.

On 16 April 1664, the new archbishop of Paris granted an audience to M. Lancelot, delegate from Port-Royal. This was how he expressed his own views on the matter:

> The king was persuaded that a new heresy was on the point of taking root in his realm. He knew how important it was to deal with it and nip it in the bud. He was more than ever determined to pursue this affair and I can assure you that, in the last meeting of the [king's] council, matters would have come to a sorry state if I had not thrown my weight against this. (160)

In the event, Péréfixe did not stop the letters-patent of April 1664 ordering the publication of the bulls of Innocent X and Alexander VII against 'Jansenism' and requiring every incumbent to sign the formulary of 1657 (201). Péréfixe was no friend to Port-Royal and he felt the pressures of Annat and the Jesuits; but he was more the subtle courtier than the obstinate theologian and he would have preferred a compromise. He rather hoped to have found one in his pastoral letter of 8 June, in which he drew the distinction between 'divine faith about the law in question and human faith as concerns the facts in dispute' (160).

Without hesitation, the archbishop made his way on 9 June to Port-Royal de Paris with this letter to begin a canonical visitation of the convent. 'Regularity', according to Racine, 'he greatly admired.' (89) But by the 14th the visitation was not progressing as well as it had begun. Péréfixe installed Michel Chamillart, an Ultramontane priest and a notorious casuist, as the nuns' confessor. The nuns refused to accept the nomination. On 11 July they sent, through the offices of Philippe de Champaigne, a declaration carrying their signatures and restating the distinction between law and facts in the case. The archbishop found himself in a ridiculous position. The king refused to countenance what he regarded as a revolt. The eyes of France were upon the nuns' determined stand. And yet the edict upon the formulary did not specify female monastic houses as included in its terms. Péréfixe turned the whole matter into a question of *amour propre*, not always the best guide for someone without the robust attitudes of a Louis XIV.

On 21 August, he again visited Port-Royal de Paris and, for almost five hours, humiliated the nuns, treating them as rebels. He had no compunction in addressing the abbess, Madeleine de Sainte-Agnès de Ligny, Séguier's niece, in these terms: 'Be quiet! You are nothing more than a proud and stubborn little woman, without the sense to see that you meddle in matters which you do not understand in the slightest. You are nothing more than a stuck-up slip of a girl, a poor fool, an ignoramus, who doesn't know what to say!' (160) To this he added: 'You are as pure as angels and as proud as Lucifer', and finished with a flourish: 'Off with you! Be off with you! You will see me again this side of the grave; and, let me tell you, it will be soon.' (160) In the mean time, they were forbidden the Sacraments.

The promised day of judgement took place on 26 August. The archbishop arrived 'accompanied by the civil lieutenant, the *prévôt de l'Ile*, the city-watch and other commissioned and non-commissioned militia and over 200 archers' (89). Twelve nuns, including the abbess, mère Agnès Arnauld and mère Angélique de Saint-Jean (Arnauld), were taken prisoner and despatched to various convents. Three of those deported were Arnauld d'Andilly's daughters. Before stepping into their carriages, the twelve nuns demanded the blessing of a hermit. Upon the rest, the archbishop imposed a Visitandine nun as prioress. But Péréfixe only managed to obtain seven signatures to the formulary. These meagre results, however, did not stop the archbishop from proceeding to impose his will upon Port-Royal des Champs on 15 November.

Persecution rallied the Augustinians and did nothing to staunch the flow of Jansenist literature which so diminished the stature of the king's former tutor. The pope showed no enthusiasm over the matter, so, in the hope of bringing it to an end, Louis XIV asked Rome for a new bull upon the formulary, and Alexander VII signed on 15 February 1665 *Regiminis apostolici*, which was accompanied by a newly drafted and draconian formulary (160). On 13 May, Péréfixe required its signature in his archdiocese and, on the 17th, he came to Port-Royal de Paris to enforce it. However, those who had been formerly non-compliant refused and so did four nuns who had signed in 1664. Chamillart had no better success. Then, upon the king's advice, the archbishop thought he had found a compromise. Those who signed the new formulary could remain in Paris at the faubourg Saint-Jacques. But those who refused to comply, and those who had been taken prisoner and deported elsewhere, would be taken to Port-Royal des Champs and kept there under surveillance, cut off from the outside world and denied the Sacraments (160).

One might imagine that this represented a victory for Péréfixe, but nothing was further from the truth. The pamphlets of Nicole took over from where the *Provincial Letters* had left off. Senior figures at court and amongst the judges shared the mental world of Augustinianism. From January 1662, Port-Royal enjoyed the protection – albeit with compromising *frondeur* associations – of the duchesse de Longueville, Condé's sister. 'Jansenism' was taking root. Amongst the episcopacy, the most Augustinian in their leanings – Arnauld, Bishop of Angers, Vialart, Bishop of Châlons, Caulet, Bishop of Pamiers, and Pavillon, Bishop of Alet – were also the most inspiring, the ones who applied the decrees of the Council of Trent with the greatest thoroughness. In Pavillon's case, Le Tellier bravely reminded the king of that fact (168). The dispute went far beyond the boundaries of the Parisian archdiocese or the relationships between Paris and Rome. Louis XIV, by a declaration of April 1665, imposed the bull *Regiminis apostolici* upon his realm. The text included 'the formulary which must be subscribed to by all clerics, both secular and regular, and including women in religious orders concerning the five propositions' (201). Pavillon, Choart de Buzanval, Bishop of Beauvais, Henri Arnauld and Caulet, who had already refused to sign any of the preceding texts, published the pontifical declaration, 'but sent an accompanying pastoral letter which took the opposite point of view' (130). This exasperated Alexander VII, who set about having the rebels expelled, before he died and was replaced by Pope Clement IX in 1667.

The advent of a new pope changed things. Despite the king's fixed opinions and his confessor, Louis XIV was not prepared to take matters too far, to press too harshly upon a few obstinate nuns or to expel prelates of acknowledged worth. He also recognized that the Parlement and the Council were Gallican enough to become Port-Royal's supporters, particularly when an Ultramontane formulary took the place of a national one. He also thought, with Lionne's encouragement, that the negotiations upon the *indult* issue had a better chance of succeeding if Clement IX was handled with tact. The latter, as a gesture of goodwill, granted the king in March 1668 the rights of patronage to the Three Bishoprics and followed this grant with three others in April, according him such rights not only in Roussillon and Artois, but also in the newly conquered regions of Flanders (130). Then, without either accepting or denying the distinction between law and fact, but contenting himself with ambiguous statements of obedience, he put an end to the quarrel over the Five Propositions, at least for the time being. Under Alexander VII, upon the pretext of combating heresy, Rome and the French king had pushed a minority of the clergy in France to the brink of a schism. Thanks to Clement IX's sensitivity, this had been put to one side by the autumn of 1668. To save Péréfixe's embarrassment, the negotiations took place in his absence. The new dispensation became rightly known as the *pax Clementina*. Louis XIV accepted it for as long as the question of the regalian rights did not stir up other issues.

PEACE IN THE FRENCH CHURCH

The peace which broke out in the French Church (1668–79) was a compromise, corresponding to a high point in the reign. It could only ever be a truce, because Louis XIV could scarcely distinguish between the supporters of Port-Royal and the disciples of Calvin, judging them both equally dangerous for a 'well-regulated monarchy'. 'One might say', wrote Sainte-Beuve, 'that, apart from the brief period following the signing of the Peace of the Church, Jansenists always had Louis XIV as their declared enemy . . . The so-called Church peace was, in reality, a truce, already violated in Louis XIV's mind well before its breakdown in 1679.'

Against Sainte-Beuve's views, which are retrospective, may be set those of a medal which the king ordered to be struck, carrying the date 1669 and the legend: 'RESTITUTA ECCLESIAE GALLI-CANAE CONCORDIA . . . *Concord re-established in the French Church.*' The accompanying commentary in the *Metallic History of the Reign* was a masterpiece of careful drafting:

> There had arisen amidst the theologians in France such bitter disputes about the nature of grace that their animus began to provoke a considerable scandal and there were fears that things would go from bad to worse. The king acted in harmony with the pope to eradicate these seeds of division. The Holy Father drew up various letters to the prelates of the realm and His Majesty published edicts which restored the Gallican Church to its former tranquillity. This is the subject of this medal. An open bible may be seen upon an altar and across it lie the keys of St Peter and the sceptre and hand of justice to represent the concordat between ecclesiastical power and royal authority. The radiant dove is the symbol of the Holy Spirit, who presides over this act. (71)

Clement IX drafted a papal bull on 28 September 1668 which expressed satisfaction with the French bishops for having signed the anti-Jansenist formulary *'pure et simpliciter'*, but did not publish it before Lionne had intervened to modify the wording so that 'purely and simply' read as 'sincerely'. And then, on 13 October, the unexpected happened when the papal nuncio in Paris received several known Jansenists and, embracing the great Antoine Arnauld, declared: 'Monsieur, you have a pen of gold with which to defend the Church.' (216) Ten days later, a Council decision admitted the distinction between fact and law. It forbad the king's subjects from 'attacking or provoking one another over events in the past', 'from using such terms as heretics, Jansenists, semi-Pelagians, and from writing about such controversial matters' (216). These were wise moves, and one can only regret that God had not seen fit to send His servant Clement twenty years sooner.

Seen from afar, the conflict was provoked by excessive zeal's bringing into conflict two elements of the Counter-Reformation. There was no need to identify the Five Propositions and send them to Rome, and, in 1653, it would have been better if Rome had buried the matter. Even the distinction between the facts and the law was hardly satisfactory, since, even if only two of the propositions could be found explicitly stated in the *Augustinus*, it certainly contained the essence of all five implicitly. But then, this essence was to be found in the works of St Augustine himself and was it important, let alone legitimate, to condemn Augustine? Should the attractive doctrine of attendant grace drive out the theocentric doctrine of the efficacy of grace? If libertines would have doubted the legitimacy of such a move, what would Christians have made of it?

Several days after the decision of the Council, well-informed courtiers learnt of Turenne's conversion to Catholicism, under Bossuet's influence. He was a foreign prince and the king's cousin; it was abjurations like this which left Louis XIV believing that the number of Huguenots was ever diminishing. This was the autumn of what seemed like a general peace, even as regards the Protestants. Port-Royal's friends, too, were among its beneficiaries. Louis XIV received Arnauld on 24 October with politeness, and, on the 31st, Sacy and Fontaine were released from the Bastille, where they had been since 1666. A few days later still, the king received Sacy, Pomponne and the archbishop. On 15 February 1669, under the weight of Sacy's influence, the nuns at Port-Royal des Champs decided to sign the formulary, on the 18th they were admitted to the Sacraments and, on 13 May, the Council decided to separate the two establishments of Port-Royal de Paris and Port-Royal des Champs into two separate monastic houses (31), and this gave a stay of execution for a further ten years to the Port-Royal outside Paris. The culmination of the Peace of the Church was in September 1671. Lionne was dead, and the king chose as his successor the nephew of the great Arnauld, M. de Pomponne, ambassador in Stockholm, and wrote to him personally: 'You will receive this letter with very mixed emotions. Surprise, joy and embarrassment will all attend you because you will not have expected me to make you my secretary of state, being so far away in the distant north.' (227) Surprise was also felt at court when Louis XIV granted an audience at Versailles to Pomponne's father, the elderly Arnauld d'Andilly, who had come to thank him for the honour bestowed on his son. To the young king, the veteran presented a flattering speech, and the king, prolonging the audience, praised Pomponne and then spoke in praise of Andilly's stature as a man of letters.

Neither Arnauld d'Andilly nor his brother Antoine nor their

friends had, in consideration of the Peace of the Church, held up or stopped the publication of the great tomes of these years. In 1668, P. Quesnel's *Words of the Incarnate Word of God . . . Drawn from the New Testament* was followed by Lancelot's *New Arrangement of Holy Scripture into an Order so that it may be Read Each Year in its Entirety . . .* In 1669, appeared the first volume of Nicole's *Perpetuity of Faith Concerning the Eucharist*. At the beginning of the following year, it was the turn of Pascal's *Pensées*, posthumous fragments from a great work of Christian apologetics which this polymath had dreamt of writing. In June 1670, another posthumous work saw the light of day, Saint-Cyran's *Considerations upon the Sabbath and upon Festivals*. The same author's *Christian Instructions* was published in 1671 and that, also in 1671, was succeeded by Quesnel's *Summary of Gospel Morality* and by Nicole's *Legitimate Prejudices against Calvinists* and the first volume of his *Essays on Morality*. In 1672, appeared the first of the thirty volumes which made up the important translation of the Bible by M. de Sacy.

The court and the capital were not obliged to read any of these works, but there were many there who counted themselves sympathetic outsiders. After several years of peace in the Church, the *Messieurs* in Port-Royal des Champs enjoyed the support of a large part of the elite. Some openly joined their ranks, like the marquise de Sévigné, a talented and effective recruit. In January 1674, she visited the convent outside Paris and was filled with enthusiasm:

> This Port-Royal is a veritable Thebes, a paradise set amidst a desert wherein every strain of Christian devotion is displayed. It is a holiness reflected in the countryside around up to a mile away. There are five or six hermits of unknown background, living like penitents in the tradition of St John Climacus. The nuns are angels upon this earth . . . I assure you that I have been overwhelmed by this divine solitude. (96)

It was in that same year, 1674, that the infatuation for the 'broad hats', as the Jesuits were called, also became manifest. As long as the truce lasted, the mutual competition between the two camps stimulated the French Church and its theologians, preachers and teachers. For every Lancelot and Nicole in the ranks of Port-Royal there was a Bouhours (who published his *Conversations between Aristes and Eugenia* in 1671) amidst those of the Jesuits. If the Jesuits were proud of Bourdaloue in their order, the Augustinians had great hopes of the preaching power of père Soanen.

The truce was the more remarkable since it lasted throughout a long military conflict, and, paradoxically, the coming of peace abroad would bring an end to religious harmony at home. On 5 February 1679, the final treaties of Nymwegen were signed and, on 15 April, the duchesse de Longueville, Port-Royal's protectress, died. On 18 November following, the king dismissed Pomponne, and religious enthusiasm and misplaced zeal once more came to the fore.

12

The King's Arms

KINGS 'owe a kind of accountability for all their actions to the whole universe and to all posterity, but they cannot be always constrained to render account to all and sundry immediately without damaging their greater interests and being forced to reveal the secret intentions of their conduct' (63). At three centuries' remove, we should be in a position to weigh these 'interests', understand these actions and divine the motives for them, but it requires an effort of explanation rather than judgement.

A VISIBLE FORCE: THE ARMY

Louis XIV was reported as saying on his death-bed: 'I have often gone to war too lightly and pursued it for vanity's sake.' (26) A beautiful baroque confession; the style of devotion demanded that the penitent exaggerate his sins. Of course, the fifty-four years of personal rule saw almost thirty-three years of armed conflict. But should one not remember that this is to be compared with the armed struggle waged by the cardinal ministers who, from 1635 to 1661, had kept France at war for twenty-four of the twenty-six years, and from whom Louis XIV had inherited the kingdom? Should one not remember that the Austrian subjects of Leopold I, who reigned for forty-seven years, only enjoyed seven years at peace?*

The 'parade ground' (164) was of enormous importance. If

* I am grateful to Professor Jean Bérenger for this point.

the finances of the state were in a deplorable condition upon Mazarin's death, this was because of the prolonged war against Spain, a war which had tripled the taxes and had provoked popular revolts which added to the victims and the devastation caused by the conflict against the Habsburgs. But, if in 1661 the administrative revolution brought about by Louis XIV and Colbert was accomplished without a crisis, this was undoubtedly because of the development of state institutions under the imperative demands of war. It is thus permissible to argue that this war which affected the second third of the century contributed to the forging of a more modern state.

In 1635, the royal army was composed of scarcely more than 25,000 men; upon Richelieu's death it comprised over 100,000. The cardinal left to Louis XIV a policy of maintaining the big battalions. At the time of the peace in 1659, the French army was theoretically made up of 250,000 men. Le Tellier took advantage of the truce to 'reform' this force: the household forces of the king were limited to 10,000 men, the infantry to 35,000 and the cavalry to 10,000, a total of 55,000 officers, under-officers and soldiers. The secretary of state for war taught the king the art of selective dialysis.

The king was not yet five years old when Le Tellier was appointed (on 13 April 1643) to the post of secretary of state for war. His relatives Louvois (d. 1691) and Barbezieux (d. 1701) followed him in office, a succession which brought together talent and responsibility in one family for fifty-eight years. By the time of Mazarin's death, the young king had 55,000 crack troops and an incomparable military instrument. Michel Le Tellier had worked constantly to upgrade the army's administration, overseeing the 'accounts for war, both ordinary and extraordinary, both within and without the realm' (165). He checked the treasurers' accounts, watched over the army intendants (a post which he had himself held), encouraged the commissioners for war and streamlined the arrangements for troop movements. 'It was a Herculean task' (165), given the uphill nature of the job. The military commanders had no experience of giving way to an administrator, of sacrificing their pride to 'the men of the pen'. Company commanders found it easier to suborn the war commissioners than to muster the required number of troops to make up a company. At every level there was resistance to change, so much so that 'by the middle of the seventeenth century, the army was only partially a royal, permanent institution of state' (165).

Under the watchful eye of Le Tellier, whose efforts the king supported, the struggle continued, above all in the wake of the Peace of the Pyrenees when a shower of regulations attempted to nationalize and discipline the army. The ministry for war was itself provided with an outline structure before 1662, the year in which, by a royal letter (*brevet*) of 24 February, Louvois became officially his father's collaborator. Le Tellier was never able to push reforms as far as he wished, and Louvois, secretary of state for war on his own from 1677 to 1691, had no greater success. The generals still resented the directives of first under-secretaries (*premiers commis*), and even the orders of ministers. Recruitment was enfeebled by two old problems: the venality of commissions for officers and conscription. But positive results were achieved. At the summit of the administration, the king had a well-regulated department of state at his disposal. In 1665, the functions of the war department were divided between five sections. One looked after military regulations, a second after personnel, a third handled military despatches to and from ministers, while a fourth oversaw the movement of troops. The final section was charged with army pensions and food supplies. Each section had a first under-secretary (Colbert himself had experience in this department between 1648 and 1651). The first under-secretary was, therefore, a senior administrator and generally given letters of nobility. The war commissioners were more tightly controlled, and the number of musters was increased to eradicate *passe-volants* or fictitious soldiers merely there to pass muster. Louvois' task was to follow the path already sketched out for the control of the commissioners, who were essential to the modernization of the army.

Le Tellier's greatest achievement was to ensure Louvois as his successor. Louvois quickly gained the king's confidence, securing influence between 1663 and 1667 in the ministerial team, and was associated with all the regulatory measures decided upon during those years. From 1667 to 1677, M. de Louvois was the minister's copartner. Throughout these ten years, Le Tellier and his son shared the burdens of office. Le Tellier remained in the ministry concentrating upon administration and discipline. Louvois' preference was for tactics and the technical side of war, and he was more itinerant (114). Le Tellier, albeit a man of the robe, was one of the most subtle courtiers of his generation (97).

Louvois, brought up to ministerial life and a born administrator, only imposed his will upon generals because he channelled his frustrated military vocation in this somewhat curious way. From the Le Tellier association emerged, around 1666, an army rather different from the units which had fought the Thirty Years' War for France. It was a royal army. Beginning in 1656, the king nominated the infantry officers. He left the office of colonel-in-chief of the cavalry in being, but emasculated its powers. Henceforth, it was the monarch who appointed not just the marshals of France, the commanders-in-chief of armies and the brigadier-generals, but every officer down to the colonels. The king and his ministers also introduced a greater order into the ranks. From 1661 onwards, the lieutenant-colonel became the regimental commander-in-chief (165). Also, the administrative importance of the major gradually increased. The principles of a military hierarchy were clearly visible from 1653, and they were progressively implemented. In order, for example, to prevent a rapid expansion in the numbers of officers, the king decided that the officers of disbanded or 'reformed' companies who wished to retain a degree of military involvement should be maintained on half-pay 'in reserve'. At the same time, the ambition of abolishing venality (Louvois would limit it to colonels and captains) inspired some preliminary measures intended to serve as a model. In 1664, venality was suppressed in the four companies of the royal bodyguard, the elite force amidst the royal household troops.

Louis XIV and Le Tellier appreciated how important the daily conditions of army life were. An ordinance of 20 July 1660 laid down the rules for the regular payment of troops. Another (in 1665) regulated troop movements and billets (*étapes*). A third governed the length of military campaigns and a fourth the calibre of ammunition. But, above all, the king and his minister appreciated the importance of the use of psychology in any military system. Up until 1708, their forces lacked any organized system of medical provision; but, from 1647 onwards, dozens of ordinances were issued which laid down the system of precedence governing the corps, for the regular troops as well as for the household troops. In the latter, the bodyguards were the premier division, followed by the household cavalry or *grande gendarmerie* (made up of the *gendarmes* and *chevau-légers* of the king), the musketeers, the other household cavalry or *petite gendarmerie* (composed of the *gendarmes* and *chevau-légers* of the queens of France, Monseigneur and Monsieur), the French guards and the Swiss guards. Among the regular troops, the French troops had precedence over regiments of foreigners. In the French infantry, precedence belonged to the six 'Veteran Corps', 'who marched in the following order: Picardy, Piedmont, Champagne, Navarre, Normandy and the Marines. There were also six auxiliary veteran regiments, created a little later on, which were named after their colonels' (138). The other regiments followed, with the date of their creation determining their precedence. In this way, an *esprit de corps* was gradually instilled in the army. In 1666, an infantry soldier proudly belonging to the veteran corps would have reckoned himself the superior of a 'master' (*maître* was how soldiers addressed one another), even a sergeant (*maréchal des logis*), in a regiment of more recent creation. How, in a century so attached to status, would it have been possible to remove it from the army? With hierarchy, selection, organization and competition already being instilled in them, there only remained, as the king recognized, the need to increase numbers and, in December 1665, he created thirty-seven new cavalry regiments (165). This move alarmed Spain and the whole of Europe.

A SECRET WEAPON: THE NAVY

The power of France's armies was manifest in the victories which preceded the Peace of Westphalia and that of the Pyrenees; but the same could not be said of the navy. 'In 1660, the French . . . navy had only nine ships of the line, and even then they were of the third rank, to which one should add three fly-boats (for a total of twelve ships) and a few galleys.' (237) This is why the naval force which Colbert assembled in the years after 1661 may be termed the king's 'secret weapon'.

The navy did not emerge from the waves like Venus, and what is regarded as its inception was, in reality, its reformation. The awakening of France's maritime potential was, in fact, Richelieu's achievement; for he, with his imaginative grasp, had understood that the oceans represented a strategically important space. In a period when a naval vessel was not very different from a merchant vessel, the cardinal saw how naval force had to be linked to mercantile ambition (276). He was only partially successful: France's lack of a strong naval tradition, the archaic divisions of its admiralty and the priority accorded to the defence of the landward frontiers during the wars against the Habsburgs did not favour success. Geographical constraints also played their part: whilst the English were, by their island existence, bound of necessity to be good mariners, and the Dutch relied for their wealth upon the sea, the French coastline was divided between the 'Levant' (the shores of the Mediterranean, where the galley ruled the waves) and the 'Ponant' (from Bayonne to Dunkirk). But Richelieu had not laboured in vain. He nationalized the navy and, in his role as *grand maître, chef et surintendant général de la navigation* (from 1626), he began to dominate the four separate admiralties of France, Guyenne, Brittany and Provence and to replace their judicial and defensive mentality with a sense of overall strategic command. So, although his plans for harbours did not get very far, since Brouage silted up repeatedly, and although his plans to build ships remained insufficient, he had set up an impetus which may be measured in the success of Colbert's efforts.

From 1660, Colbert concentrated on the Mediterranean galleys; but, from September 1661, he was *de facto* in charge of both the Levant and Ponant seas. From the end of 1665, he was the equivalent of a secretary of state for the navy, and this was his position formally from 12 November 1669, when he attained the peak of his naval powers (273). Until 1683, Colbert directed the navy, and his son, Seignelay, would continue his policies of prudent financial management coupled with bold strategic thinking. However, it is now generally thought that Louis (1690–99) and even more Jérôme (1699–1715) de Pontchartrain were the most worthy continuators of this newly established tradition.*

Colbert's career is ample testimony to Louis XIV's concerns for the navy, and the extension of Colbert's powers in this area to those of a minister was one of the important acts of the first phase of the personal rule. The king's devoted interest in Dunkirk, purchased from England in 1662 and visited by Louis in 1680, was not for its political, military and religious significance alone, but also because of its naval importance. From 1661

---

* This conclusion has been taken from the works of Professor Charles Frostin (183–7).

to 1683, Colbert worked alongside the king on naval matters – at least 4,000 hours of contact – and yet how many authors have repeatedly said that naval affairs hardly mattered to Louis XIV! It was, of course, the case that his personal involvement as an active commander of armed forces was limited to the army. But how could Colbert have spent so much, equipped and fortified so many arsenals and harbours, constructed so many ships, over-turned so many cherished habits and tormented the lives of so many officers and sailors without the regular support of the king? Upon Colbert's death, the navy was composed of 112 ships of the line, 25 frigates, 7 fire-ships, 16 corvettes, 20 fly-boats (237) and 40 fighting galleys (293), 45 more ships than the English Royal Navy and 220 vessels overall in active service.

To have built up a naval force like this in twenty years implied the development of a competitive spirit, created by Colbert, and with the king as its arbiter and patron. The best naval comman-ders in service in 1683, such as Amblimont, Coëtlogon, Relingues and Villette, and, among the squadron commanders, Amfreville, Châteaurenault and Jean Gabaret, as well as Lieutenant-General Preuilly, were recruited from the army. There were, inevitably, some failures: the comte d'Estrées, for example, a lieutenant-general in the army, joined the navy and became (somewhat prematurely) a vice-admiral before putting his squadron on the rocks in 1678 in the West Indies (274). But the navy, although put together very quickly and faced with experienced competition, soon acquitted itself well in combat.

Officers and captains were not everything; sailors were also needed, and Colbert attempted to abandon the appalling system of press-ganging naval recruits, by introducing, in 1669, the system of 'classes' – a forerunner to naval enlistment –, which was designed to recruit sailors with, at least, a certain mini-mum of competence by means of conscription. This was an imaginative scheme, although, in the provision of naval adminis-trators, Colbert largely copied Le Tellier. By order of the king, these administrative officers (intendants, commissioners, stores-attendants, marine scribes) enjoyed a status higher than that of their equivalents in the army. Trained, disciplined and more ship-shape than the vessels they administered, they managed the arsenals at Brest, Toulon and Rochefort (created in 1666 to replace Brouage) as well as others at Dunkirk, Le Havre, and Marseille, the home-port for the galleys.

Many have criticized the 'tyranny' of these administrators without any sense that a Relingues or a Gabaret would never have been able to manage the finances of a naval port, just as the intendants would not have known how to command a squadron in war. The administrators of the navy, mostly *gens de la robe*, had immense powers, powers indispensable to the nationalization of the fleet under Louis XIV. Colbert used an enlightened nepotism in keeping an eye upon his administrators. He appointed his cousin Jean Colbert de Terron as a commissioner-general in 1661 and, in 1666, Terron was intendant-general of the Atlantic fleet (posted at Rochefort). The minister made another cousin, Michel Bégon (1638–1710), an intendant of the French West Indies in 1682, and later an intendant at Rochefort, whilst Michel's brother, François (1650–1725), was created an under-secretary to the naval treasurer at Toulon (126).

SHIPS OF THE LINE AND GALLEYS

There is an intriguing painting by Jean-Baptiste de la Rose in the museum at Versailles which portrays Seignelay, duc de Vivonne, the general of the galleys, and M. Brodart, the intendant, being shown the construction of a galley in kit-form at Marseille in the autumn of 1679. It took less than a day to construct (202). Colbert and Seignelay were obsessed by these beautiful ships. In Mediterranean waters their efficiency remained remarkable; for galleys could sail into the wind without tacking and had none of the complexity of old-fashioned triremes. They were light and manœuvrable, thanks to their lateen sails and the sleekness of their hull design. They had crack officers at the helm and the oarsmen were convicted criminals, mostly army deserters. When becalmed, they could proceed using oars, which assured them an advantage over sailing vessels. But their artillery could only fire in line with the ship.

So long as they stayed in the Mediterranean, the galleys enjoyed a stay of execution – the last galley left Marseille as late as 1748 – and besides, adversaries such as the Spanish, sworn enemies like the Turks and friends as well, such as the pope and the Knights of Malta, continued to build galleys. This was why Louis XIV made it a matter of prestige and built the *Réale*, as large, beautiful and fast as the Spanish *Réale*, and encouraged his ministers to arrive at a fleet of forty galleys to outclass the ships of the Catholic king. The Colberts adopted the attachments of their master and, equally impressed by the beauty of these ships, they entertained for thirty years the dream of employing some squadrons of galleys in the Atlantic. This was why galleys, invariably useless there because of their hull designs, sometimes appeared in the Atlantic ports of Rochefort and Dunkirk.

In the Atlantic, on the other hand, broader-bottomed hulls were the centre of the attentions of the minister and the king's shipyards. Determined that France be the equal of Holland and England, Colbert wanted results, and quickly, in terms of quality, speed and prestige. A first-rate master carpenter had to construct a ship in five months. For the construction of robust and seaworthy ships, he had recourse to industrial espionage, and attracted Dutch shipbuilders to France. It did not take long for French master craftsmen with experience to become more specialized naval engineers. By the end of the reign, it was the English who were trying to pirate French naval designs. As the navy developed, the skilled constructors in the arsenals could refer to books such as Dassié's *Naval Architecture* (1677) or *The Theory of the Construction of Vessels*, written by de Tourville (and published in 1697 under the assumed name of Paul Hoste).

Colbert wanted ships with a turn of speed. Around 1670, a carpenter wrote to him that he had drawn up designs for the hull of a frigate based upon the proportions of certain fish (276). Royal prestige demanded impressive vessels, and the minister was also concerned with the elegance and majesty of the designs. There were elaborate bowsprits with faces on them and crenellated transoms to the rear (146). The ships of the line at the beginning of the personal rule were decorated by Le Brun himself, as with the *Soleil Royal*, constructed at Brest in 1669 and sunk off Cherbourg in 1692 with part of the fleet under the command of M. de Tourville. Others included carvings by Puget. However, technical prowess was of pre-eminent importance. There was a sustained attempt to adapt ships to the tasks for which they were destined. The Colbert clan discovered and protected the famous Petit-Renau, a Basque whose full name was Bernard Renau d'Elissagaray, who 'invented a machine to trace the template of a vessel's hull and then effected the design of small ships armed with large cannon which fired along the ship's axis' to a range of nearly two miles (274). Duquesne turned this into a powerful weapon in the bombardment of Algiers in 1682.

To solve the problems faced by the variety of the equipment that was required, Colbert and Seignelay set in hand, at least in the three principal arsenals, at Brest, Rochefort and Toulon, 'an industrial environment' (276), which brought together sawmills, foundries, rope-yards, sailmaking shops and other facilities. But Colbert had only partially persuaded Louis XIV of the potential of maritime effort. The minister and his monarch had, in any case, grasped that the Dutch and the English enjoyed too great a lead in the commercial sector. The idea of balancing the naval force with the mercantile marine was thus abandoned. Where Colbert showed himself more far-sighted than Richelieu was in gaining the king's approval for naval growth. Without trying to compete directly with the major maritime powers, France could invest in naval hardware and, in this sector, compete with its rivals. The king and Colbert went one better than dreaming of a great naval force: they built it, and, within a few years, saw it operational (1664–74). The risks came, obviously, when it was put to use.

AN EFFECTIVE WEAPON: DIPLOMACY

'Did Louis XIV undertake the direction of foreign policy himself? An elementary question since the reply is immediately: yes.' (281) Nothing assumed a greater importance than negotiations, alliances and treaties. It was in relation to other states that prestige and glory were to be measured. Diplomacy was, *par excellence*, the weapon to wield in the protecting of his patrimony. Governing the kingdom might involve delegation of power, but nobody else could be entrusted with the conduct of foreign affairs. And, as if to leave no one, from Monseigneur onwards, in any doubt, he gave diplomatic matters pride of place in his *Mémoires*.

Four ministers were involved in the shaping of diplomacy in the course of the personal rule: Lionne (d. 1671), Arnauld de Pomponne (disgraced in 1679), Colbert de Croissy (d. 1696) and his son Torcy (politely dismissed in 1715). But, beyond these figures, many other advisers influenced policy, including Turenne, Colbert, Louvois, Chamlay, Chamillart, the chancellor Pontchartrain, and even the comte de Bergeyck. But the king remained in charge of the final decision to be taken and of its execution (281). Responsibility for decisions in foreign affairs should be seen as entirely his.

On the eve of the War of Devolution, Louis imagined the conflict with Spain as a 'vast battlefield' offering him 'signal opportunities'. But he qualified this immediately with the remark that 'The grandeur of our courage should not make us neglect how rational thought may be of assistance' (63); thus it was the case that the king's *gloire* symbolized that of the nation itself, a nation of Sancho Panzas as well as Don Quixotes. *Gloire* was to be achieved by the defeat of the House of Austria, both in the Spanish peninsula and in its empire, a conflict in which everything seemed to be working in France's favour. France's demographic vitality did more than compensate for the economic advances of the Low Countries and England. The emperor had retreated, Italy was divided, and the Most Christian King had defeated His Catholic Majesty in a long war. During the triumphal entry of Louis and Maria Theresa into Paris in 1660, a typical inscription, upon an arch adjacent to the statue of Henry IV, compared the young king to his grandfather and ran: 'Both gave their people the benefits of peace; but the latter extended it to the whole world, pacifying all the nations through his good offices.' (281)

Nothing assisted this more than the support of French clients abroad. The King of France was rich enough to undertake a systematic effort 'to purchase the loyalty of princes and ministers abroad. One might say that the whole of Europe was purchasable' (281). In the Holy Roman Empire, princes and bishops rivalled each other to be placed on the subsidy list. But France also despatched sacks of *écus* to the restored King of England, Charles II, to the discontented elements in Hungary, to the King of Poland and to his Swedish allies. In return, the French government hoped to frustrate the English parliament, play the German princes against the emperor, and sustain doubtful allies. Up to the Peace of Nymwegen in 1678–9, Louis' diplomacy used this method of operation, although the ministers of the Sun King were not at all surprised by the fickleness and deviousness of those who thought themselves insufficiently rewarded.

The Swedish example is instructive in this respect. France showered largesse on this country of less than three million people. Sweden enjoyed rich pickings in the Peace of Westphalia in 1648, and the favourable Treaty of Oliva in 1660 was brought about through Mazarin's good offices. In addition, France, 'Sweden's historic ally', signed a trade treaty with it in 1663. But all this did not stop Sweden from negotiating with England in 1665 and 1672 and with the Dutch in 1675 and 1679. Sweden sold itself to the highest bidder. At the beginning of 1668, it joined the Triple Alliance and its English and Dutch partners promised it 480,000 rix-dollars in silver. However, its anti-French stance remained purely theoretical, providing that it continued to receive subsidies from Paris. In 1672, the same Swedish government assured France that they would intervene against the German princes and even against Dutch shipping in return for an annual payment of 400,000 *écus*, rising to 600,000 in time of war. This time, they carried out their promise, thanks to Pomponne, although it cost them dearly (257).

After Nymwegen, things were not so easy. The Reunions were not well regarded in the Holy Roman Empire. Catholics held it against His Most Christian Majesty that he had not gone to the defence of Vienna against the Turkish threat. Protestant princes never forgave him the Revocation (1685). Willing clients were less easily sustained. In any case, such a policy was ruinously expensive and France's finances were creeping towards a disaster. But in the 1660s, all this was far away. French diplomacy had no need of secrecy; exploiting its considerable prestige, it browbeat here and seduced there, always and everywhere making its presence felt.

ACTS OF MAGNIFICENCE

With eighteen million subjects, a growing army and navy, a reformed administration, an impressive clergy and its intellectual standing, France was destined, in an age when destiny mattered, to demonstrate and even to abuse its great power. To these positive elements which enabled Louis XIV to inaugurate his personal rule in Europe like a general sounding the advance should be added the negative elements, those which set the scene in Europe for the advance to occur.

Emperor Leopold I lost all direct influence over the princes of the empire. From 1662, he was faced with the Turkish threat. In Madrid, the dynastic future rested with the Infante, the puny future Charles II, born on 6 November 1661. In London, as Louis XIV wrote in his *Mémoires* for 1661: 'Cromwell was dead and the king restored'; the marriage of Monsieur to Charles II of England's sister helped to retain the Stuarts within the French king's orbit (63). Well-directed pensions would do the rest. In the Low Countries, the restless, Protestant House of Orange, with its imperialist leanings, was temporarily out of power. The office of stadholder no longer existed and the patricians of Holland directed the republic. Jan de Witt, 'the grand pensionary', was warmer towards France than the stadholders and the Orangist party had been. The princes of Italy were either allies or afraid. There were contacts in the Levant, Hungary, Russia and Poland. Before assembling all his other reinforcements, his army of 150,000 men and his navy of 100 ships of the line, Louis XIV was already far along the road of impressing upon Europe the image of a formidable king. His 'acts of magnificence' were designed to give every chancellery in Europe the measure of his personal rule.

On 10 October 1661, Baron de Watteville, the King of Spain's representative in London, forcefully denied to Louis XIV's ambassador, the comte d'Estrades, the honour of precedence customarily accorded to the French ambassador. Louis expelled from France Count Fuensaldagna, Philip IV's ambassador and then, when the King of Spain proposed to recall Watteville and to have his ambassadors absent themselves from all public occasions in London, Louis replied by demanding that the undertaking not to 'compete' with French envoys should be extended to all the courts of Europe. On 4 May 1662, the French king accepted, in a formal audience whose proceedings were minuted by the four secretaries of state, the apologies of Spain. This 'joyous theme' became one of the subjects of the official history of the kingdom, depicted in a medallion ('JUS PRAECEDENDI ASSERTUM CONFITENTE HISPANORUM ORATORE XXIV MARTII M. DC. LXII, *The rights of precedence confirmed by the Spanish Ambassador's Undertaking*' (71)). It would also be the subject of a panel in the Hall of Mirrors (*galerie des glaces*) at Versailles, prepared from a sketch by Le Brun, depicting 'France and Spain as two women easily recognizable by the symbols, Spain in the form of someone presenting her apologies and whose emblem, a lion, is crouching at the feet of France, who has Justice standing close by, holding up her finely balanced scales, indicating her approval for what was happening' (53b).

The humiliation of Spain might have been sufficient as final proof of French hegemony in Europe, but Louis XIV had other ideas. In the course of 1662 alone, he was seen to try to overthrow Duke Charles IV of Lorraine by means of a secret treaty,* to lay down the law to the Papacy over the trivial matter of the Corsican guard, and finally to impose *de facto* upon the King of England a new precedent regarding the hoisting of the flag on board naval vessels. If Charles II had been less desperate for subsidies, this dispute might well have provoked a war. But he needed them, and it is clear that, in the 1660s, the French king, in pursuing 'his own whims', was leading events, sensing the moment when not to push matters too far. Would that this sense had been maintained!

* See ch. 13.

13

Glorious Endeavours

A COMMON reproach of the Sun King is to point out the length of 'his' wars: six years for the Dutch War, ten for the War of the League of Augsburg, thirteen for the War of the Spanish Succession – the war for the queen's rightful inheritance (1667–8) being regarded as 'no more than a military manœuvre'. Clearly, to some, there is a mystical proportion between the number of years that a war lasted and the number wounded or killed. If it were accepted that the wars ascribed to him took place in circumstances favourable to France and with beneficial results, these criticisms would have little force. It is also often forgotten that Louis' predecessors fought or engaged in 'their' wars in circumstances which were much more desperate, with internal security in question and the realm threatened with invasion. Nor should the results of these conflicts be ignored. It is still widely believed to be the case that France lost much in terms of territory by the terms of the Peace of Utrecht (1712–13); but it is a simple exercise to draw a map of the limits of France in 1715 and subtract the frontier limits of 1661: the difference is a measure of the results of war. In 1667, warfare was discussed in terms purely of the king's glory, not even distinguishing it from that of the realm. The search for glory, in and for itself, did not then seem to be an empty quest. As Montesquieu said, monarchy was founded upon honour – nothing in its pursuit could be regarded as fruitless.

TASK FORCES

The formalism of great treaties of pacification tends to make the division between war and peace too neat. In the seventeenth century, the distinction was less legalistic. Statesmen did not wait until a declaration of war before commencing hostilities; nor did they fight on until the whistle before starting to negotiate peace. A peace treaty was often only a cease-fire. War was sometimes more like peace in disguise and peace, more often still, an armed truce.

These terms, 'war' and 'peace', are too abstract and do not adequately describe the experience of the smaller states on the frontier. What, for example, of the relations between France and the unfortunate duchy of Lorraine? How should one define the situation of its inhabitants between Louis XIV's accession and his death? Was there the least difference between the policies of one Bourbon and those of another? When in 1633 Louis XIII provoked the abdication of Duke Charles IV of Lorraine and occupied the duchy, this was already the third French invasion of it. Since 1552, Metz, Toul and Verdun had been under occupation and, by the terms of the Peace of Westphalia, they became sovereign French territory. Scarcely had Duke Charles IV been reinstalled in his duchy than, in 1641, he began again his hostilities against Louis XIII, leading to the fourth French invasion of the region and its occupation until 1661. The second occupation under Louis XIV (1670–97) was for the same reason as the first – to teach Lorraine a lesson for having allied with the Imperialists against France – coupled with a new consideration, France's annexation of neighbouring Alsace. As for the third occupation of Lorraine under Louis XIV (1702–14), its dates are significant: faced with a European coalition and an emperor who contested Philip V's succession to the Spanish Crown, and with French territory stretching into Alsace, no statesman could have surrendered to the empire or its allies those lands which dominated the eastern march of the kingdom.

When Louis XIV's personal rule began, the balance of forces lay in France's favour. For nineteen years, it had occupied the duchy. For thirteen years, its sovereignty in Metz, Toul and Verdun had been undisputed. A *parlement* in Metz had been established in January 1633 with pioneering and aggressive intentions (it would be the instrument of the Reunions). No one took

Duke Charles IV seriously. He had abdicated and then retracted his abdication. He had been left out of the Congress of Westphalia. He had been the prisoner of the King of Spain. The Peace of the Pyrenees left him only a fragment of his former duchy. And, at the close of 1660, he was in Paris begging for assistance. Louis and Mazarin agreed condescendingly at the Treaty of Vincennes (28 February 1661) to restore the duchy of Bar to him, subject to an obligation to pay homage to the French king. However, such agreements fooled no one. Louis XIV needed Lorraine too much and Charles IV had played the Imperialist card too often for his own good.

With Mazarin barely in his grave, the duke rendered homage to the French king on 22 March 1661. France had cut the duchy in two and Nancy had no fortifications left standing. Nevertheless, Charles IV carried on in support of Louis XIV, his nephew and heir, although there was no love lost between them. By the Treaty of Montmartre (1662), he arranged for Lorraine and Bar to revert to the French Crown and, in the meantime, he ceded Marsal to France as his pledge upon the agreement. However, in 1663, before French troops moved to take over Marsal, Louis XIV learnt that Charles IV had strengthened the garrison there. As his predecessors Henry IV and Louis XIII had done, he ordered its siege.

Marsal was not large, but it commanded the approaches to Metz and Nancy. From 1632 onwards, it had been at the heart of all the negotiations between France and Lorraine. If he had to go to war to secure it, Louis XIV had decided that it was worth the effort, and that it merited his going to Marsal to supervise the siege in person. So, having celebrated the feast of St Louis in the Louvre, Louis XIV departed for Châlons on 25 August. By the 30th, he was at Metz. On the 31st, he reviewed the troops of the maréchal de la Ferté-Senneterre, who was preparing to tighten the grip of the siege. A demonstration of force was all that was needed. On Monday, 3 September, Charles IV came to Metz to sign a new agreement. Marsal became French, a victory which it was easy to present as won without a fight.

Upon Louis XIV's instructions, a portion of the French army was always ready for service. This was eighty years earlier than Frederick the Great's system, the one which assured the successes of his campaigns. Without the French contingent under the comte de Coligny, Montecuccoli would never have so easily defeated the Turks of the grand vizier Köprülü at St Gotthard and Vienna would not have been spared (1 August 1664). Also in 1664, it was a French force of 6,000 soldiers, this time under the command of M. de Pradel, which seized Erfurt and returned the town to the authority of the Archbishop of Mainz. Some months later, Louis XIV sent a small army to aid the United Provinces. A defence treaty between the two countries had been signed in Paris on 27 April 1662. And now, taking advantage of the Anglo–Dutch confrontations, the Bishop of Münster had invaded the republic with 25,000 men. At sea, France tried out Colbert's fleet and lent assistance to the Dutch in the Caribbean in 1666. These four initiatives had the common political purpose of demonstrating the value France attached to its allies. They also had a military purpose: the naval and land forces of the Most Christian King could strike at will. Behind it all lay a sense of global strategy. Although Louis XIV's discretion prevented him from saying it openly, it is clear that the early military dispositions of the personal rule represented the king's preferred forms of campaign, the lightning strike rather than the war of attrition. Was this not Frederick the Great's ideal, but carried out a century earlier?

THE QUEEN'S RIGHTS OR SUPERIOR STRENGTH ?

Mignet analysed the reign of Louis XIV around the theme of the Spanish succession. This is to impart to Louis a simplicity of thought and an obstinacy which are only to be found in ideologues and not in pragmatists. Besides, when Europe learnt at the beginning of September 1665 that Philip IV was going to die leaving a sickly child of only four years of age, no statesman imagined that the succession to the Madrid throne would keep the world in suspense, at times seeming imminent and at others remote, until November 1700. In the weeks following Philip IV's demise, the chancelleries of Europe were obsessed with the health of Don Carlos, now Charles II, and preoccupied with Philip IV's will conferring the regency upon his wife and the inheritance upon his son. It reiterated that Maria Theresa was eliminated from the succession, as stipulated in the treaty of 1659. If the male line died out, the whole inheritance would pass

2 ANNE OF AUSTRIA was thirty-eight when she gave birth to Louis XIV. Until then her position at court was difficult. By the time of Philippe de Champaigne's flattering portrait, her penchants for gambling and ballet-dancing, as well as her piety, were well known. When regent, she relied heavily on Mazarin. (*Collection Moussalle*)

1 (*Previous page*) LOUIS XIII presided over profound changes in French government and society, changes which Louis XIV, who was loyal to his memory, made permanent. In this painting, Rubens suggests Louis XIII's rapid changes in mood by portraying him in a warrior's costume and courtier's ruff. (*Collection L. Deveen*)

3 THE BIRTH OF THE 'DIEUDONNÉ', occurred on the morning of 5 September 1638, in the château of Saint-Germain-en-Laye, just outside Paris.

4 LOUIS XIV WITH HIS WET-NURSE. Although Louis was wet-nursed, Anne of Austria, according to a contemporary account, 'rarely leaves him' and 'takes great pleasure in playing with him and wheeling him in his carriage in fine weather'.

5 LOUIS XIV IN INFANT CLOTHES and wearing, in this painting by
Denut Claudel, the blue riband and the insignia of the Order of the
Holy Spirit, into which he was invested by his father.

6 (*Opposite*) VERSAILLES, A PERPETUAL BUILDING-SITE. J.-B. Martin
here used rising ground to the east to record the developments. In the
foreground, the king surveys plans for a reservoir (*c*.1689). In the
background, to the left, is the avenue de Paris and, to the right, the old
town of Versailles. (*Musée de Versailles*)

7 THE FRONDE IN PARIS. 'Advice with a *frondeur* presents to Parisians, whom he exhorts to rebel against the tyranny of Cardinal Mazarin', an engraving from a *mazarinade* of 6 January 1649. The court was in Saint-Germain preparing for a siege. On the 7th, the sovereign courts were ordered to leave Paris. The stage was set for civil war.

8 (*Opposite*) CARDINAL JULES MAZARIN. Mazarin's influence on Louis XIV's political, spiritual and intellectual formation was profound. In this magnificent *ad vivam* painting by Philippe de Champaigne are conveyed the cardinal's exquisite refinement and his firmness and self-effacing subtlety. (*Musée Condé, Chantilly*)

9 THE TEN-YEAR-OLD KING, dressed in royal stole and mantle, in the year of the Fronde, portrayed here by Henri Tortellin. (*Musée Condé, Chantilly*)

10 PLENIPOTENTIARIES FROM FRANCE, THE NETHERLANDS AND THE EMPIRE PLEDGE THEMSELVES TO PEACE AT MÜNSTER (24 October 1648). This agreement, years in the making and part of the Peace of Westphalia, was the basis of France's dominant influence in Germany in Louis XIV's reign.

BOURBON-CONDÉ
(Louis II, le Grand)
1621–1686

11 THE SCHOOL OF MARS: LOUIS II DE BOURBON-CONDÉ. The 'Great Condé' early enjoyed a heroic military reputation. His initial loyalty in the Fronde ensured Mazarin and Anne of Austria their freedom of manœuvre. Juste d'Egmont's portrait of him, in full armour and grasping a marshal's baton, was probably painted at about that time. (*Musée Condé, Chantilly*)

Lespagnol sourd en france

Il luy met bien la bague au doigt
Mais quand au point du mariage
Il est sourd et fort mal adroit
a faire cet apprentissage

13 CARICATURE OF THE PEACE OF THE PYRENEES (1659). The Peace gave the details of the marriage contract of Louis XIV and Maria Theresa. It was widely thought, as this engraving suggests, that Spain (a deaf pantomine clown) would be unable to pay the compensation it stipulated for the loss of Maria Theresa's right to succeed to the Spanish throne. (*Bibliothèque Nationale*)

12 (*Opposite*) THE BATTLE OF THE DUNES (14 June 1658). The French military victories in Flanders in 1657–8 opened the way to peace negotiations with Spain. In this dramatic representation by La Rivière, Turenne leads the French forces in the battle which led to the capitulation of Dunkirk (depicted in the distance). (*Musée de Versailles*)

14 LOUIS XIV'S TRIUMPHAL ENTRY INTO PARIS (22 August 1660) was the last time a French king made a traditional 'Joyous Entry' into his capital. It was a celebration of peace, of the king's plenitude of power and of his marriage. In this engraving of 1661, the queen's carriage, drawn by Danish greys, precedes the king's.

15 JEAN-BAPTISTE COLBERT, whose letters provide ample evidence of his extraordinary energy and grasp of and attention to detail, was the greatest administrator of the Bourbon monarchy.

16 EARLY MEMORANDUM FROM HUGUES DE LIONNE. The king's foreign minister was quick to recognize, and appreciate the significance of, Louis' aptitude for government. Here he asks for rooms in the Louvre so that he and his secretaries might work more discreetly on royal business. Louis' comments are in the left-hand margin.

17 NICOLAS FOUQUET, 'THE SQUIRREL', marquis de Belle-Isle, was responsible, as superintendent of finances, for raising funds for France's war-effort in the 1650s. He was later attacked for his personal wealth. In 1661, Louis XIV had him arrested. He was prosecuted, found guilty and imprisoned for life. (*Bibliothèque Nationale*)

18 FRANCQIS-MICHEL LE TELLIER, MARQUIS DE LOUVOIS, succeeded his father as secretary of state for war after a long apprenticeship. He was a force at court for thirty years. Though harshly judged then and later for the *dragonnades* and the destruction of the Palatinate, his political and administrative talents were considerable. (*Musée de Versailles*)

19 JEAN-BAPTISTE POQUELIN, KNOWN AS MOLIÈRE. His plays set the moral tone for Louis XIV's court, and he amply recorded his admiration for the king. Louis applauded his social criticism and humour, and rewarded him despite contemporary criticism. (*Comédie Française*)

to Margaret Theresa, the king's younger daughter, who was promised in marriage to Emperor Leopold.

French diplomacy had to take account of all these unfavourable elements. But Louis XIV could turn the war between the English and Dutch (1665–7) to his advantage, and, meanwhile, his entourage set to work to restore the rights of Maria Theresa. The first argument was that of 'compensation'. The 500,000 *écus* dowry, promised in 1659, remained almost totally unpaid. If the articles upon the dowry had remained null, why should the same not also be true for the articles of renunciation? However, if the articles of renunciation were valid, then compensation in the form of territory would be necessary for the absence of the dowry.

The second argument was that of 'devolution'. According to the customary law of Brabant, in cases of more than one marriage, the inheritance passed to the children from the first marriage. Thus Maria Theresa, a child by a first marriage, should be given the inheritance of Brabant to the exclusion of Charles II, who was a child by Philip's second wife. What Louis XIV's jurists did not say was that devolution was only applicable in private law. The idea of devolution was developed in a book entitled *A Treatise upon the Rights of the Most Christian Queen to Various States in the Spanish Monarchy*, which indicated the various demands which led Louis XIV to the brink of war. Using the law of devolution, France demanded fourteen provinces or fiefs: Antwerp, imperial Flanders, Malines, Limburg, Upper Gelderland, Brabant, the remainder of Artois, the Cambrésis, Hainaut, the Namurois, Roche-en-Ardenne, Arlon, and a small part of Luxembourg, with part of the county of Burgundy (215). The law of devolution was really only a pretext. The concern for glory was evident and the deeper momentum was for the frontiers, a momentum continuing from preceding reigns.

It is now obvious that Louis XIV was making large demands in the hopes that he would secure a part of what he asked for. Nibbling away at the Low Countries, he never dreamt of a common border with the United Provinces. He knew that any occupation of the mouth of the Scheldt would make allies of the English and the Dutch, both Protestant countries and the 'maritime powers' of Europe. With Lionne's assistance, Louis XIV played a delicate game, threatening Spain but reassuring London and The Hague at the same time.

With his ultimatum and a plethora of legal justifications to hand, the King of France broadcast his claims abroad in the early spring of 1667. At the end of April, a peace conference at Breda brought together England, the Dutch, Sweden, Denmark and France. The negotiations dragged on; but there was still everything to play for, although the reconciliation of London with the United Provinces threatened the realization of French plans. On 8 May, Louis XIV sent a summary of the *Treatise upon the Rights* . . . to the queen regent in Spain. On the 9th, he also sent a copy to the States General in the Netherlands, along with a letter explaining why the peace negotiations had stalled (201). The Dutch were so alarmed that they attempted a coup against England: on 13 June, Ruyter sailed his fleet up the Thames estuary. On 31 July 1667, the Peace of Breda was concluded.

Philip IV's widow refused the French demand. She refused to give any concessions, 'not so much as a village or a hamlet in the Low Countries' (113). The response took no account of the accumulation of forces favourable to Louis XIV, who, for months, had been buying and constructing ships, founding cannon and setting up supply-points, garrisons and artillery magazines. The preparations were in no great secrecy and unhurried. On 19 January 1666, Turenne reviewed 10,000 troops in Picardy, whilst the king, not content with a march-past of his household troops and a few regiments, witnessed manœuvres for himself. Colbert complained about the cost of these troop reviews (113). To add prestige to this martial academy, organized by Louvois to indicate the progress already accomplished in the army, Louis was accompanied by a number of courtiers. Grosbois, Mouchy, Moret, Fontainebleau, Conflans, Colombes and, above all, the plain at Houilles served as display-grounds for the troops. On 5 and 6 May 1666, the household cavalry (*gardes du corps, gendarmes, chevau-légers*) as well as the French and Swiss guards marched past the king and queen, Monsieur and many courtiers. But the king's applause was reserved for Monseigneur, who, not yet five years old, marched at the head of the Dauphin's regiment. From 8 January 1666 to 22 April 1667, Louis XIV spent no less than twenty-two days in reviewing his troops (167).

'THE KING TAKES PLEASURE IN THE CONQUEST OF
FLANDERS' (96)

The assault on Flanders was begun in May 1667 by an army of 50,000 trained men. The governor of the Spanish Low Countries, Castel-Rodrigo, only had 20,000 soldiers. He knew that, 'barring a miracle' (113), he would be defeated. He could only garrison the fortresses as best he could.

The king did not contradict the advice of those with experience. He accepted Turenne's strategy and discovered the abilities of Vauban. He ruled, but did not direct, his armies. Part of the court and the government were on hand to appreciate how things went. Louis left Saint-Germain on 16 May and, from the 20th to the 24th, he reviewed his troops at Amiens in the presence of the queen (whose rights the soldiers were championing), the duchesse de la Vallière (the letters-patent for the dukedom of Vaujours were issued during the month, but she had ceased to please the king) and Athénaïs de Rochechouart (marquise de Montespan, a star in the ascendant). On 25 May, this small court arrived in Compiègne, and, from 8 to 14 June and from 20 July to 4 September, the queen, accompanied by others from the court, returned to Compiègne to celebrate a conqueror who seemed to come straight from the pages of Ariosto. Had the heroes of the Enchanted Isle taken, perhaps, the Low Countries as a kind of stage? Were not 'the queen's rights' a kind of pledge in a martial tournament?

These baroque exploits followed, it seemed, the dramatic conventions of Aristotle. There was 'unity of place and action' (Flanders, under Louis' authority) and even time, for the fortresses which were besieged were unable to resist the French onslaught or the science of its military engineers. D'Aumont took Bergues, Furnes, Armentières and Courtrai. Turenne accepted the surrender of Binche, Charleroi and Ath. The king directed the siege of Tournai, a town which would thereafter be close to his heart. The breach was opened up on the 22nd and the town surrendered on the 25th, its castle on the following day. The attack and capture of Douai took less than five days. Louis was present on 2 July when his army invested the town. It capitulated on the 6th and the king made a triumphal, albeit discreet, royal entry on the 7th. Since it was the inheritance of the queen that was being fought for, Louis and Maria Theresa made a further, formal entry into Douai two weeks later. However, strongholds were falling like ripe apples. On 1 August, Oudenaarde, besieged by the maréchal d'Aumont, surrendered and, the next day, Louis took Alost. On 10 August, he was within reach of Lille, one of the most strongly fortified towns in Flanders. It took less than nine days from the opening up of a breach in its walls to its capitulation, signed on the night of the 27–28 August (167). Vauban had played a major part in the success of the siege.

In the course of this martial summer, the court and the army were able to assess the king as he picked up his trophies. The marquis de Saint-Maurice gives us in his letters something of a living sketch of the king. It is the picture of a prince enjoying the game of war, with its risks and drudgeries. If necessary, 'he slept on the straw'. 'He spent the whole night under canvas and only went to bed as day broke' (3 July); he 'went to his tent, but only retired to bed at dawn' (18 August). In his councils of war, 'he issued his orders very deftly'. 'His army and its conquests occupy his whole mind.' He was 'decisive in danger and as poised as a dancer at a ball'. He risked his life, and his courage set an example:

> [In the siege of Lille, he] was all night and half the next day on horseback within range of the enemy cannon, visiting every tent and gun battery, although not the trenches, because the army officers did not want him to. A day or so back, knowing how dangerously exposed they were, he [the king] said to them: 'Since you want me to take care of myself for your sakes, I also want to make sure that you look after yourselves for mine.'

He looked 'weather-beaten and thinner', and wore 'buff and had his hair curled'. But he also appeared to be 'well turned out': 'He spent a lot of time dressing. He had his moustache curled and sometimes spent half an hour before the mirror arranging it with wax' (93). This was what a hero in the style of Ariosto, adapted to the Versailles stage, understood by the martial arts and how he prepared for the sweeter fruits of victory to come.

The rapidity and decisiveness of the French advance in the Low Countries disturbed Europe. It provoked frantic talks at Breda, a *rapprochement* between England and the United Provinces and then, finally, the Triple Alliance of The Hague (January–May 1668). The Dutch, English and Swedes threatened France with war if it held on to the conquests of 1667. In return, Louis XIV's agents responded with fair words and *écus*. M. de Grémonville, Louis' ambassador in Vienna, persuaded Leopold to accept, on 19 January 1668, a 'partition treaty', without the knowledge of Spain and its colonial empire.

Louis XIV hastened forward to his next project – to seize Franche Comté – without awaiting the outcome of Grémonville's treaty negotiations or those for the alliance at The Hague. Condé, the governor of Burgundy, was preferred by Louvois to Turenne and became the man of the moment. In December 1667, he arrived at Dijon to complete the preparations for a new lightning campaign. As for the king, he left Saint-Germain on 2 February 1668 and arrived at Dijon on the 7th to learn of the capitulation of Besançon. The prince de Condé had taken possession of the town without firing a shot. Salins also had no stomach for a fight, so Louis XIV appeared before the gates of Dôle, the provincial capital, on 10 February. The town surrendered on the 14th and opened its gates to Louis, who, accompanied by Condé, celebrated a *Te Deum* there, whilst Louvois, taking charge of things in a decisive fashion, dictated the text of the oath of loyalty which the town affirmed to the Most Christian King. The siege of Gray followed and Louis XIV arrived there on the 15th, receiving its surrender on the 19th, before heading back to Paris (167).

The inhabitants of Franche Comté had dreams of an impossible neutrality, and were sometimes bitter about the turn of events. They realized that the lightning campaign had been preceded by a process of persuasion among the provincial notables, and spoke of treason in their ranks. When the French withdrew their troops, they would light bonfires and proclaim Charles II of Spain their ruler. But when Spain, recovering some of its energies, enforced its rule, they complained of it once more in their habitual way.

Conquest without danger was not to be triumph without glory for Louis XIV and Condé. Whilst campaigning, they had assured the realm of a vital pawn at the negotiating table to secure 'the queen's rightful inheritance' in the circumstances created by the reconciliation of the maritime powers. Without the acquisition of Franche Comté, the Anglo-Dutch accord would have deprived France of its conquests of 1667. Thanks to it, Louis could conclude a favourable peace whilst posing as the generous victor. From the end of February, the Dutch offered their services as mediator. The intricacies of the negotiations increased as the intransigence of the Spanish pushed Jan de Witt into greater sympathy with France. At Saint-Germain, Louis XIV persuaded the hawks (Louvois, Turenne and Condé) to accept the point of view of the doves (Le Tellier, Colbert and Lionne). On 15 April, the preliminary accords to the pacification were signed.

The treaty was concluded at Aix-la-Chapelle on 2 May after intense, but not long-drawn-out, negotiations. The King of France agreed to restore Franche Comté to King Charles II of Spain, but, in return, he gained some useful possessions. Bergues and Furnes completed French dominion in maritime Flanders. The acquisition of Binche and Charleroi gave France the upper hand in Hainaut. But the greater part of the territorial acquisitions lay in French Flanders. The latter was not a discrete province but a collection of towns, with 'their own *bailliages*, *châtellenies*, governments, *prévôtés*, *appartenances*, dependencies and appendages' (215) – places such as Armentières, Menin, Oudenaarde, Tournai, Courtrai, Ath, Douai, and Lille. These towns were quickly fortified by Vauban, thus helping to put together the famous military 'iron curtain'. It constituted one stage in the conquest of the southern Netherlands. It was of no consequence, therefore, that there was no 'natural' frontier. It was for the diplomats, the military engineers and the generals of the king to extract the best from what had been achieved. And it was for the king to win the hearts of his new subjects. It was a bitter irony that the heart of the French acquisitions obtained at Aix-la-Chapelle were made in Walloon Flanders, which had no customary law of devolution. The 'rightful inheritance of the queen' would turn out to have been something from the pages of some chivalric novel.

'THE PATH OF HONOUR'

Louis XIV's crossing of the Rhine at Tolhuys on 12 June 1672 at the head of an army moving against the Dutch had everything of the chivalric about it. Voltaire said that it was 'one of those great events which would stay in the minds of men'. Bossuet called it the 'wonder of the century and of the life of Louis the Great'. In reality, two regiments of Dutch infantry without artillery and 500 cavalry without a stomach for a fight fled at the approach of 20,000 French troops, who, far from swimming across the river, forded it at a convenient spot. But the French preferred the legend to the real story. This is how one can measure the king's popularity and the success of his propaganda. But we should not underestimate the risks which he took, on other occasions, when the drudgeries of war took him away from the life at court: ninety-seven days away in 1672, one hundred and sixty-six in 1673, sixty-nine in 1674, seventy-two in 1675, eighty-four in 1676, ninety-three in 1677, sixty in 1678.

There is no substance to the view that, while Henry IV was a soldier and 'Louis XIII loved the army and battles', Louis XIV was nothing more than a 'parade-ground general' (158). Nothing made Monsieur in any way his superior.* Up to the end of the Dutch War, Louis displayed real qualities as a strategist and tactician. From the moment he entered a campaign, he commanded respect and symbolized the energies of the nation. He continued the tradition of his father and grandfather in leading 'his army in person' (159). Clausewitz would recognize that, by combining political and military decision-making, valuable time was thus gained. Contemporaries were aware of the value as an example to others of the risks he ran.

'To reinforce the tranquillity of his peoples', Fléchier wrote in 1673, 'he went on campaign himself . . . believing that, in justice, he owed it to his subjects to show them the path of honour.' (39) This was why Louis XIV shared in the arduousness and danger of serving-officers and soldiers, and when, later on, their battles appeared on medallions, in engravings and in tapestries, though the king's glory was writ large for propaganda purposes, it was never a complete fabrication.

To encourage others down the path of honour, Louis XIV increased the size of the nobility by ennobling soldiers to encourage a sense of loyalty and reinforce solidarities. From Maastricht (on 17 May 1672) to Ypres (13–26 March 1678), the king's schedule was motivated by scarcely any other consideration. The Dutch War, for which the king is so often criticized by historians, also fostered loyalty and patriotism and perhaps deserves, therefore, to be judged less severely.

* This is, however, the paradox maintained by Philippe Erlanger in *Monsieur, frère de Louis XIV* (1970).

THE INEVITABLE CONFLICT

The Dutch War, whatever Fénelon may have imagined, had no other cause than Louis XIV's thirst for glory. One can but refer to that 'vade-mecum' of French propaganda, the *Metallic History of the Reign*, which summarized the matter in contemporary terms thus:

> As soon as the Dutch recognized that they were in a position to do without French assistance, they dreamt of turning their forces against her. They fomented the discontent of neighbouring powers and concluded the famous treaty known as the 'Triple Alliance' with Sweden and England. Then, without any regard for what had been agreed upon trade and navigation with them in 1662, they refused rights of entry to a whole range of French export goods or levied high tariffs upon them. They even dared to put on public monuments boastful titles such as arbiters among sovereigns, defenders of the law, reformers of religion, masters of the sea; and they never missed an opportunity for giving the king particular matters for complaint. (71)

Such a text has the merit of evoking the 'political, economic and religious' (165) grievances which provoked and justified a widespread sentiment in Catholic circles in France. But it is one-sided, ignoring how much the Dutch had been exasperated by the Colbertian tariffs of 1667. Above all, it neglects the religious and the other economic and political circumstances behind the conflict which had been building up since 1648. The vaunted toleration in the United Provinces makes one forget that the Netherlands shared with Geneva and Scotland the privilege of being a Calvinist bastion. Those who say that France should have worked on an alliance with the Netherlands to restrict English power are accepting a Protestant logic. If William of Orange had died young, another stadholder would have excited the antipathy of his compatriots towards the French monarchy. And if the stadholdership had been eliminated, another grand pensionary would have replaced Jan de Witt and pushed France towards war. Behind the political frictions and economic competitiveness lay the barely disguised antagonisms of the Reformation and Counter-Reformation.

In political terms, the Spanish Netherlands lay between France and the United Provinces, not only territorially but also morally. The Hague was not unaware of the fact that France, following Mazarin's death, had aspirations to nibble away at these provinces, which were badly defended by Madrid and an easy target for the armies of Louis XIV. The more France ate into the region, the less the southern Netherlands would constitute a barrier between them. In this respect, Aix-la-Chapelle was far from having reassured the Netherlands. France had Lille and would progressively move northwards, manifesting its aim to go on doing so. So, to a republic of Calvinist merchants, more adept at trade and navigation than at land-based campaigns, the Catholic King was to be preferred to the Most Christian King as a neighbour.

The economic conflict would be a trigger. After 1668, Colbert was on the hawks' side. He had to a certain extent restored the king's finances, but reckoned that his protectionist tariffs had not achieved much. Holland must be eliminated, and Colbert therefore supported Louvois (165). Louvois was also a hawk. Having been associated with his father's post of secretary of state for war since 1662 and having had the reversion on it since 1655, he became its leading partner in 1670 (165). In two years, Louvois had everything prepared. The troops were well paid, and the start of the campaign, before the enemy had a chance to prepare any riposte, was flawless. When the war began, the magazines at Dunkirk, La Bassée, Courtrai, Le Quesnoy and Lille, Rocroi, Thionville, Metz, Nancy, Breisach and Pinerolo were stocked for six months (165). Nothing laid the foundations for a lightning campaign better than this logistic preparation.

It did not take long for Louis XIV to appreciate the worth of this young minister. He consulted him on strategic decisions, and accepted his advice on tactical matters too. Louvois participated in the councils of war, and attempted to impose his points of view upon famous captains such as Condé and Turenne. 'Before Maastricht in 1673, he was the real major-general in the army. He proved it by the lucidity and precision of the orders he gave. The presence of Louvois in an army guaranteed that the troops would be well turned out [soldiers were just beginning to become used to wearing uniforms], and there were times when Louis XIV required him to travel with an army when the result of an operation lay in doubt.' (165)

To his talent as an organizer, Louvois coupled that of a global strategist. He arrived at the title of minister on 1 February 1672, having served as a temporary minister in the department of foreign affairs. He persuaded the king in 1674 to restrict the freedom of initiative allowed to generals in the field. Inaugurating the 'overall strategy of the cabinet', he made himself no friends among the older army chiefs of staff, but established, in the king's name, a more-modern conception of warfare. The death of Turenne in 1675, Condé's disenchantment, and the institution of the 'table of ranks' (*ordre du tableau*) (also in 1675), to regularize promotion and command structures, favoured this revolution, which, although it was criticized fifty years later by Saint-Simon, was, without a doubt, an indispensable step forwards.

PRAEVIANS VICTORIA (71)

On 6 April 1672, Louis XIV declared war on the United Provinces. On the 23rd, he delegated powers to the queen 'to command in the kingdom during his absence' (201). By the middle of May, he had entered enemy territory. The places which lay under siege were stronger than those in the southern Netherlands. The troops were readier to resist, even though the Dutch were divided between Jan de Witt's republican party and the Orangists. They also had to face at sea an Anglo-French coalition. Through the good offices of Madame, the French king had obtained from Charles II the secret Treaty of Dover (June 1670), which was given official blessing in Paris in February 1671. In neglect of the Triple Alliance, England agreed to support France's war-effort in the event of a conflict with the United Provinces. The moment had come to put the agreement into practice. The result was the Battle of Sole Bay (7 June 1672), a bitter engagement in which seventy-eight vessels under the Duke of York and thirty ships under the comte d'Estrées and Duquesne did not do themselves justice. The seventy-five Dutch ships of the line were under the command of Ruyter whilst the Anglo-French force lacked discipline, training and tactical sense. After the semi-defeat of Sole Bay, it is readily understandable that the crossing of the ford at Tolhuys was a welcome relief. On the day following that, 13 June, the Dutch abandoned their 'barrier fortresses' along the IJssel. In twenty-two days, Louis XIV's armies had taken forty towns. 'Amsterdam even discussed whether it should surrender its keys; and almost the whole of Holland felt itself threatened, in only as much time as it took to cross from one part of the country to the other.' (71) This was a joint achievement of the king, Monsieur, Turenne, Condé and Luxembourg.

The achievement would have been still more important had Louis listened to Condé's advice and sent the cavalry to take Amsterdam. Turenne's advice had been overly cautious. The monarch and Louvois had concentrated too much on glory, forgetting that it was not so valiant to rout an army of 27,000 men with one of 150,000. The hopes of achieving a 'lightning campaign' in two months were dashed on 20 June. That day, the Dutch took the risk of opening the sluice-gates at Muiden. 'For three whole days, the water poured in over the low-lying land and Amsterdam became an island in the Zuider Zee.' Behind the flooding, according to Clausewitz, a 'spirit of resistance could build up in its most classic form so that every attack was bound to end in complete failure' (216). The 50,000 soldiers, some led by Condé and others, following, by the duc de Luxembourg, did not succeed in 'penetrating beyond the flooding, although it [Amsterdam] was only defended by 20,000 men' (159). As soon as the sluices were opened, the Dutch forgot their quarrels. There seemed to be a sacred bond between de Witt and William of Orange. Additional levies reinforced their small army and sailors agreed to serve on land. The grand pensionary showed himself to be the master of the crisis, and this despite the fact that the Orangists stirred up the populace against him. He desperately sought diplomatic allies. Spain had encouraged the Dutch mercenaries in its Flanders army to return to swell the ranks of the Dutch army. The Elector of Brandenburg, whose fortresses on the Rhine Louis XIV had occupied, agreed to send 20,000 troops to assist the Dutch, and the emperor likewise agreed to send troops. This was why, when the envoys from the United Provinces presented themselves before Louis XIV on 29 June, they did little more than play for time. They offered him the Rhenish towns which had already fallen, Maastricht and Dutch Brabant, sufficient to put the future defence of the Low Countries in jeopardy and far too much to be credible. Following custom, Louis XIV demanded more: the whole of the south of the country, the retention of all lands under French occupation, Maastricht and Bois-le-Duc. The French allies, England, the

Archbishop of Cologne and the Bishop of Münster, should also be recompensed. The republic would have to agree to suspend the tariffs put on French goods as a reprisal to Colbert's, give France an indemnity of twenty-four million *livres*, and tolerate the Catholic religion. The Dutch had five days in which to indicate their acceptance. Louis XIV heard nothing.

THE COMING TO POWER OF WILLIAM OF ORANGE

William of Orange became stadholder of the republic on 8 July. By force of necessity, the States General brought to an end the burgher republic and the dominance of the grand pensionary. They returned to the half-monarchy of the Princes of Orange, the destiny of that paradoxically aristocratic republic of the United Provinces. William, then aged twenty-two, was 'more ambitious than de Witt, more devoted to his country and more stoical in adversity' (112). He hated Jan de Witt, the bourgeois clan of Amsterdam and the pacifists, as well as popery, France and Louis XIV. His hatred hardened him, making him into one who could lose battles but still win wars. This zealous Predestinarian Calvinist was himself predestined to become English.

The prince had scarcely taken command before the war intensified. The Dutch dug new dykes and the French king's army was halted before Bois-le-Duc. On 22 July, the emperor joined the anti-French coalition. Then, on 20 August, a mob of zealots massacred Jan de Witt and his brother Cornelis, 'tolerant', bourgeois Amsterdam standing by whilst its populace slaughtered the most cosmopolitan of its elite. The Orangist party had gained the upper hand.

From 1 August, Louis XIV had returned to Saint-Germain, leaving the French forces in Holland in the hands of the duc de Luxembourg, a commander who clearly outclassed William of Orange, as the Battle of Woerden proved (12 October). But the French army could only besiege those fortresses where there had not been flooding. For their part, the Orangists reaped the harvest which de Witt had sown. They had the emperor, the Elector of Brandenburg, the King of Spain and several other princes as their allies. The emperor sent 40,000 men and the Prussians invaded Cologne and Münster. This meant that

Louis XIV had to divide his forces, sending Montal to relieve Charleroi (22 December), whilst, on the Rhine, Turenne prevented the Imperialists from joining the Orangist army. Münster and Cologne still had to be relieved if France wanted to retain its allies, reliefs which Turenne struggled to achieve from January 1673 onwards. By June, Frederick-William had signed a convenient separate peace with France.

The second year of the war brought Louis XIV only two satisfactory results: the retreat of the Brandenburgers, thanks to Turenne, and the taking of Maastricht (29 June) by Vauban and the French king after thirteen days in the trenches. Condé had no spectacular successes in Holland, and Luxembourg could not prevent Orange from taking Naarden so he was ordered to withdraw, a process completed by the end of the year. On the French side, doubts began to mount. A congress 'of peace' was held in Cologne in June, and this demonstrated that French ambitions had narrowed in the course of twelve months of war. In August, under imperial pressure, the anti-French coalition was strengthened: Leopold promised to become more actively involved, while the queen regent in Spain officially declared war on France and the Duke of Lorraine put himself at the head of an army. The king's greatest commanders, Condé, Turenne and Luxembourg, were in dispute with Louvois, finding it hard to accept his overall direction, which left to the military commanders only matters of secondary importance. Among the anti-French allies, relationships were scarcely more cordial – Montecuccoli disliked the stadholder and they quarrelled bitterly.

Less than two years after it had begun, the war had become European in scope, outgrowing the United Provinces and changing its character. It no longer best suited France's military capacities. Numerically, France (whom England abandoned in February 1674) was overtaken by the allied armies. But Orange was not a great military commander. Louis XIV 'attended to all the tasks of a general, down to the last detail' (224), and Turenne and Condé intensified their military endeavours. A rallying of talents was vital in order to meet the crisis. France had left its episcopal allies weary (Paderborn, Osnabrück and Münster), the Duke of Neuberg was exasperated, the Palatinate ravaged (through the imprudence of Turenne and Louvois), Cologne stranded and the alliance with Mainz in tatters. In addition, Brandenburg rejoined the imperial side on 1 July 1674.

Louis XIV only had Sweden and the Elector of Bavaria to count on as allies. Despite this, however, there were still victories to be had on the battlefield and Louis XIV was about to conquer Franche Comté, which had been virtually his for the asking in 1668.

THE GLORY OF THE KING AND HIS COUSINS

In the spring of 1674, the king, waiting to play his aces, bided his time under cover of the armies of Turenne and Condé. The acquisition of a French-speaking province of great strategic importance and the completion of that conquest (thanks to Vauban) in less than three months were the measure of the gamble which Louis XIV successfully took. Besançon capitulated in May, Dôle on 6 June. Louis XIV let the maréchal de Navailles take Gray, the duc de la Feuillade Salins and the duc de Duras the fort of Joux. But no one was allowed to share in the glory of the conquest of Besançon. (Adam Frans van der Meulen, in his *Siege of Besançon*, painted it all in brilliant colours, but the future capital had held out for twenty-seven days (102).) On the other hand, the king, not able to be everywhere at once, relinquished to his illustrious cousins the glory of triumphs on other fronts.

Condé mustered the garrisons recalled from the Dutch offensive, cut off the Paris road to the 60,000 men under the Prince of Orange and won the bitter engagement at Seneffe (11 August): 107 flags or standards were captured from the allies. The French forces suffered 8,000 casualties, but the Orangist army suffered 12,000. Divisions within the coalition partners began to give France the upper hand.

Another cousin to the king, the vicomte de Turenne, demonstrated even more dramatically in the same year, 1674, the military strength of the French realm. His first triumph preceded that at Seneffe. At the beginning of the year, the marshal covered the operation in Franche Comté. Then he struck out towards the north and, learning that Imperialists and the Duke of Lorraine were awaiting reinforcements from the duc de Bournonville in the Palatinate, he crossed the Rhine at Philippsburg on 14 June and routed, at Sinzheim, the army of Duke Charles V of Lorraine,* and the imperial forces under Count Caprara. But, with only 15,000 soldiers, he could not remain in the lands of the empire indefinitely, not even by ravaging the Palatinate. He therefore crossed back over the Rhine and drew up his forces at Wissembourg. However, he found his position had scarcely changed: his troops outnumbered, he was forced onto the offensive – which suited his temperament –, hoping to forestall the arrival of the great elector. This was why Turenne surprised Bournonville outside Entzheim (4 October 1674), harassing him continuously for over eight hours and killing 3,000 of his men, before the imperial army was constrained to retreat towards Strasbourg.

The French army in Alsace, eventually reinforced, increased to 30,000 men, but the imperial forces were still twice as numerous. The maréchal de Turenne retained the initiative during this long campaign by his genius for mobility and the endurance of his soldiers. The viscount stubbornly held onto Alsace, although he pretended to leave it to dig in in Lorraine and spend the winter there. He crossed the Vosges from east to west on 30 November, leaving the Imperialists, the Duke of Lorraine and the Brandenburg troops free to range unhindered from Erstein to the Sundgau. In mid-winter, and at the head of 'the best-disciplined and most tireless' infantry in Europe (95), he reached Belfort in under twenty-seven days and hustled the Imperialist cavalry at Mühlhausen on 29 December, before confronting the great elector at Turckheim (5 January 1675). It was at this moment that, as Clausewitz neatly put it, Turenne 'confounded the plans of his adversary as well as its troops' (159). They were so demoralized that, less than ten days later, they recrossed the Rhine.

'What do you make of our sweet success', Bussy wrote to the marquise de Sévigné on 20 January, 'and the superb victory of M. de Turenne in forcing a retreat beyond the Rhine on the enemy? This campaign gives us a good breathing-space and a good moment for celebrations at court.' (96) The victor of Turckheim was recalled to receive the king's congratulations. The marshal rather hoped to retire before his personal dispute with Louvois made his autonomous command of an army impossible. But Louis XIV would hear none of it and sent him

* In reality, he was Prince Charles of Lorraine. He would only officially become Charles V and Duke of Lorraine in 1675.

back to the Rhine army on 11 May as the only person capable of holding Montecuccoli. The result was what later experts in the strategy of war consider his master-stroke.

It is true that this confrontation was unique. Turenne and Montecuccoli were generally regarded as the best strategists of their generation. They had the same generosity of spirit, the same faith, the same detailed knowledge of the terrain and the same care for their armies. 'Both reduced war to an art-form.' (112) Turenne assembled his troops at Sélestat. On 27 May, he camped about two and a half miles from Strasbourg in order to impress upon this town how fragile its neutrality really was. Then he crossed the Rhine at Kehl, and there followed two months of manœuvring. Montecuccoli evaded the enemy and Turenne went in hot pursuit. The imperial field marshal then advanced upon him with superior military might when Turenne was unfavourably stationed. It was Turenne's turn to turn away. Marches and counter-marches followed in turn without coming to an issue. The French army had to compensate for its inferior numbers by much greater mobility, by decisive leadership from its commander and by the discipline of its hardened troops.

Eventually, Turenne spotted a moment to attack the Imperialists to his own advantage, near Sasbach (on 27 July); but, in the course of a reconnaissance with his artillery officers, he was killed by a stray cannon-ball. His nephew, the duc de Lorge, led the army back across the Rhine, whilst Louis XIV sent Condé to bring the advance of Montecuccoli to a halt in Alsace, which was once more suffering from an invasion (August and September 1675). After this last successful mission, the prince de Condé retired to his château at Chantilly. Montecuccoli also abandoned armies and battlefields, 'saying that someone who has had the honour of fighting against Mahomet Köprülü, the prince de Condé and Turenne should not have to sully his glory by fighting commanders who are only just learning' (258). In this way, the three masters of the art of war took their leave of the battlefield. But the death of Turenne contributed something to the development of national sentiment. The marshal's body was brought back amidst distressed crowds. 'Everywhere the bier passed', wrote Mme de Sévigné, 'there were tears, emotion, crowds, processions, forcing them to travel by night.' (96) It was Louis XIV's will that Turenne's body should be interred at Saint-Denis, like Charles Martel's and du Guesclin's. On 10 January 1676, Fléchier presented the funeral oration in the Church of Saint-Eustache. The Parisians filled the nave and, thereafter, generations of schoolchildren learnt by heart a paean of praise for the warrior, the Christian, the king's lieutenant and the servant of France. 'He who embodied the glory of the nation to its furthest extremities', having 'above all embraced the cause of the glory of the king, the desire for peace and zeal for the public weal' before dying, 'struck down in his triumph.' (39) It has been said that, with the disappearance of Turenne and the retirement of Condé, Louis XIV drew back from a pattern of mobile warfare. But this ignores the role played by the duc de Luxembourg, Condé's rival. It is also to forget that France and Bourbon Spain owed their security later in the reign to two commanders, Vendôme and the maréchal de Villars, the military experience of both of whom was gained under M. de Turenne.

COMBAT BY LAND AND BY SEA

From the summer of 1674, Louis sought an acceptable peace. He thought the bourgeois of Amsterdam would not be displeased to return to the negotiating table; but the king's overtures were met with the refusal of the stadholder, who was obsessed with 'his own reputation and advantage' (216). To compensate the emperor for his hostile alliance, Louis XIV played the card of allying with the emperor's enemies, the malcontents of Hungary, sending their leader Thököly reinforcements and subsidies (206). He favoured the election of Sobieski to the Polish Crown in 1674 in order to spite Brandenburg-Prussia and aid the Hungarians. In the Mediterranean, France offered the Sicilians in Messina, then in revolt against Spanish dominion, some assistance. But the war itself did not slacken its pace. France's allies proved somewhat cumbersome. Swedish intervention kept the great elector away from the Rhine, but it earned France the hostility of Denmark. And the Swedish king was no strategist. His forces would be defeated on land at Fehrbellin (1675) by the Prussians and at sea by Tromp, who was allied to the Danes (1676), and the great elector seized Stettin from them (1677).

But although these northern allies did not, strategically, live up to expectations, they still remained an important force, the proof that Pomponne was a remarkable foreign minister. Was Louvois as good a minister of war? The question has to be asked, in view of his 'cabinet war-strategy'. The latter should be seen as a kind of modern joint chiefs-of-staff command; but it has to be admitted that this institution was still in its infancy in 1675–6, when its effectiveness was patchy. The death of Turenne removed a problem for Louvois. The retirement of M. le Prince in the following autumn was the displacement of the Great Condé. But he was not replaced by Louvois' favoured candidate, the maréchal de Rochefort, who, in September 1676, had to surrender Philippsburg to the Duke of Lorraine. Even those generals who had the most experience and renown, Schomberg, Créqui and Luxembourg, were not always victorious. On 11 August 1675, Créqui was defeated by the Duke of Lorraine; in September, he was made a prisoner of war. His revenge would come not long after, with, in October 1676, the taking of Bouillon and, in November 1677, the operation to liberate Freiburg.

In the Low Countries, the king awaited his moment for several sieges: Dinant, Huy and Limburg (1675), Condé (1676), Valenciennes and Cambrai (1677). The maréchal d'Humières took Aire, and Monsieur forced Bouchain into a capitulation in 1676. For his part, Schomberg constrained William of Orange to raise the siege of Maastricht on 26 August 1676. Orange's obstinate determination was greater than his military grasp, which was why, on 11 April 1677, one finds him at Cassel surrendering, under the military onslaught of Monsieur and Luxembourg, 5,000 men, 3,000 prisoners, 13 cannon and the military standards and baggage.

The surprising feature of the final phase of this war lay not in feats of arms on land; when M. de Luxembourg was victorious at Cassel or M. de Créqui took Freiburg, he only confirmed his already established military reputation. The same was not true of the French navy. After the mediocre results of Sole Bay and the Texel, the French fleet began to show its seaworthiness and fulfil the promises which Colbert had made for it. In 1674, as soon as England made peace, the Dutch tried to deliver a knock-out blow against the French navy. They divided their force of over 150 ships into two squadrons. One, under Tromp, attempted a landing in France in June 1674. The other, commanded by Ruyter, tried but failed to take the French island of Martinique. It was in the Mediterranean, however, where

Louis XIV had his most decisive naval success. On 11 February 1675, Duquesne, with Preuilly's assistance, put the Spanish fleet to flight, in the sea off Stromboli, a victory which enabled the French to resupply the rebels in Messina, although the Dutch ships came to reinforce those of Spain. Ruyter led his fleet towards Messina. Duquesne had wind of his movements and blocked his passage near the islands of Lipari (January 1676). The savage and indecisive encounter which resulted has been called the Battle of Alicudi. A few days later, the Spanish and Dutch vessels regrouped and sought to engage the enemy again; Duquesne did not withdraw. The result was the Battle of Agosta. Happily for Louis, Ruyter was only second in command to the Admiral of Spain, Dom Francisco de la Cerda. Moreover, although the Dutch ships were well provisioned and well armed, the Spanish vessels lacked both powder and ammunition. The latter vessels constituted, however, the ships at the centre of the line awaiting the moment to intervene. The battle which took place in the open sea off Agosta was a limited engagement between the two sections of the fleets in the van. The French commander of the leading squadron was the chevalier de Valbelle. The result was a considerable defeat for the Dutch. They lost five vessels and Ruyter, severely wounded, died soon after. The United Provinces lost the most remarkable admiral of his generation. In the following June, Duquesne eliminated the Spanish fleet in a raid on Palermo. It was no longer the era of indecisive battles. Louis XIV's fleet had become pre-eminent in the world. Its successes gave the king's plenipotentiaries at Nymwegen a position of strength which the abandonment of the Sicilian venture did not weaken and which would be further reinforced by Louis XIV's astonishing military campaign of 1678.

GHENT OR THE LIGHTNING CAMPAIGN

'What say you about the capture of Ghent?' wrote Mme de Sévigné to Bussy-Rabutin on 18 March 1678. 'A French king has not been seen there for a very long time. Ours is truly admirable and deserves to have better historiographers than two poets.' These poet-historians, neatly dressed, padding around among the generals, followed the court 'on foot, on horseback, up to their ears in mud, sleeping (as the poets would say) by the light of Endymion's fair mistress' (96). The king had nominated them in October 1677 after Cassel, since it then seemed important not to give Monsieur the chance to rival the glory of the king. Boileau, already weary before his departure, was the laziest of historiographers. Racine was more diligent, and exploited his experiences in his *Historical Summary of the Campaigns of Louis XIV from 1672 to 1678* (90). We also have his notes taken before, during, and after the siege of Ghent. These are the work of a good writer and they vividly recall the experience of *blitzkrieg*, a form of warfare very different from the siege-warfare which had become characteristic of the Dutch War, a 'knock-out blow' like that which Frederick the Great would use, and for which Clausewitz would provide the theory.

Ever since the marriage of Mary Stuart, Charles II's niece, to William of Orange (in November 1677), the negotiations at Nymwegen had begun to take a turn for the worse. England, once the arbiter, had become judge and party to them. On 10 January 1678, the stadholder secured England's signature to an alliance with the Netherlands and, a few weeks later, England joined the anti-French 'confederates'. Louis XIV, with Louvois' assistance, replied by a show of force which would give Charles II second thoughts before accepting fully the Orangist lure. It had to be a limited offensive, for fear of engendering greater antipathy amongst the burghers of Amsterdam and raising the wind amidst the 'popular' party in London. The maritime powers were soothed by the withdrawal from Messina, whilst, at the same time, an army of 100,000 men was mobilized for a destination unknown to the coalition.

Whilst his enemies took up winter quarters, Louis left Saint-Germain on 7 February 'with all his court'. He spent two days at Sézanne before arriving on the 15th at Vitry, which celebrated the event: 'Inhabitants very loyal: fireworks . . .', wrote Racine. From there, it was on to Sermaize: 'A foul place. Scarcely space for the king's arm-chair in his room.' The king then continued, towards Commercy, as though he were heading towards Metz. But, here, to cover his tracks: 'The rumour at court today is that we are to return to Paris.' In fact, the court went on to Toul, where 'We passed a day. The king toured the town, visited the fortifications and ordered two bastions to be built towards the river.' Everything seemed to suggest that Louis XIV was going

towards Nancy, instead of which, he took the road towards the
north and arrived in Metz on the 22nd.

'Great zeal among the inhabitants of Metz for the king.' Louis
conferred there with Créqui and sent him on to Thionville, letting everyone think that this was his destination. 'The enemies,
alarmed and uncertain of his route, are in a continual panic. The
Germans, who had scarcely arrived in their winter quarters,
have been obliged to reassemble. The town of Strasbourg has
discussed whether it should send envoys to the king. Trier thinks
it is to be sacked and Luxembourg is certain that it is about to
be besieged.' But, after two days in Metz, the king made his
way back westwards to meet Monsieur in Verdun. The rumour
that he was about to besiege Namur began to gather weight as
he marched towards it at least as far as the little fortress of
Stenay.

At this point in Louis XIV's march, the governor of the
Spanish Low Countries was at his wits' end.

> He saw the French contingents coming and going everywhere; he
> knew that, from the heart of Flanders to the Rhine, the king had
> supplies everywhere. He had no idea which fortresses to reinforce
> and which to abandon. If he reinforced one, he would leave
> twenty others unprotected. In the end, he decided to strengthen
> the weakest by recalling all his forces from Flanders and putting
> them in the towns of Hainaut and Luxembourg.

This was a cardinal error and it was followed by another, which
was to run down the garrison at Ghent and build up the forces in
Ypres, which was where d'Humières was actively engaged. This
was when 60,000 French troops, 'assembling from different locations', gathered around Ghent, the king soon to be at their head.
Among the Spanish, the attack was a complete surprise. The
king, apparently, had never considered an attack upon Namur
or Luxembourg. The speed and secrecy of the preparations were
miraculous. Leaving the queen at Stenay, the king rode hard
towards Flanders, covering over 150 miles in three days, eating
'under a market stall', drinking 'the vilest wine in the world',
sleeping in a farm, and so exhausted at Saint-Amand 'that he
could scarce mount the stairs to his chamber'. Near Valenciennes, he paused for a moment's relaxation and showed Racine
'seven towns within sight of us, which are now his', adding:
'There is Tournai, a town worth my making an effort to hold on

to'. This was the moment when the king heard the news that the siege of Ghent had begun.

When Louis XIV arrived before Ghent on 4 March, he found the city already invested by d'Humières. The day after, trenches were dug, on the 9th the city surrendered and on the 12th the citadel capitulated. Its elderly governor, Francesco de Pardo, had a garrison denuded of rations and had no resources to resist the larger forces commanded by the king, Humières, Lorge, Schomberg and Luxembourg. The efforts to open the sluice-gates and so cut off French communications failed. His words to Louis XIV were: 'I surrender Ghent to Your Majesty; I have nothing more to say.' The victor sent Lorge off towards Bruges, whilst he and Luxembourg went to take Ypres, the key to the whole of Flanders. On 25 March, Ypres and its citadel together surrendered (90).

These contests took place between unequally matched forces and this must detract from the French achievement. But the campaign's conception and execution by Louvois and Louis XIV and his marshals were worthy of the late commander Turenne. This was the moment for Louis XIV to show that he knew how not to push his good fortune too far. He did not pursue the enemy as far as Ostende or go further north towards the United Provinces. On 31 March he was back at Amiens, and on 4 April at Mouchy, the campaign concluded. It had left the English hesitant about their future course of action, and strengthened the opposition of the burgher oligarchs in Amsterdam to the stadholder; there were mutual recriminations between England and the United Provinces. The capture of Ghent and the overthrow of Ypres were the vital ingredients for peace. At that moment, the sentiments of Bussy-Rabutin seemed less excessive: 'You ask me, Madame, what I think about the seizure of Ghent. I know not what to think, for I am lost in wonderment. I would echo what Voiture told the king, namely, that if it would please him once in a while to dismantle a siege then it would give his admirers time to catch their breath and help them savour all the different things that are happening.' (96)

Siege-warfare was markedly different from fast-moving campaigns. What was remarkable here was the effort to implant surprise in the slow rhythms of siege-warfare. 'In the seventeenth and eighteenth centuries,' according to Clausewitz, 'the siege was the essential pivot around which war revolved and the unexpected encirclement of a stronghold was a frequent goal, constituting a particularly important and special feature in the art of war; but, of course, this unexpected siege only happened rarely.' (159) Such success would be difficult to match. One year after Cassel, the king showed that he was a better strategist than Monsieur.

THE GLORY OF NYMWEGEN

Besides its strategic and tactical importance, the Ghent campaign determined the nature of the pacification. Louis XIV laid down his conditions: Sweden should recover its former territories; Spain should surrender Aire and Saint-Omer, Cambrai, Bouchain, Condé and Valenciennes; the Dutch should recover Maastricht, but should renew their trade treaty with France; all treaties must be agreed to before 10 May 1678. This 'ultimatum' was harsh towards no one save Spain; but the Dutch were so finely divided over the matter that they were given until 15 August to decide. Subsidies offered to Charles II kept England reassured for the moment. All hung in the balance because of the intransigence of the great elector and Denmark, both disinclined to give up their acquisitions to Sweden; and, under the pressure of public opinion, Charles II of England signed an alliance with the United Provinces on 26 July. A renewed and more intensified war was avoided, thanks to concessions by Sweden and some neat diplomacy by the French envoys. On 14 August, Orange still thought an attack on the army of the maréchal de Luxembourg near Mons worthwhile, but it was repulsed, and this violation of the embryo peace had no lasting effect. The first conventions, signed on 10 August, established a truce between Sweden and the Low Countries and a Franco-Dutch commercial accord, as well as peace between His Most Christian Majesty and the States General of the United Provinces. France gave up Maastricht; but, in return, Catholic worship was retained there. The war against Holland had ended in a stalemate. The same was not the case with the war against Spain. In the name of his legitimate brother, Charles II of Spain, the regent, Don Juan, was constrained to accept Louis XIV's demands. Franche Comté was to become French. The Spanish Low Countries would be partitioned. To reassure The Hague, France handed back its more northerly conquests – Courtrai, Oudenaarde, Ath, Binche and Charleroi – thus establishing a 'frontier as a line on the map' (236), the beginnings of the *pré carré* which Vauban had pressed for since 1675 (215). Three frontier areas were consolidated, corresponding to three 'bulges' inwards along the valleys of the Scheldt, the Sambre and the Aire rivers (236). Louis XIV, thanks to Saint-Omer and Aire, turned Artois French. He annexed Cassel, Bailleul, Ypres, Werwick, Warneton and Poperinghe in Flanders and took possession of Valenciennes, Mauberge, Cambrai, Bouchain, Condé-sur-l'Escaut [Scheldt] and Bavay in the southern part of Hainaut (215). To establish this new defensive frontier, the skills of Vauban would be required, but he would not find it difficult to fortify Menin in place of Courtrai and to strengthen Mauberge to replace the loss of Charleroi. But, in reality, the fixed territorial frontiers envisaged at Nymwegen were not the result of the application of a doctrine. France retained its forward positions in Philippeville and Marienburg, both strengthened with the addition of Charlemont.

On 5 February 1679, two other treaties were also signed at Nymwegen, one between the emperor and Sweden, and the other between the emperor and France. Louis XIV retained Freiburg, but surrendered his claim to Philippsburg. He offered to cede Lorraine to its duke, but on conditions which were so humiliating to the duke, now an imperial ally, that he preferred the prospect of exile. The great elector and Denmark would have continued hostilities against Sweden; but, without the support of the emperor, and with Dutch interest also waning, the Danes and the Prussians had to accept France's conditions for peace, becoming henceforth, in consequence, its opponents. By the Treaty of Saint-Germain (29 June 1679), the great elector withdrew from Swedish Pomerania, and, at Fontainebleau in November, Denmark accepted the French ultimatum. The 'peace in the north' was to show the King of France as 'the defender of his allies' (71). It tied up the loose ends of Nymwegen.

The following year, the city of Paris gave the king the title of 'Great', henceforth inseparable from his name when it appeared in inscriptions. This marked the zenith of the reign. Emperor Leopold had accepted all France's diplomatic conditions. The King of Spain had agreed to marry Monsieur's daughter, Marie

Louise, known as Mademoiselle d'Orléans. The whole continent appeared to be under France's sway.

'King Louis the Great', wrote the abbé de Choisy, 'reached the pinnacle of human glory with the signing of the Peace of Nymwegen. After myriad demonstrations of his military leadership and his personal valour, he lay down his arms amidst his victories and, contenting himself with his conquests, gave peace to Europe upon terms highly satisfactory to him.' (24) Voltaire put it this way:

> The king, at this moment, was at the peak of his greatness. He had been victorious since the beginning of his reign, had taken every stronghold that he laid siege to, had proved himself superior in every way to the united strength of his adversaries, and was held in awe throughout Europe for six years in succession, before he finally became its arbiter and peacemaker. He added Franche Comté, Dunkirk [*sic*] and half Flanders to his domains and, what must be accounted the greatest of his strengths, he was king of a contented nation, an example to other nations. (112)

Such a situation could not last. Louis had made too many enemies, particularly the determined Prince of Orange, who, although he had been given back his possessions within France at Orange, accepted an imposed peace with an ill grace. In addition, the King of France, flushed with his success, imprudently provoked his former enemies and created new ones. In the period after Nymwegen, the victor over the coalition should have considered more carefully the maxim of an old *frondeur*, the duc de la Rochefoucauld (d. 1680): Il faut de plus grandes vertus pour soutenir la bonne fortune que la mauvaise.*

---

*It is easier to bear misfortune than success.

14

Passions, Charms and Fancies

BEFORE WE judge, we should listen to the evidence; and it would be unfair to take the case for the prosecution without hearing that for the defence. The king's defence of his love-affairs may be read in the margins of the *Memoirs for the year 1667*.* The king sought to explain to his son how he came to decide upon the title of duchess for his mistress, Louise de la Vallière, and to legitimize their child, Mlle de Blois.

The king accepted that this kind of affair 'was not a good thing to follow', that it was a bad example. 'A prince should always be the model of virtue and it would be better were he to be inured from the failings of ordinary mortals, particularly since there can be no hope of such matters remaining undetected.' He hoped to have 'diminished the consequences' of these 'aberrations' by having taken two precautions. 'One must ensure', he said, 'that the time taken up by one's passions should never be to the prejudice of the work in hand', since the latter presupposed 'strenuous effort'. But Louis XIV also mentioned a 'second, rather more delicate matter to put into practice, which is that, in opening our hearts, we should retain the mastery of our minds, that we should separate our affections as lovers from our decisions as sovereigns, and that the beauty which inspires pleasure in us never has the freedom to interfere in our affairs nor in those of the men who serve us' (63).

---

* This was a part of the text of the *Mémoires* of Louis XIV which was not retained by Louis XIV in its final version.

THE TIME FOR AMOROUS ENCOUNTERS

The time for romance began in July 1661 in that fine summer at Fontainebleau as Fouquet fell from grace. Courtiers learnt 'that La Vallière was the king's mistress and that it was a serious affair, since Louis had shrouded it in such great secrecy' (213). Contrary to appearances, Louis always tried to keep his amorous liaisons secret. He did this primarily in order to spare a little the feelings of the queen. This was why he put such a high value on the complete discretion of someone like Saint-Aignan and why he harshly penalized such indiscretions as Vardes' attempt to alert Maria Theresa by means of an anonymous letter in Spanish. Throughout the queen's lifetime, Louis returned to her each night. But the care taken over secrecy had a more-general significance: it symbolized the need to protect a certain royal freedom of action. Like all royal favours, the privilege of being the king's mistress was exceptional, revocable at will. Although the court and others discreetly avoided mentioning a favourite by name, this was partly because the king did not have favourites in the pejorative sense of the word. To this extent, Louis XIV practised what he preached, although not without causing tears, since the best way of hiding a new mistress was openly to display the former flame in her company, even making sure that they were seen, together with the queen, as a threesome.

This was an effective stratagem. Mme de Sévigné, who kept herself well informed, was constantly in the dark from 1667 to 1680 as she tried to work out who was the current mistress, and how much favour others had. Even today, we do not know for sure whether the liaison between the king and Mme de Soubise went further than an intimate friendship. On the other hand, although the offspring of these affairs were kept apart from the court, and although the rendezvous remained well-kept secrets, the king did not disguise within polite company that they took place. The overall result is that we are as much in the dark as Mme de Sévigné over the exact scale and chronology of the king's love-affairs. They did not follow one another lineally. On the other hand, one can see the consequences in terms of the decorative emblems and monuments which these affections inspired the king to create. For Louise de la Vallière, he set his heart on the success of the Tuileries entertainment of 1662 and of the festivities of the *Pleasures of the Enchanted Isle* in 1664, and made 'all that was surprising and frivolous in the first château at Versailles' (291). Without the high favour of the marquise de Montespan, it would be difficult to imagine the 'grand royal entertainment at Versailles' of 18 July 1668, the Bathroom Suite, the porcelain Trianon and the garden groves there, and Clagny. On 7 August 1675, Mme de Sévigné wrote to Mme de Grignan: 'We have been at Clagny. What should one say? It is an Armidean palace . . . undoubtedly the most beautiful, surprising and enchanting novelty imaginable.' (96)*

Yet this passion for secrecy was only partially respected. One would have had to have been blind to have ignored the affair between the king and Athénaïs de Rochechouart. For, while Louis' affection for La Vallière (*c*.1661–7) had been little more than adulterous – Louise was not married, refused any suggestion of a marriage of convenience to cover things up, tried to hide her pregnancies and her childbirths, and even won the queen's sympathies – things were different with Mme de Montespan. The length of this liaison (*c*.1667–81), the number of the children which resulted from it, her distinguished parentage and her keen intelligence kept her in the public eye. Colbert complained of the expenses which His Majesty's friend engendered. The queen, too, often affronted by Athénaïs, spared no sympathy for her. But the king's attractions towards her were so strong that the reign of Mme de Montespan continued long after the abandonment of their physical affections.

Churchmen took it in turns to exort the king to better things, but without much result. They had to say something because adultery lay on both sides. Mlle de Rochechouart was no longer single. She had been married off in 1663, at the age of twenty-three, to the marquis de Montespan of the House of Pardaillan. It was a poor match, and she found her spouse's perpetual near-bankruptcy an irritation. So she had no great difficulty in accepting the advances of a king less timid than Louise de la Vallière had found him. Montespan did nothing to hold on to his wife, even when opportunities arose to take her back to the provinces. He became something of a little jack-in-the-box, popping up to give the king a lecture once at Saint-Germain, arranging a Mass

---

* Armidea was one of the heroines of Tasso's epic poem *Jerusalem Delivered*. She seduced Rinaldo by entertaining him in her enchanted gardens and delightful palace. The subject was frequently painted by seventeenth-century artists.

of solemn mourning for his wife after her death, coming to Paris almost every year from 1670 to 1686. A despot would have despatched this indiscreet cuckoo to the fortress at Pinerolo. Louis XIV played the gentleman, even to the extent of promoting Louis-Antoine de Pardaillan, the marquis and *marquise*'s son, to become, first an army commander, then a director-general of buildings and then, finally, a duke and peer of the realm. It is understandable that the children born of these love-affairs occupied a special place in his affections. He not only loved them and gave them brilliant prospects, but also wanted the two families, the two sets of offspring, to become one family. How Jupiter would exploit that!

THE LEGITIMIZED BROOD

Two of Louise's four children lived beyond infancy: Mlle de Blois (Marie-Anne de Bourbon, 1666–1739) and the comte de Vermandois (Louis de Bourbon, 1667–83). The first Mlle de Blois was legitimated by letters-patent of May 1667 creating for her mother the duchy of Vaujours la Vallière on behalf of 'our daughter Marie-Anne' (2). The Parlement registered the patent, bluntly referring to her as 'the natural daughter of the said seigneur and king'. At the age of seven, she made her début, 'dressed in black velvet studded with diamonds like a lady' (213). Six years later (1680), she had the honour to marry Louis-Armand de Bourbon, prince de Conti, the Great Condé's nephew. The comte de Vermandois had already been conceived when the Parlement legitimized his sister, on 14 May 1667. He was born at Saint-Germain on 2 October. Legitimized by letters of February 1669, subsequently registered, he was made admiral of France in the following November. His early death, two months after that of Colbert, increased Louis XIV's concern for his second brood of illegitimate offspring.

Madame de Montespan had eight children by the king, four of whom attained adulthood. All four were made Bourbon and were legitimized. Three were married into the royal dynasty. It would have been difficult to have bettered the treatment their father gave them. Louis-Auguste, duc du Maine, born in 1670, legitimated in December 1673, was in turn colonel-in-chief of the Swiss guards (1674), lieutenant-general (1692) and grand master of the French artillery (1694). He was married in 1692 to the turbulent Anne-Louise-Bénédicte, daughter of Henri-Jules, prince de Condé. Their *salon* in the pavilion at Sceaux would be the very epitome of civilization, a transitional environment between Versailles and the Parisian sociability of the Enlightenment. The duc du Maine, who suffered from a minor ailment (Madame christened him 'the lame'), was serious and pious, and the favourite of his governess, Mme Scarron, the future marquise de Maintenon; he was the great hope of the *dévots* and on intimate terms with Monseigneur and with his cousin the duc de Vendôme.

Louise-Françoise de Bourbon, Mlle de Nantes, born in 1673 and legitimized that same year, began the trend towards princely marriages for the illegitimate children: in 1685, she married Louis III, duc de Bourbon, the grandson of the victor of Rocroi. Her younger sister, Françoise-Marie de Bourbon, called Mlle de Blois – like her half-sister – was born in 1677 and legitimized in November 1681. On 18 February 1692, she married, much to the outrage of her future mother-in-law the Princess Palatine, Philippe II d'Orléans, Louis XIV's nephew and later the regent. Louis-Alexandre, comte de Toulouse, their young brother, was born in June 1678 and granted letters of legitimacy in 1681; he was the only illegitimate child of Louis XIV to make do with marriage into a ducal family (he married a Noailles) (2). Created admiral of France in 1683, following the death of the comte de Vermandois, he performed his duties conscientiously and commanded a naval fleet in 1704 (274).

The eldest children by the marquise de Montespan, particularly the future duc du Maine and the comte de Vexin (1672–83), were kept discreetly away from the curiosity of the court and the capital. From 1669 onwards, the devout Mme Scarron had been appointed to take care of these children. She was known as 'the Indian princess' because of her childhood in the East. Of Protestant stock, Françoise Scarron was the granddaughter of Agrippa d'Aubigné, Henry IV's faithful friend, a great poet and a dubious noble. She had married Scarron, a writer with a more decidedly bourgeois background. She was widowed young and, ambitious, she grasped the extent to which the opportunity of raising the king's children was a mark of favour, although she had no inkling of the heights to which it would lead her nor how quickly she would make her way at court.

From 1669 to 1673, Françoise Scarron's task was to be discretion itself; Mme de Montespan and even the king were taken in by her piety and knowledge. The future Mme de Maintenon and her young charges lived a cloistered life in Paris and then, later, in 1672, near Lagny whilst the king was away on campaign (213). But Louis XIV was dissatisfied with this clandestinity and the ambiguous status of his children. With the marquis de Montespan still alive and the father of two Montespan children, what was the status of Louis-Auguste and Louis-César, not to mention the future Louise-Françoise, whom Athénaïs was then carrying and who would be born on 1 June 1673?

In the course of the summer, everything was sorted out. The comte de Saint-Paul died when with the army as it crossed the Rhine. By his will, he had asked his mother, the duchesse de Longueville, to obtain the legitimation of a bastard son, the chevalier d'Orléans. For the king, the request could not have come at a more opportune moment. Louis signed letters-patent declaring the chevalier d'Orléans the comte de Saint-Paul's son, but making no mention of the mother (213). He then made use of the same text in drafting letters-patent in December, which were registered on the 20th in the Parlement, legitimating the duc du Maine, the comte de Vexin and Mlle de Nantes. Nothing now stood in the way of Françoise d'Aubigné's going to Saint-Germain with her protégés. The king could see them and coddle them. Everything leads one to suppose that, from 1674 onwards, he paid court to the governess from time to time, but already with a definite purpose in mind. It took some time before Mme de Montespan's jealousy was aroused. For his part, the king realized how much Mme Scarron cared for the duc du Maine and the little child's preference for his governess to his own mother. He showered favours upon the granddaughter of Agrippa d'Aubigné, giving her a pension with which she acquired Maintenon in 1675. A courtier would have had to have taken leave of his senses to have referred to her as 'the widow Scarron' then. Mme de Maintenon had entered the mainstream of French history.

FROM SCANDAL TO EDIFICATION

Many authors have shown righteous indignation at the very mention of the Sun King's amours. Nineteenth-century bourgeois Jansenism is mainly to blame, for the contemporaries of Louis XIV believed more and moralized less. Protestants, Jansenists and *dévots* professed themselves to varying degrees scandalized, but the king's confessors put their wisdom to work to sidestep the problem. The churchmen most involved, such as Bossuet in 1675, were aware that any interference was likely to be counterproductive. In any case, Bossuet was unconvinced that the ribaldry of popular songs should be taken seriously. The court, Paris and expressed opinion reacted towards Louis XIV's mistresses just as their predecessors had reacted towards Henry IV's. They were all beautiful women, Mlle de la Vallière, Mme de Montespan, Mme de Ludres and Mme de Fontanges. They gave satisfaction to the king and pleasure at court. They did not become involved in politics. They encouraged the arts – they were almost a branch of the fine arts themselves. For these reasons, a certain popular indulgence was assured towards the suitor of so many beautiful females.

This indulgence was not irreconcilable with Counter-Reformed religious attitudes. The believer knew that the flesh is weak. The sinner knew that the sins of the flesh do not incite one to add to them the mortal sin of blasphemy. Carnal sins were pardonable – the Bible gave that assurance and baroque pictures repeated it through representations of Mary Magdalene, the sinner whom Christ saved. On the other hand, the king and his subjects recognized that the Bible also said that a sin against the Holy Spirit, a sin against faith and hope, was unpardonable. If the seventeenth century is known as the age of saints, this is not because everyone in France was worthy of a halo, but because mortal sin against the Holy Spirit had become less common. Other, carnal sins may have appeared more frequent, but this did not upset the seventeenth-century economy of salvation. The important thing was that Christ saved sinners. He was the giver of the grace which infused the vast tomes of the theologians, inspired the pamphlets of the apologists and animated the conversation of the fine ladies.

All this was common ground, but the king still had to shoulder his responsibilities, and his mistresses had to decide whether to submit or seek flight. There is every evidence to show that the king and his consorts had a sense of sin and felt remorse. They all tried to reconcile their sense of carnal wrongdoing with their religious practice, and heeded the advice of their confessors. Mme de Montespan was not alone in feeling racked by remorse. 'Her sense of sin', according to Saint-Simon, 'never left her in peace. She often went from the king to pray in her study; nothing would make her break a fast or a day of abstinence.' When she left the court, she spent her days in the Saint-Joseph mission which she directed. She gave 'almost all she had to the poor. She worked several hours each day on their behalf, doing the daily round of common tasks . . . her mortifications were unceasing.' (94)

Mademoiselle de la Vallière had given the others an example to follow. She fled the court on 24 February 1662, two days before the first of the Lenten sermons that Bossuet preached at the Louvre, retreating to the Convent of the Visitation at Chaillot. She made a second escape on Ash Wednesday in 1671. Colbert had to come and seek her out at the Convent of Sainte-Marie at Chaillot. In 1674, she was eventually given permission to enter the Carmelite Convent of the Incarnation. A year later, she took her vows under the name of sœur Louise de la Miséricorde. She died there in 1710, leaving behind for the edification of contemporaries her *Reflections upon God's Mercy* (1680) (118). What became of Mme de Ludres, the 'beautiful and unfortunate' rival to Mme de Montespan? She retired to a convent in 1677. What of Marie-Angélique de Scorailles, duchesse de Fontanges, who was equally beautiful and unfortunate? She left the court to join the Parisian convent of Port-Royal, dying there three months later (28 June 1681). Her retirement inspired a mordant *rabutinade* from Bussy-Rabutin: 'If this goes on, a sure way for beautiful young girls to gain salvation will be by lying in the arms of the king. I reckon that, just as he says to those he touches for the king's evil: "The king touches thee, may God heal thee", he says to the girls he loves: "The king kisses thee, may God save thee."' (96)

With Mme Scarron, the pattern was inverted. From 1674, Françoise d'Aubigné received from Louis the first signs of what were known as 'the ultimate favours'. She managed to persuade herself that, in accepting these embraces, she was doing God's work, snatching the king from Mme de Montespan and Mme de

Fontanges, and bringing him back to the queen to satisfy her in her old age. She was Esther, charged with a mission to lead Ahasuerus back to righteousness. Mme de Maintenon talked the language of the king's salvation. She 'sacrificed' herself, a new Mary Magdelene, sinning that the king might be saved. The beauty of it all was that, where previous mistresses had banished all trace of hypocrisy, the *dévot* mistress thrived on it. In the end, though, things were no different for Françoise d'Aubigné than they were for the others, now neglected or disgraced, who had slept in the same bed: it was to a convent – her foundation at Saint-Cyr – that she retired, upon the king's death, to contemplate things eternal.

A NEW WITCH-HUNT

Louis XIV's amorous escapades, excused by his subjects, have been blackened by a trend in historical interpretation which associated the 'reign' of the marquise de Montespan with the events known as the *affaire des Poisons* which burst upon the public in 1679. On 12 March, the police arrested a certain Catherine Deshayes, Dame Monvoisin, called La Voisin, upon suspicion of witchcraft. On the 17th, there was a further arrest, of Adam Coeuret, alias Dubuisson, alias the 'abbé Le Sage'. Under cross-examination, some disquieting evidence emerged. On 7 April, with the active encouragement of M. de la Reynie, the lieutenant of police, Louis XIV set up a special tribunal, with a brief to judge the *affaire des Poisons* involving La Voisin. It met in the Arsenal and was given the awe-inspiring and archaic name of the 'Chambre Ardente' ('burning chamber'). It included magistrates of the highest rank, having as its president Boucherat (a future chancellor) and Bazin de Bezons and La Reynie as its summing-up judges. The solemnity of its proceedings, the secrecy and the subject in question all conduced to give an impression that the king wanted to see justice done expeditiously, without leaving any loopholes for the guilty. The proceedings were like those of the assize courts or *grands jours* (207).

The preliminary hearings dwelt upon abortions, magic, prognostications, *maleficia*, Black Masses and other sacrilegious acts; but the essence of the case – as the name by which it is still known suggests – lay in poisonings. Saint-Simon wrote that, 'It seems that there are, at certain moments, crimes which become the fashion, like clothes. Poisoning was *à la mode* at the time of La Voisin and Brinvilliers' (94). According to Voltaire, poisoning, 'the revenge of the coward', was not used 'during the terrible events of the civil war. Instead, it was the fate of France to find itself infected with this crime at a time of glory when habits had softened under the emollients of pleasure' (112). The year 1670 exemplified this combination – a year of pleasure, glory, rumours of poisonings, poisonings actually taking place, and an attempt to soften the penal code. In May 1670, the 'triumph of Mme de Montespan was made public during the king's trip to Flanders'. On 17 June, the marquise de Brinvilliers poisoned her brother, Antoine d'Aubray, civil lieutenant in the Châtelet prison (she had already killed their father by the same means in 1666). She struck once more, in September against another brother (188). Toxicology was then, of course, in its infancy and when someone of note died suddenly the death was attributed to poison. Thus, on 30 June 1670, no sooner had Bossuet pronounced, 'Madame [the duchesse d'Orléans] is dying, Madame is dead' (14), than the rumour of a possible crime took root and the matter even began to look like an 'affaire'. Lastly, in August, came the publication of the ordinance on criminal procedure, instigated by Colbert (82), codifying the laws and rendering them more humane. Historians have often coupled the published version of this text with Colbert's own instructions to stop witch-hunts.

The marquise de Brinvilliers was condemned to death in her absence in 1673, but not arrested until March 1676, in the Low Countries. Her trial before the Parlement lasted from 29 April to 16 July. The Parlement dragged its feet because the judges were reluctant to let the details of crimes committed within their own social orbit appear in public. There are many lessons to be learnt from this prelude to the *affaire des Poisons*. Some were religious: the death of the murderess on 17 July profoundly affected Paris. She had been converted in her last hours of life by the abbé Pirot. Mme de Brinvilliers had appeared 'contrite, her heart remorseful, hoping for a pardon'. She had even declared: 'I would like to be burnt alive to make my sacrifice more meritorious.' (188) The other considerations were political, and rather more troubling. Brinvilliers had been arrested upon Louvois' orders. Then, in the course of the trial, one line of inquiry led to the inculpation of M. Reich de Pennautier, the *receveur général du clergé*, Colbert's client. He was subsequently released for lack of conclusive proof, but it was still the case that uncorroborated testimony came close to convicting a financier who enjoyed the protection of Cardinal Bonzi, Archbishop Harlay, the duc de Verneuil and Colbert. Behind the Brinvilliers affair lay, in the shadows, another element of the Louvois–Colbert quarrel. The difficulties into which M. de Pennautier fell demonstrated the dangers of guilt by association. If it were proven that one had known a murderess, one would be suspected of some complicity in the affair. The same tendencies would reappear in the Voisin affair, the tendency to compromise someone of greater importance than oneself and a settling of old scores between two of His Majesty's ministers.

Despite her heinous crimes, the marquise de Brinvilliers remained a figure in high society. The underworld surrounding La Voisin was altogether more unsavoury. 'The old habit of consulting an astrologer, to draw up a horoscope, to find the means to render oneself irresistible, still flourished among the people and even among the greatest individuals in the land', wrote Voltaire. And he added: 'Le Sage, La Voisin and La Vigoureux made a living from the curiosity of the ignorant multitude. They predicted the future; they conjured up the Devil. If that were all that they had done, they would have earned no more than ridicule from the Chambre Ardente.' (112) Thus, the maréchal de Luxembourg had asked Le Sage for horoscopes, unaware of the fact that he also peddled Black Masses. Le Sage was not, in fact, an abbé at all, but there were others who were priests and who were experts in black magic, sorcery and *maleficia*.

'Black magic', wrote Furetière, 'is a detestable art which employs the invocation of devils and uses them to accomplish things beyond the forces of nature.' In 1679, people believed in God and feared Satan. Needless to say, La Voisin and Le Sage committed their crimes in a way which suited an age of faith. From amidst the flames of her pyre, La Voisin cried out 'Jésus, Maria'. ('This was perhaps a saint', wrote Mme de Sévigné.) Before this, Monvoisin and her accomplices and friends had testified to a whole variety of crimes and misdemeanours, pro- vided a full range of false information (La Voisin claimed to have buried 2,500 children in her garden), and inculpated a large number of clients by their confessions, denunciations and implausible circumstantial details. One might have expected it all to have awoken La Reynie's critical instincts, but this was far from the case. He took it all in, from the sale of 'inheritance powder' to the conjuring up of devils and the holding of Black Masses. His Christianity blocked his critical faculties. He forgot that, in all cases of witchcraft, the suspects confessed to crimes even more dreadful than those that they were accused of, making it a matter of pride, knowing that they would gain time, and perceiving that it would be in their interest to complicate the affair. It then would occur to them to incriminate people of importance in the hope of either obtaining their protection, or pushing the judges to call a halt to the investigation and thereby winning an automatic pardon.

The special tribunal became overwhelmed with suspects, prisoners and witnesses. La Voisin's female companions were called Leroux, Trianon, Chapelain, Françoise Filastre and La Vigoureux. The men were, besides the notorious Dubuisson-Le Sage, the abbés Mariette and Guibourg, the 'chemists' Vautier and Leroy and others. As the confessions multiplied, their clientele appeared to grow. From 10 April 1679 until 21 July 1682, the special tribunal in the Arsenal met 210 times, heard the cases of 442 suspects, ordered 367 arrests, executed 34 individuals, sent 5 more to the galleys and banished a further 23. The judges had taken a particular interest in those involved who were of some social standing. La Reynie regarded such persons as setting a bad example and therefore as deserving to be treated with severity. For some time, the lieutenant of police had the king on his side. But the magistrates in the Arsenal refused to condemn those accused who were from their own social station: Mmes de Dreux, de Poulaillon and Le Féron were released with the lightest of penalties. On the other hand, as soon as it seemed that they were on the track of some courtiers, they began to manifest some energy. But, like La Reynie, they lacked prudence and critical sense. They did not notice that Louvois, although it was not his department, was interfering at every stage, visiting prisoners, and compiling personal reports to the king. They apparently did not realize that most of the seigneurs and ladies who were being compromised were Colbert's friends or clients. In approaching this appallingly handled lawsuit, historians must follow the lead marked 'enemies of Louvois, friends of Colbert'.

The disturbing role played by Louvois in this persecution was noticed by the maréchal de Luxembourg. This great soldier, a Montmorency, spent fourteen months in the Bastille followed by several months under house-arrest. Yet everyone knew that the minister had M. de Luxembourg in his clutches. Luxembourg was accused of having poisoned a member of the bourgeoisie and then his mistress. Subsequently, there would be testimony to the effect that he had practised witchcraft. Finally, 'Le Sage said that the maréchal duc de Luxembourg had made a pact with the Devil in order to marry his son to the marquis de Louvois' daughter'. Since the House of Montmorency had links with the royal house of France, one can readily appreciate how stupid the accusation really was. The Luxembourg affair would end with the confessions of the marshal's intendant, who, the only guilty party, was condemned to the galleys.

Encouraged by La Reynie and Louvois, the king intervened in the cases of the principal suspects. The honour of the French nobility seemed to him to be being compromised. In 1680, the *président* Boucherat was given to understand that, 'We, the tribunal, judge affairs upon proof; for the king, strong circumstantial evidence will do'. Circumstantial evidence there certainly was against the marquise d'Alluye and the vicomtesse de Polignac. Two *Mancinettes* (Mazarin's nieces) were held under suspicion. Marie-Anne Mancini, duchesse de Bouillon, who was supposed to have made use of her young lover to rid herself of her husband, replied to the accusation by presenting herself before the tribunal with, on one hand, the duc de Bouillon and, on the other, the duc de Vendôme, her supposed accomplice. She replied to La Reynie with studied insolence and then retired, her dignity intact. Her sister Olympe, comtesse de Soissons, was more compromised and less clever; she was advised by the king to go into voluntary exile. If the king intervened in this way, it was because the investigation and trial were outside normal justice, and more in the realm of discretionary powers. Seeing the widening circle of suspects, the king sought to punish the guilty whilst trying to keep the scandal within bounds.

But this effort seemed to rebound when rumours – followed by accusations – began to involve the marquise de Montespan. This was the logical outcome of criminal trials with political overtones: the really culpable saw that their own guilt would be mitigated if their accusations carried political implications. Still blinded by his sincere enthusiasm, La Reynie once more forgot the need for prudence. He forgot that he was not the minister in charge of the police (in 1680, Colbert held that post). He continued to advise Louis XIV to 'get to the whole truth', without considering who the inquiry might implicate or the repercussions which its proceedings might have.

THE MOTHER OF CAESAR'S CHILDREN IS ABOVE SUSPICION

As soon as Athénaïs' name was first mentioned, Louis XIV forbade the clerks to the inquiry the use of registers to take down the questioning, requiring them to use loose sheets of paper. When it was mentioned a second time, he required the tribunal not to concern itself with individuals who might associate the name of Mme de Montespan with their inquiry. Judges worthy of their profession could not accept such prohibitions, and the king, for his part, could not stand back and see the mother of his legitimized children compromised. The only other way forward was to suspend the commission in the Arsenal and disperse the suspects in various châteaux, thus saving the skins of Le Sage, Guibourg and La Voisin's daughter Marie-Marguerite Voison, who had all implicated the *marquise*. Their bold lies had brought them great rewards.

The hostile testimony against the king's favourite had begun with the replies of Le Sage to the lieutenant of police. La Voisin, it seemed, had met two servants of the marquise de Montespan, a chambermaid by the name of Catau and a girl called Mlle des Oeillets, who had overheard them discussing poison. La Voisin repeatedly denied the allegation, but La Reynie teased numerous bits of detail out of La Filastre, Guibourg and Voisin's daughter. From this information, it seemed that, from 1667 to 1679, Mme de Montespan had been in contact with La Voisin, obtaining from her all kinds of *maleficia*. In 1667, Athénaïs had bought charms to work the disgrace of Mlle de la Vallière and stimulate Louis XIV's love for her. The following year, she was a party to a strange ceremony performed by the abbé Mariette designed to strengthen the king's affections for her. There followed numerous other encounters, particularly for the purchase of aphrodisiacs. So far, the circumstantial evidence is credible; Mme de Montespan was stupidly imprudent to have toyed with the likes of La Voisin and Dubuisson. She compromised herself and her piety in calling on these parodies of religious practice. But horoscopes, charms and the use of 'potions' were all common enough measures.

Sensing La Reynie's interest in revelations, her accusers had the fiendish notion of elaborating and inventing new crimes. Louvois was seen visiting Le Sage in prison. La Filastre then claimed that poisonous powder had been supplied by her to Mme de Montespan, although she would deny it just before being tortured. Marguerite Voisin then used her ingenuity to affirm that the *marquise* had wanted to poison the king and Mlle de Fontanges towards the close of 1678. But, at that date Mme de Montespan knew nothing of the favours granted to her would-be rival. And why should she want to kill Louis XIV? Colbert needed to employ only a little persuasion to prove to the king the absurdity of the accusation.

The crowning infamy was reached in the 'revelations' of the abbé Guibourg. Black Masses had been said, with the willing assent of the favourite, in 1667, 1668, 1675 and 1677, with the intention of fortifying or winning back the king's affection for her. On these accusations, La Reynie had only one comment to make: 'It was impossible, morally speaking, that Guibourg was mistaken in his testimony, or that he had invented what he said about a pact with the Devil, and what he chanted over her stomach in the course of these Masses. He lacked the intelligence and ingenuity to invent it all.' (207) It would be charitable not to subject this logic, from someone who is sometimes claimed as the father of modern policing, to too rigorous a scrutiny. There are telling arguments which indicate that the insinuations of this priest were mere calumny. The testimony of Mlle des Oeillets supports her mistress's innocence; and it is clear that the original accusations were threadbare, scarcely credible in themselves. Secondly, Athénaïs' best defence rests in her piety. It is conceivable that Mariette had once said an irregular *Veni Creator* over her, but it is barely credible that this pious woman had undressed before a conjuror and become associated with his diabolical dealings. In any case, the king had provided the *marquise* with a personal bodyguard, which kept a discreet watch on her comings and goings (217). It is difficult to imagine how she escaped so often for these long sabbats without the king being told what was happening. Finally, neither Saint-Simon nor Voltaire regarded Mme de Montespan as in any way culpable.

It was undoubtedly the case, though, that Louvois and, above all, M. de la Reynie had done irreparable harm by not looking for hard evidence but going on circumstantial possibilities and encouraging the king to do the same. They planted suspicions in his sub-conscious mind for which Athénaïs would suffer the consequences. Louis and Athénaïs had a stormy encounter in mid-August 1680 which introduced a new note of bitterness into their relationship. Louis must have concluded that his attractive mistress had been imprudent in resorting to shabby charms and love potions. But he also kept tucked away in a casket (whose contents he burnt only in July 1709) the incriminating documents from the witnesses at the trial. One may refuse to believe that one's mistress was out to commit murder and yet find one's worst suspicions returning to plague one on sleepless nights. One may refuse to entertain the notion that a scion of the Mortemart family would have had anything to do with this blasphemous nonsense and yet not entirely banish the possibility from one's mind, albeit that thirteen years of close relations might make it painful.

If Louis had believed in his mistress's guilt, he would not have waited eleven years (1680–91) before making her leave the court. He would not have kept the *appartement des Bains* at Versailles, nor would he have provoked Mme de Maintenon, by paying his daily visit to the mother of the duc du Maine and the comte de Toulouse. The progressive and delicate erosion of favour gives us the firmest conclusion we have upon the difficult matter of the *affaire*.

The marquise de Montespan's crime was not attempted homicide, or a sin against the Holy Spirit. Her 'crime', stemming from her imprudence, was to connect the king and the royal lineage with the outpourings of a collective madness – a political, rather than a moral error. 'The human race would be in an all too sorry state', wrote Voltaire, 'if it were as common for it to commit crimes as atrocious as those it dreamt of committing.' In the end, it was the mixture of responsibility and innocence in Mme de Montespan which determined the royal response: 'All the external signs of friendship and consideration were maintained, although it offered her no consolation.' (112)

It is again to Voltaire that one looks to end a chapter upon the king's love-affairs. 'Louis XIV regarded it as sufficiently honourable', he wrote, 'that none of these liaisons had any influence upon things in general and that his affairs, whilst they created flutters at court, never disturbed his government. Nothing proves to my mind better that Louis XIV had a soul as large as it was sensitive.' He added: 'I would even have suggested that these court intrigues form no part of the history of the state, had not the great century of Louis XIV rendered everything a subject of interest and had not the veil of discretion been lifted by so many historians who, for the most part, had little respect for it.' (112)

15

The Tedium of the Armed Peace

THE TREATIES of Nymwegen made the King of France the arbiter of Europe. This much is accepted by all historians. And contemporaries, especially the great elector, understood the position. At Nymwegen, as at Aix-la-Chapelle and later at Ryswick, Louis XIV did not require that he retain all his conquests. But some authors have gone a stage further by claiming that Louis wanted to recover what he had lost there later on, by diplomatic means. This is why it is worth investigating the king's foreign policy, in the light of circumstances 300 years ago. Did the king, the arbiter of Christendom, seek to become its overlord?

DID LOUIS XIV LAY CLAIM TO UNIVERSAL MONARCHY?

Under the cloak of glory, Louis kept a sturdy sense of what was necessary for the defence of France. A glance at the map of the Reunions is sufficient to understand that they were the product of neither obstinacy nor imperialism. They were a way of using the alternating pressures of law and brute force in order to complete the military 'iron curtain' of an extensively fortified frontier. If one individual more than any other encouraged the king towards this end it was Vauban, the least aggressive of the military strategists. The Reunions of 1680 onwards do not justify the degree of criticism they have incurred for Louis XIV. They were associated by the Huguenots with two brutal acts: the Revocation of the Edict of Nantes (1685) and the second invasion of the Palatinate (1689). Louis became 'the new Turk amidst the Christians', *Mars Christianissimus* (221), a disciple of Machiavelli who sought a universal monarchy (180). This caricature would be the starting-point for an extensive historical debate. Today, we can afford to look at things more calmly, and the legends are beginning to be reassessed, thanks to the efforts of Ragnhild Hatton (197). It can be shown that most historians have separated the principles of Louis XIV's diplomacy from its practice and forgotten to compare it with the foreign policy of his contemporaries, and have thus made no allowances in their analyses for circumstances.

The principles of French diplomacy were those of France's public law, which rested upon two fundamental tenets: first, the law of succession, the unwritten constitution of France, and, secondly, the inalienability of the royal domain. These rules required the sovereign to cede no territorial rights belonging to the monarchy of which he was the current incumbent. But 'to cede nothing' did not rule out the aggrandizement of the realm, either following a defensive war or 'by the exercise of military power when the adversary refused concessions during negotiations' (197). Besides, the fundamental laws required the king to protect his people. To strengthen the defensive arrangements on the frontier was one of the functions of a conscientious monarch. What was not contained in the constitution was to be found in the oaths of the consecration; the King of France was obliged to defend them all.

Those who criticize Louis XIV for his robust foreign policy are wrong to ignore the behaviour of contemporary monarchs. For too many historians, Louis XIV's *gloire* is interpreted as inordinately cynical, imperialist and Machiavellian. But the extraordinary length of the reign should be taken into account and, as soon as one ceases to look at Louis XIV in isolation, some sense of proportion emerges. 'If we compare Louis XIV with his peers, the other crowned heads of Europe of his day', writes Ragnhild Hatton, 'there are not many disparities between them.' His diplomacy obeyed the same criteria, came up against the same obstacles, and was attempting to resolve the same problems as 'those of all the sovereigns of hereditary states in early modern Europe'.

Let us look beyond the frontiers for a moment, to Vienna, London, Turin and Madrid. Emperor Leopold I was not an innocent in foreign affairs. He was the mainstay of the League of

Augsburg and would be the firebrand of the years from 1700 to 1701; he dreamt of restoring the empire of Charles V, and became embroiled in the conquest of Hungary. Should he not have forfeited the approbation of history? His forty-eight-year-long reign was almost as prolonged as the personal rule of Louis XIV himself. The case of William of Orange scarcely needs elaborating. Stadholder from 1672, king of England from 1689 to 1702, William III was more cynical, imperialist and Machiavellian than his adversary in France ever was. By deposing his father-in-law at the end of 1688, he infringed both law and equity. However, when it was suggested to Louis XIV that he might eliminate so formidable an enemy by having him murdered, he stoutly refused even to consider it. It is not so clear that William of Orange, convinced of his imagined role as a latter-day Gideon, was as respectful of the laws of God and of the life of Louis. The other sovereigns of the period, too, were neither saints nor nineteenth-century liberal statesmen. Up to the making of his will, Charles II of Spain put his hatred of France before solidarity with the Catholic princes and the interests of Spain. Victor-Amadeus, Duke of Savoy, whose reign would last as long as Louis' personal rule, was a diplomat without any scruples whatsoever. He began wars in one camp, only to finish them in another, and his career has more in common with the Louis XIV of black legend than with the Louis XIV of real life.

Finally, there are some events which, for mysterious reasons, historians insist on reviving, like the reopening of an old wound. But 'there are things they would rather hide. Forgotten is the destruction of Susa or Persepolis when it comes to writing Alexander into history as the model of all models' (238). 'It was, of course, the case that the systematic destruction of palaces and churches in a region of Europe which was so highly civilized [the Palatinate in 1689] was bound to have an impact upon Louis XIV's contemporaries and their successors.' (197) But how many pages do we find devoted to the ravages conducted by others? Does one hold against Queen Anne the destruction caused in Bavaria by Marlborough? Fifteen years after the ravaging of the Palatinate, the English used the same brutal tactics. Thereafter, this course of action became more common, and it was no longer the King of France who was taking the initiative. Peter the Great devastated Lithuania to hold back Charles XII's advance in 1707 and 1708, and did not even spare Russia itself.

For his part, Charles XII burnt a number of villages of the Ukraine in 1708–9, whilst, in 1711, his general Stenbock destroyed the town of Altona by fire. It is possibly the case that Louis XIV had, in 1689, reawakened the old practices of the Thirty Years' War. But which historian, English, Russian or Swedish, is entitled to cast the first stone?

In the conflicts in time of peace, the King of France did not differ much from other monarchs, save in his effectiveness. England once hoped to declare war on Denmark over a matter of honours at sea. At the conference at Nymwegen, the Dutch stubbornly refused, on account of their intransigent Calvinism, to accept Pope Innocent XI's usual title of 'His Holiness'.

Louis XIV's personal rule had been inaugurated by certain 'acts of magnificence' which had been judged indispensable to the king's prestige and that of the realm. But then there was only a relatively limited army and a navy still in the making. In 1679, France was more populous, more prosperous and better armed. The country had such an outstanding military and naval pre-eminence, and so evidently high a diplomatic prestige, that any sovereign with such an opportunity would have abused that power, even whilst retaining it within limits. This was precisely what Louis XIV went on to do. The 'acts of magnificence' in the period after the Peace of Nymwegen were never gratuitously undertaken.

THE FRONTIER SPIRIT

The primary motive for the Reunions of towns, seigneuries and territories was neither the king's ambition nor his obsession with glory, but, rather, his overriding concern for the frontiers. He thought he inspired Vauban, but in fact he often found that Vauban inspired him. This military engineer had, like all great entrepreneurs, something of the visionary in him. In 1689, for example, he would propose to Louis XIV a plan to turn Paris, lacking fortifications since 1670, into a military bastion surrounded by two walls. Louis XIV had the good sense to turn it down. But when it came to the question of the frontiers, realism and moderation were ignored in favour of the strongholds dear to the king's heart: Dunkirk, Tournai and Landau. Thus, the king and his commissioner for fortifications urged each other on, oscillating between pragmatism and less objective stances. The result was the corridor running round the realm which is known as the military 'iron curtain'.

Already in 1667, Vauban had demonstrated his siege-craft before Louis XIV. Although he was only granted the title of commissioner of fortifications in 1678, he carried out the duties of the post from 1668 (141). During the periods of peace, he toured the frontier, 'visiting the frontier towns, drawing up projects, considering the overall situation and deluging the minister with plans proposing various schemes, decisions and productions whose scale took on a political dimension' (141). The king took to him, listened to his advice and rewarded him handsomely. In 1692, Louis XIV granted Vauban a recompense of 40,000 *écus* (26). One of the medals in the *Metallic History* was devoted to this theme of defence: SECURITATI PERPETUAE, '150 fortresses or garrisons built or fortified from 1661 up to 1692'.

From 1668 to 1677, the king fortified, with Vauban's assistance, the northern frontier: Landrecies, Philippeville, Arras and Lille, then Menin, Condé, Dunkirk, Douai, Calais, Montreuil and Le Quesnoy, with, to the east, Verdun. After Nymwegen, Vauban's scope increased. The Dutch War had taught him the weak points in the fortifications which he had constructed, or which had been captured, and he set to work to repair or reconstruct them. In one year alone, 1679, he undertook work for Louis XIV in the north at Mauberge, Saint-Omer, Avesnes and Valenciennes; in Lorraine at Montmédy, Longwy and Phalsburg; in Alsace at Huningue; in Franche Comté at Besançon and Salins; and in the south at the forts of Bellegarde and Prats de Mollo, at Montlouis and Villefranche-de-Conflent, and finally at Toulon. Huningue protected upper Alsace thanks to its five new bastions. Montlouis and Villefranche defended the Conflent and Roussillon, and Prats de Mollo held the Vallespir. In 1680, there were improvements undertaken at Ambleteuse, Aire, Sedan and Bayonne; in 1681, at Thionville and Ré; and in 1683, at Belle-Isle, Brest, Gravelines and Binche. In 1685, it was the turn of Blaye and Saint-Jean-Pied-de-Port; in 1687, Belfort and Blamont; in 1689, La Rochelle, Camaret and Bouchain; in 1690, Fort Chapus and Oleron. Vauban henceforth had the ear of the king for the defence of maritime sites as, from the beginning, he had it for inland fortresses.

The king took a personal interest in developments. Although

The Tedium of the Armed Peace

sparing in his travels, he never refused when it was a matter of
fortifications. He was to be seen inspecting them, criticizing or
admiring the ramparts, bastions and earthworks. In 1662, he
took in Gravelines and Dunkirk. In 1667, he inspected Binche
and Charleroi. In 1670, it was the turn of Saint-Quentin, Landrecies, Le Quesnoy, Arras and Douai. On the eve of the Dutch
War, his trip to Flanders was with no intention other than to
test the forward lines of defence. In May 1671, Louis surveyed
the improvements at Dunkirk and inspected Bergues and
Oudenaarde and, the following month, visited Tournai, Ath,
Charleroi and Philippeville. In July, it was the turn of Le
Quesnoy. During the war, he took in Philippeville, Arras and
Lille (1673), Auxonne (1674), Condé (1675), and Calais,
Gravelines and Lille (1677). On 26 February 1678, he gave the
orders to improve the fortifications at Verdun.

Following Nymwegen, the royal inspections were based upon
the gigantic enterprise involving the military 'iron curtain'
(141). In one month, July 1680, Louis XIV inspected Boulogne,
Wissant, Calais, Aire, the fort at Saint-François, the fort at
Saint-Louis, Gravelines and Dunkirk. In August, he visited
Menin, Condé, Valenciennes, Cambrai, Landrecies, Avesnes,
Mauberge, Philippeville, Charleville, Mézières, Sedan, Stenay
and Montmédy. Between 14 October and 5 November 1681, the
king visited the fortifications of Sainte-Marie aux Mines,
Breisach, Strasbourg, Marsal, Nancy and Longwy (167). In
the mathematics of the subject, he became as knowledgeable
as Vauban himself. They were both architects, both delighting
in the beauty of form united to the efficiency of defensive
purpose.

There was another harmony also visible during these visits,
that of the king and his people in the process of rendering the
frontier impregnable. Immediately concerned were his subjects
in the newly conquered provinces. But the whole realm was the
beneficiary, and especially Paris, an open city. The educated
part of the nation took a particular interest in the frontier
improvements. Besides, in the 1680s, defence-work and castella-
tion were all the rage. The art of fortification was even being
taught by the Jesuits in the rue Saint-Jacques in Paris and in
numerous Oratorian colleges.

Although there were fortresses without Reunions, there could
be no Reunions without fortresses. For, like a stronghold, a

region reunited to France by Louis XIV 'made neighbouring princes and states jealous'. *Inde irae.*

A RASH OF REUNIONS

Had Spain possessed a clearly expressed law of succession, there would have been no War of Devolution. If the marches of the Holy Roman Empire had not been subjected to a law whose threadbare nature had been revealed in the Peace of Westphalia, the king would not have been able to pursue the Reunions. But the Treaty of Münster had been full of ambiguities and obscurities, and Louis had the advice of excellent legal opinion. It was legitimate to take advantage of the pacification to straighten out the frontiers, leaving them less open to outside aggression. Louvois was ready to carry out his orders. But to justify such pretensions, a competent and somewhat cynical lawyer would be needed. M. Colbert de Croissy, already associated with the new political mood, was much more the man for the job than the marquis de Pomponne. So, on 18 November 1679, Louis thanked Pomponne for his services and replaced him with Croissy.

The new minister, already in his fifties, was a good jurist. He had been *président* of the superior council at Ensisheim (1657) and *président* of the Parlement of Metz (1662). He had enormous diplomatic experience: the king had sent him as plenipotentiary to Aix-la-Chapelle, he had been ambassador in London (1668–74) and he had been an ambassador to the Congress of Nymwegen in 1678. He knew the marches to the east of France intimately, since he had been intendant in Alsace (1656), whilst his judicial career in the Parlement of Metz had taken him to the Three Bishoprics. He knew every detail of the clauses of the treaties of Westphalia, which had been in no way clarified by the Peace of Nymwegen. It only remained to put this knowledge to work.

In 1679, Pomponne prepared the ground. France continued to be the suitor for Charles II of England. A costly treaty of alliance was signed with the great elector (in October), and another with the Elector of Saxony (in November), whilst the proposed marriage between Monseigneur and Marie-Anne of Wittelsbach seemed to secure the alliance of Bavaria.

The technique of annexation involved exploiting the law to

obtain legal decisions favourable to the annexation of territories to the realm on the basis of a possible interpretation of feudal law and old treaty engagements. In September 1679 and August 1680, the Parlement of Besançon annexed Montbéliard in this way, taking no account of the complaints of the Duke of Württemberg. In Alsace, a province where the duc Mazarin, its governor until his disgrace in 1673, let French influence decline, military pressure was used to reinforce the decisions of the council of Breisach. The imperial towns, even Colmar, had to swear their allegiance to the French king. Then:

> in January 1680, the seigneurs and towns who were tenants-in-chief of the fiefs attached to the guardianship of the Ten Towns and the provostship of Wissembourg, were summoned to do homage to the French king, among them being the Margrave of Baden and the Duke of Zweibrücken. The council, by a decision of 22 March, declared the royal sovereignty over these fiefs as 'constant' ... leaving the way open for other towns, amongst them Strasbourg itself, along with other seigneurs and the nobility of lower Alsace, to be summoned to present their homage. After a new decision of August 1680, only Strasbourg itself retained any independence in Alsace. (216)

This, at any rate, was the opinion of Louis XIV, Croissy and Louvois. The emperor and the German princes did not share it.

In Lorraine, French activity was more subtle. The prelates of the Three Bishoprics were required to render homage to the king and present a list of their fiefs. The bishops accepted the former, but declined to undertake the latter. 'For over a century, their predecessors had so poorly maintained their rights in the bishoprics, that their vassals had totally forgotten their duties. The bishops therefore begged His Majesty, since they did not want to be parties and judges in their own case, to define the extent of their rights by means of a legal tribunal.' (216) This was what the king had been waiting for, and he instituted a 'lawcourt' in September 1679 to investigate the 'rights, lands and seigneuries constituting parts of the temporal patrimony of the bishoprics and clergy of Metz, Toul and Verdun, usurped or alienated, their appurtenances included . . . following the treaties of Münster and Nymwegen' (216). The judges were so enthusiastic in their efforts that they succeeded in annexing the same fief twice. They annexed the *bailliage* of Pont à Mousson and Forbach in the Sarre, which, together, constituted a small province on their own. Just as the Duke of Württemberg had complained about the annexation of Montbéliard, in this case it was the turn of the Elector of Trier, who protested to the emperor. To his complaints before the imperial Diet (July 1680), the French ambassador replied that the king was only exercising rights which were lawfully his following the Treaties of Münster and Nymwegen.

The Diet continued to protest, and three electors indicated their hostility towards France – the Elector Palatine, the Elector of Bavaria and the Elector of Saxony. Louis XIV replied by taking up Frederick-William's suggestion to increase his subsidies to Brandenburg (11 January 1681) and added the promise of military support in the case of conflict. At the same time, and again with the help of funds, he continued to have Charles II and the Duke of York at his behest, insisting that the King of England abandon his alliance with Spain.

The most intriguing and only lasting annexation came at an opportune moment and was a masterstroke. The seizure of Strasbourg upset the German princes and stirred up the chancelleries of Europe; but Louis XIV had calculated rightly that it would not result in a widespread war. The Spanish did not dare to oppose in public the imposition of Catholicism upon a Protestant stronghold. Besides, they hoped to take advantage of it elsewhere, in the Low Countries. The emperor found that he was torn between his Catholicism and the necessity of pleasing his Lutheran vassals; and, in any case, he had a revolt in Hungary on his hands, which was being fomented secretly by the French as well as more openly by the Turks. The empire, as Sourches described it, was 'A great body, difficult to stir into action', and could only express its disquiet. Thus, instead of a coalition, there was only, in 1681, one clear adversary, the Prince of Orange.

Strasbourg, as the capital of Alsace, which was virtually French by the terms of the Treaty of Münster, had been refused neutrality by Louis XIV at the negotiations of Nymwegen. He considered that the town had taken the emperor's side during the Dutch War: in 1674, the magistracy of Strasbourg had, in fact, called upon the emperor for assistance. Following Turenne's victories, Strasbourg declared itself once more neutral, but, when Turenne died, it opened its gates to Montecuccoli. At the beginning of 1679, the town was occupied by the imperial troops. At the close of spring, the king decided to take possession of this important bridgehead. In June, he sent Louvois to prepare the ground. Why should the King of France be overly concerned to provide a legal justification of his actions when Strasbourg had shown how it interpreted neutrality? Louis began discreetly to assemble all the necessary equipment for an expedition.

However, events moved on. During the summer of 1679, Strasbourg dismissed the imperial troops within its walls. Towards the close of 1680, it attempted once more to declare itself a neutral power. France refused to accept this. At the beginning of September 1681, not only had the king made all the necessary preparations, but they had all been accomplished in secrecy. All that was needed was a pretext for invasion, and Strasbourg imprudently provided this. An imperial envoy and reinforcements were expected to arrive in the near future, and everything suggested that Strasbourg's neutrality would once again be abandoned. On the night of 27 to 28 September, three regiments of dragoons, under the command of Asfeld, arrived to take possession of the bridgehead, and, to the alarm of the magistracy, 'announced the arrival of Louvois the following day and Louis XIV within the week' (165). On the 30th, following fruitless negotiations, Strasbourg capitulated to Louvois. According to custom, the king confirmed the town's privileges, although he required that the cathedral return to the Catholic rite. The capital of Alsace had fallen without a single shot being fired in anger.

Louis XIV ratified the Strasbourg capitulation at Vitry on 3 October. On the 6th he was at Bar-le-Duc, on the 11th at Saint-Die, and on the 13th at Sélestat. The French king, who sought to impress his new subjects, arrived in Strasbourg, on the 23rd, in a golden coach, pulled by a train of eight horses. 'All the steeples, as well as the sound of 300 cannon, greeted him . . . After the *Te Deum*, the king held court in impressive fashion at the residence of the Margrave of Baden-Durlach. Several foreign princes came to present their respects' (216).

As the troops marched into Strasbourg, others occupied Casale, the capital of Montferrat: 'thus one might conclude that the French king surpassed Caesar because, in one day, he took both the Po and the Rhine' (216). Casale commanded the Spanish duchy of Milan and kept watch over Piedmont. Despite the double-bluff of Count Mattioli (the one known as the 'Iron Mask'), Louis XIV had obtained from the Duke of Mantua in return for a pension the right to garrison this fortress.

THE COLD WAR

Spain had not, however, accepted the losses sustained at Nymwegen. At the beginning of 1680, the marquis de Villars wrote: 'The Most Catholic King evinces a hatred against France which verges on madness.' (110) By August, all the talk was of the likelihood of renewed conflict. In the autumn, there were various naval incidents; but the principal clash occurred in the Low Countries. The tribunal in Metz declared the reunion of the county of Chiny to France, but the Spanish remained *in situ*. Louis XIV thus ordered the invasion by his cavalry of a few locations in Flanders, Hainaut and, above all, Luxembourg. By the spring of 1681, the county of Chiny was in French hands. By then, the tribunal in Metz had discovered the rights this county had to demand the feudal recognizance of Luxembourg, which had hitherto been immune. Whilst discussions took place, the shadow of Louis XIV's armies was cast over them. In February and March 1682, Luxembourg was under threat. But, as Sourches said, 'The king made his most heroic gesture, even in the light of other similar notable and great occasions.' On 23 March, he raised the blockade of Luxembourg and accepted the King of England's mediation. The Turks were advancing in Hungary, and the Most Christian King had no wish to appear to exploit that.

By the end of March, two camps were already making their appearance in Europe, although England stood to one side. Openly, Louis XIV's included Brandenburg and Denmark; secretly, it also embraced the Turks and the rebels in Hungary. The other took the form of a triple alliance: Sweden, whom the French encroachments upon the duchy of Zweibrücken had more than exasperated, and the Dutch contracted an alliance on 30 September 1681; the emperor joined in February 1682. This formidable conjunction became a quadruple alliance in May 1682 with the addition of Spain. In September 1682, the 'League of the Princes of the Rhine' was formed, a coalition which Louis XIV affected to despise, but, in fact, feared.

The truce between Louis XIV and Charles II of Spain did not prevent antagonism between the two countries. In October 1682, the marquis de Preuilly, who had anchored at Cadiz with four ships, refused to dip his flag in salute to the Spanish admiral 'although the English admiral, who was also there, had already dipped his' (97). Not only was the incident in Spanish waters, but the Spanish admiral had eighteen vessels at his command. Preuilly had set himself against hopeless odds; 'but the Spanish admiral did nothing to attack him and, raising anchor, went and stationed his fleet further away' (97).

The truce would help, or so the French king imagined, to strengthen the Reunions and make them stick. The emperor had enough to do in the east, and, towards the close of 1682, whilst Louis XIV pestered the Diet to give its recognition to the Reunions, even that of Strasbourg, the rebels in Hungary held the country in their grip. In the spring of 1683, there were around 300,000 Turkish soldiers in Belgrade. On 14 July, this army, commanded by the grand vizier Kara Mustapha, appeared at the gates of Vienna, which had been abandoned by the emperor. The whole of the western European part of Christendom seemed in dire peril. In August, the papal nuncio approached the French king to ask him to intervene. Fair words were all that he was offered by way of reply. Why should Louis XIV sacrifice France's good relations with the sultan? All the king had to do was prolong the truce on a longer-term basis, one which would enable the empire to maintain its position in the east without its troubling powers to the west.

In fact, in 1683, the emperor was the recipient of precious assistance – in January from Bavaria, in July from the Elector of Saxony. Although the Duke of Brunswick only sent 600 cavalry, Leopold's principal ally, John Sobieski, King of Poland, arrived at the head of 29,000 Poles, Lithuanians and Cossacks. When it came to the Battle of Kahlenberg on 12 September, Sobieski commanded 65,000 troops and forced the Turks to retreat (123). But Louis XIV did not wait until Vienna was saved to complete the Reunions. It was no longer the Rhine which obsessed the king, for Strasbourg represented the limits of France's ambitions there, but rather Luxembourg. So, before Vienna had been relieved, France let the governor of the Spanish Netherlands know that, since the government in Madrid had not recognized French rights, as stipulated in the tribunal at Metz, an army would be billeted in his provinces and at their expense. Louvois ravaged the Spanish Netherlands, extracting a ransom of three million *livres*. An exasperated Charles II of Spain declared war on 26 October; but he had more than met his match.

Fortunately for Louis XIV, Emperor Leopold was kept occupied in eastern Europe. To the west, the French king offered assurances to the burgher oligarchs of Holland which restrained William of Orange's more bellicose stance. France agreed that it would cease all hostilities if Spain ceded Luxembourg. In the meantime, the French army took Courtrai and Dixmude, ravaged Brussels and Bruges, and bombarded Luxembourg. In March 1684, it was the turn of Oudenaarde to be devastated. On 4 June, the Prince of Chimay offered Luxembourg's capitulation to the maréchal de Créqui. Spain found itself in an unenviable position. Abandoned by the United Provinces unless it accepted France's conditions and neglected by the emperor despite the menace to him of 120 French squadrons in Alsace, it bowed before the inevitable and signed the truce of Ratisbon.

THE AMBIGUITIES OF A TRUCE

Two treaties were signed at Ratisbon on 15 August 1684, one between France and the empire, and the other between France and Spain. There followed a twenty-year truce, during which Louis XIV would retain Strasbourg and Kehl, which were imperial cities, and also Luxembourg, Beaumont, Bouvines and Chimay in the Low Countries. Reactions in France were exultant, since many had been disappointed by Nymwegen. The Reunions were thus considered as the just reward for France after too many concessions. The poets took up their lyres; the Academicians and preachers dusted down their traditional eulogies. Racine published his *Idyll upon the Peace*, in which Peace (*pax gallicana*) thrust all the blame for the recent conflict upon Spain:

> What benefits have they won, these haughty ones
> Who threaten all the world with martial war?
> Behind their frontiers, they are confined once more;
> And that proud pinnacle [Luxembourg], once
> Of all their ambitions the utmost peak,
> Now, through our success in arms, becomes a barrier. (90)

'Barrier' was a revealing word since, the more Louis XIV enfeebled the Spanish Netherlands, the more he weakened what
the Dutch called their 'Barrier'. But the French king pursued
this policy in order to construct his own barrier, what would
be known as the *pré carré*. Since the death of Turenne (1675), a
defensive strategy had evolved (123); and it was unfortunate if
this was seen by others as having aggressive overtones.

From 1681 onwards, the king had given Vauban the task of
consolidating recent gains. In 1682, Vauban created and fortified Sarrelouis. In the following year, the citadel at Strasbourg
seemed to emerge from the ground, although, in fact, it came
from the Rhine:

> all the equipment had been prepared in upper Alsace, and all the
> stones for the citadel were shaped there. These were then shipped
> down the Rhine to Strasbourg and there they were turned over-
> night into a fortress which, alongside the large number of other
> fortifications of the same nature constructed in similar haste,
> ensured that none of the king's enemies would frustrate him in his
> new conquests. (71)

The French king utilized the weapon of surprise because he
realized that the emperor, and the empire in general, would not
stand idly by and watch the construction of a fortress built to
stand for centuries in a city where he had been granted rights for
only twenty years. With Sarrelouis and Phalsburg, Sélestat,
Breisach and Huningue, the defensive works at Strasbourg consolidated the frontier, becoming a guarantee of protection to the
area in question, but not a sign of genuine peace.

On Spain's part, the peace was nothing more than a truce.
France feared the reconstitution of the empire of Charles V upon
the death of Charles II of Spain, and Louis XIV intended to
advance the rights of the Dauphin to the Spanish succession.
There was soon a new *casus belli*. Up to 1685, Spain had tolerated
the presence of foreign merchants at Cadiz, although they
infringed upon Spain's monopoly of trade with Spanish
America. Preuilly often stationed some ships there to protect
French commercial interests. But, in 1685, Spain put such puni-
tive taxes on transatlantic trade that they threatened the interests of those who traded there. In June 1686, another squadron
was sent to Cadiz to require 'the Spanish to abandon the new
tariffs on all merchandise from the West Indies' and to ensure

that the French could continue to 'accompany the fleet which left every year to search for silver and gold in Peru' (216).

Disappointments multiplied in 1685. Louis XIV tried in vain to assert the rights of Madame Palatine, the sister to Charles, the Elector Palatine, who had died on 26 May. D'Avaux attempted without success to build up the burgher oligarchs in Holland against the stadholder; he had to work against the migration of Protestants from France and the Revocation of the Edict of Nantes. By preventing the great elector from undertaking a conflict against Sweden, the King of France forfeited his support. But in respect of England, nothing was altered. French subsidies allowed the Stuarts to become independent of Parliament, and Louis XIV sent James II a present of 500,000 *livres*. But the loyalties of the new monarch acted to the prejudice of France as soon as he tried to bypass Parliament or abolish the Test Acts, which prevented dissidents – Catholics and Presbyterians – from holding public office. And his Francophone attitudes did not stop him from signing a treaty with the United Provinces on 27 August 1685. If we add to this, the agreement between the United Provinces and Sweden (January 1686) and the alliance between Sweden and Brandenburg (February), then the progressive isolation of France becomes apparent.

It was the Protestant countries in Europe which took the initiative, since the Revocation exasperated their peoples. But the Catholic countries, apprehensive of the power and pre-eminence of France, were quickly persuaded to join them in forming a league.

FRENCH PRESTIGE

Everything contributed to French prestige, France's military might, its laws, its artistic achievements, its literature and the universal use of its language. In the chancelleries of Europe, what was not drawn up in Latin was drafted in French. The statesmen of Europe spoke the language of Racine and Bossuet. The depth of French scholarship, the richness and universality of French literature, the examples set by French fine art and the achievements of Versailles and Paris imposed French norms in many spheres. It was a form of cultural imperialism.

In the period between the Dutch War and the Ten Years'

War, France made its presence felt throughout the world, enjoying a hegemony which inspired both admiration and fear. And, in order to keep a vigilant watch for that admiration turning into envy and that fear turning into hatred and open hostility, the king and Louvois ran a 'secret military diplomatic network' which complemented, especially in Italy and the Danubean lands, the official network, run by Croissy (165). Information networks and channels for infiltration were operated by soldiers in disguise, acting as a form of prototype secret service.

Louis, whose sense of propaganda bordered on genius, also made intelligent use of propagandists. Eustache Le Noble, one of them, was the author of a Gallican broadsheet entitled *The Political Touchstone* which defended Louis' interests against Pope Innocent XI. Another, with greater imagination, was Gatien de Courtilz, sieur de Sandras (1644–1712). He wrote the *Memoirs of M. d'Artagnan*, which inspired Dumas's *Three Musketeers*, and was a devoted acolyte to Louis XIV. Courtilz de Sandras also published a squib entitled *The Conduct of France since the Peace at Nymwegen*, a blatant and hollow attack which provided the same pamphleteer with the opportunity to write in the opposite vein a *Reply to the Work Entitled: The Conduct of France* (1683). Three years later, Sandras 'took up residence in Holland, where he published *The Political and Historical Mercury* every month. He became, however, so notorious an advocate of France that he had to leave the country' (165).

Up to the end of the reign, Louis XIV supported patriotic and officially sponsored writers who were capable of defending him against his critics at home and abroad. Donneau de Visé, famous for his foundation of the *Mercure Galant* in 1672, would be amongst the most tireless and effective propagandists for the regime. His *Memoirs towards a History of Louis the Great* (1697–1703) ran to ten folio volumes. It was in the aftermath to the Peace of Nymwegen that this propaganda effort was at its most active. Anti-French polemicists repeatedly found that their thunder was stolen by the shrewd counter-polemicists who protected Louis.

Nothing, however, could match the steady and continuous influence of the king's representatives, the ambassadors, soldiers, sailors, missionaries and explorers. Diplomats enjoyed the magnificent life-style which went with representing a nation with a sense of destiny. When the marquis de Lavardin was

preparing to join the embassy at Rome in March 1687, Louis
XIV gave him 20,000 *écus* for his expenses and a salary of 24,000
écus a year. Celebrating the birth of the archduke, five years
previously, the resident diplomats in Vienna authorized various
firework displays. That organized by the marquis de Sébeville
did not go unnoticed, for, above the display, there was 'a sun at
the heart of the royal device with, at the centre, the inscription:
Fulget ubique'. Eight months after Louis' entry into Strasbourg,
this was 'a considerable talking point' among Imperialists (97).

During the Reunions and the Spanish conflict, Louis might
have been more aggressive. He had the largest army in the
world; his troops were 'finer than ever' (42). The military
reforms undertaken after Nymwegen by Louvois retained the
services of almost all his officers. The peacetime forces were
retained in wartime readiness. In the meantime, parade-ground
barracks were increased in numbers (97) and the fortresses were
reinforced. On the eve of the Ten Years' War, at the end of 1688,
Louis XIV confirmed that he could muster a force of 300,000
men, and this was not an idle boast. Experts confirm that the
French army was more easily mobilized than any other fighting
force in Europe: 'The king was obeyed to the letter and it would
only take *a moment* . . . to order his troops on the march.' (42) The
naval forces were also at their zenith. Whilst the Dutch and
English cut back on their armaments and training (228), 'the
king had a navy more numerous and better than [that of] any
other European prince' (97): 118 ships of the line, 19 frigates, 11
fire-ships, 10 gunships, 21 fly-boats and 10 smaller vessels, 'a
total of 189 ships' (237). The realm lacked sailors, particularly
after the Revocation, but the arsenals had been replenished, the
higher levels of the naval hierarchy were in an excellent state –
Duquesne, Preuilly and Tourville were all lieutenant-generals;
Gabaret, Villette and Châteaurenault squadron leaders –, and
its squadrons dominated the seas.

Colbert and Seignelay also fostered naval administration and
armaments. At Toulon, the new dock could 'easily hold 100
warships'. The Toulon roads were covered with gun emplace-
ments 'to protect it from the assaults of any enemy'. At Brest,
the quays were lined with new magazines and naval workshops,
and 'could take up to fifty large ships, not counting frigates
or other smaller vessels'. Six hundred cannon 'protected the
entrance, so that the naval forces of the king were completely

secure there' (71). To train the officers to command these ships, the government no longer relied on makeshift arrangements. In 1683, Colbert created 'three companies of marine guards, veritable naval colleges, stationed at Brest, Rochefort and Toulon' (276). Their cadets studied mathematics, astronomy, hydrography, good manners . . . and dancing.

These naval officers were then given every opportunity to prove their talents. No other power then challenged French supremacy in the Mediterranean. In 1684, during the Spanish conflict, Relingues, commanding *le Bon*, pinned down thirty-five Spanish galleys with just that one ship. In 1680 and 1681, Duquesne mastered the Barbary pirates and bombarded Chios; in 1682 and 1683, he shelled Algiers, using a new kind of bomb developed by the engineer Renau. In May 1684, it was Genoa's turn to be attacked for having provisioned Spanish ships (274). The comte d'Estrées took over from him and bombed Tripoli (June 1685) and Algiers once more (July 1688).

FAR-OFF SEAS, DISTANT LANDS

Naval operations in the Mediterranean inspired fear and brought Louis XIV economic and political advantages. French trade with Spain often came close to interloping. Muley Ismael, the Sultan of Morocco, ceded commercial facilities to France in a treaty of 1682. French warships sailed the oceans whilst French missionaries took Christianity to the Far East. Without the Jesuits, inheritors of the legacy of St Francis Xavier, and the Parisian seminary for missions abroad (established in 1663), the 'rise of France as a colonial power in the eighteenth century' would not have occurred. The Jesuits held Confucian philosophy in high regard, thought the cult of ancestor worship and other oriental rites harmless, and wanted to integrate Chinese words or expressions such as *Tien-tchou* (the Lord of Heaven) into the catechism in place of 'the God of Abraham'. The Seminarists provided the Papacy with missionaries to the kingdoms of Tongking and Cochin-China; they were opposed to such compromises and denounced the maxims of Confucius as 'false, foolhardy and scandalous' (58). The former stressed efficiency, the latter orthodoxy; but both worked for France as well as the Lord of Heaven.

At the same time, France expanded its presence in West Africa. An edict of June 1679 confirmed the privileges of the Senegal Company, granting it a monopoly in bartering for slaves to supply West Indian planters. Despite disagreements between various administrators, the exploration of the interior, between Senegal and Niger was a great achievement (129).

Despite the French presence in Siam (1686) and the patchy successes of the Senegal and East India companies, the zone for expansion in the seventeenth century was not the Indian Ocean or the western and southern Atlantic, but America. At the time, the emphasis was on the Caribbean islands (Santo Domingo was French and to it were added Martinique, Guadeloupe and Cayenne). In 1687, the French West Indies supported 19,000 Europeans and 28,000 slaves. But Louis XIV and Colbert had vision enough to foresee the longer-term interest which would develop in colonies on the American continent: 'Canada', Acadia, the Hudson River, Labrador and the Great Lakes.

Here, the English occupied the neighbouring lands and, with less space at their command, numbered 200,000 by 1693, whilst the French Canadians only numbered 12,000. Rivalry between the two groups was endemic. While France and England enjoyed reasonable working relations in Europe, the 'thirty years' war' – as the inhabitants of New France (Canada) christened the hostilities which began in America in 1693 – continued and was brought to only a temporary halt by the Peace of Utrecht. During these disputes, d'Iberville took some English trading-posts on Hudson Bay in 1686 and received the governorship of the whole of northern Canada from Louis XIV (274). To sustain this French presence, the twin policies of expansion and settlement were adopted. Colbert had long been interested in the latter. Frustrated by the fact that the French seemed unwilling to acquire snow-clad acres in Canada, and anxious to ensure that the province had the means to increase its trade and defend itself against aggression, he hoped for the co-operative exploitation of the province in conjunction with the native Huron peoples. This bold strategy ran up against three insurmountable obstacles: the colonists had no desire to marry Huron squaws, the Catholic Church feared a progressive paganization of the country, and the king, sharing the prejudices of the clerics, opposed his minister's ideas. New France would increase its native population only through conjugal unions between the colonial Canadians themselves.

A second way of fortifying His Majesty's lands, and a way of attracting new immigrants, was to explore and open up virgin country. Jolliet and père Marquette opened up the route for these explorations. They reached (1673) the waters of the Mississippi and then travelled down it, not as far as its mouth, but far enough to realize that the great river was not a new route to China but probably led into the Gulf of Mexico (274). Robert Cavelier de la Salle (1643–87), originally from Rouen, landed at Montreal in 1667 and continued exploration in the face of Jesuit hostilities – they wanted to turn southern Canada into a 'new Paraguay' – to a successful outcome. In 1678, he engaged the services of Henri de Tonty, known as Iron Fist, and twenty-one young Frenchmen: officers, clerics, a surgeon and even a notary. Thirty-one Indians acted as their escort. They set out in December 1681 and reached 'the great river' Messchacebee in January 1682 at latitude 38°. M. de la Salle christened it the 'River Colbert'. He embarked on 13 February and descended on the spate until he arrived at the village of Arkansas on 14 March. He claimed the land in the name of His Majesty and called it 'Louisiana' in the king's honour, erected a commemorative column, and then continued the descent of the river. On 9 April, they arrived at the river mouth, sang a *Te Deum* and confirmed in a parchment registered before a notary that they had claimed possession, on behalf of the king, of 'this land of Louisiana, its seas, harbours, ports, bays, adjacent cliffs and all the nations, peoples, provinces, cities, towns and villages, mines, fish stocks, rivers and waters within the said Louisiana'. They returned to Quebec on 2 November 1683, 'without losing a single man' (79). Cavelier de la Salle later fell victim to bad luck and imprudence. Assigned a small fleet by Seignelay in 1684, he failed to locate the mouth of the Colbert River by sea and ended up in Texas, where he was assassinated (274). But d'Iberville and the other explorers had established the route for their successors and it was no mean achievement to have put Colbert's and Louis' names on the face of the as yet mostly unexplored American continent.

GALLICAN FEVER

Hundreds of miles away from the French Mississippi, a very different conflict was reaching its climax. The only point they had in common was that, both in America and in Europe, they were about the king's glory and the realm's prestige. This is how one should approach the battle over the *régale*, and the thunderbolt of the Four Articles in 1682.

The *régale* was 'a customary right, appertaining to the bishoprics in northern France, permitting the king to stand in for a deceased bishop in order to benefit from the revenues of the vacant see and nominate to all non-parochial benefices' (131). The sums involved were modest; a dispute over such a matter therefore had to be one involving the underlying principles.

The origin of the dispute lay in the declarations of 10 April 1673 and 2 April 1675, which regarded the *régale* as applicable throughout the realm. Pope Clement X wisely ignored these two decisions; but two Augustinian bishops in the French Midi, Pavillon, Bishop of Alet, and his friend Caulet, Bishop of Pamiers, refused to accept this extension of the king's rights and even excommunicated interloping clerics nominated by the king. Their archbishops censured them, but they appealed to Rome. However, the new pope, Innocent XI, did not overawe Louis XIV, despite his multiple briefs (1678, 1679, 1680) demanding that the king annul his regalian declarations. Pavillon's death in 1677 did nothing to change the situation.

The Assembly of the Clergy held in 1675, under the presidency of Archbishop Harlay, had refused to support the Bishop of Alet; that held in 1681, despite Louis XIV's efforts to calm ruffled feelings, condemned 'the threats issued by the pope against the Eldest Son of the Church' (131). This was in reply to the third brief issued by Innocent XI, which had spoken of possible censure of the king. At this assembly, the issue became passionately debated. Archbishop Le Tellier demanded the calling of a national council of the Church. Cardinal d'Estrées, the king's councillor at Rome, proposed that Louis XIV should threaten the Holy See by summoning just such a council of the Church. When Louis was asked, by some forty bishops, to call an extraordinary Assembly of the Clergy, it was seen as yet another way of putting pressure on the Papacy. But the pope refused to negotiate, and so nothing stood in the way of the holding of this emergency assembly of bishops, which took place in Paris towards the end of October 1681. Once in session, they took advantage of the tensions between Rome and Versailles to affirm their Gallicanism, irritate the pope and also disturb the Most Christian King. If anyone was carried away by the rhetoric of Gallicanism in February 1682, it was Charles-Maurice Le Tellier, not the French king.

Louis XIV did not draft the declaration of the Four Articles which emerged from the Assembly of the Clergy (the *Declaration of the French Clergy on Ecclesiastical Power*). In its first article, it stated 'that St Peter and his successors in the Church at large, vicars of Jesus Christ, have only God's authority to act in spiritual matters'. This was the theory of the two kingdoms, from which it was deduced that 'kings and sovereigns may be in no way constrained by any ecclesiastical power over temporal matters'. Their power in those areas, according to the thirteenth chapter of the Epistle to the Romans, remained absolute. The second article recognized 'the plenitude of power that the Holy Apostolic See and the successors of St Peter have over spiritual matters', whilst accepting the superior authority of councils of the Church. The third article wished to ensure that 'apostolic power was exercised following the canons [of the Church], inspired by the Holy Spirit and consecrated by the general respect in which they are universally regarded; that the regulations, customs and constitutions of the realm and Church in France should apply to their full extent' and be inviolable – a restriction upon pontifical authority, even in spiritual matters. The final article expanded on the second article, saying that, 'Although the pope has the principal role in matters of faith, and although his decrees are binding upon each and every Church, nevertheless, his decisions are not unalterable, unless they also have the consent of the whole Church' (106).

These articles, drawn up by Bossuet and approved by the assembly on 19 March, perhaps came close to expressing Louis XIV's basic views on the matter, but they did not conform to his public declarations on it. All too many people hoped to be able to feed the flames of this controversy: the Parlement, the Sorbonne, and a group of prelates. At the heart of them stood the Le Tellier clan, the chancellor and his two sons (130), one of whom was Archbishop of Reims (Charles-Maurice), and the other (François-Michel) minister for war. Some commentators have even drawn a comparison between the conflict with the Papacy and the policy of the Reunions (168). But the declaration of 1682 fell short of the Gallicanism espoused by the Le Telliers. The Four Articles represented a compromise. Papal infallibility would only be universally recognized in the Catholic Church in 1870. Two centuries before the Vatican Council of 1870, there was a whole range of nuances available in the definitions of the temporal and spiritual powers of St Peter's successor, and also in those of the frontiers between Papal power and the authority of Church councils.

The compromise turned out to be too Gallican for the French king. In reality, Louis, like Colbert, rather hoped for an end to this wearisome dispute, as is clear from his own response. He made sparing use of the theses of the 1682 assembly. On the one hand, he signed a declaration on 20 March imposing the doctrine of the Four Articles in all schools, but, on the other, he sought to appease Rome, aware of its indignation and of disquiet in his own entourage. Cardinal d'Estrées soothed Innocent XI, and the pope, having the sense to admonish the Gallican prelates without condemning the King of France, did not attempt further to menace the king or his realm. In return, Louis XIV issued a *lettre de cachet* on 29 June which brought the troublesome Assembly of the Clergy to a close (130).

> It was not all over yet, however. Louis XIV had nominated to vacant bishoprics two deputies to the assembly who had signed the Four Articles. The pope refused their canonical installation. Cardinal d'Estrées took it upon himself to request no further papal bulls, for as long as the pope refused to issue them to former members of the Assembly of the Clergy of 1682. In this way, a further dispute arose from the ashes of the 1682 assembly, that of the canonical institution of bishops nominated by the king to vacant bishoprics. (131)

The Revocation of the Edict of Nantes in October 1685 did nothing to appease the Papacy, although the king hoped to gain a twofold advantage from it: first, by its demonstrating his devotion to Catholicism, and, secondly, by its convincing the pope that the Church in France needed its full complement of clergy to preach to the 'nouveaux convertis' (newly converted) and that it was not the moment to leave episcopal sees unfilled (130). In fact, two political matters arose which merely heightened the tensions between Rome and Versailles, one concerning 'quarters with diplomatic immunity', the other the electorate of Cologne.

The first quarrel broke out when the duc d'Estrées, the French ambassador in Rome and brother to the cardinal, died there on 30 January 1687. The French ambassador had, up until then, enjoyed 'immune diplomatic quarters', exempt from the jurisdiction of the pontifical authorities – other embassies no longer enjoyed this right. By a papal bull of 12 May, Innocent XI suppressed this immunity; but Louis XIV ordered the marquis de Lavardin, France's new ambassador, to act as though immunity still existed, despite the threat of excommunication. So Innocent XI considered Lavardin 'excommunicate, refused him an audience, and swiftly left the king and his ministers in no doubt that they would also incur the penalties contained in the bull of 12 May' (130).

The second quarrel concerned the see of Cologne. On the death of its incumbent, the canons met on 19 March 1688 to vote for his successor, but they were divided between those who sustained Clement of Bavaria, the emperor's candidate, and those who sustained Egon von Fürstenberg, Bishop of Strasbourg, the French king's candidate. Since there was no majority in favour of either, the choice was left to Innocent XI, who confirmed Clement of Bavaria's nomination. Louis regarded this as a hostile act, and Franco-Papal relations were broken off until 1693 (although Innocent XI died in August 1689). French retaliation was not long delayed. Avignon was once more seized and the Parlement of Provence declared it reintegrated into the realm, and then, to head off an imperial offensive, the king sent his troops to occupy Cologne whilst Monseigneur laid siege to Philippsburg. This provided William of Orange with an undreamt-of opportunity of setting sail for England and deposing James II. Thus, upon the pretext of the *régale*, came the attack on the Palatinate, which was followed by the dethronement of the English king and the Ten Years' War, the first act of 'the second Hundred Years' War, from 1689 to 1815' (239).

16

Louis and his Servants

THE PEACE of Nymwegen was weighted too much in France's favour and could only be a truce. Yet this moment of ascendancy, coming between Louis' offensive wars and the subsequent wars of survival, provides an opportunity to examine the system which made this undeniable political triumph possible. For, although it would be unjust to deny Louis' personal responsibility for this success, he did not act alone. The conception and perseverance were the king's, and to these he added the art of associating the elite to his projects, the art of commanding and of expecting obedience. But, at the same time, the quality of his subjects' collaboration with their prince's initiatives was noteworthy. Like him, they cultivated a Christianized conception of honour, an elitist conception of how to follow God's law. For the king, the primary form of honour was glory; to his subjects, honour established the primacy of service.

THE HONOUR OF SERVING

The king, the nobility and all willing subjects understood the inseparability of honour and service. Honour demanded service and to serve was an honour. Preaching to the court on Maundy Thursday 1676, Fléchier proclaimed: 'You know, gentlemen, how praiseworthy an ambition it is to serve the king; this honourable servitude and the burdens of royal service are preferable to freedom, however enticing; services to kings are in themselves honourable and bring their own rewards.' (39) 'Honour', added Boileau, 'is like a steep and boundless island', whose inhabitants were not to be deterred in their desire to serve the king and state. In the sixteenth and early seventeenth centuries, Frenchmen who said 'I serve' or 'I am in service', often noblemen, meant military service. The nobility inherited a prejudice in favour of the profession of arms, and the Capetians, 700 years old in 1687, were a warlike monarchy before becoming administrative. But, after 1661, the determination of the king had begun to change people's values and, after twenty years of constant effort, the transformation was complete. Antoine Furetière's *Universal Dictionary* declared that, from now on, the robe would challenge the sword as the sole embodiment of service. Admittedly, the long tradition of army service meant that the sword was still strongly associated with the idea of service: 'To go and serve the king', said Furetière, 'means joining the army.' But he added: 'It is also said that this ambassador in the robe *served* well in securing this treaty, or that intendant *serves* well.' Under the heading of *serviteur*, the robe overtook the sword, and civil service was mentioned first: 'This magistrate and that captain are good *serviteurs* of the king and have always worked for his interests.' This change was the result of twenty years of Louis' personal rule. Modern France was being born.

To the robe went 'pride of place', according to La Bruyère, while the sword took the greatest risks on the battlefield. The two estates or professions became rivals. 'The nobility', La Bruyère continued, referring to their military role,

> risk their lives to ensure the safety of the state and the glory of their sovereign, while the magistrates relieve the king of part of the burden of passing judgement on his people. Both are sublime and admirably useful functions. Men are capable of no acts more noble and I do not understand how the sword and robe have come to despise each other so much. (48)

Although the king appeared to show greater regard for military exploits – and Dangeau and Sourches paid most attention to transcribing speeches he addressed to soldiers – this was merely a matter of policy and *politesse*. The value placed by the king on the Colbert and Louvois clans illustrates the position of the robe. Louis chose councillors of state from among the *maîtres des requêtes*; he named the *premiers présidents* of the sovereign courts and received their oaths; and he granted pensions to *présidents*, long-serving councillors and first under-secretaries of ministries (97). Thanks to these favours, robe and sword became united in royal service. Emulation replaced animosity, not only between the different branches of service, but also within the military estate. Even with a name like 'Molé', illustrious in the Parlement, less so in His Majesty's household, it was possible to obtain a command in the king's guard (97), whilst the Colberts were so eager to be killed in battle that they appeared to try to deprive the House of Choiseul of its position as the leading supplier of the glorious dead.

THE CRUCIBLE OF SERVICE

For Louis XIV, the concept of service was not confined within particular social classes, as may be seen by the way in which men of different social backgrounds were brought together in the army. The first duty of a *gentilhomme* was to risk his life for his country. We have already seen the king himself in the army while still a minor, and we shall shortly find a cluster of Bourbons at the front.* The most illustrious generals were of princely blood: Turenne, the king's cousin and grandson of William the Silent, buried alongside du Guesclin in the basilica at Saint-Denis; Condé, a first prince of the blood; Vendôme, Louis' first cousin once removed. If ever anyone, despite his faults, embodied the idea of service, it was the prince de Condé. On 10 December 1686, just before he died, he wrote to the king:

> I have spared nothing to serve Your Majesty. I have tried to fulfil willingly the duties to which my birth obliges me, by my sincere devotion to Your Majesty's glory. It is true that, at one moment in my life, I behaved in a manner which I have been the first to condemn, and for which Your Majesty was gracious enough to pardon me. Since then, I have tried to make good this error through my unbroken fidelity to Your Majesty. My regret is that I have never been able to perform enough great acts to deserve the favour which you have always shown me. (57)

The chevalier de Quincy wrote of Vendôme that 'he was like a hero, a great and honourable man', gifted with a perspicacity

* See ch. 23

and bravery which he seemed to inherit from Condé. 'He was a great citizen and a good Frenchman, devoted to his prince with such dedication that his private affairs suffered greatly for it. Adored by his soldiers, he served only for his glory, and that of the king and his country.' (88)

Behind these leaders, the high nobility could not shirk its responsibilities. In the marquise de Sévigné's circle in 1672, 'everyone mourns a son, a brother, a husband or a lover'. In 1677, a wounded nobleman was afraid of being branded as a shirker when his convalescence appeared prolonged (96). When war seemed imminent in 1688, young courtiers thought only of throwing themselves into battle. 'All the young people, those in employment as well as those who were not, asked for the king's permission to follow Monseigneur.' (97) The competitive spirit was so strong, rising to a peak at the time of the League of Augsburg, that even churchmen of noble birth yearned to don a military uniform. Dumas' Aramis in *The Three Musketeers* was not a purely fictional creation. In November 1689, 'the abbé Soubise, becoming the head of his family after the death in combat of his brother, the prince de Rohan, left the Church and entered the king's musketeers', expecting to be given command of a regiment. On 30 August 1692, following the death at the front of the marquis de Hocquincourt, of the Monchy family, the abbé de Hocquincourt went to Versailles to ask the king to grant him the regiment which had been commanded by his three brothers, all of whom had been killed in the previous eighteen months (26). But he made the mistake of appearing in ecclesiastical robes, thus causing Louis to delay giving him an answer. The Rohans were dukes and princes. The Monchys, whose ranks included a marshal of France, were courtiers. But what should we make of this news, recorded by Dangeau? Louis, he wrote on 2 April 1695, 'has given a little abbey to the abbé de Sanguinet, who has had *thirteen* brothers killed in royal service'. The king succeeded in converting traditional loyalties and the pervasive sense of public duty into patriotism and in making this transformation in many different social milieux.

Louis always respected his humbler servants. Later on, the king recounted at his *lever* on 30 April 1712, how the marquis de Mézières and forty carabineers had been ambushed and how, fortunately, after two hours' fighting, the small detachment had got the better of eighty enemy hussars. Not for the first time,

Louis exploited the latest news to provide lessons in courage and loyalty. In this instance, according to Sourches, 'the king expounded at length the praises of the carabineers and their officers, all of whose names he knew, and, in particular, a certain Lieutenant Saint-Antoine, who was a soldier of fortune' (97). Honour was rendered to all combatants, regardless of rank or origin. From 1668 onwards, Louis was preoccupied with the fate of his former soldiers, especially those disabled in service. In 1670, he announced the construction of a military *hôpital*, the Hôtel des Invalides, and building work began immediately. By 1674, the main part of the huge edifice was ready for use, to be inhabited by former soldiers and disabled veterans. In 1676–7, the building was adorned by two fine churches: Saint-Louis and the Church of the Dome (165). The *Metallic History* rightly talks of this as 'a royal magnificence', a masterpiece of Bruant and Mansart's, Louis' greatest building project in Paris. The king only visited Paris sixteen times between April 1682 and his death, yet, on five of these visits, he called in on his old comrades in arms: 1 May 1682, 19 and 20 May 1701, 14 July 1701 and 28 August 1706 (97). The last visit was to inaugurate the Church of the Dome; but, in July 1701, Louis had 'inspected it down to the last detail and had seen the officers and soldiers having supper' (97). Familiarity with the building has perhaps tended to obscure its originality, unique throughout the world. No one has evoked this great Escorial of royal, military and charitable endeavour better than Chateaubriand in his *Spirit of Christianity*:

> The Invalides is composed of three main buildings, forming, with the church, a large square. What taste is displayed in this simplicity! What beauty in the courtyard, nothing other than a military cloister, where art mingles warlike and religious ideals, combining the image of a camp for former soldiers with the comforting evocation of a hospice! It is at one and the same time a monument to the God of War and the God of the Gospels . . . In the front courts, everything evokes the idea of combat: ditches, glacis, ramparts, cannon, tents, sentries. Further in, the hubbub fades away, to be lost entirely inside the church, where a profound silence reigns. The religious building lies behind the military ones, an image of rest and hope amidst a life full of danger. The age of Louis XIV understood, perhaps uniquely, this moral affinity, and, in the arts, did what it felt obliged to do, nothing more, and nothing less . . . One senses that a nation which built

such a palace for its soldiers' declining years, had been blessed with the power of the sword as well as the sceptre of the arts. (153)

THE KING'S EXPECTATIONS

Louis XIV expected a kind of perfection in those who gave him service and felt entitled to demand it for himself, the monarchy, the Christian religion and France, embodying in himself the needs of the nation, the state and the people. The king commanded in the name of higher interests, and his subjects obeyed in deference to these imperatives. It was accepted that the elite should always be available and prepared to serve. In a country where mobilization on the spur of the moment and obligatory national service were out of the question, the elite was expected to be always at the ready to answer an imperative command and even to anticipate the king's order. This was the schedule of conditions imposed by honour in an unequal society. Mme de Sévigné wrote on 10 August 1677: 'The news of the siege of Charleroi [invested from the 6th by the Prince of Orange] has sent all the young, even the lame, hurrying to serve.'

The king supervised the intellectual, technical and moral education of his future senior civil and military servants; if he did not ask them to be ascetics, he demanded, however, certain basic moral standards. The entire politics of service was shown in May 1701 when the king granted a cavalry regiment to the duc de la Feuillade and a command in his guards to the marquis de Flamarens. To La Feuillade, Louis announced: 'Monsieur, up to now I have been dissatisfied with your conduct, and this has forced me to show you the marks of my discontent; now that I see you are following a better path, I am inclined to show you favour, and I therefore begin with the grant to you of the Tournelle regiment in the hope that you will continue to behave wisely in future.' (97) To Flamarens, he declared: 'You have always shown wisdom, and I give you command of the English guards with permission to sell your office in the company of dragoons, as you have begun to, because I am assured that you will continue to conduct yourself well.' (97)

His apprenticeship over, a servant of the state was required to show, in thought and deed, a combination of qualities which, taken together, made up the morality of public service. These were an understanding of the task in hand (which meant devotion to the public good, a sense of honour and a sense of solidarity), competence, discretion, disinterestedness, discipline, fidelity and heroism. The most important of these was the first. The king's servant was not an automaton. One could not obey king and state without also considering the general interest. Mme de Sévigné commended royal service to her son-in-law, the comte de Grignan, a military commander in a frontier province, adding: 'But it is necessary also to handle carefully the susceptibilities of the Provençals, so as to be able to make sure that the king is obeyed in that country.' The king's lieutenant should be the embodiment of the king's honour. If he found himself cut off from higher authority, he was required to put honour before his own conception of the common interest. Neither M. de la Boulaye, governor of Exilles in 1708, nor the comte de la Mothe, governor of Ghent in 1709, understood this (97). They earned the wrath of the king by surrendering these towns. Finally, good servants had to live in harmony one with another. In 1707, Louis had to waste his energies reprimanding the minister Chamillart and the maréchal de Catinat, requiring them to make peace with each other (26).

Competence was not in short supply when a spirit of emulation was fostered: Colbert, Louvois, Seignelay, Vauban and the Pontchartrains were proofs of that fact, not to mention the marquis de Chamlay, Louis' right-hand man. On 18 June 1695, the courtiers attending the king's *coucher* heard this verdict from the king on his latest meeting with Chamlay: 'We have been considering what the enemy may now do; we have no need of maps of Mons, Namur and Charleroi; we know these places well, having studied them so closely together.' (26)

His early training under Mazarin had taught Louis the value of discretion among colleagues, a sense of secrecy which might be called duplicity by those less appreciative of it. Persistent questioning might elicit a great deal of information from Croissy, and some from Pomponne: 'but, as for M. de Pontchartrain, it would be easier to get blood from a stone; he turns everything into a mystery' (24). This made him the perfect minister, just as Bontemps, a veritable wall of silence, was the perfect valet.

Disinterestedness, another virtue appreciated by Louis, must appear to us a rather relative quality. The king's servants had their rewards, and contemporaries were well aware of the immense fortunes accumulated by Colbert and Louvois. But the king alone decided what the rewards of office were to be, and service without remuneration was not precluded. Some ministers went heavily laden with the fruits of office, but there was never an automatic benefit from services rendered. It was well known that some forms of public service could be expensive. When the colonel of the Vaisseaux regiment took his leave of the king in 1701, he passed this off with humour: 'Sire, poor d'Entragues stands before you; he will be eating soldiers' rations during the campaign, but he will nevertheless serve Your Majesty more genuinely and assiduously than all the rest.' Louis replied: 'I have provided for this, granting you a pension of 3,000 *livres*.' (97)

Discipline, the virtue of hierarchical obedience, was particularly appreciated, and was expected above all from the military. Every year in the early spring the king ordered all commanders, inspectors and colonels to return to their stations and return home only when their jobs had been done. When a war began, they would be ordered to rejoin their companies a few days later. So important was this discipline to the king that refusal to obey took precedence over duels and accusations of sodomy as the principal reason for punishment by temporary exile from his court (297). One affair in 1685 illustrates how even disobedience towards Louvois led to disgrace, was an act almost constituting treason. Louvois declared to Lord Hamilton, brother of the comtesse de Gramont, 'that the king was unhappy with him because his regiment was mediocre. Hamilton replied that, though some companies were bad, the rest were in good shape and, furthermore, that even if his regiment was a bad one, he should not be held to blame for it'. After all, what were inspectors for? The minister retorted that:

> colonels were given enough authority to assume responsibility for their regiments. But Hamilton replied that he could see that his services were not appreciated by the king and that, since the Duke of York had become King of England, he would enter his service, and he should know that he would willingly return to the country whence he came. M. de Louvois replied that the king forced no one to remain in his service, and immediately reported this conversation to His Majesty, who was offended by it and said that it was only out of respect for the comtesse de Gramont that her brother was not sent to the Bastille. (97)

Fidelity complemented obedience and was another virtue held in high esteem. Based on the assumption of a tacit agreement to let bygones be bygones, it demanded a supreme sacrifice from a loyal servant. No one was more faithful to Louis XIV than former *frondeurs* like Turenne, Condé, Luxembourg and Vauban or former Protestants like Pellisson, Montausier, Villette and Duquesne's two nephews. The faithful servant had a different conception of time from that of the egotist or the *arriviste*. The duc de Vendôme, for example, spent four years at the front, from February 1702 to February 1706, eschewing winter quarters, supporting Philip V in Italy, and gaining victories at Santa Vittoria and Luzzara (1702), San Sebastiano (1703), Cassano (1705) and Calcinato (1706) (292). There was no age limit upon fidelity. At a time when a man of fifty was considered old, it nevertheless seemed natural for Duquesne to be placed in command at the age of sixty-four of the squadron which bombarded Genoa in 1684, and for the seventy-two-year-old Villette to lead the vanguard of the naval force at Velez-Malaga in 1704.

Fidelity, inspired by emulation, was the fount of heroism, and the ultimate goal of service was to be heroic. Nor was heroism a military monopoly. We should not be afraid to speak of heroism even in the case of the much reviled Nicolas de Lamoignon, sieur de Basville and intendant of Languedoc from 1685 to 1715. After the Camisard war, he wrote to Fléchier:

> The work of an intendant is so dreadful these days, Monsieur, that if I were to be beginning my career now I would avoid it at all costs. In my twenty-three years of service I have merely saddled myself with troublesome burdens, endless difficulties to be overcome, not one moment of peace and tranquillity, and I have forgotten entirely what it means to have peace of mind, the only true happiness in this life. (117)

Nevertheless he stayed where the king had sent him and stood firm.

The armed forces provided countless examples of courage and fidelity, and those who deplore the endless wars of Louis XIV should bear in mind the concept of honour. We shall leave elevated examples to one side – men such as Vendôme, laid to rest in the Escorial by Philip V, whose throne he saved, or Turenne, of whom Mazarin said there was only ever one such individual in several generations (171) – in order to examine the more human figure of Louis-François de Boufflers (1644–1711), of whom it was said that he lacked the subtlety of mind to invent a heresy, but whose life showed him as the bravest of marshals, the epitome of the heroic service which the king desired. A cadet at eighteen and a colonel at twenty-five, he was constantly in action and was frequently wounded. Louis made him a brigadier in 1675, a brigadier-general in 1677 and a lieutenant-general in 1681, and invested him with the Order of the Holy Spirit in December 1688. In 1694, he was made a marshal and the governor of Flanders. In 1695, he defended Namur against the Prince of Orange for two months. Such honours did not go to his head or encourage him to rest on his laurels (Sourches once said that marshals of France 'think only of being in action'). Despite being a duke, captain of the royal bodyguard and chevalier of the Golden Fleece, Boufflers rushed to Lille in 1708 and defended it against siege for seventy-four days, only surrendering 'after repeated orders' (2). This earned him a peerage. But he dreamt of greater glory and asked to serve under Villars, and on 11 September 1709 he converted Malplaquet, where he replaced the injured Villars, into something of a victory. The kingdom rejoiced in his honours; for, when awarded to such a warrior, they embodied the bravery of all its soldiers (135).

THE KING'S REWARDS

Louis XIV enjoyed granting rewards, promotions and honours, retaining for himself the power to raise up and to lay low. 'The king grants favours as he pleases', inclined more 'to indulgence than severity', but used both as a means of government (42). It was not a good idea to ask for favours at an inopportune moment. The answer could easily be a 'we shall see', which was tantamount to a refusal. An untoward request diminished the king's pleasure and that of the beneficiary. After the death in 1708 of Tilladet, a colonel in the dragoons, his brother asked Louis for his regiment. The king replied: 'I shall grant it to you; but I would have done so more gladly had you not asked me for it, as I had intended to give it to you anyway' (26). The king reacted sharply to threats of resignation. On 16 December 1692, the comte de Châtillon, a colonel in the cavalry, told the secretary of state Barbezieux that, if not made a brigadier-general, he would quit the army. 'The marquis de Barbezieux reported to the king what the comte de Châtillon had told him, and His Majesty ordered him to accept his resignation, which he did.' (97) Saint-Simon was more discreet when he retired in 1702 'for reasons of ill health', but Louis was not fooled.

The king made promotions without risking making mistakes, because he was well informed. When raising a young, high-born captain or an old lieutenant-colonel to the rank of colonel, he may not always have known the candidate, but he had a dossier on him, the minister's information being added to his own prodigious memory. When it came to creating generals, he knew the party involved personally and the services he had performed, as well as those of his forebears, his brothers and his cousins. Every element was then taken into account. But he also valued new blood, soldiers of fortune such as Julien or the 'baron Le Gall', who became a lieutenant-general, and was the victor of Munderkingen in 1703, his bravery showing nobility even though, as subsequently appeared, he had never been officially ennobled.

The game of rewards was so personalized that the court was in a state of constant agitation about the audience granted by His Majesty to this or that ambassador, general or sea-captain. Did the king appear welcoming or annoyed? How long did the audience last? How did the beneficiary look as he left the chamber? The barometer of credit rose and fell in response to such impressions. After Ramillies in 1706, for example, the maréchal de Villeroy 'was very well received by the king, but everyone thought he looked very disheartened' (97). Louis made sure that the courtiers were kept guessing. Sourches records that, at Fontainebleau on 12 October 1690, 'the comte de Tourville arrived at court and some said that he was received rather coolly by the king, others that he had reason to be content'. They were neither right nor wrong, as transpired three weeks later when 'M. the comte de Tourville had a very favourable audience with the king'. The sovereign's opening words were: 'Monsieur, it is time to bring to an end the coolness which I have shown towards you since Fontainebleau' (97).

Depending on circumstances, military leaders and diplomats were received by His Majesty 'courteously but coolly', 'very courteously', or 'with many signs of friendship' (97). Louis might hardly talk to Vendôme one day, yet, at the following audience, 'they laughed a lot together' (97). In early 1702, the king chose to ignore the maréchal de Catinat, but, on 6 December, he 'embraced him several times' (97). This display of esteem towards collaborators cost nothing, but was regarded as respect beyond price. Louis shunned speeches and pointless words; he knew how to combine the minimum of gesture with an economy of language. In 1709, he welcomed home his ambassador Amelot, who had returned after several years in Madrid. Amelot made his bow, and the old king 'placed his two hands on his servant's shoulders, as if to embrace him', and then, as they entered his study along with Torcy, said: 'Monsieur, I believe you are as delighted to be home as I am to see you here again.' (97) This laconic exchange was a sign of great esteem. The recipient of these embraces valued them as much as an admission to an order of chivalry. For the system of service was chivalric after the heroic and baroque custom of the age.

As far as monetary rewards were concerned, the very act of granting them meant as much as did the sums involved. On 25 July 1688, for example, Louis gave 'a pension of 2,000 *écus* to M. de Lamoignon, *avocat général* in the Parlement of Paris, who hardly had any great need of it, for he was already well enough endowed, and one day would get two millions [*livres*] from his wife, the daughter of M. de Voysin, a councillor of state' (97). During the War of the League of Augsburg, the king economized on pensions and gifts, saying on one occasion: 'It is little enough to a man in your position, but, at present, I am unable to offer you more.' (97) At other times, a few kind words sufficed. In 1707, he informed the marquis de Thianges, nephew of Mme de Montespan, that: 'Monsieur de Thianges, everyone has long been aware of your valour in war, but the way in which you have won over all Brittany to my service gives me much more delight.' (97) Louis was equally discriminating in short speeches accompanying the bestowal of offices and places in government. In 1685, having decided to give to Boucherat the chancellorship, left vacant by the death of Le Tellier, Louis told him: 'Monsieur, I have always seen in you such honesty and capacity that I have chosen you to be chancellor. I now hand you the seals. You and I may do much good or evil with them. My intention is only to make good use of them, and, because I am assured of your intentions, I entrust them to your care with pleasure.' (97)

Louis' way of inviting people to serve, and his honours to those who performed well, created rivalries among servants, who were each trying to excel the others in enthusiasm. Other monarchs admired the consequences – consequences which turned Louis into the most readily obeyed sovereign in Europe – although they did not always understand the formula and could not always reproduce Louis' brilliant execution of it. Their successors in the eighteenth century who came to be known as the 'enlightened despots' would be more skilful. By opening his service to commoners, Louis remodelled his nobility, spurred on his administrative elite and created a shifting geometry in the relations between the two groups. He gave the lie to Chateaubriand's later opinion that 'an aristocracy passes through three ages: superiority, privilege and vanity'. The aristocracy patroned and nurtured by Louis XIV lived all three simultaneously. The will of the prince declared that superiority lay with the old nobility, bullied and supervised by their king so as to ensure that they rediscovered their loyalty and zeal, and with the talented commoners promoted by Louis in his service. The world of vanity contained two hemispheres: one inhabited by new nobles, mostly financiers, whose services were indispensable, but who were thought insufficiently civilized for courtly life; and the other by nobles of ancient lineage, of whom Saint-Simon was the archetype, who, turning their backs on service, sought refuge in a world of pseudo-historical fantasy or labyrinthine ceremonial for its own sake. In general, the aristocracy justified its privileges and sustained the king. Who could claim as much for the kingdom under Louis XV?

Despite appearances, the king, unable to deprive unworthy nobles of their privileges or to ennoble every deserving commoner, had to compromise. He knew that if merit alone were the criterion, the nobility and the administrative elite would be one and the same, and, also, that society could not be changed by decree and that reform had to be effected in small doses. His system of rewards operated within the existing hierarchy. Those promoted were absorbed into the accepted elite, itself a product of several centuries of development. An intermediate state, a kind of antechamber to nobility, had always existed between commoners and the second estate, and Louis enlarged it for his servants. When noble titles were examined, those in military service were exempted from having to produce theirs, and Louis granted honorary positions endowed with privileges and exemptions from taxation to the best of his collaborators, thereby demonstrating that they stood on the brink of being ennobled. Racine, an Academician since 1673 and historiographer royal since 1677, was made a gentleman of the bedchamber in 1690, thus becoming a courtier and thereby conferring nobility on the profession of the man of letters, until then rather looked down upon in the highest circles (262). His new status brought with it the title of *écuyer* and exemption from the *taille* and from the payment of *franc-fief* (137). In 1693, the king created a new order of chivalry, the 'royal and military' Order of St Louis, entry to which was not restricted by birth and was therefore a particularly useful way of blending the different elites. Similarly, the riband of St Michael was distributed more widely, revitalizing this decoration and no longer reserving it to the nobility alone. The king granted it to his most gifted architects and painters as well as to Samuel Bernard the banker.

One more step up the ladder and faithful servants were deemed worthy of ennoblement. This might be through office: the principal offices in the sovereign courts, treasurerships (La Bruyère, Racine and Regnard all profited from these) and some magistrates' posts (including those in Lyon and Toulouse) all raised their holders above the rank of commoner. Louis liked to put his personal stamp on as much as possible and attached more importance to individual grants of nobility. He used them because 'in these, the grandeur of kings appears most clearly, making the people of ordinary birth equal alongside the great lords of a kingdom' (49). Those considered worthy of nobility displayed a wide range of talents and 'capacities': artists (Le Nôtre in 1675, Robert de Cotte in 1702), doctors (the surgeon Mareschal in 1707), engineers (Riquet, the man behind the Canal des Deux Mers, in 1666) and bankers (Samuel Bernard in 1699). But the military were still predominant. In letters-patent of January 1674, Louis ennobled two brothers, both merely military captains, François Magontier *de* Laubanye and Yriex *de*

Magontier, the former after twenty-four years' service and the latter after more than twelve. Both had been wounded three times, had risked their lives in the king's service, and had amassed brave deeds aplenty to 'provide much evidence of true valour, courage, experience and wise conduct in war' (288). Their uncle, Pierre Magontier du Cloret, first captain of the Razilly regiment, and two of their brothers, Pierre Magontier de la Borderie, ensign in the Champagne regiment, and Jean Magontier du Cloret, lieutenant in the Saint-Vallier regiment, had been killed in His Majesty's service. The ennoblement of these two remaining brothers thus constituted the recognition of 'nearly 200 years' of faithful service, and the letters granting them nobility, each with a preamble echoing like a fanfare of trumpets, seemed like a succession of posthumous citations for bravery (288). The navy also earned a prominent place for its officers among those thus rewarded. By making nobles of the chevalier Paul (1649) and captains Mathurin Gabaret (1665), Job Forant (1668), Jean Bart (1694) and René Duguay-Trouin (1709) (274), Louis rewarded those who had performed beyond the call of duty to the greater glory of the king.

Even after ministers and other servants had attained noble status, there were yet further honours which could be found for them. The first might be to raise the standing of their fiefs. This was not to be despised, especially by financiers seeking to remove themselves from the tax system. If the king transformed a seigneury into a *comte*, even if the holder was not yet officially ennobled, jurists considered that the king, who could not be held to be mistaken, had to all intents and purposes ennobled him. Membership of a royal order could follow, especially that of the Order of the Holy Spirit, which represented a social status much aspired to below the small circle of peers but above the rank of ordinary gentlemen.* In his *Mémoires*, Louis expounded the philosophy of the blue riband:

> I ended this year [1661] and began the next with the creation of eight prelates and sixty-three chevaliers of the Order of the Holy Spirit, there being so many of these because places had remained vacant since 1633 . . . but I would have liked to elevate even more people to this honour, since I find that a prince has no greater

* Members of the Order of the Holy Spirit were required to prove four degrees of nobility, i.e., that their paternal great-grandfathers were already noble.

pleasure than to be able to reward people of quality who have satisfied him without placing any additional burden on the most humble of his subjects. No reward costs the people less and none touches noble hearts more than these distinctions of rank, which are the prime movers of all human actions, especially of the greatest and most noble. Moreover, this is one of the most visible attributes of our power, to be able, if we so wish, to attach an infinite price to something which, in itself, is nothing. (63)

The next promotions, aside from a few isolated nominations, occurred twenty-seven years later, on 31 December 1688, after a new generation had been given time to emerge. This time there were seventy-four new members. The timing of these rare elevations calls for an explanation. In 1689, Mme de la Fayette remarked upon the omission of three dukes, Ventadour, Rohan and Brissac: 'These three were very rarely at court, and nor did they go to war.' In short, they shirked the king's service. As for Sourches, he noted: 'These promotions surprised the whole court and made them realize the extent of M. de Louvois' standing, for over half the places were given over to military men.' According to Sourches, the minister had made three observations to the king. Firstly, war was being prepared and the king 'ought not only to win the hearts of his principal military leaders by investing them with the Order [of the Holy Spirit], but also to encourage those following them to spare no effort in trying to get it for themselves'. Secondly, since His Majesty was having difficulty in recruiting ambassadors, he should consider that the reasons for this might be sought in their inadequate rewards. Thirdly, the blue riband could be an excellent way of honouring 'truly converted Huguenots' (97). The rewards of service thus reconciled recognition of noble birth with the promotion of an elite based on merit, and subsequent nominations underlined the policy of rewarding merit. The nominations of Tallard (1701) and Marsin (1703) were somewhat complaisant, but those of Revel (1703) and Villars, Châteaurenault and Vauban (1705) were impeccable (2). The promotion of 1711 was also exemplary: the comte de Médavy had routed the Imperialists at Castiglione; the comte du Bourg had beaten Mercy at Rumersheim; Albergotti had done all that was open to him in the siege of Douai; and the marquis de Goësbriand had defended Aire-sur-la-Lys during two months of trench warfare. The highest honour which could come one's way was to be made a duke and peer, as were

Boufflers and Villars. The king did not reward individuals to excess. Even at the risk of upsetting the victor of Denain, he did not re-establish the office of Constable of France. Though showered with honours and sharing in the king's glory, no servant of the state could rise above a certain level. He who served, however heroically, was only after all doing his duty.

17

Conquests Within

THE AGGRESSIVE peace was not a triumphant imperialism but rather France's attempt to secure strong frontiers. New conquests could only take place within the kingdom, a policy carried forward by Louis and his talented collaborators. The power, unity and coherence of France were to be consummated through a consistent but diversified programme.

> A kingdom is well governed when these objectives are pursued without hesitation: (1) to increase its population; (2) to make sure that everyone works according to his capacities for the better cultivation of the land; (3) to ensure that the people are well fed, providing that they work; (4) not to tolerate the indolent or vagrant poor; (5) to reward merit; (6) to punish disorder; (7) to maintain royal sway over all corporate bodies and all individuals, no matter how powerful they are; (8) to govern personally with moderation, so that the king does not act against the law, haughtily, violently, capriciously or feebly; (9) not to be dominated by any minister or favourite. (224)

This definition of the duties of a good head of state, which might have been taken from Louis XIV's *Mémoires*, is in fact from a text of 1701 by Fénelon for the young Philip V and seems to imply that these nine points constitute a very different policy from that pursued by the King of France.

Louis, while following a rational overall design, did not attempt to impose it uniformly. He had neither a logical nor an abstract intellect; he preferred common sense, and recommended it to his son. France was a remarkably diverse kingdom, the North being generally more literate and industrious, whilst the Midi preserved its particularities of language, civilization and sensibility. Regions where Protestantism remained a dynamic force contrasted with provinces influenced by the Counter-Reformation. The *pays d'états* were distinct from the *pays d'élections*. Internal frontiers hindered the transportation of merchandise and a thorough knowledge of the fiscal system was necessary in order to comply with the complex rules of the *gabelle*. The North followed customary laws; the South written law. Frontier provinces were controlled by the secretary of state for war, the rest were administered by three separate ministerial departments, whilst each newly conquered province – Alsace or even those which had been occupied for a longer period, such as Lorraine, Luxembourg and Pinerolo – constituted a special case. Furthermore, royal power was divided between the military authority of the provincial governors – still more important than often realized –, the religious authority of the incumbents of bishoprics in the king's gift, and civil power, which largely lay in the hands of the intendants. Yet, if this general picture holds true for, say Perpignan, it definitely does not apply to Dunkirk. What is applicable to Marseille is untrue for Rennes. Not only should modern concepts of centralization and state administration be employed with great care when discussing Louis XIV's kingdom, seventeenth-century France should not be equated with its twentieth-century counterpart, but with the under-administered expanse of Peter the Great's Russia, with seventeenth-century Spain, with the patchwork princedoms of the Holy Roman Empire or with the provinces inherited by the Elector of Brandenburg, scattered between the Rhine and the Oder. France under Louis XIV was more homogeneous, more united and more easily governed than these other lands, but it was neither centralized nor under direct state control. The people would not have accepted that, the king did not wish it, and his intendants would have been deprived of their power if they had tried to enforce it.

THE *COMMISSAIRES DÉPARTIS*

By the end of the reign, the civil administration of the provinces of France was the responsibility of the thirty-one *commissaires départis*, otherwise known as 'intendants of justice, police and finance'. 'Justice' was a reminder that they were magistrates and enjoyed judicial authority; 'police' meant that they were administrators; and 'finance' signified their financial responsibilities and supervision of the economy. As this makes clear, commissioners, although assigned personally by Louis, were nevertheless obliged to obey orders from several agents of the king. The intendant of Alsace, for example, was responsible to Louvois in the administration of the frontiers and to Colbert in financial affairs (223), while 'justice' put him in contact with the chancellor. There were eighteen intendants in the so-called *pays d'élections*. Their task was the easier one – save in Protestant areas –, for their provinces were those where taxes were collected directly by the Crown. Thirteen more served in the *pays d'états*, where taxes were voted by provincial Estates, or in the new provinces. Three were councillors of state, whilst twenty-seven were *maîtres des requêtes*, leaving only one intendant who held neither post.

Intendants were the strongmen of the provinces. Since the death of Mazarin, they had eroded local liberties to extend their authority. They competed with governors and bishops, in terms both of their administrative responsibilities and of prestige. Everyone knew that *Monsieur l'intendant* was the king's man. Louis liked to maintain contact with his envoys. He would often receive them before their departure; sometimes he would summon them back for consultations. He always knew how successfully or unsuccessfully they were operating. He could dismiss the incompetent, promote those who deserved it to a better province and make his intendants councillors of state. The king set great store by his brief encounters with his commissioners, as illustrated by one of these meetings, at Versailles in 1711. After his *lever*, Louis received Maignart de Bernières, intendant in Flanders: 'You have often sent me bad news during this past year and I am grateful to you for it because I wish to be told the whole truth, no matter how unpalatable it may be. But I hope that this year you will have better news to send me.' The commissioner, having assured the king that, thanks to the money raised by the controller-general Desmarets, everything would be ready for the coming campaign, added: 'If anything is amiss, Sire, the fault will be mine, and I alone should take responsibility for it. I am prepared to assure the subsistence of your army from 15 March, wherever it may be in Flanders.'

To keep intendants constantly aware of their position as the king's men, Colbert persuaded Louis not to leave them too long in the same post and to grant intendancies for three years only. But, after Colbert's death, Louis tended to reduce transfers between posts: Basville remained at Montpellier for thirty years, between 1685 and 1715. Commissioners became identified with their provinces, besides being agents of the Crown. Whilst remaining government representatives, they also became the defenders of local interests and, as long as they did not allow this to override their original purpose, they could gain a certain room for manœuvre, proportionate to their distance from Versailles.

Although there were only thirty-one of them, all known personally to the king, an intendant's principal relationship was with his relevant minister, who told him what the king wanted and encouraged and admonished him. Administrative formalities did not exclude familiarity, as is shown in the correspondence between Louvois and Le Peletier de Souzy, intendant of Lille from 1668 to 1683 (226). Le Peletier's family were clients of the Le Telliers, serving no doubt to accentuate the personal character of these exchanges. Louvois, redoubted throughout Europe, told his correspondent, 'I am entirely your servant', whilst troubling him with personal requests. He ordered Souzy, at various times, to send him carnations, pheasants' eggs, chickens, turkeys, cows and a bull. Private life intruded upon political considerations. Souzy complained of gout and the minister replied: 'The certain way to cure gout is to be careful when it comes to women.' (226)

In fact, there were other methods of supporting one's aristocratic diseases. All that was required was a good income, such as Souzy and his colleagues all enjoyed. The intendant's duty was to uphold royal prestige. His origins in the officeholding aristocracy, his fortune, his income (the intendant of Montauban received 18,000 *livres*) and his personal qualities all assisted him in overcoming the distrust of the provincial nobility, in winning over the merchants and in persuading people to pay their taxes. The first intendant of Brittany, M. de Pomereu, was appointed, in 1689, for his capacity as a diplomat. His successor from 1705 to 1715, Ferrand, kept open house with a staff of servants worthy of a duke.

These administrative seigneurs cut very different figures from that cut by the modern prefect, but there were others with more-modest retinues. In 1710, the intendant of Alsace at Strasbourg managed with six – himself, two secretaries and three clerks (223) – and only five subdelegates represented him at the local level. The power of the *commissaires départis*, therefore, should not be exaggerated. There was a wide gap between theory and practice. The intendant had to infiltrate royal authority into diverse areas of responsibility, eroding the powers of the bureaux of finances over highways and construction projects, keeping a close eye on the judicial and administrative roles of the seigneurial courts and, in local affairs, controlling the *communautés d'habitants*, which were responsible for village affairs. Yet if we are tempted to characterize these encroachments as despotic, we only have to look at a *pays d'état* such as Brittany to see the limitations imposed on the intendant's power by the interplay of provincial influences. In reality, his authority was essentially that of an arbiter, and, in this capacity, he was once again personally the king's representative. The nostalgic idea that 'If only the king knew' all would be well was a central component of popular attitudes and the intendant, though he may have annoyed the magistrates and sections of the bourgeoisie, was there to reassure the mass of the population on this point. Thanks to him, the king was 'present in his province'. In a monarchy where the king was the incarnation of sovereignty, his local presence had to be equally personalized.

What irritated ordinary people was not the power of the state as such but its abstract, inaccessible and thereby harsh and implacable character. As long as inhabitants of Auch or Grenoble were able, like those of Saint-Germain, to present their petitions to the king's representative, they had grounds for optimism. If their seigneur was over-zealous about his rights, with a priest and over-scrupulous seigneurial judge as his accomplices, the only source of help lay in the intendant. The failings of which he was accused by others, such as looking down on minor country noblemen, keeping too close a watch on the military and persecuting the Huguenots, were virtues in the eyes of the peasantry. The only intendants likely to lean too far in the wrong direction were those who set themselves up as social leaders in their provincial capitals, men such as d'Aguesseau, Lamoignon, Saint-Contest and Chamillart.

It was not easy to be a good intendant. After 1679, the *commissaires départis* had responsibilities extending far beyond questions of military supply and billeting, the militia, military provisioning and road maintenance. The thorny question of Protestantism was also within their remit.* The way in which the Huguenots were treated depended on the intendant's state of mind and outlook. Marillac, intendant in Poitiers, would be for ever identified with the vicious *dragonnades* of 1681. Le Gendre of Montauban multiplied 'imprisonments, fines, constant insults and perpetual threats' against the 'nouveaux convertis' between 1700 and 1704 (224). Basville, on the other hand, had to overcome his inner reservations, and his letters show the selflessness of a responsible senior administrator (117).

SECURING AND SUCCOURING THE LOYALTIES OF THE NEW PROVINCES

Between the treaties of Münster and Nymwegen, France grew, temporarily with the acquisition of the Tournaisis, Lorraine, Philippsburg, Breisach and Pinerolo and permanently with that of Artois, Alsace, Walloon Flanders, Franche Comté, French Hainaut and Roussillon. These territories, containing the towns of Dunkirk, Lille, Mauberge, Valenciennes, Metz, Strasbourg, Dôle, Besançon and Perpignan, were to count for more in France's destiny than were some of the central provinces. Yet in the annexed provinces, all the usual problems became doubly difficult for the king, his ministers and his local agents. Economic questions were more complex: whilst the peasantry had to be handled carefully so as to prevent revolts against new taxes, it had to be made certain that troops were kept supplied. Fortified towns, military camps and garrisons all had to be assured. In addition, there were religious problems, accentuated in Alsace by the language differences. With hindsight, we tend to simplify the question. We know that Lorraine was lost in 1697 and that the Duke of Savoy regained Pinerolo; but, when these territories were occupied by the French, the future was unknown. Even after Nymwegen, no one could know that France would absorb Walloon Flanders, whilst Franche Comté, conquered in 1668, would be lost, reconquered in 1674 and then annexed in 1678. There was no way of knowing that Strasbourg,

* See ch. 21.

reconquered in 1681, would be made definitively French in the next treaty of pacification. Nobody, either among the occupiers or among the occupied, knew whether any annexation would become permanent. One might be tempted to imagine, seeing how Louis treated Alsace so indulgently and Lorraine so harshly, that he had some intuition about their futures, but one would be misled by retrospection if one did so, for the eastern and northern borders continued to be temporary and provisional.

In general, Louis trod very carefully at first. The keynote was reassurance. In 1668, Louvois wrote to the intendant at Lille: 'The king has confirmed their privileges and we must keep our word until they give us some reason for breaking it.' (226) The intendant, Le Peletier de Souzy, obeyed this order so punctiliously that he became attached to Flemish interests and earned his reprimand in 1670: 'I advise you not to imagine that you should be trying to spread in the province a better opinion of the king's rule than he himself wishes it to have; rather you should remember that, in order to ensure that His Majesty is content with you, you should not serve him better than he desires.' The intendant should try to promote assimilation and integration, as underlined in a letter from Colbert to Souzy: 'His Majesty's intention is, as far as possible and proceeding little by little, to bring the customs of the province into conformity with those of the kingdom.' For the kingdom was not a mosaic, like the empire, and Louis did not want a constitution which would be different in every region, as in the United Provinces. Whilst not expecting complete uniformity, the king was seeking unity.

The cement of this unity was Catholicism. Pride in becoming French was a rarity. For the Flemings or the Comtois, the King of Spain was a distant figure and his administration did not lie heavy upon them. Louis, on the other hand, was a disturbingly close neighbour, preoccupied with conquest. France possessed a modern administration, an established tax system, and an effective method of military recruitment. To be ruled by France was a costly privilege. For many years, Spanish agents had spread anti-French sentiments and they had found a receptive audience. At Lille, the artisans and certain religious orders harked back with nostalgia to the era of Spanish rule (225). For them, whilst the Catholic King had always been an obedient son of the Church and a promoter of the Counter-Reformation, the 'Most

Christian King' had shown himself ambivalent in matters of faith. Even though he promised to exclude the 'religion prétendue réformée' from the new provinces, he was still a proponent of civil toleration. Swearing loyalty to him might be interpreted as a sign of complicity with heresy. Louis was aware of this, and it is possible that the more ardent Catholicism of his new subjects was one of the motives behind the Revocation of the Edict of Nantes. After 1685, the hearts and minds of Flanders, Hainaut and Franche Comté would be won for good.

THE KING AND HIS AGENTS AT WORK

The king's presence was assured not only through his intendants, tax-collectors and military commissioners, but also through aesthetic, utilitarian and humanitarian projects. The aesthetic became the façade for the grandiose and the utilitarian – even Versailles was free of the notion of art for art's sake. The towns fortified by Vauban or, like Neue-Breisach, built by him were finely constructed because that was seen by Louis' agents as the natural complement to the glory of king and state. Their inhabitants were in the best position to judge, with their own eyes, that taxes had not been paid in vain.

The state did not neglect the more remote provinces, as was demonstrated by the Canal des Deux Mers, 'the wonder of Europe', constructed between 1666 and 1681. This financial and technological masterpiece, stretching from the Garonne to the *étang* of Thau, saved navigators a 2,000 mile detour. It was the brainchild of the financier and engineer Riquet, who dreamt up this 'highway from the western to the eastern sea' (42) and found the capital, help and time necessary to dig across 150 miles and build dozens of bridges and locks, employing in the process 10,000 workers. He conquered both the Montagne Noire (the canal rising 432 feet) and the objections of Colbert, who was eventually persuaded of the canal's commercial and strategic importance. It was opened on 2 March 1681 by the intendant d'Aguesseau. The construction of Sète had cost one million *livres*, the canal itself fifteen million, to be paid for from tolls, with one third coming from the royal treasury. The outlets were in upper Languedoc, which provoked complaints in lower Languedoc. But the beneficiaries were many: the king, the tax system, the provincial Estates, dioceses and towns, merchants, seamen and, above all, the cereal growers. Easy and economical transportation of grain completed what has been called the 'maize revolution' (181).

But the king's presence was demonstrated, just as his concern for the dispossessed was shown, above all, through the construction and maintenance of *hôpitaux*, among which that of Paris was the most renowned, the largest and the most elaborate. Known as the Salpêtrière, its fine architecture may still be admired. The growing hoards of vagrants during the Fronde, the initiatives of Vincent de Paul and the active collaboration of pious lay people induced Mazarin to obtain Louis' signature on an edict of April 1656 providing for 'the establishment of a *hôpital général* for the enclosure of poor beggars in the city' (201). In 1670, Bruant took over from Le Vau and Le Muet as chief architect. The building is like a town in miniature. The octagonal chapel is a masterpiece, as the king had intended. As at the Invalides, he wanted to associate the prestige of the state with works of charity, glorifying the Gospel and the monarchy at the same time. To Fléchier, the Hôpital Général de Paris was 'one of the greatest works of this age' (39). Beggars, the unemployed, vagabonds, prostitutes, abandoned children and the mentally ill were all admitted. The idea was not to isolate the poor in order to protect the rich, but, rather, to restore human dignity to those on the fringes of society and to transform an anti-social mass, thrown together by ill fortune, into a healthy community. Europe understood the message and built copies of the 'Infirmary' elsewhere, although Spain, which seemed to flaunt its beggars, appeared scandalized. In France, the success of the Paris experiment encouraged Louis to adopt the idea elsewhere. In a declaration of June 1662, he ordered that a *hôpital général* be founded in 'every town and large village' (201). Urban communities obeyed with varying degrees of enthusiasm and success, often economizing by combining the new *hôpital* with the old *hôtel-Dieu*. Nevertheless, a flood of legislation, edicts and letters-patent created rules for these provincial institutions and, during the terrible winters of 1693, 1694, 1709 and 1710, these establishments saved thousands of lives. When the ground was frozen hard, a place to sleep and something to eat, despite the harsh rules and regulations, were preferable to aimless wandering.

Listing examples of the public services created or developed by Louis XIV would mean writing a history of the kingdom rather than of the king. Yet how many there were! 'It is to Colbert [and thus to Louis XIV] that we owe the first specialized administration of roads, known thereafter as the *Ponts et chaussées.*' (151) The controller-general, in charge of this huge network, became a true minister of public works. After 1668, Colbert ensured the regular financing of the principal highways. He gave direct instructions about construction and repair, but at the same time devised an overall strategy, laying out plans for roads connecting Paris with the frontier towns, the royal arsenals and also the provincial capitals. The Paris region, because of the court, and the frontier regions, for strategic reasons, absorbed the largest slice of the budget, but the whole kingdom profited from Colbert's vigour (151).

Louis XIV's road network, perfected during the eighteenth century, was not created exclusively for the benefit of the court, armies, merchants and the mounted constabulary. Numerous stage-coaches and mail-coaches also made use of it. The stage-coaches made frequent stops; they were cheap but slow. Diligences were faster. 'Diligences', wrote Furetière, 'are boats or coaches which go to certain busy places in less than the time taken by others. To go from Paris to Lyon by diligence takes five days' (42), about sixty-two miles a day. In 1715, this diligence could be boarded at the Hôtel de Sens. But those who needed to go more swiftly than the diligence – soldiers, king's envoys, nobles or rich merchants – caught the mail-coach, using the post houses which covered the kingdom. The so-called 'horse post' was particularly active between Paris and the frontier regions. Louvois, who was responsible for it from 1668 to 1691, made it an excellent public service and also organized a messenger service without equal in Europe and a letter post, the speed and accuracy of which surpassed those of all previous arrangements (165). The state benefited from this, whilst Louvois' various responsibilities, for war, fortifications and the administration of the frontier zones, as well as the superintendency, gave him the power to investigate the contents of letters. This *cabinet noir* provided Louvois with police powers permitting him to challenge Colbert on his own ground. The public, whilst they may have been irritated by having their letters opened, were content to make use of a postal service. Mme de Grignan in Provence received the letters in which Mme de Sévigné kept her up to date with court gossip and the latest rumours in the capital in only five or six days. 'The general order of the posts . . . both within and outside the kingdom for the year 1715' occupied no less than ten densely printed pages of the *Royal Almanac*. And the fact that, in the immediate aftermath of a long war, internal and international communications could be assured with such regularity and precision illustrates the administrative and technical advances carried out by the absolute monarchy. But this success was itself the vector of a wider progress in civilized living.

EDUCATION AND CIVILIZATION

In the age of Louis XIV, whatever such quintessential Parisians as Furetière, Molière, La Bruyère and others may have thought, the provinces, thanks to the stage-coach and the letter post, became less parochial. Regularity of communication and speed of information, so valuable to the regime, kept the attention of the inhabitants of the provinces fixed upon developments at the centre, whilst creating the desire to emulate them. Provincial *bailliage* judges knew within the week the ideas, speeches and style of their grander colleagues in the Parlement of Paris. Priests and their Catholic faithful benefited from the non-residence of their bishops, whose travels to and from Paris brought to their bishoprics news and ideas, wider perceptions and a fresh awareness.

The French language itself was carried by the posts from Versailles and Paris into smaller towns and villages. In a country where patois or dialects had been maintained and where schoolchildren learned Latin words sometimes before French ones, new forms of expression penetrated the provinces relatively quickly, their novelty less of a hindrance. Words and concepts created in Paris – such as *savoir vivre* or *savoir sans morale* – spread, according to Bouhours, 'through people of breeding coming to Paris almost every year and taking the latest novelties back with them' (15). Through neighbourly contact, imitation and snobbery, the town notables and the people at large became influenced by these linguistic fashions and usages. Noblemen living in towns visited country squires. Seigneurial officials copied their masters. Pedlars carried more than just merchandise in their baskets. Books of devotion opened up 'not only the internal life of the spirit, but also the manners and language of polite society'. Pellisson, given responsibility for the reconquest of souls in the Protestant regions, defended and fostered the use of the French language in prayer books after the fashion of the Académie française. At the end of the reign, the first editions of Jean-Baptiste de la Salle's best-seller, *The Rules of Etiquette and Christian Civility*, taught the best manners, creating a code which was a slightly simplified version of that of the nobility (135).

The mobility created by improvements in transport also influenced education. Public schooling, strongly encouraged by the king, was developed, not under state control but through the driving force provided by provincial towns and their authorities, the clergy and the *communautés d'habitants*. It was not standardized or universally available: the North was more literate than the South, towns more than the countryside, boys more than girls. Everything depended on local initiative and parental motivation. Secondary education achieved a high standard, stimulated by the use of Latin and competition between the Jesuits, Oratorians and Doctrinarians. The larger colleges taught the humanities, whilst also training the royal servants of the future. Applied mathematics, the art of fortification, fencing, equestrianism, dancing and even heraldry created young gentlemen prepared for the noble life and military service. 'In 1715, 200 French towns possessed a college.' (294) But the immense development of popular educational provision is even more striking. New teaching-orders were founded during this fifty-year period, the great names of this endeavour being those of père Barré in Normandy, Démia in the diocese of Lyon, and Roland and his successor Jean-Baptiste de la Salle at Reims. These schools were not reserved solely for boys. The most remarkable initiatives concerned the daughters of the poor. Barré's 'Mistresses of Christian Charitable Schools', Démia's 'Assemblies of Ladies of Piety' and the girls' schools in Reims all did outstanding work. De la Salle's 'Brothers of Christian Schools' perfected a simplified pedagogy for use in their schools, the first of which was established in 1680. In their classes, pupils learned to pray before learning to read, and only began Latin once they had mastered French.

The king granted or declined to issue letters-patent for the creation and regulation of colleges, seminaries and schools, as well as for the statutes of teaching-orders. In the provinces, the intendant, often in conjunction with the bishop, played a decisive role in the promotion and maintenance of schools. But only in the field of technical education did the French state seize the initiative. 'Colbert's royal manufactories all had courses for apprentices.' (294) Then, towards the latter part of Louis' reign, came a transformation. A royal edict of April 1695 and a declaration of 13 December 1698 ordained the creation of an elementary school in every parish. These instructions were in connection with the catechism imposed on the children of *nouveaux convertis*. Religious, anti-Protestant regulations founded universal schooling 183 years before Jules Ferry's compulsary, free and lay schools, except that, in many parishes, classes did not always operate and the punishments reserved for uncooperative parents remained unenforceable. Louis' measures promoting these schools did, however, bear some fruit. In the diocese of Montpellier in 1715, eighty per cent of parishes in some archpresbyteries had schools (189). The same diocese in 1716 contained a total of eighty-eight boys' schools and forty-seven girls' schools (189). The combination of a zealous bishop, Colbert de Croissy, and a dynamic intendant, Basville, had put the declaration of 1698 into effect. Thus the fight against ignorance was not the least important aspect of the conquests within. However, the king did not ignore his capital.

THE IMPORTANCE OF PARIS

The king had his own way of winning people over to his rule. He never visited the Midi after his marriage, but he was frequently seen at Amiens, Arras, Dunkirk, Lille, Reims, Metz, Toul and Verdun. At first sight, he seems to have neglected Paris too: it was no longer his normal residence after 1666, and he was rarely seen there after 1672. Yet Parisians had in their midst Monsieur, to whom his brother had given the Palais-Royal, and, above all, Monseigneur, who was frequently attracted to the capital by its entertainments. This distribution of roles seems to have been intentional. Louis himself willingly played the dual role of protector of Paris and promoter of improvements. Through Colbert in his capacity as minister for Paris, the king acted as overseer of the capital's health, well-being and beautification. Private initiatives by parishes, religious houses and aristocrats played a part as they emulated one another, yet always in harmony with royal wishes.

In Paris, as elsewhere, the early years of Louis' personal rule were marked by feverish activity. Colbert still hoped to install his master in Paris and make the Louvre-Tuileries complex into the world's most impressive palace. In 1662, the Vigaranis completed the Tuileries theatre, that renowned 'Auditorium of Mechanical Devices', capable of holding 6,000 spectators and entertaining them with complex baroque ballets. Between 1660 and 1678, work continued on the Louvre, notably on the Cour Carrée, and from 1664 to 1666 on the Tuileries, where Louis occasionally spent the winter months. In 1665, soon after the departure of Bernini, a French project for the east colonnade of the Louvre was approved and Claude Perrault, with the assistance of François Dorbay, constructed his masterpiece between 1668 and 1672 (198). But plans for an avenue leading to this façade were abandoned. The king's interest was no longer sufficiently engaged by his Parisian palaces and he would never have agreed to the demolition of the Church of Saint-Germain-l'Auxerrois. The Louvre remained unfinished, exposed to the elements, yet bearing enough of Louis' imprint to be acknowledged as a contribution to his glorification.

The 1660s saw the construction of several other prestigious buildings: the Collège des Quatre-Nations (1662–72), the Gobelins manufactory (1666) and the Observatory (1667–72).

The year 1670 seems to have been a particularly important one. With Colbert's collaboration, Louis, still basking in the glory of the treaty of Aix-la-Chapelle, decided to make Paris an open city and began to demolish the ramparts. The word *boulevard*, hitherto applied to fortifications, acquired a more pacific sense. Under Louis' patronage and Colbert's instructions (but partly financed by the municipality and under the architect Blondel's direction) the laying-out of the Boulevard began. 'This new avenue, on top of the boulevard [rampart], is 1,200 *toises* long [a Parisian *toise* was about six feet in length], running from the porte Saint-Antoine to the porte Saint-Martin, and was constructed in 1670 by an order of the Council issued on 7 September that year, and by another, of 11 March 1671 . . . In order to ensure easier access to the rampart for coaches, a forty-eight feet wide ramp was built.' (18) It has been too often said that the demolition of the ramparts was the king's revenge for the Fronde. Parisians understood that the opening-up of Paris was connected with the strengthening of the northern frontier and that, if the king endowed them with avenues and triumphal arches, then they had the benefits twice over. Also in 1670, Colbert lengthened the Cours la Reine through the Champs-Elysées and the Avenue du Roule, whilst Bruant took charge of the construction of the Hôpital Général and began building the west façade of the Invalides.

But these works represented Louis' farewell to Paris. No longer able to tolerate the invasion of his gardens or the unwanted encounters on the Cours la Reine, he divided his time from 1672 onwards between Saint-Germain and Versailles (167). This detracts from the merit of his gift of the Louvre to letters, the arts and the public, but enhances that of the works which he continued to patronize. The year 1672 saw the start of the construction of the porte Saint-Denis (completed in 1673). 'No other gate has been built with such magnificence.' (18) Designed by Blondel, it stands seventy-two feet high and celebrates the crossing of the Rhine and the seizure of Maastricht. In 1674, Colbert ordered Bullet to built the porte Saint-Martin, a triumphal arch with three passages through it and 'with rustic bosses' celebrating recent victories, particularly the conquest of Franche Comté.

The projects of the king and his minister were not, however, confined to civilian buildings, for they also sponsored religious architecture. Aside from the construction or refurbishment of chapels, major churches like Saint-Sulpice, Saint-Louis-en-l'Ile, and Saint-Jacques du Haut-Pas were built under their auspices. It would require a whole book to describe the splendid buildings erected by individuals during this period of feverish construction, stimulated by the arrival in Paris of provincial financiers and maintained by rivalries between the court, the robe and financiers.

In his projects for the improvement of roads and gates, Colbert relied heavily upon the *prévôt des marchands* Claude Le Peletier. And Blondel and Bullet contributed their technical knowledge. Together, these two architects drew up a plan for the capital which constitutes one of the first examples of town planning based on an existing ground-plan.

But the *prévôt des marchands* was equally preoccupied with

standards of living, a concern shared by the lieutenant of police. On matters of public cleanliness, the orders of the two officials were sometimes complementary and sometimes in contradiction. According to Furetière's dictionary, some progress was made: 'The *boueurs*', he wrote, 'are required to clean the streets twice weekly.' (42) Such, at least, was the theory. In reality, the inhabitants still emptied their chamber-pots through their windows, whilst every butcher let blood flow out into the streets and those on the riverside by the Petit Pont threw offal and carcasses into the Seine. Endlessly reiterated ordinances demonstrate the concern of both king and municipality, the negligence of the Parisians, and the blind eye turned in practice by the administration: one order requiring proprietors to construct latrines was repeated at least three times. Street-lighting, which first appeared in 1662, progressed thanks to the lieutenant of police. The quays were the Town Hall's responsibility. With Colbert's encouragement, the banks of the Seine were improved, and everyone admired the quai Le Peletier, a technical triumph for Bullet. The paving of Paris, a protection against sewers, came under the aegis of the treasurers, but the king intervened to regulate the pavements' quality and size (64). To keep the capital supplied with water, Colbert exploited new springs at Vaugirard and Saint-Cloud. Since the Samaritaine pump was barely sufficient for the area of the Louvre, he had another one built at the Pont Notre-Dame and, in 1671, Louis ordered the repair of the twenty-two public fountains in Paris and the construction of fifteen new ones.

After 1675, public building in Paris became less frenetic. Versailles was expensive and Colbert had less power and enthusiasm. Between his death in 1683 and the end of the reign only three monumental public works were commissioned in Paris. The first of these resulted from the private initiative of François d'Aubusson de la Feuillade, duc de Roannez, marshal of France and the king's friend. He commissioned from Mansart the design for a 'place des Victoires' as a setting for a replica of the statue of Louis XIV by Desjardins which he had given to the king after Nymwegen. Work started in 1685, was officially 'inaugurated' by Monseigneur on 28 March 1686 and was completed in 1690. The statue of the king was encircled with inscriptions by Régnier des Marais, permanent secretary to the Académie française. At the same time, the foundations of the Pont Royal were laid, on 25 October 1685. It was designed by Mansart, in emulation of the Pont-Neuf, and its construction was supervised by the Dominican friar François Romain. Taking up La Feuillade's challenge, Louis decided in 1685 to create the place Louis-le-Grand, work on which began in 1686 on the site of the demolished Hôtel Vendôme. This work was interrupted in 1691 by the death of Louvois, and in 1699 the king conferred responsibility for its completion upon the city of Paris, which immediately contacted some rich financiers. The equestrian statue at its centre was erected on 13 August 1699 with 'much pomp and ceremony. The duc de Gesvres, governor of Paris, escorted by guards in brand new uniforms and accompanied by town councillors in full regalia, presided at its dedication, for which a new kind of apparatus, never before seen on such occasions, was used. That evening, a grand firework display was held on the river, opposite the Great Gallery of the Louvre' (18). The history of this public square is a good example of how Louvois, exploiting his influence alongside Mansart's personal financial initiatives, could press Louis forward. War expenses forced the king to set his ambitions aside for the moment, but he accepted a compromise in the form of an agreement with the municipality and the participation of private finance, thus satisfying his *gloire* without irritation to taxpayers. The population at large did not hold it against the king that he was hardly ever to be seen in Paris. Parisians were clear-headed and rational, and, in any case, any true Parisian knew that only Parisian tastes and opinions really mattered.

PUBLIC OPINION

Despite the power of the monarchy and the dominant position of France after Nymwegen, it is obvious today that the weak point of the whole edifice lay in the inadequate rapport between government and people. The king knew that a public opinion existed and, even though it was no longer *frondeur* after 1653 and lacked a philosophical component before 1690, he still had to take it into account. He was also aware of the apprehensions of the inhabitants of the new provinces. And he recognized that public opinion would tolerate his mistresses but not necessarily his confessors (112). Finally, when it came to the question of

whether or not to accept Charles II's will conferring the crown of
Spain upon Philippe, duc d'Anjou, Louis sought the advice of
merchants and businessmen. Examples of this kind of consultation are plentiful throughout the reign. Greater harmony was
created around three factors: the hereditary monarchy, with the
mutual affection between king and loyal subjects; the calming
influence of Catholicism;* and, after the Fronde's turmoil, a kind
of understanding between Louis and the majority of his people.

    Although a kind of public opinion existed, it lacked freedom of
expression, especially when it was hostile (229b). The press was
never free. The *Gazette de France* and the *Mercure* contained
only adulation and submission towards the king; nor did the
Journal des savants risk causing offence. Books were censored, and
despite Paris's being an intellectual centre of universal influence,
the lieutenant of police still searched for subversive literature,
either imported from Holland or printed clandestinely in France
with false imprints of London or Amsterdam. But this censor-
ship should not be exaggerated. Dutch journals circulated in
secret, and people delighted in reading, copying and singing
ballads, rhymes and satires which seemed to come straight off
the streets of Paris (91). Furthermore, as Nerval was to remark
nostalgically, pamphleteers in those days chose their own
censors.

    At the more elevated level of political advice, subjects could
not express their opinions as easily. In Assemblies of the Clergy
and in the king's councils, opinions were free but their expression was muted, and those expressing themselves were not ordinary subjects. As the king's agents, there were bound to be
restraints. Chambers of commerce and the bureau of commerce
of 1700 expressed the point of view of some merchants, but they
were only concerned with one aspect of policy. All that remained
were the Estates, in those provinces where they still existed.
Their deputies voted so-called *dons gratuits* taxes and could talk
freely. Neither those of Languedoc nor those of Brittany saw
themselves as passive; they were politically conscious and
shouldered administrative responsibilities.

    On the whole, the machinery worked. The king thought that
he had done his duty to his subjects as long as he was informed
about their feelings. In serious crises, as in 1695, 1709 and 1710,

---

* The point is Jean-Pierre Babelon's (119).

he appealed directly to public opinion, for example in the preambles to edicts. In less extreme circumstances, he used the bishops, whose pastoral letters reached throughout the kingdom. But, as would be seen under Louis XV and Louis XVI, although the king paid attention to public opinion, he did not provide it with sufficient channels through which to express itself. Louis XIV cannot be blamed for not having ruled in the following century, but there might be some regret that his political intelligence had not been more prescient. Between the Peace of Nymwegen and the League of Augsburg, he might have saved the monarchy in the long term. For only the king could have reformed the absolute monarchy, and concessions could have been made from a position of strength rather than under pressure.

If he had been capable of the thought that for the monarchy a state of grace was not eternal, Louis could have earned his sobriquet 'the Great' by creating structures for associating different groups with his authority and by forging a common interest through the free expression of public opinion. But he did not even consider extending the system of provincial Estates, not so much because of the headaches given him by the Bretons as because Estates appeared to be outmoded institutions. To have let the *parlements* off the leash and to have accepted the desires of the Parisian *parlementaires* to imitate their counterparts in London would have been to re-create the conditions of 1648. It would have meant granting legislative power to self-interested notables with no popular mandate, their pretensions based merely on their having bought offices. In theory, Louis could have revived the Estates General. With a strong monarchy and a healthy financial situation, this was feasible. But, in practice, many obstacles stood in the way. Having been frequent and useful in the sixteenth century, the Estates General had not met since 1614, a gathering which had not left warm or lasting memories. Seventy years later, who would want them back? The arguments against extending the provincial Estates applied also to the Estates General. They would have seemed a living anachronism. This is what Furetière had to say about them in his *Universal Dictionary*: '*Estates* also means an assembly of the different orders of the kingdom, called to reform disorder in the state and to pacify troubles within the state.' (42) For the present, there were no troubles or disorders, and reforms were a matter for the king. Also, the conflict with the Netherlands created a further problem. That nightmare of the king's, the Protestant United Provinces, a federal republic which gave succour to his adversaries, was the embodiment of Estates General. The calling of such a body in 1680 would have appeared as the emulation of this disturbing regime. The only remaining option for associating national representation with monarchical sovereignty was an Assembly of Notables. But the preoccupations of such an assembly can readily be imagined. It would have raised the banner of Gallicanism, which was the last thing that Louis wanted, despite his skirmishes with Innocent XI. The notables would have called for action against the Huguenots, but Louis needed no encouragement in that direction. So it is difficult to blame him for not 'liberalizing' the *ancien régime*. Louis XV would, in this respect, have more to answer for.

THE WEAKNESS OF THE OPPOSITION

The extent, duration and influence of opposition to Louis XIV have often been exaggerated. Opposition was nourished by religious argument; political opposition was only a byproduct of this. Even before the Revocation of the Edict of Nantes, the Protestants formed the natural opposition group. The king treated them as such, whilst they themselves were essentially presbyterian and not always royalist. After the Revocation, only the most devout among them would be able to muster manifestations of loyalty to the monarchy. As for the Augustinians, they became 'Jansenist' because that is what they were called; the way in which they were treated made them a fertile terrain for possible opposition. But was their spiritual independence really politically inspired? And was their tendency towards open-minded study of the Bible really a danger to the monarchy? Arnauld, Racine, Mme de Sévigné and even Quesnel were all among Louis' admirers. All the 'Jansenists' put together would not make up a force comparable to the Duke of Burgundy's *camarilla*, including, as it did, Beauvillier, Chevreuse, Fénelon and Saint-Simon.

If literary historians are to be believed, a party of *libertins*, or sophisticated agnostics, were laying the foundations for the Enlightenment. Yet there is nothing to prove that La Mothe le Vayer was an agnostic and much to indicate that we have been mistaken about *libertinage*, just as we once were about Bayle's beliefs.* The abbé Gaussault was nearer the truth when he pronounced this judgement on the age in his *Reflections on the Different Characters of Men*: '*Libertinage* does not mean denying the fact of religion, but rather implies not living in accordance with its laws and maxims. They know what they should believe and what they should do, but that is where it stops; they believe, but unfailingly neglect to do what they ought.' (39) Père Camaret wrote along the same lines, affirming that: 'Jesus Christ is not universally obeyed with the fidelity due to him. But Jesus Christ is still king.' (145) Even if groups of *libertins* (in the philosophical sense of the term) did exist in France, it would still require to be proved that they were engaged in political activity hostile to the regime. Even the *libertin* Philippe d'Orléans was not a member of the opposition. In Spain, he was not tempted by personal ambition to be so and, whilst in France, the possibility of his succession to the throne obliged him to be cautious, and this also constituted his best strategy.

Opposition was more likely to be found among the *dévots*. The Jansenist sympathizer Saint-Simon and the Ultramontane Beauvillier, Chevreuse and Fénelon all subscribed to a 'political Augustinianism'. In 1712, all four appeared to be preparing for the next reign. But they had to act prudently. Fénelon was tucked away in his diocese and Saint-Simon was kept under careful surveillance by the king, but Chevreuse was in an influential position, albeit not in an official capacity, and Beauvillier was a valued minister.

These groups and individuals had neither an identity of views nor a common programme. One finds critical tendencies and indifference, a few republicans among the former Protestants and a majority of royalists. Saint-Simon and Fénelon criticized the absolute monarchy, but the noble utopia which they envisaged was supposed to strengthen the Crown. Such groups and individuals formed part of the intelligentsia and therefore their views attracted attention; but numerically they were few and they enjoyed no connections with the provinces or relations with the lower orders. This fact was, however, attenuated by the foundation of academies such as those at Villefranche (1679), Nîmes (1682), Angers (1685), Arles (1689), Toulouse (1694),

---

* i.e., before the appearance of the remarkable thesis of Elisabeth Labrousse (208).

Lyon (1700), Caen (1705), Montpellier (1706) and Bordeaux (1713). Versailles and Paris did not stifle the rest of the kingdom. But these societies had not yet gone in the direction which they would take in the eighteenth century. They were *bien pensantes* and loyalist. Louis granted them letters-patent and thus demonstrated that, even at the time of Mme de Maintenon and père Le Tellier, he was far from being obscurantist.

As far as the people were concerned, it was safer to be loyal, and their patient acceptance of his rule betrays a real affection for the king. The countryside was tranquil after the Breton revolt of 1675. (The Camisard war was neither political nor social, but religious, and ignited by prophetic millenarianism.) The peasantry subscribed to that Catholic unity which supplied the cement to the sense of French national identity, a cement which the Revocation of 1685 reinforced. Bishops and priests denied the king nothing. When a battle had been won, France sang a *Te Deum*; when things were going badly, the people were mobilized in prayer. In such conditions, news travelled in less than three weeks from the sovereign to the most distant inhabitant in the kingdom. Victories created enthusiasm, defeats concern. France was saved on its frontiers between 1709 and 1712 thanks to a mobilization that was requested by the king but obtained because the clergy supported it. After years of war, harsh winters, epidemics and deaths, higher taxation and the demands of military service, in a never changing regime where the king had exhausted all his credit, the popularity of the regime is not to be gauged by a few sporadic revolts, but by the astonishing fidelity and patience of those who lived under it.

18

The Consolidation of the Court

O N 20 APRIL 1682, Louis XIV bid adieu (on the pretext of
some forthcoming building work there) to Saint-Germain,
where he had spent the winter. On 6 May, it was learnt that the
king, the queen, Monseigneur and the Dauphine had left Saint-
Cloud for Versailles, which was itself still being built, neither the
Hall of Mirrors nor the Mansart wing having yet been completed. Louis had considered the move for some time. Versailles,
the setting for fêtes and amorous affairs, had long been his obsession. For the past twelve years, he had been tired of the Tuileries
and, despite his extensions to Saint-Germain, that château was
no more his own creation than was the Louvre. It was no mere
coincidence that the court had already taken up residence at
Versailles in 1674, 1675 and 1677. Now the king's personal
preference merged with his plans for a more ordered, more distinct and more resplendent court. Louis' political designs were
more important than the charms of the Versailles gardens or
Mansart's seductive embellishments. Just as Le Nôtre's art disciplined nature, the art of Versailles served to discipline the
court, the king's creation.

THE COURT SYSTEM AS IT APPEARED

It did not take long for ambassadors to inform their government
about the primacy of Versailles. Princes, great nobles and artists
came to observe and admire Louis' creation. Such was the success of Versailles that, for a century, sovereigns throughout
Europe attempted to erect replicas of it. The original was domin-

ated by the quest for glory, to which everything had to make its contribution: the grandeur of the setting, the nobility of the architecture, the beauty of the new buildings, the symbolism of Apollo, the majesty of the king and the quality of his entourage, as well as the splendour of the ceremonial and the receptions. Versailles was to be identified with national celebration. The Duke of Burgundy (1682), his brother Philip V (1683) and Louis XV (1710) were all born there; the Dauphine (1690) and the Duchess of Burgundy (1712) both died there. Great festivities would mark the births of Burgundy and his brother, the marriages of the duc de Bourbon to Mlle de Nantes in August 1685, the prince de Conti to Marie-Thérèse de Bourbon in 1688, and the future regent to Mlle de Blois in 1692, and the birth of the Duke of Brittany in 1704 (242). But the public remembered and posterity would recall, above all, the receptions given to distinguished visitors from abroad.

Such was the case with Louis' reception of the Doge of Genoa in May 1685, when he subjected him to a ceremonial abasement. On Tuesday, 15 May, the Doge, dressed in red velvet and flanked by senators in black velvet, made his entry into the Hall of Mirrors. On the 18th, he was shown round the interior of the château and showed his admiration by declaring: 'A year ago it was Hell; now it is Paradise.' (26) Then he was shown the Menagerie, the Grand Canal and the Trianon. On the 23rd, the Doge, Lercaro, attended Louis' *lever*, visited the stables, gardens and fountains, and then watched the court dance until midnight. Dangeau wrote that he had never seen a more sumptuous ball. The Genoese took their leave on Saturday, 26 May. A year later, Versailles saw the 'notable reception' of the Siamese ambassadors in the *grande galerie* (Hall of Mirrors) and, in 1699, the audience for the Moroccan ambassadors. To receive the Persian ambassador on 19 February 1715, the old king wore a black and gold outfit so heavily embroidered with diamonds that he had to change out of it before dinner. The Hall of Mirrors was furnished with four tiers of seats 'filled by more than 400 magnificently dressed ladies'. Louis mounted his throne with the Dauphin to his right under the watchful eye of the duchesse de Ventadour, the duc d'Orléans to his left, and, on both sides, 'all the princes of the blood ... according to their rank'. At the foot of the throne, Coypel was ready, crayon in hand, to capture the historic moment, whilst M. de Boze of the Academy of Inscriptions concentrated on the 'composition of a true account of the ceremony' (26). 'Never', wrote Saint-Simon, 'has the king espoused such magnificence.' (26)

These images traverse the centuries. Doges, envoys from Muscovy and ambassadors from distant lands provided the occasions for courtly, royal and politic display, mounted for and by the court. Everyone played a part: Dauphin, *fils de France*, princes of the blood, royal officials and dignitaries of the household. The first gentleman of the chamber in residence and the captain of the king's bodyguard were both kept busy, under the command of the *maître des cérémonies de France*, of the *grand prévôt de l'Hôtel* and of the presenters of ambassadors. Each official's position was determined by the regulations of the court, perfected by long usage. Continuity prevailed over change, and respect for the rules laid down to create an impression of magnificence gave the court a 'classical', logical and refined appearance. Writers described the splendours of Versailles in terms of a ballet, as though court and ballet were synonymous. But a ballet presupposed hierarchy and discipline, so, if this comparison was valid, it was inevitable that Louis XIV's court was, above all, hierarchical and probable that nobles living in the king's entourage were so well 'domesticated' that they became merely objects of the royal will. This was what appearances suggested. The *Ceremonial* of 1682 was already a weighty volume, and it continued to expand. Its study obsessed certain individuals such as Monsieur and Saint-Simon. It was based on the existence of ranks and helped to draw the distinctions between them. After the king, came the Dauphin, then Monsieur, followed by the *petits-fils de France* and then the princes of the blood. This is, however, only a superficial impression. Each category did not comprise merely a single rank; there was a protocol to be observed within each group and the king arbitrated on this whenever either necessity demanded it or there were disputes. Thus, on 4 March 1710, he had to make a decision on the question of the relative positions of the princesses, and he attached so much importance to it that he opened a meeting of the council of ministers the next day by announcing his decision (103). From then on:

> daughters in direct line of the royal branch will all be addressed as Madame and will take precedence over all other princesses of the royal family, even if they are not married. Similarly, the daughters of Mme the Duchess of Burgundy will take precedence

and Madame the dowager princess [Madame Palatine], and the princess who will marry M. the duc de Berry; in collateral branches of the royal family, married princesses will take precedence over the unmarried. In addition, Mme the duchesse d'Orléans, *petite-fille de France*, will take precedence over the daughters of M. the duc de Berry until they are married.

The same principle will apply 'between the other princesses of the blood, so that Madame la Duchesse and married princesses of the blood will take precedence over Mademoiselle because she is only an unmarried princess of the blood'. De Tourcy, whose analysis this is, concluded that: 'The king's purpose in this ruling was to re-establish peace within the royal family.' (103) Only a historian like Jean-François Solnon could comprehend this complex text at first reading,* and today it is impossible to grasp the total significance of these hierarchies and ranks. On the same occasion, Louis specified the titles of several princes. 'It has been said', reported Sourches, 'that the duc de Chartres should be known as Monsieur le Prince [as the head of the House of Condé has been called], but this is false, and he will keep his present name, enjoying all the prerogatives, nevertheless, of first prince of the blood. As regards the duc d'Enghien, we have learnt that, out of respect for the memory of the prince, his father, he will take the title of Monsieur le Duc only after his father's funeral.' (97) Princes of the blood came ahead of legitimized royal bastards, but the stations accorded the *légitimés* preoccupied their father from 1694 to 1715, feeding speculation and infuriating Saint-Simon. The uncertainty surrounding their future position, and their rapid rise in royal esteem, provided a focus for reflection on the king's authority.

After the princes, prominence was given to the dukes, amongst whom the first rank was reserved to the peers (one group, the 'foreign princes', claiming superiority over the rest), followed by the hereditary dukes and then the so-called dukes *à brevet*. Between this ducal elite and the commonality of the nobility, Louis gave special prominence to the chevaliers of the Order of the Holy Spirit. Finally, among the courtiers, there was a tendency to consider the *logeants*, those resident at Versailles, as a cut above the mere *présentés*.

Yet this can all be misleading. Neither rank nor etiquette was

* See the work of Jean-François Solnon (272b).

enough to justify some privileges, such as the place assigned to individuals at the ceremonial *lever*, where favour and credit were crucial. All these gradations created an appearance of hierarchy within the nobility. Only duchesses, for example, had a right to the *tabouret*, that is, to be seated in front of the queen. But precedence did not determine everything. Certain posts formed a parallel hierarchy. A minister was more envied than a duke; the *prévôt de l'Hôtel* could enjoy credit equal to that of a prince; a historiographer royal or gentleman of the chamber had direct access to the king. Saint-Simon pretended to be unaware of these facts, but other contemporaries were conscious of them. Those who persisted in likening Louis XIV's court to a machine knew that no astronomical clock had a more complicated mechanism than Versailles.

USING THE COURT TO GOOD EFFECT

In fixing his residence at Versailles in 1682, Louis inaugurated something beyond new buildings, although at that time the southern wing and the stables were completed, and work on the chapel, the final constructions at Marly and the building, just beginning, of the *grand commun* were all proceeding apace. For the court, the novelty lay in the impressive enlargement of the setting. For more than thirty years, the king had been preoccupied with avoiding the conditions which might lead to a new Fronde, and the courts at the Louvre, the Tuileries and Saint-Germain had been organized with this in mind. The higher nobility, attracted and captivated by the glamour of court life, was kept under surveillance. The king had persuaded the aristocracy that its vocation lay not in independence but in the service of the state, which to aristocrats meant military service, with its glory, duties and honour. For the previous twenty years, the courtier had been a soldier, and if he was also a master of the wardrobe, gentleman of the chamber or *grand écuyer tranchant*, this was an additional honour, extending the range of his service.

The first military campaigns of the reign, especially the Dutch War, sealed in blood the pact binding the nobles in his entourage to the king. Later wars only served to confirm the courtier's desire to serve. Several former *frondeurs* died in battle, including Beaufort in 1669 and Turenne in 1675. Others died worn out by their efforts, like Luxembourg, the *tapissier de Notre-Dame*, in 1695. More blood than ever was spilled. The priority given to military service, and the ease with which Versailles allowed the king to determine the quality of service given him, show the true extent of the court's role. During the winter season, the court might be distracted by the marquis de Dangeau's gambling profits, or the latest duel or adultery; but, come the spring, attention switched to the forthcoming dangers, exploits, wounds and deaths. 'After Malplaquet in 1709,' the Princess Palatine wrote, 'Versailles was full of bandages and crutches.' (87) The higher nobility justified a large part of its privileges through the risks encountered in war, and the price was paid, without hesitation, in blood. Often attendance at court was merely the prelude to death on the battlefield. Balls, masquerades, gambling, the joys of love, the games of pall-mall, hunting and carrousels represented, above all, the warrior's rest, and if the term 'warrior' seemed incongruous when applied to these beribboned aristocrats, it became justified when they joined the armed forces.

The armed forces were commanded by the greatest in the land – princes of the blood, *légitimés* and 'foreign' princes –, and, when victorious generals came from lesser stock, like Boufflers or Villars, the king made them dukes and peers. It makes little sense to deplore the fact that aristocrats such as Condé, Conti and Vendôme were excluded from the king's council or that officeholders headed the government. Louis made each group serve according to its abilities. The high nobility was at home in military service, whilst ministers from the robe did enough for the king and the kingdom to earn their honoured place at court. The transformation was completed at Versailles in 1682 when Louvois finally gained ascendancy over Colbert and the *plus grands* such as Condé finally submitted to the king and displayed the kind of discipline requisite to a more modern state. What did it matter if Condé remained at Chantilly or that the ducs de Rohan, Brissac and Ventadour turned their backs on Versailles? None of them gave a thought to reviving the Fronde. Periods of enforced idleness, intrigues, and even the three cabals revealed in 1709 were mere surface ripples compared with the tidal wave of 1648. Versailles was Louis' revenge for the Fronde, a vengeance with political and moral purpose whose ultimate beneficiary would be the state.

Yet it might be argued that the court was not composed

merely of gentlemen in service. It encompassed the old, the very young and many ladies. It is impossible to discern the fine line which divided the court nobility from the 'nobility at court' and give the precise number in each group. The court nobility, the exact number and composition of which are unknown, suffered (or so we are told) from three vices: the trammels of etiquette, domestication and *déracinement* or the abandonment of their provincial roots. Furetière was ignorant of the word *étiquette* in 1690. Court ceremonial was only slightly more elaborate than it had been under Henry III, though it was exaggerated somewhat after the move to Versailles. Louis had long been attracted to it, since it satisfied his sense of order. Ceremonial possessed political and also aesthetic value, and kept the courtiers occupied. It is significant that Monsieur was its high priest. Louis preferred to see his brother busy settling ceremonial matters rather than dabbling in plots. The same applied to the dukes, the great nobles and their companions: in bickering over matters of precedence, they had no time for intrigues. Dangeau's *Journal* and Sourches' *Mémoires* record these squabbles, although they never attained the importance of those chronicled by Luynes under Louis XV. Moreover, the ceremonial at Versailles was less Olympian than that at other courts. Whilst in Vienna, Madrid or London one knelt before the prince or walked backwards in front of him, at Versailles a bow was more common (135).

The word 'domestication' dates from Louis-Philippe's reign rather than Louis XIV's and it gathered pejorative overtones which would have astonished Louis' boon companions, who were elated rather than humiliated by the idea of service. They took it as an honour to belong to the king's house or *domus* (their Latin was better than ours), and, in the seventeenth century, to be the *domestique* of a great prince was not demeaning to commoners but rather conferred privileges upon them, endowing them with a kind of intermediary status between that of a noble and that of a commoner (137). In addition, domestic duties were generally but one form of service among many others. It was possible to be a marshal, a provincial governor and a captain in the king's bodyguard at the same time, or else a general, an ambassador and a first gentleman of the chamber. The courtly vice was not idleness but pluralism.

As far as the 'uprooting' of the nobility by the king is concerned, it did happen that nobles became too attached to courtly

life and cut themselves off from their familial and local attachments. The comte de Tessé, having decided in 1710 to visit the
estate which gave him his title, wrote: 'I had not been there for
thirty-two years and I found it without doors or glass in the
windows, except in one tower, where there was only one room up
five sets of stairs.' (101) But Furetière only used the word *déracinement* in an agricultural context. He included the verb *déraciner*
('to uproot') in its moral sense, but gave it a positive value:
'*Déraciner* is applied figuratively to moral matters, meaning to
remove the source of an abuse.' (42) Establishing the most
powerful men in the kingdom at court meant uprooting their
propensity for revolt. Not that we are dealing here with the
nobility as a whole, a group numbering 12,000 families and some
200,000 individuals, but only with 'the great personages of the
realm'. If, at the end of the reign, Versailles and its dependencies
housed around 10,000 people, half of them commoners, the court
was therefore composed of about 5,000 nobles. The system of
seasonal 'quarters' meant that active service lasted not for a year
but for three months twice yearly, and therefore these 5,000
nobles represented as many nobles again in effect. But if the king
retained 10,000 members of the nobility at court, he was still
'uprooting' only five per cent of the whole class.

DISTRACTIONS AND RESTRICTIONS

Those who chose to participate at court had little to complain
about, since their duties and distractions tended to coincide.
If the obligations of service did not detain one, then the king
expected one's presence. Being on hand from the *lever* to the
coucher increased one's opportunities of being rewarded with a
position, a pension, an invitation to Marly, or just a friendly
word to make one feel the centre of attention. In the case of the
last, the king would greet one with a 'Good morning, Monsieur
de So-and-so . . .', showing that he had singled one out. Waiting
on the king was generally worth the effort, whilst an 'I shall not
notice him' acted as the final curtain to a courtier's ambitions.
There were many opportunities to show oneself to the king, on
the way to and from Mass, at table (known as *au grand couvert*)
and at *appartements*. But the surest method was to be present in
the morning. His Majesty's *lever* took account of 'the various

degrees to be observed in admittance to it, only allowing entry at the start to those with rights to attend what is called the *petit lever*, to the servants of the chamber' (98), and to a handful of the most privileged. Those admitted at this initial stage, the *grandes entrées*, attained this favour either by virtue of their offices (the first gentlemen of the chamber and the grand chamberlain, for example) or because of their credit (the *légitimés*). Beneficiaries of the *premières entrées*, such as Condé, Villeroy, Beringhen, the *lecteurs du roi* and the Dauphin's tutors, had access at the conclusion of the *petit lever*. This list reveals a mixture of birth, merit and favour. A third wave brought in other important figures, such as the captain of the guards and the *premier maître de l'Hôtel*, whilst the fourth stage, known as the *entrée libre*, let in the courtiers, 'among whom some were often singled out, according to their current standing at court, in preference to the rest'. The four categories, then, were really five. But it is more accurate to say six, because members of the royal family made their entries *par les derrières*. They avoided the filtering process and presented themselves to Louis before the *grandes entrées* arrived.

Many of the courtiers' lodgings were small and uncomfortable. Only a few were equipped to provide acceptable meals or receptions. But since it was understood that the king honoured one simply by one's being received, it would have been bad form to have made a fuss. By the king's command, the court was rather austere, pious and reserved, although, after the arrival of the Duchess of Burgundy, the old king partially restored entertainment to its former prominence. Royal banquets, carnivals, balls, concerts and ballets helped to make Versailles more hospitable. Out of doors, hunting, pall-mall and promenades on foot, on the canal or on sleighs enlivened court life, while indoor distractions were provided by the *appartements*, conversation, billiards and dancing.

Throughout his reign, the king made the park, with its walks, woods, canal, Orangery and Menagerie, available to courtiers, and, on occasions, his huntsmen, carriages and sledges too. He opened up the grand apartments, not even keeping the music to himself: the musicians of the chapel, the king's chamber, the *écurie* and the military bands were also public servants (122). Their fanfares and symphonies formed a marvellous accompaniment to court life.

This description of court life omits gambling, which, it is said,

Louis encouraged in order to impose on his nobility a more debilitating dependence. The reality was less complex. Louis banned duelling by repeated edicts. He also discouraged the 'ultramontane vice' (homosexuality) and, after his second marriage, adultery too. He reduced the number of spectacular entertainments. There were only a limited number of ways of attracting the aristocracy to court, of entertaining them and of preventing their intrigues. They had to be offered distractions which were neither immoral nor tedious. The game of *hoca* was already all the rage in 1675 at Versailles. In 1678, *bassette* was in vogue. Between 1681 and 1689, fortunes were won and lost at *reversi*. After 1693, the court imitated Paris and adopted *lansquenet* (135). These games were based on chance. Skill only intervened in deciding how much to stake and when. But the whole kingdom was tremendously keen on this kind of exercise. Sometimes the city followed the court, sometimes the court copied the city; but the provinces always echoed and prolonged these fashions.

THE SUN KING'S SATELLITES

Such a glittering court had to be well ordered. This was evident throughout the seventeenth century, even when memories of the Fronde had faded and court life became more routine. It was a political fact that, although a despot might live in isolation, a monarch needed to be surrounded by reflections of himself. The king, though absolute, presided over a government with a collegial structure, and the more powerful the minister, the more his reputation contributed to the king's glory, and that of the kingdom. The same applied to the court. For Louis, continuing in the tradition of the Valois kings, the court was an indispensable instrument and reflection of the prince. It constituted a system of glory serving the king and making the reputation of the kingdom. The queen played an indispensable role and, after her death, Louis did not seek to give France a second queen. The young and largely unrecognized Maria Theresa 'had a good figure . . . and might even have been called beautiful, although she did not possess an attractive personality . . . She appeared to be consumed with a violent passion for the king and otherwise was attached only to the queen her mother-in-law . . . and subject to much grief because of her extreme jealousy regarding the king' (49). With Anne of Austria's death in 1666, Maria Theresa lost a valued friend, but she retained her patient meekness and her Spanish piety. She also retained her Spanish accent ('She called the *sainte Vierge* [Blessed Virgin] *Sancta Biergen*' (87)). Shy and loving towards the husband who betrayed her, she was far from unintelligent. It needed a great deal of virtue, serenity and intelligence to make the best of things over twenty-two years, at times neglected in favour of more renowned beauties and at others obliged to stand smiling at their side. Her sister-in-law, Madame, who occasionally thought her almost ridiculous, nevertheless called her the 'good queen'. Sensible to her kindness, Louis ended his nights by her side and liked to calm her with sweet nothings. Charles V's granddaughter lacked the physical charms and conversational ease which might have ensured her a more agreeable private life. Yet she was a good wife, a model of devotion, a symbol of delicacy and the only pain she caused the king was by her death, on 30 July 1683.

Louis de France (1661–1711), the Dauphin, known as Monseigneur, was the most popular member of the royal family and the favourite among the Parisians. Through him, the hurt caused by king's absence from the capital was assuaged. A lover of spectacle, Monseigneur found in Paris what was missing at Versailles. When he fell ill, the ladies of Les Halles paid him visits. When he joined the army (as in 1688), he was engulfed by attention and gratitude, with junior officers and soldiers devoted to him. He had inherited his father's qualities. He too had intelligence without pedantry. Like Louis XIV, he enjoyed stimulating company and showed an equally lively taste in his collection of paintings, medals, coins and antiques. The father embellished Versailles and Marly, whilst the son did the same at Meudon, where he had succeeded Louvois. And Louis XIV and Monseigneur both appreciated good food, war, horseriding and hunting. Yet the king had to be endlessly prudent, whilst the Dauphin could burn the candle at both ends, restraining with difficulty his impatience and energy. He was not a *gastrolâtre*, but he had an enormous appetite, a *grand gosier* (42), which stimulated a worrying tendency to apoplexy. His physical energy seemed inexhaustible. He hunted wild game, especially wolves, almost every day; he was excellent at pall-mall, dominated *courses de bague*, and took endless risks. He was not one of those princes who went to war just to show off, and took such risks in 1688 and 1689 that the king was forced to forbid his heroic excess. Monseigneur took to extremes the combination of taste and action inherited from his father. Like Louis XIV, the Dauphin married a rather effacing, dreary and devout princess, and, again in imitation of his father, he contracted a further marriage. Mlle de Choin, whom Louis de France installed at Meudon with the same pre-eminence that the king bestowed on his Mme de Maintenon, possessed to a similar degree her refinement and amorous experience. The select company received by Monseigneur and his second wife at Meudon was amongst the most exclusive in the kingdom. It was an open secret that the king liked to join them, Meudon not being far from Versailles. The Dauphin, recognizing his filial duty as well as his social responsibilities, managed to reconcile his position as heir apparent with his desire for autonomy. He was a member of the royal council of finance and council of despatches from 1688 and of the council of ministers from 1691. In the War of the Spanish Succession, he lent faithful support to his son, Philip V. It was unfortunate that his premature death prevented this gifted dauphin from succeeding his father, for he would, perhaps, have made the best of kings.

The princes of the third generation also played leading roles. The Duke of Burgundy (1682–1712), the second dauphin, and his brother Anjou (1683–1746), the future King of Spain, combined their mother's piety with firm Bourbon traits. The former was a trial to his tutor, Fénelon, whilst the latter would become a living example of courage and will-power. Flanked by his young wife (Marie-Louise-Gabrielle of Savoy, d. 1714), a Jesuit confessor (père Daubenton) and a mistress (the princesse des Ursins), Anjou displayed remarkable decisiveness and lucidity as Philip V. In defeat, he retained his confidence. Driven out of Madrid, he later returned there. On the point of losing Spain, he prepared to continue the struggle in the Spanish Americas. When the fate of Spain and of Europe at large lay in the balance in 1709 and 1710, his resolution was apparently greater than that of his grandfather.

Amidst all these virtues, seemingly drawn from a Corneille play, Philippe d'Orléans (1640–1701), the king's brother, known as Monsieur, appeared more like a hero from one by Racine. Though eclipsed by Louis XIV, he should not be underestimated. A century earlier, his somewhat Valois characteristics would have allowed him to cut a fine figure. He was adaptable, cultivated, refined, sensitive and courageous, and shared Henry III's exaggerated piety and tendency to ambiguity and indecision. Fickle in love, he found it hard to choose between the chevalier de Lorraine and his wives, and yet, whilst no saint, he never missed a Lenten or Advent sermon. On Palm Sunday 1678, in the Church of Saint-Sulpice in Paris, Bourdaloue pronounced an encomium on the prince, recalling that 'on this liturgical date, Sunday, 11 April 1677, he had been victorious at the Battle of Mont Cassel', an affair which Louis XIV had tried to consign to oblivion.* He always held his younger brother in an affection tinged with jealousy at his military exploits. Rather than being an Alexander or a Caesar, Monsieur had to be content with sharing the renown of his successes in the Dutch War with the duc de Luxembourg. Like Monseigneur, Monsieur enjoyed life in Paris and took the king's place there. His town residence was at the Palais-Royal, his country retreat at Saint-Cloud. Less esteemed than the Dauphin, he was 'more popular than highly regarded', although he enjoyed a reputation for charity (195). His second wife, the Princess Palatine, constantly complained bitterly about him, but always forgave him. Her position as the wife to a homosexual was not an enviable one. In 1672, she called him 'the best man in the world', and, though her opinion of him soon went downhill, to the end 'Liselotte' said that he was 'more to be pitied than hated' (87).

The king's two sisters-in-law, so different from each other, shared nothing in common beyond, perhaps, that excess of personality which Monsieur lacked. The first Madame was Henrietta of England (d. 1670), her husband's cousin. Granddaughter of Henry IV, and known mostly for Bossuet's oration for her funeral ('Madame se meurt! Madame est morte!' (14)), she possessed great charms and, in 1661, the king came close to a love-affair with her. Mme de la Fayette admired her quick wit and, because of her abilities, she was chosen for a mission to England.

Madame Palatine (Elizabeth-Charlotte von Wittelsbach) knew herself that she was no *belle* – not even Rigaud could glamorize her –, but, like Henrietta, she fell in love with her

* See ch. 13.

brother-in-law. Like Louis XIV, she was addicted to the open air, to riding and hunting. In November 1709, she claimed to have run more than 1,000 stags. Her affection for Louis made her despise Mme de Maintenon, whom she referred to as an *ordure* in her letters. The king did not enjoy having to sanction this German correspondence, choice elements of which were revealed to him by La Reynie, and which presented France as a frivolous kingdom and Versailles as the den of iniquity. The princess adored sauerkraut and beer soup, loved the theatre and was always ready for a country walk or a hunt. She adored the Psalter and Lutheran chorales which she had heard before her precipitate conversion to Catholicism. But she detested everything else, despised Monseigneur, hated the duc du Maine, whom she called 'the bastard', and was jealous on all matters regarding the king. She criticized Catholic devotions and priests and any church service which lasted for longer than a quarter of an hour. She attacked Paris, Marly, the war, French cooking, gambling and all libertinism, of both mind and manners. Her correspondence has to be treated with caution.

It would be wrong to take in a pejorative sense the idea of the Sun King's 'satellites', as though the members of the royal family had lost their independence and had been condemned either to sulk in their tents or to revolve around Louis. None of them sacrificed their personality, nor were they forced to submit to liaisons against their wills or to ostracism. Even when Vendôme fell from grace, his close relations, Monseigneur and the duc du Maine, continued to visit him. The friendship of these three, to some extent the pillars of the kingdom, was enough to justify Louis XIV's forms of sociability.

Around these stars revolved a cluster of asteroids – princes of the blood, 'foreign' princes, dukes, table companions, regular courtiers and 'gentlemen of passage' who kept their provinces informed of the splendours at court. They came, went, looked, listened and made themselves visible. Ceremonial did not favour every one of them; but, at a time when and in a place where disputes over precedence preoccupied magistrates, treasurers of *rentes* and war commissioners, town *échevins* and *syndics*, and masters and journeymen in guilds, confraternities and journeymen's associations, we may be sure that, if Louis XIV had not so ordered his court, the king's satellites would have invented a ceremonial for themselves to satisfy their own self-esteem and the renown of Versailles.

In Lavisse's school textbook, *The New First-Year History of France*, we read that 'Louis XIV spent countless sums of his subjects' money to satisfy his pride; his courts and the palaces he built, especially at Versailles, cost an enormous amount, which must be added to his military expenditure.' The only truth in this sentence lies in the final clause. War did indeed strain the budget, accounting in 1683 for 56.7 per cent of total expenditures. But who is to determine that this was money wasted? In the same year, that which saw Colbert's demise, the king's buildings only accounted for 6.27 per cent of state spending or 7,222,000 *livres* (238). Versailles represented a fraction of this sum, the château, park and dependencies costing 1,855,000 *livres* that year (45). Even if we were to add to this the 846,000 *livres* of expenses on the works at Marly, the Versailles system only represents 2.35 per cent of national expenditure, one third the amount spent on fortresses (238).

Versailles was 'a work of peace and the essential construction was carried out and the greatest expenses incurred whenever peace was proclaimed' (291). The Salon de la Paix has a symbolic meaning. During the War of Devolution, 536,000 *livres* were spent over two years at Versailles. With the return of peace, expenses rose rapidly once more: 676,000 *livres* in 1669; 1,633,000 in 1670; 2,621,000 in 1671 (45). Total expenditure on Versailles during the five years of war from 1673 to 1677 amounted to 4,066,000 *livres*. After Nymwegen, the king felt no further need to economize and the costs of Versailles rose to 4,886,000 *livres* in 1679 (45). The Ten Years' War soon put a stop to further new construction. Waterworks apart, the expenditures on Versailles recorded in the accounts of the *bâtiments* amounted to 6,104,000 *livres* in 1685, 2,520,000 in 1686 and 2,935,000 in 1687. War preparations forced restrictions in 1688, reducing the total to 1,976,000 *livres*. In the years from 1689 to 1697, Versailles only cost the state 2,145,000 *livres* (45). Looked at objectively, these are not astronomically high figures. From 1661 to 1715, Versailles cost no more than 68 million *livres*. If we add to this

4,621,000 *livres* for the water-pump at Marly, and even the cost of other waterworks, on the River Eure or the aqueduct at Maintenon, 8,984,000 *livres* in total, we arrive at less than 82 million. This was an important sum, but not much more than the budget deficit for the single year 1715, which amounted to 77 million *livres*.

In relation to the political and artistic influence of the court, it is scarcely relevant to count the cost at all; for, as Pierre Verlet put it: 'It may be readily agreed that Louis XIV enriched France through Versailles . . . Louis XIV's expenditures gave the world a château that one cannot help but admire.' (291)

19

Images of Versailles

'Louis XIV endowed France with new provinces ... but that was a long time past. Versailles is still standing.' (291) A great effort has been made to restore at least part of the château's interior décor. Yet, however splendid it may now seem, the park can only give us a rough impression of the original splendour created by Le Nôtre. The château, however delicately restored, is but a symbol. For, even if Versailles were to recover its former gardens, furnishings, art-collections and original decorations, it would still remain a shell, empty of the everyday life of king, courtiers, government, messengers, guards, musicians and kitchen boys and of the ceaseless activity of its artistic manufacturers.

APOLLO'S WORKSHOPS

When the king and court arrived at Versailles in 1682, the château was 'full of masons' (97). When they returned in November, they settled in in the midst of what was then a building site. Behind his unruffled exterior, Louis was growing impatient. He was an architect with a grand design who imposed a kind of asceticism on himself and on others, never satisfied and never at rest, betraying a perfectionism which, emerging from an apparent disorder, shows a creative and alert mind at work. In 1684, the *grande galerie* or Hall of Mirrors was still not clear of scaffolding (291), yet Mansart's plans had been drawn up in 1678 and Le Brun had begun the ceiling murals in late 1679. In 1684, the superintendent spent 34,000 *livres* on the workers' lodgings (45), and, in 1685, Dangeau estimated that the works in the park, château and its dependencies gave employment to 36,000 workers. When the court finally settled in, the façade of the 'château neuf', or Hall of Mirrors, was completed and Mansart put the finishing touches to the wings of the ministries on the town side. The place d'Armes, enclosed in part by the stables – practical buildings as fine as palaces – was nearing completion. The southern wing was habitable, but the northern wing would only be constructed between 1685 and 1689. Inside, the Grand Staircase or *escalier des Ambassadeurs* was freshly decorated, but two more years' work remained to be done to complete the Hall of Mirrors, the Salon de la Paix and the Salon de la Guerre. Meanwhile, Mansart continued to oversee the construction work on the *grand commun* from 1682 to 1684 and contemplated the planned building works for the superintendency which were to take shape in the period from 1683 to 1690 (291).

Everything came together to stimulate innovation: the growing number of *logeants* to be housed in Mansart's wings; the proliferation of services, necessitating the construction of stables, kitchens and water cisterns; and the changing lifestyle of the royal family. Monseigneur's changes of apartment are a case in point. The rooms which the Dauphin occupied before his marriage were on the ground floor beneath the queen's apartments, and were already his third set of quarters. The king wanted to provide him with more space and so he was provided with vast apartments in the new southern wing, now called Monseigneur's Wing.* After the death of Maria Theresa, the Dauphin was relocated for the last time. His wife inherited the queen's apartments in 1684, whilst he occupied the corresponding space on the ground floor, and this fifth set of lodgings was soon 'regarded as one of the marvels of Versailles' (291). On 8 January 1689, when the exiled James II visited Louis XIV for the first time, his host let him stand at the top of the Escalier de la Reine and admire with his connoisseur's eye the 'paintings, porcelain and crystal' with which the heir apparent had decorated that space (291). Symmetrical with the *appartement des Bains* or Bathroom Suite in the northern wing, the Dauphin's rooms included a vestibule, a guardroom, an antechamber 'with blue hangings and furnishings' and a bedroom, also decorated in blue, with two

---

* Today the Princes' Wing.

windows overlooking the gardens. Then came the *salon* or 'grand cabinet', which was a corner room with three windows overlooking the southern terrace and three others giving a view towards the water gardens. The Dauphin received visitors in it, but in 1686 there was scaffolding here as well because Mignard was painting *Apollo and the Virtues* on the ceiling. The *salon* led into a *cabinet* decorated in gold by Cucci and housing the prince's collections, as well as into a mirrored *cabinet* where Boulle created 'marquetry and bronzes', consoles and *scabellons*. Blue was the dominant colour here too. The Swedish architect Tessin admired this suite greatly and recorded that 'it is attributed entirely to the genius of Monseigneur' (291).

The Dauphin was not the only one to move his lodgings several times. The king himself set an example in mobility. From 1684 to 1701, his bedchamber was not the central room overlooking the Cour de Marbre but another one, more to the south. It was only in 1701 that he settled in his former *salon*, the room in which he was to die. It was situated midway between the antechamber of the *grand couvert* and the billiard room, opening directly onto the Council chamber. This was, as it were, the artistic culmination of the reign, a grand outburst of arrogance following Philip V's accession to the Spanish throne and an embodiment of the imposed royal prestige.

At the Escorial, the chapel was at the heart of the palace and, in the French-influenced Europe of the Enlightenment, princely residences provided the Church with the same privileges. Louis XIV, on the other hand, did not grant the Almighty a prime site (253). At Versailles, the chapels were invisible. The last to be built, designed by Mansart and constructed under the direction of Robert de Cotte, was more elaborate than the king's bedchamber, but less imposing. Begun in 1689 and consecrated in 1710, the chapel was only completed in 1712. Neither Bossuet nor Bourdaloue ever preached there.

During the thirty years between the arrival of the court and the king's death, a continuous series of new works and improvements made Versailles into a permanent construction site. The passage of time and evolving royal taste changed conceptions and styles. From around 1690 onwards, the ostentation of Le Brun's apartments gave way to a taste for more intimate interiors, 'a more graceful décor created by Jean Berain the elder, André-Charles Boulle, Lassurance and, in particular,

Pierre Le Pautre' (142). A similar evolution may be detected in the park, to which the king attached great value, and of which he was architect, gardener and stage manager.

THE KING VISITS HIS GARDENS

In the 1690s, 'at the very moment when the setting of Versailles, having taken its definitive shape, displayed its most dazzling splendour',* Louis drew up a *Guide to the Display of the Gardens at Versailles* (the *Manière de montrer les jardins de Versailles* (62)). In twenty-five crisp paragraphs, this guidebook laid down a fixed itinerary which provides testimony to the satisfaction of their creator and the simple tastes of their owner and devotee. With this little book in hand, we may follow the paths taken by His Majesty's guests – the King of England, the Elector of Bavaria, or the wife or this or that minister.

The king had mastered his passion for fresh air, trees and flowers and, in collaboration with Le Nôtre, transformed his gardens into a work of art. Neither in the *Guide to the Display*, nor in the park itself, do we find provision for aimless strolling around. The visitor was not encouraged to be lulled by Nature's charms; he was required to submit himself to a ritual. 'Each movement and step conformed to a predetermined pattern, planned, calculated and measured as if to some well-planned choreography.'†

'Leaving the château through the vestibule of the Cour de Marbre, the visitor comes upon the terrace from where, standing at the top of the steps, he may peruse the layout of the parterres, the ornamental lakes and the fountains.' From the start, the ornamental pools and fountains which brought the park to life were laid out before the visitor. Water from Marly was laid on to keep them supplied, whilst, to increase the flow, Louis invested money, sweat and tears in the Eure canal.‡ 'From there, proceed directly to the top of [the Bassin de] Latone and pause to study [the statue of] Latona, the [Bassin des] Lézards, the ramps, the statues, the Royal Avenue, Apollo and the canal and, from there, turn round to admire the parterres and the château.' The *bassins*

---

* Raoul Girardet in his preface to the *Manière de montrer les jardins de Versailles* (62).
† Raoul Girardet, ibid.
‡ e.g., the machinery at Marly cost 514,000 *livres* in 1682 and 846,000 in 1683.

of Apollo and Latona still survive, as does the Grand Canal. It is possible, therefore, to use the king's guide rather than a modern tourist's one, so long as one uses one's imagination to re-create the vanished pools and woods. Louis then invited the connoisseur to turn left, where, standing in front of the Dauphin's quarters, he might admire the Daybreak fountain with its bronze animals, and then to stop once more, before Sarrazin's *Sphinx and Children* to contemplate the parterre of the Midi; 'and then one proceeds to the top of the Orangery, whence one may look over the beds of orange trees and the lake of the Swiss Guards'. This ornamental lake commemorated the fidelity of the king's guards and records how they had dug, under difficult conditions, the pond where His Majesty sometimes went fishing. Then came an ascent between the bronzes of Apollo and Antinous,* before 'one pauses on the projecting terrace, whence Bacchus and Saturn may be viewed'. Then the visitor descended in order to visit the orange-tree garden, its fountains and avenues of orange trees, planted by the late M. de la Quintinie, and, finally, the Orangery itself.

The next stop was the maze. Built twenty years previously, it still amused the king, and visitors regarded it as one of the most remarkable in the world, with a seemingly infinite number of paths, groups of lead statues (described in quatrains by Benserade), an Aesop by Le Gros and a Cupid by Tuby. Most of the statues represented fabulous animals, ensconced in surroundings of shells and spurting water out at each other. One might imagine, according to Perrault, 'that they were in some way endowed with speech, as in the fables'. Escaping from this labyrinth past the statue of Bacchus, the visitor next admired the Salle de Bal,† a beautiful 'grove' ideal for dancing, music and taking refreshments. From there the visitor was to go once again to the 'viewing-point of the Bassin de Latone', for Louis found this a suitable point from which to contemplate the whole park. To one side lay the Lizards, the Bassin de Latone and the château, whilst, to the other, were the Royal Avenue, the Bassin d'Apollon, the Grand Canal, 'the shrubberies, Flora and Saturn, with Ceres on the right and Bacchus on the left'. After this general survey, the visitor discovered the trees around the pool

* Antinous was the Emperor Hadrian's favourite. He was drowned in the River Nile in AD 130.
† This glade still survives.

at the Girandole, turned round 'towards Saturn' and walked towards the Mirror and Ile Royale pools. Following in the king's footsteps along the path between these pools, he would admire the flowing waterfalls of the Mirror and, 'arriving lower down, one may pause to study the plants, shells, pools, statues and porticoes'.

The next feature, known as the *salle des Antiques* or Water Gallery, seemed somewhat Italianate and outmoded to the king. The *Guide to the Display* describes it briefly, already looking forward to 1704 when Louis, continually adapting and renewing his creations, ordered the removal of this oblong shrubbery with its ponds and marbles separated by orange trees. The Colonnade, on the other hand, built by Mansart in 1685, was much more up to date.* 'One enters the Colonnade and goes right to the centre, from where one may study the ring of columns, the bas-reliefs and the pools.' On leaving the Colonnade, the visitor was invited to admire Domenico Guidi's group *La Renommée du Roi* and then to make his way towards the Royal Avenue, pausing before Apollo.

To add to the visitor's pleasure, Louis recommended several halts to give different perspectives on the same features: the château, statues, ornamental pools, shrubberies, fountains and lawns. But Le Nôtre and the king alone could enjoy the 'groundwork' of the conception. They worked together with what Saint-Simon christened 'this pleasure and pride in the compulsion of nature'. Where there had once been merely a sandy upland, marshes or moorland, without trees or fresh water, a controlling idea, planning, years of study and effort, skill and determination created a miracle, 'a triumph of will', according to M. Girardet, 'which was also a victory for the spirit of discipline' (62).

Moving on to the Dômes, later known as the fountain of the Bains d'Apollon, visitors were urged to walk around 'to admire the statues, pavilions and bas-reliefs', especially the large group *Apollo Tended by Nymphs*, the work of Girardon, Marsy and Regnaudin, which was then in the process of being installed, as well as the Encelade fountain, by Marsy. The next clearing, known as the Salle du Conseil, stood until 1706. It had twelve sides with eight pools and a lawn in its midst. From the Salle du Conseil, the itinerary proceeded to the statue of Flora and thence

---

* It still exists.

to the Montagne d'Eau, a fountain in rock-work at the heart of the grove of the Star. The next feature worthy of note was Le Nôtre's Théâtre d'Eau. The peristyle surrounding it provided an intriguing novelty, each pillar appearing to be supported by a jet of water. From there, the king led the visitor to the Marais grove. Until its destruction in 1704, this baroque ensemble, built for the marquise de Montespan, entranced spectators. From the centre of the pool rose a tree made of bronze with tin-plate leaves. The pool was encircled with artificial reeds and this decorative vegetation threw out water continuously, an ingenious device which justified the king's advice that one walk right round it.

The visit proceeded with the spectator's entering the grove of the Three Fountains to study the Dragon and Neptune pools before admiring, in the copse of the Arc de Triomphe, 'the diversity of fountains, the expanse of water, the figures and the different water effects'. The Allée d'Eau or Allée des Enfants, completed in 1688, led to the fountain of the Bain des Nymphes, designed by Perrault and decorated with bas-reliefs by Le Gros, Le Hongre and Girardon. 'From there, the visitor proceeds to the Pyramid, where he should pause for a moment, and then ascend towards the château by the marble staircase' from the northern parterre framed by Coysevox's *Venus* (1686) and the curious antique statue known as *The Grinder*. At the top of these stairs, the visitor should glance behind him 'to see the northern parterre, the statues, the vases, the crowns, the Pyramid and as much of Neptune as is visible', before leaving the park.

Thus was constituted the ideal visit to His Majesty's gardens. The *Guide to the Display* lives up to its title. There was no need to enumerate every fountain, marble statue, bronze, and bas-relief, each vase of porcelain or box of orange trees, in order to re-create for us this luminous, noisy and colourful park, in which, when it was open to the public, the king required a guard to protect him from the crowd. An appendix, also by Louis, proposed a complementary itinerary taking in the Menagerie, the King's Garden, the Jardin des Sources and especially the Trianon. This itinerary required several trips on the Grand Canal.

THE GRAND CANAL SQUADRON

Visible from the terrace, with their rigging standing out at the end of the Royal Avenue, displayed before diplomats and princes and made ready for courtiers, the boats on the canal stood ready as though for a long voyage – perhaps to the East Indies. The king had no better means to demonstrate his interest in naval matters both at home and abroad than the little ships on the Grand Canal which symbolized his fighting fleet. Louis liked to follow the evolution of the Versailles flotilla, commanding and supervising its construction. Like his larger projects, it demonstrated his practical intelligence.

His Majesty's miniature ships were used for cruises through the park and during concerts and firework displays. They were not fantasies but working models with the relative dimensions, designs and riggings of ships of the line. The fleet on the canal also included a few English-style pinnaces, several launches, a Neapolitan style felucca and, most significantly, three miniature warships, constructed in 1685. These were the *Dunkerquoise*, a large ship of the type used by the *capres*,* assembled by Flemish carpenters, the *Réale* and the *Grand Vaisseau*. The *Réale* was a replica of the genuine galleon *Réale*, pride of the Marseille squadron. The original was decorated by Puget, her small sister ship by Tuby and Caffiéri. Riggings, awnings, hangings and bulwarks were resplendent in gold, silver and blue. As for the *Grand Vaisseau*, the marquis de Langeron, inspector of shipbuilding, was in charge of its design and construction. Wood had to be brought from Amsterdam and twenty-two carpenters were employed to build it. Despite its name, the *Grand Vaisseau* was merely a small frigate, equipped with thirteen cannon from the Keller foundry. So, just as the naval forces of the kingdom were divided between the galleys of the Mediterranean and the smaller vessels of the Atlantic, the king could choose between the *Réale* and the *Grand Vaisseau* for his cruise on the canal, until the day when M. Fagon, fearing the effects of humidity on His Majesty's rheumatism, forbade further expeditions.

It is difficult to imagine the activity on this stretch of water, with its numerous landing-stages. The Venetian gondoliers wore taffeta, damask or crimson brocade with silver or gold braid,

* This was the name given to the privateers of Dunkirk.

whilst the sailors, dressed by the *filles bleues* of Versailles, almost equalled them in elegance. They all inhabited the village of Petite Venise, built specially for them. The permanent personnel numbered about fifty. In 1687, the *bâtiments du roi* paid the wages of a captain, master, mate and second mate for the galley, four carpenters, two caulkers, a storeman, twenty-six sailors and fourteen gondoliers (45). This flotilla stood ready on the canal for cruises and concerts until the end of the reign.

THE BEAUTIES OF THE CHÂTEAU

It is unfortunate that Louis XIV did not also compile a guide to the interior of his palace. If we were to have visited it in around 1701, the logical place to have started would have been at the Grand Staircase or *escalier des Ambassadeurs*. Completed in 1678 at the time of Nymwegen, it provided a résumé of 'the triumph of the king and of his artists' (291). Le Brun, Van der Meulen, Jacques Gabriel, Girardon, Le Hongre, Desjardins, Tuby, Caffiéri, Coysevox and a score of others contributed their talents. Turning left at the top of the right-hand wing of the staircase, the visitor reached the Salon de Vénus, which was decorated in marble – the Grand Apartment, prepared for receptions, justly merited its reputation for magnificence. Then came the Salon de l'Abondance, leading through to the Cabinet des Médailles. To the right at the top of the left wing of the Grand Staircase was the Salon de Diane or billiard room. In this room stood the Bernini bust of Louis XIV in a décor which rivalled that of the Salon de Vénus. Mars then replaced Diana in the mythological spectrum, but the Salon de Mars was designed as a ballroom. The use to which each room was put during royal receptions transformed its official title into a short-hand version. There followed the Salon de Mercure or state bedchamber (*chambre du Lit*) and then the Salon d'Apollon or throne room. This majestic series of linked rooms, which the king found too cold to inhabit, looked out onto the gardens. On the other side of the central parts of the château, the Duchess of Burgundy, in succession to the Dauphine, occupied the corresponding apartments: a guardroom, antechamber, *grand cabinet* and bedchamber. The two structures were joined together by the complex made up of the Hall of Mirrors and the two corner rooms – the Salon de la Paix on the princesses' side and the Salon de la Guerre on the king's side.

The *grande galerie*, the king's pride and joy, was not the first of its kind. Louis had already built one at the Louvre and one for Mme de Montespan at Clagny. But the Hall of Mirrors eclipsed its rivals in its unprecedented size (*c.* 239 by 34 feet), its magnificence and its symbolism. Even at the end of the reign, stripped of the silver furnishings which were sacrificed in hard times, the gallery continued to dazzle visitors (291), who all understood that it was a 'work of monarchical and national glorification' (243). The ceiling paintings, executed or supervised by Le Brun, depicted 'in a direct fashion, the glorious or beneficial actions of the first eighteen years [of] personal rule, from 1661 to the Peace of Nymwegen' (53b), the restoration of order within the kingdom, the king's wars, diplomatic successes, the great achievements and the acts of justice and charity. 'The subject of the central picture is *The King Ruling by Himself.*' (243) By order of the Council, historical themes had replaced those of Hercules and Apollo and, in accordance with Colbert's wishes, 'the French style' had prevailed over the antique or the Italian. The use of mirrors marked the success of an industry by then capable of competing with Murano. Mansart placed 'opposite each of the huge bays which looked out over the park at Versailles a second window, furnished with the reflecting power of its mirrors. Thus the gallery, which overlooks the gardens on one side, is also open to them on the other, at least in appearance, *per speculum in aenigmate* [allegorically by means of a mirror]'. Louis and Mansart placed this 'masterpiece of baroque illusionism' (243) in the position of glory in a classical palace.

The king's guardroom overlooking the Cour de Marbre was reached from the Escalier de la Reine. It communicated with the Salle du Grand Couvert, which was furnished with a gallery for musical accompaniment for the king's meals. From here, the courtier reached the Salon de l'Oeil-de-Boeuf, which was created in 1701 by the conjoining of an antechamber and the king's former bedroom. This room was admired for its gallery, 'the curve of which was decorated on the king's orders with a kind of frieze in plaster bas-reliefs representing children's games' (291). As with the Menagerie and the Trianon, Louis XIV, Mansart and Cotte here prefigured the elegance of the eighteenth century, envigorated with a sense of youthful abandon and with open access to the garden. An usher would introduce the courtier into the king's bedchamber (*chambre du Roi*), the alcove of which backed onto the Hall of Mirrors. The king preserved a large portion of the original décor, but ordered Robert de Cotte to update and enliven it with a 'white and gold ensemble of cupids, trellises and flowers'. He supervised other improvements – door locks, espagnolette bolts and, for his bed, a balustrade – ordering, for example, 'that the rear arches be knocked through so as to be able to pass cords through them for the raising and lowering of curtains, and to arrange it all neatly' (243). The king did not lose his obsession with small details even in old age. If 'kings build for eternity' (42), then the minutiae were of great importance. From the *lever* to the *coucher*, the king's bedchamber, the soul of the court, was open and accessible. Under the pretext of honouring the king, courtiers tended to turn this room into a public square. The king's bed and its balustrade had to be protected. Guards and officers of the bedchamber patrolled or stood guard outside this enclosure, the only refuge for privacy. Such an arrangement was an image of the French monarchy, neither Olympian nor intimate. For those who appreciated its symbolism, the canopy above the bed was a sign that the French kingdom watched over the king's rest. The bedchamber gave access to the Council chamber. This ample room, decorated with mirrors, gemstones, three Poussins and sculptures by Caffiéri, was also used for audiences. There was also an alabaster table to admire, and a harpsichord decorated with paintings (291). For more-intimate meetings, Louis preferred the Cabinet des Perruques.

The king felt the need for greater intimacy, as was demonstrated by the construction of Marly. At Versailles, he had an 'inner apartment', constructed between 1684 and 1701. In place of the marquise de Montespan's former lodgings, the king created rooms free from the restraints of the palace yet equivalent to the Grand Appartement. They comprised the Cabinet des Chiens, the Salon du Petit Escalier, the Cabinet des Coquilles, the Cabinet aux Tableaux and the *petite galerie*, framed by two *salons*. The *petite galerie* was Mignard's masterpiece. Le Brun's *grande galerie* was filled with hordes of courtiers, but Mignard's *petite galerie* was reserved for the king, his family 'and a few distinguished guests', such as the Prince of Denmark, in 1693, and the Elector of Cologne, in 1706. On the ceiling, a child representing the Duke of Burgundy symbolized France, flanked by Minerva and Apollo and surrounded by gods, Virtues, Hours and Cupids. It was no coincidence that the arts too were portrayed in this tableau, for the *petite galerie* was conceived as an incarnation of royal patronage. Here were placed the most beautiful canvases in the royal collection (291), and Louis 'could enjoy the sight of a great number of rare masterpieces' (291) on a rotating basis. The *Mona Lisa* was therefore occasionally to be seen there.

After 1701, economy seemed to be the rule at Versailles. The only major expenditure at the end of the reign was on the chapel. Its building and decoration took over twenty years and the ageing monarch ended up offering to God 'the most extraordinary of palatine chapels' (291). In place of the marble proposed by Mansart, Louis XIV and Robert de Cotte preferred stone from the Ile de France. Instead of repeating the familiar décor, they created a new style for the new century. Yet it was one which recalled the Middle Ages, with the Sainte-Chapelle haunting the imagination of its architects. The sobriety of the stonework contrasted with the exuberance of the statues, in which their creators – Pierre Le Pautre, the Coustous, and Robert Le Lorrain – prefigured the age of the Enlightenment. Like all churches of its time, the royal chapel presents a catechism in images. The vault, the Lord's domain, is dominated by the Creation, whilst the Resurrection is located above the altar. The dove of the Holy Spirit flies above the royal gallery, whilst the monarchy is symbolized by Charlemagne and St Louis at Prayer. The king's customary place was in the gallery facing the altar, whilst his family occupied the seats below. Louis attended Mass daily, to the accompaniment of a motet. Whilst fêtes provided a wonderful spectacle, the king – in his devotions as in every other aspect of his life – never neglected the day-to-day routine.

THE KING'S TIMETABLE

The king's life was monotonous. Leaving aside his occasional travels, his autumn hunting at Chambord or Fontainebleau and, until 1693, his time at the war-front, there was little variety to Louis XIV's schedule. The arrangement of weeks, days and hours appeared regulated as if by clockwork. To avoid too much repetition, Dangeau summed up 'the king's activities' for 1684 at the end of the *Journal* for that year. His Majesty enjoyed virtually no private life. The work-load was so exhausting that his time was dedicated almost entirely to public business. Louis got up and went to bed late, the opposite ends of the day being reserved for ceremonial (the *lever* and *coucher*). Woken at about half past eight, he would preside over a section of the Council between 9.30 a.m. and 12.30 p.m. On Sundays, there was the council of ministers or *conseil d'en haut*, which was the most important organ of the Council, the one where the crucial decisions were taken. The king asked for opinions from each minister of state – Le Tellier, Louvois and Le Peletier making up the Le Tellier clan, with Croissy as sole representative of the Colberts – and then made up his mind, usually following the majority decision. The same council also met every other Monday with the council of despatches, when the correspondence between government and intendants was analysed. The king presided over the Dauphin, Monsieur, the chancellor, the maréchal de Villeroy (head of the council of finances), the ministers, the secretaries of state (Seignelay and Châteauneuf) and the controller-general Le Peletier.

The royal council of finances, often referred to simply as the 'royal council', the successor to the superintendency of finances, was held on Tuesdays. His Majesty presided, assisted in theory by the chancellor, in reality by Monseigneur, by the maréchal de Villeroy, by the controller-general, and by the two 'councillors of the royal council of finances'. The controller-general was, as we have seen, Le Peletier, and the other two were Pussort, Colbert's uncle and a noted legislator, and Boucherat, friend of the late M. de Turenne and a future chancellor. The council of ministers met again on Wednesdays and Thursdays, and a second council of finances met on Saturday mornings. Friday mornings were rather different, given over to a *conseil de conscience*, which was not a section of the king's council at all. It was a council in name alone, a legacy of Mazarin's era, and should rather be seen as an important part of the 'king's work'. This was where the affairs of the Church were discussed, especially in respect of benefices. The king received Harlay de Champvallon, Archbishop of Paris, to discuss plans for the revocation of the Edict of Nantes, and then his confessor, père de la Chaize, to talk mostly about the attribution of benefices. Later in the reign, Louis would sometimes have a free morning, which he would spend walking or sometimes out hunting.

On normal days, the king left the Council chamber at around 12.30 p.m. He would then 'inform Mme the Dauphine that he was ready to go and hear Mass, and the whole royal family would join him there, when there was excellent music' (since 1683, Delalande had been *sous-maître* of the chapel). After the service, Louis visited the marquise de Montespan. He then went 'to dine in Mme the Dauphine's antechamber. The gentlemen of the chamber served him. Monseigneur, Mme the Dauphine, Monsieur and Madame, Mademoiselle and Mme de Guise, and occasionally the princesses of the blood, dined with the king'. After the meal, Louis would pay a visit to his daughter-in-law, and then take a stroll. He needed this walk, on which he was sometimes escorted by ladies, possibly even a short hunt. Sometimes His Majesty went shooting, but he preferred to chase deer, on horseback if he was fit, in a barouche when afflicted by gout. But these *après-dîners* of fresh air were merely interludes. The second half of the afternoon was devoted to matters of state. Twice a week, Louis worked with Seignelay, mostly on naval affairs. Three or four evenings were taken up with Louvois' dossiers concerning military matters and the superintendency of buildings. The foreign minister, Croissy, as well as the controller-general, had to be content with less regular meetings.

There had always been councils at the French court and private conversations between the king and his chief ministers were not an innovation. The art of Louis XIV lay in transforming habits into institutions. The *appartements*, which adorned the evenings at court, were also a novelty, symbolizing the king's ability to put even distractions to the service of his glory and his policies. The word *appartement*, in the sense of a royal reception, was a neologism, barely making any appearance before 1674. 'Over the past few years,' wrote Furetière, 'it has been said that an *appartement* was being held by the king, meaning a festivity or merry-making to which the king treated his court on several evenings in his apartments, which were superbly furnished and lit, with music, balls, dancing, meals, games and other magnificent distractions.' (42) After the permanent shift to Versailles, His Majesty received his guests on Tuesdays, Thursdays and Saturdays. On those days, the *salons* were open from seven o'clock in the evening. The king, passionately fond of billiards, played until around nine, his partners being friends such as Vendôme, the comte d'Armagnac and Gramont, not forgetting the *parlementaire* Chamillart. After billiards, the king called on Mme de Maintenon until supper, after which the ball began. Louis was no kill-joy. Gamblers played for high stakes; theatre-lovers were given plays; and balls filled the carnival season. Today such receptions seem completely natural and it is difficult to comprehend why they were so admired and celebrated at the time. A medal was struck in 1683 to mark COMITAS ET MAGNI-FICENTIA PRINCIPIS, *the affability and magnificence of the prince*. The commentary underlined this innovation: 'The king, in order to increase the pleasures of his court, wished for his apartments to be open on certain days of the week. There were large rooms for dancing, gaming and music. Others offered all sorts of refreshments, available in abundance, and the greatest pleasure was that here the enjoyment was in the presence of such a great king and good master.' In this palace where mythology set the style, the Academy of Inscriptions and its engraver created suitable sponsorship: a Muse oversaw concerts, Pomona watched over the drinks and 'Mercury presided over the games' (71). In reality, it was the king who did the honours, seeing their usefulness to the state. To Louis XIV, performance was a service. In 1686, afflicted by a fistula, he took this to heroic lengths. One day, when he had suffered more than usual the surgeon's tortures, the Dauphine begged him not to hold an *appartement* that evening, saying that she was incapable of dancing when she thought of his condition. The king replied: 'Madame, I wish there to be an *appartement* and for you to dance there. We are not like private persons; we must devote ourselves entirely to the public. Go and do this with good grace.' (97)

On days without an *appartement*, the king spent the early evening with Mme de Maintenon, and then 'came back to take supper with Mme the Dauphine'. From there, he would go to Mme de Montespan, according to his strategy of maintaining rivalries between several favourites. At midnight, he retired for the ceremonies of the chamber. 'The *petit coucher*', Dangeau noted, 'was usually finished by half past midnight, one o'clock at the latest.'

The king, who began and finished his day with a prayer and never missed a Mass, gave a prominent place to religious duties; his daily round consisted of a well-regulated proportion of spirituality, physical effort and intellectual endeavour, the last being inseparable from public affairs. But it would be wrong to limit the political domain just to meetings of the Council, the mastering of dossiers and ministerial and diplomatic audiences. The time devoted to ceremonial was also a matter of state concern and political obligation. It was a question of keeping an eye on the *grands*, maintaining their devotion, stimulating competition. Through it, the king won fidelity, the court gained prestige, and good servants reaped rewards. On the other hand, the role accorded to women, accompanying the king on his promenades, going with him to Marly, holding *salons* with Mme de Maintenon, gave the court the element of courtesy which might otherwise have withered. In a palace which no longer had a queen, it seemed a good idea for the king to maintain a triple female presence, with the Dauphine, Mme de Maintenon and, for a while, the marquise de Montespan sharing the role.

RETREAT TO MARLY

It seems curious that Louis XIV, having fled the Paris crowds to his retreat at Versailles, should then retreat from Versailles to the solitude of Marly. If Versailles had remained what it had been in 1664, Marly would not have been necessary. By building this further palace and the place d'Armes, Louis could overcome the disadvantages of an enormous residence. He wanted the largest number to take pleasure in Versailles and had thus alloyed its pleasure. Now he wished to take refuge at Marly, which was built on a scale which Versailles had lost. Soon, however, he was forced to protect this reconstituted and fragile pleasure.

Marly was built, under Mansart's direction, between 1679 and 1686, and Le Nôtre was also involved in its conception. As at Versailles, the king had to wrench things from their natural course. Marly was not designed as a château but as a 'small country house' called the 'Pavillon du Roi' surrounded by twelve pavilions for his guests, the 'Pavillons des Seigneurs'. His Majesty's residence, in the centre like a sun, was dedicated to Jupiter and the satellite lodges to Saturn, Apollo, Mercury, Diana, Minerva and other divinities (198).

The buildings seem to have been specially designed with festivities in mind. The carnivals there were especially splendid, that of 1700 being outstanding, with seven masquerades, including one in a Chinese style. The Philidors composed the music for this, and the Duchess of Burgundy appeared as Flora, the princesse de Conti as an Amazon and the duchesse de Chartres as a sultana (242). Admiration for the splendours of Marly may be detected even in the writings of Saint-Simon and Madame Palatine. The king stayed there about twelve times a year, inviting fifty to sixty guests on each occasion. 'The rules date from August 1685: visits to Marly took place at first from Mondays to Thursdays, later from Tuesdays to Fridays or Wednesdays to Saturdays at irregular intervals' (242). The royal family were accounted as permanent guests. Officials of the household – high officers of the Crown, heads of offices, the chief physician (*archiatre*) and *lecteurs* – were prominent on the guest-lists. Racine, a gentleman of the chamber, was a member of this select group. Not many places remained for the ladies of the court and their husbands. Hunting was one of the recreations, as were outdoor games: *anneau tournant, portique, trou madame*, and pall-mall, which was much appreciated by Monseigneur with his taste in rough sports. Indoors, *brelan* and billiards were played. On holidays, theatre, opera, lotteries and dancing made Marly the least solitary of retreats.

The king was usually content to inaugurate the entertainment and then retire in order to work. But he did not tear himself away from outdoor recreations. Louis supervised the planting of the park, inspected the parterres and visited his estate. In April 1709, Dangeau reported: 'Thursday the 18th, at Marly – The king promenaded in his gardens. Mme de Maintenon was in her chair alongside the king's small carriage and, in a further carriage, were Mme the princesse d'Harcourt, Mme de Caylus* and Mme Desmarets, and the king took pleasure in showing his gardens to the latter, who had never visited Marly before.' (26) In November, the same honour was accorded to the Elector of Bavaria.

The king put on a coat and conducted the elector on foot to the edge of the terrace, from where he could see all the fountains gushing forth in the lower gardens. From that point, turning left, he showed him all the splendid forests of Marly, as far as the fountain of Diana and, walking still further, which caused his

* Madame de Caylus was a frequent visitor at Marly.

servants to be concerned about another attack of gout, at length he called for a little two-seated carriage, which he had commissioned to be constructed for his promenades with the Duchess of Burgundy, as he himself told the elector, and, clambering into it first, he bid the elector to get in too. The latter demurred for some time, but the king at length persuaded him to climb in and took him to the Eperon which looks out over the magnificent reservoir which retains all the waters of Marly. From there, they went to the side where the garden lay and he showed him all the beauties of the woods and, coming to the avenue of the Grand Cascade, he descended from the carriage and accompanied the elector to the foot of the fountain, the most beautiful in Europe. From there, he took him to see the carp ponds and then they made their way back via the same gate through which they had left. (97)

Mme de Maintenon disliked Marly, but her husband the king retained his affection for this gracious residence until his death, and courtiers appreciated the pleasures of visits there, dedicated as they were to pleasure, beauty and gracious living.

20

The King at Prayer

IN THE nineteenth century, it became the fashion to divide Louis XIV's reign into two halves. Various turning points were proposed: the fistula of 1686; the Revocation of the Edict of Nantes in 1685; the introduction of a stricter religious style of devotion at court in 1684; the secret marriage of 1683; or the king's return to a more respectable private life in 1681 (207). But such a simple pattern does not accurately fit the reign. Furthermore, it is by no means evident that the king's moral conversion should be seen as a return to the faith: for Louis had never, in fact, deserted it. Cardinal Fleury told Voltaire that Louis 'had a blind faith' (112). 'He knew nothing whatsoever about the differences between religions', wrote Madame Palatine in 1719, adding that 'His confessor told him: "Those who are not Catholics are heretics and damned", and he believed it without further consideration.' (87) In other words, his sister-in-law was criticizing him for not accepting Protestant freedom of enquiry. She thereby granted him his certificate of Catholicity – for no one in the seventeenth century placed Rome and Geneva on an equal footing. It is true that the Princess Palatine accused the king in several of her letters of being ignorant of Scripture: 'The late king knew nothing whatsoever of the Holy Scriptures.' But she was merely underlining the differences between the two confessions. If, in reality, Louis had read little more than the Gospels and the Psalms, this did not necessarily mean that he was ignorant of the contents of the Bible. The king was a reflection of his people and his times. His creed was contained in his recitations of the *Paternoster*, of the *Credo* of the Mass and of the *Confiteor* which preceded confession, in the anthems and motets of his chapel and in the hymns of the ceremonies in which he took part (the *Te Deum*, jubilees and Vespers, among others). When a point of doctrine troubled him, he consulted his confessor. He meditated on the Word of God like most Catholics of his generation by listening to sermons.

ELABORATE EULOGIES AND STERN TRUTHS

Louis XIV, who attended Mass daily, submitted in the same spirit twice a year to hearing and meditating upon the truths of the faith and the commandments of its law. This was partly a matter of fashion. The *Mercure galant* described the great success of the Lenten sermons of 1682 as follows: 'The court and Paris, who spare no effort in associating the most elaborate gallantry to their holiday festivities, do the same when it comes to their displays of devotion at times of piety. Never has greater assiduity been seen than during these Lent-tide sermons.' (195) This coincided with Louis XIV's installation at Versailles and his return to conjugal fidelity. Between 1661 and 1681, seven complete Advent and Lenten 'stations' were preached at court by the Jesuits, and sixteen by the Oratorians. Between 1682 and 1715, the proportions were reversed, with thirty-four preachers from the Society of Jesus and only thirteen from the Oratory. Yet continuity was the hallmark here, as elsewhere. Because the king had mistresses, this did not mean that he was less of a believer. True, he neglected to follow in their entirety the Lenten sermons of 1662, preached by Bossuet in the Louvre; for he was too preoccupied by the flight of Louise de la Vallière. But he attended some of them, even on weekdays, and, bearing no grudge against Bossuet, he invited him to preach again in 1665, 1666 and 1669. In 1672, Louis asked for the cancellation of the sermon for the first Sunday in Lent on the grounds of mourning, and, on 25 March, with the Dutch War about to break out, Bourdaloue found himself preaching before the queen alone. In 1674, however, when the king appeared totally immersed in his pleasures, he followed a good number of Bourdaloue's Lenten sermons.

After his secret marriage, Louis became assiduous in attending sermons and a good listener, willing to recognize good oratory when he heard it. The Jesuit *père* Gaillard was invited to preach at court more than a dozen times, and was first among the king's preachers, ahead of Mascaron and Bourdaloue, although his reputation does not now place him in the front rank of orators of his generation. It is not surprising that pères Quinquet, Fromentières and Massillon were each invited back to preach three times, Cosme and the abbé Bossuet four times each, Le Boux more than five times, La Rue more than nine times, and Mascaron, Bourdaloue and Gaillard more than twelve times each. Louis XIV was a creature of habit: like his subjects, he enjoyed repetitious eloquence and the preachers exploited this. They changed the allusions at the beginning and the compliments at the end, but, for the bulk of the sermon, often repeated themselves. The compliments sung the monarch's praises, and those of his victories and treaties, and also praised the *régale*, the persecution of the Protestants and the Revocation of the Edict of Nantes. The triumphalism was, in reality, tempered by the common sense of the king and his courtiers, who all knew how to take rhetoric and propaganda in their stride, and also modulated by the preachers, who knew how to Catholicize glory and turn it to God's account. Fléchier's compliment made towards the close of Advent in 1676 sums up this eloquence *ad usum regis*:

> You, O Lord, who hold the hearts of kings in Your hands, and who, according to Your Scriptures, grant Your salvation to kings, fill with Your grace this day him to whom I have declared Your truth; he would prefer me to address these vows to You rather than to sing his praises; to You he gives all glory, for it comes from You and belongs to You alone. If he is enlightened in his counsels, it is Your wisdom which enlightens him; if he is prosperous in his good works, it is Your providence which guides him; if he is victorious in his wars, it is Your sword which protects him. Your hand crowns him in the midst of such prosperity with which You have blessed his reign; all that remains is for us to ask You to grant him that which he himself asks each day, his salvation. You have strengthened his throne against so many enemies in league to attack it. Strengthen his soul against the many objects of passion which surround it. He has victories still to win, more precious than those already gained; and You have crowns to give him more precious than those he wears. The immortality which the centuries seem to herald is but a small thing unless he has that which You can grant him beyond all ages. Consecrate his many royal virtues with as many Christian virtues. Increase the

fount of devotion which you have engraved on his soul and make
him as holy as You have made him great so that, having reigned
in tranquillity through You, he may at the last reign eternally
with You. (39)

Nobody ever preached better to Louis XIV, neither Mascaron
celebrating Nymwegen on All Saints' Day 1679 nor Bourdaloue
praising Ryswick at Christmas 1697 and transforming his final
compliment into a 'farewell to the king' (195). But many
preachers equalled its boldness. The Lent stations began with
the Candlemas sermon, devoted to the theme of purity, those of
Advent with preaching on holiness on All Saints' Day. However,
before 1683, it was difficult for a preacher to celebrate holiness
and purity without the listener's sensing innuendo, so great was
the distance between the king's life and the ideals of holiness and
purity. None of the preachers wished to appear censorious.
Rather, they used the 'privilege of the pulpit' without abusing it,
accepting that they could not refuse to talk about ambition,
pride or even adultery just because the sermon was being
preached before a proud and adulterous king. It was up to the
prince to heed the explicit or implicit message they offered and
mend his ways. Equally, it was incumbent on courtiers and
Parisians not to search for innuendo where none was intended.
The king gave his preachers the same freedom he allowed his
confessors. They were not allowed to criticize his policies, but
discreet and courteous criticism of his morals was permitted, if
politely and briefly presented. The court was given to understand that Mascaron, by delineating a conqueror during one of
his Lenten sermons in 1675, had incurred royal displeasure. But,
six years earlier, the same preacher had been rather more audacious in the exordium of a sermon 'On the Word of God':

> Kings and great ones on earth rarely hear the truth. As one
> wishes to convert them without incurring their wrath, and
> because Scripture itself ordains that we should proclaim the truth
> before princes whom it also requires be treated with respect, as
> Nathan, making David aware of his adultery and homicide, used
> the ways and means which God's Spirit put before him, so it is
> that the truth is only displayed before them with a prudence
> which the great should recognize for what it is. (195)

Mascaron preached this sermon in 1669 and Louis XIV made
him Bishop of Tulle in 1671.

Between 1661 and 1715, the king sat through over a thousand Advent and Lenten sermons, dutifully until 1682, piously thereafter. The court knew that it was his custom to 'follow the orator fixedly, leaning his chin on the top of his cane, and resting his two hands one on top of the other on it' (195). In 1695, the Princess Palatine described the concentration with which Louis listened: 'His Majesty will not let me doze through it. As soon as I nod off, the king nudges me with his elbow and wakes me up.' (87) We cannot know the king's heart in these matters, but it is beyond credibility to imagine that his attentiveness was purely his looking out for censorious allusions. Whether he liked it or not, twenty-six times a year (not counting Sundays and holydays) Louis listened to morality being preached, the mysteries of the faith celebrated, theological virtues praised, cardinal sins condemned, the gifts of the Holy Spirit enumerated. The king, who was often said to be ignorant of theology, was subjected for sixty years to revisions of his catechism by teachers of the highest calibre. This Counter Reformation homiletics propounded the Tridentine catechism. To Protestants, this was more Catholic than Christian. But seventeenth-century Protestants did not always perceive that these sermons were based on Scripture and abounded in biblical citations. The eloquence and rhetoric, commonplaces and repetitions, and cumbersome and archaic expressions could not hide the positive theology behind them, of which the king was the first and principal beneficiary.

DAVID AND ST LOUIS OR APOLLO AND JUPITER?

It is easy to suggest that these sermons did not deter Louis XIV from deceiving the queen. But this is to forget the essence of the seventeenth century, 'its hallmark, a faith which was not engulfed by morality' (212). Furthermore, the court preachers, although it took them a long time to amend His Majesty's private life, had eventually succeeded by 1683. Morality was not everything though. Madame Palatine still refused to recognize her brother-in-law's piety as late as 1686: 'The king thinks himself devout', she wrote, 'because he doesn't sleep with young women any more.' From a different standpoint, the French had already accepted the king's piety twenty years previously, despite his lapses. Lenten and Advent sermons did not suddenly work a transformation of Louis into a dutiful monarch. But they constantly preached God's law, the indispensable basis to a moral life, reminded him of the essence of the faith and, finally, educated him to the limits of greatness. If Louis did not imagine himself as Apollo or identify himself with Zeus, then it was because of his Christianity.

If we were to stop passing moral judgement on Louis XIV, then his authoritarianism would become less surprising, especially in comparison with the despotism, vanity and excess of modern dictators, no matter of what political persuasion or significance. What needs to be stressed is the relative moderation, the genuine restraint and the reasonableness of Louis XIV despite his wielding so much power for so long. He owed these qualities to his religion, and if the role of his confessors is undeniable, that of the preachers was even greater. In their sermons, they exalted David, the Lord's anointed, as a model for the king. That David should have been an upstart was not important or may even have restrained Bourbon pride. That he should have been a sinner, however, was of importance, since David's sin reminded the king that God put faith and hope before the problems of the flesh. It also demonstrated that the powers of princes were not unlimited. Jupiter changed laws as he pleased, Apollo followed his fancies, but a Christian king, David's heir, had to account before God for his actions. The conditions laid down in this divine law emerged from the Old Testament through the preachings of such orators as Mascaron and Bourdaloue.

Although David was their model for Louis, churchmen did not hesitate to reinforce their teachings by reference to a French prince, St Louis, the venerated king from whom the creator of Versailles was descended (150). The panegyric was much appreciated in the seventeenth century as a form of religious eloquence. Bossuet, Bourdaloue, Fléchier and Mascaron competed in it. St Louis' day, 25 August, was also Louis XIV's feast-day as well as that of the army and, in practice, a kind of national holiday when the king would listen to the recital of the virtues of his pious ancestor. St Louis was commemorated at court and in Paris, in small towns and in army camps. Whilst the royal preachers reminded the king that he should emulate his ancestor, other clerics preached to his subjects about how a prince should behave. Some of these were sycophantic, but there were also some truly inspired orators, among them Fléchier. His sermon of 25 August 1681 at Saint-Louis en l'Ile was a model panegyric (39). The only person of note missing from the audience was Louis XIV himself, though we are assured that he heard the substance, or a résumé, of it not long afterwards. Fléchier preached on a text from Proverbs: 'The king's heart is in the hands of the Lord.' He began without any preface by denouncing princes who lived without devotion:

> When the hearts of kings are in their own hands, and God, through a secret judgement of His providence or His justice, abandons them to their own devices, then, alas! intoxicated by their own grandeur, they forget the One who made them great. They have no law and nothing to restrain their wills but the will itself. Everything which panders to their whims seems permissible, and worldly pride, the vanities of the world and the pleasures of their senses occupy all their minds.

A denunciation of 'depravities' and 'passions' followed, along with a condemnation of flattery. These dangers were contrasted with the happy state of things which flourishes 'when the king's heart is in the hands of the Lord'. Rather than take as his main theme the virtues of Louis IX, Fléchier stressed the faults which the saint had avoided, thus allowing himself the opportunity to moralize for the benefit of Louis XIV. There were three vices almost integral to the position of sovereign rulers. 'An *amour propre* which tethers them to their own glory, interests and whims, making them indifferent to all else; an illusion of independence which induces in them a belief that they can do whatsoever they please; and a worldly spirit which they hold onto in many ways, and which pushes them towards irreligion or, at the least, towards apathy.' St Louis had avoided 'these three corruptions', and the implication was clearly that his successors should do likewise. A eulogy of Louis IX had become an object-lesson for the ruling monarch. Had he divested himself of *amour propre* and vainglory? Was he aware that the law of God, natural law and the laws of the kingdom transcended his will? Was he immune to the 'worldly spirit'? This panegyric was a masterpiece. It should be understood that this kind of eloquence represented an attempt at the continuing education of the king.

As the Lord's anointed, the Eldest Son of the Church and Most Christian King, Louis bore a heavier crown of responsibility than that which he had worn at the consecration. As the prophet Nathan's successors could not admonish him all the time, they had to seek to educate him by indirect means, putting before him the biblical image of David, author of the Psalms, repentant sinner who knew God, and the medieval image of Louis IX, the embodiment of the honour and glory of France. Thanks to this, Louis the Dieudonné did not take himself to be a god. On the first Sunday in Lent 1703, père Lombard preached before the king on the text: 'You shall worship the Lord your God and have no other gods but Him.'

> [The orator] vividly demonstrated how both great and small were obliged to serve God above all else. He even went so far as to address himself sharply to the courtiers and soldiers and, having run through the details of how they behave, of their daily conduct, and the dangers to which they were thus exposed, he showed them all that this would not gain them their salvation, etc., so that the majority of his audience, alarmed by this strict morality, said aloud to one another as they left following the sermon: 'So we must abandon the king's service to work for our salvation!'

Some claimed that Louis was so angry with Lombard that he banned him from the pulpit. His fellow Jesuits, however, were upset by the uproar and counselled their colleague to tone down his remarks, whilst père de la Chaize apologized to the king. Louis replied that:

> [he was] most surprised by this false rumour that was being put about, seeing that père Lombard had preached the truth, that he was satisfied of that fact, that he knew full well the difference between himself and God and that he had no pretensions of passing for a god, that he was delighted that the preacher had let it be known that his subjects should dedicate that which they did in his service to God and not to him. (195)

The king had received the lessons of the preachers well, as well as their invocations of David and St Louis. Père Lombard finished his Lenten sermons, but he was never invited to return.

THE 'INTERESTS OF HEAVEN'

Tartuffe, as is well known, took upon himself, *motu proprio*, the 'interests of Heaven'. When Louis XIV dealt with these matters, he believed himself to be fulfilling his duties as king and exercising his regalian rights. Since 1516, choosing bishops had been one of the monarch's most important religious prerogatives. The Concordat of Bologna, by giving the King of France power over appointments to bishoprics, created the risk that arbitrary choices would be made. Louis XIV, however, made few mistakes and, from the beginning, took his task seriously. After the move to Versailles, he announced his decisions about the distribution of benefices five times a year, upon the great feast-days (26). In his *Mémoires*, he wrote that 'perhaps the king has no more taxing problem' than the choice of prelates. Careful consideration was necessary, the merits of each candidate required assessment. 'I have always believed that three things should be taken into consideration: knowledge, piety and exemplary life.' (63) He favoured doctors of the Sorbonne and preachers, seeking to appoint the most suitably edifying clerics.

Such precautions made their impact, and 'the reign of Louis XIV was, during the early modern period, the one in which birth counted least in appointments to the episcopate' (282). The Choiseuls and Clermont-Tonnerres were from the higher nobility, d'Argouges and La Bourdonnaye from prominent houses, and the Colberts, Bocharts de Saron and Phelypeaux from the robe; but there were also many bishops from more-humble origins. Malézieu and d'Aquin were almost *roturiers*, whilst Anselin, Vallot, Mascaron and Fléchier came from the lower strata of the bourgeoisie. To these, we should add the great prelates preferred by Richelieu, Mazarin and Vincent de Paul – Pavillon, Caulet, Vialart and Henri Arnauld, Bishop of Angers, all Jansenists and all worthy (284) –, making it obvious that the image of the courtly bishop, young and ambitious, abandoning his diocese for the distractions of Paris, is a misleading one. This is an area in which legends abound. Towards the close of the reign, Saint-Simon reproached the king for having filled sees with 'bearded scruffs from Saint-Sulpice', supposedly under the protection of Beauvillier. In reality, these disciples of M. Olier are nowhere to be found (224). Others have said that Louis was scrupulous in not promoting Jansenists, yet the eminent Fléchier and Noailles were Jansenizing Augustinians and the real Jansenists like Choiseul, Bishop of Tournai, Soanen and Colbert de Croissy were not driven into obscurity. Père de la Chaize did not have it all his own way in his Friday meetings with the king.

The disposal of other benefices was doubtless less rigorous. Courtiers who made Versailles their way of life needed canonries for their brothers, abbacies for their nieces and priorates for their nephews. The system of *in commendam* provided the justification for a simony which would be regarded as deplorable now. Often a convent was run spiritually by a devout, bourgeois nun whilst the temporal rights to it were administered by a well-born but less devoted abbess. Yet an individual such as Rance showed the better side of the bestowal of benefices. As a courtly *abbé*, he had accumulated ecclesiastical positions, until the death of his mistress caused him to quit the worldly life and change his way of living. After several years, he settled down at the abbey of La Trappe, the abbacy of which he held *in commendam*. He reformed it with vigour, persuading several other Cistercian houses to join the 'strict observance'. His death was an edifying spectacle: 'He died on the ground,' according to Saint-Simon, 'lying on straw and ashes.' The case of Rance, albeit exceptional, followed the spirit of that generation. He was not alone in renouncing the court for the cloister. The correspondence of the marquise de Sévigñe and the memoirs of Dangeau and Sourches recall ministers and soldiers, royal servants and highly placed members of the robe abandoning their earthly honours in order to attend to their salvation. From Arnauld d'Andilly to the minister Le Peletier, it was a regular occurrence.

Looking at the distribution of benefices, we may see how often Louis XIV favoured the interests of Heaven. In the period of his greatest conquests and emotional affairs, as in the succeeding more bigoted era, Louis avoided the worst and often chose the best. But, in his relationships with the various religious orders and congregations, his interventions did not always have the most positive results. He placed too much confidence in the Jesuits, almost obliterated the Eudists and upset the Oratorians for good, not to mention his persecution of Port-Royal.

The case of the Jesuits would be worth a book in its own right. The Society of Jesus, with its allegiance to the Papacy alone, its grip on the post of royal confessor, and its enhanced position as spiritual director to the great and educator of the elite, undeniably exercised an excessive degree of influence on the king. Pères Annat (1654–70), Ferrier (1670–74), de la Chaize (1675–1709) and Le Tellier in the final years of the reign enjoyed more credit than any individual minister. Annat was fiercely anti-Jansenist and La Chaize fanned the flames of royal hostility towards both Port-Royal and the Huguenots. Ferrier was perhaps the most moderate. Le Tellier was the most disturbing. His colleague La Rue is supposed to have said of the latter that 'père Le Tellier drives us all on so fast that I fear he may trip us all up'. Le Tellier distorted Louis' last years, bringing upon his master the degree of discontent which fostered the 'black legend'. In 1715, popular opinion was summarized in a refrain:

> You might, our great king, beheld with awe,
> Have followèd Jesus and his law
> And not loved so much his Society. (91)

Posterity has accepted these strictures, but it should not be forgotten that the Jesuits led the way in the foreign missionary effort, in which France predominated, and in the development of public education in Louis XIV's reign – they had 108 educational establishments in 1711 –, not to mention their contribution to scientific research and erudition – even Voltaire men-tioned the names of thirty-two of them in his compendium on Louis XIV's reign. Nor should we ignore the fact that the Jansenists, despite persecution, were always the more influential party within the French Church and that the Society of Jesus, whose reign was also in this world, was of great use to the king. The abbé Le Gendre wrote in 1690 that 'Just as the Jesuits had been Austrian during the hegemony of the House of Austria, so they have become French once France gained its ascendancy under Louis XIV not just over this house but also over all Europe.' (54)

Whilst Louis thus gave a privileged position to the Jesuits, he had no reason to give similar encouragements to a smaller, rival institution, Jean Eudes' Congregation of Jesus and Mary. Eudes, despite having as his brother the historian Mézeray and being a fervent Catholic missionary in the Normandy countryside, had every reason to think that his creation risked destruction. Louis XIII's letters-patent of 1642 had only granted it a temporary privilege. Anne of Austria, once Eudes' most useful supporter, was no longer alive. And, after 1673, he had become the object of persistent attacks. He was denounced for having introduced into the liturgy 'new feasts in honour of the hearts of Jesus and Mary', of having confused veneration for the Virgin with the memory of his former collaborator, Marie des Vallées, and of having undertaken to support Rome in no matter what circumstances. Between 1674 and 1678 he suffered all manner of tribulations and his supplications remained unanswered. It required the intervention of the Archbishop of Paris to put an end to all this and, on 16 June 1678, Jean Eudes was finally presented to the king, at Saint-Germain. Louis XIV approached the old man 'with a friendly look on his face' and let him speak. 'Sire,' said Eudes, 'I am here at Your Majesty's feet to thank you most humbly for the goodness you have shown me in permitting me the honour and consolation of seeing you once more before I die and to tell you that there is no man alive with more zeal and ardour for your service and interests than myself.' He then asked for the prince's 'royal protection'. Louis XIV replied: 'I am very pleased, père Eudes, to meet you. I have been told much about you and I am sure that you have done much good in my kingdom. Continue your good work. I shall be happy to see you again and I will serve and protect you on all possible occasions.' (47) The Congregation had been saved, but its founder had waited four and a half years for the reassurance which he was given.

THE TRIBULATIONS OF THE ORATORY

If the Eudists had failed to secure royal protection or had disappeared, it would have been difficult to hold the king to blame, for he was under no obligation to give urgent attention to the cult of the Sacred Heart of Jesus. All reformers inevitably encountered obstacles. It is less easy, however, to understand why Louis showed such long-standing severity towards a flourishing institution like the Oratory. Unfortunately, the Oratorians were regarded as the rivals of the Jesuits. Their seventy-two colleges were as good as those of the Jesuits and they possessed some excellent seminaries. The Oratory had fewer scholars and writers than its competitor, but arguably it surpassed it both in depth of scholarship, with Malebranche and Richard Simon, and in pedagogical effectiveness, with Mascaron and Massillon. The Jesuits, with their pretensions towards fighting *ad majorem Dei gloriam*, seemed to imagine that they held a monopoly in such things. Perhaps the Catholic Church needed these creative tensions, creative of new styles of religiosity; but Louis XIV would have been better advised to have confined himself to being an umpire between them. Surface tensions are not always the symptoms of a deeper crisis.

Why should the followers of Loyola have become so favoured and those of Bérulle so distrusted? Religious questions were, of course, a contemporary obsession. *Marquises* discoursed about the doctrine of grace as eloquently as theologians of the Sorbonne. Theology had transcended the ecclesiastical forum and become a subject for general debate, like politics today. Louis XIV shared the tastes and predelictions of his contemporaries, but he also had a mania for meddling in everything, reminiscent of the excessive zeal of his great-grandfather, Philip II, for the 'interests of Heaven'. His confessors told the king that the Oratory was rubbing shoulders with heretics in its adoption of the philosophy of Descartes and its sympathy for Port-Royal. True, the general of the Oratory had tried hard to satisfy the king. When Innocent X condemned Jansen's Five Propositions in 1653, père Bourgoing had endeavoured to bring his flock into line. As for père Senault, general of the Oratory from 1663 to 1672, Louis XIV respected him, and the Oratory enjoyed a decade without harassment. The Oratory's leaders were, however, rather different from its rank and file fathers, and, in 1661, several Oratorians had felt the fury of royal displeasure. In the following year, pères du Breuil, Juannet and Séguenot were exiled by royal *lettres de cachet*; for, although they had signed the anti-Jansenist formulary, they had done so only with reluctance and with mental reservations. Similarly, a number of regent teachers, dissatisfied with Thomism, had replaced Aristotle and Aquinas, sometimes with Plato, but more often with Descartes. Such audacity appeared an outrage to Archbishop Harlay (in office in Paris from 1671) and also to père de la Chaize. The death of Senault and the election of père de Sainte-Marthe, general of the Oratory from 1672 to 1696, sparked off another, longer conflict, fed alternately by accusations of Jansenism and Cartesianism.

In 1675, two decisions of the Council supported the University of Paris against the Parlement and banned the teaching of theses based 'on the principles of Descartes'. In the same year, renewed accusations of Jansenism appeared against the Oratory. The general himself, Sainte-Marthe, did not hide the fact that he was a follower of St Augustine. Every means of harassing the Oratorians appeared legitimate. Lamy, an Oratorian professor suspected of Cartesianism, was now accused of teaching subversive politics and dismissed from his post at Angers by a *lettre de cachet* of 10 December. Two years later, his successor, Pelaud, suffered official displeasure through the same process. Despite the protection of his bishop, Henri Arnauld, he was condemned on 17 September 1677 and exiled to Brive. In the same year, the king acted against père Poisson, a commentator on Descartes. Within the Oratory, the situation was confused, with Oratorians opposing the circular letters of their congregation as well as the decrees of the king's council. Louis XIV, for his part, by his intervention turned Jansenists into Cartesians and some Cartesians into quasi-republicans.

In the autumn of 1678, there were signs of a peace within the Church and the assembly of the Oratory tried to appease the king by imposing on all its members a formula which condemned both Descartes and Jansen. Sainte-Marthe sent père de Saillant, a friend of Harlay, to report on this assembly to His Majesty. On 26 September, Louis XIV received the Oratorian at Saint-Germain: 'Well, is it over? – Sire, the assembly has ended in accordance with Your Majesty's intentions. – But was everyone unanimous? – Yes, Sire, it ended unanimously, with all in agreement.' The next day, Louis continued the interview in this Napoleonic fashion: 'So, Monsieur, tell us who your officers are, their names, origins and characters.' Then, on matters of doctrine: 'These are matters of faith about which I know nothing. You are wrong if you take me for a theologian. – Sire, Your Majesty may permit me to tell you that I do not think I am mistaken. Monseigneur the archbishop has assured us that Your Majesty is so perceptive that you always succeed in putting your finger on the important matters and invariably correctly.' Louis smiled and continued reading the Oratory's report. He came to the section dealing with the philosophy of Descartes, 'which the king had forbidden with good reason. – Yes, for very good reasons. Not that I wished to prevent its being taught to Monseigneur, but I do not wish it to be made the basis for a doctrine' (214). Despite the smiles, however, the exiles were not recalled. Louis still bore a grudge against Lamy, calling him 'your little man from Angers'.

Relations went on being strained between Louis and the Oratorians for the rest of the reign. The king and his confessor continued to suspect them of heterodoxy. And it was true that neither the philosophy of Malebranche nor the rationalist exegesis of Richard Simon nor the biblical commentaries of Quesnel would enter the 'middle way'. But everything happened as though the Oratorians had rebelled intellectually, as though they had been forced into accentuating their tendency towards independence. After the armed peace came war. The triumvirate of Louis XIV, Harlay and La Chaize tried to obtain the resignation of Sainte-Marthe. The king exiled him twice; but the general resisted until 1696. The king's anti-Protestant policy saved the Oratory; in need of missionaries in 1685, the king rediscovered the Oratorians. The resignation of Sainte-Marthe and the election of a more accommodating general also soothed matters a little. La Tour, by origin Spanish, was held in high regard by the king. He managed to avoid the accusation of Jansenism, whilst retaining his sympathy for Soanen, Noailles and Quesnel. Thanks to him, the Oratory survived the rest of the reign unscathed.

The surveillance of congregations, the inquisition which filtered reports about obscure regents through to Versailles, does not display Louis at his best. Under the façade of God's honour, the king's vanity is more apparent than the king's glory. It was no longer a question of religion or politics but of maintaining order. The 'interests of Heaven' coincided too neatly with the interests of the Jesuits and royal authoritarianism. Louis XIV's only excuse lay in the sincerity of his convictions.

THE PREFERRED PATH OF DEVOTIONS

Following the way outlined in the Tridentine decrees, the king's concern was to fight the Reformation, support Thomism and oppose Jansenism, which, an embattled and impassioned product of the Counter Reformation, threatened to turn into a caricature of it. That is why Louis XIV acted so harshly towards dissidents. Like all Christians of his generation, he was intolerant. There was but one Truth, and to tolerate error would be to undermine that Truth. But intolerance did not necessarily mean fanaticism. Voltaire understood this distinction and, in 1702 and 1704, fanaticism was not the hallmark of Louis XIV or his followers but of the Camisards. One may be forced to adopt extreme measures without necessarily professing extreme doctrines. The king's position was that of Bossuet, half-way between the dogmatic and moral extremes. This led to the famous 'middle way' advocated in the funeral oration for Nicolas Cornet in 1663: 'One must walk in the middle'.

This middle way had an outcome in practice which can be traced through Louis' devotions. After his death, there was considerable debate over whether he had worn a hair-shirt (87). Since 1661, his subjects had noted that he attended Mass daily. As a mere gentleman he might have been content with a Sunday service alone, but he saw it as his duty to attend Mass daily so that his French subjects would themselves go every Sunday. He 'only missed Mass once in his life' (24). At Versailles, the king had himself carried to Mass when he had gout. If he was ill, he would hear the office from his bed. Following Madame Palatine and Saint-Simon, it has become the convention to pour scorn on Louis XIV's rather rustic way of following the service. As the books of prayers for the liturgy were being distributed, he would say his rosary. But Madame Palatine saw things as a Protestant, and Saint-Simon as a snob. In fact, there is something rather touching in this haughty prince behaving like the most humble of his subjects and preferring the attitude of the Publican to that of the Pharisee. François de Sales recommended daily attendance at Mass, but did not insist that one should follow the liturgy. To him, the Mass was 'the sun of spiritual exercises', the best way of coming into contact with it being to 'meditate on its mysteries' (41). The rosary was nothing other than a meditation upon the mysteries of the Christian faith. That is why the king's confessors did not bring it into contention.

Louis' piety rose in a crescendo, everyone remarking on it after the emergence of Mme de Maintenon. After the death of Maria Theresa it became even more evident. On Easter Monday, 3 April 1684, the king, during his *lever*, 'spoke in strong terms about the courtiers who had not performed their Easter duties and said that he valued highly those who had done so conscientiously' (26). In March 1685, 'His Majesty founded a *salut* for Sundays and Thursdays in the chapel of Versailles' (26). In April, the court learnt that Condé, who was rumoured not to have taken communion for seventeen years, had performed his Easter office (97). In May, the king admonished Madame Palatine through his confessors – the Princess Palatine was said to have laughed with the princesse de Conti about the admirers attracted to her 'ladies' (87). The following year, in June 1686,

Madame Palatine tells us that the *dévotes* at court were embracing bigotry, and, on 1 October 1687, she wrote: 'The court has become so tedious that it is insupportable.'

The chronicle of activities at Versailles becomes sometimes a record of Louis' pious devotions. A 'Christian under siege' – Pierre Gaxotte's description – from the attentions of his wife, his confessors and the parties of *dévots* (in 1709–10, the Maintenon party and the Burgundy-Beauvillier-Chevreuse group, with Monseigneur alone leading the moderates) (94), Louis multiplied his religious exercises. He began to take communion at least five or six times a year. He spent all Holy Week in prayer, listening to sermons and attending services. On Maundy Thursday, he washed the feet of the poor; on Good Friday, he adored the cross; on Easter Saturday he took communion and touched for scrofula; and on Easter Sunday he went to Mass and Vespers, not to mention Benediction (26). He performed all the jubilees, despite their frequency, going on foot to visit each station of the cross. The *Gazette de France* reported it all, stressing His Majesty's 'good days', those when he took communion. These 'good days' entailed confession, attendance at Vespers, a long talk with his confessor, then Mass, touching for scrofula, then Vespers once more and a sermon. The disposition of benefices, also determined on 'good days', only involved a relatively few individuals, but the royal touch was populist and the king never shirked this religious and royal obligation. Even when ill, he touched dozens of sufferers, in normal times receiving around two thousand on each occasion. Sourches, who noted down these details, also revealed the sense of pious obligation with which Louis carried out this task.

We tend to see the king as a bigot, so bound up in his devotions that he strayed from his 'middle way'; but, in reality, he never departed from it. It has been said that he imposed a moral order; but it had its own rationale as well. The higher nobility did not become pious overnight, as Madame Palatine confirmed whilst, at the same time, deploring both bigotry and homosexuality. Against certain practitioners of the 'ultramontane vice', including members of the Houses of Lorraine and Bouillon, friends of Monseigneur, Louis took action in 1682 (97). They were even accused of perverting His Majesty's children. Yet their punishment was not too extreme, merely a few months' exile from Versailles. Louis displayed the same moderation in the matter of court theatre. Mme de Maintenon and all the *dévot* clans would have liked to see the king ban plays and ballets at court, but he refused to banish them from his palaces. When the *marquise* wished him to become a kind of Savonarola, he replied that his late lamented mother had enjoyed the theatre and she had retained her virtue intact, having even consulted the doctors of the Sorbonne and obtained their consent.

Louis was obsessed with his own salvation, but not easily persuaded to excess. He kept Mme de Montespan at court until 1691 and granted rather indiscreet favours to their children in 1694 and 1714. He remained moderate in matters of religion until his death, admiring Mme de Maintenon's piety whilst not always sharing her zeal. He listened to the advice of pères de la Chaize and Le Tellier, but by no means always followed their more intemperate advice. In the final analysis, common sense, rather like that of Henry IV, preserved Louis from exaggerated piety, puritanism and superstition. He had not really changed since the day in 1682 when he begged the queen, the Dauphine, the Villeroys, Charost, Créqui and several others to stop attributing the recent earthquake in France to the anger of the Almighty, with God thereby validating the declaration of the Four Articles (97). Louis and Bossuet displayed the same good sense in dealing with the so-called 'Quietism' affair. The king and the best theologians in the kingdom did not try to stifle mysticism; rather they sought to demonstrate Fénelon's imprudence, the dangers of popularizing (as in the case of Mme Guyon) a religion freed from all dogma, and the folly of trying to lead unprepared souls onto higher spiritual planes. It is a pity that Louis XIV did not follow the middle way in the question of pluralism. As regards Protestantism, however, he had little margin for manœuvre.

21

Religious Cohesion, National Unity

A FTER NYMWEGEN, Louis XIV appeared at the height of his prestige. The *Universal Dictionary* recorded: 'The King of France is the arbiter of peace and war. Europeans see him as the greatest and most powerful king in Europe. He is called the Most Christian King. Louis XIV is the greatest king there has ever been since the foundation of the monarchy.' (42) These formulae help us to comprehend the crises which developed in the 1680s. For two princes refused to accept this hegemony: the emperor and the pope. The pope was the more discontented, accusing the French of trying to make a fundamental law out of the king's independence *vis-à-vis* the Papacy. Innocent XI, pope since 1676, refused Louis XIV's extension of the right of the *régale* and, by a papal brief of 1678, ordered him to withdraw the texts of this abusive augmentation of his powers (131).

Everything had thus been prepared for the termination of the Peace of the Church which had given a breathing-space to the Protestants, and had permitted the Augustinians to publish some monumental works and the French Counter Reformation to reach its zenith with the most respected prelates (Pavillon, Bishop of Alet), the most pious nuns (the Benedictines of Faremoutiers), the most learned monks (Mabillon), the most educated and enlightened clergy (Voltaire listed sixty-five of them in his *Century of Louis XIV*), the ablest theologians (Bossuet, Arnauld) and the most brilliant Christian philosophers (Malebranche). Protestantism was, however, struggling simply to maintain its position. Instead of ignoring Innocent XI's provocations and maintaining a religious peace which might have transformed the war between the Jesuits and the

Oratorians into peaceful competition, and instead of perpetuating the slow decline of a Protestantism which had become intellectually stagnant and the adherents of which might have been attracted to the magnet of a revived Catholicism, the king was determined to replace long-term evolution with the imposition of his will. Jansenism would pay the price of the clash with the pope, and the persecution of the *prétendus réformés* would be the result of the breaking of that peace. Between two *Te Deums* in praise of the Peace of Nymwegen, observers would have noted some disquieting events taking place, including a declaration against 'relapsed heretics and apostates', the death of the duchesse de Longueville, protectress of Port-Royal, on 15 April 1679, a further papal bull on the *régale*, and, finally, the disgrace, on 18 November, of Pomponne, the Augustinian party's representative on the king's council.

Louis, of course, had not yet read Furetière in detail; but he was constantly reminded that he was 'the most powerful prince in all Christendom'. Whilst all Europe was being forced to submit to his hegemony, was this most powerful of kings to be restrained by an aggressive pope? And why should he persecute the Protestants just because the friends of Port-Royal annoyed him? The motives were not so very different. Could Louis go on being the most powerful prince in Christendom whilst allowing a religious dualism of a kind permitted by no other king? Could the greatest king in the world not find some mechanism to overturn an 'already elderly edict of pacification and a text dictated by circumstances', sealed with yellow wax like royal acts of lesser significance (119)? On the other hand, if the quarrel with Rome were to grow more intense, the king could only win with the support of his clergy, a clergy which was partly Jansenist. In order, therefore, to obtain their compliance, he had to take account of their predelictions and sentiments and fulfil some of their aspirations. Their oldest, most entrenched wish – more a matter of instinct than rational design – was the achievement of unity through the extinction of Protestantism.

HATRED OF HERESY

Nothing had, in fact, changed since the day of the consecration when Louis XIV had sworn to extirpate heresy and the Bishop of Montauban had stressed that this was an oath he should put into practice. Nothing had changed since that day in 1660 when the king had received the delegate of the Reformed synod so frostily. The king's anti-Protestantism, sustained by his confessors and the Archbishop of Paris, had not altered, and neither had that of the people, who were even more hostile than the king towards dissidents. In the Midi especially, the *prétendu réformé* was often the seigneur of the community or a manufacturer, the 'papists' being the poor. Protestants were educated, with even the most humble possessing a bible, while Catholics only rarely possessed a catechism or a missal. Protestants tended to look down upon Catholics, seeing them as being ignorant of the Word of God, superstitious and idolatrous, and as often sanctifying laziness in the guise of celebrating evangelical poverty. Catholics, encouraged by their clergy, envied and hated Protestant arrogance, the pride which caused them to keep their hats on when processions passed, and to refuse to kneel in church, pray for the intercession of saints, or go on pilgrimages and keep fasts. Catholics had their revenge when a mission arrived in their locality and the *prétendus réformés* were forced to stay in their homes, as though besieged.

Amongst the bourgeoisie, the nobility and clergy, it was less a question of hating heretics than of denouncing the heresy which threatened the faith and eroded the nation. For, although Catholic complaints against Protestantism were primarily religious, they were also political. Furetière showed this dual state of mind, and his definitions read like proverbs, echoing the received wisdom of his generation. Protestantism, presented first as a heresy and a sect on the margins of the Church, is then denounced as an obstacle to the unity of the kingdom. The misunderstanding began with the sources of faith. 'The heretics abuse Scripture and corrupt its meaning.' Protestants were schismatics: 'The Huguenots left the Catholic Church.' Above all, they were heretics: 'The doctrine taught by Calvinists has been condemned', and 'the dogmas of the heretics are, for the most part, blasphemous'. 'Our poor lost brethren', not content with denying transubstantiation, 'make use of specious arguments' and opposed many points of doctrine. Notably, they refused to 'honour images, relics and the memory of the saints'. Consequently, they 'cause disruption in the discipline of the Church'. The trouble was not, however, restricted to ecclesiastical matters. 'Heresies, as a rule, provoke great conflagrations in kingdoms.' Memories of the religious wars of the sixteenth century and the uprisings in the time of Louis XIII were still alive. 'The Huguenots', wrote Furetière, 'stirred up many troubles' and 'the heretics abused the edicts of pacification.' He then cited his examples in the present tense: 'Heresy is the cause of troubles and dissensions in a state'; 'People of different countries and religions have difficulty living together.' This was the justification for the universal nostrum *Cujus regio, ejus religio*. Even though the Protestants, the adherents of the *religion prétendue réformée*, no longer constituted a state within the state, they still preserved a particularism which perturbed the sense of national identity. The Dutch War had illustrated this when some French Protestants had barely disguised their sympathy for William of Orange.

Politics and religion were inextricably interwoven. The structures of the Reformed Church irritated and perplexed Jansenists, Jesuits, bishops and peasants, even artisans and labourers. It was presbyterian, each parish running its own affairs, and was governed by a regime of synodal assemblies. Each parish appeared a republic in miniature. Although Calvin's *Institution of the Christian Religion* had been dedicated to Francis I and had advocated submission to the king, all Calvinists were thought of as republicans. Furthermore, the examples of Geneva and the United Provinces helped to give direction to French Protestantism and taint it with democracy. The vicomte de Turenne, who would readily have accepted an Anglican-style hierarchy or a Lutheran mode of political submissiveness, condemned the presbyterian system, and this incompatibility became one reason behind his conversion to Catholicism in 1668.

PERSECUTION OF THE 'HERETICS'

More than a decade had passed since Turenne's conversion. The king had counted on winning over the Protestant aristocrats, but he realized that this was only proceeding at a slow pace. A number of state servants, the maréchal Schomberg, for example, were tempted to abjure, but their wives remained obdurate. The king was well aware of this, although he failed to grasp how Protestants, especially in France, were insensitive to arguments

based upon the principle of hierarchy. He also failed to grasp
how much of a contradiction was implied in being both Protestant and French. The Huguenots had already endured the
closure of Protestant places of worship between 1659 and 1664, a
more rigid interpretation of the clauses of the Edict of Nantes,
Catholic missions and the *caisse des conversions*, run by Pellisson,
which used the revenues of the *régale* to reward Protestants who
abjured (261). Emigration had been forbidden. Some read but
others ignored the bibles translated for their benefit (230), the
catechisms and works of controversy designed to indoctrinate
them. Fervent Calvinists clung to their own bibles, their own
forms of worship and their pastors, while the less committed
moved closer towards the majority religion.

In the normal course of events, France would probably have
become wholly Catholic at some date between 1730 and 1760.
But the king would be in his grave by then. He was impatient to
accomplish the unity which he wanted to be the crowning
achievement of his reign and, since 1679, had determined to
bring it to pass. The determination to destroy French Protestantism dates from then, and the Revocation has to be understood in
the context of the measures taken from around that date to make
the Huguenots' position less and less endurable. The year 1679
saw the introduction of severe penalties against relapsed heretics
and apostates and restrictive regulations concerning abjurations.
In July, a further support to the guarantees given in the Edict of
Nantes was removed when the *chambres mi-parties* in the *parlements*
of Toulouse and Grenoble were suppressed (201). An act of June
1680 forbade all conversions from Catholicism to Protestantism,
whilst another in November required magistrates to visit the
bedsides of all sick Protestants in order to attempt their conversion. A few months previously, Protestant women had been forbidden to become midwives. In 1681, the knot was tightened still
further. On 18 March, Louvois authorized the use of the *dragonnades* in Poitou (261). This was a means of conversion recently
dreamt up by the intendant Marillac: instead of imposing the
burden of billeted soldiers upon tax-evaders, it was reserved for
Protestants. In April, however, it was learnt that *nouveaux convertis*
were to be exempted from this duty for two years. On 17 June,
the king decided that the children of Huguenots could choose
Catholicism from the age of seven and that their parents would
be forbidden to have them educated abroad in the Reformed

confession. Throughout 1681, zealous intendants imitated Marillac. They sent in optimistic lists of conversions, and Louis XIV, taking his desires as the reality, persuaded himself that their numbers would be increased if repression were increased.

The year 1682 saw the proliferation of the *dragonnades* and the strictest possible application of the Edict of Nantes. In the summer, two or three Protestant places of worship (*temples*) were 'legally' demolished every week (135). Furthermore, royal legislation decreed that Huguenots' illegitimate children would be brought up according to the Roman Catholic rite, prohibited the emigration of sailors and artisans, and banned Protestants from the professions of notary, *procureur, huissier*, sergeant and bailiff. On 14 July, the state reinforced the ban on emigration – confiscating the goods of all offenders. A declaration of 30 August forbade Protestants' assembling outside their *temples* and without the presence of a pastor. An edict of 7 September specified the risks run by Protestants who emigrated; another bequeathed to *hôpitaux* the legacies left by Protestants to the poor (201). With all these measures in force and the *dragonnades* in full swing, one can see how the statistics provided by intendants and bishops encouraged the king. As soon as he made his first mistake, in taking the large number of 'conversions' at face value, he was condemned to go on believing in them, to go on encouraging the policy of abjurations and to go on being duped by his own agents.

In March 1683, an edict decreed the punishment of public apology (*amende honorable*), followed by banishment, for any Protestant minister who accepted a Roman Catholic convert into his Church. On 22 May, a declaration created a special place for the informers of the king's police in each *temple*. On 17 June, another decided that the children of *nouveaux convertis* should be educated in the Catholic faith. The year 1684 was even harsher upon what was left of Protestantism in the kingdom. June saw a succession of restrictive laws, one of which renewed the ban upon private worship. In August, an edict banned Protestant ministers from serving more than three years in the same place, and a declaration reduced the number of meetings of consistories. Finally, a declaration of 26 December forbade all Protestant services where the local community consisted of fewer than ten families (201).

Louis XIV's councillors now had to use their imaginations in order to invent new coercive measures, and the unhappy history of 1685 was to demonstrate that they were not deficient in that regard. On 20 January, a declaration reduced still further the powers of Protestant magistrates still holding posts at Metz. In February, another royal act laid down the punishments for pastors 'who have allowed people into their places of worship to whom the king had already required them to forbid entry'. After 16 June, marriage abroad was no longer to be permitted – Protestants were not explicitly mentioned, but the edict was clearly aimed at them. Two days later, a declaration prescribed the demolition of places of worship where pastors had celebrated mixed marriages or used expressions which might give offence to Catholics. On 9 July, Protestants lost their right to employ Catholic servants. On the 10th, the king forbade their becoming lawyers' clerks and, the following day, the Bar itself was closed to them. On the 25th, Huguenots learnt that they were no longer to attend religious worship outside the *bailliages* in which they resided. Then came an edict forbidding all Protestants to preach or write works of polemics or theology. On 6 August, a declaration excluded Protestants from the practice of medicine and, on the same day, Louis XIV decided that Protestant ministers were not to reside within fifteen miles of places where Protestant worship was forbidden. On 14 August, it was decreed that the children of Protestants had to be taught by Catholic tutors. On the 20th, the public learnt that half the goods of Huguenot emigrants would be given to those who had denounced them (201).

The enumeration of these acts of harassment indicates that, so far as persecution was concerned, little was left to accomplish by the end of September 1685. Only the empty shell of the Edict of Nantes remained. While it is difficult to comprehend Louis XIV's intransigence in destroying a form of dissent which was becoming progressively enfeebled as time passed, it is easier to understand the logic behind revoking the terms laid down at Nantes. The Edict of Fontainebleau, dated October 1685, made known on the 18th and registered by the Parlement on the 22nd, appeared as the legal incarnation of an 'already established fact'. Since there were no longer (in the eyes of the law) any Huguenots remaining in the kingdom, the legislation granting them privileges had no longer any legal rationale. Therefore the edict banned the public exercise of the 'religion prétendue réformée'. Pastors were to convert within two weeks or leave the kingdom. Children of adherents of the *religion prétendue réformée* were to be baptized into, and brought up and educated in, the Roman religion. *Emigrés* were given four months within which to benefit from an amnesty and recover their confiscated property. Besides this, the edict reiterated the previous ban on emigration. Leaving the kingdom and sending goods abroad were absolutely forbidden 'with the penalties of the galleys for men and confiscation of all worldly goods [*de corps et de biens*] for women'.

Despite 1,450 condemnations to the galleys, the most powerful king in the world could not prevent emigration (69). It robbed the kingdom of some 200,000 subjects, many of them educated, active, rich and industrious. He was no more skilful in forcing consciences or persuading souls to yield. The Revocation brought in its wake the miserable spectacle of forced communions, half-truths and sacrilege. How was it that there was no warning from Bossuet, Bourdaloue, père de la Chaize or Harlay de Champvallon to Louis XIV of the risks? A veil of mystery still obscures this political error and religious crime.

RESPONSIBILITY FOR, AND COMPLICITY IN, 1685

The Edict of Fontainebleau cannot be considered in isolation, for the intensification of persecution had started in 1679 and thereafter gradually increased. For this reason, it would be naïve to see it as Louis' revenge on the emperor, who, since Vienna had been saved from the Turkish threat in 1683, had once again come to occupy the centre of the European stage. This was at best a secondary consideration. In Counter-Reformation France, politics took second place to religion. The dream of unity had obsessed the king since 1649, not just since 1679. The circumstances of the Revocation, of the final hammer-blow, are less important than the causes of a persecution which had been intensifying over the preceding six years.

The king was absolute and should take complete responsibility. He shared legislative authority with no one. Even though the chancellor Le Tellier countersigned the Edict of Fontainebleau, this was not a co-signature: the royal stamp stood alone, just as it had on the succession of reiterated edicts which had stifled French Protestantism and which the Revocation would revive. The king had been imbued, since his consecration, with the sacred character of his role. He had been convinced, by the catechism of his childhood, by the conversations with his confessors, by sermons, that the Reformed religion was heretical and therefore satanic. He stood in lineal descent from the Council of Trent (1545–63), the fount of early modern Catholicism. If the *prétendus réformés* were destined for the eternal fire, was it not both a humanitarian and devout action to use every means to ensure their salvation? Like his subjects, Louis was permeated with Augustinianism, and St Augustine, irritated by the Donatist schism, had justified forcible conversions by interpreting strictly the *Compelle intrare* of the parable of the great supper. Whilst religious unity in France had useful political consequences, to Louis it seemed the essential prerequisite to religious order. Unaware that 'religion is the only truly effective counterweight to the abuse of supreme power',* Louis did not hesitate to place his formidable authority behind what he held to be the true religion. In this case, it was no longer a counterweight, and its own authority reinforced his absolute power. That is why persecution was also a political act, since there was no effective politics other than that based on religion.

Since Louis' hostility to Protestantism had taken shape during his early years, the complicity of those who brought him up – Anne of Austria, Mazarin, Péréfixe, Paulin and Archbishop Marca – should be acknowledged. In the 1670s, Pellisson had managed to persuade the king to prefer conversion by kindness, but this had been a change of tactics and not of strategy. It is true that, up to the end of the Peace of the Church, nothing irreparable had yet been promulgated. As long as he did not force consciences, the drive for unity could be justified. The change came in 1679. But Louis did not act alone. All those with authority around him encouraged the sovereign to stiffen his resolve towards unification. Bishops and intendants struggled with the facts, rivalled each other in their despatches and fought to be the one who announced the most remarkable rates for conversion. There was, inevitably, a touch of sycophancy and a propensity towards the 'pious' lie, but they were sincere enough, and, as in the case of the intendant du Maître, thought that they were obeying the divine command of the *Compelle intrare*. Confronted with their reports, the king's critical faculties failed him. He wilfully believed that religious unity was being forged and

---

* Honoré de Balzac.

added ambiguous conclusions to the ambiguity of the messages which he received. Barring a complete reversal of trends, the Revocation had become inevitable. The statistics of the missionaries and the *dragonnades* only served to speed up the process.

In the preparation of the Edict of Fontainebleau, it is easy to identify the king's accomplices. They were Harlay, Archbishop of Paris, the king's confidant every Friday and theologian of the Counter-Reformation, and Le Tellier, the countersignatory of the Revocation. Then there was also the skilful père de la Chaize, who was less aggressive but equally determined. Too much the courtier to play a leading part, he let Harlay do most of the work. Louvois carried out rigorously a policy which was not of his choosing (165). For her part, the marquise de Maintenon rejoiced at the conversions, but found the constraints used against her former co-religionists repugnant. Neither Seignelay, who shared the pragmatism of his father Colbert and his contacts with Huguenot men of affairs, nor Châteauneuf, on whom adherents of the *religion prétendue réformée* relied, had any real influence on policy. Least guilty of all was Basville, and Louis had been wrong not to ask him for his views. 'I was never in favour of revoking the Edict of Nantes', wrote the intendant of Languedoc at a later date, 'and I was never consulted about it.' (117) Finally, the complicity of the people at large, especially of the lower orders, as well as of the clergy, from bishops down to parochial clergy, should be noted. For the Revocation, as a religious rather than a political act, was also a popular measure.

'MIRACLES OF ZEAL'

We have become so accustomed to deploring the Revocation that it is difficult for us to conceive the immense enthusiasm which it aroused among French Catholics. The instigators of the Edict of Fontainebleau, confident that they had a mandate from Heaven, were not at all tormented by their consciences. On 16 October, Louis XIV finally overcame all his hesitations: 'I praise God', he wrote to Harlay, 'for the abjurations of so many skilled people at Grenoble these past few days. Their professions of faith according to the Council of Trent assuage all the doubts aroused by their acts of conversion.' (179) On 7 November, the king wrote: 'I am persuaded that God will consummate in His glory the work which He has inspired in me.' The preparation of the edict was the last important act of chancellor Le Tellier. 'God has reserved for him', said Bossuet, 'the accomplishment of the great work of religion; and, sealing the revocation of the famous edict of Nantes, he said that, following this triumph of the faith and fine monument to the king's piety, he was no longer worried about ending his days.' (14)

To the end of the reign, churchmen showed their satisfaction, even enthusiasm, for the Revocation. 'All the sermons', wrote Madame Palatine in 1700, 'contain great compliments to the king for his persecution of the poor Protestants.' Bossuet proclaimed Louis a new Constantine, another Theodosius, a second Charlemagne, applying to him what the fathers of the Council of Chalcedon in 451 had said of the Emperor Marcian. Bourdaloue thought that the Edict of Fontainebleau was the crowning achievement of a king predestined to greatness. At the end of his sermon for All Saints' Day 1686, he exclaimed:

> I address a king whose particular character is to have known how to make all things possible, or even easy, when it was necessary to carry through his projects, whether for the glory of his crown or the glory of his religion. I address these words to a king who, in order to triumph over the enemies of his state, has accomplished miracles of such renown that posterity will not credit it, because they are more true than credible, and who, in order to triumph over the enemies of the Church, is today performing such miracles of zeal that we who witness them can scarce believe our eyes, so much do they exceed our hopes. I am speaking to a king raised up and chosen by God for things of which his august ancestors did not even dare to think, because he alone could have planned them and carried them out. This zeal for the interests of God and the true worship of God is, Sire, that which sanctifies kings and which should be the apogee of your glorious destiny. (16)

The exchange between the marquise de Sévigné and Bussy-Rabutin captures the popular satisfaction. 'You will no doubt have seen', wrote the former on 28 October 1685, 'the edict by which the king has revoked that of Nantes. Nothing is more sublime than its contents and no king has ever done, or will ever do, anything more memorable.' Bussy went further, rising from tactics to strategy: 'I admire', he replied, 'the king's conduct in destroying the Huguenots. The wars against them in the past and the massacres of St Bartholomew served to increase and give vigour to their sect. His Majesty has sapped this little by little, and the edict which has just been proclaimed, supported by the *dragonnades* and the Bourdaloues [*sic*], has been the *coup de grâce.*' (96)

It might be imagined that these individuals represented only a narrow section of opinion; but the further one descends down the social scale, the greater the manifestation of Catholic delight. In Paris, capital of the Catholic Holy League (*Ligue Sainte*) a century earlier, the Revocation propelled the king's popularity to its apogee. The abbé de Choisy recorded on 30 January 1687 that the king had attained 'the heights of human glory when he came to dine at the Hôtel de Ville after his illness; he saw how he was beloved of his people. Never had so much adulation been manifested. The acclamations were never-ending. He was in his carriage with Monseigneur and the royal family. A hundred thousand voices cried out *Vive le Roi!*' The king was under siege from the acclamations of artists and men of letters. Sculptors, such as Coysevox, composers and engravers competed in this exaltation of the reconquest of Christian unity, and Fontenelle won the Académie française's poetry prize: Calvinism in defeat was a 'hydra vanquished' or Python slain by Apollo. La Bruyère praised the king in 1691 for having banished a 'false cult, enemy of the sovereign power', and for having accomplished Richelieu's plan for the 'extinction of heresy'. Everyone remembered the couplet from Racine's *Esther* of 1689:

> The warmth of zeal, which inflames and devours him quite
> To spread Thy [God's] glory, glows from sunset to first light.

WAS A MODERATE SOLUTION STILL POSSIBLE?

It is easy to set history to rights. But, in the case of the Revocation, there is such a profound gap between the satisfaction evinced by the French population in the seventeenth century and our unanimous disapproval in the twentieth that it is legitimate to try to imagine what Louis XIV might have done to satisfy the majority and carry through his aims, whilst avoiding the worst consequences. In theory, the king who, in the context of Catholicism, adopted 'the *via media*' would have been well advised to apply the same approach to the sectarian divide. Hypothetically, he could have rescinded the Edict of Nantes without violating consciences. One may even imagine how Protestants might have been forbidden to hold state offices, as long as other professions remained open to them. The king might have forbidden the exodus of capital, whilst not seeking to prevent emigration.

Following on from these hypotheses, the Protestants would have split into three groups, according to their attachment to particular styles of belief. One group would have opted for Catholicism. In a less oppressive atmosphere, the *nouveaux convertis* would have been incorporated into the majority religion. Persuaded by less-militant missionary endeavour, enlightened by friendly persuasion, instructed by catechisms and encouraged by the *caisse des conversions*, they would have been fewer in number, but more completely converted, than the *nouveaux convertis* in fact were. After all, the theological shifts of the Counter Reformation had rendered some of the polemics of the sixteenth century obsolete (261). Furthermore, the form of Catholicism centred around Port-Royal offered an attractively Augustinian outlook. Nor should one ignore the argument from national identity. The great figures of French Protestantism were proud of France, its king, conquests and influence. Duquesne and Bayle, for example, were, and would remain, loyalists. Why should an ordinary young Protestant not have preferred his king to Calvin? In mixed marriages, the love of a fiancée often led to conversion. In the context of the 1680s, souls could be influenced by patrimonial affections.

On the other hand, other Protestants, obsessed by the question of worship, would have fled abroad, paying the price of separation in order to practise the religion of their fathers each Sunday, to sing the Psalms of David to the music of Loys Bourgeois and to use the *patois de Canaan*, that distinctive diction embellished with scriptural citations. This is what Lucrèce de Brignac, a noblewomen from the Cévennes, did in 1701. Leaving her husband, the baron de Salgas, 'with six children on his hands', she made her way to Geneva in order to participate in public worship (147). If freedom to emigrate had been granted, several thousands or tens of thousands of Protestants would have done the same as Mme de Salgas, without risking the galleys or weakening the kingdom with a massive exodus.

The third, larger group would have been content with family worship. An option denied Catholics, this was reconcilable with

Calvinist rites. Centred round a bible and presided over by the head of the family, a Sunday service could be performed anywhere. In this fashion, consciences might have been respected. In order to preserve their fatherland, their property and their way of life, all that Protestants would have been required to do would have been to adopt a practical theology similar to that of the Mennonites.

But who would there have been to give the king the necessary advice? Séguier, Le Tellier, Bossuet, Bourdaloue, La Chaize and Harlay, none of these advisers would ever have proposed this course of action to His Majesty. The clergy would have regarded toleration of domestic worship as an infringement of their privileges, a scorning of the Mass, an incitement to the open examination of Scripture, and an aggravation of the 'sacrilegious' character of the Protestant eucharist. Churchmen would have preferred the presence of their Protestant rivals to that of Protestants deprived of their ministers. The political objections would have been equally compelling. Before 1685, with the Protestant *temples* open, it was easy for the state to infiltrate its informers into the Protestant movement. But if every Protestant house had become transformed into a chapel, who would have kept the king informed about references to public affairs? Toleration of private worship, in short, risked engendering plots and creating a propaganda network favourable to William of Orange and a threat to France.

One of the reasons for the policy adopted in fact was the impracticability of this more liberal option. In order to understand the choices as they appeared to contemporaries, we must leave our own century behind us and immerse ourselves in the seventeenth century. According to the then prevailing notions, if Louis XIV had conceded the rights of emigration and private worship to the Huguenots he would have stirred up, especially in the conquered provinces, the opposition of nineteen million Catholics. Bishops, monks, priests, and the ordinary faithful would have supported such a concession only with reluctance. Emigration would have been less and, with it, the Refuge would not have been of such significance, but could the networks of complicity have been dismantled and the Huguenots have become more loyal? Only Louis XIII could have abolished the Edict of Nantes whilst avoiding the horrors of that of Fontainebleau and, in so doing, he would not have left this poisoned legacy to his son. In 1629, after the subversive war in the Midi, it would have been seen as logical and *de bonne guerre* to have abolished the provisional and recently accorded privileges of 1598. But this had not appealed to Richelieu, who needed to treat the Protestant princes of the empire with consideration. Among those implicated in the bringing about of the Revocation, Louis XIII and his minister should not be entirely neglected.

THE BALANCE SHEET OF THE REVOCATION

The Sun King's contemporaries were too eager to praise the work of this 'new Constantine', this 'new Theodosius'. But historiography has painted the Edict of Fontainebleau in too sombre a light. The truth lies somewhere between the two extremes. If the Revocation occupies the prime position among the reign's liabilities, its consequences were not entirely negative. The Edict of Fontainebleau brought as many advantages to France as it did disadvantages.

Six unfavourable consequences may be enumerated: first, the *nouveaux convertis* would also be *mal convertis*. Robbed of leadership by the conversions of the nobility and of spiritual guidance by the expulsion of their pastors, the Protestants became seemingly more attached to their beliefs and preconceptions, their way of life and their identities, than the king and his councillors had conceived. Secondly, Catholic Easter communions, now obligatory, were, for the *nouveaux convertis*, often forced and sacrilegious. Even without their ministers, the Protestants could still read the words of St Paul: 'He who eats the bread or drinks the cup of the Lord in an unworthy manner shall be guilty towards the body and blood of the Lord.' They could put this alongside Christ's warnings: 'All sin and blasphemy will be forgiven, but blasphemy against the Holy Spirit will not be pardoned.' Thirdly, more than had been the case previously, French Protestants (who would regard France's defeat as the hope of a return to the Edict of Nantes) would look like the *parti de l'étranger*. Fourthly, the revolt of the Camisards would contribute to France's difficulties and the burdens of war. Fifthly, with the emigration of 200,000 Protestants, the country weakened its demographic base and lost an economic, social and intellectual elite. Finally, France's enemies – Prussia, the United Provinces,

Great Britain – gained more than France lost. The Refuge Galli-
cized Europe, but strengthened the host countries and reinforced
their hostilities towards France.

There were, on the other hand, an equal number of favourable
consequences to consider: first, in abolishing the edict, the king
had returned to the traditional rules of French public law.
Secondly, he was no longer in breach of the oath which he had
taken at his consecration. Henry IV had never troubled to
amend his legislation and Louis XIII had only taken half-
measures. Thirdly, religious unity, the ideal of the reign and the
obsession of the clergy, was attained, even if more in theory than
in practice. Fourthly, national unity was reinforced. Louis XIV
had bound the episcopate, clergy, urban notables and people
more closely to the king and the state. This consensus would be
more apparent in 1709 when the monarch called for mobilization
against the invader. The rush to arms of the military and civilian
populations between Malplaquet in 1709 and Denain in 1712
can only be explained by the spirit of this new-won union. It was
no longer the alliance of throne and altar, but the alliance of
throne, altar and people. Fifthly, the Edict of Fontainebleau
completed the conquest of the hearts and minds of the more
Catholic of the conquered provinces. Spanish agents in Flanders
and Franche Comté had tried in vain to contrapose fidelity to the
Catholic King, champion of the Counter-Reformation, with the
compromises of the Most Christian King, guarantor of civil
toleration. The contrast had now evaporated: committed
Catholics in Lille or Besançon would have little hesitation in
collaborating with the 'restorer of altars'. Finally, from the
beginning of the War of the Spanish Succession, France, in
the persons of Louis XIV and Philippe duc d'Anjou, possessed
the necessary religious components for winning the throne in
Madrid and the war in Spain. Under the regime of the Edict of
Nantes, Philip V would have encountered the same obstacles as
Napoleon did in 1808. Indeed, he would possibly not even have
been designated as his successor by Charles II of Spain.

FALSE NOTES

Even before the Revocation, perceptive individuals had doubted
whether the real number of conversions coincided with the

administration's triumphalist enumeration. One might cite Sourches' commentary on the *dragonnades* of 1685: 'The *dragonnades* thus achieved more conversions in one week than the missionaries in a whole year ... The method of conversion was somewhat novel, but it achieved good results and, if the conversion of the older generation was not entirely sincere, at least the children were surely won over.'

A fortnight after the promulgation of the Edict of Fontainebleau, news began to flood into the court. Bishops, administrators and soldiers were forced to admit some regrettable errors. Louis was made aware of the limits to the effectiveness of the new legislation. On 5 November, he wrote to the Archbishop of Paris:

> We should not have imagined that everything would pass off perfectly smoothly from the beginning. We must, as you have well observed, give every consideration to the *nouveaux convertis* of good faith, arouse the ardour of the indifferent through education and use the law against those who relapse. Time and the diligence of the bishops and labourers [the missionaries, workers in the harvest for the Lord ...] will do the rest, with God's help. As for myself, I shall leave nothing undone in the accomplishment of my duty. (179)

Fénelon was perhaps alone among the French Catholics in assessing the consequences of these constraints. He weighed up the effects of the violation of consciences and the violence used and wrote to Bossuet on 8 March 1686: 'Those of this sect who are left will fall little by little into indifference with regard to the external practice of religion, and this should make us apprehensive. If we wished to make them abjure Christianity and follow the Koran, we would merely have to send in the dragoons ... It is an awesome fount for future ferment within the realm.' (261)

Nevertheless, the numbers of 'conversions' rose by leaps and bounds. Missions continued and the distribution of books intensified. Between October 1685 and January 1687, seventeen Parisian booksellers delivered 160,000 catechisms, 128,000 copies of the *Imitation of Christ*, 148,000 copies in translation of the New Testament and 126,000 Psalters, in all over half a million volumes (230). Printers made their fortunes. The *nouveaux convertis* were to be assailed by this propaganda. The king was besieged by inaccurate reports, just as before the edict.

The bishops deliberately misrepresented things, in both word and deed, and by omission. The intendants lied through misplaced enthusiasm. In early 1700, Le Gendre, intendant of Montauban, assured the king that 'not a day passes without my conducting five or six *nouveaux convertis* to Mass', and claimed that he used 'mildness with the reasonable amongst them'. If his despatches are to be believed, he only employed severity against the recalcitrant. Twelve months later, this same intendant found it 'marvellous to behold churches which were empty a year ago now filled with people'. Montauban, citadel of Calvinism, had become the first town 'to set a good example after having been an object of scandal for so long'. In reality, Le Gendre had used mostly repressive means, and the conversions, so portentously announced, only existed in an imagination dictated by his desire to flatter the government. In 1704, a priest signalled the progress of clandestine Protestant worship: 'This', he wrote, 'is the result of the imprisonments, fines, frequent insults and continual threats used by M. Le Gendre.' Montauban is but one example among many. It would be possible to draw up similar dossiers for Sedan, Normandy, Saintonge, Poitou, Guyenne, the Vivarais and Dauphiné. Individual intendants preferred either the use of severity or the use of persuasion, but everywhere the two went hand in hand. The worst-affected regions were those where the king's agents and the local bishop joined forces in order to justify their remarkable statistics. Basville was far from being the worst offender. In the midst of the Camisard war, he wrote: 'I shall always believe in winning over the heart, where religion dwells, and in employing the gentlest methods.' (117)

Between 1689 and 1697, and again between 1702 and 1713, a certain number of Protestants believed that Louis XIV's enemies would force him to re-establish the regime of the Edict of Nantes. Amongst French Catholics, on the other hand, the partisans of this belief could have been counted on the fingers of two hands. The most notable amongst them was Vauban; but the king took no notice of his opinion on this issue. Even if Louis had come to believe that he had committed a political error in 1685, he would have judged it dangerous to revoke the Edict of Fontainebleau. Lamoignon de Basville criticized the Revocation in private, but thought that, in the face of European opinion, it was impossible to undo what had been done. The only solution was to apply the law firmly, humanely and intelligently (117).

Louis was not unintelligent. The death of Harlay in 1695 rid him of one of his evil geniuses. The contradictions between the intendants' despatches, the bishops' and missionaries' letters, and the reports from his agents made him guard against excessive optimism. The revolt of the Camisards in 1702 made a great impression on him. But the failure of Montrevel, the 'burner of houses', to tame the revolt in the Cévennes struck him even more deeply. It was no coincidence that Louis replaced Montrevel with Villars. In less than eight months, between April and November 1704, the latter transformed the situation. 'It is well known how Villars inaugurated a new system and how, by combining humanity and firmness, by talking for the first time of clemency and forgiveness towards a people fanaticized by suffering, he created a general respite.' (112) On 6 November, Fléchier, Bishop of Nîmes, wrote: 'You are right, Monsieur, to congratulate yourself on the tranquillity which we enjoy at present. There is no more killing or burning and the roads are almost completely safe. Most of the fanatics are surrendering with their arms.' (39) After 1704, the 'crossing of the desert' would be less harsh for many Protestants. But who will ever know how many consciences had been bullied and how many forced communions had been sacrilegious? Forced communion was no longer a question of policy or favourable occasion. Even in those times when the Protestants held fast to their roots and the Counter Reformation was ablaze with fire and fury, the authorities did not practice this 'brutal intercommunion'. The logic of the Revocation had led the Most Christian King to be the godfather to tens of thousands of sacrilegious acts.

22

The Ten Years' War

THE WAR which began in 1688 originated, superficially, in
Louis XIV's quasi-legal annexations or Reunions. These
had been intended, however, as a means to avoid war. The
Palatinate affair provided the pretext, although the plan for a
'Glorious Revolution' to restore Protestantism at the English
court predated the French assault on Philippsburg. The great
land-battles, such as Fleurus, Steenkerke and Neerwinden, seize
the limelight, but the war was won and lost at sea. Too many
conventional ideas shield from us the reality of this conflict,
which was baroque and paradoxical, but, in many respects,
foreshadowed more modern forms of warfare.

Numerous authors have depicted the war as provoked by an
imperialism emanating from Versailles, although they contradict themselves when they nevertheless call it the 'War of the
League of Augsburg'. The league put together at Augsburg on 9
July 1686 between the emperor, Sweden, the Duke of Bavaria
and Spain, and reinforced by the Elector Palatine on 2 September and then subsequently by Victor Amadeus, pretended to be
for the maintenance of the Truce of Ratisbon. But its adherents
were tied to the United Provinces, England and Brandenburg.
These reinforcements made it a European league, lacking only
the adhesion of Denmark. It can only be interpreted as an
intimidatory move against France. But the signatories to the
coalition were clever enough to issue declarations which
emphasized peace and the status quo, whilst Louis XIV,
Croissy, Louvois and Vauban had been openly pursuing the
quite opposite policy since 1679 of 'aggressive defence' (165).

THE FALL OF JAMES II

Politically, the weak point in Europe was in Great Britain. Louis and Croissy had been aware of this since the accession of James II. Charles II had irritated many of his subjects by his private life and his authoritarianism; but his conversion to Catholicism had been kept a secret. His brother was quite different. The former Duke of York practised a militant 'popery'. Although he succeeded Charles II in February 1685 without difficulty, this was because his second marriage was childless. He would be succeeded by one of his daughters, Mary or Anne, both of whom were Protestant, the elder being married to William of Orange. This explains the failures of Monmouth's rebellion in England and Argyll's in Scotland. The royal prerogative was maintained. But this loyalism did not last. The new king piled error upon error, and to such a degree that, within three years, Protestant opinion had turned almost entirely against him. He installed Catholic worship in the queen's chapel, sent an ambassador to Rome in 1686, attracted Catholic regular orders and a Jesuit college to London, sacked his most Anglican ministers and promoted into senior positions in the government Catholics such as the Duke of Tyrconnell, Lord Deputy of Ireland. By publishing, on 14 April 1687, the (first) Declaration of Indulgence, which exempted Catholics and Nonconformists from the Test Acts, he not only angered the Established Church, Parliament and the man in the street, but also annoyed Nonconformists by lumping them together with papists. Nor was the dissolution of Parliament on 12 July destined to win over the population. Thereafter, nothing went his way. Whilst he made deals with Holland, public opinion was calling him an accomplice of Louis XIV, and he narrowly escaped being held responsible for the Revocation of the Edict of Nantes.

By 1687, James II's fate was sealed. William fostered his contacts in England and waited for the right moment to intervene. Louis XIV was aware of this and tried to warn his cousin; but he was not believed. 'From this moment, the majority of Nonconformists and many Anglicans saw the Prince of Orange as the protector of public liberties and the Protestant religion.' (271) Several months later, the same was true of the majority of Anglicans. The second Declaration of Indulgence was published in May 1688, and seven bishops, including the Archbishop of

Canterbury, having refused to publish it from their pulpits, were put on trial – their acquittal on 10 July was greeted with great rejoicing. But the most decisive event was the birth of a Prince of Wales on 20 June, James Edward, son of James II and Mary of Modena, baptized by a Catholic priest. The Protestant succession was compromised. Even those Englishmen least attracted by William of Orange now hoped for his intervention. On 10 July, seven leading figures, including Compton, Bishop of London, launched an appeal to the stadholder in the name of 'nineteen twentieths' of the British people. The Glorious Revolution had begun. It awaited the landing of the Prince of Orange. James, for his part, did exactly what was required of him to assist it. Not content with refusing Louis XIV's help, he repudiated it. *Quos vult perdere dementat . . .*

Up until this moment, Louis XIV had committed no errors. He could not give assistance where it was rejected. But he had underestimated the strength of William of Orange and the weakness of his English cousin. Like him, he did not think that the admirals of the Royal Navy would betray the ex-Duke of York who used to lead them into battle. This explains his decision to attack the Palatinate whilst the stadholder was occupied in his English expedition. Louvois and Chamlay saw in this 'the surest method of achieving a lasting peace' (271). They were making a great mistake: William would be the master of the game; James II would demonstrate his incompetence; French troop movements in the Rhineland would encourage the Dutch to support the Prince of Orange; and, finally, far from striking fear into the empire, the French adventure would succeed only in driving the princes away from the old League of the Rhine.

No chancellery could have predicted the course of the Glorious Revolution. On 10 October 1688, William of Nassau launched a double proclamation, one for England and the second for Scotland. On 14 November, he embarked at the head of 15,000 men and eventually landed at Torbay. James II, with his army of 40,000, did not even try to bar his way. He took flight on the night of 20–21 December, was arrested, and fled again on 2 January 1689, with the tacit complicity of his son-in-law, who had no intention of becoming a Cromwell. On 23 February, a Declaration of Rights was read out at Whitehall, forming the charter for a monarchy restored to its traditions, whilst the crown of 'England, France and Ireland' was offered to Prince

William and his wife Mary. The coronation took place at West-
minster on the 21 April. Eighteen months later, with Ireland
subdued, William III was the master of the situation.

Louis XIV took pity on his cousin, welcomed him at Saint-
Germain, and left the château to him. The town would be
inhabited by Jacobites, faithful to the exiled monarch, a restless,
gallant little group, eager for revenge and cultivating their illusions and prejudices. The presence of the Stuart king and the
Jacobite refugees would weigh upon France and influence
events. A Jacobite card could perhaps be of use politically, and
anything which could be done to support the partisans of the
Stuarts in the British Isles was a point scored against the coalition. On an emotional level, monarchical solidarity came into
play: Louis XIV tried in vain to interest Charles II of Spain in
the fate of the dethroned king. But the exiles were poor advisers.
They put forward a distorted picture of England, Ireland and
Scotland, and encouraged the king to risk his ships and his men
in a highly unlikely landing and restoration. The disappointment of 1690, the defeat of La Hougue in 1692 and the failure in
Scotland in 1708 were all part of the Jacobite project. The
marquis de Chamlay was perhaps not wrong in preferring to
carry the war to the borders of the Holy Roman Empire.

EUROPE AGAINST FRANCE

'This is the greatest war that a king of France will ever have on
his hands', affirmed the comte de Rabutin (96). The war was
waged by Holland (26 November 1688), the empire (December)
and Frederick III of Brandenburg (January 1689). The destruction of the Palatinate led to the adherence of the Elector of
Bavaria (4 May). By mid-April, France and Spain were at war,
and, on 17 May, England declared war on France. Even Sweden
was, at least officially, in the German-Dutch camp. In theory,
Louis XIV's enemies possessed superior forces – on land,
220,000 soldiers as against 150,000. The French navy was the
biggest in the world, but with fewer vessels than the combined
forces of the maritime powers and Spain. Since the raising of the
siege of Vienna in 1683, the emperor had regained his authority
within the empire. The sinews of war were supplied by William
of Orange's sleeping partners: the merchants of Amsterdam and

London. The coalition partners had enough resources to be able to distribute 'subsidies to the rather hesitant smaller princes' (165). Finally, other countries were still undecided; the Duke of Savoy joined the coalition in June 1690.

But Louis' enemies had their weaknesses too. 'Each went his own way, forgot his promises, neglected the general aims of the war and looked after his own interests.' (271) The King of Spain did not rush to send his troops to the Low Countries. The Turks were still a threat to the emperor. Savoy was not strong enough to defeat Catinat. Even Orange, so determined to succeed, was far from possessing Louis' resources. In the British Isles, he had to take account of a suspicious Parliament, the Irish and the Jacobites too. In Holland, he did not enjoy the consistent support of the notables, with their republican spirit.

The coalition's troops were not without strengths. The English fought valiantly. The Imperialists had been battle-hardened in the Turkish war. Hatred of France spurred on the Spanish, Dutch, Lorrainers and Palatines, whilst Huguenots like Schomberg lent their support to the enemies of their former homeland. Each of these armies eventually adopted the technical innovations promoted by Louvois. On the other hand, it was a coalition worthy of Babel: nations, languages and religions stood side by side without having adequate reasons to co-ordinate their tactics or harmonize their war-aims. Finally, the general staffs were neither as efficient nor as competent as the French one. Louis-William of Baden was no Montecuccoli, and neither was the Elector of Bavaria. William III, often defeated, although formidable in his tenacity and determination, was a special case. The only gifted general in the imperial camp was the Duke of Lorraine, Charles V, but he died on 18 April 1690.

In contrast to the diversity of the enemy stood French unity. Here a sovereign 'commanded alone, with no obstacles and without protest ... served by a nation which understood the perils, ready for full military and financial effort' (271). The king united in his person political, strategic and tactical authority. He made mistakes, but he was obeyed and could impose an effective overall strategy. At the beginning of the war he could rely on two extraordinary individuals – Louvois, the organizer of victories on land, and Seignelay, who ran the navy – who served him 'with complete devotion'. Seignelay was to die in 1690 and Louvois in 1691, but the naval divisions and regiments over which they had presided lost none of their valour. Alongside the prince and his ministers, the great technicians played a decisive role: Bonrepaux in the navy and Chamlay, one of Louis XIV's most skilled collaborators, in the armies. The commanders were of high quality. After the retirement of Duquesne, Tourville was seen as the greatest naval commander of his time. Châteaurenault was a 'lucky' leader. And numerous squadron chiefs and captains were good tacticians, not to mention the privateers tempted out of port by the progress of the war. The land armies had a great captain in the maréchal de Luxembourg, emulator of Condé, three excellent seconds-in-command in maréchal de Lorge, Turenne's nephew, the patient Catinat and the courageous M. de Boufflers, and a master of the art of siege warfare in Vauban, whilst the future commanders-in-chief of the Spanish war, Vendôme and Villars, earned their spurs.

The demands of war did not diminish French political activity in Europe. Louis XIV released propaganda, distributed subsidies and encouraged alliances to the rear of the enemy – with the Turks, and the 'malcontents' in Hungary, led by Thököli. Similarly, as in the Dutch War, the king sought suitable occasions for negotiations. In the summer of 1692, after the victory at Steenkerke, emissaries began to explore the terrain. Unlike William of Orange, Louis did not have the plunderer's instinct.

A STRING OF VICTORIES

That the war should have begun with the destruction of the Palatinate was, therefore, all the more embarrassing. It tarnished the reputation acquired by Monseigneur in the surrender of Philippsburg in October 1688. It caused enduring damage to the reputation of Louvois, even though the worst excesses, the despoliation of the castle at Heidelberg and the tombs of the Electors Palatine there, were not committed until 1693, two years after his death.

Amidst the interminable sieges, France notched up victories. On 1 July 1690 at Fleurus, the maréchal de Luxembourg, at the head of 35,000 soldiers, crushed Waldeck's army of 50,000 Dutch and imperial troops. 'Eight thousand prisoners, six thousand dead,' wrote Voltaire, 'two hundred flags and standards, cannon, baggage, the flight of the enemy – such were the signs of victory.' (112) Seven weeks later, on 18 August, it was Catinat's turn when he cut the Savoyard army to pieces at Staffarde. 'The French army lost only three hundred men; that of the allies, commanded by the Duke of Savoy, lost four thousand.' (112) On that day, Victor Amadeus lost all his duchy except for Montmélian, leaving the way open to Piedmont and the county of Nice.

The year 1691 was less spectacular, but Catinat seized Villefranche, Nice and Montmélian, and, on the Low Countries front, Luxembourg beat Waldeck at Leuze against heavy odds. In June of the following year, Louis XIV, assisted by Vauban and protected by Luxembourg's army, personally took the town and then the castle of Namur. Racine wrote a prose account of the occasion: 'In five weeks, he captured a place which the greatest captains in Europe had thought impregnable.' His colleague Boileau, an occasional historiographer, wrote, for his part, an *Ode on the Seizure of Namur*. On 3 August, Mars offered the victory, not to the king, but to his stalwart lieutenant, Luxembourg. Steenkerke was a true 'battle among the nations': William of Orange commanded an army consisting of Spanish, English, Dutch and German troops. The fiercely contested encounter lasted from 8.30 a.m. until 12.30 p.m. It was an infantry fight which turned France's way when the French attacked 'swords in hand, with the princes of the blood at their head' (71), overcoming all obstacles and tearing the enemy infantry to pieces. The news reached Versailles the next day at 10 p.m. The maréchal de Luxembourg had taken 1,200 prisoners and 10 cannon and had killed 8,000 enemy soldiers. 'This great news gave the king enormous satisfaction.' (97)

In reality, the battle had not been entirely decisive and William III had been able to retreat. But the effect on morale, with Luxembourg's overcoming his illness in order to give orders and the glorious charge of His Majesty's cousins, was considerable. 'Monsieur le Duc, the prince de Conti, Monsieur de Vendôme and their friends found the roads lined with people on their return. Acclamations of joy verged on the ecstatic. Women pressed forward to catch a glimpse. Men wore lace cravats at that period, over which they took great time and trouble, but the princes, dressing hastily for the battle, had just thrown theirs around their necks. Women now wore ornaments modelled on these, known as *steinkerques*. All new jewellery was *à la steinkerque*

(112). Overcome by the spirit of emulation, Lorge defeated Charles of Württemberg at Pforzheim on 17 September.

The year 1693 occupies a rather more important position in French military history. On 27 March, the king promoted seven commanders to the rank of marshal, including Catinat, and, on 10 May, he created the royal and military order of St Louis. The combatants responded to these honours: Tourville was victorious at Lagos on 27 June, Luxembourg at Neerwinden on 29 July and Catinat at Marsiglia on 4 October. At Neerwinden, Luxembourg once against faced the Prince of Orange, this time but a few miles from Brussels. Once more, the battle was fiercely fought, with charge following charge. Luxembourg, M. le Duc, the prince de Conti and the duc de Chartres personally led the assaults. As at Steenkerke, the *furia francese* won the day. 'Few battles were more deadly', wrote Voltaire. 'About twenty thousand were killed: twelve thousand on the allied side and eight on the French.' Luxembourg showed himself a 'great general' (159). At court, 'the king is beside himself with pleasure, as are all the ministers, at the grandeur of this action' (90). On 4 October, the maréchal de Catinat justified his new rank by defeating Victor Amadeus of Savoy at Marsiglia, a victory made the more distinguished by the fact that he was pitched against, among others, the talented Prince Eugene of Savoy, son of Olympe Mancini.

It is customary for historians to pause at this point, as if worn out by so many pitched battles, in order to philosophize about the war. They point out the deceptive nature of its victories. But the same authors also condemn siege warfare, judging it worth nothing more than to flatter a prince. If siege warfare was worthless, and pitched battles hardly more significant, how could combatants like Louis XIV have waged war at all? The point of view is at once ingenuous and magnanimous. From the comfort of his study, the historian discovers that war is cruel, that cannon kill and that great captains may be overtaken by events. The pace of events, a kind of Tolstoyan reality, spurred on someone like William of Orange, making of him, despite adverse circumstances, a man of war like Turenne, Luxembourg, Vendôme, Tourville and Boufflers. Or like the old king himself. Louis XIV only retired from the command of his armies in 1693, and Saint-Simon, who had resigned at the age of twenty-seven, reproached him for it. But we should recall that his first campaign had been in 1650 and that he only stepped down after forty-three years of military service.

Although Louis XIV should not be called to account for ceasing to play the general, he was guilty, having equipped France with the finest fleet in its history, of putting it to such poor use between 1689 and 1692. A navy was an instrument of glory but should have also been an essential element in strategy. In 1688, His Majesty's was the most important in the world, technically highly proficient, accustomed to life at sea, battle hardened and well trained. It was capable of carrying out a variety of tasks: policing the Mediterranean, neutralizing the Spanish galleys, defending the colonies, escort duties, transport, fighting in squadrons. Was it really necessary to transport James II and 1,200 men to Ireland to reinforce Tyrconnell's 36,000 followers? That is what was asked of a division commanded by Gabaret in March 1689. Should not munitions and reinforcements also have been sent to Ireland? This happened in May under Châteaurenault, and he succeeded in immobilizing Herbert's twenty-four vessels in Bantry Bay. The king's navy carried out its orders. If James II, having entered Dublin on 3 April, did not succeed in disciplining the Irish, then that was his own fault.

Louis XIV liked fleets, but he understood little about the sea. He moved squadrons around on a map in the way that he organized the marches and counter-marches of his land armies. He thought that, despite winds and tides, insufficient numbers of sailors, failures of quartermasters or shortages of stores, a time-table could be followed. It was a constant gamble, especially when it meant moving Mediterranean vessels into the English Channel. His ministers did their best, particularly Seignelay, who got the king to sign the important naval ordinance of 15 April 1689, and even Pontchartrain. But their weakness was that they remained jurists and bureaucrats, and consulted other bureaucrats, such as Bonrepaux, rather than listening to some competent seamen, such as Nesmond and Villette. The British Admiralty was still far from being perfect, but in London sailors worked alongside administrators and gave them the benefit of regular advice.

For Louis XIV, the results were disappointing. The king, believing James II's reports, thought that Ireland could be the base for a reconquest of England. The correct decision would have been to ask Châteaurenault to sail round the Irish coast to stop 'Dutch Billy' from landing and dislodging his father-in-law, and to provide the French expedition with a squadron by way of reinforcement. The wrong decision having been taken, the only real hope for the Stuart cause lay in sending Tourville in the spring of 1690 to help the dethroned king and cut William III off from the mainland. Instead of which, on the day when William, with the aid of Schomberg (who was killed in the battle), crushed the Irish on the banks of the Boyne (10 July 1690), the fleet commanded by Tourville was confronting the Dutch and British squadrons off Beachy Head, some 375 miles away. Furthermore, dissatisfied with their vice-admiral (who had destroyed a ship during the battle and fifteen more in the pursuit), the king, the minister and the court taxed Tourville with faint-heartedness for not having sailed up the Thames and bombarded London. To have attempted such an exploit with a fleet worn out by a hard fight would have been madness. Instead of haggling over the glory of the victor of Beachy Head, the French government would have been better advised to support suffering Ireland.

The following year, the plans thought up by Louis XIV and Pontchartrain for naval warfare were no better. Limerick, besieged by the Prince of Orange, was abandoned, and Tourville was given a role which was not even that of diversion. In the event of a meeting, Tourville was only supposed to attack from a position of superiority. He was expected to carry out two contradictory tasks: to defend the coasts and to capture a large convoy coming from Smyrna. He performed the first admirably and, instead of the ships from the Mediterranean, he seized the Jamaica convoy. Above all, he 'master-minded the so-called open-sea campaign, a master-stroke of tactical skill, in the course of which he was at sea for fifty days [from May to August 1691], deceiving the English squadrons' (274). However, the court continued to deplore the vice-admiral's prudence and his propensity for disobedience. Châteaurenault's squadron meanwhile escorted the 12,000 survivors of James II's army to Brest in November, in accordance with the terms of the surrender of Limerick.

There was no question of slackening the pace in 1692. A

council of war was presided over by Louis XIV on 13 February which brought together James II, Pontchartrain, the comte de Tourville, Gabaret, d'Amfreville and Châteaurenault in order to determine the operations of the fleet (26). Unfortunately, this operational committee, in which seamen were permitted to offer their opinions, was an exceptional occasion, and the plan eventually decided upon was the product of landlubbers. The idea was to capitalize on the growing unpopularity of William III and to land, under James II's command, twelve Irish battalions and nine French battalions (assembled at La Hougue), and a corps of cavalry, a small amount of artillery and provisions (gathered together at Le Havre), on the English coast. The exiled king, who was in continual contact with the other side of the Channel, sometimes with important figures such as Malborough, fantasized about a British fleet ready to rally to the legitimate sovereign, and imagined that the beaches would be black with Jacobites ready to welcome him back. This was a delusion: the Jacobites were numerous but scattered, faithful but wary, ready to rally to a cause which had been won but not to risk death or imprisonment to help such a hazardous enterprise. The more audacious amongst them, those prepared to sacrifice their lives in a noble cause, were also deplorably talkative. The comings and goings of messengers and the intemperate declarations of these heroes made secrecy impossible. Yet the landing needed discretion.

The plans went as follows: the naval contingent commanded by Tourville was to gather at Brest and get under way in April, before the preparations of the Dutch and English fleets were completed. In fact, they only set sail on 12 May. This armada was supposed to include the Levant squadron under d'Estrées, which in fact only arrived after the battle. That of Rochefort, under M. de Villette, did arrive on time, but, on the other hand, not everything was in readiness, even at Brest, and Tourville, ordered to make haste, gave the orders to set sail, leaving Châteaurenault with twenty as yet unarmed vessels unable to join him. The navy was supposed to take the infantry on board at La Hougue and to protect the heavy transport at Le Havre. It was then supposed to conduct all these forces to the other side of the Channel, a technically delicate operation. If the enemy fleet opposed them, Tourville was ordered to fight whatever the odds. These arrangements were not as absurd as they might seem. If d'Estrées had arrived on time, he would have taken charge of the landing fleet with Tourville as cover. The tasks of the convoy and the battle fleet would thus have been divided. But when the Mediterranean vessels did not arrive, everything was left to chance. The provocative nature of the instructions sent to Tourville reflects the king's lack of confidence in his vice-admiral and also indicates the confusion between naval and army tactics. On land, as Turenne had proved, battles could be won against armies twice as strong. At sea, this was almost unthinkable.

If Louis XIV, who was going to war in Flanders, had been content with such hazardous arrangements, this would not have been so very serious. Unfortunately, the king and Pontchartrain came up with the idea of installing at La Hougue a trio of commanders with full powers. This triumvirate appears similar to Georges Dumézil's Indo-European triad, with James II as Jupiter, Bellefonds as a sixty-year-old Mars, spoiling for a fight, and Bonrepaux as Quirinus. None of them was a seaman – James II had forgotten all that he had learnt as Duke of York. The commanders all thought as landlubbers. Moreover, if we imagine a naval theatre running from Brest to Le Havre, how could the small boats carrying orders be expected to find the *Soleil Royal*, the admiral's superb vessel with its 104 cannon, in order to transmit his latest orders on time? This is precisely what went wrong. The triumvirate, learning that the enemy fleets had joined forces, and realizing, too late, that the British commanders would remain faithful to William and Mary, gave the order to abandon the whole enterprise. That order never arrived. With 44 vessels and 3,100 guns, Tourville attacked 98 enemy ships armed with 7,100 cannon off Barfleur on 29 May 1692 at 10 a.m. He began his assault 'like a madman', said Bonrepaux, who once again was a bad judge. Tourville attacked because his courage had been put in doubt, because he had admirable support, because the wind stood in his favour, and because an offensive was the only way of compensating for the imbalance in the forces. The battle, led by Tourville, Villette, Nesmond and Coëtlogon, lasted twelve hours. At ten o'clock at night, fog caused a lull in the fighting. 'Not one French ship had rendered its colours, not one had been sunk [on the other hand, one English and one Dutch vessel had been scuttled]. This extraordinary result was the strongest indication of military spirit and valour which could have been provided by a navy.' This was the judgement of Admiral Mahan (228).

The retreat was nevertheless inevitable, albeit hampered by damage to the *Soleil Royal*, which the admiral was reluctant to leave behind, as well as by sluggish and variable winds and by the absence of a port at Cherbourg. Twenty-seven vessels managed to reach Brest, twenty-two by sailing round Raz Blanchard, three by audaciously hugging the coast of England, and two others, commanded by Nesmond, by sailing all the way round the British Isles. Two vessels reached the arsenal at Le Havre. The fifteen others were condemned to destruction, as if to compensate for the Anglo-Dutch losses at Beachy Head in 1690. Three large ships, crippled by too much damage, M. de Machault-Belmont's *Triomphant* (seventy-six guns), the chevalier de Beaujeu's *Admirable* (ninety guns) and the *Soleil Royal*, pride of the navy, found a precarious refuge under the batteries of Cherbourg, where they would be destroyed by enemy fireships.

Tourville, by then aboard the *Ambitieux*, could forge a course to Saint-Malo for only twenty-two of his ships. A victim of changing currents, becalmings and changes of wind and forced to lose anchors in order to escape from pursuers, he found himself off the coast near La Hougue with twelve vessels, all of which deserved a better fate. On 2 June, the English and Dutch moved in for the kill aboard 200 small boats and dinghies, attacking the six vessels close by the fort at Ilet. Tourville, Villette and Coëtlogon led an impossible defence, and were unable to prevent the burning of their ships. On the following day, the six others met the same fate. The *Ambitieux, Merveilleux, Magnifique, Foudroyant, Fier, Fort, Tonnant, Terrible, Gaillard, Saint-Philippe, Saint-Louis* and *Bourbon* were burnt and sunk.

Under the gaze of the agitated Bonrepaux, M. de Tourville had been forced into the sacrifice of these ships. Throughout the battle at Barfleur, he had shown, according to Villette, 'what possessing the character of a hero means'. He had obeyed the king's orders to attack at all costs. But glory in victory means little and true heroism is shown under adversity. Here, lacking adequate orders, their commander was forced to accept the destruction of the best ships in his fleet in the course of four days. Then, 'with no complaints and without regrets, he organized the rescue operations and guided the marines to shore'* whilst the pyre of his burning ships lit up the evening sky across the bay.

'THE NAVY IN ITS SPLENDOUR'

It has become conventional to ignore the glory of Barfleur in favour of the disappointment of La Hougue and to consider it all as a terrible defeat – a legend which persists to this day. Contemporaries judged events differently. France's adversaries had lost sixteen vessels off Beachy Head;† two years later, the French in turn lost fifteen. This was far from dishonourable. Moreover, La Hougue was less an allied victory than a triumph of adverse winds and tides. When the king received Tourville, he judged the situation correctly. The courtiers expected him to upbraid the unfortunate vice-admiral, imagining some *Vare, legiones redde.*‡ Louis XIV, having reproached Tourville for a lack of daring, would today surely crush him with a contemptuous silence. To general surprise, the king said: 'I am entirely happy with your conduct and with all the navy; we have been defeated, but you have earned glory, both for yourself and for the nation. It has cost us some ships, but this will be put to rights during the coming year, and assuredly we will defeat the enemy.' (26) The following March (1693), Tourville received a marshal's baton, an honour rare in the navy. On 27 June, he justified his master's confidence by winning the victory of Lagos.

The harsh winter of 1693 pushed naval strategic plans for the invasion of England into the background. Although the king, his minister Louis de Pontchartrain, Vauban, and several others were by then thinking primarily of waging war on commerce, this was not in order to forget La Hougue, but in order to adapt to circumstances. England and its Parliament, and Louis XIV and his ministers, had begun to grasp the costly nature of naval warfare. In France, a success helped to justify the new tactics. In the spring of 1693, 200 ships laden with merchandise were proceeding towards Smyrna, escorted by English and Dutch vessels.

---

* La Varende.
† Less at Beachy Head itself than in the ensuing pursuit. Some authors even speak of seventeen vessels lost in the encounter.
‡ 'Varus, return my legions to me' – according to Suetonius, the words of Emperor Augustus upon being told of Publius Quinctilius Varus' defeat and death in Germany.

Taking or destroying them would strike a great blow at the British economy. Tourville therefore camouflaged his vessels in the port of Lagos, attacked and sank several Dutch ships and then scattered the squadron. 'This first success struck fear into the enemy fleet. They dispersed and fled in confusion to Cadiz and Gibraltar. They were pursued vigorously right under the cannon of these two forts. Seventy-five vessels were taken, burnt or sunk, and twenty-seven were escorted to Provence.' (71)

A year later, in June 1694, the first victory at the Texel, which earned Jean Bart his noble title, became a symbol of government activity against food shortages. A medal proclaimed the fact: *France supplied with wheat by the king, after the defeat of a Dutch squadron* (71). The famous Dunkerquois, a privateer turned regular captain in 1689, had created 'a war tactic based on the use of divisions of light and manœuvrable frigates, a kind of prefiguring of the submarine packs in the Second World War' (274). He struck terror into the seamen of the United Provinces, who were not easily impressed. In 1692, he had destroyed eighty of their fishing smacks. Now he brought off the most remarkable exploit of his career. The court learnt of it at His Majesty's *lever* on Monday, 5 July 1694. In order to feed his kingdom, hard hit by two harsh winters and a general dearth, Louis XIV had bought enormous quantities of wheat in Poland. 'In order to ensure its transportation, it was carried by Swedish and Danish vessels, whose neutrality allowed them to trade freely throughout Europe.' (71) On 29 June, when Bart set out with six frigates to escort this convoy, he found it being inspected by eight Dutch ships. With scant regard for his relative weakness and without even returning their cannon-fire, Bart boarded the Dutch vice-admiral's ship and captured it. His little squadron took two other vessels, put the rest to flight, and returned to Dunkirk with its prizes and thirty merchants. Eighty ships carrying cereals continued on to Calais, Dieppe and Le Havre under the noses of the English. 'This action', Dangeau commented, 'is most renowned for Bart, most useful to the state, and gave the king great satisfaction.'

Whilst so many writers, from Fénelon to the present century, have added the misfortunes of war to the horrors of famine, it should be stressed rather that, thanks to the king, Pontchartrain and these seamen, success in naval warfare attenuated the effects of the 'disordered seasons'. In any case, the image of a monarch so attached to the vaingloriousness of arms that he neglected the welfare of his subjects is inaccurate. The device on the commemorative medal of the first victory at the Texel is worthy of repetition: *France supplied with wheat by the king, after the defeat of a Dutch squadron.* The academicians responsible for it, reflecting an evident concern, placed the useful above the glorious, the civil above the military, the common good above everything else.

Medals celebrated the victories of Luxembourg at Neerwinden and Catinat at Marsiglia, and actions at sea were not neglected. Between 1693 and the Peace of Ryswick, celebratory medals were struck in abundance. One associated the ships of the comte d'Estrées and the galleys of the bailli de Noailles with the capture of Rosas in Catalonia on 9 June 1693. Another depicted the abject failure of the English landing at Brest on 18 June 1694. A third portrayed how Relingues and Bart resisted the bombardment of Dunkirk in August 1695. A fourth (*Treasures of the Indies seized from the enemy*) celebrated privateering activities: 'During the war more than 5,000 Dutch and English ships were captured with all their cargoes.' A fifth praised the second victory at the Texel, won by the chevalier Bart: 'Thirty merchant vessels and three warships burned or captured near the Texel on 18 June 1696.' A sixth celebrated the taking of Carthagena in the Indies by Pointis on 4 May 1697. A seventh evoked the contribution made by d'Estrées' squadron to the taking of Barcelona by Vendôme on 10 August 1697. An eighth recalled previous feats and commemorated the events of the year. A ninth implied naval victories in its title – *France invincible. War fought successfully for ten years, 1697* – whilst the commentary evoked them as it showed the coalition armies unable to breach the frontiers: 'The king alone took the strongest towns of the Low Countries and Catalonia, won many battles on land and sea, and has only been victorious in order to make peace.' (71)

Throughout the war, France was, with its victory at Beachy Head balancing the bitter disappointment at La Hougue, at least the equal of the coalition of maritime powers in the encounters at sea. And it won on points if flexibility in tactics is taken into account, with combined operations, escort duties, attacks on convoys, and harassment of enemy commerce. Contemporaries were aware of this. Dangeau and Sourches never omitted to relate the arrival of news of the navy at court and the celebration which accompanied good news.

The king and Pontchartrain did not wait until the end of hostilities to demonstrate their concern for the navy. From 1693, the public was made aware of it. A medal of this date, celebrating both Rosas and Lagos, bore the device SPLENDOR REI NAVALIS (*The navy in its splendour*). Fifteen or seventeen months after La Hougue, France did not indulge itself in self-pity, because it knew it was a major naval force. At almost the same moment, another naval medal was struck: VIRTUTI NAUTICAE PRAEMIA DATA (*Titles of honour granted for skill in the art of navigation*). Although the Order of St Louis, founded that same year, was intended to honour the navy as well as the army, Louis XIV and Pontchartrain inaugurated specific awards, especially for port officials, naval officers and sailors, to set alongside the crosses of St Louis, which were generally given to the members of the general staffs.

> The king's particular attention to everything concerning the navy kept it in the flourishing condition to which he had raised it. As he always rewarded the valour of even the least of his soldiers, he wanted good sailors and skilful pilots to benefit from his liberality. With this in mind, and to stimulate a noble spirit of competition amongst them, he had medals struck which were awarded to those who had performed the greatest services, and they wore this honourable and public testimony to His Majesty's satisfaction and their services. (71)

These views are confirmed by modern statistics. La Hougue was but a sideshow which posterity has artificially linked with changes in naval strategy. Both before and after La Hougue, Louis XIV's France possessed 'a formidable fighting navy which remained, until 1715, to all intents and purposes, the best in the world' (239). Right up to the Peace of Ryswick, the king and Pontchartrain pursued an immense programme of rearmament. France possessed 132 ships of the line in 1692, 135 in 1696, and 137 in 1697 (237). It would be mistaken to criticize their tactical deployment in these decisive years. A navy was not solely to be used in formal engagements, and the successes of Forbin, Bart and Nesmond in commercial warfare cost the enemy dearer than any hypothetical confrontations between the fleets, as was proven by the complaints of British merchants and leaders, and the decreasing bellicosity of the Dutch. A coalition of the two fleets was needed to save England from invasion and defeat. It was at

Nymwegen probably that Louis' armies appeared at their most puissant, and at the time of Ryswick that his navy was at its strongest.

By 1694, the burden of war was weighing ever more heavily upon the belligerent nations. In England, the stocks of the chartered companies were consistently falling in value, and indirect taxes, despite being greatly increased, were insufficient for the needs of public finance, necessitating a recourse to loans. Jacobite plots accompanied this restless public opinion. The Tories, supported by the gentry and ministers of the Established Church, called for peace. The only positive development was the creation of the Bank of England, granted its charter on 24 July 1694, a bank of issue, the credit of which was placed at the disposition of the state. In France, the controller-general Pontchartrain, who had enjoyed the confidence of the financiers since 1689, had run out of expedients. More a lawyer than an accountant, he had done well to mobilize the resources for a costly war which had lasted for over five years. Now, at the beginning of 1695, he reluctantly decided on the imposition of a new tax, the *capitation* – which, however, only brought in twenty-six million *livres* in that year. It had the non-fiscal advantage, however, that it was imposed upon the entire civil population, including the nobility, and associated the whole people with the fiscal effort, and thus with national defence.

In 1694, operations dragged on in wearisome fashion. Virtually nothing was achieved in Italy or Germany. Noailles had some successes in Catalonia, winning the Battle of Ter on 27 May and taking Palamos and Gerona. In the Low Countries, under the nominal command of Monseigneur, the duc de Luxembourg executed a forced march of 100 miles in four days (22–25 August) which led to the closure of the frontier from the Scheldt to the coast and saved the fortified coastal towns that were being threatened by enemy fleets. Unfortunately, Orange recaptured Huy in September, a disappointment which indicated that the war was far from over. Neither the emperor nor William III, nor yet the King of Spain, had any intention of withdrawing. In response, Louis XIV created several dozen new regiments in November 1695. The visible weariness of the coalition came up against French determination not to surrender, as was shown by the victory of Vendôme and the army of Catalonia over the Prince of Darmstadt on 1 June 1696. The French desire to arrive at a reasonable peace settlement also marked out these months of transition. There was no shortage of negotiations, willed on by Louis XIV. Croissy was forced to undertake them (he died in July 1696) and, taking his place, his son Torcy completed his training. No progress was made in the course of 1695. The emperor was so intransigent that talks were broken off almost before they had begun. Nevertheless, the king pursued discussions with the United Provinces. Its claims remained negotiable. The Dutch wanted Louis XIV to recognize Orange as 'His Majesty the King of Great Britain and Ireland' and accept a new 'barrier' of garrison towns in the Low Countries. But William III broke off the negotiations.

Yet the 'Grand Alliance' was not in good shape. Spain seemed exhausted and, as for the Duke of Savoy, he desired nothing save a separate pacification. Louis XIV surrounded and neutralized him. Victor Amadeus lost Savoy and Nice, but still retained Piedmont, although the presence of the French at Casale was a threat. In theory, the French could have forced him to cede Nice and Savoy to them, but this demand would have led to increased activity in Italy by the emperor. In practice, French diplomacy was extremely skilful. The influence of the young Torcy and the wisdom of the old king amongst those who sought conciliation triumphed over the 'sticklers'. In the secret pact of 29 June 1696, and the Treaty of Turin (29 August), the Piedmontese monarchy was treated not as a defeated enemy but as an ally. France surrendered not just the duchy, Nice and Villefranche, but also Pinerolo, the hinge to the whole frontier system. The Savoyards would reinforce the French armies in attacking Lombardy. If successful, they would gain Milan, a long-established aspiration, and France would receive the duchy of Savoy by way of exchange, a Francophone region of considerable strategic importance. To seal the reconciliation, a marriage was arranged between the fourteen-year-old Duke of Burgundy and Marie-Adelaide of Savoy, who was not yet eleven, the wedding taking place on 7 December 1697.

The abandonment of Pinerolo was a shrewd act on the part of Louis XIV. The Treaty of Turin irritated the emperor, worried

William of Orange and determined Charles II of Spain against intervening in Italy. The entire burden of the war now fell upon a divided England and a far from united United Provinces. Louis understood that the maritime powers now had reasons for not maintaining their intransigence. He informed William that, in exchange for peace, he would recognize him as 'King of Great Britain'. Gratified, the Prince of Orange gave the Dutch a lead, brought pressure to bear upon the emperor, and, ignoring the wishes of the Spanish king for the present, agreed to a peace conference with Louis XIV on 4 February which finally opened at Ryswick on 9 May.

Like all conferences of its kind, the meeting of ambassadors in this village near The Hague did not proceed smoothly. The Spanish wanted a return to the clauses of the Peace of the Pyrenees. The emperor laid claim to Strasbourg and the whole of lower Alsace and wanted a restatement of the relevant clauses of the Peace of Münster of 1648. The Dutch insisted on the urgent necessity of a commercial agreement. It was the emperor, however, who most disturbed the proceedings at Ryswick. He proved so inflexible that, by the end of August, Louis XIV was forced to warn the congress that he would retain control of Strasbourg. It was not, however, merely a question of settling the rights and wrongs as between the idea of a German Rhineland and the modern concept of a French Alsace. Another *casus belli* emerged over the elective throne of Poland, vacant since the death of John Sobieski in 1696. Two candidates had entered the lists: the prince de Conti, cousin to Louis XIV, and Augustus, Elector of Saxony, supported by the empire. Leopold I was all the more aggressive because the Prince of Saxony seemed to be the favourite, and all the more intransigent because his general, Prince Eugene of Savoy, had just succeeded in driving back the Turks. But his hardline attitudes worked against him, and, whilst most of the treaties were signed on 20 and 21 September, peace between France and the empire was not concluded until 30 October.

SANTO DOMINGO AND ALSACE

'The moment decreed by Heaven for the reconciliation of the nations has arrived; Europe is at peace. The ratification of the treaty which my ambassadors concluded recently with those of the emperor and the empire has put the seal on the re-establishment of this tranquillity which everyone has desired.' (59) Thus wrote Louis XIV in a letter to the Archbishop of Paris on 5 January 1698. His diplomats had shown great accommodation and each party could claim to have made some gains. A decade of cruel warfare had ended in a victory for reason. Yet the treaties of 1697 are generally described with reference to an exhausted France, worn out by royal ambition and victim of an agonizing struggle on land and at sea. The king is held responsible for abandoning his conquests and returning to the situation of Nymwegen in 1678 after a pointless war. Less demanding critics refer to it as an 'empty peace'. All agree that it was the beginning of a decline. These assertions are hardly surprising; for, if the Peace of Ryswick had been more advantageous, if Torcy and Pomponne had not made so many concessions on the advice of the king, if Lorraine had not been restored to its dukes, no doubt the 'cynical acquisitions of the *réunions*' would have been deplorable, and Louis XIV a megalomaniac.

The facts contradict these hostile comments. It would have been difficult in 1697 to have made much of the king's ambition, given that it consisted of fighting only for the retention of Strasbourg and Tournai. For four years, he had sought a peaceful resolution, being never a proponent of war at all costs. In the spring of 1697, Fléchier wrote: 'Apparently, we are to enjoy peace, for the king, through religion and the grandeur of his soul, wants to give to each what he thinks is his due. I have no doubt but that the desire to bring relief to his people has led him to satisfy his enemies at a time when he would have been capable of overcoming them. This is a great historical moment.' (39) France probably did show signs of exhaustion. The winters of 1693 and 1694 took their toll. But the coalition powers were also extremely weary. They were discouraged by French successes. On 20 April, Carthagena, one of the richest ports in the West Indies, had surrendered to the siege by Pointis' squadron and the privateering activities of Captain Ducasse. On 5 June, Catinat had taken Ath. During the summer, three armies had lived at the enemy's expense and that of the maréchal de Choiseul had advanced onto German soil. On 10 August, Vendôme accepted the surrender of Barcelona. On 5 September, d'Iberville captured Fort Nelson in Canada. The plenipotentiaries from Versailles had been in a strong position when they signed the accord at Ryswick. The compliments paid the king upon his moderation were not mere flattery. Some of his adversaries would have liked to return to the clauses of Münster or the Pyrenees, but they had to content themselves with those of Nymwegen. Louis XIV returned the bridgeheads at Philippsburg, Kehl and Breisach to the empire. He gave up the Reunions outside Alsace, such as Trier and Montbéliard. He returned Lorraine to its ruler, whilst retaining Longwy and Sarrelouis. Content with a return to the customs of 1664, the United Provinces surrendered Pondicherry. Making careful use of Louis' rights to the succession of Charles II of Spain, his ambassadors treated Spain with indulgence, negotiating only for the exchange of occupied towns. France returned Gerona, Barcelona, Luxembourg, Charleroi, Ath, Mons and Courtrai, whilst retaining the eighty-two towns and villages which together made up 'French Hainaut'. The gains in Hudson Bay were returned to England. The Prince of Orange, once depicted as a kind of Antichrist, now became in official French eyes 'His Majesty William III, King of Great Britain'.

Louis XIV had thus made concessions, but the balance struck in 1697 was a positive one. The treaties dislocated the coalition and brought France closer to the Spanish succession. They confirmed two large acquisitions. The first was recognition by England and Spain of French sovereignty over Santo Domingo, what is now the Dominican Republic. This strategic base, the domain of buccaneers, would become a magnificent plantation colony which would make eighteenth-century France the world's leading producer of sugar. The second was lower Alsace (the Ten Towns, the Reunions, the landgravate and Strasbourg). 'Strasbourg,' wrote Louis XIV, 'one of the principal ramparts of the empire and of heresy, united for ever with the Church and my crown; the Rhine established as the barrier between France and Germany; and, most important to me, the practice of the true religion authorized by a solemn engagement entered into by sovereigns of different religions, these are the gains of the recent treaty.' (59) This vital text confirms the national and pragmatic character of the king's endeavours. The Edict of Nantes had been revoked in France, but French interests demanded religious pluralism and civil toleration (an Edict of Nantes in reverse) outside the frontiers of the kingdom. The royal letter recorded that, while the Reunion of Strasbourg dated from 1681, its acquisition could only be dated from 30 October 1697, the day when the emperor gave up one of the 'ramparts of the empire'. This definitive annexation granted to Alsace the conditions for its unity and put an end to the ambiguities of Westphalia. The French, accustomed to shifting-frontiers, did not comprehend the importance of the acquisition of lower Alsace. But the elite in the empire suffered from this amputation. Leibniz, despite being a Francophile, was furious over the cession of Strasbourg, seeing it as prejudicial to the 'ancient rights of the empire' (221).

The Peace of Ryswick, though it appeased the Duke of Lorraine, reassured Spain and soothed the Dutch burgher oligarchs, was nevertheless a victory for France – more decisively so than Steenkerke or Marsiglia. His Majesty's soldiers and sailors had died not merely for the sake of honour. Mme de Maintenon rejoiced at the news of these treaties, as did her nuns at Saint-Cyr. But peace with the empire on 30 October was greeted with the greatest rejoicing, popular rather than royal. Since 9 October, Louis XIV had every reason to be concerned about the prince de Conti's chances of becoming King of Poland. So, sensibly exploiting his talent for propaganda, the king masked his disappointment behind the ceremonies for peace. On 12 November, he ordered a *Te Deum* at Notre-Dame in Paris, which was sung on the 16th. On the 25th, he received at Versailles delegations from the Parlement, the other sovereign courts and the city of Paris. On the following day, it was the turn of the *grand conseil* and the University of Paris. On the 27th, the Académie presented its compliments (26). On the other hand, the *Te Deum* 'for the three treaties' was sung without ceremony on the 24th in the royal chapel (97).

Ryswick, from the preliminary conversations through to the final *Te Deum*, was a peace based upon compromise. Some compromises mask defeat, but that was not so in this case, as contemporaries recognized or divined. 'The king', wrote Dangeau, 'gave peace to Europe upon conditions which he wished to impose. He was the master, and all his enemies acknowledged this and could not forbear from praising and admiring his moderation.' (26)

23

Psychological Warfare

THE SIGNING of a general pacification closes a chapter, but that does not prevent us from pausing for a moment's reflection on the war which had ended. That war, the War of the League of Augsburg, is very informative. The coalition had been more formidable than that in 1678. Bussy-Rabutin took in the magnitude of the confrontation when he wrote: 'Bellefonds, Choiseul and Montrevel did not return to active service because of M. de Louvois' death; it took the greatest war which a King of France will ever have to face to bring these men back.' (96) But Rabutin did not realize how the nature of warfare had changed. At the moment when France had 'brought its political state and standing army to the peak of perfection' (159), the military aspect was but one aspect of the war. Louvois and Louis understood the essence of what would lie behind one of Clausewitz's axioms: 'War is nothing other than the pursuit of state policy by other means.' (159) The Dutch War had implied this and that of the League of Augsburg had made it self-evident. Two heads of state applied the rule: William of Orange, the soul of the League, and Louis XIV, who waged a 'war against all the powers of Europe' (90).

THE BOURBONS AND THE ARMY

The emperor did not choose to occupy himself with the martial arts and Charles II, King of Spain, would have been incapable of doing so. Only William III and Louis XIV commanded armies. This union of political and military power did much to improve French efficiency and promote the king's glory. With William of Orange having taken advantage in 1689 and 1690 of the example he had been set, it was essential for Louis XIV to return to the front. He did not hesitate to do so in 1691, 1692 and 1693. This gave him a tactical advantage. In May and June 1692, the king commanded his own army whilst sending orders to the maréchal de Luxembourg to keep the lid on the siege at Namur, the culmination of which the king hoped to reserve for himself. In terms of morale, the presence of the prince was beyond price. When he inspected his regiments, he stimulated a sense of national identity and encouraged the valour of his officers and soliders. At Gévries on 20 May 1692, Louis did not satisfy himself with a mere tour of inspection of a few units; he reviewed all 46 battalions and 90 squadrons of his own army as well as Luxembourg's 66 battalions and 209 squadrons. 'This was', wrote Racine, 'surely the greatest spectacle that there has been for centuries', with 120,000 men 'together in four lines' drawn up before the King of France, who needed eight hours to complete the inspection. Racine, a mediocre horseman, had given up three-quarters of the way through. He wrote to Boileau: 'I was so exhausted, so dazzled by the brilliance of the shining swords and muskets, so deafened by the sounds of the side-drums, swords and kettledrums, that, if the truth be told, I let my horse carry me through it.' (90)

But, while the king commanded the parade, his cavalry and soldiers could also be assured that they would often see him exposed to danger. This was well known in the military camps. Boileau wrote to Racine that, whilst he had enjoyed his account of the siege of Mons in March 1691: 'I must confess, however, that I am mystified by the degrees of risk to which the king subjects himself ... How it is possible that a prince who organized the siege of Mons so well should take so little account of the preservation of his own person?' The king remained faithful to this sense of duty. If the upstart Prince of Orange was not afraid to come under fire, how could a descendant of St Louis not be seen to be taking the same risks? At the attack upon the château at Namur on 13 June 1692, the king led his regiment personally, giving 'his orders within musket-range'. He was barely protected by three gabions, all the more dangerous for being crammed full of loose stones.

Yet Louis was not alone behind these feeble defences. With him were his son Monseigneur, his brother Monsieur, and his illegitimate son Toulouse – four Bourbons, including the king and two of his possible successors. Events showed that the risk was real. A musket-ball aimed at the king was turned aside by a gabion and 'bruised the arm of M. the comte de Toulouse, who was, so to speak, under the king's feet' (90). It may be imagined what a hole a volley of shot might have made in the royal house of France. Furthermore, these were not the only princes to be found in the front line. The prince de Condé and duc de Bourbon were in that same army, whilst a few miles away, among the maréchal de Luxembourg's troops, the rest of the princes of the royal family were to be found: the duc de Chartres, the prince de Conti, the duc du Maine and the duc de Vendôme and his brother. The only absentee was the nine-year-old Duke of Burgundy.

It is easy to underestimate this mobilization of Capetians and give Vauban all the credit for the successful sieges of Mons and Namur. Contemporaries were more clear-sighted, rendering unto Vauban what belonged to Vauban, and unto the king what was the king's. The latter assumed the responsibility for exposing his family to danger. He had shed tears when, on 25 September 1688, Monseigneur had left Versailles for Germany (97). He assigned Beauvillier to him 'to temper his youthful ardour' (49), and, with the assistance of Vauban and Catinat, laid out his tasks for him. The capture of Philippsburg and other fortified towns was only the purely military aspect of the expedition; it was more important that he live up to his father's esteem. 'In despatching you to command my army, I am giving you the opportunity to demonstrate your worth. Make it known throughout Europe so that, when I am dead, they will not notice the death of the king.' (26)

On 19 October, the king read with pride his son's letter reporting the siege in minute detail. 'There were few men in France', wrote Sourches, 'who could write on such a subject in this concise fashion and with such order, precision and clarity.' The *président* Rose, His Majesty's secretary and a highly cultivated individual, had no hesitation in comparing 'Monseigneur's style with that of Caesar's *Commentaries*' (97). Three days later, Louis sent a courier to the Dauphin ordering him not to put his person in such grave danger. Soldiers and officers were not slow to praise Monseigneur's valour and how he allied this virtue with 'a decency, a charm and a liberality which enthralled everybody' (97). On 1 November, news of the capture of Philippsburg reached the court in the midst of a sermon by the Jesuit Gaillard. The king was so delighted that he interrupted the preacher and ordered a prayer of thanksgiving and only allowed the reverend father to continue after a quarter of an hour. On the 28th, Louis postponed a sermon by the same preacher and left to give his son a spectacular welcome at the porte Maillot. From that moment on, he preferred to have Monseigneur at his side during campaigns, not out of jealousy, but in order to ensure that his life was not put at too much risk.

These exploits were relayed to the country at large. Everyone from dukes to peasants was given to understand that the descendants of Henry IV were still valorous and that Versailles had not softened their sinews. The king did not despatch soldiers to their deaths whilst remaining secure in his own palace. Nor did he spare himself or his immediate family. Serving the king meant following him. He participated, understood the concerns of the artillery, engineers, cavalry and dragoons. A better general than William of Orange, Louis XIV also rose above him in personal prestige, whilst the presence in the armies of eleven descendants of Henry IV was excellent propaganda against the rest of Europe. The cohort of Louis XIV at its apogee was not a luxury to be dispensed with, since psychological warfare became of greater importance during the War of the League of Augsburg. In this type of conflict, every element counted, whether royal or national, military or political, civil or religious, elitist or popular. In 1688, France had more than just armies and navies arrayed against it.

WHEN PROTESTANTISM PREACHES CRUSADE . . .

The Ten Years' War has its curious aspects and Voltaire was right to stress its paradoxes: 'In this war, Louis XIV took up arms against his brother-in-law, the King of Spain, against the Elector of Bavaria, whose daughter he had married to his son the Dauphin, and against the Elector Palatine, whose state he devastated after having married Monsieur to the Princess

Palatine. King James was chased from the throne by his son-in-law and daughter . . . Most wars between Christian princes are some form of civil war.' (112) If Voltaire had been of a more religious persuasion, he would also have mentioned the presence of three Catholic sovereigns (the emperor, the King of Spain and the Duke of Savoy) fighting alongside the Protestant powers against Louis XIV and James II. Once again, the Catholic King and the Most Christian King were opposed to one another, whilst, at the opposite extreme, the intemperate William of Orange, who was exasperated by French Catholicism, could entertain an alliance with intolerant Spain.

William III was skilful and obdurate. Throughout the war, he mounted an effective political campaign of what we might describe as indoctrination or disinformation. His hatred of Louis XIV augmented his abilities. From time to time, William spread false reports designed to demoralize the French army and people, using Huguenot refugees in Holland as a relay station. He could sometimes count on Protestants who remained in France, *nouveaux convertis* who were *mal convertis*, who envisaged the war ending in negotiations that would compel Louis XIV to re-establish the Edict of Nantes. There was a symmetry between these Huguenots and the Jacobites faithful to James II, who laid their plots whilst moving around on the other side of the Channel in France. In both cases, their lack of political lucidity and their impetuosity succeeded only in fomenting disorder; for neither the Protestants of Languedoc nor the Scots had the means or the will to welcome a landing-force and help it to succeed.

In place of military assistance, the French Protestants and *nouveaux convertis* offered psychological support. They were eager to identify Louis XIV as a latter-day Nebuchadnezzar and the League of Augsburg with the execution of God's justice. The immorality of James II's dethronement by his son-in-law did not strike most contemporaries. In late October 1688, there circulated throughout western Europe a *Prayer for the Success of the Arms of the Prince of Orange*, the work of Bishop Burnet, who had fled from England on the accession of James II, but who was preparing to return in triumph. It said that the Catholics 'wanted to destroy the truth' of the Word of God and to 'establish an idolatrous cult; abominable to the Lord'. On the other hand, the cause of the Prince of Orange was God's cause:

Assemble the kings and princes who serve you in purity to defend
your cause: render them victorious over your enemies. And You,
God of battles, make their hands skilful in fighting, and cover
them with Your protection. We ask this grace of You, in particular, in favour of my lord, the Prince of Orange . . . Uphold his
cause, for it is Yours, and give him the grace to be victorious over
all his enemies . . . Command the sea and its impetuous waves to
become level in his presence; keep contrary winds locked away
and allow no breath of air unfavourable to him.

Three further pages follow in a similar vein. William was the
new Joshua, a Zerubbabel. God, in answering the prayers of the
faithful, would grant him 'the strength of a Samson, the joy of
Gideon and the victories of David'. He was the pillar of the
Church and it was therefore appropriate that angels 'gather all
about him'. The prayers of the righteous would, God willing,
allow this prince to succeed in his enterprises, assisted by his
wife Mary, the Stuart princess, 'the Esther of his age' (97). In
the midst of this martial prayer, the Church was invited to sing
that most warlike of David's Psalms: 'Let God arise, let his
enemies be scattered', 'Hallelujah, Hallelujah', 'Safety and
strength belong to our eternal God'. The Protestants turned a
usurpation into a crusade. Huguenot refugees in Holland
worked innumerable variations on the theme of the new crusade
and the victory of the People of God over the Philistines. The
pastor Jurieu alone published *The Fulfilment of the Prophecies or the
Coming Deliverance of the Church* (1686), *Apology for the Fulfilment of
the Prophecies* (1687), *Continuation of the Fulfilment of the Prophecies*
(1687), *Portents of the Decadence of Empires, with Several Curious
Observations Concerning Religion and the Affairs of the Times* (1688)
and *Examination of a Libel against Religion, against the State and
against the Revolution in England* (1691) (180).

In a Europe where the elite spoke French and where forty per
cent of the population were Protestant, such invective had a
considerable impact. And for those who might have found the
comparison between Louis XIV and Nebuchadnezzar excessive,
the devastation of the Palatinate seemed to confirm it. From 26
November 1688, when Louis XIV gave the order to raze
Mannheim to the ground, until 23 May 1693, when the
maréchal de Lorge allowed the destruction of Heidelberg castle,
the French lived up to the image spread by the pamphlets. The
result, as always when terror does not succeed in paralysing a

population, was the opposite of what was intended, in this case by Louvois. Far from terrorizing the empire, the sack of the Palatinate united it against France. The ruins of Heidelberg castle marked a tactical error in the psychological offensive and a military defeat for the apparent victors. The *Te Deum* at Notre-Dame in Paris on 27 May was in vain. Louis had committed one of the gravest errors of his reign. In 1693, Europe thought it had forgotten the excesses of the Thirty Years' War, but now the country claiming to be the seat of refined civilization, whose king claimed the title of the Eldest Son of the Church, put the clock back half a century under the pretext of protecting one of its frontiers, ruining a peaceful country because the king's sister-in-law wished one day to be its ruler. The scale of the crime could readily be appreciated, although the error was graver than the crime. The exaggerations of Protestant polemic were over-shadowed by the excesses of the French troops.

. . . THE CATHOLICS OF FRANCE SUPPORT THEIR KING

That the sack of Heidelberg deserved a Requiem rather than an act of thanksgiving did not occur to Louis XIV or Archbishop Harlay. Notre-Dame rang out with the trumpets of *Te Deums*. In November 1688 this hymn celebrated the seizure of Philipps-burg, in June 1690 that of Ath, in July 1690 the victories of Luxembourg at Fleurus and of the fleet at Beachy Head, and in August 1690 the victory of Catinat at Staffarda. In April 1691, one ceremony praised Catinat's seizure of Villefranche, Nice and Montalban, whilst another did the same for Louis XIV's cap-ture of Mons. In January 1692, there was another *Te Deum*, for the capture of Montmélian, and in July of the same year there was a further celebration, for the king's victory at Namur. In August, another rang out in celebration, of Luxembourg's vic-tory at Steenkerke. In May 1693, thanks were rendered for the unfortunate actions at Heidelberg, in June because Noailles had taken Rosas, and in August after Luxembourg had crushed Orange at Neerwinden. In October, one commemorated Catinat's victory at Marsiglia, whilst a second marked the capture of Charleroi by Luxembourg. The year 1694 was taken up with the successes of Noailles: Notre-Dame celebrated in June the Battle of Ter and the capture of Palamos and in July the fall of Gerona.

If any group had been likely to lose confidence in the righteousness of the French cause and its success in arms, it would not have been the French clergy, who had been appeased by the declaration of the Four Articles in 1682 and who had fully approved of the Revocation in 1685. The Revocation had been one of the causes of the War of the League of Augsburg and the clergy were therefore inevitably supportive of the king. Whilst for Bishop Burnet, William of Orange was the new Joshua, to the Church of France, Louis XIV was the new David. Dozens of examples might be cited as proof of this solidarity between the Most Christian King and his people (*pars catholica*) and of the supervision of the people by the clergy, but here are just a couple, both dating from 1693, the terrible year of great hunger. The first is provided by the Bishop of Nîmes, Fléchier. In a speech to the Estates of Languedoc, he analysed the union of the throne, altar and people. He affirmed that:

> Religion is the mother of subordination and order. It tempers the powers of kings with goodness and binds the fidelity of subjects with conscience. It places the hearts of the people in the hands of their kings through a voluntary submission; and it places the hearts of kings in the hands of God through an essential dependency. It represents the grandeur and empire of God by the images of princes, and the image of the humility of Jesus Christ in their subjects. It teaches some to bow low through goodwill and others to rise to the throne through faith. From this mutual comprehension spring both good order and public contentment. (39)

The second is to be found in the Christmas preaching of père Bourdaloue at the end of Advent in 1693. The orator exclaimed: '*Da pacem, Domine* . . . Give peace, O Lord, to Your people.' But the God of peace was also the God of battles, so that, whilst Louis XIV should love peace, the preacher did not urge pacifism upon him. Peace was to be wished for the king and the kingdom, but a peace based upon the victory of the one that had re-established religious unity in France:

> For without forgetting the holiness of my ministry, and without fear of my being accused of bestowing false praise upon Your Majesty, I must, as a preacher of the Gospel, give thanks to Heaven when I see in your person, Sire, a conquering king, and

the most conquering of kings, who nevertheless uses all his glory to be recognized as a peace-loving king, and distinguished as such among all the kings of the world. Before this Christian audience, I must render solemn thanks to God when I see in Your Majesty a victorious and invincible monarch whose only desire is to pacify Europe and who puts all his efforts into working for this and contributing towards it, and whose only ambition is to succeed in this task, and who is, because of this, the visible image on Earth of Him whose nature, according to Scripture, is to be at once the God of battles and the God of peace. (16)

Only seven and a half months had elapsed since the violation of the tombs of the Electors Palatine.

For French Catholics, from the marquise de Maintenon to the poorest labourer, from bishops to mere curates, and from men of letters to peasants, William III was so much the incarnation of heresy and venomous hatred that it seemed their duty to oppose him. The Prince of Orange had fallen into a trap of his own devising. He who had preached the anti-papal crusade was now the victim of a pro-Roman one. To some he was guilty of unorthodox morality. Clerics and laymen denounced his treachery towards James II. In 1690, La Bruyère described the English expedition in terms very different from those in Bishop Burnet's epic account. He summed up the Orangist revolution in this laconic fashion: 'A man says: "I will cross over the sea, will rob my father of his inheritance and then throw him, his wife and his heirs out of his lands and his estates." And then he does as he says.' In the normal course of events, princes throughout Christendom should have condemned the usurper and shown solidarity with his victim. But everything had happened as though the majority of them had said to the Prince of Orange:

'Cross over the sea, rob your father, show the whole universe how a king may be chased out of his kingdom like a minor lord from his château or a farmer from his smallholding, that there is no difference between us and ordinary people (such distinctions are wearisome), and teach the world how these people over whom God has given us dominion may abandon us, betray us, give us and themselves over to a foreigner, so that they have less to fear from us than we do from them and their power.' (48)

In early 1689, the court and Paris echoed to the phrase attributed to the Prince of Orange: 'I will perish or I will set his

Versailles ablaze!' 'A speech', comments Sourches, 'of such insolence that only he could be capable of it.' The following year, William was grazed by a bullet at the Battle of the Boyne, and this, mingled with the news of the death of Schomberg, sparked off a rumour in Paris on 27 July of the prince's death. It was never discovered who was responsible for spreading the false report, but 'from midnight, they began making bonfires and showed all the signs of rejoicing which would herald the birth of a king' (97). Even the marquise de Maintenon shared this hatred towards William III. She wrote to Mme de Fontaines, on 3 January 1696: 'I forgot to tell you that the Princess of Orange has died of smallpox; if such a thing had happened to her husband, I doubt that I would have forgotten to tell you of it.' (66)

THE ABBÉ DE FÉNELON STANDS APART

This animosity towards William did not prevent the existence of a peace party. It had two representatives close to the king: Mme de Maintenon and the duc de Beauvillier. The former easily shed tears about war: 'We never grow tired of petitioning for peace; my only pleasure is the prospects in sight for its achievement' (18 January 1691); 'Let us pray for peace; nothing is so terrible as war' (24 September 1691); 'I hope that God will be assuaged and that we shall have peace' (10 March 1693). But she was neither defeatist nor unwaveringly pessimistic. She never ceased to talk the language of peace to Louis XIV, but she listened to his replies. The king told her that he did not wage war for the pleasure of it and that the best peace is that which succeeds victory. The duc de Beauvillier, a minister, was also close to the king and also urged Louis XIV to make concessions. At Rocroi on 16 June 1693, he presented the king with a *Memoir . . . Recommending a Means of Concluding Peace*. The text began without any preface save these words: 'I assume from the beginning the absolute necessity of making peace. The king is fully convinced of this.' Like many people, this pious minister had been strongly affected by the wheat crisis, which had accentuated his tendency to support the peace party in the Council. Now Beauvillier proposed negotiations with the emperor, William III and the princes of the empire. France would surrender Freiburg, Mont-

Royal and Philippsburg, would cede several Reunions, raze Landau, retain Sarrelouis and return Lorraine with the exception of Nancy. The plan was realistic and prefigured the terms of Ryswick. Beauvillier was ever the statesman and royal servant. The same could not be said of one of his colleagues, the abbé de Fénelon.

Fénelon, tutor to the Duke of Burgundy whilst Beauvillier was the duke's governor, became renowned for the success of his missions in Saintonge, enjoyed the protection of Mme de Maintenon and the patronage of Bossuet, and had up until then had no reason not to praise Louis XIV. And yet, as the king prepared to bestow high ecclesiastical office upon him, this *abbé*, under the guise of peace, wrote several texts attacking both the monarch and his policies. The Duke of Burgundy was the first to discover this with the *Adventures of Telemachus*, which the public only learnt of in 1699. This dialogue between Idomeneus and Mentor contained one amongst many criticisms:

IDOMENEUS: No, I have never found anyone who loved me enough to risk my displeasure by telling me the unvarnished truth.

MENTOR: If you have been misled until now, it is because you have wanted to be. You are afraid of honest counsellors ... When you discovered flatterers, did you drive them away? (35)

Then, in the spring of 1694 – Fénelon would be consecrated Archbishop of Cambrai by Bossuet at Saint-Cyr on 10 July 1695 – the tutor and ideologue secretly composed an apparently open letter, entitled *To Louis XIV. Remonstrances to this Prince on Several Aspects of his Administration* (36). The future Swan of Cambrai dipped his pen in vitriol, but kept the resulting letter to himself. There is no doubt that indiscretion would have landed him in the Bastille. Not content with criticizing the king, he had also attacked the Archbishop of Paris and his protectress, Mme de Maintenon. He had written a civil-war tract.

The 'remonstrances' began with a triple falsehood, since Fénelon assured the king that he wrote 'neither out of grief, nor out of ambition, nor out of a desire to meddle in high politics'. On the contrary, up to the death of the Duke of Burgundy, the future archbishop would be a leading member, along with the ducs de Beauvillier and de Chevreuse, of the cabal around the

Dauphin's son, who was ready to appoint him as his first minister. According to Fénelon, the king had been led astray by flatterers and urged on by his ministers and had let the traditional ways of the kingdom decay in order to promote himself as an absolute monarch. 'One talked no longer of the state or of government, but of the king and his pleasure.' Fénelon criticized the extreme adulation of the monarch and the 'monstrous and incurable luxury' of the court, contrasting it starkly with the impoverishment of France. Then the tone became harsher and the sense of grievance stronger. The king's despotism disguised the tyranny of his ministers, 'harsh, haughty, unjust, violent, men of bad faith'. They had urged Louis XIV into declaring war on Holland, causing France to become an object of hatred. This war, born of the 'motives of glory and vengeance', was the 'source of all the others'. The vanquished had only signed the Peace of Nymwegen with 'knives at their throats', so that all the king's conquests 'were, from the beginning, unjust acquisitions'. Fénelon admitted to no mitigating circumstances, neither *raison d'état* nor border security. 'Here is proof enough, Sire, that you have spent your entire life outside the paths of truth and justice, and, consequently, outside that of the Gospel.' The present war was the consequence of this injustice, of the bitterness of the ravaged, of the iniquity of the Reunions. And the coalition powers aimed to 'wear [France] down over a period of time' in order to escape from an otherwise inevitable servitude.

'Yet your peoples, who should love you like your children, and who have, up till now, been fascinated with you, die from starvation ... Consequently you have destroyed half the real force inside your state for the sake of making and retaining vain conquests elsewhere.' The people, according to this critic, had abandoned their patterns of obedience. 'Sedition is, little by little, rising up everywhere .. If the king, it is being said, had the heart of a father for his people, would he not gain in glory by giving them something to eat and giving them a breathing-space after so many evils, rather than by hanging on to a few frontier posts, which are the cause of the war?' It was, therefore, advisable to surrender all the conquests gained since 1672, including Cambrai. But, Fénelon declared, it would appear that Louis persisted in his conquests. Neither Mme de Maintenon nor Beauvillier had been able to turn him to the ways of peace: 'Their weakness and timidity do them no honour.' The king's obstinate desire for glory was, in Fénelon's eyes, the negation of Christianity. He went so far as to write, in prophetic fashion: 'You love not God; you do not even fear Him with the fright of a slave; it is Hell and not God that you stand in awe of. Your religion consists but of superstitions and a few superficial rituals. You are like the Jews of whom God said: "Whilst they honour me with their lips, they are far from me in their hearts." '

Citing these pages addressed to Louis XIV, although he never set eyes on them, saves us the trouble of refuting them. Not even Saint-Simon reached such heights of bad faith. Fénelon knew that the rigour of the winters of 1693 and 1694 was not the king's doing. Nor could he have been unaware of what the marquise de Maintenon continually asserted: the king's constant preoccupation with the suffering of his people. Finally, it is impossible that he was ignorant of two further facts: the entire administration had been mobilized for eighteen months in the struggle against food shortages; and this priority provoked a change in naval tactics in 1693 – everything was done to ensure that neutral ships carrying grain reached French ports safely, and also to capture those of the enemy. When Fénelon wrote: 'Popular revolt, which has been unknown for so long, has become frequent', he was doubly mistaken. He confused the perfectly comprehensible disturbances provoked by the high price of bread in two harsh years with significant revolt. And he pretended not to understand that real popular revolts had become far less significant in Louis XIV's reign despite the fact that they had been frequent and violent under Richelieu and Mazarin (7).

In itself, this letter of 'remonstrances' is of no importance. Such is often the case with texts of which it is said that they are only of historical interest. It shows, nevertheless, that there were moles burrowing under the gardens of Versailles. Opposition to Louis XIV remained covert. When it was expressed in attenuated form by, for example, Beauvillier or Françoise d'Aubigné, it provided topics for discussion. Even if the marquise de Maintenon was an irritant to her royal spouse, he still listened to her. Even though Beauvillier voiced repeated dissent, the king, who admired his honesty, took account of his opinions. But closet conspiracy by such courtiers as Fénelon and Chevreuse, who, it was imagined, might one day be the councillors of 'Louis XVI' (the Duke of Burgundy), was more serious. It was the more ominous in that it appeared to be progressive, when, in reality, it was conservative, demonstrating the same ambiguities as *parlementaire* opposition. In the midst of war, the king had no need of faint hearts like these.

THE GREAT MOBILIZATION

The kingdom was swept along by a sense of loyalty. Not many of the traditional Catholic subjects of France were perturbed by the abbé de Fénelon's scruples, or were concerned about the destruction wrought upon the lands between the Rhine and the Neckar. They listened to their priests on Sundays, whilst clergy and laymen alike savoured their unwholesome satisfaction at the Revocation. The popularity of Louis XIV at the beginning of 1687 should not be underestimated. Such a degree of esteem would not have been dissipated in twenty-four months. There was no reason why warfare should excite such enthusiasm. In 1688, it was good news for serving officers and the merchants who sponsored privateering activities. But, within less than a year, the French began to understand that the war-effort was the responsibility of every individual in society. And the king himself, the object of renewed acclamation, set an example.

The war was fought outside French frontiers, save for the bombardment of western ports by the allies. The peasants did not, thus, bear the brunt of it – the hardship from the bad weather of 1693 and 1694 was bad enough. Only young males of modest social status were likely to join the army. At the start of the war, the king had 100,000 men in the field, with as many again in arms within the kingdom. Over the years, he had to increase those forces, with the result that voluntary and impressed enrolment, which provided the majority of the regular troops, was intensified. Moreover, on 29 November 1688, Louvois established a new method of recruitment, the lottery, by which the militia were to be chosen. Militia regiments served until 1697, but it needed the loyalism of the period to enable France to sustain this embryo form of national service. The navy was similarly greedy for men, although the universally hated system of the press-gang was shown to be both unpopular and inadequate. Louis XIV's 'Ordinance . . . on the naval forces and arsenals' of 15 April 1689, which revived the 'system of classes', was, thus, highly opportune (81).

The well-to-do, magistrates and town notables were called upon in other ways; for the *ancien régime* always found a way, when it was necessary, to tax those who could afford to pay. In early 1689, the king imposed further financial burdens upon financial officials, transformed certain posts which had been exercised on commission into regular offices for sale, and found new expedients to extract money from both officeholders and those wishing to acquire offices. In November, the Estates of Languedoc 'offered' a *don gratuit* of three million *livres* instead of two (26). Finally, in December, a devaluation hit those who hoarded gold coins.

The military nobility was called up or volunteered in spectacular fashion. Letters-patent of 26 February 1689 convoked the *ban et arrière-ban*. The poorer rural nobles thus mobilized could only serve as 'the worst troops in the world', as Vauban put it (136). No matter. The act of convocation was a clarion-call: the peasantry would comprehend that the *hobereaux* were not above the law. But gentlemen from families with uninterrupted military traditions answered the call with greatest alacrity. The best flocked to court, colonels 'à la bavette', whose rough clothes would be stained in blood, thirty-year-old generals and forty-year-old marshals. The merchants of the rue Saint-Denis who, through jealousy or fear of being cuckolded, habitually sneered at courtiers would have to understand what a blood sacrifice entailed. In the two years between July 1690 and August 1692, the House of Hocquincourt lost three of its number, all colonels. He who wished to please the king would be the first to go to war in the spring and the last to return in the autumn. In early 1696, Louis XIV reproached the duc de la Ferté for having been the last to depart and the first to return (97).

The entire kingdom was thus called on to show solidarity, which was sealed in the fiscal sense by the *capitation* of 1695.* But what did the king do, apart from sending his subjects to war, whatever their age? Was the capture of Namur his only contribution to national defence? In fact, not content with his dangerous service (along with other members of the royal family) at the front, he also imposed heavy sacrifices upon himself. In 1688, 'his building projects, upon which he lavished immense amounts, gave him infinite pleasure' (49). From 1689, the king

---

* See ch. 25.

cut back upon this kind of expenditure. On 2 December 1689, Dangeau wrote: 'The king removed many horses from his greater and lesser stables, causing a saving of up to 100,000 *écus* a year.' Louis could not put the key to Versailles under the mat, close Marly and the Trianon and shut himself away in the Tuileries, under the pretence of setting an example in the saving of expenditure. This would have been a sign to Europe that France was on its knees. But, in the absence of such dangerous and excessive gestures, Louis XIV did what he could in the circumstances. Building-expenses, which totalled 7,389,375 *livres* in 1688, were halved every year, falling to 3,571,552 in 1689 and 1,569,781 in 1690. The war, through shortages of money and manpower, led to the dismantling of works on the River Eure. In 1688, these had cost 1,932,376 *livres*; in 1689, expenditure fell to 871,731; and, in 1690, it was limited to 40,000 (45). It is clear that Louis did not lightly abandon works which he saw as his own to create and supervise; he sacrificed them for the sake of the state and the nation.

In order to prolong the effect of these economies, the king issued a 'Declaration regulating works and tableware of gold and silver' on 14 December 1689, which ordered that all the nation's silverware be handed over to the Mint. His Majesty set an example: on 3 December, the courtiers learnt that he 'was melting down all his fine silverware, despite the richness of the ornamentation, even the filigrees' (26). The silver furniture of Versailles, of the most remarkable quality, was carried off to be melted down between 12 December 1689 and 19 May 1690. During a period of five months, the king watched these works disappear little by little, 'cabinets, tables, *guéridons*, coffers, arm-chairs, seats, stools, benches, two 'alcove balustrades', chimney decorations, mirror frames, candelabra, arm-rests, chandeliers, bowls, vases, urns, ewers, flasks, washbasins, trays, salt-cellars, flower-pots, *cassolettes, caisses d'orangers*, litters, pails, cages, writing-desks, glove-boxes, stills, spittoons' (26). Only seven years had elapsed since the king's move to permanent residence at Versailles, and already the Hall of Mirrors and the apartments, emptied week by week by furtive removal men, were like a town house repossessed by the bailiffs. The war being waged was a total war, and it demolished all kinds of privileges. In 1690, the main privilege of the King of France consisted in being at the front line, even whilst at Versailles.

24

Portrait of the King

LOUIS WAS at the height of his glory after Nymwegen and by the time of Ryswick the king's character had attained its definitive composition. At the age of fifty-nine, he still possessed, despite attacks of gout and the absurd obsessions of his physicians, a robust constitution, sustained by exercise and plenty of fresh air. He was absorbed by public affairs. In less than nine years, between 1683 and 1691, he had lost his best ministers (Colbert, Seignelay and Louvois); but he did everything possible to minimize the damage. He governed the country more, and regimented himself completely. 'He is very orderly in all things and uses the hours of the day with such regularity that one always knows the times of his *lever*, his dinner, his visits, hunting, audiences, Council meetings and his *coucher*.' (86) He was a prisoner of the system which he himself had ordained, condemned to follow his timetable in public, almost every hour of the day. The king was required to smile or remain impassive before the court, diplomats, the kingdom and Europe. Every inflection of his physiognomy was scrutinized, every aspect of his bearing a matter for remark. Sourches, for example, says that 28 July 1704 was 'a day on which nothing happened, but, because the king appeared uncharacteristically downcast, the courtiers whispered among themselves that he must have received bad news from Germany' (97). In short, the royal sphinx did not have the right to knit his eyebrows without some interpretation being placed upon it.

In 1697 as in 1707, and in 1686 as in 1986, Louis was judged by appearances. Portraits were painted of him, flattering canvases like those of Rigaud, or cruel as some of the passages in

Saint-Simon, but all lacking in a sense of depth. One shows the king in the full panoply of glory, another portrays him as a despot, but neither reveals him as a human being. A portrait only shows the immediate moment. Yet it is by no means certain that, in opposing the official portraits, we should seek to create an alternative flesh-and-blood portrayal or reply to a caricature with a rose-tinted watercolour. It is preferable to let Louis XIV present himself through thirty years of his own words and gestures.

DIRECT AND PLAIN SPEAKING

The *Mémoires* only really deal with the early years of the reign and, moreover, de Périgny and Pellisson had applied their talents and style to His Majesty's prose. The king's letters are useful so far as they go, but they are more informative about politics than about his inner thoughts. Furthermore, though Louis signed them, he was not, strictly speaking, their author. The relative paucity of the written word from Louis is not surprising; for, just as the king educated himself through conversation and listening, so he expressed himself more thoroughly in talking. His words gain in authenticity and quality from this. The abbé de Choisy is witness to this feature in his own *Mémoires*: 'I shall report', he wrote, 'even his least significant words, for they always possess a certain piquancy which gives them force and charm. He is truly a master of speech and may serve as a model of eloquence to the French people. His off-the-cuff responses put scholarly addresses into the shade.' There follow some 'expressions of Louis XIV', too good to be accounted entirely genuine. The abbé and Academician concluded: 'In all the kingdom, the king is perhaps the man who thinks most succinctly and expresses himself most agreeably.' (24)

We do not possess the king's confidential conversations, his dialogues with Mme de Maintenon, his confessor, his ministers, the people in his service or the royal family (with the exception of Madame (87)). But what has been preserved is rich beyond price: the miniature discourse pronounced at the *lever*, before or after Mass, at dinner, at supper, or more rarely at His Majesty's *coucher*. From 1681 to 1715, the marquis de Sourches, *grand prévôt*, and the marquis de Dangeau, a privileged courtier, noted such pronouncements on a daily basis. They hardly come into the category of 'historic utterances'. But then the 'historic utterances' that exist are rarely authentic, whereas when Dangeau reports Louis XIV as saying to the duchesse de Berry (15 June 1712), 'We are both a little too fat to ride together in the same barouche', the sentence has the ring of authenticity.

The king was sparing in his use of words and never went to extremes of oratorical flourish. Contemporaries appreciated each phrase, knowing the value he placed on the laconic expression. His favourite sentence was the shortest: 'I shall see' – a useful device for princes to employ and one which Gaston d'Orléans had used during the Fronde. But for Louis XIV brevity was of the essence. No writer or member of the Academy of Inscriptions could have improved upon formulas such as these: 'Monsieur, that is not advisable for either of us'; 'Monsieur, here is your king'; 'Monsieur, our affairs proceed very well'; 'I make you my physician in chief.' To someone urging him to renewed conflict, the king replied: 'Monsieur, we are not here for that.' To an old friend fearing his sovereign's coolness: 'Enter, M. de Lauzun; we are all friends here.' To a messenger: 'Monsieur, you always bring me good news.' To the members of the council of state: 'Messieurs, you pronounce about war, and I about peace!' (25)

It is instructive to count up the number of sayings attributed to the king between 1681 and his death. Dangeau and Sourches report 443, all sentences designed to be repeated, commented on, and amplified. One might have imagined two or three hundred cases of 'I wish' or 'I demand' or simply 'I have decided'. But if we count rather than just make assumptions, the results are rather different. Of the 443, 308 are expressions of kindness and 81 are neutral. Only 54 are expressions of authority, anger or criticism. And if we count the number of cases of 'I give' (48 of them) and 'I accord' (6 of them), we find that they equal that 54 . . .

THE KING AND HIS FRIENDS

'The manner of giving', according to Corneille, 'is worth more than what one gives.' This axiom guided the actions of Louis XIV, as Berwick testified: 'He was the politest man in his kingdom; he knew his language to perfection, and, in his replies, was so obliging that you imagined that you were receiving twice what you actually were, whilst when he refused you, it was impossible to formulate a complaint. There has not been a more human king in the history of the monarchy.' (10) The sovereign should be judged at close quarters and without prejudice. Madame Palatine, for her part, endorsed this picture of Louis' consideration. On 3 January 1705, he was moved to behave towards her thus:

> Yesterday the king paid me a visit. I thanked him humbly for the 2,000 *pistoles* which he had been kind enough to send me. He told me very politely that he had deliberately not come to see me on New Year's Day itself for fear that I would think that he had come to receive my thanks. The truth is that no one in France is as polite and accommodating as the king. When he is affable, one can love him with all one's heart. (87)

It was universally recognized that such consideration was often shown towards the most humble. To a valet who, in the midst of winter, presented him with an ice-cold shirt, the king said, without reproaching him: 'You will give it to me burning hot in the midsummer heat.' Racine, who recorded this incident, also reported this characteristic anecdote: 'A gatekeeper in the park, who had been told that the king was to go out of the gates for which he had responsibility, was not there and it took a long time to find him. As he came running up and was scolded and abused, the king said: "Why are you making fun of him? Don't you think he has suffered enough by holding me up?"' (90)

The king, who is regarded as unapproachable, loved and needed to feel that he was appreciated. It must be admitted (as Montesquieu did, for example) that Louis XIV was shy, almost as reserved as he had been at the age of twenty, and also sentimental and loyal to his friends. 'There was nothing proud about him,' said Berwick, 'except in his appearance . . . [, and] he knew how to put you at your ease in his company.' (10) He did not take advantage of his superior position, and hated it when people were petrified in his presence. Racine, honoured by an invitation to Marly in 1687, understood this: 'He did me the honour of speaking to me several times, and I came away as I always do, that is to say very charmed by him and annoyed with myself, for I never find myself more tongue-tied than during those moments when I most want to show my mettle.' (90)

20 'THE KING GOVERNS PERSONALLY, 1661'. Designed by Le Brun (*c.*1681), this central ceiling-panel in the Hall of Mirrors portrays Louis XIV in Roman armour (but wearing the French king's mantle) guided by Minerva (wisdom). Below are images of joy in his rule. Female figures in ominous storm-clouds represent Louis' foreign enemies. (*Musée de Versailles*)

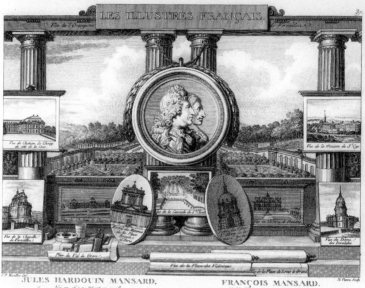

21 JULES HARDOUIN-MANSART co-ordinated the building projects at Versailles. In the Orangery (background of the engraving, with some works by his uncle François Mansart that elaborated the basis of French classicism), an awesome, almost military, sense of engineering was deployed. But the Hall of Mirrors best displays his genius.

22 VERSAILLES. Part of the immense façade of the south front as seen across the first parterre. To the original design by Le Vau, Mansart added the enclosed loggia of the central section and the windows of the Hall of Mirrors. The sculptured figures around the *bassins* of the parterres represent the rivers of France.

23 THE 'GRANDS TRAVAUX'. Colbert, charged by Louis XIV with reorganizing tapestry- and carpet-weaving, created the Royal Manufactory of the Gobelins, which employed hundreds of craftsmen to make not only carpets and tapestries but also furniture, goldware and silverware. (*Bibliothèque Nationale*)

24 EVENING FIREWORK DISPLAY on 9 May 1664, the third day of the famous festivities called the *Pleasures of the Enchanted Isle*.

25 LOUIS XIV'S TOURNAMENT OF 1662 in Paris honoured the Dauphin's birth on the site marked by the place du Carrousel. Three to four hundred courtiers, in five regiments, the first, the 'Romans', led by the 'Roman Emperor', Louis XIV, wore splendid, ornate costumes by Gissez.

26 SÉBASTIEN LE PRESTRE, MARQUIS DE VAUBAN, was, after the Fronde, commissioner for fortifications. In 1667, he directed Louis' Flanders sieges. Later, in overall command of fortresses, he carried through a massive building-programme. A military engineer of genius, he also had interests in statistics and economics. (*Collection du Louvre*)

27 THE NEW FORTRESS AT SAINT-MALO (now the Fort National) was part of Vauban's extensive project of 1689 for the development of the port. It dominated the port's northern access and proved its value during the War of the Spanish Succession. (Drawings of the southerly and northerly elevations.) (*Archives departementales de l'Ile et Vilaine*)

28 THE MILITARY 'IRON CURTAIN'. The second perimeter defences, here depicted, of the new fortress at Besançon, the newly transferred capital of the recently acquired province of Franche Comté, were part of the military 'iron curtain' created by Louis XIV and Vauban.

29 LOUISE DE LA VALLIÈRE, in her younger days an exceptional horserider and noted singer, was Louis XIV's mistress from c.1661 to 1667. Here she was painted by Mignard with her two surviving children by the king, Marie-Anne, the first Mlle Blois, and Louis, later comte de Vermandois, both legitimized. (Musée de Versailles)

30 FRANÇOISE, MADAME DE MONTESPAN, known as 'Athénaïs'
because of her wide intellectual interests, was Louis XIV's mistress
from *c.*1668 to 1681. Four of her children by the king reached adulthood
and were legitimized. Mignard here painted her (*c.*1675) with the
eldest of them, Louis-Auguste, duc du Maine. (*Musée de Blois*)

31 'LA SAINTE-FRANÇOISE' was how Louis XIV teasingly referred to Françoise, Madame de Maintenon. Witty, intelligent and pious, she became his wife in the 1680s and was the valued companion of his later years. In this painting by Mignard (c.1694), she holds a book of devotions. (*Musée de Versailles*)

32 CATHERINE MONVOISIN, NÉE DESHAYES, KNOWN AS LA VOISIN, was at the centre of the notorious *affaire des Poisons*, which involved prognostications and conjurations implicating various prominent figures at Louis XIV's court. She was burnt at the stake in 1680. (*Bibliothèque Nationale*)

34 PHILIPPE, DUC D'ORLÉANS, THE KING'S BROTHER. Monsieur was frequently overshadowed by the king, although he played a role in Paris and at court. His sexuality was ambivalent, but his sense of rank and decorum was rigorous and he never missed a Lenten or Advent religious observance. (*Musée de Versailles*)

33 (*Previous page*) JACQUES-BÉNIGNE BOSSUET, BISHOP OF MEAUX, supervised the education of Louis XIV's eldest son, the Grand Dauphin, from 1670 to 1679. At the time of this painting (1683), Bossuet was about to become involved in efforts to mediate between Louis XIV and the Papacy. (*Private Collection, New York*)

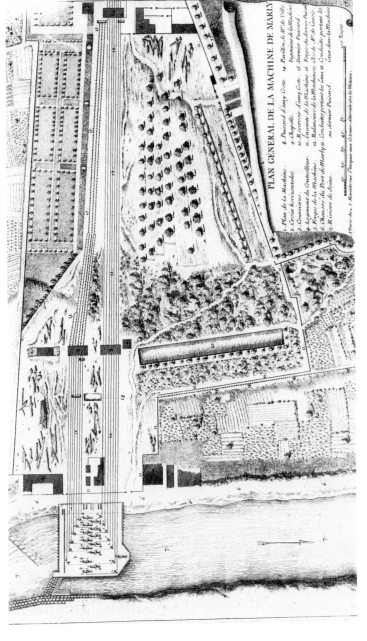

PLAN GÉNÉRAL DE LA MACHINE DE MARLY

1. Plan de la Machine.
2. Grüe horizontale.
3. Courriere.
4. Logement du Controlleur.
5. Frqoc de la Machine.
6. Chaussée du Port de Marly.
7. Rivière de Seine.

8. Puisard d'amy Coste.
9. Chapelle.
10. Reservoir d'amy Coste.
11. Incente de la Machine.
12. Balancier de la Machine.

14. Pavillon de M. de Ville.
Ingenieur de la Machine.
15. Dernier Puisard.
16. Frqoc du dernier Puisard.
17. Ecole M. de Ville.
18. Conduite portant les eaux
au dernier Puisard.

13. Frqoc du dernier Puisard.
19. Conduite portant les eaux
dans la Machine.

A Paris chez I. Mariette rue S.Jacques aux Colonnes d'Hercule et à la Victoire.

35 THE MARLY MACHINE. When the local sources of the water for the fountains of Versailles were no longer sufficient, a gigantic and cumbersome machine was built at Marly on the Seine. It raised the water 525 feet, using the river's current to winch up buckets attached to chains. (*Bibliothèque Nationale*)

36 THE EDICT OF FONTAINEBLEAU (18 October 1685), revoking the Edict of Nantes, outlawed Protestantism in France. In the preamble, illustrated here, Louis XIV claimed that he was accomplishing what Henry IV had intended. Widely applauded in France, it was a gross political blunder in the context of his foreign policy aims. (*Archives Nationales*)

37 THE HUGUENOT REFUGEES. Under the Edict of Fontainebleau, Protestants were forbidden to leave the realm on penalty of being sent to the galleys (in background here). Nearly 1,500 suffered that fate, but at least 200,000 found refuge in Switzerland, Holland and England (left and background here).

38 LOUIS XIV IN THE COSTUME OF A PENITENT, PROCLAIMING HIMSELF AT THE HEAD OF THE 'HOLY LEAGUE' OF AUGSBURG (1686). A satirical print of the French king, hiding within a sinister penitent's cowl, proclaiming himself, for his own political ends, at the head of this league of European princes.

39 THE DESTRUCTION OF PORT-ROYAL DES CHAMPS (29 October 1709). The climax of the long quarrel with the 'Jansenist' nuns there came when a squad of musketeers was ordered by the lieutenant of police to close the convent. The buildings were not destroyed until 1710 and the chapel until 1712.

40 THE BATTLE OF HÖCHSTÄDT (20 September 1703). The French forces under Villars combined with the troops of the Elector of Bavaria to overwhelm the imperial forces under Field Marshal von Stirum, who lost 14,500 soldiers and all his cannon and baggage in the encounter. (*Bibliothèque Nationale*)

41 THE PEACE OF UTRECHT (12 April 1713) brought the wearisome last war of Louis XIV's reign to a close. In Paris, its publication was marked by a formal procession to Notre-Dame, in which the king played a prominent part.

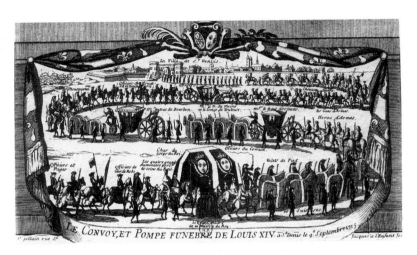

La Ville de St Denis.

LE CONVOY, ET POMPE FUNEBRE DE LOUIS XIV a St Denis le 9.^e Septembre 1715

42 LOUIS XIV'S FUNERAL CORTÈGE. Nine days after Louis XIV's death, his body was brought to Saint-Denis. At the head of the procession went the duc du Maine and the comte de Toulouse, followed by the regent and then the coffin and the royal household. The new king was never present at the funeral of his predecessor. (*Bibliothèque Nationale*)

43 (*Overleaf*) LOUIS XV, King of France, 1715–70.

The king's servants were often his friends. 'The king', wrote the abbé de Choisy, 'loves tenderly those who serve his person; and, if he promises them a favour, he remembers to carry it out, and does not count the cost. He overwhelms them with kindness as though they were always in need of it. When they make mistakes, he treats them as men; and when he is well served, he treats them as friends.' (24) One cannot improve on this summary. And Louis XIV treated ministers, dukes, people of repute, artists and dining companions with the same tact. It would take less time to count those ministers whom the king merely supported than to enumerate those to whom he displayed friendship. His friendship came in different forms and in varying degrees. Louis XIV admired Mazarin, protected Seignelay and Torcy, and turned Colbert and Louvois into his accomplices. He treated Chamillart and Villeroy the younger as his close friends. The public could not help but notice such visible amity.

But did Louis, as Fénelon suggested, surround himself merely with flatterers? It is the case that there were sycophants at Versailles; but those courtiers who told him the truth, and not necessarily the truth he wanted to hear, have received rather less attention. These Catos required royal friendship in order to carry out their tasks, and were dispersed around within the wide circle of Louis' affinity. The best known were the duc de Montausier and the maréchal de Bellefonds, both great magnates; but someone of more modest origins provided for Louis XIV, for over twenty years, an echo of the *France profonde*. His name was Vauban and he had spent most of his life in the lower ranks, only becoming a marshal at the age of seventy. However, 'there was no one alive who made his feelings known so freely to the king and his ministers, and he earned the right to do this by only saying what he thought was most useful to the service of the state, of which he was the most ardent champion' (97). Sourches does not mention the king's friendship explicitly, but it was implied.

The monarch liked contented servants and victorious generals (Turenne, Luxembourg, Vendôme, Villars) and he was sad when forced to punish the shortcomings of his servants (Villeroy, Chamillart), for he let his feelings intrude into a domain where pragmatism should have reigned supreme. The result was that Louis often preferred fidelity to efficiency, as Chamillart showed for a decade between 1699 and 1708. Fidelity was both a noble virtue and a useful alibi. This virtue flourished among ministers, justifying dynasties and placing the Phelypeaux above the Colberts and the Le Telliers. It blossomed around the royal person. If the king had an elderly physician (Fagon), old chaplains and old valets (Alexandre Bontemps), this was because he did not relish new faces and liked the company of his experienced servants (97). He showered rewards upon his valets, especially the Bontempses, father and son. The elder Bontemps was not merely first valet, intendant of Versailles and governor of Rennes. Until his death in 1701, he was His Majesty's confidant and friend. He knew all the details of the king's emotional affairs; doubtless more than père de la Chaize did. He knew the mysteries of the court; the minister of the king's household would have learnt much in questioning him. Few state secrets eluded him; Bontemps' head contained a quantity of information comparable only to that possessed by M. de Torcy or Mme de Maintenon. But his prudence and respect for His Majesty's friendship were such that he let nothing slip.

Amidst this gossipy court, where secrets escaped and were traded and often distorted, three men remained as impassive as statues. They were the king, chancellor Pontchartrain and M. Bontemps. In a world where indiscretions led to the disgrace of the likes of Vardes, Bussy-Rabutin, Lauzun or Madame Palatine, one man was the very incarnation of discretion: once again it was Alexandre Bontemps. To say that the king and his chief valet were linked by ties of affection only gives a feeble idea of their relationship, which constituted, in all conscience, forty years of connivance, a complicity which approached symbiosis. Louis' solicitude reached its peak when, on 13 January 1701, Bontemps fell into 'an apoplexy, and the king showed great concern, wishing to be given the latest news at every moment, even if he was with the marquise de Maintenon'. Four days later, the old retainer died, 'universally mourned by the great and the humble, and the king gave him this rare and touching compliment, saying that he had never spoken ill of anyone and never let a day go by without saying a good word about somebody' (97). Louis XIV had gained much from this socially unequal friendship, which had taught him more than his Jesuit confessors or Mme de Maintenon had about the meaning of charity and care for one's fellow man.

If we were to establish a directory of Louis XIV's acquaintances, we would find that great personages (the duc de Vendôme, the prince d'Armagnac, Turenne) were less numerous than we might have expected at first sight and departmental ministers only slightly less exceptional (Colbert, Louvois, Chamillart, Chamlay). Nor would members of ducal families fill its pages (Saint-Aignan, Lauzun, La Feuillade, the duc de la Rochefoucauld, Villeroy the younger, Villars). Almost the entire space would be occupied by artists (Lully, Mansart), men of letters (Molière, Racine, Pellisson), table companions and servants (Périgny, Rose, the Bontempses, Fagon). These friends were highly unlikely to engage in plots. The king overawed them, and enjoyed showering favours upon them. But such friendship can only be reciprocal, and on at least one occasion, the king was the recipient of a servant's gift. In early May 1693, Sources noted: 'At this time, the famous Le Nôtre, who was the leading man of his time for creating gardens, gave all his pictures, his bronzes and his porcelain to the king, and this present was estimated to be worth 100,000 *livres*.' (97) What Louis had refused from Mazarin, he accepted, thirty-two years later, from Le Nôtre (who did not die until 1700). There must have been more than one courtier, more than one Parisian, who pondered hard on this apparent contradiction. André Le Nôtre would have appreciated Voltaire's remark that: 'The friendship of a great man is a gift from the gods.' For his part, the king, if he could have known it, would have agreed with Chamfort's maxim: 'In great matters, men show themselves as they find it appropriate to do so; but, in small matters, they reveal themselves as they truly are.'

THE KING AND HIS PHYSICIANS

The intimacy afforded by the king allowed his friends to sample his simple tastes. But they were a select group and were required to maintain their discretion. The bulk of the French people had a less complex picture of the prince. For them, the man scarcely emerged from behind the image of the sovereign in glory. However, Louis XIV displayed for all to see the most private domain of all, that of his health. His courtiers knew everything; his doctors kept nothing to themselves. Even His Majesty's bowel movements were discussed. Sources noted his 'bowel hurry', and both he and Dangeau spare us no detail about his 'medicines' or regular purges. These purges were one a month at first, then every three weeks later on, if his health was normal. On occasions, they became even more frequent. In May 1692, Mme de Maintenon tells us, His Majesty was purged 'six days consecutively' (66). Nothing was less common at this time than a good intestinal equilibrium. The aristocrats rode to horse too often and did not eat enough 'roots' (vegetables), although the first factor did not apply in Louis XIV's case after 1683. Shortly after the death of the queen, he dislocated his arm. After that, he rode less often and followed the hunt in a light carriage. Sourches reported that in 1697 many were worried lest the king was being purged too frequently, 'but he gave the reason himself, saying that he took virtually no exercise and that he ate a lot, which naturally meant that he accumulated many humours' (97). Although he so enjoyed walking, he was condemned to view his gardens from a 'chariot'; excellent horseman though he was, he had often to resign himself to being carried or pulled.

From 1681 onwards, in fact, Louis XIV suffered from that aristocratic illness *par excellence*, the gout. Everyone knew and he made no attempt to conceal the fact. Within seven years, the attacks had become so serious on occasion that His Majesty was obliged 'to go about his château of Versailles in an armchair on wheels' (97). Later, Fagon prescribed frequent medicaments to prevent these attacks of gout, but to no avail. What a spectacle the panoply of the royal gout presented before ambassadors: the chair on wheels for the interior, the light barouche for deer-hunting, and the 'chariot' for the park! The latter was the least discreet of all, 'an armchair set on a wide board covered in Russian leather mounted at the back on two small wheels, and, under the board at the front was a very small wheel which turned in all directions, like a pulley, to which was attached a sort of rudder, with which the king steered himself wherever he wanted to go, having chair-carriers who pushed the contraption from behind' (97).

The most powerful monarch in the world was not out to display any false shame by flaunting his infirmity. Nor did he become angry with the physicians who were incapable of curing his enteritis and could not even rid him of his tapeworm. He endured their tortures patiently. On just one day, in April 1701, they drained from him 'as a precaution, five bowlfuls of blood'

(87). Louis was by then sixty-two years old. His sister-in-law noted: 'The reason why the king is so transformed is that he has lost all his teeth.' In extracting his upper-left molars, the dentists had also pulled out part of his palate (190). He would gain the reputation for having been a soft man; but, to us, he appears stoical. Even whilst suffering from a cold, he took his walk 'in his gardens until very late'. Even with a fever, he would rise at his usual hour, changing nothing in the ceremonial of the *lever*, then preside over a Council meeting. This submission to the Faculty of Medicine, this acceptance of illness and remedies, this constancy in putting the duties of monarch before the desire for a little peace and quiet appeared throughout the painful year 1686, 'the year of the fistula', when the surgeons joined the doctors in tormenting their illustrious patient. In 1685, the court talked of nothing but afflictions in embarrassing places. 'Previously unknown, they [anal fistulae] have become so common in France over the past ten or twelve years that all the talk is of people who have had the big operation performed.' The feathered seats of carriages were blamed, as was an excess of stews, and the evil was also attributed to 'ultramontane debauchery'. Louis XIV's fistula would result from 'an abscess, the consequence of excessive horseriding, hunting, walking, travel and warfare' (190). Dangeau noted on 5 February 1686: 'The king was rather incommoded by a tumour on the thigh.' Sourches interspersed his information with commentaries which take some sorting out. If he is to be believed, a number of sufferers had already submitted to 'the big operation' and 'unhesitatingly'. The king, on the other hand, 'accustomed to his comforts' and readily 'upset by the smallest things', postponed the necessary surgery. Sourches admitted that the 'big operation' could be 'very dangerous'. Yet it was the king's medical entourage who exaggerated the dangers, above all the chief surgeon, Félix, who was unlikely to perform it with complete success. D'Aquin and Félix, therefore, undertook 'to assuage this tumour by imperceptible sweating, a ridiculous and very dangerous undertaking'. But, since the affliction was not responding, Félix administered a lancet cut to the king, and then applied 'cauterizing stones to enlarge the wound'.

Suffering both from this malady and from gout, Louis XIV not only was unable to mount a horse but was obliged to appear in public much less, leading to rumours of his imminent death.

March saw a further incision and more cauterizing. The illustrious patient remained uncured, but could walk a little by the 30th, going from his chamber to that of Mme de Maintenon, and could mount his carriage on 9 April. The court rejoiced on the 13th to see His Majesty touch 1,500 sufferers from scrofula. Their delight was premature. On the 20th, Félix had to apply further cauterization, condemning the king to three days in bed. May saw the promise of better things to come. The king seemed happier in himself and he could walk easily. He was advised to go and take the waters at Barèges and he announced his departure. However, the court put on a long face and some objected to the tiring nature of the journey and the doubtful outcome, so the cure at Barèges was cancelled. But 'palliative remedies' continued to have no effect and Louis decided to undergo the 'big operation'. Louvois had encouraged him in this in order to put an end to speculation. But the operation remained an affair of state with, theoretically, only six people in on the secret. These were Monseigneur, Louvois, the *marquise*, père de la Chaize, d'Aquin and, of course, Félix.

On 17 November, Louis had been 'in great discomfort' whilst walking at Versailles and summoned his doctors for the following day.

On the 18th, eight o'clock having sounded, they entered the king's bedchamber and found him sleeping soundly, a great sign of his inward composure in a situation where others would have had so much anxiety. When he had been awoken, he asked whether everything had been prepared and whether M. de Louvois was in his antechamber. When told that M. de Louvois was there and that everything was prepared, he knelt by his bed and prayed to God. After which, having got back up, he said aloud: 'My God, I place myself in Your hands.' And, getting back onto the bed, he ordered Félix to begin the operation, which he did right away, in the presence of Bessière, the most skilled surgeon in Paris, and of M. de Louvois, who held the king's hand throughout the operation, for Mme de Maintenon stood near the fireplace.

The king did not cry out, but said only 'Mon Dieu!' when the first incision was made. When the operation was almost completed, he told Félix not to spare him, but to treat him as he would the humblest individual in the kingdom, which obliged Félix to give him a further two cuts. After which, having applied the first dressing, he bled him from the arm, and was never so

pleased with an operation as with this one, for he had done it to
perfection ... (97).

The official *lever* was only delayed for sixty minutes. Those privileged to enter were surprised to learn of the operation and to
hear 'all the circumstances' from the king himself. In the afternoon, Louis presided at a Council meeting.

By 2 December, His Majesty was eating almost normally,
taking 'a little meat' and drinking some wine mixed with water.
But by the 7th, calluses had formed which 'completely prevented
the cure'. The surgeons 'decided therefore to make new incisions
and to remove those calluses, which they did, but this could not
be carried out without causing the king great pain and even
giving him a touch of fever. However, he continued to see
everybody two or three times a day, not wishing to shirk this
duty even on the day of this cruel operation' (97). In theory,
these incisions were to be the last. On the 9th, Dangeau wrote:
'The surgeons assure us that there is no further cutting to be
done.' (26) But on the 11th the *marquise* wrote: 'The king suffered
today for seven hours as if he had been on the wheel, and I am
afraid that his pain may recur tomorrow.' (66) The success of the
cure was only assured two days before Christmas.

This cure, wrote Sourches, 'gave great joy to everybody'. The
Protestants apart, they all rushed to show their contentment.
'The musicians of the chapel decided to sing a *Te Deum* for his
convalescence in the parish church at Versailles. The Blessed
Sacrament was displayed, and M. the Bishop of Orléans, first
chaplain to the king, officiated in the presence of Monseigneur,
Mme la Dauphine and the whole court.' (97) On Christmas
Day, Bourdaloue 'gave the most touching sermon one could ever
wish to hear ... He addressed the king towards the end, and
spoke of his health. In truth', wrote Mme de Maintenon,
'everybody was much moved, or so it appeared to me, for one
could see that his heart was speaking as well as his voice.' (66)

Firecrackers and services of thanksgiving resounded
throughout Paris and the kingdom at large in January 1687. The
Gobelins manufactory celebrated a Mass at which père
Ménestrier preached a 'panegyric to the king'; the master-
scribes funded a *Te Deum* (195). Paris forgave Louis XIV for
having turned his back on it for fifteen years. And the provinces
did not want to be left behind: on 20 January, Bossuet officiated

in his cathedral at Meaux, which was filled with 'all the public dignitaries', and celebrated the royal cure with a *Te Deum*. On 30 January, the welcome given the king in Paris was one of the high points of a long reign. The tempo of everyday life soon resumed. On 15 March, the court learnt that His Majesty was riding once again (26), a 'great joy for him and all his servants' (97), because this minor event put the seal upon the king's convalescence. His sufferings had made of 18 November 1686 a kind of turning-point in the history of surgery. From then on, the lancet and the scalpel were less frightening, and the 'big operation' became fashionable. His Majesty's friends seemed to demand it, including Dangeau in 1687 and Vendôme in 1691.

The episode of the king's fistula did not have, in reality, the importance which Michelet was to attach to it, but it was never-theless a revealing one. It showed the popularity of Louis XIV in the aftermath of the Revocation, a popularity to which the lower orders made the greatest contribution, despite taxation and war-fare. It revealed several of the king's qualities: his common sense, patience, endurance, piety and kindness. It is instructive to imagine the monarch, undergoing the operation without anaes-thetic, gaining strength and reassurance from holding the hand of a minister. The operation revealed the boundaries of princely pride. He had to obey the physicians, rather than give them orders. He was in their hands, which were rather less reassuring than those of Louvois. By asking Félix to treat him like an ordinary patient, he was deliberately forgoing the privileges of his position, as if purges, surgeon's knives and cauterizations were there to remind him that man is but dust. Christian kings, though they might have been sinners, were not gods on Olympus. When Louis XIV placed himself in the hands of the surgeons, he was implicitly resigning himself to the decrees of providence. He was putting himself in what the Bible calls 'the strong hand of God'.

IN PRAISE OF THE CHINESE PORTRAIT

A study of Louis XIV's friendships is fully justified in a chapter dedicated to the king's personality. Looking at medicine and surgery might be less justified were it not for the way in which the king willingly consented to, and good-naturedly suffered, his doctors' ministrations.

There are several ways of conceiving the portrait of a distinguished personage, for no portrait is a mere likeness. Houasse's equestrian *Louis XIV*, begun in 1674, portrays warlike glory; the most noble of Rigaud's portraits epitomizes sovereignty. It is Jupiter preceded by Mars. From the inception of the reign, artists garlanded their royal 'subject' with objects of symbolic value. Without leaving the château of Versailles we can follow the changing face of the king, inseparable from a thought or an action which the artist is trying to embody in his portrayal of the king's physiognomy. Testelin's portrait of Louis (1648) shows a ten-year-old king seated on a throne and holding a crown of laurel in his right hand. Yet it is not the glory of Lens which holds our attention, but rather the attributes of sculpture and painting which are laid out before the throne. Apollo joins Mars. Garnier's *Louis XIV* (1672) is a painting within a painting: the king, in armour, reigns within his oval frame, whilst the whole presides over a disorderly collection of fruit, books and parchments, surmounted by a collection of musical instruments. The protector of the arts and letters contemplates their scattered attributes. With Van der Meulen (*Louis XIV at the Siege of Lille, The Crossing of the Rhine*, etc.), military props replace those of the artistic academies. Mars moves into centre stage in front of Apollo. It is not until 1706 and the realistic medallion modelled in wax by Benoist that we see the old king, toothless and wasted by age, and discover Louis XIV represented plainly and unadorned by symbols (202). For the king's contemporaries were imbued with rhetoric, influenced by preciosity and passionate about mythology, and they liked to savour the movement of eye and mind between the subject of a portrait and his surroundings. Each ordinary still-life or undistinguished addition to these canvases was there to shed light on the subject. Let us draw a veil over the rhetorical flourishes and embellishments habitually used in written portraits. Even Boileau was not immune to them.

There is a party game called the 'Chinese portrait' or 'Chinese roulette', which Jean Cocteau considered to be a literary genre. The idea is for the questioner to guess the identity of a preselected member of a group by asking questions framed as analogies, such as 'As what kind of flower do you see this person?' or 'As what form of musical instrument?' The portrait takes time to emerge and the clearer and more honest the answers, the more revealing the portrait. Therefore, having answered the question 'As what kind of medical patient do you see this person?' it would be interesting to have the answers to two others about Louis XIV: 'As what kind of reader do you see him?' and 'As what kind of collector?'

A LAZY READER

The king's reputation for intellectual laziness is well known, especially as regards his reading habits. Madame Palatine and Saint-Simon both did much to ensure that such an image was etched into the collective memory. But the question of intellectual laziness is separate from the question of reading.

Louis XIV did read less than his cultivated contemporaries. Even as a child he preferred activity to meditation and enjoyed reading less than he did conversation. In 1677, Pascal's friend Méré published a treatise *On Conversation* (72). And Saint-Evremond wrote: 'However much pleasure I take in reading, that of conversation will always be more palpable.' (92) In the case of a sovereign, such contrasts were attenuated. A king had people to read to him, and they were educated individuals, able to comment on those pages which His Majesty had particularly enjoyed hearing. Such a man was Périgny (d. 1670), whom Louis XIV judged to be worthy to educate the Dauphin, Bonrepaux another. The king often used other regular companions, for example his historiographers, so that one day it might be Pellisson, another Racine or Boileau.

Racine and Boileau had been charged since 1677 with writing the history of the reign. At first they had taken their task seriously. 'When they had written something of interest,' Louis Racine tells us, 'they went and read it to the king.' (90) This would take place in Mme de Montespan's apartments, where the king went to gamble, and in the presence of Mme de Maintenon. Mme de Montespan liked Boileau and Mme de Maintenon preferred Racine. 'When the king arrived at Mme de Montespan's suite, they read him something from his history and afterwards the gambling commenced' and Mme de Maintenon slipped into the background. On the other hand, if the king was ill and called the historiographers to him, they would find only Mme de Maintenon present for the start of their reading, with her rival putting in an appearance later. Thus they were the first to know of the great credit enjoyed by the widow of M. Scarron.

Under the protection of Mme de Maintenon and appreciated by the king, Racine benefited from the privilege of *entrées* and quickly became His Majesty's favourite interlocutor. The king 'liked to hear him read and found that he had a singular talent for bringing out the beauty of the works he read'. One day, Louis asked his historiographer for 'some book which would amuse him'. Racine proposed Plutarch's *Lives of Illustrious Men*. 'It's old-fashioned' said the king, thinking of Amyot's translation. Racine replied that he would modify certain turns of phrase and modernize it, and he succeeded so well that the king made no secret of his delight and seemed to savour every detail. But this arrangement, though it placed Racine on intimate terms with the king, aroused jealousy: 'The honour received by the reader without a title caused the official readers to whisper against him.' The king preferred the author of *Andromache*, asking him one day 'who was the greatest of all writers who had honoured France during his reign'. 'Molière', replied Racine. And the king, who, although he had protected Molière, was nevertheless not free from the prejudice of the *dévots* against theatre people or from the literary prejudice against comedy, replied: 'I do not believe it, but you know more about such matters than I do.' (90)

The preference for listening to the best minds in the kingdom reading to him rather than flicking through an octavo volume smelling of glue in between audiences was not, then, a sign of a closed mind. The king's curiosity remained alert and, at the age of sixty, he still appeared eager for knowledge and new under-standing. On 23 September 1699, for example, when the court was at Fontainebleau, Louis observed an eclipse of the sun and, at his command, 'the celebrated Cassini of the Observatory brought him a sky-map of the eclipse, in which he could see the different ways in which it had been seen wherever in the world it had appeared' (97). This anecdote shows the king's lively intel-lect and also his taste for graphic representation. A lover of drawings and paintings, coins and medals, architecture and parks, of whom it was said that he had a pair of compasses in his eye, he had every reason to prefer visual explanation to the bookish. Not that he looked down upon libraries. The King's Library in Paris, direct ancestor of the Bibliothèque Nationale, 'contained very many interesting volumes' (42). And the registration of copyright, begun by Francis I, only started to be seriously observed during his reign.

At Versailles, amidst so many *objets d'art*, Louis could not do without a reading room for ever. But for twenty years, descriptions of the château are virtually silent about books. It is not certain that the king kept the hundreds of poems, addresses and sermons which were dedicated to him. According to Primi Visconti, his readers only presented him with a sample of these works, for Louis preferred 'the reading of histories and good books' (86). Apart from some valuable manuscripts, the shelves of the king's *cabinet privé* only contained a few hundred volumes, mostly about numismatics. This all changed in November 1701. 'His Majesty', wrote Mansart, 'has ordered to be made in the recess of the *cabinet carré* adjoining the oval *salon* to the end of the *petite galerie*, some cupboards at leaning height, forming a table above, of which all the windows will be filled with glass, so that all His Majesty's rare books may be seen' (203). The king's books were not measured by the yard. Chosen items were put on display.

Louis liked books, but not just any books. He wanted them to be 'big, sumptuously bound, richly illustrated, if possible with miniatures in bright colours'. He preferred vellum and calligraphy picked out with gold. The courtiers knew this and so did ambassadors, and they were eager to offer him manuscripts of this type. In 1684, the king ordered a splendid new binding to be made for Anne of Brittany's *Book of Hours*. The floral manuscript pleased a prince who loved flowers. He also ordered the completion of the *Velins* of Gaston d'Orléans, a collection of nature paintings. In 1700, he gave 10,000 *livres* to Joubert for '400 drawings of rare plants, birds and animals, painted in miniature on vellum, to be included among the books of His Majesty's *cabinet*'. Mazarin, Fouquet and Colbert all had the same passion. Louis made it into a royal style and a national taste. The king was here cherishing his love of nature and 'Colbert his obsession with science. This dual interest was to 'enliven illustrated books and help French publishing completely to revive itself'. Whilst the king took the greatest pleasure in looking at art books, showing them to the ladies and admiring the richness of their bindings, Colbert encouraged the multiplication of artistic, scientific, historical and geographical plates. He mobilized the scientific academicians as he did the members of the Academy of Inscriptions. By the production and circulation of the *Cabinet du Roi*, he wished to serve the king's glory, develop scientific curiosity and celebrate the artistic grandeur of the reign.

But, while the modest library of Versailles was transformed into the *Cabinet du Roi*, all propaganda and prestige, and while Colbert spent 116,975 *livres* in 1679 merely for the engraving of plates for it, we may still imagine that the king would, on occasion, consult some of the non-artistic works in his reserve stock. In fact, he kept by his side Thomas Hobbes' *Elements of Politics*, J. Baudouin's *Perfect Prince*, Madaillan's *Portrait of the Political Governor*, and even, later in the reign, Vauban's *Dîme royale (Royal Tithe)*, despite the fact that its publication had irritated him. He possessed treatises on, and abridged works of, history, which he had adored since childhood, as well as treatises on theology and controversy (203). The king was certainly not as ignorant on these matters as, through modesty and prudence, he pretended to be,* and as Saint-Simon and Madame Palatine claimed. Why did he keep these austere works with their plain covers by his side instead of the illuminated plates of his collections? It would have been strange if, at a time when lords and ladies, clerics and bourgeois, discussed divine grace, the Five Propositions and the Four Articles, Louis XIV had not had works on these topics read or explained to him. His lazy reading habits did not mean that he was reluctant to acquire knowledge.

AN ENDEARING COLLECTOR

A similar openmindedness and lack of pedantry may be seen in the king's attitude towards the arts. For public consumption, Louis appeared the political patron. In private, he is better understood in the guise of collector. There are several kinds of collector. There are those who buy for vanity's sake, without judgement. At the other extreme is the maniacal hoarder of artistic works who knows more about painting than painters do and could never admit the slightest error. Louis XIV, to whom the best of the collections of the Louvre, the Bibliothèque Nationale and the Cabinet des Médailles are owed, avoided

* See ch. 20.

either extreme. If he amassed many fine works of art for the sake of his own and the nation's glory, his own pleasure was also involved. Moreover, he sought guarantees by taking the best advice. He pretended to no infallibility, but he was a connoisseur, as everyone was aware. Foreign courts and personalities wanting to please him knew that he enjoyed receiving *objets d'art*.

Such was the case with the eminent Swedish architect Tessin the younger, who, in 1700, decided to offer Louis XIV a *St Jerome* by Correggio. The intermediary was Cronström, the 'commission secretary' of the Swedish ambassador to France. Thanks to Cronström's notes and letters, we may follow the encounter between Louis and this canvas and hear the commentaries of the king and witnesses of the scene. Following enquiries, the King of France informed the Swedish secretary that he was prepared to receive the painting as a gift. M. de Torcy, therefore, conducted Cronström into the *petits appartements* of Versailles. Bontemps 'had the picture taken into the king's *arrière-cabinet*'. The canvas was placed on an armchair whilst the king heard Mass. He returned, accompanied by Monsieur and the Duke of Burgundy, and sent Torcy to find the Swede. 'I found His Majesty', wrote the latter, 'preoccupied with studying the painting attentively. He addressed me curtly at first, without letting me speak, saying: 'Connoisseurs pronounce it very fine.' Louis' combination of modesty and graciousness was not always in evidence. Thinking that the king was alluding to the question of authenticity, Cronström told Louis XIV what he already knew: that the picture had been presented to M. de Torcy, who had taken the advice of an expert, the sieur Forest, of the painter Roger de Piles and of Mansart. Torcy said: 'M. Mansart found it very fine.' The king interjected: 'I can easily see that it is very fine, but I do not know enough to be able to discover all its exquisitenesses.' Monsieur, addressing the Swede, asked: 'Are you the one who is presenting it to the king?' Cronström replied: 'The Baron of Tessin is its presenter.'

Cronström intimated that it would give Tessin the greatest pleasure to learn that His Majesty had received his gift as a mark of zeal and veneration. The king replied with laconic politeness: 'I accept it with pleasure and beg you to thank him on my behalf.' Cronström recalled the painting's history: Tessin had discovered it in Copenhagen in 1690 at the sale of the goods of a former ambassador, Baron Lerk. The king: 'The draperies are in a different style from those in Correggio's other paintings, but, since it is a sketch for the larger picture which is said to be at Parma, that is hardly surprising.' Cronström: 'This is the original, rather than a sketch, and the sureness of touch in the draperies shows that it was done a long time before the large painting.' The Swede then took from its packing-case a print reproducing the Parma *St Jerome*, and brought to Louis XIV's notice:

> the malice of those who doubt that this one is earlier than that in Parma, pointing to St Jerome's left foot, the lion, the trees and branches, the light on the sea, St Jerome's right foot, etc., all things which had been added on the large picture and the print, and which persuaded His Majesty on the point: after which [Cronström added] as I wished to retire, he reminded me once more to thank you [Tessin] on his behalf. The affair is thus concluded as graciously as it possibly could be and, thank goodness, without any hitch or impediment. (56)

The king was, therefore, an *amateur*. He enjoyed a direct and delicate pleasure from watching painters at work and from scanning a canvas. But he did not rush to judge, qualified his opinions and did not trust to first impressions. He saw nothing wrong in taking advice; nor was he concerned about thinking aloud in front of witnesses when confronted with the perennial problem of originals and replicas. Yet he had a shrewd eye, a rich experience and excellent taste. The preceding anecdote is, therefore, most valuable. It reveals a character at the threshold of the soul where Pascal located and celebrated the spirit of delicacy. Before this *St Jerome*, the king showed that, at the age of sixty-two, he was far from senile, and that he was gracious, spontaneous, agreeable, and attentive to others' sensitivities. He formed his opinions and put them forward without imposing them on others. He was not Apollo but an *honnête homme*, like an elderly marquis remarried into the robe in search of a quiet private life.

THE UNCROWNED QUEEN OF VERSAILLES

She remained a mysterious figure, obscured by walls of friendships and hatreds. Her career was incredible; her success paradoxical; her situation at Versailles unique. Many points in a life without personal drama remain obscure. She was like ivy clinging to an oak tree. We shall probably never know whether she was more intellectual than intelligent, more devout than bigoted, or more sincere, more spontaneous, less devious, less egotistical, or less *arriviste* than she appears. She is interesting to us at this point merely for what she reveals about Louis XIV.

Was he right to have married her? It is amusing to see writers of progressive views criticizing the king for marrying beneath his social station, whilst moralists tend to forget that a consequence of his marriage to Mme Scarron, the king's secret wife after 1683, was that he ceased to take mistresses. It was Antoine Arnauld, scarcely over-indulgent towards the king, who justified his sobriquet of 'great' in his sane conclusion on the matter. In 1688, he wrote: 'I do not see what is wrong with this marriage, which has been contracted according to the rules of the Church . . . May it please God that his directors of conscience never give him any worse advice.' (20) In the long term, the king sacrificed something by this marriage. Like his last confessor, his secret wife attracted criticism, irritated public opinion and lessened the monarch's popularity. But, in the earlier days, Mme Scarron was irreplaceable. She rendered null and void La Bruyère's judgement: 'A king lacks for nothing except the pleasures of a private life.' (48)

At the most practical level, it seems clear that Françoise was still youthful and one of the most attractive women in the kingdom. Like her friend Ninon de Lenclos, she seemed immune to the ravages of time. She was beautiful and did not dress forever in black as iconography always portrayed her, but wore fashionable clothes, and liked blue dresses. She had the capacity to satisfy the king's needs and keep him from other amorous encounters. As the widow of an invalid who was full of vitality, how could she have been maladroit in the giving of caresses? But did she share her husband's pleasures? It is hard to be certain on the matter. She often appeared curt and cool, and she alternated caprices and quarrels so readily that we may imagine her as, at the same time, artful and indifferent, a characteristic of the courtesan. But the important point is that the king did not deceive her and never gave a thought to paying visits to other alcoves. Such fidelity in a vigorous man who loved women cannot be explained by devotion alone.

Private life, however, was not restricted to the alluring domain of the god Eros. That is why Mme de Montespan enjoyed royal favour for so long, and why Mme de Maintenon had no rivals. With the lively Athénaïs, the king could make fun of the ridiculous ceremonies he had to endure in public (49). He could talk about Molière's comedies and Racine's tragedies. In the marquise de Maintenon's apartments he could ask questions, converse and listen. Already in 1680 Mme de Sévigné said that their conversations were 'so long as to set everybody thinking': 'They lasted from six o'clock until ten.' And in the same year: 'She introduced him to a new world which had been unknown to him, the enjoyment of friendship and conversation without constraint and without petty quarrels; he seemed to be charmed by it.' (96) From the end of 1683 onwards, they talked every day, at length and on all subjects: buildings, entertainments, religion. They could not avoid talking about other people. She received 'the visits of the great'. She wrote in 1707: 'The courts of France and England often do me the honour of being in my chamber.' (66) Ministers' daughters and dukes' sons about to get married were presented to her, as they had been to the queen. She would form an opinion about them and then pass it on to her husband.

This game went on for thirty-two years, and her judgements of individuals inevitably encroached on the political domain. Madame Palatine in 1680 accused her future sister-in-law of spreading disunity: she annoyed the queen, irritated the Dauphine, stirred up ill feeling between Louis XIV and Monsieur (87). Later, Madame Palatine accused her of being responsible for her (Madame Palatine's) disgrace, calling her an *ordure* and a *pantocrate* (*sic*) in letters which amused the courts of Germany but displeased the king. It is true that Mme de Maintenon had her wits about her and that, helped by age and her growing credit, her influence was sometimes unfortunate. She did not like Monsieur, nor Monseigneur, who reciprocated her dislike. She pretended to like the Duchess of Burgundy because she thought it would please the king. On the other hand, she always championed the duc du Maine. As far as politicians were concerned, it was said that she did not care for Louvois and favoured the Colbert clan, especially Beauvillier and Chevreuse, that is to say the supporters of the Duke of Burgundy. Like Maine, Burgundy was enough of a *dévot* to be in the *marquise*'s good books. When Burgundy and Vendôme accused each other of losing the battle of Oudenaarde in 1708, she took the prince's side. If Saint-Simon is to be believed, in 1709 Mme de Maintenon commanded a clan which included Beringhen, Bignon, the valet Blouin, Boufflers, MM d'Harcourt and d'Huxelles, François de la Rochefoucauld, the Pontchartrains, the maréchale de Villeroy and her son, and finally Voysin, whom she supported against Chamillart (220). In 1714, scandalmongers said that a triumvirate was running affairs, over the heads of the council of ministers, comprising Mme de Maintenon, père Le Tellier and Voysin, who had just been made chancellor (224).

Such accusations and insinuations were both true and false. They were false in that the king did not let himself be led by the nose. Mme de Maintenon knew that her voice did not count once matters in which she was interested 'have become affairs of state'. She once wrote: 'I do not govern père Le Tellier' (66), and she had no pretensions to govern Louis XIV, only of enlightening him. The *marquise* did not meddle in politics, but everyone was sure that Beauvillier owed his considerable credit only to her (224). Similarly, she promoted Voysin, who had administered the temporalities of her house at Saint-Cyr since 1701. She did not interfere in politics, yet she did not hide her irritation at the credit enjoyed by Louvois. She did not meddle in politics, yet the promotion of the king's legitimized sons in 1694 and 1714 was done with her blessing, and the king's disastrous will in 1714 owed much to her obsessive insinuations against Philippe d'Orléans and her no less obsessive eulogies of the duc du Maine.

The *marquise*'s feelings did not always tally with the good sense that Louis XIV sought from his wife. She had Fénelon made an archbishop, but Quietism made her regret her initiative. She pressed for Noailles to be appointed to the archiepiscopal see of Paris, but the dispute over Quesnel's book caused her to quarrel with him. If we raise the level of the debate, was it right or legitimate that, in an organized court, at the head of a self-regulating monarchy, there should have existed a person, without a mandate other than the monarch's affection, through whom ran the 'channel of favours'? Sometimes the *marquise* gave good advice – when she was not obsessed with her pious intrigues or overcome with pacifist yearnings.* She liked and

* See ch. 28.

supported Boufflers, a captain as brave as Bayard. She protected and defended Villars. So, paradoxically, this devout defeatist helped to save the king's domain.

A setting and a timetable suiting this unusual situation had to be found. This was not a difficult task; no sooner was the court installed at Versailles than the queen discreetly passed away. From 1684 onwards, the true queen of the great château 'in its greatest splendour' was 'whether one likes it or not, Mme de Maintenon' (291). The king installed her on the same floor as his own new apartments, overlooking the Cour Royale, at the top of the Escalier de la Reine. From his antechamber, Louis XIV had easy access to the apartments of the 'secret queen'. He only had to pass through two antechambers, decorated in red (the *marquise* only liked blue (152)), to reach Mme de Maintenon's chamber, 'a large deep room on the corner of the Cour Royale'. Here, the king had his work-table near the *marquise*'s bed (66), as well as his commode. Every day, His Majesty went about his work in the presence of someone who, twelve years earlier, had been merely a widow from robe society and governess of the royal bastards. The famous chamber was furnished and draped with green and gold damask, alternating with red damask. The bed was in an alcove 'crowned by four bouquets of white egret feathers'. Several tables and bureaux were used for work with ministers. Nothing could be more routine. What is striking is the *marquise*'s position, so arranged that she would miss nothing of what was said but without appearing to be involved in any official capacity (and also so as to protect her from draughts). One must imagine 'a large niche, at the front of which she settled herself', this niche containing 'a bed covered with cushions'.

Ministers had to get used to this arrangement and this silent presence. On 8 October 1708, at Fontainebleau, or so Sourches tells us, Torcy 'was closeted for three-quarters of an hour with the king in the marquise de Maintenon's room' (97). Each minister had to weigh his words carefully, taking account of the occupant of the niche. As she was busy with her embroidery, it only needed a moment's inattention and a sentence, heard out of context, might be enough to discredit him. The *marquise*, who corresponded with the Curia and received presents from the pope, she to whom Alexander VIII sent papal briefs ('To our dear daughter in Jesus Christ, the noble lady of Maintenon', 18 February 1690) and whom he had charged with protecting his nuncio at a court where her merit had allowed her 'to acquire justly a favour approved of by everybody' (97), possessed great privileges. In 1694, she was made spiritual superior of Saint-Cyr; a papal brief 'allowed [her] to enter all the convents of France'; and a permission from Mgr de Harlay gave her the same rights throughout the diocese of Paris (66). The king kept her up to date about everything. Only the council of ministers was barred to her. Yet the *marquise* 'was not born for public affairs' (20), as her niece Caylus correctly reported. Madame Palatine, therefore, was not wrong to protest against 'this frightening power' which was bestowed upon her (87).

This is what Sourches thought in 1686: 'One could have no more doubts about Mme de Maintenon's policy. She gave her protection to each minister in turn, to get them to work in her interest, and balanced their authority, making them equal one with another, without allowing any of them to raise himself too high above his competitors.' (97) What would he have written at the beginning of 1715? Yet the beneficiary of so many privileges complained about the restrictions of court life. The house at Saint-Cyr was her beloved creation, where she ruled as a mistress. She had drawn up the regulations for this boarding-school which was reserved for noble young ladies without fortunes. She would inspect their classes and their recreations, join them in their prayers and dine in their 'refectory, preferable to royal banquets' (66). She wanted to turn them into ladies, not silly or scatter-brained creatures. 'I like women to be modest, sober, gay, capable of both serious conversation and *badinage*, polite, mocking but in a manner which hides praise, with good hearts and bright conversation, and simple enough to admit to me that they recognize themselves in this portrait, which I have drawn without plan, but which I consider to be approximately correct.' (66)

At Saint-Cyr, founded in 1686, transformed into a regular Augustinian nunnery on 30 September 1692, and where Mme de Maintenon would retire after the death of the king and was to die in 1719, the 'secret queen' could relax. She recounted her life in biblical terms to her young ladies. There she had staged the tragedy which she had commissioned from Racine. *Esther* was played on 26 January 1689 before a delighted Louis XIV and a number of select guests. 'The way in which she resists was so highly praised!', exclaimed Mme de la Fayette. 'Madame de Maintenon was flattered by the writing and the staging. The play shows in its way the fall of Mme de Montespan, and the rise of Mme de Maintenon, the only difference being that Esther was a little younger and less affected in matters of piety.' (49)

The Louvre houses a testimony of the new Esther's 'affected piety'. When the new Ahasuerus commissioned from Mignard, known as 'the Roman', a tenth portrait of himself, he had the painter do one of Mme de Maintenon at the same time. Françoise d'Aubigné, so the marquise de Sévigné tells us, 'is dressed as St Francesca the Roman. Mignard has made her more beautiful, but tastefully, without any false rouge or white face-powder, without her appearing too young, and, without all these perfections, he gives us a face and physiognomy which words cannot express: lively eyes, perfect grace, without finery ... No other portrait is its equal' (96). Where the Princess Palatine saw only malice, hypocrisy and stubbornness, Mignard – who in painting the king tried to show his mind and his soul through his gaze – revealed not only the marquise de Maintenon but how the old monarch liked to imagine her, as his faithful wife.

A PORTRAIT SKETCHED

The king who reigned so long and gave so much of himself to the public remains barely known. After three centuries there are still debates as to the depth of his intelligence and little agreement as to his personality. The 'black legend' is, in part, responsible for this. There can be no doubt that Fénelon, Jurieu and Saint-Simon still influence our judgements. But so does that failing denounced by M. Michel Déon: the refusal to recognize true greatness (29).

There were two personalities within Louis XIV. The private man cultivated friendship, seeking to love and be loved, and liked beautiful women and pretty faces. It is too facile to set up a contrast between the years of the young mistresses and those of Mme de Maintenon; they were all delectable, attractive and agreeable companions. Here, too, Louis wanted to love and be loved, although he yearned for intelligence as well as distraction. 'The king's private existence ... is a *sanctum sanctorum* to which mere mortals are not admitted', mortals including his worthy but dull sister-in-law, Madame Palatine (87). Louis presided here, accompanied by a carefully chosen lady: Mme de Montespan or the second Mlle de Blois or the marquise de Maintenon. In retreat from the pressures of Versailles or the constraints of Marly, the king guarded jealously the private life of an *honnête homme* and a conversationalist. 'I should confess', he once declared in confidence, 'that I have a liking for people of spirit.' (87) And the private man, once in a small group, could be relaxed, enjoying a dry sense of humour. He could be a good listener. Madame Palatine once recalled how a Swiss guard had stopped her from walking at night in the park at Versailles (after thirty years of service, he only knew his orders: 'I have never asked whether the king had a wife, children or a brother; it does not bother me'). 'I made the king laugh heartily in relating this dialogue to him.' (87)

His pleasures and problems were of a piece with this private life, and this is why they have been wrongly interpreted both then and subsequently. When he left the Tuileries for Saint-Germain in 1666 it was to flee the ghost of his dead mother. Each new birth in the family gave him great pleasure and he was stricken with grief at each death. But propriety and *raison d'état* both prevented any effusive demonstrations. Sourches summed this up when he wrote of the birth of the Duke of Burgundy in 1682: 'The king's joy was very great; but, since he was so undemonstrative, he did not let it so appear at large.' (97)

While the public man appears to have ruled his family with a firm hand, the private man was indulgent towards his relatives. He was never content with Monsieur's character defects, but neither did he despise him, despite his perennial disapproval of the practitioners of the 'ultramontane vice'. In early 1701, Madame Palatine thought she was in terrible disgrace; but, three months later, Monsieur died and she was forgiven: 'I know nothing of your letters,' he told the Princess Palatine, 'I have read none of them and the very idea was a product of Monsieur's imagination.' (87) While the public man appears domineering, the private man knew how to obey. He followed the decrees of his confessors – too closely with Le Tellier – and obeyed the dictates of his physicians. While the public man seems haughty, the private man made an effort at humility, and succeeded. In his instructions to the Dauphin, the young king had written: 'Although we take a legitimate pride in our rank, modesty and humility are also no less praiseworthy.' (63) In his conversations with his uncrowned queen, the elderly king willingly listened whilst she told him: 'Sire, what you have done is wicked and you have been very wrong.' When Mme de Maintenon sought to return to the subject the following day, Louis replied: 'Make no excuses for me, Madame, I was very wrong.' (66) Perhaps the *marquise* protests too much:

> Was I not correct to say that he is humble? He does not flatter himself; does not think that he is all-important; is under no illusions that another would not do just as well, and even surpass him in many particulars; takes no credit for the achievements of the reign, seeing them as the result of God's providence working through him; shows less pride in a year than I do in a day. (66)

Even allowing for exaggeration, Mme de Maintenon's testimony is of the greatest importance. At an age when, generally speaking, faults become sharper and defects more accentuated, towards the end of an interminable reign, Louis XIV, resisting the confirmation by his reign of the superficial notion that absolute power corrupts absolutely, strove towards Christian virtues and the amendment of his life. However, it is possible to see how one can be misled into measuring the king by his public persona alone, which belonged to the position he occupied rather than the man.

One domain of the hidden garden remains closed from us: that of his conscience. The king who was described by the Venetian ambassador in 1660 as 'extremely pious' and of whom it was believed late in life that he wore a hair-shirt (87) also pursued an illicit love life for twenty-two years. How did he reconcile his faith to his actions? 'Your heart will never be at peace with God as long as this violent passion, which has kept you separated from Him for so long, reigns there', wrote Bossuet to him in 1675 (106). He knew that his heart belonged to God, and that it was 'never at peace'. Torn between two kinds of love, he never really chose between them. But he always knew repentance. Following the example of his pious subjects, he practised daily reading of the Lord's Prayer: 'Forgive us our trespasses.'

The precise dividing-line between the king's private life and his official existence is impossible to determine. Even Louis XIV's physical appearance belonged to both worlds. He could be seen at close quarters often enough for visitors to know his height – he was probably of medium stature. But his customary deportment and his concern to appear majestic almost hypnotized contemporaries. Mademoiselle depicted him as a kind of giant (1658) and Venetian ambassadors describe him as 'of great stature' (1664) and 'very tall' (1680). Hébert, the *curé* at Versailles, wrote as late as 1710: 'He is very tall and well proportioned, being six feet tall or as near as makes no difference and his bulk is proportionate to his height.' (75) This last remark at least was true; Louis had thickened out since the 1690s.

Yet he took exercise. Like Madame Palatine, he adored walking. 'Promenades,' wrote Primi Visconti, 'the gardens and flowers are his most habitual forms of relaxation.' (75) He enjoyed horseriding as well. Like Monseigneur, he preferred hunting on horseback, the traditional pastime of kings, to shooting or falconry. But this hunting was done in order 'to distract his mind and to maintain the vigour and lightness of a body which tends naturally to grow fatter' (1683) (75). It was never permitted to interfere with His Majesty's work; Louis XV and Louis XVI were not to display the same restraint.

Louis XIV took care of his appearance and placed his body in the service of his kingship. His physicians did not recommend regular baths, but his body was rubbed down with toilet water every day, whilst he would sometimes change his shirt several times a day (97). The marquis de Saint-Maurice said 'that he is very clean and takes a long time in getting dressed; he has a curled up moustache and sometimes he spends half an hour in front of a mirror waxing it' (93). At war he was content in 'a short-sleeved cotton shirt and a drugget jerkin' (93), and Spanheim records that the old king generally dressed simply (98). However, in the first half of the reign, he knew how, when the circumstances demanded it, to dress up for the occasion. On 2 December 1684, after a hunt, the king changed for the *appartements*, and the court saw him in an outfit which shone with 'what seemed like twelve million diamonds' (26). This did not prevent him from listening meditatively, the following day, to an austere sermon from père Bourdaloue. The king ate too much, because his physicians could not rid him of intestinal parasites; but he drank next to nothing. He detested tobacco (94). With the exception of an amorous temperament, inherited, perhaps, from Henry IV, Louis held his body in check.

Contemporaries were at one in admiring the king's composure. Others around him found such control more difficult; Monsieur could scarcely restrain his emotional outbursts, while Condé had an appalling character. Even Montausier found self-control difficult. Throughout the fifty-four years of the personal rule, Louis only became extremely angry three times: with Colbert, with Lauzun and with Louvois. When he did lose his temper, those present would gaze at each other in astonishment. On one occasion, in 1675, he was heard to say *mezza voce*: 'My God! People who like a quarrel are so hateful! For myself, I think there is nothing more stupid!' (96) Shortly afterwards, he gave 'a thousand favours' by way of reparation to the young duke who had provoked this outburst. Normally, Louis saw the retaining of a cool head as the pre-eminent princely virtue. In public, said Primi Visconti, 'he had all the gravity of a king in a play', even when having to listen to nonsense, and conducted himself 'in such a manner that one did not know when he had won and when he had lost' (86). This is also how the Venetian ambassador described him during the Dutch War, and it is how he would appear to have behaved later in the reign. When the court learnt of the surrender of Landau in 1702, a place close to the king's heart, 'consternation appeared on all their faces; only the king showed a heroic steadfastness' (97). After the reverse at Turin in the autumn of 1706, Madame Palatine assures us that 'he shows great firmness of soul in his unhappiness'. In 1708, he manifested 'the same courage and spirit of calm' (87) after Oudenaarde.

> I am the master of myself as of the universe;
> I am, and wish it so.

To the new Augustus, this mastery implied an exquisite royal courtesy. People spoke of his 'habitual politeness', which, given his position, was remarkable, and said that he showed 'every possible *honnêteté*' (96). No one showed a greater degree of 'decorum' in replying to an ambassador's compliments (97). 'He is most precise as to his replies and speaks with such affability that he never says anything which might give offence unintentionally. One will not find a prince in history who has retained propriety, honesty and an engaging air towards everyone better than he has done.' (75)

In the half-closed world state affairs, during the long hours devoted to public business in the Council or the reading of *liasses*, his ministers appreciated the courtesy which helped to get the work carried out efficiently and placed him closer to his servants. Whilst talking to his artists, from Le Nôtre to Mansart, the king seemed to give suggestions rather than orders. But, in the case of Louis XIV, this kind of courtesy, a remnant of chivalry in an age of baroque self-discipline, was elevated from a virtue into being a component of *raison d'état*. His tact and *politesse* constituted 'a certain style of command, which made it clear to others that he was the master and that they should obey him' (30). So wrote the princesse des Ursins, who was far from ignorant of political affairs. It was part of his conception of grandeur and glory that he should be, like the heroes of chivalric romances, without pettiness. When informed in 1676 that he would no longer be troubled by vice-admiral Ruyter, he replied: 'One cannot help but be touched by the death of a great man.' (112) Or again, on the death of Charles V of Lorraine in 1690, he launched into a panegyric of his enemy, 'as if to put on record that, although great men are capable of competing one with another, they are nevertheless incapable of ever demeaning themselves by displays of envy' (97).

Grandeur and glory – state ideals and not matters of personal vanity – required other virtues from Louis XIV: courage in war and peace, equity (he knew how to punish, pardon and forget) and secrecy. The king's enemies condemned this latter quality, calling it 'dissimulation'. In fact, it was self-evident that high politics required secrecy. At most, it might be worth examining his use of the famous 'I shall see', which some individuals held against him. The royal 'Je verrai' stopped him from committing himself lightly. It was preferable for Louis XIV, when confronted with seven candidates for the post of organist in 1693, to say 'I shall see' and then, a week later, to choose François Couperin, rather than pick a candidate there and then, merely in order to appear to be infallible.

The king's 'Je verrai', which so irritated Saint-Simon, leads us naturally to the question of his intelligence. How could a prince with a mediocre intellect have written, even with the assistance of Colbert, Périgny and Pellisson, the *Mémoires* for the education of Monseigneur? Surely only Marcus Aurelius and Frederick the Great have written better in that genre. How could he have presented so many precise, witty, and effective speeches, without authoritarianism, bombast or banality? How could he have tolerated Colbert's remonstrations or Louvois' curtness? How could he have displayed so amply that good taste in literature, architecture, painting, sculpture and music? How could he have created a political and artistic style, or have chosen such able ministers, such good poets, such effective administrators and such brilliant artists? How, indeed, could he have given his name to a century?

But if our reflections about such a remarkable character and its achievements were not enough to persuade us as to the quality of the king's intellect, as against the testimony of the talented but resentful Saint-Simon, other authorities may also be cited. Madame de la Fayette saw in Louis XIV 'one of the greatest kings there has ever been', almost 'the most perfect', and only reproached him for one thing, the discretion which made him too 'sparing with the intellect with which Heaven has endowed him' (49). The abbé de Choisy, himself endowed with a keen intellect, called Louis 'an extraordinary genius' (24). Finally, Leibniz spoke of him as a 'great intelligence' and 'one of the greatest kings who ever lived' (87).

25

Was France Changing?

THOUGH THE king himself changed little, the same could not be said of the kingdom. It is conventional wisdom that there was a 'European crisis of consciousness', a sort of prologue to the Enlightenment, around 1680, with Richard Simon's *Critical History of the Old Testament* appearing in 1678. From this work it is clear that Louis XIV's misgivings about Cartesian philosophy were not misplaced. On the other hand, we do not find the king, despite the surveillance of the book trade, making any serious effort to hold back a process of secularization which, in any case, appeared to be overshadowed by the brilliance of the Counter Reformation between 1670 and 1680. There was no intended irony in Voltaire's verdict on Fontenelle: 'He can be regarded as the most universal intellect to emerge in the century of Louis XIV.' (112) His *Dialogues of the Dead* (1683) and *On the Plurality of Worlds* (1686) appeared before Bayle's *Historical and Critical Dictionary* and were more subversive. We now are aware of the fact that Pierre Bayle was a fideistic Protestant respectful of the Bible (208), but it would be difficult to portray Fontenelle as a serious Christian. This did not prevent him becoming a member of the Académie française in 1691, the Academy of Sciences in 1697, and the Academy of Inscriptions in 1701. He was even appointed as permanent secretary of the Academy of Sciences in 1699. The king was the patron of all these bodies, and could have vetoed any of the elections of this unbeliever.

To comprehend the relative freedom to be found in the kingdom of France, we should remember that, in Spain, the Inquisition was still omnipotent. On 30 June 1680, the Plaza Mayor in Madrid was the setting for a solemn and terrible *auto de fe*, preceded by a series of religious rituals, readings of sentences, abjurations and public recantations by eighty-six Jews and Marranos, 'relapsed' or Muslim, already judged and condemned by the Holy Office. Eighteen of them were burned. Charles II watched the whole of this horrific spectacle. 'The king's demeanour', says a chronicler,

> was a source of great comfort to the fervent and of extreme confusion to the less assured, whilst making a great impression on all present. It was something truly worthy of the admiration of posterity. From 8 a.m. His Majesty did not move from his balcony, suffering no discomfort from the heat or disturbance from the crowd, and not being bored for one second throughout such long proceedings. His devotion and zeal so dominated any fatigue that he never left his place, even for a quarter of an hour at dinner time, and, when the *auto* ended . . ., the king asked whether it was really all over and whether he might now leave in full assurance of a clear conscience. (110)

If we compare the Most Christian King with his cousin, the Catholic King, the former emerges, despite the persecution of Protestants and Jansenists, as a paragon of tolerance. Measured by such standards, Louis XIV may pass for a moderate head of state. His empiricism saved him from many excesses. His contemporaries had been aware of this since the League of Augsburg, and since the death of Louvois in 1691, an event often thought (albeit inaccurately) to have been a turning point of the reign.

DID DECLINE SET IN AFTER 1691?

Mme de Sévigné had been correct: that dominant minister had been one of the great figures of his age.

> So M. de Louvois is dead – this great minister, such an eminent man, whose position was so important, whose *moi*, as M. Nicole would say, was so extensive and who was the centre of so many things! How many matters, plans, projects, secrets and interests to be sorted out, how many wars started, intrigues started, chess moves accomplished! – Ah, my God! Give me a little time; I would like to check the Duke of Savoy, checkmate the Prince of Orange? – No, no, you won't even have a single moment.

And Sourches noted: 'He was a man whose genius was capable of anything, whose mind was admirably organized, and who brought an indefatigable application to the smallest matters.' Louvois may have opposed Colbert on many occasions, and their spirits may seem contradictory or complementary, but they were, in fact, on the same level. Their kind of genius, invaluable to the king, lay in the combination of the capacity for synthesis with the most meticulous attention to detail. Mme de Sévigné was not alone in believing that the death of Louvois would cause almost irreparable damage. The king knew of these beliefs, or soon came to sense them.

Everyone waited for his reaction. When an envoy from James II presented his condolences, the king replied: 'Monsieur, tell the King of England that I have lost a good minister, but that his affairs and mine will not suffer as a result.' (26) This speech contained a triple message. The Most Christian King was reassuring his cousin that, even without Louvois, the dream of a Stuart restoration was still alive. Secondly, Louis XIV always kept his eulogies short. In an age of lengthy flights of oratory from the pulpit, the king made funeral orations with few words. That for Vauban in 1707 would be no warmer than those for Colbert, Seignelay and Louvois. The prince may have been sentimentally attached to his collaborators, but such friendships did not require public expressions of affection. Finally, it was a political necessity that an absolute monarch should never appear helpless or bewildered. The inhabitants of the kingdom and the chancelleries of Europe had to be persuaded that there was never a power vacuum.

Furthermore, in 1691 cemeteries and crypts were filled with individuals who had seemed unique. Among the illustrious departed were saints (Vincent de Paul, Pavillon, Jean Eudes), statesmen (Lionne, Colbert, Seignelay), great artists (Lully, Le Brun), soldiers (Turenne, Condé, Créqui) and seamen (Duquesne). But replacements soon appeared for these out-standing men. The French saints would now be Jean-Baptiste de la Salle, Marguerite Bourgeois and Grignion de Montfort; the artists Mansart, Berain, Delalande and Boulle; the seamen Tourville and Châteaurenault; and the soldiers Luxembourg, Catinat and Vendôme. Were ministers to be the exception?

It is sometimes claimed that this was so. For many, 1691 marks a turning-point. An age of mere clerks would replace that of the viziers; the distinguished administration of the Colberts and Le Telliers would be succeeded by administrations with a lack of ministerial talent. Saint-Simon's gallery of unfair portraits is partly responsible for this. Chamillart was portrayed as 'sensible, hardworking, but hardly enlightened', Barbezieux as making the king accustomed to 'postponing his work when he [Barbezieux] had drunk too much or when there was a card-game which he did not want to miss', and Desmarets as intoxicated by ministerial power. Châteauneuf was to him the equivalent of 'the fifth wheel of a chariot' in the government, whilst chancellor Voysin was 'thoroughly ignorant, as well as unaccommodating, without sparkle or *savoir-vivre*'. Jérôme de Pontchartrain, minister for the navy, appears in the duke's *Mémoires* as 'a most detestable and contemptible individual, and looked upon as such, without exception, by all France and by all the foreigners who came into contact with him in his official capacity' (94). Saint-Simon gives a pass mark to La Vrillière and distinctions only to the chancellor Pontchartrain, Beauvillier and Torcy. From this has emerged a black legend: that Louis XIV chose mediocrities in order to impose his own will. But this is contradicted not only by the king's acknowledged virtue – his capacity to choose the right man – but also, above all, by an examination of the facts. Neither the composition of the council of ministers nor the succession of ministers between 1691 and 1715 reveals sustained mediocrity. There was certainly a temporary decline, and at a particularly difficult time, but it was made up for by the quality of the top-ranking public servants of the last years of the reign.

Heading the Council at the beginning of 1691 were, Louis XIV apart, the conscientious M. Le Peletier, Croissy, Louvois and Louis de Pontchartrain. By the end of the year, with Louvois dead, he had three replacements: Monseigneur, Beauvillier and the marquis de Pomponne. The Council gained in numbers and wisdom. Monseigneur was intelligent and cultivated, courageous and faithful, and experienced in political affairs. Between 1691 and his death in 1711, he occupied a key position in the council of state, particularly during the Spanish war. The duc de Beauvillier, also head of the royal council of finances, was gifted 'with a sound, exact and penetrating mind, whose full capacities were not apparent to many, because of the narrow limits which he placed on them, through his natural good sense, and which were restrained further by a solid piety which was his dominant characteristic throughout his life and which grew ever stronger' – or so claimed Saint-Simon in his additions to Dangeau's *Journal* (26). Governor of the Duke of Burgundy and Colbert's son-in-law, friendly towards Fénelon but more rational and honest, something of a pacifist but presenting the views of his conscience, a *dévot* but an adversary of Port-Royal, the admirable and irritating M. de Beauvillier lent moral security to the Council. His honesty made up for his intellect. From 1691 until his death in 1714, he strove to live up to the king's confidence in him, without siding with the Colbert clan. The third new minister of 1691, Simon Arnauld, marquis de Pomponne, who had been in disgrace since 1679, re-entered the government by the front door. This resourceful diplomat was able for the few years until Croissy's death in 1696 to counterbalance annexationist diplomacy. The council of ministers of 1709 (the king, Monseigneur, Burgundy, Beauvillier, Torcy, Pontchartrain, Desmarets and Voysin) or of 1714 (the king, Beauvillier and then Villeroy, Torcy, Pontchartrain, Desmarets and Voysin) held its own. But could the same be said of the main departments of state?

Two of the most important underwent crises: finances, between 1699 and 1708; war, from 1701 to 1709. They shared the same head, Michel de Chamillart, the king's partner at billiards and companion. His weaknesses as a minister should not be exaggerated, for the shadow of his predecessors, Colbert and Louvois, makes him appear in a dim light. Yet Chamillart could not hope to be their equal, even with Le Peletier de Souzy in charge of fortifications, and with Desmarets, as director-general of finances after 1703, making up for his inadequacies as controller. At a time when the kingdom was under attack from all Europe, the combined functions of war and finances were no sinecure. Louis XIV, having at last realized that Chamillart had risen to the level of his incompetence, provided him with more-acceptable successors. Voysin, replacing the billiard player at the war department, was not so suspicious of people of merit. Excited by his task, 'capable of great attention to detail' (as Louvois had been) and 'very sound' (10), he managed to keep the armies at full strength until peace came. For his part, Desmarets, a distinguished nephew of the great Colbert, raised in the seraglio of public office and private business, used his connections among financiers to associate them with the national effort. By exploiting expedients, justifiable to the extent that they were effective, he always managed to find the resources to sustain Voysin's armies and Pontchartrain's naval forces.

Recent work has provided us with a new image of the Phelypeaux de Pontchartrains, father and son, novel to such a degree that many judgements about the navy and the role of the central institutions must be modified.* It has shown that Colbert's huge department remained in competent hands. Following Colbert and Seignelay, Louis and Jérôme de Pontchartrain exercised their administrative duties skilfully, throughout a difficult period, duties which encompassed the king's household, the navy, commerce, the colonies and the clergy. Louis de Pontchartrain, chancellor between 1699 and 1714, also restored the former importance and distinction of the chancellorship, not seen since the last days of Séguier. 'Never such lightning grasp', says Saint-Simon about him, 'so much effortless charm in conversation, so much delicate and quick-witted repartee, so much ease and solidity in work, such despatch, so quick an understanding of men, such a knack in handling them.' Something like the brilliance of Lionne grafted on to the genius of Louvois. The latter had proved to be far from irreplaceable.

Until 1713, the king hardly suffered at all from the absence of Louvois. In the council of ministers he was easily replaced. At the head of his department the great administrator was only missed between 1701 and 1709. The King of France's reply to his English cousin had not been mere bluster. When the later ministers – the Pontchartrains, Torcy, Desmarets, Voysin – are referred to as 'epigones', this term should only be taken in its chronological sense. The pejorative sense may only be applied to the choice and retention of the mediocre Chamillart. But this should not be taken as a sign of despotism but of weakness.

MERIT REWARDED AND THE LEGITIMIZED PROMOTED

Many, writing about the promotion of the king's legitimized children, have associated weakness with despotism. It caused Saint-Simon to fly into an apoplectic fury. It upset legitimists

---

* This is the direction of the research of Professor Charles Frostin (183–7).

and horrified puritans. In fact, this measure was taken in wartime, as if to associate it with another form of advancement, that which rewarded military prowess. In the case of the comte de Toulouse, it was perhaps a question of payment in advance. At the moment when the weight of an interminable war was added to a succession of atrocious winters, the top of the social hierarchy was visibly transformed, as if in reaction. Torn between the privileges of birth and the legitimate rewards for services rendered, the higher ranks of the kingdom seemed to be undergoing the pains of childbirth. The king, anxious to revitalize national energies, introduced more and more meritocracy into an aristocratic system. In 1693, the nomination of the low-born Catinat as a marshal of France did not go unnoticed, no more than did the foundation of the Order of St Louis. This red riband, which directly prefigured the imperial Légion d'Honneur, created a spirit of emulation in the armies. While it could not claim to be a rival to the blue riband of the Holy Spirit, it did have the significant and peculiar characteristic of being open to all.

When he shaped and remodelled the elite in this way, the king was not playing with change for change's sake. Louis' interests were those of the state. If birth had retained an almost total monopoly on the great offices and commands, France, confronted by a strong coalition, would not have had the resources to match it. But if merit had replaced it too abruptly, the country would have lost part of its traditional values. So the king struck a balance, in his usual empirical manner, between these two components. When merit justified birth, augmenting its natural influence, Louis was entirely happy. He appreciated the true value of the association of nobility and success, 'condition' and talent. This applied, in the civil branch of service, to the *premier président* Lamoignon. On the military side, Louis always had a great captain, as remarkable by reason of his origins as for his prowess: Turenne, grandson of William the Silent; then Luxembourg, from that remarkable military dynasty the House of Montmorency.

After serving the king at Fleurus and Steenkerke, Luxembourg helped his master to carry his legitimized children to the heights. In January 1694, the marshal was engaged in a lawsuit. He claimed a place among the peers, a claim which was contested by Saint-Simon. There could have been no better public demonstration that the hierarchy was never rigid. Nor could anything have been more favourable to the interests of the king's natural children. Louis had already married Mademoiselle de Blois to Philippe II d'Orléans, the future regent, on 18 February 1692, and the duc du Maine to Anne-Louise-Bénédicte de Bourbon-Condé, on 19 March. This raised them *de facto* almost to the same level as the princes of the blood. The next step was to achieve this *de jure*, and this was what the king did in 1694. Contrary to the accusations of Saint-Simon, the king did this by degrees. M. de Harlay took charge of the operation. Intelligent and enterprising, this highly placed magistrate knew his public law well. He knew how quickly to go and that he could not go too far.

There was no better means of soothing legal opinion than by citing precedents, and this was not the first time that a King of France had legitimized his natural children and given them privileged positions. Two lineages had been placed on an almost equal footing with the princes: the Longuevilles, descended from Charles V, and the Vendômes, from Henry IV. Now, while the dispute between Luxembourg and Saint-Simon was in full spate, the last of the Longuevilles died, on 4 February 1694. The ducs de Longueville, descended from Dunois, the uncle of Louis XII, had occupied an intermediary position between the princes of the blood and the dukes and peers. This policy of raising legitimized children to high rank, begun by the Valois, had become an institution under Henry IV. By letters-patent of 15 April 1610, the Béarnais had given to his legitimized son, César de Vendôme, 'the first rank and precedence' behind the princes of the blood. The Parlement registered this act on 4 May – just in time, for the king was assassinated on the 14th. In eighty-four years, MM de Vendôme had only exercised their precedence on four occasions. But now that the Longuevilles had disappeared, the Vendômes tried their luck, with *président* Harlay operating on their behalf.

On 16 March 1694, Louis-Joseph de Vendôme, grandson of Henry IV's legitimized son, nephew of the duc de Beaufort, and first cousin once removed, and friend, of the king, presented the Parlement of Paris with a request to be allowed to enjoy his ancestral precedence over the dukes and to follow directly below the princes of the blood, basing his claim on the royal act of April 1610. He expected to gain satisfaction, thanks to M. de Harlay, and thereby to gain the right to assume command over the marshals of France. In fact, although Louis XIV and the *premier président* gave open support to Vendôme, this was primarily in order to remind public opinion of what Henry IV's policy had been. The duc de Vendôme's coat-tails covered the sons of the marquise de Montespan, and the edict of 1610 was only wielded in order to prepare the way for another ordinance, one intended to glorify the destiny of Louis XIV's legitimized children.

As proof of this, we need only consider the chronology of the rapidly unfolding and interconnected events. On 4 May, M. de Vendôme presented a second request to the Parlement, designed to overcome the opposition of the princes of Lorraine. The very next day, 5 May, the king enacted letters-patent according to the duc du Maine and the comte de Toulouse rank and precedence immediately below the princes of the blood. The justification for this decree was based on the royal act of April 1610 and the rank accorded to César de Vendôme (61). On 8 May, the Parlement registered this text. On 8 June, Vendôme was received into the Great Chamber (2). From now on, after the Condés and the Contis, would sit Maine, then Toulouse and then Vendôme.

These procedures were perfectly legal. The rights to legitimize, ennoble and modify rankings were all regalian. As long as the *légitimés* were not declared capable of succeeding to the throne, the constitution was respected and the law of succession safeguarded. The duc de Saint-Simon's moods (he no longer acknowledged M. de Luxembourg) were of no importance. Moreover, as Voltaire showed, the people forgave their king for having engendered a flock of natural children. They would not be bothered about one more rank or degree of precedence.

'THE KING WISHES, AT ALL COSTS, TO SEE HIS PEOPLE MORE CONTENT'

'As luck would have it, the second part of Louis XIV's reign was to a large extent a period of climatic adversity.' (220) Fortune deemed that periods of bad weather would coincide with those of war, and that these problems should follow the Revocation of the Edict of Nantes, so that many Protestants saw them as the consequences of the wrath of God. However, the king was not to blame except for misplaced simplification. But that did not bother Fénelon, and nor did it worry Michelet, who apparently relished the calamities which added to the miseries of warfare. Yet, not only was Louis XIV incapable of commanding the elements, he was never indifferent to the sufferings of the poor. From the beginning of his reign, he took action to help the most vulnerable. In the *Memoirs for the year 1661* we read: 'Nothing seems more urgent to me than to relieve my people, to which I am compelled by the misery of the provinces and my compassion for them.' (63) These were not idle words, for at the same time the king decided to lower taxes. 'Every father of a family wishes for the good of his house', and therefore, thought Voltaire, it was natural for an absolute monarch to be preoccupied with the prosperity of his subjects.

Neither court ceremonial nor the move to Versailles prevented Louis XIV from being informed about conditions in the realm. He could rely on work with his ministers, the despatches of the intendants, petitions, reports from his secret agents, and personal contacts established during his journeys and military campaigns. Above all, the king had a remarkable informant in Vauban, the progenitor of applied statistics, who, in 1678, had invented a method of demographic calculation. This was intended to ensure that Louis XIV would:

> know the precise number of his subjects, the true state of their riches or poverty, what they did, how they lived, the state of commerce and employment, whether it was good or bad, for what each *pays* was suitable, the good and bad areas, what their quality or fertility was, including the value and yields of the land, how many inhabitants the kingdom could feed from its own resources and without help from its neighbours, whether it was in as good a state as it could be [, etc.] (177)

Eight years later, in 1686, the future marshal published a *General and Simple Method for the Counting of Peoples*, while the intendants of the central provinces set about calculating the number of 'hearths' in their *généralités*. They performed their task unceremoniously, but the king and Vauban (as his *Dîme royal* of 1707 would show) did not separate the economic from the social.

It almost seems as if Sébastien Le Prestre de Vauban had a premonition about forthcoming difficulties. After 1687, began what is now called the 'mini ice-age', thirty disastrous years, lasting until 1717. The winter of 1693 was catastrophic, causing an appalling famine. The year 1694 was no better. A respite was only perceptible between 1704 and 1708. The 'great winter' of 1709, almost as harsh as that of 1693, started another period of immense cold. This ruined crops, brought hunger to the countryside, and forced people to migrate through desperation. Famine killed directly, but was even more destructive in lessening the resistance to disease of a thus under-nourished population. The number of victims of the crisis of 1693 and 1694 has been estimated as 2,000,000; for 1709 and 1710 as 1,400,000. The movements of people engendered by food shortages, far from easing the problem, only made it worse. If famine hit the countryside, epidemics ravaged the towns, because of their densely packed populations, the use of polluted water, and generally insanitary conditions. The spring of 1694 was almost worse than the preceding winter. The tale of *Tom Thumb* (1696) reflects the horror of those terrible years.

The king and his administration reacted swiftly. We have seen how their concern to get food for France led to an intensification of the war on trade and an unprecedented effort to protect maritime convoys carrying cereals. Jean Bart and his crews fought at the Texel not for glory alone but also to feed the kingdom. In 1693, Pontchartrain started an inventory of cereals and a census of the mouths to be fed, completing his figures with further calculations in 1694 (177). These investigations were not mere flights of fancy. Behind Pontchartrain stood the king and, if the controller-general had it in the back of his mind to prepare fiscal expedients, the king and his minister wanted above all to know the extent of the damage caused by shortage of food and to find a remedy. The intendants of the less affected provinces were asked to provide aid to the *généralités* which were suffering more; lower Languedoc was urged to go to the help of upper Languedoc (181), assisted by the Canal des Deux Mers, which had been opened in 1681.

Mme de Maintenon, while never tiring of lamenting the horrors of war, never ceased to emphasize how much Louis was sensitive to the evils of the times and the sufferings of the poor: 'He knows about the misery of his people; nothing is hidden from him; we are searching for all the means of relieving it' (14 October 1692). 'The king wishes, at all costs, to see his people more content' (10 March) (66). To his natural benevolence, *raison d'état* and the concern about population, a sign of good government, the king added Christian impulses.

HIS MAJESTY'S SUBJECTS AND THE COMPLEXITIES OF FRENCH SOCIETY REVEALED

Despite the harsh circumstances, the king could not, as in 1661, reduce the tax burden. On the contrary, the war demanded more taxation. But Louis and Pontchartrain made the distribution of the burden less unfair. The poor would pay more willingly if they realized that the *grands* and the rich were no longer being spared. This is what happened. On 18 January 1695, a royal declaration created a *capitation*, an annual poll tax, new to France and to a degree radical (because the nobility had to pay it), despite its being copied from central Europe. Saint-Simon thought that Pontchartrain had his doubts about it; but it could not have been said that Louis XIV did. Throughout 1694, he followed the preparatory work of the *capitation*. If the rich paid, this was because the king wanted it so. This novelty, which made the new tax part of an overall policy, is sufficient to indicate the importance of the *capitation*. The new tax of January 1695 assisted public finances, and, through its records, we have information about the structure of the French *ancien régime* as well as about the achievements of Louis XIV's social policy (138). This information is provided not so much by the royal declaration as by its graduated scale of payments; for Chamlay (the inspiration behind the expedient) and Pontchartrain's clerks (who carried it out) were fully aware of the nuances of the social hierarchy.

It was neither three orders (clergy, nobility, third estate) nor two opposing groups (privileged and commoners, rich and poor, the powerful and the powerless) who were taxed; instead it was twenty-two 'classes' of taxpayers. These contained no less than 569 ranks, corresponding to offices, estates, grades and professions. The first class, which included most notably the royal family, ministers and the principal financiers, was taxed at 2,000 *livres*; the second, dukes and the *premier président*, at 1,000 *livres*; the eighth, which included brigadier-generals and the councillors of the Parlement, at 200 *livres*; the fifteenth, including the *greffiers* of the *présidiaux* and *rentiers* of medium-sized towns, at 40 *livres*. The last of all, that of simple soldiers and minor domestic servants, only paid 1 *livre*. Since the *capitation* was a tax neither on capital nor on revenue, but one based on rank, the assessment presents an X-ray photograph of French society, taken two thirds of the way through the reign.

The population of the kingdom was neither a society of orders based on protocol nor a class society ruled by money. The division of the nation into three orders no longer corresponded with social reality. That is why the first class of the *capitation* took in a good number of financiers of common birth. The hierarchy of *fiefs de dignité* no longer made sense, except for the primacy of the ducal houses. Marquises, counts, viscounts and barons were all of the same rank: the king placed them in the seventh class, along with the *contrôleurs des postes*. As for 'gentlemen having neither fief nor château', they were in the nineteenth class, alongside gamekeepers. Yet French society was not dominated by economics. No matter how rich a *receveur des tailles* (seventh class) may have been, he was still below even a penniless lieutenant-general in the army (sixth class). In fact as in law, the monarchy was based on honour, and honour had a value which could not be measured in *écus*. The hierarchy, therefore, was not linear. It worked according to four criteria: position or *dignité* (through which maréchal de Bezons, of modest origin, could command the most aristocratic of lieutenant-generals); power (which placed ministers alongside princes of the blood); wealth (a vice-admiral came behind a treasurer of the navy), and consideration (the 'je ne sais quoi', beloved of père Bouhours (15)). Herein lay the mainsprings of the *ancien régime* (138).

The texts of 1695 are equally informative about the immediate situation. Although the combination of power and money clearly favoured the world of finance, it is surprising to see the tax-farmers general (*fermiers généraux*) placed above the dukes. Saint-Simon, the easily offended representative of the ducal class, did not denounce this as a 'scandal' and we may notice, therefore, the extent to which, after thirty-four years, Louis had remoulded French society. The primacy of public service is so great that the business world is eclipsed, not appearing above the eleventh class. For the men of 1690, modernity lay less in industry and commerce than in the renovated institutions and administration to which the king and his ministers had devoted so much attention since 1661. Since then, though war services continued to be honoured, the pen, the robe and finance had come to rival the army. In each of the higher classes we find the same mixture: the military, the pen and the robe, and finance. This demonstrated that the court could not sustain a hegemony over the entire robe class and that the robe could not hope to dominate the whole of the financial world. It also showed that the sword, the robe and finance, understood in their professional sense, were the pillars of the state, the dominant, complementary and competing forces of society. Such was the revolution imposed by the will of Louis XIV.

Finally, the value of the assessment of 1695 is shown even in its details. One of the supplements which were adjoined to it concerned the grades of the navy. Its truth cannot be doubted, with Pontchartrain combining the departments of finances and the navy. And the text proves that the navy did not perish at La Hougue. Through this document we may perceive the vitality of the arsenals and the squadrons, and the effectiveness of the ordinance of 1689. The parallel importance of the new tactic, the war on trade, is no less remarkable – no captain or crew member of the corsair vessels is forgotten. The fact that in the middle of a war, the overworked services of a minister could draw up, purely for a fiscal expedient, one of the most profound texts of French administrative and social history shows the quality of the king's political intelligence and of his administration.

THE DUKE OF BURGUNDY'S KINGDOM

In 1697, with the war still proceeding, the intendants demonstrated once again the solidity of the administrative texture of France. The opportunity was provided for them by Beauvillier. He wrote to the intendants in his capacity as governor of the Duke of Burgundy. He and Fénelon had educated the young prince in religion, Latin, history, geography, politics and the art of war. We know the history syllabus established by the duke: the histories of England and northern Europe (1695), of Germany, Lorraine, the Low Countries and Savoy (1696), of Italy (1697), of the Iberian peninsula, the Indies and Africa (1698), of eastern Europe (1699), and finally of France (1700) (224). In order to complete this last rubric and prepare the Duke of Burgundy for his profession as king, Beauvillier needed the help of the provincial administrators. That is why he engaged their services in early 1697.

The *Memoir . . . for the Instruction of Monseigneur the Duke of Burgundy* was intended to provide a complete picture of each province: situation, geography, navigable waterways, climate, production, forests, stock-rearing, mines, 'marshes to be drained', a picture of the inhabitants calculated by town, village and parish, religious, legal and cultural institutions, the state of the Church, a description of the nobility, 'the magistrates of the towns, their reputation, talents, credit and goods', agriculture, manufactures and 'the number of workmen', ports, trade and commerce, 'the number of sailors and merchants, the number of foreigners settled there', fishing, 'income, where and how, and expenditures, where and how. – Consult old registers to ascertain whether the population used to be more numerous than it is now, the cause of the decline; whether there were Huguenots, how many left. – Customs duties, tolls and *gabelles* of each place, stages, ordinary lodgings [of soldiers], winter quarters.'

This type of statistical inquiry was not novel: in 1664, Colbert had despatched his famous *Instruction* to the *maîtres des requêtes*. The significance lay in the importance given to demographic questions and in the zeal shown by the respondents. Although not officially responsible to Beauvillier, the provincial administrators, despite having little help, were eager to provide replies. These were completed at Beauvillier's request by 1698, and were occasionally modified between 1698 and 1701 on the intervention of Pontchartrain and Chamillart. The memoir for Hainaut ran to fifty-three pages (46), that for Brittany sixty-seven dense pages (8), Champagne two hundred and twenty-nine (17), the intendancy of Paris three hundred and ninety-seven pages (13). Boulainvilliers was to bring all this documentation together in his *État de la France* (1727). These memoirs, so ahead of their times, fixed the image of the kingdom. They allowed Vauban to estimate the population at 19,094,000 souls, an underestimate of some ten per cent (177).

What is striking today, but what the king, clergy, ministers and intendants could only have guessed at, is the demographic revival after the disasters which had added their weight to the high rate of infant mortality, a rate which meant that only one child in two would reach the age of twenty-five. We know there was striking mortality in 1693 and 1694. But, now, from 1695 onwards, a demographic recovery is perceptible, with marriage and birth rates rising sharply. Over the whole decade between 1690 and 1700, there was neither growth nor loss; but in the longer term a slow population growth is perceptible. Between 1675 and 1705, the kingdom gained a million inhabitants (177). Such indices would obviously not appear in the intendants' reports of 1698 and 1699, but these texts do show the advance of the state. The precision of the answers by comparison with those of 1664 is a sign of the enhanced capacity of public service. By 1698, the administrative monarchy had been created: the king was by then better informed and better served. However embryonic the bureaucracy may appear to modern eyes, it had achieved a singular degree of efficiency.

THE MODERNS DEFEAT THE ANCIENTS

The French were aware of the modernity of the state. They could take pride in it, and the *capitation* had just turned it to good account. But the fertile decade of the 1690s also witnessed the debate between the Ancients and the Moderns and the dispute between Bossuet and Fénelon, the latter dispute being a particular instance of the former debate. The dispute between the Ancients and the Moderns was remarkable for having crystallized a certain area of literary activity in France for thirty years, for having been sparked off by the reading of Perrault's poem 'The Century of Louis XIV' at the Académie française on 27 January 1687, and for having worked for the glory of the king and his patronage. Both camps endeavoured to flatter His Majesty. Perrault and his allies (Fontenelle, Houdar de la Motte, the abbé Terrasson, the abbé d'Aubignac and the abbé de Pons) held that the century of Louis XIV was superior to that of Augustus. Before becoming the guiding thread of Voltaire's work, this theme was propagated in Fontenelle's *Parallel between the Ancients and the Moderns* (1688–97) and his scintillating *Digression on the Ancients and the Moderns* (1688).

But the champions of the Ancients, led by Boileau and with La Fontaine, La Bruyère, Racine, Huet and Mme Dacier in the ranks, whilst asserting the superiority of the Greeks and the Romans, did it with enough talent to confirm their own standing and to contribute to the influence of Louis XIV's France at a

time when the country was pondering the true richness of its
blossoming culture. This shows the extent to which the dispute
was a meaningless argument. The partisans of Antiquity exalted
themselves with false modesty. The supporters of the Moderns
had constantly to defend themselves against jealousy, whether
real or apparent. Paradoxically, it was two fervent partisans,
both on the threshold of death, who imposed truces, Arnauld in
1694 and Fénelon in 1714. The first of these peace treaties was
celebrated in verse by Boileau:

> Perrault the anti-Pindaric
> And Despréaux the Homeric
> Have agreed to embrace each other. (11)

The second preceded the triumph of the Moderns. But at the
time of the old king's death there were as yet neither victors nor
vanquished, except for Louis XIV, whose apotheosis was
celebrated in these literary jousts.

Ancients and Moderns had worn each other out by fighting to
delay their antagonists' election to the Académie. Yet they had
respected the rules of literary jousting. Although philosophy slipped into the Moderns' camp, politics does not appear to have
influenced the fight. It is difficult to make the same claim about
Quietism. On 20 July 1698, Madame Palatine wrote:

> I assure you that this quarrel between bishops has nothing to do
> with faith; it is purely a question of ambition; religion hardly
> enters their heads and only its name remains. The verses which
> have been written on this subject are wholly true: faith alone is
> suffering. I don't know whether you have seen them; in any case,
> I have transcribed them for you:

>> In these combats where the prelates of France
>> Seem to seek after truth,
>> One says that hope is being crushed,
>> Another replies that it is charity;
>> It is really faith and no one gives it a thought. (87)

It is the fashion now not to hold Fénelon responsible, to compare Mme Guyon to the finest spiritual authors, to minimize the
dangers of Quietism and to reproach Bossuet for the form of his
polemics.* Everyone agrees in questioning the attitude of Mme

* This was the view of the late abbé Cognet.

de Maintenon – imprudent at first, and then relentless against those whose false mildness had seduced her. Madame Palatine wrote again, on 7 August 1698:

> I can well understand that mysticism is not at all for me. Mme de Maintenon understands it better than I do; everything about it is mysterious. Nothing has surprised me more, I assure you, than seeing this lady abandon the Archbishop of Cambrai, who was such a friend of hers. They often used to eat and drink together. She would go on no outing without the archbishop also being present; music, meetings of friends, he was invited everywhere, and now he is persecuted to excess. Also I feel sorry for him with all my heart, for this fine man must suffer a lot from being abandoned and persecuted by those in whom he had placed all his confidence. (87)

Madame Guyon, born Jeanne-Marie Bouvier de la Mothe, a good-looking, lively and devout widow, had been introduced by the Barnabite, père La Combe, to the 'new mysticism' of the Spanish theologian Molinos, who had defended, in a series of striking works, the doctrine of Quietism. These claimed that contemplation not only was more important than prayer but made it irrelevant, because all acts ended up by denying a more important truth: the complete belonging of the soul to the Creator. Escorted by her Barnabite, Mme Guyon travelled around preaching on this theme. She then popularized it in 1685 with a work entitled *A Short and Very Simple Method of Orisons, which may be Practised Very Easily by All*. In Paris, the couple did not please Mgr de Harlay in the slightest. Père La Combe was arrested in October 1687 and Mme Guyon in January 1688. But the preacher of pure love had cousins in the Parlement, and Mme de Maintenon persuaded Louis XIV to release the young woman.

No sooner released, Mme Guyon won over the marquise de Maintenon, the ladies of Saint-Cyr, and a chapel at the court called 'the little convent', which was run by several duchesses (Mmes de Beauvillier, Chevreuse and Mortemart, who were daughters of Colbert, and the duchesse de Charost) and to which Fénelon gave lectures. Mme de Maintenon walked about with the *Short . . . Method* in her pocket. Fénelon, who took up his appointment as tutor to the Duke of Burgundy in August 1689, enjoyed the king's favour. The only discordant voice was that of Pontchartrain, who told the king that Fénelon 'was forming at the court and almost before his eyes a party dangerous to religion, pernicious to good manners and capable of stirring up a fanaticism which could be fatal for both the Church and the state' (224). In any case, Mme Guyon, whose Quietism did not preclude a remarkable level of activity, made plain her desire to reach Beauvillier with the aid of the duchess, and the Duke of Burgundy through his governor, Beauvillier. The young prince was thus besieged by the Beauvilliers, the Chevreuses and Fénelon.

At the same time the author of the *Short . . . Method* organized her disciples: the children of pure love would be known as 'Michelins'. 'Small, joyous, cheerful, feeble, childlike', but fervently militant, they would have their hierarchy ('general, assistants, secretary, chaplain, master of novices, gaoler, porter, flower girl, portress, sacristan, *intendante* of recreations', and so on). Fénelon was the head, Mme Guyon an 'assistant' and St Michael the 'special protector'. The fact that the future Archbishop of Cambrai endorsed these games – even though Molinos, the begetter of the business, had been condemned in 1687 – shows that 'this exceptional soul' was lacking somewhat in realism. Neither Mme Guyon nor Fénelon, while aspiring to the mystic life, was suited to it. As for the marquise de Maintenon, her religion, so reasonable, could not support for long the graft of a 'pure love', with its vague and indistinct verbiage. She remained faithful to Fénelon until 1696, obtaining his nomination to the see of Cambrai in 1694. Saint-Cyr became unrecognizable. Quietism provoked a slackening of obligations, even of the rule of obedience. Ecclesiastical visitors, including the Bishop of Chartres, complained about this and Mme Guyon banned their visits.

In early 1694, Bossuet, having read *The Torrents*, a work by Mme Guyon, thought it should be condemned; on 16 October, Harlay censured the theses of Mme Guyon and père La Combe; in the spring of 1695, a commission made up of Bossuet, Noailles, Archbishop of Rouen, and Tronson, head of Saint-Sulpice, also condemned neo-mysticism, in terms which Fénelon accepted. Everything seemed in order. On 19 August 1695, Noailles replaced the deceased Harlay as Archbishop of Paris, while Fénelon was combining his tutorship of the prince with his diocesan duties. But late in 1695 the Archbishop of Paris decided to have Mme Guyon, who had started preaching again, imprisoned. Bossuet was wrong in trying to exploit his victory, while Fénelon was wrong in contesting what he had appeared to accept a year earlier. Fénelon, in taking up the gauntlet, had forgotten two facts. First, the condemnation of Quietism had merely confirmed a papal brief of 29 November 1689. Secondly, Mme de Maintenon, urged on by Godet des Marais, now shared Bossuet's opinions. The year 1696, therefore, saw two quarrels: between Mme de Maintenon and Fénelon, and Fénelon and Bossuet.

This affair, politicized by the importance of the antagonists, embittered relationships at court and in Paris for four more years, between 1697 and 1700. Even religious orders and institutions were divided. Public opinion was perplexed, as was shown by a carol of 1699:

> Hey, why write so much
> Of Cambrai and of Meaux
> When there is nothing left to say
> Which is either good or new? (287)

Because it was smothered in the nest, we may smile at Quietism. Bossuet well knew that it was not a mere trifle. It is indeed true that, in an age of baroque Catholicism, rapid condemnations were perfectly normal. Innocent texts and false summaries of a doctrine were censored. And, on the other hand, certain theses which could have been censored only led to minor controversies before the passage of time proved them justified. But the French Church and the Roman Church understood (or divined) that Quietism was harmful, anti-evangelical, anti-popular and falsely elitist. It was an intellectual vice. Better advised than on Protestant affairs, the king sensed the dangers of Guyonism, especially of Fénelon's variety. To begin with he reacted gently, but then intervened against the 'divine but fanciful' Fénelon.*

In January 1697, the Archbishop of Cambrai published his *Explication of the Maxims of the Saints*; the following March Bossuet presented to Louis XIV his refutation of Fénelon, the *Instruction on the States of Prayer*. This won him a position on the council of state. On 3 August, Fénelon, to whom the king had refused permission to go and plead his cause in Rome, left the court for

---

* The expression is Lamartine's.

Cambrai, in a state of semi-disgrace. The courtiers drew back. The archbishop was supported by Chevreuse and Beauvillier alone. In late 1697, Bossuet published a *Summary on the Explication of the Maxims of the Saints,* in which the controversy was sustained. According to Madame Palatine's résumé of Bossuet's polemical position, Quietism 'is a very convenient religion, for they hold prayer and all external devotion to be superfluous, good for the ignorant alone; while they, having given their lives once and for all to God, cannot in any way be damned; all they have to do is to say once a day "God is", nothing more; the rest of the time they need refuse their bodies nothing of what they demand', considering such physical attractions to be 'merely bestial'. This résumé was, in reality, a caricature of the extreme position of Molinos. Fénelon was more subtle, and, because his style attracted considerable praise, his condemnation was not assured.

Royal disgrace came on 2 June 1698, when Louis XIV discharged the Duke of Burgundy's household, which swarmed with Quietists. The condemnation by Rome was declared on 12 March 1699, but only just, and as a result of pressure from Versailles. But when, on 4 April, the nuncio presented the brief censuring twenty-three propositions from the *Maxims of the Saints* to the king, His Majesty found it too moderate. Dangeau reported on 12 April, not without humour: 'M. the Archbishop of Cambrai has issued a pastoral letter forbidding anyone in his diocese from reading his book: here they are pleased with this letter.' A year later the Assembly of the Clergy prepared a sort of White Book on the affair, which was now considered closed.

The apparently conservative party of the Bishop of Meaux would in future dominate the Church of France. The apparently innovative party of the Archbishop of Cambrai was merely an avatar of Gnosticism. That is why Fénelon is to be placed among the Ancients and Bossuet among the Moderns.

26

The Spanish Succession

A FTER RYSWICK, the image of Louis XIV was transformed
in some people's eyes. 'No provocation . . . a reasonable
acceptance of what was unpreventable; a desire for concord with
the other European powers in order to preserve peace.' (281) On
the surface, the responsibility for this new deal should, perhaps,
be accorded to the official animators of his diplomacy, the
elderly Pomponne (d. 1699) and his son-in-law Torcy, secretary
of state for foreign affairs since 1696 and minister from 1699. As
individuals, they were not as tough as Croissy. But a deeper
explanation lies with the king himself. His desire for *détente* was
not novel. This helps us to understand the extent to which the
Ten Years' War had been, on the French side, a defensive affair,
like the Reunions which had been one of its causes. It was in line
with the spirit of Ryswick, for victorious France could either
have prolonged the conflict or demanded more advantageous
terms. Despite his repugnance at having to bargain with William
III, the king did not hesitate, with Torcy's assistance, from
entering into the preliminary discussions about a possible partition of the Spanish succession.

'DON'T COUNT YOUR CHICKENS . . .'

Charles II's state of health seemed to be a matter of universal
concern in the last two years of the century. On 14 May 1699,
Dangeau wrote: 'The latest news from Madrid is not good concerning the health of the King of Spain.' On 12 July: 'He is
better at present.' But on 14 August: 'It is not thought that he

will last through the autumn.' On 24 August, Charles II was 'a little better', and on the 28th, 'considerably better'. This surprising recovery overturned Europe's expectations as to the likely course of events. Dangeau similarly noted on 5 November: 'The news from Madrid is that the King of Spain is much better; there is even a hope that he may soon have children.' (26) The king was an epileptic, but not yet thirty-eight years old, and his desire for offspring was still strong. On 12 January 1700, Dangeau wrote: 'The health of the King of Spain is growing more robust', but on the 19th he learnt that His Catholic Majesty had been unconscious for over an hour after having fainted. On the 23rd, the opinion at Versailles was that Charles II had 'recovered very well from his recent accident'. But on 1 March, 'the latest news from Madrid is not good so far as the health of the King of Spain is concerned'. On the 5th, Dangeau noted: 'He is swelling considerably, and it is greatly feared that he will not last.' (26) In fact, he only survived a further eight months.

The court at Madrid was a nest of intrigue. Louis XIV was hated by his brother-in-law and held in contempt by the Austrian faction. Europe was kept on tenter-hooks. The Habsburgs of Vienna kept close watch on events, hoping to be the sole beneficiaries. The three maritime powers – England, France and the United Provinces – for their part, looked forward to a partition, and sought thereby to avoid the reconstitution of the empire of Charles V. These courts frantically planned the disposition of the dying king's possessions. The immense inheritance comprised Castile, Aragon, Navarre, Belgium, the better part of Italy (Milan, Tuscany, Naples and Sicily), Sardinia, Latin America (except for Brazil) and the Philippines. Spain was poorly administered, but still counted as a fourth-ranking maritime power. It seems the case that poverty in the peninsula was on the retreat after 1680, with renewed economic growth in Catalonia. American precious metals were once again reaching Cadiz. In 1698, Charles II's preferred successor was a grand-nephew who had the advantage of being neither a Habsburg nor a Bourbon: Joseph-Ferdinand, Prince of Bavaria, son of the elector. His death in 1699 reduced the number of candidates to two: Archduke Charles, nephew of the King of Spain, born in 1685; and Philippe duc d'Anjou, born in 1683, second son of the French dauphin and grand-nephew of Charles II.

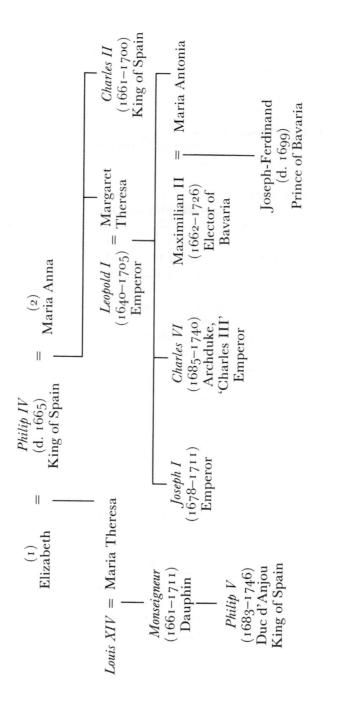

In 1698, however, there were still three candidates. Louis XIV used the comte de Tallard as an intermediary and arrived at an agreement with William III for a partition along the following lines: Archduke Charles would get Milan; Monseigneur, the Two Sicilies, Tuscany and Sardinia; Joseph-Ferdinand of Bavaria, Spain, the Low Countries and the colonies. For France, it was a question of gaining bargaining-counters in order to lay its hands upon Savoy and improve the 'pré carré' (124). The death of Joseph-Ferdinand put an end to these plans. And a further element entered the equation: the Peace of Karlowitz (26 January 1699) marked the containment of the Turks, gave Hungary and Transylvania to Leopold I, and allowed him to turn his attentions towards western Europe. Louis XIV and Torcy therefore reopened negotiations with William III. Archduke Charles would get Spain, Belgium and the Indies; the Duke of Lorraine, Milan; Naples would go to the Duke of Savoy; and Monseigneur would take possession of Lorraine and Savoy. On 5 July 1699, the emperor agreed to a partition, but on condition that his younger son would take the whole of Italy, with France getting the West Indies as compensation. But the English objected to this last clause, and Louis preferred his *pré carré*. Thus, the possibility of an agreement lapsed, whilst Louis XIV signed a new partition treaty with England (13 March 1700) and with the United Provinces (25 March). The archduke would be offered the Iberian peninsula, the Indies and Belgium. Milan would go to the Duke of Lorraine. The Dauphin would get Naples and Sicily, the fortresses of Tuscany, Guipuzcoa and Lorraine.

In all these negotiations, the chancelleries of Europe had taken no account of the Spanish, nor of their sense of national identity. In spite of the weakness of the monarchy, they did not want to accept the dismemberment of their empire. The situation in Madrid developed rapidly during 1700. Despite his weaknesses, Charles II was conscious of the grandeur of Spain and the eminent dignity of his house. He refused to stand to one side whilst the monarchy which had once been the leading power in Europe was torn in pieces. (124)

Before his death on All Saints' Day, he drew up a will (2 October) and selected a legatee.

A COUP

Charles II chose not so much an individual as a vision of the possessions of his Crown carried forward into the future as a unity. Having already drafted a will giving the entire inheritance to Archduke Charles, he let himself be persuaded by Cardinal Portocarrero to sign a new one in favour of Philippe duc d'Anjou. All idea of partition was eliminated, but the two Bourbon monarchies would remain separate. 'The news of the will in favour of the duc d'Anjou exploded like a bomb in Madrid on 2 November, spreading confusion within the Austrian faction but being generally well received by the Spanish' (124). Elsewhere, news of the will percolated abroad, and Tallard, arriving at Fontainebleau on 2 November, made known British concern; on the 5th, the council of ministers decided to retain the plans for partition and advised Heinsius of this fact. Yet a faction favourable to the Bourbon succession was forming, comprising the French ambassador in Madrid, the marquis d'Harcourt, and, at court, Barbezieux and, above all, Monseigneur, who had a direct interest at stake. One cannot say, therefore, that the King of Spain's will came as a surprise. But it forced Louis XIV and his politicians to take almost without delay one of the most momentous decisions in French history.

The process began on Tuesday, 9 November, at Fontainebleau. 'In the morning, the king being at the council of finances, M. de Barbezieux came to give him the news of the death of the King of Spain' (124) and an extract from the will despatched with the courier. 'The king changed the orders which he had given for hunting, and, at 3 p.m., ordered the ministers to come to Mme de Maintenon's apartments. Monseigneur, who had been hunting wolves in the morning, had already returned. The council [meeting] lasted until seven o'clock. Mme de Maintenon, in whose rooms it took place, was present.' (26) Not having any record of what transpired, we do not know the details of what was said by each participant (224). But the broad lines may be set out by a reconstruction, a legitimate device to enable us to take the measure of Louis XIV as he consulted and made up his mind, and one which will reveal the reasons which made him incline towards acceptance of the will. It was possible that to accept would spark off a general conflict. But by looking at the logic in 1700 we can the better comprehend Voltaire's famous affirmation: 'There has never been a more legitimate war.'

In his capacity as *rapporteur* to the council of ministers, Torcy was the first to express an opinion. He presented the two options: to accept the will of Charles II or to stick by the agreements reached with William of Orange. Acceptance of the will would lead to war, because Europe would accuse the king of aspirations towards universal monarchy. France would lose the promise of the annexation of Lorraine, a guarantee of the frontier with the empire, and all for stakes which were uncertain. Upon the advantages of acceptance, Torcy was less convincing. Beauvillier, for his part, did not try to balance the arguments. He 'concluded for upholding the partition treaty, for he was persuaded that war, the natural consequence of accepting the will, would cause the ruin of France' (104).

The chancellor too weighed up the arguments for and against. But, unlike his younger colleague, he expressed a preference for accepting the will. He thought that France did not have much to fear from the emperor, who was only suzerain over highly independent princes (he had forgotten that France had lost the support of the Turks and did not perceive that its only allies in the empire would be the Elector of Bavaria and his brother, the Archbishop of Cologne (124)). He declared himself certain that France possessed the means necessary for the protection of Spain and its colonial links. Closely connected to the merchants of the ports and to the chambers of commerce and their representatives, as well as to the other members of the council of commerce, Pontchartrain knew what this group would want. He knew that from Dunkirk to Bayonne they were anxious to increase their imports from America and dreamt of 'inundating Latin America with Breton cloth and ebony [black slaves]' (124). In any comparison between the advantages of accepting the will – an increase overseas in the prestige and profits of the kingdom and a diminishment in those of England and Holland – and the acquisition of Lorraine, which had, in any case, been neutralized after Ryswick, the latter counted for less. This left the question of England (and who could rely upon William III's good faith?) and the danger of war. But, if such a danger existed, was it not better to be exposed to it for the sake of a great kingdom rather than for the crumbs offered by a partition?

Monseigneur strongly supported Pontchartrain. He claimed 'his inheritance' all the more passionately because he was losing the hope of personal authority in Italy, preferring to ensure a great kingdom for Philippe in accordance with his uncle's wishes. Opinions, therefore, were divided. Louis XIV ended the debate and delayed his decision until he had received more information. This came on the 10th. Couriers brought details about the 'wishes of the lords and the peoples' (124) demonstrating the significance of Spanish national sentiment. On the evening of the 10th, therefore, a new council meeting decided unanimously in favour of accepting the will, with even Beauvillier coming round to the proposition. A quick decision had been necessary, and the Spanish ambassador was informed on the following day. Though Louis XIV had taken dynastic interests into consideration, the national interest had been the more significant and, though he had been inclined towards his brother-in-law's solution since the 9th, he had taken note of the divisions in the council, had waited until he knew the details of the will, and had taken time for reflection and for the winning over of Torcy.

On Tuesday the 16th, Louis XIV summoned the Spanish ambassador to Versailles, called the duc d'Anjou, and said to the former: 'You may salute him as your king.' The ambassador having presented his compliments, the king replied: 'He does not yet understand Spanish; I will reply on his behalf.' Then the doors of the *cabinet* were opened and the king spoke to the courtiers: 'Messieurs, before you stands the King of Spain. His birth has called him to this crown; the whole nation wished it and asked me for it without delay, and I granted it to them with pleasure. It is the command of Heaven.' Then he turned to Philip V and declared: 'Be a good Spaniard, that is now your first duty; but remember that you were born French and maintain the union between the two nations. This is the way to make them happy and to preserve peace in Europe.' (26) After Mass, the Spanish ambassador was heard to say: 'What rapture! There are no longer any Pyrenees.' Torcy busied himself trying to calm foreign opinion, repeatedly saying that 'the acceptance of the will was the best possible solution, because partition would have aggrandized France and provoked a war with the emperor, who had not accepted it, and with Spain, which did not want it at any price' (224). He would support the new king in a similarly effective way for twelve years, subtly and pragmatically for the most part, firmly when he thought it necessary. As for Philip V, he left for his kingdom on 5 December, accompanied by his brothers, by Beauvillier and by Noailles. On 13 January 1701, the cortège had reached Bayonne, where over 3,000 Spaniards came to meet them. Philip V reached his palace of Buen Retiro on 18 February. 'There was such a crowd of people at his arrival that more than sixty were suffocated.' (26) It seemed as if the people of Spain were happy to accept the grandson of the Most Christian King as Catholic King. This sentiment committed the future to the Bourbon cause, despite the imminent perils.

AGITATION IN EUROPE

The Bourbon solution was far from perfect. In Madrid, whilst proving himself a 'good Spaniard', Philip V needed not only French troops and ships, but also advisers from north of the Pyrenees. Cardinal Portocarrero adapted to this, but not all of the Spanish court followed him. Spain lacked politicians and military leaders of stature, although it was not admitted at the time. The young king would turn out to be courageous and determined, but to have little capacity for government. Did he not become too heavily influenced by his wife, Marie-Louise-Gabrielle of Savoy (d. 1714), and by the *camarera mayor*, the irrepressible princesse des Ursins, née La Trémoille? 'This gave to Franco-Spanish relations between 1701 and 1703 a confused and chaotic character which, because of personal rivalries between individuals with authority, reminds one of the Fronde.' (224)

Still more serious for France were the upheavals caused by a situation wished upon them all by Charles II. Louis was obliged to take precautionary measures and he could not do that without disturbing the Dutch and upsetting England. For example, the Parlement of Paris, on 1 February 1701, registered letters-patent keeping open the possibility of Philip V's succession to the French crown (201). At the same time (5–6 February), Louis occupied, with his grandson's consent, the so-called 'barrier fortresses' in the Low Countries, driving out the Dutch mercenaries. Heinsius was furious. As for William III, he exploited it skilfully to orchestrate fear of a papist plot. The spies of the maritime powers could easily discover how the King of France was 'taking precautions' against an uncertain future. On

26 January, he signed an ordinance for the raising of the militias. On 5 and 10 February, Chamillart co-signed letters-patent creating seventy-two new companies of dragoons (on the 5th) and a further twenty regiments of cavalry (on the 10th). On 15 February, as France renewed its alliance with Cologne, Louis XIV re-established the regiment of carabineers. On 1 March, he ordered the raising of 120 cavalry companies; on the 20th, he reinforced all the infantry regiments by ten men per company (201). Europe once again experienced an atmosphere of armed peace. The alliances with Cologne, with Bavaria in March, with Savoy in April and with Portugal in June completed these precautionary measures.

In the other camp, William of Orange also sought safeguards. The famous Act of Settlement, guaranteeing the Protestant succession, was pushed through Parliament in June 1701. It was an opportune measure, for William III was to die on 19 March 1702. But before that, his father-in-law, the exiled James II, himself died on 16 September 1701. Louis XIV, ignoring the terms of Ryswick, besieged by the Stuart Queen of England, the pope and the marquise de Maintenon, recognized the Prince of Wales, now James III, as rightful king. He seemed to have given way to his Catholic prejudices, to his emotions and to family feeling, committing a political error under a cloak of beneficence. In reality, matters were less simple. Although William III recognized Philip V, on 17 April, English merchants were putting pressure on Parliament, which duly voted large credits for war preparations. The States General at The Hague were in a state of high tension. As for Leopold, having assured his alliance with Brandenburg, he sent his troops to invade Milan. Catinat, short of troops, fell back before the Imperialists, who were commanded by Eugene of Savoy. Almost immediately, the emperor, England and the United Provinces signed the Treaty of The Hague (7 September). In this text, the signatories did not declare war on Louis XIV, although they did each promise not to conclude a separate peace. They wanted the separation of France and Spain, and demanded the restitution to the maritime powers of their lost trading privileges in the Spanish Indies. They divided Charles II's inheritance yet again: Milan, Naples and Sicily would fall to the emperor; and the neutralized Low Countries would become a barrier between Holland and France (instead of *Gallus amicus sed non vicinus*, there was to be *Gallus* *inimicus et non vicinus**). In the light of these events, we may understand that Louis XIV's recognition of James II's son was merely one move in a cold war.

But William III broke with Versailles, called new Parliamentary elections – which produced a Whig majority that was hostile to Philip V and France and that voted new subsidies for war – and stirred up his adopted country against the Pretender,† so successfully that, at his death, English attitudes changed little. Queen Anne, his sister-in-law, had not the means by which to change course. In Holland, Heinsius, possessing greater freedom of movement, quickly set himself up as the leader of the coalition. The emperor, emboldened by his successes in Italy, had no intention of restricting a conflict in which he was fully implicated. On 15 May 1702, England, the emperor and the United Provinces declared war on the Bourbon monarchies. Louis XIV found himself on the defensive more than ever before.

THE BALANCE OF FORCES

At first sight, Louis XIV was not in a better position than he had been in 1688. Opposing him were the emperor, the Elector of Brandenburg (shortly to be King of Prussia), the Palatinate, some other German princes, Denmark, England and the United Provinces. But such an impressive list presents the wrong impression. Although England possessed fiscal resources comparable to those of France, Leopold had three times less money at his disposal (124). England could mobilize 100,000 soldiers, as could the emperor, but the King of France already had 200,000 armed, trained and prepared. The English navy had a great reputation, but only 150 warships as against the 206 of Louis XIV's. Of course, the Dutch fleet was the third in the world, but then that of Spain should not be ignored (237). In all, the maritime forces of the two camps were in broad equilibrium. On the side of France and Philip V stood the Electors of Bavaria and Cologne, the Duke of Savoy and the King of Portugal: three advanced positions and protection on the left flank in the penin-

---

* 'A Frenchman as a friend but not as a neighbour', 'A Frenchman as neither a friend nor a neighbour'.
† James Edward or James III, son and heir of James II, King of England.

sula. Two great and four smaller powers should have been a match for three great and three medium-sized powers.

Working to Louis XIV's disadvantage would be the administrative weakness and endemic disorder of Spain, the imminent defections of Savoy (8 October 1702) and Portugal (16 May 1703), the scale of a world-wide theatre of operations, the determination of the Dutch pensionary Heinsius, and the talents and aggression of two generals, Marlborough and Prince Eugene. To these should be added the element of Protestant solidarity. The War of the Spanish Succession was a religious war. Whilst in the preceding conflicts William of Orange, for example, had not hesitated, despite his convictions, to ally himself with the Spain of the *autos de fe*, now the camps were, at least at the beginning, more entrenched. The only exception was the emperor; for, although the empire was divided, the emperor was a Catholic and, further, a friend of the Jesuits. This paradox would not help the Habsburg, surrounded by so many Lutherans, Anglicans and Calvinists, and nor would it strengthen the cause of his son Charles, compromised in religion by his own troops.

On the other hand, the kingdom of France possessed a number of assets. Tallard, Villeroy and La Feuillade were not in the same class as Marlborough and Prince Eugene; but Berwick was to turn out to be a 'fortunate' general, whilst Vendôme and Villars were aggressive, patriotic and well respected by their soldiers. Jean Bart died early in the war, but no other navy had a trio comparable to Ducasse, Duguay-Trouin and Cassard.* After thirty years of attention, Vauban's military 'iron curtain' demonstrated its strategic importance. Since the acceptance of the will, French merchants had launched themselves into the exploitation of the riches of America, large-scale slave-trading and commerce in the southern seas. It was a rich and dynamic nation which entered the war. The revival of the privateering war and the contracts between the king and its sponsors would be the proof of that. But it appeared that two other elements would play a decisive part: Philip's capacity to rally and galvanize the Spanish population, and the inexhaustible talents of Desmarets for mobilizing resources to support the burden of a war which would be cripplingly expensive.

* And the contributions of Châteaurenault, the comte de Forbin and many others should not be ignored.

Philip V's task was not an easy one. His privy purse, the *bolsillo* was inadequate. Without help, his troops were incapable of retaining his Italian possessions or the Belgian towns. The marquis de Louville, *gentilhomme de la manche*, half mentor, half spy, openly despised the Spanish and kept Versailles informed by regular despatches. France refused to send Desmarets to Philip and kept him waiting for the military adviser he requested, Puységur. And the Austrian faction was still in existence.

In the 1680s, the Spanish had often hated France (110) and Charles II's will had not changed everything overnight. An easily offended nation was being offered a choice of foreign sovereigns, French or Austrian. But the mistakes made by the archduke and his allies soon began to influence public sentiment. By September 1702, it was being said in Spain 'that the heretics had committed terrible desecration on all sides, pillaging churches, using them as stables and trampling on the Blessed Sacrament, smashing the statues of saints, dressing them up to mock them and dragging them through the streets'. When Louis XIV talked about this with his grandson's ambassador, the diplomat replied: 'All the better, Sire! All the better!' Such reports did indeed serve Philip V's cause. Now 'an infinite number of people rushed from all parts to defend religion and their country' (97).

As a descendant of the king who had brutally extirpated 'heresy' in France, and flanked by a Jesuit confessor, Philip V was well placed to appeal to his subjects with his sense of honour, his courage and even his tendency towards indolence. Though the archduke was also a Catholic prince, his troops hardly inspired the Spanish with confidence. The situation of 'Charles III' prefigured that of the French in Spain in 1808: even when his armies appeared victorious, the local population detested their presence as an occupying force. Did not the pretender's armies contain every variety of European Protestant? In their ranks could be found Lutherans from the empire, Anglicans, Scottish Presbyterians and Dutch Calvinists. This explains the success in 1703 of a medal struck in Italy for Spanish consumption. On the obverse side was the image of the duc d'Anjou: 'Philip V, by the grace of God, Catholic King.' On the reverse side was the portrait of his rival: 'Charles III, Catholic King by the grace of heretics.' (97) How could divine law not have intended the Bourbon to rule over pious Spain? It was not known how long it might take for the archduke to become Spanish. On the other hand, everyone was in agreement that Philip V would soon speak the language well and become assimilated into Castilian culture.

From the spring of 1701, Louville had requested a financial adviser from Versailles. France sent the armourer Orry, and not (as Madrid had wished) Desmarets. Desmarets, Colbert's nephew and in disgrace since 1683, was held in reserve. In October 1703, he joined the royal council and, from them on, was in effective control, being more competent than Chamillart and having a special relationship with potential lenders in the kingdom and elsewhere, including the Protestant bankers who would help to finance Louis XIV's war. In 1708, he became controller-general and then a minister. Even Saint-Simon praised this high-ranking civil servant:

> Desmarets, raised and educated by his uncle, had learnt from him all the maxims and the whole art of financial government; he had got to the heart of all its different aspects, and, since everything passed through his hands, no one knew better than he did all the tricks of the financiers, all the profits which they made in his [his uncle's] time, and, through this knowledge, what they could have made since. (94)

After 1703, Desmarets would be Chamillart's support. In the financial crisis of 1708, he restored confidence within a few days. On 4 March, the marquise de Maintenon wrote to the princesse des Ursins: 'The devaluation of the coinage, at the same time as the change of controller-general, has led to eight or ten million [*livres*] appearing in a single day. M. Desmaretz does not appear perturbed and all the businessmen are delighted by it.'

There would be no major transformations in this area of finance, neither through receipts capable of guaranteeing a whole year of cash and credit, nor through a revolution in patterns of behaviour. Expedients still flourished. But Desmarets displayed something approaching frantic zeal in his creation and multiplication of minor miracles of fund-raising, enough to allow for a spring campaign and to buy time during the long negotiations. Louis and Philip did not believe that 'the war could not be sustained and [believed] that the conditions laid down at Geertruidenberg could only have been avoided thanks to his efforts' (224). Saint-Simon accused him of taking on his shoulders, like Atlas, the burden of the world, and, to some degree, the comparison was apposite. Pontchartrain had carried the weight of the Ten Years' War; Colbert's nephew financed a longer and more gruelling war under extraordinary conditions and did so for two monarchies, not one.

AN UNSTABLE EQUILIBRIUM

In 1701, these financial problems were not yet of critical import-ance, but, on 12 March, the king reintroduced the *capitation* tax of 1695. Then, in June, an edict created two directors-general of finances to ease the burdens on Chamillart, who now had two departments, finances and war, under his overall command. Unfortunately, Fleuriau d'Armenonville and Rouillé du Coudray did not possess the talents of Desmarets.

The first three years of war were marked by French superior-ity. At sea, the defeat of Châteaurenault at Vigo, with the loss of several vessels (22 October 1702), was offset by the successes of the aggressive Coëtlogon, Forbin and Saint-Pol. In Italy, the first engagements were disappointing: Prince Eugene forced Catinat to retreat (July 1701), beat Villeroy and the Duke of Savoy at Chiari (1 September 1701), and then took Cremona and captured the duc de Villeroy (1 February 1702). On the other hand, Philip V's visit to Italy satisfied Naples, and the situation in the north changed once Louis XIV sent his cousin Vendôme there. For four years, Vendôme held Eugene in check, making up for the defection of Savoy. On 26 July 1702, Vendôme defeated Visconti at Santa Vittoria; on 15 August 1702, he gained a victory over Prince Eugene at Luzzara; on 26 October 1703, Visconti was again repulsed, at San Sebastiano; on 16 August 1705, he once again had the better of Eugene, at Cas-sano; and on 19 April 1706, he crushed Rewentlaw at Calcinato. But as soon as Versailles recalled Vendôme, the Savoyard change of sides began to influence the course of the war; Pied-mont was a wedge between France and Spanish Milan, by then under threat. The Duke of Savoy abandoned the French in late 1702, declaring war on his erstwhile allies in December.

In the Low Countries, after a raid by the maréchal de Bouf-flers as far as Nymwegen in June 1702, which provided Louis XIV's grandson with an opportunity to display his bravery, and the splendid defence of Kaiserswerth by the marquis de Blainville, who held the town for fifty-nine days, the reverses began. Marlborough, the enemy commander-in-chief, took Gueldre and Liège. On 7 November, Louis XIV gave the government of the Low Countries to the Duke of Bavaria. Most of Belgium remained in Bourbon hands until 1706, but the population, their customary loyalties disrupted and subject to the militia impositions, considered themselves under French military occupation. Nevertheless, Bergeyck, 'the Belgian Colbert', contributed towards the establishment of a provisional French-style administrative organization, whilst at the same time carrying out a stratagem that was more personal and more Spanish than it appeared. Certain towns were bitterly contested: in June 1703, Marlborough took Huy, which was recaptured by the Elector of Bavaria in June 1705, before falling once again into allied hands, in July.

Between the Rhine and the Danube, the war went well for France at first. Villars confirmed his reputation as a commander with luck on his side. After taking Neuburg, he beat the Prince of Baden at Friedlingen on 14 October 1702 and won his marshal's baton. Late that same year, the comte de Tallard took Trier and the king's troops began a new occupation of the duchy of Lorraine. The year 1703 turned out just as favourably: in March, Villars took Kehl and the elector was the victor at Passau; in April, the elector captured Ratisbon; in May, the two generals combined their forces; in June, the elector took Innsbruck; in July, the baron Legall beat Prince Louis of Baden at Munderkingen; in September, the Duke of Burgundy and Vauban accepted the surrender of Breisach; and on 20 September, Villars and the elector crushed Field Marshal von Stirum at Höchstädt.*

In all these campaigns, however, the real stake was the Spanish kingdom, where the position of Philip V had become precarious. The defection of Portugal was a heavy blow. On the 16 May 1703, the Portuguese king imitated Savoy and promised to lend assistance to the allies with an army of 27,000 men in support of 'Charles III'. On 27 December, in a treaty signed

---

* This first encounter at Höchstädt (20 September 1703), which went in Louis XIV's favour, should not be confused with the second battle of the same name (and same location), of 13 August 1704 (Blenheim), which ended with the victory of Prince Eugene of Savoy over the comte de Tallard and M. de Marsin.

with John Methuen, he opened Portugal to British commerce. This provided the means for the archduke's first attempt at winning the crown. Landed at Lisbon by the British navy in March 1704, Charles III marched towards Madrid. He was stopped by Berwick, who had been hastily despatched with 12,000 men by Louis XIV to save the Spanish king's throne. Meanwhile, the British fleet under Rooke was very active along the coast of Andalusia and in the Mediterranean. But his attempt to take Cadiz failed, although he succeeded in August 1704 at Gibraltar, which was besieged in vain by Pointis and Tessé in the following year. Only the French naval victory at Velez-Malaga on 24 August 1704 prevented the Mediterranean from becoming a British lake; but what Charles III had failed to achieve in the west in 1704 he succeeded in doing in the east in 1705. He landed in Spain, and Gerona and Barcelona rallied to him in October. Things seemed to be going very badly for the French king.

Louis XIV put a brave face upon it, however, and, whilst he rejoiced at successes, commanding *Te Deums*, he was imperturbable when the news was disappointing or bad. This phlegmatic calm earned him the admiration of the marquise de Maintenon, and even the respect of Saint-Simon. It did not prevent the king from reacting to events. He sent the Duke of Burgundy into battle. He knew how to use rewards to stimulate the enthusiasm of his commanders. In this domain, the king was generous to a fault. On 23 December 1702, he named twenty-four lieutenant-generals, twenty-five brigadier-generals and thirty brigadiers. At the beginning of 1703, he awarded forty crosses of St Louis to the navy. On 20 January, he gave the same red sash to 512 disabled veterans of the land armies. Between these two promotions, he had doubled the number of marshals of France. To the nine existing ones, he added another ten: Chamilly, 'a big fat man,' according to Saint-Simon, 'very valiant, the epitome of honour and probity, in keeping with his bulk' (26), Coeuvres, son of the comte d'Estrées, Châteaurenault, Vauban, Rosen, and MM d'Huxelles, de Tessé, de Montrevel, de Tallard and d'Harcourt. Later that same year, he added the comte de Marsin. These were the eleven of 1703 in order of promotion. The classification appeared to single out two qualities: the first five were fighting men; the remaining six were courtiers. The first group were being rewarded; the second encouraged to do better.

Louis XIV was also preoccupied, indirectly, with sustaining morale within France. Now that he was no longer at the front, this was his best means of contributing to the war-effort. Royal letters, read out by clergymen, encouraged patriotic endeavour. Depending upon the circumstances, His Majesty prescribed the celebration of a *Te Deum* or ordered ceremonies of jubilation or prayers 'of forty hours' (173). In general, the prelates acceded obediently to these requests and required priests to read out pastoral letters concerning the latest news. Thus, on 31 August 1705, Louis XIV ordered *Te Deums* in celebration of Vendôme's victory over Prince Eugene. His order was in a text of twenty-six lines (60), but the Bishop of Châlons drew up a pastoral letter of sixty lines, and this text echoed in even the smallest parish of his diocese. As for the clergy of Châlons, they were convoked on 13 September 'on leaving Vespers' in order to celebrate a *Te Deum* in thanksgiving. The text included a political and military analysis of the events, not in order to obscure the merits of M. de Vendôme, but, rather, in order to place the event in context and keep up the level of public awareness. The kingdom was short of money and its armies of provisions. But it retained its underlying morale. Such solidarity was not for nothing after 1704, for there were causes for grave concern for the future of the two kingdoms.

'THE DREADFUL DAYS'

The year 1704 'witnessed a complete European volte-face' (258). Italy was turned upside down. The Dukes of Modena, Mantua and Mirandola lost their possessions. The King of Poland was driven off his throne by Charles XII, the King of Sweden. The English took Gibraltar. La Feuillade and Vendôme won battles, but the situation in Bavaria turned out badly. Villars, who did not get on well with the elector, was delighted to be despatched to the Cévennes. His successor, Marsin, was incapable of slowing Marlborough's advance, and Tallard, who reinforced Marsin, was hardly better as a tactician. Marlborough laid waste Bavaria, and then, with the help of Prince Eugene, crushed an army of 50,000 men, which was 'commanded', if that is the right word, by the elector, the comte de Tallard and M. de Marsin, at Höchstädt (Blenheim) on 13 August 1704.

In 1705, the pendulum swung both ways. Though the archduke was acclaimed at Barcelona and recognized by Valencia and Murcia, the armies of the old French king recovered their nerve. In the north, Villars held Marlborough in check, forced the lines at Wissembourg, and halted any plans for an invasion of Champagne. 'It was one of this general's best campaigns.' (258) The year 1706, however, 'marked the nadir of French misfortunes' (258). Villars had carried out a successful campaign in Germany and Vendôme held Italy until the spring; but, from April to September, cruel disappointments followed one after another. On 16 April, Lord Galway took Alcantara. On 23 May, Villeroy and the Elector of Bavaria were beaten by Marlborough at Ramillies. Villeroy had drawn up his troops poorly: his right wing had to bear the full brunt of the battle. There were some heroic actions, and the French only lost 4,000 men; but the direct consequences were disastrous – Brabant and Flanders would be invaded forthwith – the psychological impact was severe, and the indirect effects made the disaster even worse. Louis XIV and Chamillart decided to recall Vendôme for the defence of what was left of the Low Countries. And with Vendôme gone, France lost Milan, Piedmont and Savoy within a matter of months. The decisive moment came in September, as Versailles awaited with trepidation the news from Turin. On 7 September, Prince Eugene, reinforced with Prussian battalions, defeated the army commanded by the duc d'Orléans, La Feuillade and Marsin within sight of the Piedmontese capital. All the French strongholds fell – Mantua, Modena, Casale, Chivas – and the army fell back on Pinerolo. After Höchstädt (Blenheim) and Ramillies, Turin represented the third heavy defeat sustained in twenty-five months.

The year 1707 turned out to be not nearly so disastrous. Vendôme had no difficulty in holding on to Flanders, which had become a dormant front. Forbin and Duguay-Trouin pursued a remarkable privateering campaign (274). Villars was victorious at the Battle of Stolhofen (22 May). Prince Eugene and the Duke of Savoy were forced to abandon the siege of Toulon in August. Most importantly, things changed in Spain after 25 April, thanks to the victory of Almansa in Murcia. It was a curious situation: the Duke of Berwick, marshal of France, born in England and the natural son of James II, defeated Lord Galway, the British commander, born in France as Henri, marquis de Ruvigny, a Huguenot refugee, in order to impose his candidate

upon the throne of Spain. The position of Charles III was reversed: in May, Valencia submitted to Philip V and Saragossa was
recaptured from the Anglo-Portuguese forces. In October, the
duc d'Orléans took Lérida. The Archbishop of Paris was kept
busy as Louis XIV asked for a *Te Deum* for Almansa, a second to
celebrate the birth of the Prince of the Asturias, and a third for
the occupation of the castle at Lérida. The Parisians were thus
kept informed of the hopes of the King of Spain.

As if to confirm the fickleness of fate, 1708 brought less
satisfaction to Versailles. As in 1706, disappointment and disaster came alternately and in succession. The only occasion for a
Te Deum proved to be the capture of Tortosa by the future regent;
but this exploit took place on 11 July 1708, the day on which the
French army in the Low Countries suffered a major defeat.
Moreover, it was whispered at court that Orléans had been
negotiating secretly with the English in order to proclaim himself
King of Spain, so that, even if the accusations were proved
groundless, his was a bitter victory. Discouraging news flooded
in. A Jacobite landing in Scotland in March and April, using
Forbin's squadron, failed near Edinburgh through inadequate
planning. The Flanders campaign was appalling. Instead of
entrusting the fate of Belgium to Vendôme alone, the elderly
king took it into his head to associate the Duke of Burgundy with
him. It would have been difficult to imagine a more mismatched
pair. Burgundy knew nothing of warfare; Vendôme was a
veteran soldier of fortune. Chamlay organized the campaign in
the best tradition of Louvois, that is to say, with too much detail.
The king could not determine which of the two princes should be
in command.

It was in such conditions that the French army confronted
Marlborough and Prince Eugene near Oudenaarde on 11 July.
The battle began in confusion on unfavourable terrain. It was
engaged mostly on the French right flank and was composed of
up to eight smaller encounters. At 8 p.m., nothing had been won
or lost. Vendôme was known to be a great improviser, a leader of
men, capable of transforming a situation. But, that evening,
Burgundy decided to retreat towards Ghent, making a lost
opportunity appear like a rout. The result plunged Vendôme
into disgrace for the next two years at the very moment when the
kingdom lacked military leadership of high calibre. It earned
Burgundy the secret contempt of his grandfather, left France

open to the threat of invasion and demoralized the army, though the morale of the army was restored by Boufflers' heroic defence of Lille between 12 August and 9 December.

The situation in the Mediterranean was no more reassuring. In 1707, Naples had given itself over to the archduke. The English fleet overthrew the French hegemony imposed there in 1676 when the British took Minorca in September and October. Philip V's troubles were far from over. It is understandable that Louis XIV, who had been seeking a peaceful solution since 1704, should now have been even more concerned to find a negotiated settlement. Despite Desmarets' handling of state finances, the kingdom showed signs of exhaustion. Yet the sternest test of endurance was yet to come.

THE 'GREAT WINTER' OF 1709

Besides the deteriorating military situation, financial difficulties and negotiations begun in the most unfavourable circumstances, there came a winter almost as rigorous as those of 1693 and 1694, one which became known in folk memory as the Great Winter. The autumn of 1708 had been marked by sudden fluctuations in the weather. The chevalier de Quincy noted: 'We had seven or eight days of bitter cold around St Andrew's Day [30 November]; but the weather improved so much that we were sure that winter was past.' (88) The brutal winter began on Twelfth Night, the 5–6 January 1709. In Paris, the temperature plunged to twenty degrees below zero. Madame Palatine thought on 2 February that: 'In Paris alone, 24,000 people have died since 5 January.' (87) 'Every morning the talk is of people who have been found killed by the cold; partridges have been found frozen in the fields.' Even the normally restrained Dangeau noted 'great cold', 'excessive cold' and eventually 'horrible cold'. The court was more affected than the city, Versailles being impossible to keep warm. Saint-Simon reported that wine froze whilst it was being carried through an antechamber.

In Paris, entertainments were suspended, shops closed and the Parlement prorogued. Depressing news came in from the countryside. Not all provinces were equally affected: Brittany was spared, but Anjou was so cold that 'the crests fell off the poultry' (210). Everywhere, trees cracked, vines froze, fruit trees were affected. Water-mills were blocked up with ice. Only the winter wheat proved resistant, although a second sharp cold spell would spell disaster for it. Up to 24 January, the wheat had been protected by snow. But, in the last week of January, an illusory promise of mildness was followed by a hard frost on 31 January, a thaw on 15 February, a new attack of bitter weather, and finally the real thaw on 15 March (210). Trapped under a layer of ice, enclosed by frozen snow up to three feet deep, the wheat crop was destroyed.

The French kept reminding themselves that they were not the only ones to be affected; the situation was 'the same in all the neighbouring kingdoms' (26), notably in Holland, the state responsible for prolonging the war. They had enough to eat, or, rather, there would be enough if everyone conserved his own stock and if those possessing reserves had been wise enough to sell their stock at normal prices to the king's agents or charity commissioners. But the price rise became seemingly endless. At Gonesse a *setier* of wheat cost eight times as much in September 1709 as it had done in March 1708. Everyone had some responsibility for what happened: speculators, suppliers, magistrates. Monopolies did more harm than good. From April through to September, *émotions* and pillaging were reportedly widespread. In April, wheat was being pillaged 'at Bordeaux, at Beauvais . . ., at Nogent-sur-Seine, at Orléans and in many other places, including Paris' (97). In early May, 'gatherings' and 'disorders' multiplied 'in all parts of the kingdom'. On the 4th, 100 boat-men, armed with boat-hooks, attacked the market of Saint-Germain-des-Prés (97). But 'all that totters does not come crashing down'; otherwise it would be 'Goodbye to everything!'* Such a crisis could not be solved by repressive means. The king recognized this and, building upon the precedent set in 1693, did his best to help his people.

The old monarch kept a steady hand upon the tiller. 'It is very easy to govern a kingdom from an office with a decree; but when one has to defy half of Europe after the loss of five great battles and the atrocious winter of 1709, it is not so simple.' (112) As in 1693, Louis XIV despatched grain from the less afflicted provinces to the worst-hit areas. Measures which had been taken against monopolists in 1694 were strengthened. It was ordered

---

* Orig. 'Adieu la boutique!': 'a proverbial expression . . . used of something which has failed, which is in the process of collapsing or falling down' (Furetière).

that cereals should only be sold in the marketplace and not from the place of residence. The government gave the authorities the order that 'each [authority] is to give to its poor and feed them' (210). Those causing overcrowding in towns had to return to their parishes, with only the disabled and incurably ill being admitted to *hôpitaux*. In Paris, there were more than 4,000 residents in the Hôtel-Dieu in September, and 14,000 at the Hôpital Général (241). Public distress reached disquieting proportions. Vagabonds were so numerous that the king opened 'public workshops', apparent precursors of the 'national workshops' of 1848. But the government had neglected to recall that it was not altogether a good idea to bring together large congregations of the marginal population. 'This gathering caused a sedition in Paris amongst all these beggars and the works had to be closed [by a royal declaration of 6 August]. It had been a mistake to gather together all this starving multitude. Shops were closed on many streets and this lasted through the evening.' (210)

Such public disturbances flared up again in the autumn, the season of greatest mortality. Yet Louis XIV had adopted a broader policy than the measures of 1693. By setting an example of austerity, by sending ships in search of wheat and by mobilizing the clergy and charitable organizations, the king succeeded in curbing shortages to some extent. In early June, the court learnt that His Majesty, repeating his gesture of 1689, was sending to the Mint 'all his gold service, plates, dishes and saltcellars' (87). It was essential that his subjects should recognize that their prince was demonstrating some solidarity with them at this time. The courtiers were invited to deposit their silverware with Launay, the king's silversmith, and His Majesty made public the names of the donors (101).

As in 1693 and 1694, naval tactics were deployed to secure grain provisions. Arrangements were made with Genoa. The English were cut off from the return voyage from Smyrna, whilst wheat was shipped across from Africa. Pontchartrain did not, perhaps, have all the necessary warships at his command, but he was assisted by enterprising captains such as Pas and Cassard. The months between April 1709 and the autumn of 1710 were particularly busy. In 1709, Cassard, having vanquished, one against five, an English cruising-fleet on 29 April, brought twenty-five ships to Marseille carrying cereals from Tunisia. The following year, he diverted eighty-four vessels from the Smyrna convoy to Toulon (274). Provence was saved from famine.

The king mobilized not only his ships but also the elaborate mechanisms of social assistance, half secular and half ecclesiastical, which lay under his command and which might attenuate some of the worst effects of dearth. These *hôpitaux généraux*, which have attracted so much criticism, formed a remarkable network of public assistance. Under pressure from the intendants, the priests and notables in every parish taxed all land at two *sols* per *livre* of its value in order to buy grain and feed the hungry, of whom lists had already been compiled. Soup-kitchens were also put into operation. The bishops were often particularly active. On 10 July 1709, Fléchier, Bishop of Nîmes, issued a pastoral letter 'on the subject of the shortages of wheat and the fear of dearth' (39). 'The winter, longer and harsher than usual, has devastated towns and countryside . . . Flocks have died in their pens . . . You have been caught between fear and hope for several months, searching the entrails of the land to discover the doubtful fate of your harvest . . . Rich and poor have been seized with a sudden fear of being without bread.' The bishop encouraged his flock to place themselves under God's protection. Then he denounced the selfishness and cupidity of both hoarders and hunger-rioters. He encouraged almsgiving: 'This is both charity and justice.' Everyone, especially the holders of benefices and the rich, should help his neighbour. In the atmosphere of the Counter-Reformation, such exhortation might prove invaluable.

Peasant initiatives were also of incalculable importance. The rural world was still resourceful enough to find a solution in the spring of 1709 through the planting of barley, Desmarets having forbidden the sowing of spring wheat. The frost had aerated the soil and broken it up, allowing access to nitrogen, so that there were yields to be had of twelve to sixteen *quintaux* an acre, three to four times more than normal (210). Priests could preach from the pulpit upon the proverb: 'God helps those who help themselves.'

THE ENEMY REFUSES PEACE

If Louis XIV had been governed by royal pride, he would not have been so preoccupied with attenuating the sufferings of his people. If he had been an imperialist, he would have held out for total victory. The kingdom and its conquests and Spain, with its young king, Italian dependencies and overseas empire, would have had no more determined defender. But Louis XIV knew the importance of limiting his political ambitions, disciplining his legitimate objectives, and placing the hopes for a lasting peace above the prestige of the King of France. After the second battle of Höchstädt in 1704 (Blenheim), he opened up negotiations with the Dutch. In 1706, after Ramillies and Turin, he once again made overtures, using Bergeyck and Van der Dussen as intermediaries. But Heinsius, his intransigence strengthened by the successes of the coalition, turned down the offer, proposed by Torcy, that Philip V should abandon his throne in Madrid, take that of Naples in return and retain Sicily. The following year, the conditions had changed, for the emperor held Naples; but, since Berwick had put Philip V firmly back into power in Spain, Louis XIV's emissaries hoped that the Dutch would accept the Angevin regime in exchange for 'commercial privileges in the Indies' (103). But Heinsius proved implacable: he required that Philip V renounce his claims to Spain.

The failure of the 1708 campaign in Flanders forced the elderly king to make the greatest possible concessions. The state of his troops, and, more particularly, of his kingdom and its finances, obliged Louis to sue for peace, despite all else. 'He no longer had the right', according to Frédéric Masson, 'to create difficulties about intermediaries. He had to take what could be found: an individual named Pettekum, resident of the Duke of Holstein-Gottorp. Whatever the channel used, the replies from the Dutch remained the same. As a preliminary condition to talks, Spain, the Indies, Milan and the Low Countries should be surrendered and a commercial treaty signed.' (103) The king accepted these draconian conditions and, on this basis, Torcy asked for the opening of a peace conference. Rouillé, the French plenipotentiary, should first call for a suspension of hostilities. If necessary, he should surrender, on Philip V's behalf, in addition to Spain, Belgium and the empire, all his claims to Tuscany and Sardinia, whilst retaining his sovereignty over the Two Sicilies. The Dutch would have to think over what would be a reconstitution of the empire of Charles V, to the profit of the Habsburgs. They must be made aware of the price which the King of France was willing to pay in return for peace: to return, as regards the emperor, to the conditions of the Peace of Ryswick, to recognize Queen Anne and even the Act of Settlement in England, and to expel James III from France. On 5 March 1709, Rouillé set out, carrying these concessions.

Heinsius' diplomats set out with very different instructions. Emissaries without powers were sent to meet Rouillé. They objected that Louis XIV could not guarantee the ratification of a treaty by Philip V. They told him that the United Provinces could not decide on behalf of England. They assured him that the emperor would not rest content with the clauses of Ryswick, but would want to return to the clauses of the Peace of West-phalia. France would have to surrender lower Alsace. England would want Dunkirk, the King of Prussia Neuchâtel. Louis XIV would have to restore the Duke of Savoy to his lands. Above all, he would have to give up Ypres, Condé, Tournai, Mauberge and especially Lille. Toul and Verdun would provide compensation for the Duke of Lorraine. French Protestants would be at last restored to their nationality, liberty and belongings. All these demands were not offered as a guarantee of the suspension of hostilities, but *ad referendum*.

The Dutch expected such opening moves to produce a refusal. They had a stereotyped picture of the King of France. But Louis XIV, bearing in mind his people's sufferings, accepted 'these unheard of conditions'. He wanted only to maintain Strasbourg and to be assured of Naples and Sicily for his grandson. But the deputies from the United Provinces presented new demands. Louis XIV was again expected to break off the talks. But again he accepted, trying to retain Lille and assure the Two Sicilies for Philip V. The Dutch created still more difficulties: 'They want the Spanish monarchy in its entirety and no suspension of hostilities.'

Surprisingly, the French king once more gave way, so great was his inclination towards peace. He would surrender Tournai, Lille and Mauberge, demolish Dunkirk, return to the Treaty of Münster and expel James III. Philip V would have to content himself with Naples. In exchange for such concessions, Louis required a rapid response. However, with each delay, the Dutch demands became larger. Torcy proposed that he (Torcy) should go in person, against all protocol, and sue for peace. He would be in some personal danger, without a safe-conduct, and his repu-tation would be put greatly at risk: 'a minister who signs such a treaty would be lost in the present and dishonoured before posterity' (103), but he understood the national need and the old king's confidence in him would make up for his lost honour. The abandonment of pride by king and minister had something of the heroic in it.

Louis thought that Torcy would be able to influence Heinsius and establish a basis for discussion. On 29 April, the decision for the journey was taken. On 6 May Torcy arrived at The Hague, where, between the 6th and the 28th, the destiny of Europe was decided. The pensionary was no longer alone; Marlborough and Eugene of Savoy had joined him, and, between them, they had determined upon the humiliation of France. Behind them were the envoys of the allies. 'The crows were gathering.' Every day, the coalition parties produced a new demand, claiming here a province, there a city. After three weeks, the forty articles of the 'Preliminaries of The Hague' were presented: Louis XIV was required to recognize the archduke as Charles III, possessor of the entire inheritance of Charles II. The 'duc d'Anjou' was permitted two months in which to leave Spain, failing which the allies and the King of France 'would together take suitable action'. In the meantime, Louis XIV was to withdraw all assistance to his grandson. No French prince would ever reign in Madrid. The Indies would be closed to French trade. France would surrender Kehl and Strasbourg, Breisach and Landau, retaining only the Ten Towns in lower Alsace. Louis XIV was obliged to recognize Queen Anne and the Protestant succession in Great Britain, to renounce all claims to Newfoundland and any overseas conquests taken from the British. The ramparts of Dunkirk were to be razed to the ground and its harbour filled in, the Stuart Pretender was to be expelled, and a commercial treaty was to be signed to the advantage of Great Britain.

Louis XIV was supposed to surrender his claims to the Low Countries, ceding Furnes, Ypres, Menin, Condé, Tournai, Mauberge and Lille. The customs conditions of 1664 would be re-established. Savoy would recover its lands and receive reparations. Prussia, the imperial circles and the Duke of Lorraine would present their own demands at the general conference. In exchange, France obtained nothing but an armistice for two months. Torcy could not have gone further in making concessions. He had surrendered 'even Lille, even Naples, even Dunkirk'. But he realized that the allies had demanded the impossible in obliging a grandfather to dispossess in two months a grandson of proven fidelity. The reactions of the court, which changed from favouring peace into determining upon reprisal, encouraged the king and his minister to appeal against the ultimatum of The Hague. Louis XIV had drunk from the cup of humiliation. His subjects now had to find the reply for him: *Non possumus.*

27

French Revival

S HARED MISERIES brought the king and his people closer
together. Without the famine of 1709, he would have made
fewer concessions. But the intransigence of its opponents forced
France to renewed effort, which meant the engaging of hearts
and minds and the forging of a unity between people and
sovereign.

THE APPEAL OF 12 JUNE

On 12 June 1709, a king accountable to God alone addressed
himself to the public at large so as to associate it with his objectives. Using the novel device of a letter to his subjects, which the
governors and intendants were ordered to disperse everywhere
(the bishops having already received a shorter version), Louis
XIV introduced a remarkable element of consultation into his
absolute regime. The old man had always known how to adapt
himself to the worst of circumstances and he did not let slip this
chance to rescue the kingdom. It was essential that the French
people understand that the prolongation of the war was the
result of the evil designs of the enemy.

> The hope of peace soon [wrote the king] is so widespread in my
> kingdom that I owe it to the fidelity which my people have
> demonstrated during the course of my reign to inform them of the
> reasons why they are not yet enjoying the repose which I
> intended to procure for them. I would have had to accept, in
> order to achieve this, conditions highly dangerous for the safety of
> my frontier provinces; but the more I demonstrated a willingness

and desire to dissipate the suspicions which my enemies claimed still to have of my powers and intentions, the more they multiplied their demands. (97)

These demands came not so much from a desire for a lasting peace or international stability as from a wish to encircle France with a view to future dismemberment, beginning under the cloak of a false and unilateral truce.

> I pass over in silence [Louis XIV continued] the proposal that I should join my forces with those of the league and force the king, my grandson, to quit his throne, unless he had voluntarily consented to live henceforth without a state and reduce himself to the condition of a private individual. It is against all humanity that they even should conceive of asking me to promise such an alliance with them. Yet, even though my affections towards my people are no less great than those I feel for my own children, and even though I share in all the evils which war has inflicted upon such faithful subjects, and though I have demonstrated to the whole of Europe that I want sincerely to give them the contentment of peace, I am certain that they would be opposed to accepting it upon conditions contrary to both the justice and honour of France.

The king counted on the support of his people and associated them by a kind of implicit plebiscite in one of the great choices of world diplomacy. He placed his confidence 'in God's protection'.

> I am writing to the archbishops and bishops of the kingdom to stimulate the fervour of prayers in their dioceses. And, at the same time [the king added] I wish for my people throughout the areas of your government to know from you that they would be enjoying peace now if it had depended only upon my will to procure for them a blessing which they rightly desire, but which must be acquired through renewed effort, since the harsh conditions to which I have agreed are of no use for the re-establishment of public tranquillity. (97)

This text was both emotive and skilful. In the negotiations, the Dutch had gone too far. No one in France could have accepted the prospect of the king at odds with his own grandson. Even Madame Palatine, still at heart a Bavarian, was scandalized. She wrote: 'To want to set a grandfather against his own grandson, who has always been obedient and submissive towards him, is barbarous and unchristian.' (87) Meanwhile, the people of France mobilized at the king's request. Three months was sufficient time to redress, at least provisionally, the military situation. The letter to his people was dated 12 June; by 12 September, it appeared as though the kingdom had been saved. With the sovereign and the nation behind them, the generals seemed transformed. Bezons, who until that moment had been a reluctant supporter of Philip V, decided to place four battalions at Spain's disposal. Besieged in Tournai towards the end of June, Louis-Charles de Hautefort, marquis de Surville, held the town until 29 July. On 31 August, he was still refusing to surrender the citadel unless he obtained full military honours. He only gave up, on the night of 2–3 September, when his decimated garrison had permission 'to return to France with all their arms, standards, and even cannon'. The general had decided that, if honours were refused him, he would 'blow up the citadel, go out into the city at night, cut the throats of the guards on one of the gates and leave through it, his whole garrison having promised to execute such a glorious, albeit dangerous, enterprise' (97).

On 7 August, Noailles had some success in Catalonia. On the 26th, the comte du Bourg crushed Mercy at Rumersheim, killing or wounding 7,000 men, and saving upper Alsace. Two days later, Dillon, Master of Briançon, put the enemy to flight. On 2 September, Noailles won another victory, near Gerona. Finally, on 11 September, the Battle of Malplaquet took place, the last offensive battle fought by the allies, and a truly disturbing one. The popular song 'Malbrouk s'en va t'en guerre' ('Marlborough pushes off to war'), which appeared at this time, was prophetic. Malplaquet, 'the bloodiest and most hard fought [battle] during Louis XIV's reign' (88), marked, to some extent, the end of Marlborough's invincibility.

HOPE REKINDLED AT MALPLAQUET

On 15 March 1709, the king gave Villars command of the grand army of Flanders, in which lay the last chance of preventing an invasion. Vendôme would perhaps have been better suited to the task, but he was still in disgrace. The marshal, on the other hand, had the support of the marquise de Maintenon and Chamillart, and he enjoyed the king's confidence. Louis was aware of his faults, his tiresome vanity; but also of his courage, his determination to attack, his skills as a leader, and of those faults which were capable of being transformed into positive attributes – the marshal's aggressive stance might redouble the morale of the troops whilst disconcerting the enemy.

He inherited an unenviable legacy and made the best of it. The sufferings of the troops gathered near Cambrai were incredible. The army had endured hunger to an even greater extent than the civilian population. Now the frost of an exceptional winter gave way to torrential rain. The French battalions and squadrons were short of everything: food, money, replacement horses. Rumours of peace had disheartened many officers. On the other hand, regiments were up to strength and the troops in good spirit. Villars was not deceiving the *marquise* when he wrote to her on 3 April: 'I can assure you, Madame, that the king will have a good army with which to oppose the enemy.' (295) Like the king and the marshal, the *marquise* knew the importance of the issues at stake: 'The salvation of the state', she wrote on 19 June, 'rests in your hands.' Villars told the *marquise*, with whom he felt at ease, that everything would be decided that summer; what was needed was either fruitful negotiation or a clear victory. In either case, it was essential to stand firm. To do this, the controller-general would have to find the resources and the minister provide the rations. For not only did a hungry army lose its fighting capacity and its mobility, but the enemy would quickly realize the fact and exploit it.

When Marlborough and Prince Eugene began their offensive on 23 June, they were confident. Their optimism influenced the negotiations at The Hague and contributed to their suspension. On the French side, Villars enjoyed great freedom of initiative. The king asked him, above all, to hold the line of the Scheldt. Holding a defensive position was not the marshal's greatest forte – he preferred movement. But the structure of the frontier, the directives from the court, the inferiority of his numbers and the shortcomings of the organization of supplies meant that he had to resort to defensive tactics. Villars drew up 'good lines' to close the frontier. From 26 June, the enemy tested the French defences. And, after some inconclusive engagements, Marlborough and Eugene changed tactics. Since France no longer appeared so open to attack, they returned to siege warfare, with a view to capturing Tournai, Condé and Valenciennes. The defence of

Tournai has already been referred to. Whilst this was proceeding, Villars ensured that the battle battalions did not become demoralized through inaction. If Tournai were to fall, the king would let him attempt a decisive confrontation. In the meantime, he confined them to skirmishes. And Louis XIV allowed Boufflers, governor of Flanders, to join the army and serve under the younger Villars. On 4 September, the two marshals met at Denain, acclaimed by their troops. The next day, Villars announced the orders to march.

It appeared a good opportunity. With Tournai taken, Marlborough did not dare to advance up the Scheldt. He headed towards Mons, leaving his right flank exposed to the French. Between Mons and Bavay, between the woods of Sart and La Lanière, lay the gap of Malplaquet, the gateway to French Hainaut. On the 9 and 10 September, shifting earth round the clock, the French army dug itself in. Villars had followed the king's wishes to the letter – to seek a resolution in battle but without being too provocative.

When the famous battle began, on the morning of the 11th, the positions of the two armies were the result of two manœuvres, one half-strategic by Marlborough, the other intelligently tactical by Villars. The latter protected Mons, Mauberge and Valenciennes and forced the enemy to stop their movement towards the east and to attack. At that time, no better manœuvre was known.

At 7.30 a.m., the enemy attacked the King's regiment on the French left flank. By 8 a.m., the artillery battle was in full swing. Five hundred allied guns pounded the French battalions and 'inconvenienced' the French squadrons, which were too close to the front line. The less numerous French artillery replied, firing 8,000 rounds in the course of the day, emptying the munitions reserves. Meanwhile, between 9 a.m. and midday, the troops of Marlborough and the young Prince of Orange wore themselves out against the French right wing, which was commanded by Boufflers, supported by Montesquiou. Here were located the military elite of the kingdom, the old regiments of Piedmont, Navarre and Picardy, the French and Swiss guards and the cavalry of the king's household. The Piedmont regiment lost many men, the Picardy regiment retreated, and the Navarre regiment saved the situation twice. But the weakness of the French guards was regarded with astonishment. Outflanked by the enemy, three of their four battalions fell back in disorder and ran into the horses of the king's household. However, the allies suffered worse losses. The Prince of Orange's battalions lost half their strength. By midday, the formidable French right flank was victorious. Maurice of Saxony would later accuse Boufflers of staying too fixed to his battle-lines (95). He was ignoring the fact that the enemy enjoyed a numerical superiority.

With its mixture of woodland and open country, plains and hills, the terrain dictated that the battle would be composed of separate but deadly combats. From early in the morning, the French left flank, with M. d'Albergotti in command under Villars, withstood the assaults of Prince Eugene's fifty-nine battalions. The King's regiment, attacked by twenty guns within musket-range, panicked at first but then rallied. The Champagne, Queen's, Charost and Irish regiments did their best. By late morning, Prince Eugene had failed on his extreme right wing, but was satisfied with his frontal attack. Varying his points of attack, trying several flanking movements, able to call upon fresh troops, and risking his skin, he wore down the French left wing. But the infantry only fell back inch by inch edging up the slopes of the plateau, and were then reinforced by reserves brought in from the centre by Villars. Several bayonet charges in counter-attack showed Prince Eugene that he had not yet won the day. The Battle of Malplaquet was certainly not lost by midday. The situation of the French troops was satisfactory on the right, challenged on the left and uncertain in the centre. This situation would be repeated at Fontenoy.

Albergotti and Villars had both been wounded. The marshal had been cut down in the front line, and had had to be evacuated. The loss of this leader, of which Boufflers was only informed at a later stage, and the lack of ground cover in the gap of La Louvière gave Marlborough his opportunity to break through. The French centre, diminished in favour of the left wing, had hardly any more infantry. Marlborough sent in fifteen English battalions and almost all the Dutch cavalry. The French heavy cavalry overwhelmed the Dutch squadrons, but retreated before the British infantry and artillery.

Between midday and 3 p.m. the cavalry battle between the allied squadrons and those of the king's household took place. Deprived of infantry support and with little support from the artillery, the French cavalry performed miracles. The seventy year-old comte de Gassion, the Pretender, the duc de Rohan and the best of the old nobility all led charges, and the allies were repulsed three times. Though the French guards and the King's regiment had been weak, the king's bodyguard lost more than a third of their number, forty officers and four hundred 'masters'. Unfortunately, these heroic charges ran into the squares of the British infantry and the allied batteries. They deserved a better fate and possibly they had gained a moral victory. Marlborough had encountered unexpected resistance. His 110,000 men had not been able to seize the field of battle from Villars' 70,000 men. The terrain would be theirs thanks to M. de Boufflers, who, by late afternoon, had neither the means to attempt a decisive breakthrough nor the desire to court disaster – the French artillery had only 400 rounds left. But the field of battle was only ceded with reluctance. Goësbriand, who had taken command of the left flank from M. d'Albergotti, was preparing for a fourth charge when the maréchal de Boufflers called a cease-fire.

The withdrawal of the 60,000 French survivors – about 10,000 had been killed or wounded – was not exactly a retreat. M. de Montesquiou led his troops towards Bavay. Baron Legall and Puységur took the rest towards Quiévrain. The cavalry covered their movements and none fled or straggled behind (295). The carabineers, still fresh from their charges, left their mounts and joined the infantry and dragoons to cover, in their turn, the withdrawal of the remainder of the cavalry (166). On the 12th, the French army was once more assembled in fighting formation, ten miles from Malplaquet. The enemy, who had lost 20,000 men, including a number of generals and senior officers, would not try an attack. They even abandoned the field of battle. 'The dead and dying seemed to outnumber the living; there were more than 30,000 lying in this small space . . . 20,000 wounded cried out for help which the most charitable endeavour was not able to satisfy. The victor felt the poignancy of this tragic scene, and the song of thanksgiving which Marlborough had ordered sounded like a dirge.' (295) Had the allies really gained a victory?

On the evening of the great battle, the chevalier de Quincy encountered outside Bavay, more than two and a half miles from Malplaquet, 'a man lying dead, who had apparently dragged himself this far. He had no toes on his feet. Whilst alive, how had he walked?' (88). On 26 October, Madame Palatine wrote from

Versailles: 'Daily we see officers arriving on crutches.' (87)
In the harsh autumn of 1709, neither 'the mobilization of the
humble' nor 'blood tribute' was an empty phrase.

COURAGE IN ADVERSITY

At Malplaquet, Villars and Boufflers had not succeeded in
mastering the situation, but they had performed heroically, as
had Montesquiou and some of the other leaders. Villars, in order
to inspire the left wing, placed himself at the head of the
carabineers and 'charged like an ordinary grenadier, striking
with sword in hand' (97). Gravely wounded in the knee, he at
first refused to be evacuated. The letters-patent granting him his
peerage stated: 'Our said cousin did not cease to act and give
orders, despite the pain he was suffering, until his loss of blood
and weakness forced his evacuation.' (2)

Revolutionary regimes tend to imprison or execute their
vanquished captains. Great monarchs, on the other hand,
proudly reward merit, even when it has not been matched with
good fortune. Louis XIV took this to extremes. Tourville, after
La Hougue (1693), and Châteaurenault, after Vigo (1703), were
made marshals. Now, dissatisfied with the translation of Villars'
duchy into a peerage, he lavished attention on the 'defeated'
marshal with considerable thoughtfulness. Cynics might have
seen this as merely a desire to manage carefully a competent
general, one of the few remaining military leaders capable of
halting an invasion. Others were aware that M. de Villars
enjoyed the support of officers and soldiers and was the incarnation of bravery. Everyone in the camps, the quarters and garrison towns could support the attention lavished upon him. Each
honour he received was a citation for bravery given by the nation
to every act of heroism in the army.

The king enquired incessantly about the marshal's state of
health. On 19 September, the court learnt that his wound would
take a long time to heal; on the 24th, they were warned not to be
too optimistic, the marshal having spent 'a greatly worrying
night'; finally, on the 27th, a courier arrived at Marly warning
'that the maréchal de Villars' wound was not healing well, and
that he had a morbid swelling on the back of his knee'. Concerned, Louis XIV decided to send Mareschal, his chief surgeon.

Mareschal found Villars' condition serious: 'He could not sleep ... The agonies of his wound could only be lessened with the help of opium.' (97) On 4 October, the court received a more optimistic bulletin. On the 6th, it was learnt that Mareschal had found the deepest part of the wound and that 'the ball had not pierced the bone'. On the 8th, 'all the letters from Flanders stated that the maréchal de Villars was very happy that the king had sent' his chief surgeon, without whom 'he would have been lost'. The next day, Mareschal returned to Marly, thereby reassuring the court (97). Many shared the opinion of Madame Palatine: it would be 'a tragedy if such a brave man were to die' (87).

The fuss which was made of him was far from over, even then. In the last week of October, the king learnt that his general would soon be in a fit state to be moved, and sent him a litter. Villars was transported to Versailles under the best possible conditions. On 13 November, he reached Paris 'with the king's litter following his stretcher, three or four six-horse carriages, several chairs and a large mounted escort' (26). A victorious general had not always been accorded such largesse. On the 20th, Villars proceeded to Versailles 'on his stretcher, with many cavalry, the *maréchale* following with two six-horse carriages'. That evening he was installed in the prince de Conti's apartment, 'in the middle of the ground floor' (97). The next day, M. de Villars was visited by 'a procession of men and women'. The king, for his part, was not content with receiving the duchesse de Villars 'with many marks of respect' (97), or with sending several envoys, including the marquise de Maintenon, 'to visit the injured man'. On 22 December, after the sermon, Louis XIV came to pay his respects to his old servant, taking care to demonstrate *urbi et orbi*, by the length, ceremonial and personal attention of the visit, that a faithful soldier and captain of great merit could and should be better treated than many crowned heads.

'It was a great spectacle', wrote Dangeau, 'by the numbers of courtiers and guards stationed in the gallery. The *maréchale* and her son stood at the door of the lodgings.' (26) Villars lay upon a couch. 'As the king approached him, he bowed as deeply as he could,' adds Sourches, 'the king stepping forward to embrace him.' (97). Then came the young marquis de Villars, a child of seven, to pay his respects to the king. Louis XIV ordered the courtiers to retire whilst he remained 'in the *cabinet* with the ladies and the little boy; an armchair was brought for the king and placed near the marshal's feet, so that the king could look him in the face, and the king had a screen placed in front of him so that the fire would not bother him' (97). According to Dangeau, the conversation lasted for two hours. 'It would appear that they talked of many different things.' (97) The wounded man repeatedly told the king of his wish 'to return to the campaign in the spring' (26). His hopes were too far in advance of his cure; for, on 23 April 1710, taking supper with the king, he was still having to lean 'on his crutches' (97).

These gestures were to the credit of both master and servant. For how could Louis XIV, whose nature, said Voltaire, endowed him with magnanimity, not have honoured the head of an army which had earned even the enemy's praise? The king may have read several times through the second account of Malplaquet, dated 13 September, written in the elegant style of the maréchal de Boufflers:

> Your Majesty, Sire, will have seen by my letter of the 11th of this month, dated 10 p.m., the unfortunate outcome of the action on that day, but also how this misfortune was accompanied by glory for the troops and arms of Your Majesty. I can assure you, Sire, that this glory is, in reality, greater than words can express. You will learn this even from the accounts of the enemy, who cannot sufficiently praise the bravery, determination and persistence of Your Majesty's troops, the effects of which they felt most strongly.

The allied generals paid dearly for their victory. They realized that Malplaquet was more than just another battle, that it was a turning-point of the war. 'Finally, Sire,' continued Boufflers, 'the succession of disasters which Your Majesty's armies have suffered for several years now had so humiliated the French people that one hardly dared admit to being French. I can assure you, Sire, that the title of French has never been held in higher esteem nor more feared than it is now among all the allied armies.' Marlborough and Eugene were constrained to admit the greater number of their losses, wounded, prisoners and missing. 'They speak with admiration of our retreat and the pride with which it was conducted. They say that they saw the old French in action.' (97) English officers said: 'The French have become brave once more; we are friends again.' The maréchal de Boufflers continued: 'All that I may have the honour of telling Your Majesty is that no army has for many years acquired more glory or more deserved the esteem of its master and of its enemies.'

But the final word, which should strike Malplaquet from the list of French defeats and give it its real place, should be accorded to Villars: 'If God grants that we lose another battle like that, Your Majesty may be sure that his enemies are destroyed.' (295) The king understood this perfectly on 14 September when he received Villars' 'moving and pathetic' letter, and better still on the 17th when, 'between his *lever* and Mass', he could see in his chamber at Versailles the thirty-three flags and standards presented to him by the marquis de Nangis. Unable this time to order a *Te Deum*, Louis XIV instructed the minister Voysin to have them displayed in Notre-Dame.

NOTHING WAS YET WON

It is always dangerous to celebrate prematurely. From Malplaquet (September 1709) to the close of the Congress of Utrecht (April 1713), more than three and a half years passed – long months, a wearisome mixture of expectation and anxiety. Nothing was yet won or lost. Against France stood Dutch intransigence, the enmity and talents of Prince Eugene, the ultimate hesitancy of the Spanish population, English naval superiority, and the weakness of French finances. On its side lay Louis XIV's cool head, Torcy's subtlety, the talents of Vendôme and Villars, and the solidarity behind the military effort which rekindled popular confidence in the king. At the beginning of 1710, who could have foreseen the course of the next few years? The fate of Spain, which seemed to depend upon France, would actually be decided in Spain itself. That of France, which appeared tied to that of Spain, would be directed in The Hague, Vienna and London. So many unforeseen elements interposed themselves during these three years that the marquis de Torcy attributed it all to providence. But we should also measure the significant contribution of a national genius.

Despite the harsh terms of the Preliminaries of The Hague and in spite of the relative improvement in the military situation of France, the negotiations had never been formally broken off.

Thus, on 19 November 1709, Torcy had been unofficially visited by M. Pettekum. According to the latter, Heinsius was inclined towards conciliation, more than Eugene and Marlborough. Articles 4 and 37 (dispossession of Philip V and the opening of a peace conference if the King of Spain could be disposed of within two months) were negotiable. In order to avoid the total humiliation of Philip V, French diplomats proposed a new partition. To protect himself against duplicity, M. de Torcy refused to limit the truce to two months. For several weeks, supposedly secret exchanges took place between Versailles and The Hague, with the Elector of Bavaria ('vicar-general' of the Spanish Low Countries since late 1709) and the comte de Bergeyck both creating complications in what was already an almost impossible dialogue.

In January 1710, Bergeyck hoped to conclude his own compromise peace between Madrid and the allies. As for Pettekum, under the pretext that the notables of Amsterdam seemed to him desirous of peace, he disregarded the bellicose inclinations of Marlborough and the Imperialists. He thought that the moment had come for a conference where M. de Torcy would be able to obtain a worthwhile compensation for Philip V, Sicily for example. His letter was read to the ministers on 27 January. Two days later, the Council decided to send two plenipotentiaries to the United Provinces, the maréchal d'Huxelles and the abbé de Polignac. These envoys travelled to Geertruidenberg, hoping to obtain sufficient compromise on articles 4 and 37 to allow them to negotiate.

They were soon disillusioned. On 14 March, Torcy brought His Majesty the despatches from the maréchal d'Huxelles: the Dutch repeated verbatim what they had said at The Hague the preceding year and rejected 'any shift on article 37' (103). There could be no question of compensating Philip V. Never had the enemy shown 'such condescension' or 'less appearance of peace'. Twelve days later, on the evening of 26 March, the king told his ministers the latest news from Geertruidenberg. The Dutch might consider the granting of Sicily to Philip V, but only on condition that Louis XIV join his former enemies 'to force the Catholic King to subscribe to the treaty'. Further, they demanded that the 'barrier', which would have already considerably reduced French territorial gains, be augmented by Douai, Valenciennes and Cassel. All this was separate from the demands of the allies of the Dutch. Thus, France would have to be prepared to give Charles III something equivalent to Sicily which he would amalgamate with his Spanish possessions.

Torcy, being realistic, argued for a modified acceptance of these proposals. Philip V should acquire Naples as well as Sicily. Louis XIV would join forces with the coalition to force his grandson to accept this solution, once the ultimatum had passed. If the enemy accepted this, honour would be saved – or nearly so – for the King of Spain, whilst France, desirous of peace, would achieve that objective. If the coalition refused, the king would be 'exonerated in the eyes of everyone'. If the Dutch refused to concede more than Sicily, then the plenipotentiaries should reject this inadequate proposal and refuse the support of the French armies for forcing Philip V to accept. Desmarets and Pontchartrain supported Torcy. For various reasons, Beauvillier, Burgundy and Monseigneur rejected the idea of intervention against the former duc d'Anjou, and Torcy had to elaborate a further counter-proposal for Geertruidenberg.

Three days later, on 29 March, the minister received further letters from the Low Countries. As had been foreseen, the coalition wanted to retain Naples and only offered Sicily. If the King of France desired peace, he would have to wage war on his grandson in order to force him to accept such a 'partition' (103). Nothing had been decided, either at Geertruidenberg or at the frontier where the enemy was besieging Douai. In early May, Villars, at the time of his departure, advised the king to make peace. A further important meeting of the council of ministers was held on the 11th. First, Torcy read out two letters from the plenipotentiaries envisaging 'an imminent rupture'. Beauvillier, after he had been admonished by his brother-in-law Chevreuse, spoke of the necessity of making peace: let the king, instead of fighting his grandson, offer money to the coalition partners as finance for their doing so. This proposal was reluctantly adopted, and an express courier was sent to the United Provinces.

On the evening of 13 May, the king signed the marriage contract between the duc de Vendôme and Marie-Anne de Bourbon-Condé, known as Mademoiselle d'Enghien. The reconciliation was thus complete. Vendôme's departure for Spain would depend upon the negotiations, which, however, were not going well. Since 10 May, the French diplomats had lost all hope of a compromise. Polignac was still patient, but d'Huxelles was eagerly awaiting the order to return to France. Fortunately, the king and Torcy realized that this was a trap set by the Dutch to 'throw responsibility for the collapse of the conference upon France' (103). The French envoys would stay in the Netherlands for a further two months.

Meanwhile, the French army of Flanders set off 'to attack the enemy and bring help to Douai'. Unfortunately, according to its commander, Villars, morale was not high. Such was the debilitating effect of the prolonged peace negotiations. At the end of May, a vague hope of progress emerged: the Dutch were talking of linking Sardinia to Sicily to reinforce the new possessions of the deposed King of Spain. June saw affairs drag on. Villars did not dare to go to the aid of Douai. The Council decided to offer half a million *livres* to the allies to finance the expedition against Philip V. But, on the 28th, despatches gave details of the enemy's demands: Louis XIV would himself have to make war upon his grandson. A final French counter-proposal was rejected. So a final rupture followed the Dutch ultimatum, and the plenipotentiaries arrived at Marly on 30 July. There could be no further delaying the despatch to Philip V of the man he had repeatedly requested. Louis XIV decided to offer command of the Spanish army to Vendôme, his first cousin once removed. On the 20th, the duc de Vendôme took his leave of His Majesty, 'full of hopes of success and of living up to his reputation' (103), and set out to meet his destiny, a glorious one as it transpired, and his death.

ALL SHALL PAY THEIR TAXES

The year 1710 had much in common with 1694: the second of a pair of glacial winters, war against a European coalition, dilapidated state finances, the exhaustion of expedient taxation. Dutch intransigence had made the price of peace so high that 1710 was tragic. Even though the winters of 1709 and 1710 were less lethal than those of 1693 and 1694, the situation of France in general, and of the royal treasury in particular, was desperate. The king and his ministers made every effort to find a remedy.

In the midst of the previous war, Louis XIV had accepted the principle of a revolutionary kind of tax and forced Pontchartrain to accept it.* The *capitation*, abandoned in 1698, had been re-established in 1701, but was no longer sufficient for the needs of the Treasury. The king therefore decided to create a tax on revenues, and, by a declaration of 14 October 1710, established the *dixième*. As with the *capitation*, the clergy were exempt, which allowed them to increase their 'don gratuit'. But, also like the *capitation*, the new tax made no distinction as between commoners and the privileged: all were to be subject to it. It was to be a general mobilization of energy, a global contribution to the war-effort. The king had some misgivings about that. Not that he hesitated over forcing the nobility to make the necessary sacrifice, but he knew that the less well off were already paying up to the very limits of what they could afford. So, as in 1695, the act creating the new tax contained a preamble by way of explanation, appealing to the public spirit of the people. Louis recalled his attempts to end the war; as in 1709, he declared that peace was long in coming only because of the bad faith of the anti-French allies. France would only achieve peace by making war (68). With this in mind, His Majesty had decided to create the *dixième*: as from 1 October 1710, every subject would give a tenth of his income to the common cause. Laity, 'nobles and commoners, privileged and non-privileged' were all liable. The ten per cent would be payable on, among other things, income from land, seigneurial rights, property, offices, rents and trading-profits.

On that date, 14 October 1710, a breach in the wall of privilege was opened up by the royal volition. If Louis XVI had done something similar, both financially and psychologically, in 1780 – in the course of the American War – the Capetian monarchy might have been saved (245). With the *dixième*, the king showed the poor that he was making the rich pay as well. He associated everyone with the national effort: a small contribution, the poor man's mite, contributed to the salvation of the kingdom, just as the large payment from the financier Crozat did. Yet the labourers, though they might grumble *in petto*, did not haggle over their contribution, whereas the privileged duc de Saint-Simon prevaricated, lamented and appealed to divine justice (238). Not daring to propose that the entire burden of taxation be imposed upon commoners, he tried to divorce his

* See ch. 25.

protest from self-interested rationalization and sheltered behind an apparent concern for the public weal. 'They took no account', he wrote in his *Mémoires*, 'of the difficulties caused, by the amounts of tax collected, to a multitude of men of all conditions.' (94) In particular, he denounced the obnoxious nature of one clause in the preamble to the proposed tax legislation. The text read: 'And, in order to be able to assess with fairness what should be paid as the tenth of the revenues subject to the tax, we order that proprietors of taxable possessions will furnish, within fifteen days of the publication of the present articles, declarations of their possessions to those charged with carrying this out, and in the form which will be laid down in the execution of our orders.' (68) For Saint-Simon, to 'the difficulties caused by the amounts of tax collected' was added, for 'a multitude of men of all conditions', the 'despair at being forced to reveal the secrets of their families, the turpitude of a great number [*sic*], the lack of goods made up for by reputation and credit, the cessation of which will inevitably bring ruin, the discussion of everyone's means, the destruction of families'; all this caused, it would appear, by 'these impious enumerations which have always aroused the indignation of the Creator, and caused His hand to fall upon those who had them made, and almost always stirred up striking punishments' (94). This curious biblical exegesis alluded to an episode in the career of King David, punished for having carried out a census.* A theologian might have replied to this example with that of the 'edict of Caesar Augustus . . . while Quirinius was governor of Syria',† which resulted in the birth of Christ at Bethlehem, in fulfilment of the prophecy.

Above all, if we recall the conditions towards the close of the *ancien régime*, Saint-Simon's lack of foresight appears extraordinary. Here was a most talented individual who had abandoned the army at the beginning of the most difficult of wars. Whilst courtiers risked their lives for six months of the year defending territory which had been invaded, this duke lived at Versailles, criticizing its useless opulence. And when, in one accord with his subjects, the king attempted to mobilize all the people in a common effort, the duke complained at having to pay taxes. It was individuals such as Fénelon, Boulainvilliers and Saint-Simon, more royalist than the king, who would capsize the

---

* 2 Samuel 24.
† Luke 2: 1–2.

monarchy. Louis XIV rarely broached the subject, but the disgrace of Fénelon and the polite contempt he displayed towards Saint-Simon indicate his lucidity. Saint-Simon wanted to portray the Sun King as the destroyer of the old order and the enemy to the nobility. But each phase of the reign, the *capitation* and the novelty of the *dixième* demonstrate, on the contrary, that Louis XIV was the protector of order, through pragmatic reform. His fiscal reforms of 1695 and 1710, justified by wartime necessity and accepted by the humble, reduced privileges without harming the privileged. If the Bourbons had done the same, and with similar courage, in the century of the Enlightenment, would there have been a revolution in 1789?

VILLAVICIOSA

At the moment when the king and his government were contemplating the *dixième*, the situation of Philip V was critical: on 10 September, he was forced to flee from Madrid to Valladolid. Starhemberg and the archduke were nearing the capital. Philip V could count only on his own spirit of resistance and the martial talents of his distant cousin Vendôme. Both of these, however, proved to be prodigious. In October, M. de Vendôme informed 'the duchess his wife that he was gathering his troops to march against the enemy, and that nothing would be easier than breaking their necks' (97). In late November, his opponents, aware of the increase in the Bourbon military forces and of the lack of enthusiasm for the archduke among the Spanish, left Toledo in the direction of Aragon. On the 30th, Vendôme wrote to the marquis de Sourches: 'I hope that you will soon receive some good news from Spain.' This arrived on 19 December, and was of the first importance. That Friday, the king was getting ready 'to go and relax' at Marly when Torcy burst into his *cabinet* with the despatches from Spain. On Wednesday the 24th, the Duke of Alba arrived with details of the events, all good news for the two Crowns.

These events had begun on 6 December, the day when Philip V left Madrid for Alcala and learnt that his enemy had divided their forces. Vendôme caught Stanhope at Brihuega and forced him to capitulate. This allied rearguard were taken prisoner. 'We were very surprised when we knew their numbers',

Vendôme wrote. 'There were eight English battalions and eight English squadrons, commanded by Stanhope, two lieutenant-generals, two brigadier-generals, and almost all the officers who had been sent by England to make war in Spain.' (97) If Stanhope had held out for twelve more hours, he would perhaps have been extricated by Starhemberg, who had made an about-turn to come to the aid of the English forces (9 December 1710).

But the Austrians arrived too late, and met Vendôme's army the following day near to Villaviciosa. By the evening of the 10th, Starhemberg had lost three-quarters of his army. Out of 11,500 men, just over 3,000 remained: 2,800 had been killed and 5,600 taken prisoner. He had abandoned twenty-two pieces of artillery, all his baggage, and a 'prodigious number of flags, standards and drums' (97). Philip V had spent three nights 'in the midst of the campaign, without removing his boots or undressing, in the most rigorous weather'. And, while the unhappy Starhemberg fled, Vendôme related what had happened: 'Never has a battle been so glorious for the king's arms, no victory so complete as that of Villaviciosa. That formidable army, which had penetrated as far as Madrid and threatened the whole of Spain, has been entirely wiped out in two engagements.' (97) The double victory robbed the archduke of his chance to become Charles III of Spain. It confirmed the prestige of the obstinate Philip V and the aggressive craft of M. de Vendôme. It had incalculable consequences. 'This battle of Villaviciosa', wrote Torcy, 'changed beyond doubt the affairs of Spain, and, with that, those of Europe as well.' (104) On Sunday the 28th, the king had a stirring *Te Deum* sung during Mass at Versailles (26).

In the opposing camp, disappointments mounted. On 25 January 1711, Noailles took Gerona. In April, Emperor Joseph I died. Archduke Charles was his heir, and would be elected emperor in the following October. This event, coming soon after the defeats, modified the position of the Habsburgs in the peninsula. Whilst Europe could have accepted the idea of a double monarchy, with one Habsburg in Vienna and another in Madrid, the courts now had to envisage the disturbing prospect of the reconstitution under one prince of the immense inheritance of Charles V. This concern was to dominate the negotiations between the England of Queen Anne and the France of Louis XIV. These talks were not undertaken from a position of weakness; for the defeat of Count Stanhope was reinforced by French successes at sea.

As Villaviciosa made its mark upon European opinion, and contributed to the rescue of Philip V, another war was being won, little by little – the war at sea. Too many authors have presented it as a triumph for the Royal Navy over the French *marine royale*, either after Vigo (1702) or after Velez-Malaga (1704). They are anticipating later British hegemony, underestimating the naval power of Louis XIV and forgetting that Spain depended on its overseas links for its survival. Their views are reliant upon received ideas about the importance of naval tactics, elaborated from Mahan (228) to Jenkins (204). The author of *The Influence of Sea Power in History* does not seek to conceal this. In his eyes, the War of the Spanish Succession 'contained no interesting naval action from the military point of view' (228), Velez-Malaga being neither original nor decisive. Mahan preferred manœuvres, and his admiration was thus reserved for Ruyter, Suffren and Nelson.

Contemporaries saw things differently. Louis XIV, the Pontchartrains and Philip V had a global, more rational vision of war at sea. It is true that the King of France, disappointed by La Hougue and Vigo, 'did not adapt himself', Mme de Maintenon tells us, 'to the uncertainties of what happens at sea' (65). Hence the opportunity missed by his son, Toulouse, at Velez-Malaga, and hence also his lack of enthusiasm for the Jacobite expedition to Scotland in the spring of 1708. On the other hand, he supported the war on commerce, attacks on opponents' colonies, and the escorting of Spanish ships carrying the riches of the Americas. And, in these three areas, the French commanders, sailors, officers and privateers gained success after success. Dunkirk and Saint-Malo struck terror into the English. In 1707, the latter admitted that they had lost 1,146 commercial ships since 1702 (228). And when, in May 1709, Duguay-Trouin, 'the famous privateer of Saint-Malo' (26), a captain of royal ships since 1705, was ennobled for services rendered, he had already captured sixteen warships and more than three hundred merchant vessels (274). In the autumn of 1707, he had taken a strong English convoy which was transporting reinforcements for Archduke Charles to Portugal, thereby underlining the success of Berwick at Almansa. Forbin, who became a squadron leader in 1707, had not lost the aggressive spirit which he had shown when associated with Jean Bart. He collected prizes from the Adriatic (1701–2) to the White Sea (1707). In the area of the war on commerce, the French had, since 1701, equalled, on a quantitative level, the coalition's success.

The second form of naval warfare influencing the fate of Philip V consisted of the belligerents' actions in the New World, from Hudson Bay to Cayenne. British historians attribute the victory to the British, citing the clauses of the Peace of Utrecht, by which they gained Newfoundland, Acadia and St Kitts. But this is to ignore the failure of the English attack upon Quebec in 1711 and, more especially, the ravages by French sailors and privateers in the British West Indies. In 1706, d'Iberville devastated St Kitts and Nevis. Cassard, who commanded six vessels at the age of thirty-two, was ordered to create trouble in the English, Portuguese and Dutch colonies. He returned with more than thirty million *livres* from his ravages in the Cape Verde Islands, Antigua, Montserrat, St Eustache, Surinam and Curaçao. Warming to the challenge, Cassard continued his offensive after the signing of the Franco-British truce and even after the Peace of Utrecht.

Greater numbers of French seamen were involved in the expedition against Rio de Janeiro in 1711. This affirmed the glory of Duguay-Trouin, as instigator and executant of a bold enterprise, but it would have been impossible without the agreement of the king, the support of the comte de Toulouse, and even the grudging collaboration of Pontchartrain. A pretext for the expedition was soon elaborated, namely, the murder of Captain Duclerc by the Portuguese in Rio. The real motive had long been in the mind of Duguay. Unable to intercept the annual fleet carrying precious metals from Brazil to Lisbon on the open ocean – Brazil was a colony of Portugal, but, after the Methuen treaty of 1703, Portugal itself resembled a British colony – he would take the precious cargo at its point of departure, in Rio. It was to be a repeat of the exploits of Pointis and Ducasse against Carthagena in the Indies in 1697.

Duguay envisaged one of the mixed fleets which, by a formal signed agreement, placed royal vessels in the service of 'privateers', careened, provisioned and rigged, with commanders, crews, artillery, arms and munitions, at His Majesty's expense and risk. The king had, since 1694, only retained one fifth of the value of the prizes; in 1709, he surrendered his share entirely. Amongst the investors in the company were not only the merchants of Saint-Malo, but also the comte de Toulouse. The first plans date from 30 December 1710, and, on 19 March 1711, Louis XIV and his secretary of state for the navy placed their signatures on the contract: 'Conditions accorded by the king to the sieur Duguay-Trouin, ship's captain, and to his suppliers for the provisioning of His Majesty's privateering vessels.' (277) The king provided crews, officers and ships – six thousand sailors, five hundred soldiers, seven ships of the line, four frigates, a corvette, two armed galliots and a fly-boat –, whilst surrendering any part of the prizes and imposing only a superintendent of his choice. On 9 June 1711, Duguay-Trouin's small fleet left La Rochelle and, on 12 September, it arrived off Rio. The English had not been able to intercept it on its outward voyage, nor would they on its return voyage, between 13 November and its arrival at Brest on 6 February. The French destroyed four ships of the line, two frigates, and sixty merchant ships. They lost only two, separated by storms during the return voyage. Back to Brest, they brought more than 45,850 ounces (1,300 kilograms) of gold, plus the 1,600,000 *livres* of the cargo of the two lost ships, which returned after a long detour (277). Pontchartrain argued over some details, but congratulated Duguay-Trouin: 'I am delighted for you and for the navy, which has gained great honour by this enterprise.' The news of the success at Rio gave 'visible pleasure to His Majesty' and impressed the English. Without it, would they have signed the suspension of hostilities on 17 July 1712? (277).

However remarkable the Rio expedition might appear, we should not ignore the third great task of the French navy, the constant success of its naval escorts. It is paradoxical historically that we know a great deal about the Vigo affair, of which Châteaurenault was the victim in 1702, but are less aware of the other convoys of Spanish precious metals, escorted by French vessels, crossing the Atlantic in 1703, 1706, 1708 and 1711–12, that is, in the years when it is often said that the English fleet dominated the Atlantic. Without these successful escorts, which presuppose an admiral in charge with a knowledge of information-gathering, strategy and politics as well as an outstanding naval ability, the war could not have been pursued or have developed favourably for the House of Bourbon. The marquis de Sourches wrote in 1709:

> On the 31st, Easter Day, everyone went as usual to his [Louis XIV's] *lever*, which was not until 10 a.m. There he said that he had received the good news that Chabert, leader of a squadron, had arrived at Port-Louis with the southern fleet, which was carrying riches for France, but little for the King of Spain, and that the whole fleet had arrived, with the exception of one vessel, loaded with riches, which had become separated. (97)

The thirty million *piastres* thus received permitted 'the avoidance of immediate bankruptcy' (194).

One man's name was particularly attached to the escort of galleons: Ducasse. In turn a filibuster, governor of Santo Domingo, merchant, slave-trader, ship's captain at the age of forty-seven, lieutenant-general at sixty-one, director of the Guinea Company and of the *asiento*, captain-general of the King of Spain, and finally chevalier of the Golden Fleece, this officer of Basque and bourgeois origin, whose life would inspire a generation of adventure novels, was 'one of the most distinguished leaders of Louis XIV's navy' (274) and the least acknowledged of the French commanders. In 1702, he brought 300,000 *piastres* from Carthagena to La Rochelle as a gift from Philip V to his grandfather (26). On the outward voyage, he had carried Spanish soldiers to the Americas. In 1704, he commanded a division at Velez-Malaga. On 28 October 1707, Dangeau noted: 'The news from Brest is that Ducasse has set sail in quest of the galleons in America, to escort them to Spain or to France.' And, on 1 September following, 'The king learnt at his *lever* from a naval officer, brought by M. de Pontet, that M. Ducasse was in port last Monday with the fleet from Mexico, with between forty and fifty million [*livres*] in silver', and had decided, on the advice of Desmarets, to prepare all the mints for the striking of *écus*. On 26 June 1709, Dangeau again noted: 'Ducasse, with seven warships now being fitted out with all speed at Brest, will be ready at the end of next month to conduct the new viceroy of Peru to Lima.' On 30 December 1710: 'M. Ducasse is leaving for Brest, where he will find three or four of the king's vessels ready to set sail. There is no doubt that he is going to Carthagena to bring back the galleons.' On 1 June 1711, Louis XIV created Ducasse a commander of the Order of St Louis. In March 1712, Ducasse returned a new division of galleons to Corunna. He had not stolen his Golden Fleece. If the war took a turn in the Bourbons' favour in 1712, this was because Ducasse had won the battle of the convoys.

DENAIN

It was certainly the case that the course of the war changed after Villaviciosa in 1710, that Denain in 1712 stabilized the situation in France in the North, and that by the Peace of Utrecht (11 April 1713) France attained the most vital of its objectives. But events did not proceed in a straightforward fashion. The old king lived these difficult years a day at a time, hour by hour. Chronology is not history and yet, for the king, it was more real, more intensely human – and inhuman – than history is. On 14 April 1711, the Dauphin, the kingdom's hope, died. On the following day, Louis XIV despatched Villars to command the army of Flanders. On the 17th, Joseph I died. Before the month was complete, the 'malcontents' in Hungary had made their peace with the Habsburgs.* Meanwhile, Philip V was constrained to surrender what was left of the Spanish Low Countries to the Elector of Bavaria. The only glimmer of good news came from England. Louis XIV knew that Queen Anne was weary of war, less than totally committed to the grand designs of Marlborough (the duchess had been in disgrace since 6 April 1710) and, with the Tories in power from November 1710, interested in proposals for peace. But the balance was too fragile for the King of France to attempt any sudden manœuvre. For this reason, he opposed a plan for the invasion of Germany as proposed by Villars. It was true that Prince Eugene had left the army to go to the assistance of Archduke Charles, who would be elected emperor on 12 October. Furthermore, Gassion had won a combat near Douai and Montesquiou had taken Arleux. But as soon as Marlborough decided to attack, he breached the northern frontier, besieged Bouchain in August and occupied Denain, isolating Valenciennes and Condé. Villars, who had been boasting about the excellent state of an army where 'order and

* The 'malcontents' of Hungary and Transylvania were the 'mutual allies' of France under their leader, Francis II Rákóczi (1676–1735).

discipline' prevailed, appeared paralysed. Bouchain capitulated on 12 September. Fortunately, Marlborough returned to England to attend to his political interests, and found himself disgraced (295).

Despite all these objects of concern, Louis had remained vigilant. Whilst avoiding a decisive confrontation in Europe, he pursued talks with the envoys of Queen Anne and these began again in August. At the same time, he maintained offensive actions in the colonies: on 9 June, Duguay-Trouin's squadron had set off towards Rio; on 2 December, the king would put his hand to a deal with Cassard for the pillaging of the Dutch and English Atlantic territories. France was not in a position of weakness when it accepted the preliminary proposals of London on 8 October 1711. These consisted of two pacts. One, a discreet pact (which could be communicated to Heinsius), involved, above all, a French undertaking not to unite the Crowns of France and Spain under one monarch. Guarantees about the 'barrier fortresses' were intended to appease the Dutch and the emperor. By the other, a secret treaty, Louis XIV recognized Queen Anne and the Act of Settlement.* He undertook to neutralize Dunkirk, surrender St Kitts and sign a commercial treaty. On behalf of his grandson, who was not consulted, the king confirmed the English sovereignty over Gibraltar and Minorca and even granted London the privilege of the *asiento*, of which France had been the beneficiary since the succession of Philip V.

Seen from Paris, these concessions seemed palatable when compared with the terms of The Hague (1709) or Geertruidenberg (1710). But Heinsius regarded them as insufficiently robust and it took the pressure of the Tory party, the fall of Marlborough, and the unanimity of opinion among the councillors of the Queen of England to force Europe to a peace congress. Proposed for 12 January 1712, it opened on the 29th. The emperor had given strict instructions to his emissaries. As for Philip V, the allies had not deigned to invite him. This latter point annoyed Louis XIV, but allowed elbow room to his negotiators, the maréchal d'Huxelles and the abbé de Polignac.

In short, the French king had some reason to feel relieved: the war appeared to be turning in his favour, the coalition partners

---

* i.e., the Protestant succession.

disagreed about everything, Philip V was on the way to saving his inheritance. A less experienced individual would have felt overjoyed; Louis XIV remained sceptical, and with good reason. On 6 February, Duguay-Trouin returned to Brest with the ransom of Rio; but, on 12 February, the Duchess of Burgundy died, followed on 18 February by the Duke of Burgundy and, on 8 March, by the Duke of Brittany. And, as if fate had set itself against the descendants of Henry IV, Vendôme, restorer of Philip V's throne, died in Spain on 10 June. If the old king had ceased to direct affairs in order to mourn the deaths of his relatives, he would have been held responsible for the failure of the talks at Utrecht. Instead, he retained a superficial calm, hid his grief, and did not neglect the making of decisions during these decisive days. In so doing, he ran the risk of being accused of insensitivity.

Without this phlegmatic attitude, not to mention the flexibility and firm negotiating talent of Torcy, France would not have extracted the advantages it did during the summer of 1712. From April onwards, the situation began to improve. The enemy failed in their attempt to break through. They camped near Douai, waiting for Prince Eugene, for news of the negotiations, or for orders. Facing them, Louis XIV drew up '102 battalions camped between Arras and Cambrai' (97). At the same time, things were going rather better for France at the peace conference. Letters arriving at court on 18 April confirmed 'that everything at Utrecht was confused and distrustful, that it seemed that the supposed common cause was beginning to be replaced by individual interests, that nothing was to be seen except comings and goings, that all seemed in chaos, and that one did not know what there was to worry about, so much had the firmness of the French plenipotentiaries surprised the allies.' (97)

Louis XIV was, in fact, so far from being insensitive to the losses in his family and the dangers threatening the kingdom that he laid aside all modesty when dictating to Villars his instructions on Saturday, 16 April. The king informed the marshal: 'God is punishing me and I deserve it, but let us for the moment leave our grief at domestic misfortunes to one side and see what may be done to prevent those of the state.' He entrusted his last great army to Villars, making clear his confidence in him. Then he foresaw the possibility of defeat, of the opening up of the road to Paris, and asked what would need to be done in such an eventuality. As Villars remained silent, the old king went on: 'While waiting for you to express your opinion, I will give you mine . . . I know the Somme. It is difficult to cross. There are strongholds. I would go to Péronne or Saint-Quentin, collect all the troops I could, make a last effort with you and we should die together to save the state, for I would never allow the enemy to approach my capital.' Villars, moved, rose to look the king in the face. It was no longer the proud military commander who spoke but the confidant of a great prince: 'The most glorious actions', replied the marshal, 'are often the wisest. I see none more noble than those proposed by Your Majesty; but I hope that, with God's grace, we shall not be brought to confront such an eventuality.' (295) Four days later, Villars assumed command of the army at Cambrai upon which so much rested.

Bolingbroke on the English side and Torcy for the French speeded up their negotiations, resulting in an armistice between the two nations, applicable first in Flanders (17 July) and then more generally (22 August). These arrangements had the disadvantage of having weakened French morale when Prince Eugene laid siege to Le Quesnoy on 8 June, capturing it on 5 July, and thereby threatening Landrecies. But they had the advantage of depriving Eugene of the help of British soldiers. A decisive confrontation was being prepared. Louis XIV sent the order to Villars to relieve Landrecies, leaving him free to determine the time and place of the battle which now appeared inevitable. In fact, the couriers between the court and the army crossed and carried contradictory messages. It was Louis XIV who first proposed the idea of attacking Denain, but Villars carried it out against his latest orders.

Clausewitz said: 'most sieges fail for lack of means, and the means are usually deficient because of difficulties of transport' (159). Prince Eugene's supplies were at the camp at Denain, over seventeen miles from Landrecies. But Villars' task was not an easy one. He had to 'execute a flanking march of eight or nine *lieues* [between twenty and twenty-three miles], without the enemy's knowledge, cross a river and take some well-defended entrenchments, before the enemy had time to come and attack him in the rear' (295). Secrecy was essential. Only seven officers were told of the plans. Ruse and diversion played their part.

Feigned movements made Prince Eugene believe that his adversary was advancing towards Landrecies.

Montesquiou marched the entire army at nightfall in silence to the west of the Selle. By 4 a.m. the troops had reached the Scheldt. Eugene, at last informed, did not believe that Villars was on the offensive or that the troop movements were significant. At 10 a.m. he was eating whilst Broglie moved the French cavalry across the Scheldt. Eugene only realized his mistake at noon, by which time it was too late. Denain was taken by assault and seventeen enemy battalions were destroyed (295). The allied supplies were captured, with eight cannon and 'all their flags and a great quantity of equipment' (97). The French infantry had attacked as if on the parade ground. Villars galloped, dressed in his 'lucky jerkin', encouraging his troops. Montesquiou took care of the 'details'. Prince Eugene had preserved the bulk of his army, but his heart was no longer in continuing the struggle: he raised the siege of Landrecies and abandoned his heavy artillery. The king's army took Marchiennes, Saint-Amand, Douai, Le Quesnoy and Bouchain. The time for *Te Deums* had returned. Such success persuaded the Dutch to obstruct peace no further.

THE PEACE AGREEMENTS

The main precondition for a (belated) peace lay in the separation of the two Crowns. Philip V had only resolved to surrender his claim to the throne of France in July, an act which had permitted the signing of the armistices. The formal renunciation took place in Madrid on 5 November before the Cortes and in the presence of the English and Dutch ambassadors. For their parts, the ducs d'Orléans and de Berry renounced all rights to the Spanish succession. These three acts were inscribed in letters-patent of March 1713, published by the Parlement in the presence of the allied ambassadors on 15 March.

The allies had apparently every reason to be content with these arrangements. And it is true that France and the King of Spain had been humiliated, but then the neutralization of Dunkirk and the renunciation of Tournai of 2 November had also been humiliating. If such was the price of peace, the old king was prepared to meet it. But he also knew his public law and, if his memory faltered, chancellor Pontchartrain, *président* de Mesmes and the *procureur général* d'Aguesseau were there to remind him of its principles. The ruin of Dunkirk, already a *fait accompli*, the purely formal renunciation of the rights of succession, and even the concluding of the Peace of Utrecht, which everyone was preparing to sign, were only acts of circumstance. Philip V's renunciation had a double significance: 'On the one hand, to ensure the throne for Philip V's descendants; on the other, to prevent the union of the crowns of France and Spain on the same head' (264). Yet this renunciation could hardly be binding in the kingdom, for it was contrary to its fundamental laws. According to the French public law of the *ancien régime*, 'on the death of the Capetian king, the nearest male in the order of primogeniture succeeds him automatically' (264). Torcy reminded Bolingbroke that:

> it is . . . [a] question of taking solid measures to prevent the union of the two monarchies, but we would be moving away from that desired objective and towards evils worse, if possible, than those which we would all wish to avoid, if we were to contravene the fundamental laws of the kingdom . . . This law is regarded as the work of the One who established all monarchies, and we in France are persuaded that God alone can abolish it. (264)

It was no coincidence that neither Pontchartrain nor d'Aguesseau attended the Parlement on 15 March 1713. Nor was it by chance that *président* de Mesmes called for the publication of the renunciations in a tone which showed how little he respected acts extracted by force and incapable of breaching the old constitution.

The interval between the renunciations of 1712 and their publication is to be explained by divisions between the allies. The United Provinces, continuing the intransigence of the late Prince of Orange, proved the most reluctant, though the news of the devastation of Surinam by Cassard in January 1713 provided further impetus towards compliance. Similarly, the French expedition against Rio softened the position of Portugal, leading to an armistice with Spain and France on 7 November 1712.

Utrecht was not a single pacification treaty but a series of separate agreements. The so-called 'barrier treaty' of 30 January 1713 between Great Britain and the United Provinces gave the latter several strongholds in the Low Countries. Five treaties followed on 11 April. One between France and Portugal ended their colonial disputes. A second was concluded between France and the King of Prussia: France recognized him as a king and as sovereign in Neuchâtel, whilst, in return, France's sovereignty over the principality of Orange was accepted by Prussia. By the Franco-Savoyard treaty, Louis XIV was forced to recognize the Duke of Savoy as King of Sicily, but the adjusted frontier gave Barcelonnette to France. The treaty between France and England confirmed the preliminary negotiations. Louis XIV ceded Newfoundland, Acadia and St Kitts, demolished the fortifications of Dunkirk, recognized Queen Anne and the Act of Settlement, and promised to expel the Pretender. The treaty with the United Provinces modified France's northern frontier once more. The Low Countries would go to the House of Austria. The Dutch would retain the garrisons in Luxembourg, Namur, Charleroi and Nieuport. A commercial agreement reproduced that of Ryswick. France lost Tournai, Menin, Ypres and Furnes, but retained Lille, Aire, Béthune and Saint-Venant. As for Philip V, though he had to recognize the Duke of Savoy as King of Sicily and concede Gibraltar, Minorca, the right of *asiento* and 'privileged status' to English shipping in Latin-American trade, he retained Spain and its overseas empire.*

Not quite everything was determined. The Elector of Bavaria only renounced the Low Countries in exchange for a promise to be restored to his estates. Catalonia still rejected the sovereignty of its legitimate king. Much remained to be done, but Louis XIV was far from defeated. 'If one compares', Torcy was to write,

> the Peace of Utrecht with the preliminaries proposed by pensionary Heinsius in 1709, and then the even harsher demands made by the deputies of the States General at Geertruidenberg in 1710, if one has not forgotten the state in which the kingdom found itself in 1708, 1709 and 1710, and if one remembers the fatal battles of Höchstädt in 1704 [Blenheim], Ramillies and Turin in 1706, Oudenaarde in 1708 and Malplaquet in 1709, so many disasters leading to the loss of important strongholds, these hard times only serve to show how little this peace has cost France. (104)

Emperor Charles VI, however, wanted to continue the war. Although Starhemberg left Spain in July 1713, Barcelona only

---

* The treaty with Spain followed after a three month delay.

surrendered to the Duke of Berwick in September 1714. But Villars was operating on imperial territory, and luck seemed to have abandoned Eugene of Savoy. The French took Speyer, Worms and Kaiserslautern in quick succession. After fifty-six days of siege, Landau surrendered to Villars on 20 August 1713. He now undertook the difficult siege of Freiburg. The capture of this city could make it a useful bargaining counter to exchange for Strasbourg. After a combat before the gates of the city on 20 September, Villars began the siege of Freiburg, which ended on 16 November with the surrender of the castle. After this blow, the emperor understood that it was pointless further to resist France. On 26 November, Eugene met with Villars at Rastadt.

Full of his recent success, Villars was not the perfect negotiator. But Torcy kept an eye on the victor of Denain from Versailles. Despite 'frequent and lively arguments' (113), the antagonists arrived at an agreement: the treaty between France and the emperor was signed at Rastadt on 6 March 1714; that between France and the German princes at Baden on 7 September. France retained Landau and Strasbourg and ensured that its faithful German allies, the Electors of Cologne and Bavaria, were re-established in their 'estates, offices and dignities'. The emperor renounced Spain, whilst receiving the Low Countries, Milan, Naples, Tuscany and Sardinia. The final treaty agreed by the old king was in the line of Aix-la-Chapelle, Nymwegen and Ryswick: France stayed within its legitimate pretensions.

GAINS AND LOSSES

Commenting on the treaties of Utrecht and Rastadt, M. de Torcy's great achievement and the old king's swansong, Frédéric Masson wrote:

> This long and painful war had, at times, put France in great danger. But diplomacy repaired the faults of the military in so far as it was possible. There had been dreadful days, like Höchstädt [Blenheim] and Ramillies, but there were others which may be inscribed alongside the most glorious and most renowned. France had evinced a spirit and energy which did it no mean credit, and which demonstrated that a people may always be saved when they want to be and, instead of being divided amongst themselves, remain firm around an assigned leader. (103)

Peace had been secured. It is now time to take stock, and the result is quite surprising. Many people believe that France was smaller in 1715 than it had been in 1643. Throughout the litany of wars and the details of treaties, the same names recur: Ypres, Tournai, Philippsburg, Breisach, Pinerolo. The alternation of acquisition and loss presents an impression of fragility. But this is to ignore the underlying pattern; for these venerable and magnificent fortresses and towns with shifting sovereignty attached to them mask the techtonic growth of the kingdom: ten new provinces, rights over the Crown territory of Madagascar, an establishment in Senegal, and the huge spaces of Louisiana which bore the king's name, whilst the Mississippi was known as the River Colbert.

In late August 1715, on the eve of the king's death, the territorial expansion of France since 1643, at home and in the colonies, appeared therefore almost inordinate; the losses were bearable. Utrecht forced France to surrender rights to Newfoundland (whilst retaining fishing rights), Acadia and St Kitts. Yet, despite these concessions, France overseas held a 'domain much greater than the English colonial possessions at that time' (129). It is true, however, that it was much more sparsely populated than the English colonies and that France lacked a colonial consciousness, even if Jérôme de Pontchartrain seemed close to inspiring it.*

The map of acquisitions emerges thus: Artois (1659), Dunkirk, a town close to Louis XIV's heart (1662), Walloon Flanders including Lille (1668), Aire and Saint-Omer, or the rest of Artois (1678), French Hainaut including Mauberge and Valenciennes (1678), Thionville and 'French Luxembourg' (1643, 1659), the three bishoprics of Lorraine – Metz, Toul and Verdun (1648) – Sarrelouis, the *réunion* built by Vauban and baptized by the king (1680, 1697), Landau (1680, 1714), Alsace (1648, 1681, 1697), Franche Comté (1674, 1678), the valley of Barcelonnette (1713), the principality of Orange (1673, 1713), and Roussillon and Cerdagne (1659). This was the king's *pré carré*, which, in the aftermath of Ryswick, was more homogeneous and more easily defensible. Taken as a whole, France in 1715 was not far off possessing 'natural frontiers'. This was *de facto* assured on the Rhine, between Dauphiné and Savoy, and

* This is based on the works of Professor Charles Frostin (183–7)

along the Pyrenees. Vauban died regretting the loss of Philipps-burg, Breisach, Kehl and Pinerolo. He reacted like a commissioner of fortifications. Louis XIV, more intelligently, appreciated the situation through the eyes of a politician.

Overseas, the king pursued no imperial plan, but the list of new possessions shows that the French presence was greater than it would have been if he had only followed a mercantilist policy based on immediate profit. In the West Indies, the strategic and commercial exploitation of Santo Domingo (1655, 1697) would compensate for the cession of St Kitts. Cayenne and French Guiana (1676) were not El Dorado, but they ensured that the English and the Dutch were not alone upon the coasts of Brazil. Louisiana (1682), conceded to the financier Crozat in 1712, was as yet empty of people (79), but was full of potential. In Africa, Louis had rights in Senegal (1659, 1700). The comte d'Estrées had conquered Gorea (1677, 1678). Madagascar was not the land fit for colonization of which Colbert had dreamt, but Louis XIV baptized it 'Ile Dauphine' and united it to the Crown in 1686 (129). At some distance, France possessed two ports of call on the way to the Far East, the Mascareignes – Ile Bourbon (1649) and Ile de France (1715) – facilitating contact with the East Indies. France had its first trading-posts at Pondicherry (1670, 1697) and at Chandernagor, Mazulipatam and Calicut (1701).

The acquisition of these distant lands, and the conquest of the neighbouring provinces which composed the *pré carré*, were not made without cost. Louis XIV's wars had cost the lives of 500,000 men. They brought ten provinces and an overseas empire.

28

Trials, Errors and Hopes

VOLTAIRE THOUGHT that Louis XIV's glory would have been unalloyed if the king had died immediately following Utrecht, between the signing of the treaties and the unfortunate bull *Unigenitus*. The author of *The Century of Louis XIV* was not fundamentally mistaken, but he had simplified matters. For example, all was not gloom between the spring of 1713 and the king's death. Trials and errors, but also hopes, preceded and succeeded the settlement of the treaties. Pacifism was one such test of endurance.

THE SIRENS OF PACIFISM

During the difficult years of the Spanish war, the king had to confront not only the coalition, the hatred of pensionary Heinsius, the determination of Marlborough and Prince Eugene, the animosity of the Prostestants, financial problems and the vacillation of his Council, but also the insinuations and heavy silences of the 'confraternity of pacific souls' (87). Madame Palatine claimed, albeit without any manifest enthusiasm, to be a member of this group. The abbé de Saint-Pierre, for his part, was working on a *Project for Perpetual Peace in Europe* (1713), and in 1711 circulated a first instalment (which fell on deaf ears). Some of the military commanders had come to hate the war. The maréchal de Tessé was one of them. He rejoined his army 'discouraged' (65), and wrote: 'I will avoid telling you about the war, I hate it.' (101) That is why whiffs of pacifism reached the middle ranks of the army, less patriotic than the king and less habituated to discipline than lower-ranking officers and ordinary soldiers. In January 1709, the marquise de Maintenon recorded that 'the officers are all too fond of Paris' (65). In September, on the eve of Malplaquet, peace seemed so close that parts of the army lay paralysed.

In the *Tables de Chaulnes*, written by Fénelon (36) after his discussions in November 1711 at the duc de Chevreuse's château, the plan envisaged by these plotters implied immediate peace and the renunciation of the king's conquests (224). In the council of ministers, the defeatist party was represented by the duc de Beauvillier. This pious councillor had not supported the duc d'Anjou consistently, only sustaining Madrid between 1701 and 1703 (224). Pacifists such as Beauvillier, Fénelon and Mme de Maintenon 'looked on the retention of Spain as an invincible obstacle to peace' and stuck relentlessly to this simplistic notion. They 'did not stop to think', noted Torcy, 'that, with Spain lost, France, far from having peace, after this loss would for ever after face an enemy army in Guyenne or Languedoc' (104).

Louis did not allow himself to be swayed by Beauvillier, whose 'intentions are known' (224). But he could hardly avoid the ramifications of the devout and maudlin pacifism of the *marquise*. To be sure, her husband did not consult her and ignored her advice, to Mme de Maintenon's resentment. But she kept herself well informed about many things; for the king maintained the curious custom of talking to his ministers in her presence, and from 1704 until 1714 she allowed herself the luxury of innumerable interjections. Her abundant correspondence captures their tone and context. Peace was the theme of the letters addressed to the ladies at Saint-Cyr: 'Never tire of praying for peace' (1704), 'Pray for the salvation of the king and peace' (1706), 'If God does not give us peace at any price, everything will get worse and worse' (1707). Louis's secret wife wanted an immediate peace, especially when the fortunes of war were going against the king. But she also called for it after a success like Velez-Malaga, on account of the dead and wounded (66). She toned down her desires when the situation was favourable and there was an evident chance of peace, as in 1712.

Her pacific words were not very cheering on the eve of decisive battles. On the eve or morning of Malplaquet and Denain, Saint-Cyr was on bended knee asking not for peace but for victory. For the course of events was attributed not to chance but to providence, as no one doubted it should be. But Mme de Maintenon claimed to interpret the secrets of providence. She prayed in 1704 'to obtain from God that He turn His wrath away from France, although we have well deserved it'. In 1706, she was saddened by the thought that Louis XIV and Philip V were the champions of religion but were suffering reverses. 'Our enemies are attacking both of them and are triumphant: God is the master.' (65) Such submissiveness before the will of the Almighty evidently turned into pessimism. To the *marquise* God was on the side of peace. Her letters endlessly talked of the 'salvation of His Majesty' and of praying 'for the salvation of the king', to the extent that it appeared that his salvation was tied to his desire for peace and his efforts towards it.

THE INSURGENTS OF THE DESERT

The French Protestants sang a different tune: from the benches of His Majesty's galleys came the lamentations of the Lord's people exiled by the waters of Babylon. The 'galériens pour la foi' were Protestants caught in the act of contravening the clauses of Fontainebleau: pastors who had not emigrated, preachers, participants in clandestine worship, or would-be emigrants arrested at the frontier. Their numbers have been calculated at 1,450 between 1685 and 1715, but have long been thought to be ten or twenty times more numerous than that, so great has been their impact on Reformed consciousness. At Marseille, they were watched more closely than other prisoners, but were better treated, except when the chaplains of the galley *La Superbe* had the idea of forcing rowers to kneel during Mass. However, they found accomplices, enabling them to correspond with other countries, even Holland. Some created a secret organization for correspondence and for the provision of bibles as well as the diffusion of imported propaganda. They busied themselves with teaching, catechizing and mutual assistance, and with despatching abroad tracts and testimonials about 'the Church of the confessors [of God's truth]'.

But Marseille was not France. The kingdom as a whole had, since the Revocation, seen the beginnings of a Protestant revival. 'Up to the end of the reign, repressive measures allow us to find Protestants who had not stopped being Protestants and had never abjured' (222). The 'crossing of the desert' had begun, for the brave and the stubborn: that in the Bible lasted for forty years; theirs would last one hundred and two years, until the edict of toleration under Louis XVI. Assemblies were reported from late 1685 in Languedoc, Normandy, Dauphiné and Saintonge, and in Paris. For lack of pastors, worship was led by improvised preachers. The king was gradually informed about all this, and after ten years of repression Louis XIV realized that a section of the 'nouveaux convertis' had slipped through his clutches. This explains the edict on education of 1695 and the declaration of 13 December 1698 ordering the establishment of an elementary school in every parish. Having failed to obtain a sufficient number of sincere abjurations, the king and his clergy made do with the children of the *nouveaux convertis*. But these children, returning home after school, were subjected to a counter-catechism, more biblical and polemical. Like their brothers in the galleys, the resistance of these *obstinés* successfully obstructed a supposedly invincible king. It needed only a small step for them to see in this a judgement of God, a step taken by the adherents of 'Prophetism'.

Its first manifestations, drawing on apocalyptic arguments from Jurieu's polemics, flourished in 1688 and 1689. Rome became the new Babylon. The Revocation was compared to the captivity and Louis XIV to Nebuchadnezzar. The preachers, new Daniels, preached the revolt of the righteous, the triumph of the saints, supported by God. The faithful, aroused to fanaticism, braved the dragoons and thronged to the assemblies. In the Cévennes, a poor mountainous region which would be dislocated by the revival of the *capitation* in 1701, where Reformed Christianity meant education, the confessional rupture of 1685 destroyed the rhythms of daily life and inflicted a blow to the collective consciousness to such an extent that the Psalms completely replaced popular songs. All did not remain peaceful: 1689 saw the beginnings of a rising and 1692 more troubles. The dates correspond with the Ten Years' War and the attempted Anglo-Protestant landing in the Mediterranean.

A second wave broke across the Cévennes from north to south in the summer of 1700. Prophetism was now less peaceable. In July 1702, the murder of the abbé du Chayla, known as the persecutor of the Huguenots, sparked off the war of the Cévennes, known as the Camisard war. These disturbances, like the earlier ones, coincided with a foreign war. In both cases, the insurgents were in contact with the refugee Huguenots; they hoped that the Protestant powers would force a return to the regime of the Edict of Nantes. The Camisards had skilful leaders: Jean Cavalier, Rolland, Mazel. In 1703, they stood firm against the royal armies, driving the maréchal de Montrevel into taking brutal reprisals, which, far from calming the uprising, only intensified it. For the insurrection was a holy war. The cause of the insurgents could only be that of the Eternal, the God of Abraham, Joshua, Gideon and the Maccabees. They took as their battle-song Psalm 68: 'Let God arise, let His enemies be scattered: let them also that hate Him flee before Him.' Doubt never crossed their minds. If they burned down a church, they were, they thought, destroying a dwelling-place of superstition. If they trod the host underfoot, they were suppressing an idolatrous cult. If they broke a crucifix, this was to remind the Catholics that the Lord said: 'Thou shalt not make unto thee a graven image.' The Cévenols saw themselves defending the honour of the Almighty and acting for the glory of God against the king, that unrighteous Caesar. When an entire population with such feelings supports one, one can withstand an army.

To be fair to Louis XIV, he saw that he was getting nowhere by waging outright war on the insurgents, and that Montrevel had to be replaced by a leader capable of diplomacy. In March 1704, therefore, Villars was named as commander of the troops in Languedoc. His actions combined firmness with flexibility, and quickly achieved results. Père Anselme translated it into a *Veni, vidi, vici*: 'He calmed them, and restored freedom of trade to the province.' (2) The Bishop of Nîmes, Fléchier, gives a less concise account:

> It is difficult to be certain about the future with people so corrupt and violent as these; however, they seem pacified, they are no longer killing and burning, they are returning to work and are content to sleep in their houses and to eat in peace the bread they have earned during the day. Here we have seen all their chiefs, each more depraved and destitute than the last, yet who call themselves evangelists, preachers, prophets, who have gone abroad to spread their extravagances in foreign lands. The maréchal de Villars has conducted this affair very prudently, and has calmed it without bloodshed, which has pleased us very much. (39)

Thus spoke Fléchier in early 1705. In 1708, he said: 'Violence has ceased, but error still remains and will not end in the majority of these obsessed brains until the end of the war removes their last hopes of re-establishing themselves.' (39) What the bishop called error was not at all to end in 1715, so much had the Cévennes been marked by these struggles. After the semi-amnesty of 1705, the government hardly penetrated this volatile region. The result was a toleration in practice which satisfied neither its beneficiaries nor the priests nor the Catholic population at large. It demonstrated Louis XIV's political intelligence, but underlined his limited success in the matter of religious unity.

THE DESTRUCTION OF PORT-ROYAL DES CHAMPS

The king did not find the right strategy for dealing with Augustinianism either. The dawn raid which took place on 29 October 1709 is ample testimony to this. Then it was that:

> [the lieutenant of police] M. d'Argenson presented himself at the gates of Port-Royal des Champs in the king's name. They were opened to him, and, His Majesty's wishes having been made known to the mother prioress, she assembled the chapter, so as to make them known; this lasted until midday without any disturbance or tears from the nuns, but a respectful silence accompanied by submission to his orders. The prioress asked M. d'Argenson if he would allow them enough time to collect their meagre belongings; when he replied that he had received no instructions about this from the king, but would take the responsibility himself, she thanked him, saying that, having no order, the only thing to do was to leave with nothing but a staff and a breviary. There were eight carriages and some chairs, in which all these unfortunate individuals were put. (26)

So wrote the marquise d'Huxelles, who also specified the towns and convents to which the nuns were sent. Sœur Anne-Cécile, aged eighty-seven, was despatched to Amiens, whilst the Ursulines of Mantes received sœur Euphrasie Robert, who 'is eighty-six years old and paralytic' (26). They all had refused to submit to the bull *Vineam Domini* of 1705, which forbade the 'respectful silence' which had been allowed instead of the open approbation of the eternal condemnation of the Five Propositions of the *Augustinus*.

This was a mistake, for lightning strikes at the highest places, and the high places of religion were those where the Spirit dwelt. The hardest trial for the convent at Les Champs would have been to wither and fade away, starved of the Sacraments and new recruits. The king, ill advised and stubborn, did it the honour of persecuting it in its centenary year, for the 'journée du Guichet' had taken place in September 1609.* Unaware of this perhaps, père Le Tellier, Louis XIV's new confessor, had neglected to remind him of the axiom: 'Martyrdom grants immortality.'

Since the end of the Peace of the Church in 1679 and the expulsion of Port-Royal's boarders, novices and confessors, it had been doomed to extinction. Furthermore, the exile of such leaders as Arnauld and Quesnel had debilitated Jansenism. It was difficult to run things well from abroad; messages from afar were liable to be misunderstood within the kingdom. The disappearance of the movement's leading lights seems to have left its ranks bewildered, with the result that Jansenism 'took an often grim and unpredictable turn' (282). And yet the group remained influential, and widespread in the provinces, much to Louis XIV's annoyance. But it was not possible to submit the Augustinians to the same treatment as that meted out to the Calvinists. The former were within the Roman Church, many among its greatest jewels. They enjoyed widespread support and they had joined with the Molinists in applauding the Revocation. So the king chose to strike at the head, the symbolic places, both individuals and institutions. He was encouraged by the marquise de Maintenon, herself spurred on by Bishop Godet des Marais. On the other hand, père de la Chaize had seemingly mellowed in his old age.

Louis-Antoine de Noailles, son of the duke, Bishop of Châlons, and Archbishop of Paris from 1695, had begun his period in archiepiscopal office with 'reforms; his zeal extended to the laity and not only to the clergy' (54): measures against the theatre, prying into morals, strict control of the secular and

---

* The 'journée du Guichet' was the moment, symbolic of the return of Port-Royal to the strict rule, when mère Angélique (Jacqueline Marie Angélique Arnauld de Sainte-Madeleine, 1591–1661), its reformer, refused to meet her father, save through the bars of a grille in the gates of the convent.

regular clergy. He soon seemed to have 'made himself a grand inquisitor through his zeal and his influence'. On theological matters, Noailles set great store by the opinions of Mgr Le Tellier, Archbishop of Reims, his former metropolitan; but, according to abbé Le Gendre, he consulted so many (Bossuet, the Oratorian père de la Tour, Godet des Marais) that he found himself in the position of a patient torn between the divergent diagnoses of a large number of doctors. In fact, for a period of seven years he had his pastoral letters drawn up by a Jansenist, Canon Boileau. This twin character – playing the part of a Charles Borromeo while allowing scope to abbé Boileau – turned M. de Noailles perforce into a Jansenist. When, in a pastoral letter of 1696, he condemned the *Exposition of the Faith of the Roman Church concerning Grace and Predestination* by Martin de Barcos, Saint-Cyran's nephew, he managed to denounce 'the poison of the dogma of Jansenius' (54), but then expounded his own doctrine of grace without dissociating himself from what he had condemned in the first half of his text. Many Jansenists said that Mgr de Noailles 'had only taken on the appearance of Esau in order to speak more assuredly the language of Jacob' (54). Noailles was not profoundly Jansenist, but he was sufficiently Gallican to put the brakes on those intiatives from Rome which he judged to be untimely. This may be seen in his attitude towards père Quesnel and in the way in which he took part in the affair of the 'matter of conscience'.

M. de Noailles admired Quesnel and as Bishop of Châlons had approved his *Summary of the Morality of the Gospels or Christian Considerations on the Text of the Four Gospels* (vol. 1, 1671; definitive version, 1695). The Jesuits had denounced it, and Quesnel, in exile in the Low Countries in 1684, was imprisoned from 1696 to 1703 after being denounced by the Archbishop of Malines. (He escaped and, hunted by Louis XIV's agents, sought refuge in the United Provinces.) Yet, far from associating himself with the enemies of the Oratorian, Noailles protected him. He asked him to revise his *Summary* and Quesnel complied, publishing *The New Testament in French, with Moral Reflections on Each Verse* in 1699. And, when Clement XI ordered the burning of this Jansenist work, on 13 July 1708, Quesnel, who had been made a cardinal in 1700, associated himself with the Gallicans on the Council (Torcy, Pontchartrain and d'Aguesseau) in order to ensure that the papal brief would not be accepted in France.

In the affair of the 'matter of conscience', Noailles and Bossuet searched for a peaceful solution. The Jesuits and Fénelon, on the other hand, added fuel to the fire, urging Clement XI to give a decision, and rekindled the interminable conflict. In 1702, Mme de Maintenon, frightened by the 'effrontery' of her former protégé, warned the cardinal-archbishop that he had lost the confidence of Louis XIV, who was accusing him of 'favouring the Jansenists' (216). At this moment, in fact, Louis XIV was discovering an irritating political side in Jansenism. He viewed Quesnel as the leader of a party and a leading rebel, and wanted to make peace with Rome. He detected, even in the council of ministers, collusion between Gallicans and Augustinians and feared that this would become something more permanent. After 1703, he pestered Clement XI for a bull condemning adherence to Jansenism and bringing the formulary back into force. On 15 July 1705, the pope duly published the bull *Vineam Domini*. It should have put an end to the dispute about grace; but it only succeeded in affirming the political appearance of Jansenism. Leading Augustinians like Quesnel and Boileau along with their well-placed supporters such as Colbert, Bishop of Montpellier, ceased defending the Five Propositions come what may, preferring to mobilize opinion against Rome in the name of the liberties of the French Church. Noailles was not alone in deploying this tactic.

The Assembly of the Clergy in 1705 provided Noailles with an ideal platform. According to the cardinal, the pope had refused to claim 'infallibility in the affirmation of the reality of facts, even in the area of dogma, which are not shown by revelation', and had not declared whether 'respectful silence' was or was not sufficient. Consequently, he invited his fellow bishops to 'adhere only to the decision contained in the bull, without adding anything to or subtracting anything from such a precise decision' (216). But this apparent acceptance was invalidated by the bishops' promise to accompany the publication of the text with an explanatory letter. The assembly demonstrated to the pope that the authority of the Church of France opposed his authority. Noailles and the majority of the bishops in effect subscribed to the doctrine of the future chancellor d'Aguesseau, according to which a decision taken by Rome only had force of law 'by the acceptance and unanimous consent of the entire Church'. If the Archbishop of Paris and the Bishop of Montpellier had significant reservations, then consent could not be said to be 'unanimous'. Having defied the king, Noailles was obliged to make concessions on certain points: in the end 'Port-Royal paid the price'.

Even the Jansenist sympathizer Saint-Simon defended père de la Chaize, 'the confessor, who was fundamentally a good man' (94). Racine appreciated his courtesy, his flexibility and his appreciation of fine distinctions. Mme de Maintenon, on the other hand, had taken an immediate dislike to the confessor, who was too independent for her taste. This independence emerged in the choice of certain bishops, not always Molinists, and in his attitude towards dissidents. Despite his animosity towards Quesnel, La Chaize maintained a qualified position towards Jansenists, though not towards Protestants. After his death in January 1709, Madame Palatine could write without qualification: 'The Protestants have lost their most relentless enemy, that is to say, the king's confessor, père La Chaise.' (87) Saint-Simon, however, noted in the margins of Dangeau's manuscript: 'This père de la Chaise was universally mourned.' (26) Posterity has tarnished his image, partly under Protestant influence and partly by putting him in the same category as the king's last confessor.

Père Le Tellier was not a courtier, but a controversialist: 'too violent', according to Voltaire; 'of a cruel and ferocious disposition', according to Saint-Simon. A man 'of no birth', and at first 'entirely devoted to study' (65), he had reached the elevated station of *provincial* of Paris when the king chose him (26). He was not as singleminded as his reputation suggests: he took the side of Confucius in the debate over the Chinese rites. Unfortunately, his liberalism did not extend to the French. He was undoubtedly more clumsy than malicious, having never had an open mind (65); he lacked malleability in social relations, and subtlety entirely escaped him.

Le Tellier's Ultramontanism led him to encourage the king's anti-Jansenist tendencies. In March 1709, the so-called 'council of conscience', Friday morning deliberations between Louis XIV and his confessor about ecclesiastical benefices, was revived. From that moment, Le Tellier influenced 'the personal affairs' of the sovereign. Yet, even after a year and a half of apparent intimacy, he 'did not think he had the right to interfere in certain matters which did not seem to be of his concern and, for this reason, he managed to keep quiet about them' (224). Thus wrote the duc de Chevreuse to Fénelon on 13 November 1710. This demonstrates that Le Tellier was in liaison with Beauvillier and his brother-in-law, Chevreuse, but avoided talking politics, a forbidden subject, with the king. How much did this matter to him? He was skilful enough to translate his political perspectives into theological terms, following the opposite course to that of the Jansenists. The true extent of his influence can never be known. Though the king missed père de la Chaize, he had become more rigid anyway. He was influenced here by his *dévote* wife. The miseries of war, the hard winter of 1709 and the succession of deaths in his family encouraged him to see the hand of God at work everywhere. Despite himself, he found himself drawing closer to this disagreeable Jesuit, and, whether or not Le Tellier overstepped the boundaries of his role, the damage had already been done, for public opinion thought that he had. Among the verses of the song-writers of 1715 unleashed after the king's death may be cited this couplet:

> He died, this king, a hero and a Christian,
> Albeit in the arms of a Jesuit. (91)

Le Tellier's quickly accumulated capital of unpopularity determined the decline in the king's own popularity. One of the first acts of the regent, a good politician, would be to exile this tactless and discredited monk.

One of Le Tellier's first acts had been to attack the Convent of Port-Royal des Champs in order to destroy its symbolic importance. The nuns had indeed rejected *Vineam Domini*. If they had followed Mgr de Noailles and found a way of condemning Jansen's book while remaining faithful to Saint-Cyran, they would have enjoyed a measure of support from the cardinal. But they turned down what Racine called 'tactics and condescension', an obstinacy which revived so many memories of previous debate and obstinacy that the king lost his patience. From then on Noailles abandoned these elderly rebels. 'He accepted the merger of Port-Royal-des-Champs with Port-Royal de Paris.

Port-Royal-des-Champs was abolished by a decision of 9 February 1707, a bull of 27 March 1708 and letters-patent of 14 November 1708, with the agreement of the archbishop and without protest from the diplomats of the [Augustinian] party.' (216)

The police operation of 29 October 1709, seemingly enjoying Noailles' approval, did not, apparently, disturb père Le Tellier. The public appeared similarly indifferent. Only a few delicate souls like the marquise d'Huxelles shed tears over the fate of the nuns. But soon outside sympathizers started to take the road to Les Champs, and the king, in irritation, decided to extirpate all traces of disobedience. In 1710, the Council ordered the demolition of the convent. The following year the bodies of the nuns buried there were exhumed and dispersed to nearby sanctuaries or thrown into the pit of the cemetery of Saint-Lambert. Their graves were desecrated like Catholic cemeteries in the Maghreb. In the short term, the king had won: even violence like this was the result of the theological 'middle way'. In the medium term, he was repudiated: in the century of the Englightenment, not only the Augustinians but also the *philosophes* would deploy these terrible images against him. In the long term, Louis would lose even more, as if the ghosts of the nuns would return to haunt his memory ever after.

However, men have difficulty imagining the future. In 1710, nobody knew that Port-Royal des Champs, where 'no stone lay on top of another' (Saint-Simon), would become what the king wanted to stop it from becoming, a place of pilgrimage. But everyone could see that the king was suffering such harsh tribulations that it seemed a punishment from God. After the Revocation, the Protestants had seen such justice in the fistula. What providence had in store for the Most Christian King after the violation of Port-Royal was a hundred times more cruel.

THE DEATHS OF THREE DAUPHINS

In less than a year, between 14 April 1711 and 8 March 1712, the old king would lose: his son, Monseigneur; his grand-daughter-in-law the Duchess of Burgundy; his grandson the Duke of Burgundy, the second dauphin; and, finally, his eldest great-grandson, the Duke of Brittany, the third dauphin. To these losses should be added that of the duc de Berry, grandson of the king, in 1714, and that of the duc d'Alençon (Berry's son), in 1713.

It is said that age encourages self-centredness and that the death of the young is reassuring to the old. In the case of Louis XIV, we should not ignore either his sensitivity or the fact that such a succession of deaths, cruel in any family, was traumatic for a royal house. Was the Capetian line, identified with France for 725 years, about to be extinguished? It is true that the king, preoccupied with government, warfare, food shortages and religious upheaval, did not have the time to philosophize or indulge in self-pity. He had to confront these ordeals under the gaze of his adversaries. If he displayed too much emotion, he would be suspected of forgetting the troubles of the kingdom; if he continued to fulfil his duties as king, he would be accused of inhumanity. Such was the burden and grandeur of being a hereditary sovereign.

Louis XIV's descendants died according to the order of primogeniture, as if destiny were ruled by the fundamental law of succession. The first to be struck down was Monseigneur, the prince beloved by the king, and well liked by the soldiers and by the populace at large. On the evening of 8 April 1711, at his residence at Meudon, he felt 'a great pain in the head'. Fagon and Mareschal rightly feared smallpox. On the 14th, 'at seven o'clock in the evening,' says Sourches,

> he began his death agony and expired at 11 p.m. The king immediately called for his carriages [he had not been afraid of contagion; now he set an example in taking precautions], and left Meudon for Marly at 11.30 p.m. As he approached Versailles, he came across the Duchess of Burgundy, who was riding in front of him in her carriage with several ladies. He stopped for a moment to speak to her, telling her the sad news, and then continued on his way, and was not able to go to bed until three hours after his arrival, being afraid of suffocating, so great was his grief. (97)

On 16 April, Madame Palatine wrote: 'I saw the king yesterday at eleven o'clock. He is racked by such pain that it would melt the hardest heart. However, he shows no vexation, talks to everyone with resigned sadness and gives orders with great firmness. Yet tears come to his eyes all the time and he has to stifle his sobbing. I am mortally afraid that he may fall ill himself.' In the face of such grief, the Princess Palatine herself spent all day in tears. She who had mocked the king's religious devotions and the paradoxes in his piety now admired 'such submission to the will of God that one can scarcely imagine it'. Louis XIV's only consolation was the testimony of his son's confessor that he had performed his Easter duties piously before meeting his 'Christian end' (87).

France had perhaps lost its best king. The custom of denigrating him goes back to Saint-Simon, who depicts him as an oaf. But this portrayal is a mere caricature. If Monseigneur, as he did do, devoted himself to violent exercise, collected marvellous works of art, conceived the designs for sumptuous interior decorations, presided over charming masquerades and ruled a refined circle at Meudon, this was to occupy himself in an intelligent manner during periods of enforced leisure. Whenever his father gave him responsibilities, he showed himself worthy of his confidence: courageous and popular in the army (1688), attentive and decisive in the council of ministers.

However, Louis XIV's trials were not over. After smallpox came a malignant form of measles, and, after the Dauphin, the Duchess and Duke of Burgundy departed, soon to be followed by their eldest son. The duchess died first, on 12 February 1712. She was not yet twenty-six years old. She had given the king great pleasure, for her character had lightened the atmosphere of the court. Mme de Maintenon, who disliked her, had written: 'Mme la Dauphine has surpassed my hopes: she makes herself liked by everyone and is admired by all who meet her at close quarters.' (66)

Burgundy, the second dauphin, died less than a week after his wife, on 18 February. His grandfather was not blind to his faults (a mixture of piety and pride) or his limitations – he had no capacity for command and was as yet incapable of thinking like a monarch. Fénelon, who educated him, had said of him: 'His most solid occupations are restricted to vague speculations and impotent resolutions.' (224) But the death of Monseigneur had obliged Burgundy to shoulder his responsibilities and appeared to have made him rather more mature. A month after his father's death, Sourches spoke of him thus: 'We may observe with satisfaction how M. le Dauphin, so as to learn properly about public affairs, works in private every day with the controller-general Desmarets and secretary of state Voysin.' (97) After several years of preparation, the second dauphin would have been ready to assume his probable succession. The king became more certain of this every day. But events rendered these hopes vain. The death of Monseigneur had been an event of particular public mourning. With the death of the Duke of Burgundy, 'enlightened' opinion was unanimous in lamenting the ill luck of the kingdom, deprived of its Telemachus. With the passage of time we may see that their regret was not so misguided. His evil geniuses would die before Louis XIV: Chevreuse in 1712, Beauvillier in 1714, Fénelon in 1715. Why should Burgundy not have made a good sovereign, once the influence of their ideology had been dissipated and he had come into contact with reality?

The tears of Louis XIV grew more bitter. The old king watched the list of possible successors get shorter, almost day by day. On 8 March, the third dauphin, the Duke of Brittany, died at the age of five: he had only been dauphin for nineteen days. Nothing is sadder than the death of a child. On 17 March, Madame Palatine wrote: 'Yesterday M. le Dauphin's little dog made me cry. The poor creature went to the gallery of the chapel [of Versailles] to look for his master where he had seen him kneeling for the last time.' (87)

The king found time to meditate on these tribulations. During his conversation with Villars in 1712, as he entrusted his last army to him, Louis XIV, as we have seen, recalled the sequence of three deaths, of which 'there are few such examples'. He saw the hand of providence at work. But it was not yet complete and on 16 April 1713 Alençon died, a baby twenty days old, son of the duc de Berry. On 4 May 1714, Charles de France, duc de Berry and younger brother of the Duke of Burgundy and Philip V, followed him. Up to his own death, the old king did not know whether the hand of God would strike at his house one more time. In April 1713, Tessé wrote: 'As for our dear little Dauphin, the only remnant of the finest and purest blood in the world, he is growing stronger and God will preserve him for us.' (101) And in fact the future of the dynasty did seem to rest on the frail shoulders of the fourth dauphin, Louis duc d'Anjou, the future Louis XV, who had been born on 15 February 1710.

This succession of deaths created disquiet. Some thought it was poison. Others took the liberty of suspecting, even of accusing, Philippe II d'Orléans, who was brought nearer to the crown by each death. The king declined the temptation to incriminate his nephew. But he did not resist the regalian temptation, and in 1714, as we shall see, he would try to modify the law of succession to the throne.

THE BULL *UNIGENITUS*

Suffering often induces mistakes; one error then forces others. It has been said that the Jansenist question cast a shadow over the whole reign. The bull *Vineam Domini* would have satisfied the pope provided the bishops had not slighted him by adapting it to their Gallican tastes; but it was no longer sufficient for the king, in whom feelings and prejudices easily crystallized. Père Le Tellier encouraged him and Mme de Maintenon, still the 'mother of the Church', resented the credit still enjoyed by Port-Royal. Already in 1707 she had said to one of her ladies at Saint-Cyr: 'He is very sad when he sees the progress being made by Jansenism, which is spreading in all parts of the kingdom and has won over almost all the convents.' (66)

The king promised the pope that he would reprimand his bishops and extirpate Jansenism. He required Cardinal de Noailles to send a letter of excuse to Rome about the assembly of 1705; but he could not prevent the archbishop recommending Quesnel's *Moral Reflections*. In 1710, a cabal, spurred on by père Le Tellier and Fénelon, undertook to weaken the cardinal's prestige. A condemnation of Quesnel's work, signed by the Bishops of Luçon and La Rochelle, was nailed to the door of M. de Noailles' palace, and this earned them the approval of Rome.

Louis XIV was content when the Archbishop of Paris disavowed the assembly of 1705; but, in 1711, he withdrew Fénelon's permission to publish, which the Swan of Cambrai had been putting to curious use. When the confessor was caught overtly organizing a cabal against Noailles, His Majesty unhesitatingly took the cardinal's side, but did not dare disgrace père Le Tellier. For his part, Mgr de Noailles, strengthened by the support of 'the greater part of the ecclesiastical corporations' (216), issued an ordinance against the condemnation signed by the Bishops of La Rochelle and Luçon. Urged on by a discreet cabal, the two episcopal figure-heads asked the king for 'permission to lodge an appeal with the pope'. They were merely furthering the plans of Beauvillier, Fénelon, the Society of

Jesus and père Le Tellier. The Duke of Burgundy shared their animosity towards Noailles and demanded that the cardinal show his orthodoxy by drawing up a document against père Quesnel's book. Yet it was against the Jesuits that the cardinal acted: he forbade them from hearing confession in his archdiocese. He wrote to the king on 11 August 1711 telling him that père Le Tellier was not worthy of being his director of conscience. He refused to accede to the Duke of Burgundy's demand. These intiatives merely inflamed the situation; M. de Noailles did not comprehend that, by attacking the confessor, he was insulting the king.

Louis XIV, therefore, decided to turn to Rome for help in neutralizing Noailles and anathematizing Quesnel. On 11 November 1711, an order from the Council banned the sale of the *Moral Reflections*. On the 16th, the king asked Rome for a bull condemning the book. By acting in this way, he broke with Gallican tradition: d'Aguesseau pointed this out in vain. To help the pope make up his mind, Louis promised to accept the bull that he asked for and to 'get it accepted by the bishops of France with the [necessary] respect'. The pope reacted less speedily than was expected. He had condemned Quesnel's book in 1708, and was not accustomed to repeating himself. But the first condemnation had only been the object of a papal brief, and it was possible to prepare a bull in order to clarify the points at issue. 'The book of *Reflections* was scrutinized page by page once more in order to pick out some suitable propositions.' (54) Instead of 20 or so excerpts, Rome thought it advisable to find 101 propositions to be judged as Jansenist and heretical. This was the beginning of 101 years of controversy.

It was two years before the Vatican put the finishing touches to the bull: *Unigenitus* was issued on 8 September 1713, a seeming victory for Le Tellier, Fénelon and the Jesuits, a less obvious success for Louis XIV. Until now his position *vis-à-vis* Rome had been that of a supplicant. Now he was obliged to ensure that the bull was received with respect. The government improvised, calling an 'extraordinary' Assembly of the Clergy in Paris. But of the forty-nine bishops, nine, including Noailles, made known their opposition. The pope would not get the unanimous approval he had been promised. The king had not kept his word.

THE RESIGNATION OF A GREAT CHANCELLOR

In the midst of all these difficulties, Louis XIV should have been in a position to consult more with intelligent counsellors. Unfortunately, he no longer took enough account of Torcy's advice; nor did he appreciate the true value of Pontchartrain, the chancellor. In place of the calm authority which he had shown throughout the Spanish war, when he had held firmly to the helm in the eye of the storm, he now showed an old man's authoritarianism. Was the absolute monarchy becoming absolutist? Pontchartrain complained that it was, that the workings of the system had become distorted: 'The council of ministers is now only held for form's sake . . . All the decisions are taken in private.' (224) In the *Unigenitus* affair, Louis XIV pushed events along. On 5 February 1714, Noailles and his supporters signed a letter against the condemnation of the *Moral Reflections*, and then refused to receive *Unigenitus* in Paris. On 15 February, Louis XIV forced the Parlement to register the letters-patent for the publication of the bull. The magistrates were waiting for their hour to come; but d'Aguesseau, a friend of the cardinal and the chancellor, did not hide his Gallican hostility.

Since the end of the Assembly of the Clergy on 5 February a kind of schism had been tearing the French Church apart. The majority of bishops had received the bull and decided to accompany its publication with an exhortatory 'pastoral instruction'. The others, known as the *refusants* and centred around the cardinal-archbishop, were by no means all Jansenist, but most were Augustinians and all were Gallicans. They had greater influence than their numbers indicated, and they quickly gained the support of the Sorbonne, the faculty of Reims, the majority of the lower clergy, the robe and a large number of the faithful. One of these *refusants*, Coislin, Bishop of Metz, a member of a ducal house and holder of a frontier diocese, attracted particular attention when, on 20 June 1714, he became the celebrated author of an explosive pastoral letter.

After rejecting the bull, its accompanying pastoral instruction and the letters-patent dated 14 February, Coislin decided to publish a *Pastoral Letter and Instruction . . . on the Publication and the Constitution of Our Holy Father the Pope of 8 September 1713*. This text shook the whole Church of France. In a plain and elegant style, Coislin recalled the propositions of Augustine and Aquinas on sufficient grace, did not reject the idea of an invisible Church (that of the justified) and showed the dangers inherent in a hasty condemnation of propositions 79 to 86. To the Jesuits it seemed to be 'a critical refutation rather than an obedient acceptance of the bull', and perhaps 'the most violent satire which has yet appeared against the constitution' (283). We do not know how many of the inhabitants of Metz understood a text subtle enough to contain at one and the same time 'the condemnation and acceptance of the same text'; but it soon spread throughout the kingdom, and was known and disliked by père Le Tellier, and known and admired by the chancellor.

Louis de Pontchartrain had ceased to understand the king ever since *Unigenitus* had created so many divisions in the kingdom. In his council, Louis XIV prepared what would become the *arrêt* of 5 July 1714 ordering 'that the *Pastoral Letter and Instruction* of . . . the lord bishop of Metz' be 'suppressed, revoked and annulled, as prejudicial to His Majesty's letters-patent, contrary to the acceptance of the bull by the Assembly of the Clergy of France, and tending to weaken or render ineffective the condemnation of the errors in the hundred and one propositions, as of the book containing them' (283). Pontchartrain did not see by what principles the temporal authority could condemn someone who had only exercised his rights as a bishop. He tendered his resignation. The king, who was firm in his intention to curb Gallicanism and liquidate the Quesnelian opposition, and who had never been able to put up with the smallest attempt at blackmail or intimidation, accepted it. On 2 July, the court learnt that M. Voysin, while remaining secretary of state for war, had also been made chancellor. Voysin, a protégé of Mme de Maintenon and less of a jurist, great lord and man of honour, and less independent, than his predecessor, was the kind of official who could be entrusted with any kind of mission and who could be made to sign anything. He was one of those who 'in an ecstasy of loyalism [declared] the sovereign to be above all the normally accepted rules'.

Louis de Pontchartrain belonged to an altogether different class of men. His motive for resigning had been a desire to retire and contemplate his own salvation; the refusal to put the seals on the *arrêt* condemning the Bishop of Metz had provided a suitable pretext. Louis XIV was now secretly preparing yet more disturbing texts, to which Pontchartrain, as an honest jurist with a good knowledge of public law, could never have given his backing as the principal officer of the Crown. The king was getting ready to violate the fundamental laws of the kingdom.

THE OLD KING'S ABERRATION

The famous French dictum 'One Faith, one Law, one King' remained unalterable. It was the cornerstone of the demonstration that natural law and the fundamental laws were above the king. If the sovereign were to violate the unwritten laws which served as the rules of the monarchy, then he would be violating the constitution of the kingdom, and his subjects would be released from their duty to obey him. How could Louis XIV have deliberately placed himself in this situation, he who knew the public law, had perfected the teaching of it in the universities, had on numerous occasions given way to the opinions of his ministers, and had so often consulted with competent people without seeking to impose his ideas or feelings at all cost? There are several answers to this question. The duc de Berry died on 4 May, following Alençon, Burgundy and Monseigneur. Mme de Maintenon adored the duc du Maine, or pretended to, which amounts to the same thing. Louis XIV himself had always had a soft spot for this prince. He showed little interest in the Condés or the Contis. His nephew Orléans worried him: he seemed to be lazy, debauched and even a libertine in the philosophical sense of the word; he had been the object during the Spanish war of strange suspicions, which continued thereafter. This was more a question of emotion than of reason. But we know of the part played by his feelings in the king's anti-Protestant and anti-Augustinian policies. On top of all this was the pretentious notion that his own issue, even illegitimate and born of adultery, were of better blood than that of the Orléans and the Condé branches of the Bourbon family. The excuse of senility cannot be ignored; but we may suppose that the old king was much more lucid than he appeared. Like his master Mazarin, he often had more than one iron in the fire, especially in foreign policy. Here was a chance to satisfy the *légitimés*, soothe the *marquise* and his confessor, show his authority to the Condés and Contis, hand out a warning to the duc d'Orléans, gain some time, and try to lay down some directions for the regency.

He was fully aware that a compliant Parlement had quashed in turn the wills of his grandfather Henry IV and his father, Louis XIII. There was no reason why the same thing should not happen once more if he, dying after a long and authoritarian reign, left only a dauphin still well below the age of reason. He was thinking like a politician and an old man: let others deal with tomorrow's problems. In slightly modified Christian language: I have made some preparations for the life to come; may God watch over my family and protect France! In the meantime, the king declared his two natural sons capable of succeeding to the throne (edict of July 1714), gave them the title of princes of the blood (declaration of 23 May 1715), and made them members of the council being prepared for the regency (will of 2 August 1714). This last decision arose normally from his regalian rights. The two others violated the constitution.

The law of succession, which designated the rightful king, was venerable, customary and untouchable. It encompassed several unbreachable principles: heredity, primogeniture, masculinity and collaterality, indisponibility and, last but not least, Catholicity (120). The indisponibility of the crown of France was a noble servitude of which Louis XIV had always been aware. In 1667, in his *Treatise on the Rights of the Queen*, justifying the famous 'devolution', he had stated unequivocally:

> The fundamental law of the state having formed a reciprocal and eternal liaison between the prince and his descendants on the one side and the subjects and their descendants on the other, by a kind of contract which destines the sovereign to reign and the people to obey, none of the parties can alone and as it pleases him free himself from such a solemn engagement, which assists both sides to help each other mutually. (144)

The king, therefore, may not dispose of the crown as he wishes. By decreeing in the edict of July 1714 that 'M. the duc du Maine and M. the comte de Toulouse and their male descendants, there being no princes of royal blood' (201), may succeed, the Louis XIV of 1714 repudiated the honest and juridically knowledgeable Louis XIV of 1667.

In addition, the arrangements contained in the July edict violated the principle of Catholicity, which implied 'that anyone capable of succeeding must be the issue of a canonically valid marriage' (120). But Louis had never married Athénaïs de

Rochechouart. Furthermore, at the time of the births of Maine and Toulouse, the only canonically valid marriage connected with them was that which had joined together before God M. and Mme de Montespan. However, the Parlement registered this totally illegitimate edict. To be sure, Madame Palatine remarked that there had already been enough connections between His Majesty's first and second families to turn them into one. It is possible that the king's subjects, accustomed to admiring and obeying, did not care a fig about the fundamental laws: this was the off-hand opinion of Ernest Lavisse. But it is not possible that fifty thousand professional jurists, the magistrates of the courts, eighty *maîtres des requêtes*, thirty councillors of state and six ministers were not aware of the outrageousness of this royal action. And what of the declaration of 23 May 1715? It violated the adage 'A prince of the blood is born not made' (120). Saint-Simon was wrong to talk of Maine and Toulouse contemptuously as 'bastards', but he was perfectly correct in his anger about such a violation of the Frankish constitution.

The king's last will and testament was scarcely any more defensible. Voysin, the new chancellor, had helped to draw it up in the same month of July 1714 which saw the dignified departure of M. de Pontchartrain. On the morning of Sunday the 29th, the *premier président* de Mesmes and the *procureur général* d'Aguesseau were called to Marly 'for a matter of very great importance' (26). The king charged them with obtaining the registration without opposition of the edict of July, a registration which duly took place on 2 August, Maine and Toulouse being on that day received by the Parlement with all the honours due to the princes of the blood (with, as yet, the exception of the title), in the presence of the duc de Bourbon and the prince de Conti, who were obliged to swallow the bitter pill without complaint. It was thought that Louis XIV also told them about his will. Written and signed but secret, 'sealed with seven seals', it would be entrusted three weeks later to these same *parlementaire* magistrates and deposited 'in the *chambre de greffe* of the Parlement, locked away in the wall with an iron door and an iron grille so that no one may approach it. There will be three different locks; the *premier président* will have the key to one of the locks; the *procureur général* a key to the second lock, and the *premier greffier* of the Parlement the key to the third' (26). A public edict was deposited at the same time, dated at Versailles, August

1714: it stated that the king, by his will, had made provision for the organization of the future regency during the minority of his great-grandson, selecting the composition of the council of regency. 'Nevertheless, we believe it right, for good and just reasons, not to make public in advance the choice that we have made of the persons whom we judge capable of filling such great and important posts' (26).

Among other things, this will, which, although it was kept such a closely guarded secret, contemporaries could almost piece together by applying a little intelligence and knowledge of affairs at court, confirmed the edict of July: 'Our intention is that the arrangements contained in our edict of July last in favour of the duc du Maine and the comte de Toulouse be carried out fully and permanently, so that what we have declared to be our will may never be breached.' (144) The council of regency was to comprise the duc d'Orléans, as head of the council, the duc de Bourbon once he came of age, the duc du Maine, the comte de Toulouse, the chancellor, the head of the royal council of finances, the secretaries of state, the controller-general, and the marshals Villeroy, Harcourt, Huxelles, Villars and Tallard. The duc du Maine was charged to look after 'the safety, conservation and education' of the young king, from the day of the testator's death, the military household owing him their total obedience. All matters were to be decided in the council 'by the plurality of votes', the duc d'Orléans having a preponderant voice when opinions were divided.

In theory, everything was set up to limit and control the room for manœuvre of Philippe d'Orléans. In fact, the text is so similar to the will of Louis XIII, who had encompassed Anne of Austria in a council of regency in a similar manner, that its author must have had the earlier example in mind. This confirms the idea that the old king had no illusions about the future of his plans.

THE RESOURCES OF A LARGE COUNTRY

After an enumeration of these trials, losses, half-revolts and besetting problems, it is traditional in accounts of the reign and biographies of Louis to end on a note, not merely solemn, but sombre or downright ominous. Reading some commentators, one would imagine that, on the eve of the king's final illness and death, uncertainty ruled at the top, with revolts of conscience, loss of morale in the public service and armed forces, and misery in the provinces. The exaggeration inherent in such a portrayal does not seem to worry them, any more than does the explosion of vitality under the regency, as though the latter were the product of spontaneous combustion.

In reality, the kingdom of Louis XIV was neither ruined (except for the public finances) nor anguished nor perishing. Usbeck, Montesquieu's Persian, observing Paris between the treaties of Utrecht and that of Rastadt, and far from depicting the low morale, resignation or despondency attributed by legend to the end of such a long reign, wrote: 'Men in Persia do not have the gaiety of the French: one does not see in them this freedom of spirit and this air of contentment that I find here among all estates and conditions.' (77) Yet the person holding the pen of the Persian was the same *président* de Montesquieu who was never afraid of offering criticism: he was writing under the regency and could have adopted a different tone without difficulty.

France in 1715 was larger and more defensible: right up to the Revolution no country would invade it. The advanced fortresses, Philippeville and Marienburg, Sarrelouis and Landau, and the others (like Neue-Breisach and Huningue), delineated frontiers which were clearer, more logical and almost 'natural'. With the help of the faithful Vauban, the king had created his *pré carré* and his double or triple military 'iron curtain', which made of Paris the most peaceful of open cities.

The population of the kingdom, hard hit in 1693, 1694, 1709 and 1710, had recovered successfully through a phenomenon of positive regulation, which was not merely a question of the instincts of rural proprietors. People had children if hope was on the horizon. Without this hope, there might have been demographic decline. This shows at least four things: first, that warfare had not affected France as harshly as has been said; secondly, that the recent difficulties (defeats, fiscal pressure, famine, epidemics) had not really weakened a population which was working, producing, and developing small-scale property, and had been educating and refining itself for two generations; thirdly, that the administration had been an element of protection and a factor for progress – we have been so concerned about the supposed 'financial State' that we no longer appreciate the value of the young, intelligent and effective 'bureaucracy' installed and overseen by Louis XIV; and, finally, that the subjects of the kingdom – with the exception, of course, of the 'nouveaux convertis' – had united around the old king. The Revocation of the Edict of Nantes brought them closer to him, and his own misfortunes brought him closer to the most humble of his subjects. The meeting-point of these two processes may be dated to June 1709, with Louis XIV's appeal to the people and the mobilization which was the reply to this call.

A harmonious social evolution had also been at work. The people had noted with satisfaction that since 1661 the government had ceased to be seemingly the property of the princes and the *grands*. For sixty years they had been able to see that, thanks to the king, merit had more and more challenged birth: Riquet, Forant, Fabert, the chevalier Paul, Gabaret, Le Nôtre, Jean Bart, Lully, Vauban, Colbert and Catinat were the living proof, a portrait gallery of popular heroes whose ancestors were not dukes and peers and had never gone to the Crusades. Enterprising notables had sought and found their place in the subtle and complicated *tchin* (ranking) of the officer bourgeoisie. And, in the small towns and villages, rural elites had been created that were more 'urban', less rustic. Doubters had only to study the tariff of the *capitation* of 1695, with its 569 social categories.

The poorer peasant still paid too much tax. This was a French malaise, and, as in all countries of the *ancien régime*, one apparently accentuated by the persistance of privilege (which the blood sacrifice, a French virtue, did not completely serve to justify). But he could take a little comfort from the thought that the lord of the village now paid the *capitation* and the *dixième*. He could not foresee that Louis XV and Louis XVI would clumsily release the nobility from the fiscal trap into which their predecessor had lured them.

There was still the spectacle of the financiers, real or imagined, which produced public irritation, especially in times of restriction and delayed expectations. But it only needed the government to intervene – as it would in 1716 and would have done if Louis XIV had still been alive – to restore the status quo, by bringing excessively rich financiers down to a level which produced less public irritation. The social equilibrium would be restored; the ploughman would be more content with his lot.

The kingdom which Grotius had rashly compared to the kingdom of God was far from perfect, but it is clear today, and confirmed by historical demography, that this belligerent, pious and reformist reign, ending in solemnity, hardship and a certain austerity, cannot without misunderstanding be painted entirely black.

29

The King Dies . . .

AT MIDNIGHT on Sunday, 25 August 1715, the faithful
marquis de Dangeau, installed in his apartment at the
château of Versailles, wrote: 'I have just witnessed the grandest,
most touching and most heroic spectacle that a man could ever
see.' Admitted as one of the great officers into the king's antechamber, Dangeau had just attended, a few yards away from the
royal bed, the most mournful festival of St Louis imaginable.
Inaugurated by the dawn serenade of drums and oboes, it had
ended with the ceremony of the viaticum and extreme unction.
The old king was, as his subjects did when their time came,
endeavouring to die like a good Christian, calmly and with devotion. To this, he added a delicacy and edifying serenity which
came as no surprise to those who knew him more intimately. He
would declare to Mme de Maintenon: 'I have always heard it
said that it is difficult to resolve to die. Now that I am close to
this moment, so fearful for mankind, I do not find this resolution
so painful to take.' Later, he would say: 'I place my hope in
God's mercy.' (26) To his confessor, père Le Tellier, he would
remark: 'I would that I should suffer more in atonement for my
sins!' (On 17 July 1676, the marquise de Brinvilliers, repentant
poisoner, had said prior to her execution: 'I would like to be
burnt alive to make my sacrifice more meritorious.' (188))
People knew how to die in this age of baroque piety.

'OLD BUILDINGS CAN BE SHORED UP, BUT THEY
CANNOT BE RENOVATED'

In 1706, Louis still slept 'with the windows wide open, exposed to the elements' (30). At the age of seventy, 'neither the cold nor the heat nor any kind of weather ever disturbs him' (26). This indicated to what extent, in an age when a man of fifty was called a greybeard and a man of sixty an old man (42), the king's physical stamina was admired. His face was wrinkled, but 'he still looks strong and well' (87). 'His strength is still surprising', wrote the marquise de Maintenon in 1712 (66). The king, however, faced a more fearsome adversary than illness: medicaments. The physician Fagon was perhaps, as Saint-Simon assures us, 'one of the great minds of Europe, curious in all things touching his profession, a great botanist and a good chemist', a mathematician indeed. But he was not, *pace* the author of the *Mémoires*, 'a skilful expert in surgery, an excellent physician and a great doctor' (94). He wore down his illustrious patient. Madame Palatine thought that her brother-in-law might have enjoyed a few more years of life 'had he not been purged so frequently by Fagon and . . . until his stools were red' (87).

His physical condition was, however, still apparently sound. The old king seemed as indestructible as an old oak-tree, and this was a cause for satisfaction in the kingdom. Even those who thought that the reign had lasted too long were aware that its successor would be dependant upon a dauphin not yet four years old. But Louis, who had worked, fought and hunted hard, and ridden so much, was now being gnawed at from within. That obstinate but uncoordinated, pious coalition of père Le Tellier and Françoise d'Aubigné, pestering him endlessly to think of his salvation (without comprehending that, the old king's zeal being assured, they were merely encouraging false zeal, or fanaticism and intolerance), would have been enough to unbalance even a man in the prime of life. Melancholic meditation on the fragile future of the dynasty, now that God had deprived the king of his son (in 1711) and his grandson (in 1712) would have turned anyone but Louis XIV into a depressive. But to have continued to shoulder the burdens of the incessant pressure of decision-making and the responsibilities of government would have required a truly superhuman physical stamina and morale. But then, as Mathieu Molé said: 'Old buildings can be shored up, but they cannot be renovated.' (73)

In the summer of 1715, life at the court, based at Marly since 12 June, continued in relative calm. Yet a preliminary alarm was sounded on 9 August. That evening, the king returned 'a little tired' from an afternoon's hunting in his light barouche (26). He returned to Versailles the following day, never to set eyes upon his beloved Marly again. He worked with chancellor Voysin in the marquise de Maintenon's apartments. But afterwards he was 'taken with a sudden indisposition', only moving with great difficulty from his *cabinet* to his *prie-Dieu*. The following day, a Sunday, His Majesty was determined not to change his plans. Thus, he presided over a meeting of the council of ministers and then went for a walk at the Trianon. He was not to see the Trianon again. Louis then returned to work with Le Peletier de Souzy, his director of fortifications, received the *procureur général* d'Aguesseau (a future chancellor), and handed out some high offices. It was a normal day, alternating work and leisure, a full day, but not excessively heavy. Yet Dangeau noted: 'The king does not seem very well; he will take medicine tomorrow.' After so many years of routine, how could Fagon have suggested anything else to his old master?

On Monday the 12th, His Majesty, as always, submitted docilely to his chief physician and 'took medicine'. As the king suffered pain all down one leg, Fagon diagnosed sciatica. Others made a similar error. Unfortunately, throughout the next two weeks, he never altered his diagnosis, thus confirming Saint-Simon's judgement: 'He made up his mind very quickly about everything, although in a most enlightened fashion; but once his mind was made up, he almost never changed it.' (94) However, in the afternoon, Louis XIV worked with the comte de Pont-chartrain and, despite being in agony, in the evening he went to the *marquise*'s rooms, where there was 'chamber music' (26). At 10 p.m., he took supper in his usual manner, and went to bed at midnight. On that night, Dangeau began to be worried. For the first time, he could see the debilitated condition of his royal companion: 'As he began to undress, he looked to me like a corpse. Never has a vigorous body wasted away with such suddenness to become so thin as his in so short a time. It appeared, on seeing his naked body, as if the flesh had just melted away.'

On Tuesday, 13 August, the pain forced Louis XIV to be

carried to Mass in an armchair; after the service, he received the Persian ambassador (who would leave France laden with valuable presents) in the throne room. 'The king was on his feet throughout the audience, which was rather long, and this tired him greatly.' Here, courtesy, politics and a sense of duty took him to the frontiers of heroism. Exhausted by this effort, the old monarch thought about taking a rest; but it was time for a meeting of the council of finances, and he presided over it as though nothing were amiss. He then dined normally, worked with M. Voysin, 'then he had himself carried to Mme de Maintenon's rooms, where he listened to chamber music'.

On Wednesday, 14 August, the king's thigh and whole leg were so painful that he gave up trying to walk and had himself carried in an armchair. Yet he presided over a meeting of the council of ministers, played with the ladies in the *marquise*'s apartments, and listened to a concert of 'orchestral music'. Though he dined in private, he talked with courtiers, princes and princesses before retiring at 10 p.m. (26) It became apparent at this point that, though His Majesty was still stoical, M. Fagon was at last becoming seriously concerned. 'It was decided at the king's *coucher*', wrote the faithful attendant Anthoine, 'that M. the chief physician would sleep in the king's bedchamber with M. de Champcenetz, *premier valet de chambre. . .*, and that MM Boudin, *médecin ordinaire*, Mareschal, chief surgeon, and Biot, apothecary, would sleep in the *cabinet* with the sieurs Anthoine and Bazire, *garçons de la chambre*, so as to be close at hand to help His Majesty if required.' (127) In fact, Louis had a troubled night, only managing to snatch some sleep just before dawn.

On the 15th, the king awoke at 10 a.m. Although it was a feast day ('Our Lady of Summer'), he had to resign himself to hearing Mass from his bed. In the remainder of the morning, he received in turn Voysin, Desmarets and Pontchartrain. Everyone could see that he was in pain but trying not to let it show. Yet, despite his efforts, the entourage were worried. 'Our king, alas, is unwell', wrote Madame Palatine. 'I am so worried that I am almost ill myself, not eating or sleeping at all well.' Yet, at 1 p.m., Louis dined in his bed 'with quite a good appetite'. Then he had himself carried to Mme de Maintenon's rooms, stayed there from five to nine, and listened to chamber music. He saw the courtiers whilst taking supper in his bedchamber and the princes in his *cabinet*, and went to bed at 10 p.m. That night, as on previous and succeeding nights, the king was restless and insomniac, asking constantly for a glass of water. He only slept peacefully between three and six.

Friday the 16th was typical of these trying days. The hours seemed fewer, the beautiful August day shortened. The king rose late and retired early, trying in the interval to perform his duties. He allowed no one into his bedchamber until 11 a.m., stayed in bed for Mass and dinner, but got up afterwards to grant an audience to the envoy from Wolfenbüttel, 'and then had himself transported to Mme de Maintenon's rooms, where he was entertained by the ladies and, in the evening, orchestral music' (26). The entourage thought that he was in less pain, but all observed with disquiet his unquenchable thirst. Saturday was virtually a repeat of Friday: a feverish night, drowsiness in the morning. Then Louis 'heard Mass and presided over [a meeting of] the council of finances . . . [from] his bed'. He dressed at 1 p.m. for dinner 'and, after dinner, received in his *cabinet* the general of the Order of Sainte-Croix de la Bretonnerie, and then moved to Mme de Maintenon's rooms in his armchair on castors, and worked there with M. the chancellor'. It was still a royal day's work, but reduced to a third of normal.

For the old king had not stopped working. Though allowing Fagon to watch over him again at night, he was less thirsty and had less pain, and he seemed to be more composed. He intended to spend a busy Sunday the 18th, increasing his activities, and it did indeed turn out to be a day of hope. The king heard Mass from his bed, held a meeting of the council of ministers, dined, presided over another meeting of the council, and worked with Souzy. The evenings had by now established their routine. Louis XIV waited on the *marquise*, listened to music, took supper in his bedchamber, whilst allowing the court to enter, spoke with the princesses, and went to bed at 10 p.m.

The following day, the king, though in pain, worked and listened to some music. It was still only a matter of sciatica. The medical team were out of their depth, incapable of even deciding whether their patient had a fever. Fagon said that he did not, but Mareschal suggested the contrary; Hippocrates said yes, but Galen said no. As if to prove Fagon correct, Louis spent a peaceful night from Monday to Tuesday. Few were permitted to dine with him, but, for the sake of politeness, he did admit the ambassadors. In the afternoon, he presided over a meeting of the

council of finances, and then worked with the controller-general.
Then he received guests in his bedchamber. He thought he had
found a way to suffer less pain: to lie stretched out, and have
himself massaged and then wrapped in sheets. But Fagon was
not reassured. He begged the king to agree to a collective consultation. On Wednesday the 21st, four leading lights of the Faculty
appeared. Having approved Fagon's diagnosis and actions, they
ordered a purge with cassia, obtaining a triple result, 'which',
said Dangeau, 'they regard as a very good score'. However, the
review of the royal guard had to be postponed, and the patient
remained in bed. Yet he still found the strength to preside over a
meeting of the council of ministers and then to work with
Voysin. The only change in routine was that the violins,
accompanied by the ladies, came to play in the royal
bedchamber.

At 10 a.m. on Thursday, four more physicians arrived. These
gentlemen did not know whether His Majesty had a fever, but
still 'were in unanimous agreement as to the remedies to be
prescribed'. At 7 p.m., therefore, Louis swallowed some cinchona and at night was given some ass's milk. Unfortunately,
with all the bandages around his leg, the king could not be
dressed, and, since he had too high a respect for his guards to
conduct a review in his dressing-gown, he was replaced by the
duc du Maine, accompanied by the Dauphin and the duc
d'Orléans.

Whether or not through the effects of the cinchona or the ass's
milk, the king spent a peaceful night. On the morning of the 23rd
as on every Friday morning, he held his 'council of conscience'
with Le Tellier. Still unable to dress because of the bandages, the
king, having risen from his bed, dined in his dressing-gown.
Dangeau noted: 'He was quite jovial during the meal and joked a
lot with me.' So ended the first chapter of the illness. Everyone
purported to believe that it was sciatica. The physicians prescribed their preferred nostrums and the king struggled on as best
he could.

We do not know at what point he realized that he might never
recover. Old people can sometimes sense the approach of death.
But Louis tried to brush pessimism to one side. Every day won
against illness was a day gained against the minority of the
young Dauphin.

HOW A GREAT KING DIES

It was on Saturday the 24th that the court, the king's friends and his doctors began once more to be seriously concerned. His condition had not improved. The sovereign had performed his duties. He 'dined in public, held the council of finances and worked with M. the chancellor as though he had been in perfect health'. After supper, at about 9.30 p.m., he was in so much pain that he dismissed the courtiers and did not go to greet the princesses. He asked for père Le Tellier and made his confession. His leg was streaked with marks that appeared to indicate the onset of gangrene. Whilst Louis contemplated his imminent death, and the confessor prepared him for it, the physicians could but pronounce themselves 'most perplexed'.

After a night of agony, the king prepared to celebrate the feast of St Louis, Sunday, 25 August, in the normal way. As he awoke, drums and oboes played a dawn serenade under his window, 'and he did not seem bothered by all the noise. He even asked for the twenty-four violins to play in his antechamber during dinner' (26). The drums presented this farewell to a warrior king, conqueror of Flanders and indefatigable Low Countries veteran, and the violins saluted the protector of Lully and Couperin. In the afternoon, Louis, rising once more above his illness, worked with his ministers and then saw Mme de Maintenon and the ladies. But just as the musicians were about to enter, the dozing prince was awoken by the most terrible pains. His pulse was found to be 'very poor', and he lost consciousness. When he came round, he asked for the viaticum, 'and, from that moment,' said Dangeau, 'knowing that he only had a few hours to live, he acted and gave orders like a man about to die, but with a strength, a presence of mind and a grandeur of soul never before witnessed'. A little before 8 p.m., Cardinal de Rohan, *grand aumônier*, two other chaplains and M. Huchon, the *curé* of Versailles, were admitted 'by a secret stairway'. These pious duties seemed to be so urgently required that no attempt was made to surround them with ceremony. 'There were but seven or eight torches, carried by the cleaners of the château.' (26) In order to witness the viaticum and extreme unction, the princes and household officers were in the bedchamber and the princesses in the Council chamber.

With the clergy and the others gone, Louis remained alone

with the chancellor, going over a codicil. No sooner had he finished than the *marquise* returned. So, even upon his deathbed, Louis accepted the falsely discreet and truly obtrusive presence of the woman he had secretly married. That evening, paying no attention to her or to the courtiers who were trying to invade his bedchamber, the king called those to whom he wished to give a final message. Each one drew near as his name was called, listened, and then tearfully returned to the adjoining *cabinet*. Villeroy's audience lasted seven minutes, the controller-general's two minutes, the duc d'Orléans' a quarter of an hour. It was said that the king was friendly towards his nephew, telling him 'that he would find nothing in his will with which he would not be content and committing to his charge the Dauphin and the interests of the state' (26). Then came Maine, Toulouse, the duc de Bourbon, the comte de Charolais and the prince de Conti, 'and all those princes came back into the *cabinet* with such heavy hearts and so tearful that a more touching spectacle had never been seen at court. For, since His Majesty had always loved his family tenderly, he cried when talking to all these princes, who then told this to the courtiers who were in the *cabinet*, full of affliction and rooted to the spot'. What Dangeau does not relate is that these tears and sad expressions hid feverish speculation about the future, the regency and who would be master in it. Even so, the king's piety and steadfastness, his lucidity and benevolence would have brought tears to their eyes on their own. Between the ceremony of the viaticum and the Condés' audience, the chancellor had mounted a guard. Then came surgeons and apothecaries 'to put dressings on the gangrene'. Meanwhile, the chancellor told the duc d'Orléans about the codicils. At 11 p.m., the king, exhausted, ordered the curtains to be drawn. And then the *marquise* retired to have something to eat.

On the morning of the 26th, the rooms around the bed-chamber were full of people, with the princes and the *entrées* crammed into the *cabinets*. 'At 10 a.m., the king's leg, in which several lancet cuts and incisions down to the bone had been made, was bandaged.' Mme de Maintenon was present for these painful operations. The king told her gently to leave 'because her presence caused him such emotion'. So she made a false exit; 'but after this dressing the king told her that, since there was nothing more to be done, he asked that at least he should be left to die in peace' (26).

Louis XIV, having known from childhood that 'nobody knows the day or the hour', continued to issue important messages. At noon, he called for his great-grandson the Dauphin, the future Louis XV. Having embraced him, he spoke to him thus, in a mixture of testament and confession, of grandiosity and devoutness:

> My child, you are going to be a great king, but all your happiness will depend upon your submitting yourself to God and upon the care that you take in bringing relief to your people. This means that you should avoid, as far as is possible, making war. It is the ruin of the people. Do not follow the bad example which I have set you. I have often gone to war too lightly and pursued it for vanity's sake. Do not imitate me, but be a prince of peace, and let your principal concern be to bring relief to your subjects. (26)

There followed an invitation to obey père Le Tellier and Mme de Ventadour.

This confession had been inspired by his confessor. The proof lies in the fact that the king was confessing to faults of which he was innocent. This book has attempted to prove that the wars of the reign, with the exception of the Dutch War, were wholly justified, especially the last. A king who was not the master of his own mind was expressing himself here, admirable though the noble and laconic style of expression undoubtedly was. At the same time, it is difficult not to be impressed by the Christian grandeur of this voluntary self-abasement – 'Blessed are the meek; blessed the peacemakers!' Père Le Tellier, who was neither meek nor a peacemaker, had nevertheless stimulated the rare virtues of the Sermon on the Mount in the king's soul.

After this audience, the king called for Maine and Toulouse, to whom he spoke behind closed doors, and then the duc d'Orléans. At 12.30, he heard Mass, Dangeau reported, 'with his eyes open, praying to God with astonishing fervour'. He then conversed with Cardinals de Bissy and Rohan. 'He told them that he wanted to die as he had lived, in the apostolic and Roman religion, and that he would rather lose a thousand lives than have other feelings.' He alluded to his anti-Protestant and anti-Jansenist policies. He thought them right and legitimate, knowing that he had been accused of 'taking authority too far', but knowing also and affirming that he had never acted without the consent of the Church authorities. In fact, we have no precise testimony about this important audience. But it is generally thought that the king also declared his fidelity to the Church with a show of emotion which the dignitaries of the Church would be the last to reproach in him, since they, with their mitres, crosses and theology, had stimulated that zeal within him.

Then the king motioned to the courtiers and *gens de bien* to draw nearer to his bed and said to them:

> Messieurs, I am content with your services. You have served me faithfully and have desired to please me. I am sorry not to have rewarded you better than I have. These last years have not permitted it. I leave you with sorrow. Serve the Dauphin with the same affection you have given me. He is a child, five years old, who may encounter many difficulties, for I remember having met with many in my youth. I am leaving you, but the state remains for ever. Bind yourselves to it faithfully and you may set an example for all my subjects. Be united and in conformity with one another; for in this lie the unity and strength of a state. And follow the orders my nephew gives you. He is going to govern the kingdom. I hope he will do it well. I hope also that you will remember your duty and that you will remember me from time to time. (26)

These are the king's own words and thoughts. Louis XIII had loved the people in his service, as Mme de Motteville testifies (78). His son followed in that tradition. It is touching that the audience for the dying man's farewell speech included not only great men in the kingdom, but also valets, *huissiers* and his *garçons de la chambre* (127). It is also remarkable that this speech, with the uncertainty of the regency running through it, contains the keystone of the reign: the perpetuity of the state. But service to the state meant service to the king. And it suggests that service to the king meant fidelity and zeal, but also affection. Those present, 'in tears' (26), understood this.

It remained for the king to bid farewell to the ladies. He called for the duchesse de Berry, Madame Palatine, the princesses and their ladies-in-waiting. It was a short and moving audience, but a noisy one: Dangeau wondered 'how the king had coped with the lamentations and crying they all made'. Madame Palatine, who wrote down her own impressions, is a witness:

He said goodbye to me with such tender words that I am still surprised that I did not faint on the spot. He assured me that he had always held me in affection and more than I myself had thought, that he was sorry that he had sometimes caused me sorrow . . . I threw myself upon my knees, took his hand and kissed it, and he embraced me. Then he spoke to the others, bidding them remain united. I thought he was saying that directly to me. 'In that, for all my life,' I replied, 'I shall obey Your Majesty.' He turned towards me with a smile: 'I say that not to you,' he added, 'for I know that you have no need of being reminded of it, for you are too reasonable. I am saying it to the other princesses.' (87)

The 26th of August marked the apogee of the dying king's steadfastness, grandeur, piety and sensitivity. Though he was aware of the passions and ambitions simmering just outside the doors of his antechamber, he had for forty-eight hours spoken only of fraternity, peace and concord. He had shown affection, even to the future regent, who made him nervous. But was the sensitive and delicate Louis XIV encountered by Madame Palatine and the duc d'Orléans the real one? Mortal agony is like drunkenness: it does not deform, it exaggerates. If the old king, too harassed by père Le Tellier, had been filled with the fear of death and anguish over his eternal salvation, these little speeches of 25 and 26 August might be interpreted more cynically: Louis XIV, racked by remorse and under the gaze of his confessor, was trying to win some good marks before appearing before his Maker and using any method to 'put himself in good standing'. But the king was prepared for death.

On 26 August, Dangeau noted:

One has to have witnessed this great king over these last hours in order to believe the Christian and heroic strength with which he has faced the approach of a death which he knows to be imminent and inevitable. At no moment since eight o'clock yesterday evening has he not performed some illustrious, pious and heroic act, not like the ancient Romans who pretended to defy death, but in a natural and simple fashion like the acts he was most accustomed to perform, only talking with each person about what was most appropriate to him, and with an exact and precise eloquence which he had possessed throughout his life and which seemed to have grown even greater during these past hours. Finally, however impressive he has been during the glorious course of a seventy-two year reign, he has shown himself even greater as he faces death. His good spirits and steadfastness did not abandon him for a moment, and, while speaking with gentleness and goodness to all those with whom he wished to speak, he retained all his grandeur and majesty throughout. I defy the most moving preachers to discover, with the exaggerations of eloquence, anything more poignant than all that has happened since yesterday evening, or any expressions capable of bringing to light the marks he has shown of a true Christian, a true hero and a hero king.

Between 2 a.m. and 4 a.m., as if he realized that the respite which he was being granted would not last long, Louis sifted through his papers with chancellor Voysin. Some were burnt, others given to ministers with orders. From time to time, the confessor would come to talk with him about God; Louis XIV 'had never let an hour go by since his confession without talking of piety to his confessor or to Madame de Maintenon' (26).

'DIE THEN! YOUR DEATH IS SWEET AND YOUR TASK IS DONE'

Louis had been happily inspired in taking care of essential matters during these two days. On Tuesday the 27th, he went into a decline. His leg did not reveal the internal progress of the gangrene, but the patient suffered losses of consciousness and convulsions. In a corner of the bedchamber, Françoise d'Aubigné kept up her vigil. As for père Le Tellier, he went in and out about twenty times. At midday, the king heard Mass from his bed. There was strictly limited access to his bedchamber. The first gentlemen of the chamber only made appearances when His Majesty took his broth. In the evening, the king called for Jérôme de Pontchartrain, and said to him: 'As soon as I am dead, you will issue a warrant for my heart to be taken to the Jesuit house [in the rue Saint-Antoine] and placed there, as was that of the late king, my father. I wish for no further expense.' Dangeau affirms that this order was given with the same calm with which the king, not long before, had ordered a fountain at Marly.

As if Louis had played the king enough on the 27th, on Wednesday the 28th, he lived as a private individual. In the morning, he saw two of his *garçons de la chambre* in tears. He said to them: 'Why are you weeping? Did you think me immortal? For myself, I have never dreamt that it was so, and you should have prepared yourselves long ago to lose me, given the age I am now.' (26) At 11 a.m., there appeared at Versailles a Provençal, the sieur Brun, who claimed to have with him a sovereign remedy against gangrene. The physicians felt so helpless that they accepted the drug brought by this 'charlatan of the worst kind', placed ten drops of it in three spoonfuls of Alicante wine and made the king drink it. It was an elixir 'made from the body of an animal', and it stank. But the king accepted it. He said wryly: 'I take it without any hope or desire for a cure, but I know that in my state I must obey the doctors' orders.' (26) At regular intervals, the duc d'Orléans having assented, His Majesty was made to swallow Brun's remedy. On Thursday, 29 August, the quack was even allowed to enter the royal bedchamber, along with the representatives of the Faculty. Each dose of the charlatan's elixir seemed to revive the king's exhausted body momentarily. But in the evening, the bandaging revealed the progress of the gangrene, and the king, 'although his awareness was not much more than mechanical, said that he was slipping away'.

He spent Friday the 30th in constant somnolence, 'having little more than the awareness of an animal'. The 31st saw matters deteriorate: 'the lucid moments having been very short and more of a mechanical than a rational awareness.' At 10.30 p.m. prayers for the dying were read to the king. There followed a reflex which sums up and symbolizes the strength of baroque piety. 'The voices of the chaplains saying these prayers', the marquis de Dangeau related, 'energized him, and during these prayers he recited the *Ave Maria* and the *Credo* several times and with a louder voice than theirs, but without any awareness and through His Majesty's great familiarity with them.' In an age when people prayed to God to preserve them from sudden death, who would not have wished, after a lucid death agony, to die with the *Credo* on his lips?

The end came on the morning of Sunday, 1 September, four days before the beginning of the king's seventy-eighth year. 'He rendered his soul', said Dangeau, 'without a struggle, like a candle going out.'

A few hours later the nuncio wrote:

So died Louis XIV, King of France and Navarre . . . In him were united all the royal and Christian virtues, and, apart from the follies of his youth – from which are exempted only those who, by an exceptional disposition of providence, are called to sainthood from birth – one can find no others to reproach in him. He united in his person great majesty and affability. Whilst commanding men he remembered that he was a man himself, and he had a talent for winning the hearts of all those who had the honour of approaching him. In him also, were great piety and justice, an excellent and rapid ability to distinguish the true from the false, moderation in prosperity and strength in adversity, no less capable in the arts of war than in those of peace. In the midst of the disorders of war, he made good government flourish and spread the sciences and arts throughout his kingdom. Great speed in unravelling the most complicated matters, a great talent for taking good decisions, and great resolution in executing them. All qualities worthy of forming the perfect model of a great king, and, if one adds to this his constancy in the true religion, in the confession of which he died, little else remains to be said for us to have the idea of a holy king. At least these qualities will make him live in the history of the centuries to come, when it will be difficult to find his equal. These gifts will mean that his name *in benedictione erit* for all men of goodwill. (131)

For Bentivoglio, the representative of a papacy which had threatened the King of France with divine vengeance, neither the deaths in his family nor the defeats in the Spanish war were signs of God's anger. They were the kind of ordeals ordained by providence, 'like those of the holy man Job, which should serve to reveal the strength of the king's soul and his invincible faith and to refine in the furnace of tribulations a soul beloved of God' (131). Louis' enthusiasm for 'orthodoxy' erased everything else in the eyes of the Roman Church and, to all appearances, those of the Lord. This was not an innocent opinion. The nuncio was a little quick to sanctify the destroyer of Port-Royal des Champs, the denouncer of père Quesnel, the one who had revoked the Edict of Nantes. But it has the merit, in the context of the Counter-Reformation, of revealing the emotions of a Catholic observer within a few hours of one of the most edifying last hours in a century when dying well was of importance.

We should bear this testimony in mind when we are tempted to prefer myths and received ideas to the day-to-day reality of a reign and the atmosphere of an entire century. Scarcely had the nuncio laid down his pen than the 'rabble' rushed to the *cabarets* and the 'populace' lit celebratory bonfires. But their short-sighted reactions were soon overlaid, for Voltaire was soon to demonstrate to France the measure of the greatest of its kings. 'Tacitus was already born in the Empire.'

30

... But the State Remains

L ouis XIV never said 'L'état, c'est moi', but he did write:
'The interests of the state should come first', and then, on
his deathbed, said: 'I am leaving you, but the state remains for
ever.' (26) What did these sentiments mean?

A CERTAIN CONCEPTION OF THE STATE

The French state today is a Leviathan (238). And this Leviathan
state, not content with its voracity and ruthlessness, requires
that its citizens worship it. Moloch demands voluntary and willing sacrifices. Logically, therefore, we seek the origin of this new
religion. It is now customary to attribute it in France to Louis
XIV. The king, we learn, imposed unity upon French diversity,
establishing state control over a lax administration – in short,
established state domination. Some imagine that the intendants
constituted a kind of administrative training-school, prefiguring
the Ecole Nationale d'Administration. And the growth of state
taxation at that time is universally deplored.

In reality, the state, in its administrative sense, had nothing of
the Leviathan about it in 1715. The *contrôle général des finances*
employed fewer people than does the prefecture of a small
French *département*, the Hautes-Pyrénées, today. The intendancy
of a large province employed between five and ten agents.
Ministerial departments, of necessity, employed many people,
but no one in the early eighteenth century imagined that France
had too many naval or military commissioners. Ever since the
advent of Michel Le Tellier in 1643, these 'officers of the pen'

had provided the principal army of Europe with its administrative structure. The 'bureaucracy' involved was neither gigantic nor restricting. No one knew whether the intendant of a *généralité* was irritated by the fact that the people continued to speak *patois*. Once the *communauté d'habitants* had accepted the tutelage of the intendant, the inhabitants still remained free. The interventions of the intendant furnished them with a protection against seigneurs who abused their position. French administration was the opposite of inhuman – if anything, it was too personalized.

Even the colonies, which historians portray as a kind of caricature of France's administrative defects, experienced a visible impact from royal functionaries. Marcel Giraud once wrote an important article entitled: 'Humanitarian tendencies towards the end of Louis XIV's reign.' In it, he mentioned Jérôme de Pontchartrain's intervening with Desmarets on behalf of sailors and their families and the workmen in the royal arsenals. He is seen supporting the cause of seamen held captive in England, 'these poor men who ask only for what is legitimately owed them after they endangered their lives for . . . His Majesty'. For their part, *ordonnateurs* and naval commissioners took up the cause of sailors, workmen and artisans against the collectors of the *tailles*. These agents of the state used their powers to shelter the more defenceless from constraints imposed by other departments. Pontchartrain's correspondence demonstrates 'a sort of spontaneous benevolence towards the people, for all those who are liable, because of their status, to be subjected without defence to the arbitrary whims of their superiors and the privileged classes' (193). This suggests the meaning behind the famous phrase: 'If only the king knew!' When one group of the king's officials imposed the state's burdens too heavily, other agents of the king were there to protect the defenceless. The king acts and the king knows; the state acts, but the state keeps itself in check. This was the administrative style of the absolute monarchy.

This dialectic may be seen in the process of colonization as well as in the running of the colonies. Though the king had the power to enlist sailors by force, the minister forbade the practice of impressment. 'But the solidarity between king and secretary of state is particularly apparent in their attitude towards their subjects overseas.' They applied generous principles, which 'endowed the colonial policy of the later years of the reign with a different character from that of the regency'. Louis XIV and his minister were opposed to the forcible despatch overseas of poor or criminal subjects. In 1699, Louis had refused to use compulsion to send fifty Limousin masons to work on the fortifications of St Kitts. He allowed the despatch of 'disreputable individuals', who might make a new life for themselves in the Indies or America, but on condition that they 'committed themselves by mutual agreement'. The king used his *lettres de cachet*, but did not abuse them. Even when families asked him to send a delinquent son overseas, he refused any expatriation without the consent of the person in question, thereby depriving the West Indies and Louisiana of so many chevaliers des Grieux.*

In the colonies, the king's desires ensured the pursuance of a policy of treating his subjects considerately, an attempt at social justice and the protection of the humble. Despite the great distances involved, war, and the constrasting conditions prevailing in the overseas territories, the king and Pontchartrain forbade abusive price rises and themselves violated the sacrosanct monopoly in order to prevent the inhabitants of the islands from suffering too much from the repercussions of the famine of 1709 in France. They kept a close eye on governors, officials and planters. A true habeas corpus, unknown in France, was imposed on governors, too given to arbitrary decisions. Protestants were better treated in the colonies than in France. The protection of the inhabitants entailed a limitation of abusive privileges. His Majesty, wrote Pontchartrain, wished that 'the humble inhabitants' of the islands should no longer be 'oppressed by the favour which the rich usually enjoy with those who possess the principal authority' (193). In order that administrators should understand that this was policy and not mere propaganda, the king, through his minister, took measures to ease the lot of the disinherited. In Martinique, he lightened the *corvées*, controlled land surveys, and forbade the reduction of the land of the poor under the pretext of constructing roads. He opposed the augmentation of the costs of justice. In Cayenne, the West Indies and Canada, he incorporated neglected *latifundia* into the royal domain, where they formed concessions to grant out to colonists without resources. Such examples could be multiplied. The *code noir* of 1685 provided only inadequate protection for slaves. Now

* The chevalier des Grieux, a character in the abbé Prévost's novel *L'Histoire du chevalier des Grieux et de Manon Lescaut* (1731), was deported to New Orleans, to the despair of Manon Lescaut, a young girl who had fallen in love with him.

Louis XIV and Pontchartrain clarified it considerably. Judges, administrators and planters were advised to treat the blacks humanely. The king would not allow tribunals to acquit the murderers of slaves; he opposed the colonists of Santo Domingo when they turned themselves into judges over their black slaves, since it was inadmissible that 'a Frenchman and a Christian should exercise such a tyranny'. Measures were to be taken to ensure that the slaves were properly nourished, and the colonists were to 'plant provisions' for this purpose. Finally, Pontchartrain, in the king's name, attacked the egotism of the slave-owners, the principal cause of *marronage* (193).

Ministers thus showed, during the difficult last years of the reign, that the duties of their offices did not make them heartless, and the state which they ran and over which the king presided thereby revealed its sensitive and humanitarian side. Whatever the shortcomings of the state in certain areas and its excesses on the religious question, we are dealing, under Louis XIV, and thanks to him, with a state which empowered men, not despots or robots, and the rules of which applied to other men (whites, blacks or redskins), not to impersonal entities. To be sure, 'the interests of the state should come first' (63), but it was never a question of state control or of the state as an inhuman monster or abstraction. The king and his collaborators had a certain idea of the state. It was neither tyrannical nor ideological, but in a Christian tradition, as if lit by the first rays of the dawn of the Enlightenment.

THE INSTITUTIONAL STATE

The development of this administrative monarchy moulded by Louis XIV merged with the progress, and the hold on the individual conscience, of public service in France. Commissioners and officers served 'the king *and* the state', the sovereign *and* the public. And it was the king who persuaded them of this. If his sole achievement in fifty-four years of personal rule had been the successful formation of the representatives of authority, his reign would deserve to be called great.

Without modifying the original structure of his government, which counterposed collegiate forms with ministerial departments, Louis XIV established both a balance between the central institutions and a style of government. This equilibrium was not frozen, but perpetually unstable. Nor was the style stereotyped; it was always capable of adaptation. Throughout the reign, according to the wishes of the king, the play of events, the personalities of the different ministers, the passage of time, and the force of circumstances, the balance changed and the style was modified. Louis XIV was not irreplaceable, but the secret of his success could not be discovered, dismantled and reassembled by his successors without damage. Louis XV and Louis XVI were to be the curators of a museum where paintings were no longer restored and objects never moved, and which was no longer replenished with new acquisitions. Louis XIV's effectiveness may be measured by the relative failure of his successors. Other princes of the period of the Enlightenment, those known as the 'enlightened despots', would be more alert than the Bourbons. Confronted by all too obvious problems and wanting to modernize their backward countries, they discovered the essential Louis XIV whilst ignoring the forms and details, imitating his empiricism by simplification, transposition and adaptation. For government efficiency did not result from having five secretaries of state instead of four, nor from favouring the controller-general to the detriment of the chancellor. However attractive the forms of French higher administration between 1661 and 1715 may have been, they are not sufficient to explain the success of a polity, itself the result of teamwork, and only effective because of the dynamism of its chief and the confidence placed in him by his collaborators.

If a formula were needed to express how Louis XIV guided public service, one might propose the following: 'Neither revolution nor reaction, but skilful and supple reformism.' Everything was empiricial: the conservation of old-fashioned institutions, prudence in erecting new structures. Pragmatism ruled, as under Frederick II or Catherine the Great. Louis XIV was – taking away despotism and adding religion – the first enlightened despot. There were still numerous anachronistic, and apparently parasitic, institutions around in 1715, as there would be in 1789, and the king was seemingly unconcerned. As legal tribunals, the *présidiaux* were almost useless; the *Connétablie* was as out of place as a knight of Agincourt in the Hall of Mirrors. France could have happily continued without the bureaus of finances, even though there were about thirty of them. They were supposed to administer the *taille*, the royal domain and the highways, but competent functionaries, particularly intendants, had nibbled away at their functions. In Paris, the bureau of finances had more than thirty officers, whilst a dozen would have more than sufficed.

But matters were more complex and subtle than might appear. The *ancien régime* in general, and Louis XIV in particular, showed great intelligence in respecting these aged institutions. The preservation of the *Connétablie* allowed the king, Le Tellier and Louvois to give immense powers to the *prévôts* of the armies and the councils of war, without overturning old customs. Augmenting the privileges of the *trésoriers* of France hid from public view the way in which the intendants were increasing their responsibilities at the expense of the bureaux of finances. Keeping the *présidiaux* was a way of providing openings for the inhabitants of medium-sized towns as magistrates and auxiliaries of justice, of encouraging local commerce, the hotel business and posts for servants, and of preventing too much provincial emigration to the great cities. Under the *ancien régime*, there were no institutions as such, only individual instances, institutions run by men and designed to solve human problems.

Whenever the king decided on a revolutionary measure, he was careful to ensure that he did not create a revolutionary spirit in his subjects. The lieutenancy of police of Paris, created in 1667 as the offspring of a reassuring 'conseil de police', only obtained its full powers in 1674, seven years later. The lieutenant of police remained, until the Revolution, subordinate to the minister for Paris. He only ranked third in the hierarchy of the Châtelet. Up until 1789, he had to pretend to recognize the primacy of the Parlement in matters of policing. (Nor did the king free himself from competing institutions: the *bureau de la Ville* and bureau of finances.) And yet this same lieutenant-general of police was *de facto* as powerful as the minister for Protestant affairs. He was a beneficiary of the *liasse*, that is, of the privilege of working directly with His Majesty. The innovations of Louis XIV succeeded while those of Joseph II were to fail because the former, more intelligently, always used existing forms. Sugaring the medicine is the art of great heads of state.

THE TRIUMPH OF PRAGMATISM

When we have identified empiricism as Louis XIV's golden rule, the image of power without limits melts away. In fact, in the institutions of 1715 may be found everything and its opposite. An analysis of them shows that the king did not impose a monopoly. Royal administration, ecclesiastical administration and provincial government through the Estates coexisted. It also shows that royal institutions were not necessarily state institutions, as the farming out of indirect taxation demonstrates. One searches in vain for any unity within royal administration. The 45,000 royal officeholders, who owned their offices, enjoyed an extraordinary degree of autonomy, even though they often also possessed a sense of the state and of service, and even though the king kept them in check and imposed heavy 'augmentations of payment' upon them. And yet it was they who provided the nursery for the senior public servants. Most certainly, the commissioners appointed by the king represented a kind of modernity. But they were only a minority within a public administration largely outside direct royal control. Between pure commissioners and royal officers there flourished, in 1715 as in 1661, several intermediate positions. There were great offices which were sold, but which one could not apply for personally, such as secretariats of state. There were great offices which came free, including those of the chancellor, the controller-general, and the thirty councillors of state. And there were commissions which had to be paid for.

Even ministerial departments lacked uniformity. Louis XIV and his collaborators may have introduced some significant reforms, but these were unsystematic. The secretariat of state for the king's household was something of an anachronism in 1715. On the other hand, that for the navy inaugurated, thanks to Colbert, a regime which was free of all legacies from the past, and for which ranks, a hierarchy, career guarantees and rules were established in 1689. This was unique, its only inferiority (in comparison with its English counterpart) being the absence of an operational general staff. Yet for all this, in 1715 (as in 1669), the two ministries came under the same minister. This represented the heights of pragmatism. Both Pontchartrain and Colbert were reformers so far as the arsenals and ships were concerned but men of routine when it came to the king's household service.

The secretariat of state for war, whether under Voysin in 1715 or Louvois in 1690, appears to have been somewhere between these two extremes. Venality of office survived in part. The ministers favoured the pen, but all, even Louvois, had to make room for the sword. The table of ranks diminished the opportunities for favouritism. In principle, M. Voysin was not supposed to accord privileges to courtiers; but in reality he accepted the need to advance the careers of the king's friends.

Louis XIV's government was so little constrained by general administrative principles that the administrative developments of the reign followed no overall pattern. The navy was amongst the more modern components, and this was apparent as early as 1669. And yet, for financial reasons, this was vitiated in 1706 by the creation of purely honorary commissioners. Contradictions abounded in other branches of public service. Whilst Louis kept the judicial officers in check and was irritated by the venality of so many posts, he permitted Colbert and Le Peletier, Chamillart and Desmarets to create thousands of useless offices. It was a question, of course, of wartime necessity, and the king only accepted such creations for fiscal reasons. Nevertheless, they represented a real regression. These new officials – mayors, magistrates, *receveurs d'octroi*, measurers of grain – made the last years of the reign appear a little ridiculous. A witticism attributed to Pontchartrain circulated round France and abroad: 'Every time Your Majesty creates an office, God creates an idiot to buy it.' (290) For the true 'French disease' was to be found in the sale of offices, rather than in a centralization which had hardly begun in 1715.

Louis XIV's politico-administrative empiricism, then, was far from being complete, logical, or consistent. But, while he oversaw the birth of something recognizably bureaucratic, he also set up what M. Pierre Chaunu has described as a 'meritocracy'. The king's creations (table of ranks, rank of brigadier, Order of St Louis) contributed to this, as did the social mixture within the king's service. The relative proportions of noblemen and *robins* ('men of the robe') among ambassadors would itself be worth further investigation. The role of service in the creation of new dukes, and the distribution between birth and merit in the granting of the blue riband and in the nomination of generals and marshals, both indicate the king's skill in remodelling the relationship between the administrative elite and the nobility.

Even the 'Bonnet affair' – an interminable quarrel over precedence between dukes and *présidents* which continued into the reign of Louis XV – stimulated individual and social rivalries and created a greater equality between those who claimed rank on the basis of birth and those who claimed it as a consequence of services rendered.

Among lower cadres, other forms of meritocracy made an appearance, also with the king's encouragement. Selection was fostered, as may be seen in the constitution of that remarkable body the corps of the royal engineers (128). But they usually worked against any idea of technocracy, as the operation of the arsenals demonstrates. Although marine engineers only made an appearance under Louis XV, in 1765, it was, in 1715, no longer simple master craftsmen who, as in 1669, constructed the great vessels of the fleet, but the 'engineers in ordinary to the navy', trained in post and the envy of the English and Dutch.

This victory for empiricism and rejection of technocracy characterized Louis XIV's reign and protected the state against abstraction and the people's contempt. In the France of 1715, the magistrate of an *élection* was not necessarily a law graduate, whilst his colleague in the *grenier à sel* rarely was. Both of them learnt the law by sitting on the bench. A councillor of the Parlement who entered the court at the age of twenty knew very little; but, by the time he was thirty, he would have become a zealous judge and a learned magistrate, having learnt law and jurisprudence by applying them. A *maître des requêtes* who purchased his office aged twenty-two, after passing through the Parlement, had almost everything still to learn: the law, economics, administration, provincial customs. The *maîtres des requêtes* under Louis XIV were not from any *grande école*. They were not recruited by competitive examination but chosen by the king as intendants. Their *grande école* was the university of life. They applied themselves at first to studying the Council's dossiers, and then to preparing each decision which, as intendants, they would be required to make.

The same applied in all fields of service. The future army officer was a volunteer or gentleman cadet, experienced under fire since the age of fourteen. Before 1682, there was no formal preparation for being a naval captain: one may have come from the infantry with a suitable rank, another from the merchant marine, a third may have been an apprentice seaman. Only the

Knights of Malta knew something of both navigation and the military arts. After this date, some of the officers may have been trained in the companies of the *gardes-marines*. But they had not entered it by examination, nor had they been overwhelmed by any theoretical study. They had embarked and seen action under fire.

A good number of ministers, including the Phelypeaux and the last two Le Telliers, Seignelay and Torcy, had inherited a post of secretary of state from their fathers. Louvois had obtained this privilege at the age of fourteen. If they were gifted, then all well and good; but if they were mediocre, the king removed them. If they showed some measure of ability – like Barbezieux – their training lifted them above the rest and above themselves. This was how Louis trained, observed and guided his ministers, soldiers, sailors, engineers, ambassadors, intendants and judges. His remarkable pragmatism was formidably effective.

THE STATE, IT IS FRANCE

It has been asserted that the Bourbon monarchy devalued the concept of France in favour of dynastic loyalism. This was only superficially the case. Under Louis XIV, and especially in the early years of the reign, France continued to be portrayed in effigy as a beautiful maiden holding the hand of her little sister, Navarre (199). But this representation never enjoyed the ubiquity which later was assured to Marianne by town-hall busts and postage stamps. No misogyny was implied in this reticence. At a time when figures of the Virgin Mary or Mary Magdalene were more numerous than those of Christ, why was the representation of France diminished? Because patriotism had always meant loyalism, and it was the more satisfying to answer the call of a warrior king than that of a woman representing an abstract idea. National identification meant, in practice, following the king, serving the king, obeying the king. The bystanders had seen him on the day of his consecration, the sick had felt his healing hands, the soldiers had seen him near the trenches, and the notables and common people had approached him in the gardens of Versailles. Then the king addressed himself to his people on 12 June 1709, associating them with his cares and his decisions. The French of the seventeenth century preferred obedience to the descendant of St Louis and Henry IV rather than to 'those people of mediocre condition, by whom aristocratic states are governed' (63). Whilst these latter followed only their own predelictions, or those of an oligarchy, a hereditary king thought and acted in relation to his kingdom, the patrimony of which was his alone.

This is why the presence of the king in paintings and sculpture and on coins and medals, and the ubiquitous representation of his symbol, the sun, though not tied to the pagan practices of imperial Rome, encouraged loyalism and patriotism. The king was never far away: whoever locked a coin in his coffer had earned not only his wages but also a portrait of the king. The king was never far away: M. the *curé*, especially after the Revocation, talked about him, one day asking for one's prayers for the success of the armies, the next making one sing a *Te Deum* because the duc de Vendôme had won a victory, and between two phrases of this hymn to the glory of God could be felt some patriotic *frisson* at the thought of the martial glory of the king and the country at large.

From the moment when the military took priority in the state finances, providing the fulcrum to the administration and assuring paths of glory for the young, it was the armed services which wove the fabric of national identity (218). The Church had no scruples about blessing ensigns or welcoming into its sanctuaries the flags and standards brought back by the king's soldiers. There was not a single day during wartime when the marquise de Maintenon's ladies and young girls did not pray for the king, France and the army (66). Everything merged, sometimes in a minor key, sometimes in a major one: France and the army, the king and his subjects, military service and state service, obedience to the Church and loyalty to His Majesty, the government and the nation, France and the king, the state and the king, the state and the kingdom of France.

The word 'state' constituted no abstraction. When Louis XIV took a decision in the interests of the state, he was thinking, speaking and acting in the name of France, which was, of course, a kingdom and a nation (or group of nations), but, above all, a *patrie*. Dynastic loyalism – conserving the fundamental laws of the kingdom – the union of throne, altar and people, the imperatives of national defence, the personal radiance of Louis XIV and the shared difficulties of the last years of the reign (when the people tightened their belts and the king reduced his expenditures and sent his gold and silver to be melted down) meant that in 1715 the state was synonymous with the *patrie* and with France. All those connected, by direct action, filiation, kinship, marriage, friendship or solidarity, with the government, administration, clergy, army or navy were members of the state or associated with it. Whoever had paid a single *sou* of the *capitation* had played the game of the state, as had the poor man who had prayed for His Majesty's armies.

As long as 'the old stickler' lived on, this multiform and disciplined, concrete and tangible notion of the *patrie*, this idea of the state as inseparable from the fabric of the nation, was maintained by the efforts of the king, by the sacrifices of the taxpayers, by the blood sacrifice rendered unto Caesar, by honour and heroism, by the efficiency of a well-run administrative machine, by the will of all and by force of circumstance. The king had not established state control. He had not founded an allegorical state. He had not invoked an abstract state as an alibi for egotistic endeavours. He had raised to the rank of the state the community that welded the kingdom to its prince, a state which would embody and protect France, the civilized embodiment of a notion of *patrie*. This was Louis XIV's greatest achievement. His last thought was of the state: 'I am leaving you, but the state remains for ever.' (26) It has proved an enduring, if not always recognizable, legacy.

Conclusion: *Nec Pluribus Impar*

THE STATURE of a reign cannot be measured exclusively by the criticisms voiced by a minority. Neither Fénelon's jeremiads nor Saint-Simon's critiques, nor the celebratory fire-crackers in September 1715 should be allowed to weigh excessively in our judgement. Three hundred years later, it should be possible to lay their partiality to one side. And when that is done it will be seen that the charges against Louis XIV are disproved, on almost all counts, by the facts.

Was the king really too fond of warfare? The first three wars of the reign, directed against Spain and the empire, continued the policies of Henry IV, Richelieu and Mazarin. The purpose was to loosen the Habsburg noose. Even if Louis XIV had not invaded the United Provinces in 1672, William of Orange would have become stadholder, then King of England, and leader of an anti-French coalition. Even if Louis had not revoked the Edict of Nantes, a league would have been constructed uniting Europe against a France which was too populous, too rich, too well administered, too industrious, and too commercially powerful – a France whose 'arts, arms and laws' aroused enmities. As for the Spanish war, none was more legitimate, as Voltaire affirmed.

By the treaties of Utrecht and Rastadt, France retained almost all its recent conquests. Louis XIV did not leave a closely confined country behind him. Under his rule, the kingdom had expanded, in 1648 with upper Alsace, in 1659 with Artois and Roussillon, and between 1662 and 1702 with Walloon Flanders, French Hainaut, Franche Comté and lower Alsace, not to men-

The Latin tag *nec pluribus impar* can be colloquially translated as 'one of the best'.

tion Pondicherry, Santo Domingo, Louisiana – named after the king – and Senegal.* There was much wisdom in the older accounts which judged reigns and regimes according to their gains or losses of territory. Louis XIV enlarged the kingdom. The 'pré carré' was not perfect, nor tangible, for natural boundaries are a myth; but the rectifications of the frontier and the Reunions created a defensible France, and the military 'iron curtain' remained operational until 1790.

Wars are always too long, but the duration of Louis' should be halved to take account of time in winter quarters. Battles always have too many victims, but, in this instance, such losses should be counterbalanced by the invaluable degree of security gained, providing for seventy-nine years without invasion, between 1713 and 1792. Most of Louis XIV's campaigns were fought abroad: in Spain, Piedmont, the Palatinate, the Low Countries, the United Provinces. French territory was only invaded late on and in a very localized fashion. The royal armies were composed essentially of volunteers and mercenaries. When national integrity was imperilled, the levying of the militia, a forerunner to conscription, and an amalgam of recruits and veterans, which made it a precursor of 1792 and 1813, contributed to the strengthening of national feeling, and this too compensates for the bloodshed.

Because the navy, growing in a decade from ten to one hundred vessels to become the strongest in the world between 1676 and 1705, was inseparable from the land armies, war constituted the principal industry of the kingdom. The building-sites of the naval arsenals and fortresses inland and at ports represented, for forty years, from 1661 to 1701, the greatest collective mobilization of labour since the construction of the medieval cathedrals. The development, to a degree unique at the time, of a more modern military administration brought new talents into public service. Around 1690, no other country possessed the equivalent of Colbert's navy. Everything was regulated: ranks, promotion, appointments, careers, retirement, social security. In the land armies, the domain of the Le Tellier dynasty, it is still difficult to decide which was the more important: the provisioning, the billeting, the training and supervision, the technical innovation or the troop mobility.

* See the conclusion to ch. 27 for colonial developments.

Such an effort, productive of considerable success, presupposed, of course, a constant and attentive determination. Neither Colbert nor Seignelay nor Le Tellier nor Louvois would have been able to supervise 350,000 men and hold Europe in check without the patient and lucid support of the monarch. 'The excellence of a minister has never diminished the glory of his master; on the contrary, all the honour of his achievements must reflect upon their principal originator, and all the blame as well.' (44) This is why Louis XIV's severity towards the Palatinate was so regrettable. Though the devastation was relatively small-scale, it was still too reminiscent of the horrors of the Thirty Years' War not to provoke the hostility of public opinion, even one which was kept under strict surveillance. Even though Turenne executed his orders without any scruples of conscience and even though Louvois displayed a gratuitous zeal, the excess involved in the burnt-earth practice itself was still very unfortunate. The burning of the castle at Heidelberg, for example, was a blunder as well as a crime.

Others have followed Saint-Simon in accusing Louis XIV of being too fond of his buildings.* We are delighted now to possess Versailles, to use it as a venue for conferences and for the reception of heads of state, and yet its creator is illogically accused of having spent too much money upon its creation. His Majesty's works (the Louvre, the Tuileries, the Observatory, the porte Saint-Denis, the Invalides, the Salpêtrière, the place Vendôme, Saint-Germain, Vincennes, Versailles, Clagny, the Trianon and Marly, not to mention all the smaller Versailles copied in the provinces or abroad), as well as those works encouraged by the king (Saint-Roch, Saint-Sulpice, the place des Victoires and Saint-Louis-en-l'Ile), formed the second industry of the kingdom behind that of national defence. Although their utility is not always evident now, they dazzled contemporaries. 'Excellent buildings' provide the measure of a king, a reign, a kingdom. They had undoubted political value. They were also a permanent world exhibition. Neither Francis I nor Lorenzo the Magnificent had achieved such a total dominance over, and such a happy co-operation with, the arts. Having chosen his masters of works – Colbert and then Louvois as superintendents, Le Nôtre,

---

* This reference to the buildings is a calumny of Saint-Simon's – he had never liked Versailles – and is to be found in none of the detailed and accurate accounts from Dangeau of the king's illness and death.

Le Brun and Mansart for overall plans, and Coysevox, Vigarani, the Kellers, Tuby, Berain, Boulle and others for particular projects – Louis XIV created a style which was often imitated but never surpassed.

The haste involved in certain projects, improvisation, and the climate at Versailles were responsible for illnesses, injuries and sometimes fatal accidents. But this should not form a basis for a negative verdict upon the constructions as a whole. Similarly, whilst it may be correct to deplore the cost in money and human life of the notorious diversion of the waters of the River Eure, the product of an over-large imagination despite its technical feasibility, that judgement should not distort our overall assessment. 'One only judges a great man', Voltaire reminds us, 'by his masterpieces and not by his mistakes.' There were battles fought which claimed more lives than this miserable canal. But, now, on the other hand, no treaty did as much for the prestige of France as did Versailles: palace, park and dependencies, architecture and decoration. The Swiss guards consumed by the digging of the lake which bears their name, and the soldiers decimated by their work on the Eure canal, did not die in vain; the same cannot be said for the victims of all modern wars.

The third main charge brought against Louis XIV – sometimes the principal one – is the Revocation of the Edict of Nantes. It would be better to talk of an anti-Protestant policy, since the Revocation was only the culmination of a persecution lasting a quarter of a century. Inexcusable in our eyes, this persecution was at that time not only explicable, but demanded by a Catholic majority in the nation, from the Bishop of Montauban to the most modest day-labourer. The adage *Cujus regio, ejus religio* ('The religion of a country is that of its prince') held sway in the sixteenth and seventeenth centuries. There is every reason to believe that, if the Reformation had succeeded in France, Catholic worship would have been speedily suppressed. But it failed, and the situation was reversed. Furthermore, in France, heresy had always been 'a royal cause'; the commitment to extirpate heresy (*Haereticos exterminare*) had been one of the solemn vows of the consecration since the thirteenth century. In such conditions, the Edict of Nantes can only be understood as a measure dictated by circumstances and a provisional safeguard for the Protestant minority in the kingdom. Henry IV was so conscious of this that the act was sealed with yellow wax instead of the green seal reserved for important edicts (119). If the Béarnais had lived another twenty years, perhaps the position of the Protestants would have been very different. After the risings in the South (1621–9), Louis XIII would have had no problem in revoking the Edict of Nantes, but he rested content with abolishing its political clauses. Richelieu needed to mollify the Protestant princes of the empire. Civil toleration, though it continued to violate the principles of French public law, was maintained.

Such toleration was also contradicted by contemporary theology. Just as, in the Reformed camp, pastors consigned papists to eternal damnation, Catholics could only foresee the flames of Hell for the 'prétendus réformés'. Therefore, rough treatment and violence here below to save dissidents from an eternity of suffering appeared legitimate, even charitable. It was the application, following St Augustine, to conversion of the *Compelle intrare* of the parable.* Nurtured by a pious Catholic mother, catechized by a Jesuit hostile to all the principles of the Reformation and confessed and preached at by clerics and orators anchored in the reconquest theology of the Counter Reformation, Louis XIV had only to let his conscience speak, for him to regard the Protestants with abhorrence. The demand of Catholic opinion, of the clergy, bourgeoisie and people, for one sole religion in France, and the king's perennial suspicions of the democratic ecclesiology of Calvinism, were grafted onto a primitive and primordial revulsion, based on the catechism of the Council of Trent.

With regard to his kingdom, Louis XIV had the best of reasons for wanting to put an end to religious dualism: theological motives – accentuated by his title of Most Christian King and the consecration at Reims – legal imperatives, and the weight of opinion. However, he made a twin error. Within the kingdom, he failed to comprehend that Protestantism was slowly disintegrating and that it would be enough to ignore it. And then, misled by the statistics provided by bishops, intendants and missionaries, he did not predict that the Revocation and its awful consequences would revive a sense of conviction and strength of belief amongst French Protestants. Abroad, where the restrictive measures taken between 1660 and 1682 had not been the subject for widespread condemnation, the longer the

* Luke 14: 23.

time that passed, the more the virtually unique religious regime in France gained a symbolic value. The enfeebled, diminished and restrictive toleration of 1683 and 1684 could still lie in the reflection of the Edict of Nantes. The result was that the Revocation struck Protestant peoples abroad like a bolt from the blue. After eighty-seven years, the regime of the Edict of Nantes had contributed to the image others had of France, whether in a negative sense (as with Charles II of Spain) or positive sense (as with the Elector of Brandenburg).

To the king's crime, in which nineteen million French people were, in some sense, accomplices (*Sanguis ejus super nos, et super filios nostros**) – the crime of compelling consciences in the name of the same Lord – were added, therefore, two political blunders, two grave misjudgements. But none of this would have occurred if Henry IV had lived or if Louis XIII had revoked the Edict of Nantes in 1629 as a punishment for the damaging rebellion in the Midi. Following the logic of this argument, and taking into account the religious intransigence of the century, the persecution of the Protestants was inevitable (which is not to say that it was excusable). In terms of the sensibility of the period, nothing is more easily explained. But if Louis XIV must assume his responsibility in the matter, then it is surely the case that the chancellor Michel Le Tellier, Archbishop Harlay de Champvallon, père de la Chaize, the cardinals and bishops and the Assembly of the Clergy of France must assume some of the blame.

It is a matter for each individual to assess the results of the reign, to weigh the positive (a more modern, enlarged and powerful France, with a flourishing cultural heritage) against the negative (700,000 poorly converted 'nouveaux convertis'). To the latter, it is scarcely worth adding the aqueduct of Maintenon when there is Versailles to set towards the former. And the king's mistresses, as Voltaire stressed, are worth not much more than a footnote in the overall assessment.

> He had his faults, the sun has its sunspots
> But it still remains the sun.†

One may not warm to Louis XIV, one may even detest him.

---

* 'Their blood is upon us and upon our descendants.'
† From the verses of père de la Rue (reproduced in an appendix in the original French edition).

But it is difficult not to respect, with his grandeur and his weaknesses, his glory and his mistakes, the king whom the German-born Protestant Leibniz described as 'one of the greatest kings who ever lived' (87).

References

The bibliography of this subject in French is so immense that it is impossible to present it accurately in a selective fashion. The following titles are therefore only intended to provide the sources for particular quotations or ideas. Works are published in Paris unless otherwise indicated.

PRIMARY SOURCES

Where a primary source is contained in the *Nouvelle Collection des mémoires relatifs à l'histoire de France* (eds Michaud and Poujoulat, 1866) that collection is referred to as 'Michaud and Poujoulat'.

1 *Almanach royal pour l'an mil sept cent quinze* . . . (1715).
2 Anselme de Sainte-Marie, Pierre Guibours, *Histoire généalogique et chronologique de la maison royale de France et des grands officiers de la couronne* (9 vols, 1726–33).
3 Arnauld, Abbé Antoine, *Mémoires* . . ., in Michaud and Poujoulat, vol. 23, pp. 475–556.
4 Arnauld d'Andilly, Robert, *Mémoires* . . ., in Michaud and Poujoulat, vol. 23, pp. 363–474.
5 Ballard, Christophe, *Brunettes, ou Petits airs tendres* . . . *mêlées de chansons à danser* (3 vols, 1703–11).
6 Barthélemy, Edouard de, *Madame la comtesse de Maure, sa vie et sa correspondance* (1863).
7 Bercé, Yves-Marie, *Croquants et nu-pieds. Les soulèvements paysans en France du XVIᵉ au XIXᵉ siècle* (1974).
8 Bérenger, Jean and Meyer, Jean, *La Bretagne à la fin du XVIIᵉ siècle d'après le rapport de Béchameil de Nointel* (1976).
9 Bérulle, Pierre, Cardinal de, *Discours de l'état et des grandeurs de Jésus* . . . (1623).

10 Berwick, James Fitzjames, Duke of and maréchal de, *Mémoires ... écrits par lui-même ...*, in Michaud and Poujoulat, vol. 32, pp. 303–466.

11 Boileau, Nicolas, *Œuvres complètes* (1966).

12 Boislisle, Arthur Michel de, *Correspondance des contrôleurs généraux des finances avec les intendants, 1683–1715* (3 vols, 1874–93).

13 Boislisle, Arthur Michel de, *Mémoires des intendants sur l'état des généralités dressés pour l'instruction du duc de Bourgogne*, vol. 1: *Mémoire de la généralité de Paris* (1881).

14 Bossuet, Jacques-Bénigne, *Œuvres* (ed. Velat, 1961).

15 Bouhours, Père Dominique, *Entretiens d'Ariste et d'Eugène* (ed. G. Radouant, 1920).

16 Bourdaloue, Père Louis, *Œuvres complètes ...* (4 vols, ed. Saint-Dizier, Agen and Bar-le-Duc, 1864).

17 Brancourt, Jean-Pierre, *L'intendance de Champagne à la fin du XVIIe siècle* (critical edition of the *Mémoires* 'for the instruction of the Duke of Burgundy ...') (1983).

18 Brice, Germain, *Description de la ville de Paris et de tout ce qu'elle contient de plus remarquable*, 9th edn (4 vols, 1752).

19 Bussy-Rabutin (Roger de Rabutin, comte de Bussy), *Histoire amoureuse des Gaules* (ed. A. Adam, 1967).

20 Caylus, Marthe de Mursay, comtesse de, *Souvenirs de Mme de Caylus ...* (ed. Noël, 1965).

21 *Cérémonies faites et observées au sacre et couronnement du roy Louis XIV en la ville de Rheims le dimanche 7 juin 1654 ...* (1654).

22 Challes, Robert, *Mémoires de Robert Challes, écrivain du Roi* (ed. Augustin-Thierry, 1933).

23 Challes, Robert, *Voyage aux Indes d'une escadre française (1690–1691)* (ed. Augustin-Thierry, 1933).

24 Choisy, François-Timoléon, abbé de, *Mémoires ...* (ed. Mongrédien, 1979).

25 Currat, Geneviève, *Les paroles de Louis XIV* (unpublished *mémoire de maîtrise*, University of Paris-Nanterre, 1983).

26 Dangeau, Philippe de Courcillon, marquis de, *Journal ...* (19 vols, eds Soulié and Dussieux, 1854–60).

27 Darricau, Raymond, *Contribution à l'historiographie d'Anne d'Autriche. Oraison funèbre de la Reine, prononcée au Val-de-Grâce le 9 février 1666, par Guillaume Le Boux, évêque de Dax* (Aire, 1966).

28 Delassault, Geneviève, *Choix des lettres inédites de Louis-Isaac Le Maistre de Sacy (1650–1683)* (1959).

29 Déon, Michel, *Louis XIV par lui-même* (1983).

30 Des Ursins, Anne-Marie de la Trémoille, princesse, *Lettres inédites ...* (ed. Geffroy, 1859).

31 *Deux siècles de jansénisme à travers les documents du fonds Port-Royal d'Utrecht* (1974).

32 Drouhet, Jean, *Les œuvres de Jean Drouhet, maître apothicaire à Saint-Maixent* . . . (ed. Richard, Poitiers, 1878).

33 Durye, Pierre, baron, 'Le Roy de glorieuse mémoire', *Gé-Magazine* no. 5 (March 1983), pp. 48–9.

34 Estrées, François-Annibal, maréchal d', *Mémoires* . . . (ed. Bonnefon, 1910).

35 Fénelon, François de Salignac de la Mothe-, *Les aventures de Télémaque fils d'Ulysse*, new edn (1837).

36 Fénelon, François de Salignac de la Mothe-, *Ecrits et lettres politiques* . . . (ed. Urbain, 1921).

37 Ferrière, Claude-Joseph de, *Dictionnaire de droit et de pratique* . . ., 4th edn (2 vols, 1768).

38 Fléchier, Esprit, *Mémoires de Fléchier sur les grands jours d'Auvergne* (ed. Y.-M. Bercé, 1984).

39 Fléchier, Esprit, *Œuvres complètes de Fléchier, évêque de Nîmes* . . . (2 vols, ed. Migne, Le Petit-Montrouge, 1856).

40 Forbin, Claude, chevalier de, *Mémoires du comte de Forbin* . . . (ed. Boulenger, 1934).

41 François de Sales, St, *Introduction à la vie dévote* (2 vols, 1934).

42 Furetière, Antoine, *Dictionnaire universel* . . . (3 vols, The Hague and Rotterdam, 1690).

43 Goubert, Pierre, *L'avènement du Roi-Soleil. 1661* (1967).

44 Gracián, Baltasar, *L'homme de cour* (trans. Amelot de la Houssaye, 1924).

45 Guiffrey, Jules, *Comptes des bâtiments du Roi sous le règne de Louis XIV* . . . (5 vols, 1881–1901).

46 Hasquin, Hervé, *L'intendance du Hainaut en 1697* (critical edition of the *Mémoires* 'for the instruction of the Duke of Burgundy . . .') (1975).

47 Jean Eudes, St, *Lettres choisies et inédites* . . . (ed. Berthelot du Chesnay, Namur, 1958).

48 La Bruyère, Jean de, *Œuvres complètes* (ed. Benda, 1951).

49 La Fayette, Marie-Madeleine Pioche de la Vergne, comtesse de, *Histoire de Madame Henriette d'Angleterre*, followed by *Mémoires de la cour de France pour les années 1688 et 1689* (ed. Sigaux, 1965).

50 Lambert, Anne-Thérèse de Marguenat de Courcelles, marquise de, *Œuvres morales* . . . (ed. L. Colet, 1843).

51 La Porte, Pierre de, *Mémoires* . . ., in Michaud and Poujoulat, vol. 32, pp. 1–57.

52 La Rochefoucauld, François, duc de, *Œuvres complètes* (ed. Martin-Chauffier and Marchand, 1964).

53 Laudenbach, Hélène, *Chroniques de Port-Royal* . . . (1946).

53b *Le Brun à Versailles* (catalogue to the exhibition in the Musée du Louvre of October 1985–January 1986) (1985).

54 Le Gendre, Louis, *Mémoires de l'abbé Legendre, chanoine de Notre-*

Dame, secrétaire de M. de Harlay, archevêque de Paris . . . (ed. Roux, 1863).

55 Le Gras, Mgr Simon, Bishop of Soissons, *Procès verbal du sacre du roy Louis quatorze du nom* . . . (Soissons, 1694).

56 L'Epinois, Solange, 'Louis XIV, Corrège et l'appréciation des œuvres d'art', *Gazette des Beaux-Arts* (July 1965), pp. 103–4.

57 *Lettres du XVIIe siècle* (ed. Henriet, 1945).

58 Loew, Jacques and Meslin, Michel, *Histoire de l'Eglise par elle-même* (1978).

59 Louis XIV, *Lettre du Roy écrite à monseigneur l'archevêque de Paris pour faire chanter le* Te Deum *en l'église Notre-Dame, en action de grâces de la paix conclue avec l'Empereur et l'Empire* (1698).

60 Louis XIV, *Lettre du Roy écrite à monseigneur l'évêque comte de Châlons, pair de France* (requesting a *Te Deum* for the victory at Cassano) and *Mandement* (for the same) (n. p., 1705).

61 Louis XIV, *Lettres patentes en faveur des enfans naturels du Roy, pour avoir rang après les princes du sang* (1694).

62 Louis XIV, *Manière de montrer les jardins de Versailles* (ed. Girardet, 1951).

63 Louis XIV, *Mémoires* (ed. Longnon, 1978).

64 *Louis XIV et l'urbanisme parisien* (1984).

65 Maintenon, Françoise d'Aubigné, marquise de, *Lettres à d'Aubigné et à Madame des Ursins* (ed. Truc, 1921).

66 Maintenon, Françoise d'Aubigné, marquise de, *Lettres historiques et édifiantes adressées aux dames de Saint-Louis* (2 vols, ed. Lavallée, 1856).

67 Mancini, Hortense, duchesse de Mazarin, and Marie, Princess Colonna, *Mémoires* . . . (ed. Doscot, 1965).

68 Marion, Marcel, *Les impôts directs sous l'ancien régime, principalement au XVIIIe siècle* (1910).

69 Marteilhe, Jean, *Mémoires d'un galérien du Roi-Soleil* (ed. Zysberg, 1982).

70 *Mazarin, homme d'Etat et collectionneur, 1602–1661* (1961).

71 *Médailles sur les principaux événements du règne entier de Louis le Grand, avec des explications historiques* (1723) (*The Metallic History of the Reign*).

72 Méré, Antoine Gombaud, chevalier de, *Œuvres complètes* . . . (1930).

73 Molé, Mathieu, *Mémoires* . . . (4 vols, ed. Champollion-Figeac, 1855–7).

74 Molière (Jean-Baptiste Poquelin), *Œuvres complètes* (5 vols, ed. N. Chaix, 1864).

75 Mongrédien, Georges, *Louis XIV* (1963).

76 Montecuccoli, Raimondo, Count of, *Mémoires de Montecuccoli, généralissime des troupes de l'Empereur* . . . (1751).

77 Montesquieu, Charles-Louis de Secondat, baron de, *Lettres persanes* ... (1930).

78 Motteville, Françoise Langlois de, *Mémoires de Mme de Motteville*, in *Collection des mémoires relatifs à l'histoire de France* ..., vols 38 and 39 (1847) (covering the years from 1648 to 1658).

79 *Naissance de la Louisiane, tricentenaire des découvertes de Cavelier de la Salle* (1982).

80 Nemours, Marie d'Orléans de Longueville, duchesse de, *Mémoires* ..., in Michaud and Poujoulat, vol. 23, pp. 604–60.

81 *Ordonnance de Louis XIV pour les armées navales et arsenaux de marine* (1689).

82 *Ordonnance de Louis XIV, roy de France et de Navarre, pour les matières criminelles, donnée à Saint Germain en Laye au mois d'aoust 1670* (1670).

83 Ormesson, Olivier Le Fèvre d', *Journal* ... (2 vols, ed. Chéruel, 1860–1).

84 Patin, Guy, *Lettres du temps de la Fronde* (ed. Thérive, 1921).

85 Perrault, Charles, *Les contes de Perrault* (illus. by Gustave Doré; ed. Stahl, 1971).

86 Primi Visconti, Jean-Baptiste, *Mémoires sur la cour de Louis XIV* (ed. Lemoine, 1908).

87 Princess Palatine (Elisabeth-Charlotte of Bavaria, duchesse d'Orléans, often called Madame Palatine, or simply Madame), *Lettres de Madame, duchesse d'Orléans* ... (ed. Amiel, 1981).

88 Quincy, Joseph Sevin, chevalier de, *Mémoires* ... (3 vols, ed. Lecestre, 1898–1901).

89 Racine, Jean, *Abrégé de l'histoire de Port-Royal* (ed. Gandon, 1926).

90 Racine, Jean, *Œuvres complètes de J. Racine* (preceded by an essay on his life and works by Louis Racine), new edn (n. d.)

91 Raunié, Emile, *Recueil Clairambault-Maurepas. Chansonnier historique* ..., vol. 1 (1879).

92 Saint-Evremond, Charles de Maguetel de Saint-Denis de, *Critique littéraire* (ed. Wilmotte, 1921).

93 Saint-Maurice, Thomas-François Chabod, marquis de, *Lettres sur la cour de Louis XIV* ... (2 vols, ed. Lemoine, 1911–12).

94 Saint-Simon, Louis de Rouvroy, duc de, *Mémoires* (7 vols, ed. Truc, 1953–61).

95 Saxony, Maurice of, Marshal and Count of, *Mémoires sur l'art de la guerre* ... (Dresden, 1757).

96 Sévigné, Marie de Rabutin Chantal, marquise de, *Correspondance* (3 vols, ed. Duchêne, 1972–8).

97 Sourches, Louis-François du Bouchet, marquis de, *Mémoires du marquis de Sourches sur le règne de Louis XIV* (13 vols, ed. Cosnac and Pontal, 1882–93).

98   Spanheim, Ezéchiel, *Relation de la cour de France en 1690* . . . (ed. Bourgeois and Richard, 1973).

99   Tallemant des Réaux, Gédéon, *Historiettes* (2 vols, ed. A. Adam, 1960–1).

100 Taveneaux, René, *Jansénisme et politique* (1965).

101 Tessé, René de Froulay, maréchal de, *Lettres* . . . (ed. Rambuteau, 1888).

102 *Textes et documents sur l'histoire de la Franche-Comté*, vol. 2: *XVIe et XVIIe siècles* (Besançon, 1965).

103 Torcy, Jean-Baptiste Colbert, marquis de, *Journal inédit* . . . *pendant les années 1709, 1710 et 1711* (ed. Masson, 1884).

104 Torcy, Jean-Baptiste Colbert, marquis de, *Mémoires du marquis de Torcy pour servir à l'histoire des négociations depuis le traité de Riswick jusqu'à la paix d'Utrecht*, in Michaud and Poujoulat, vol. 32, pp. 517–735.

105 *Traité de la majorité de nos rois et des régences du royaume* . . . (2 vols, Amsterdam, 1722).

106 Truchet, Jacques, *Politique de Bossuet* (1966).

107 Turenne, Henri de la Tour d'Auvergne, vicomte, prince and maréchal de, *Lettres de Turenne* . . . (ed. d'Huart, 1971).

108 Vallot, Antoine, Aquin, Antoine d' and Fagon, Guy-Crescent, *Journal de la santé du roi Louis XIV, de l'année 1647 à l'année 1711* . . . ed. Le Roi, 1862).

109 Vauban, Sébastien Le Prestre, maréchal de, *Project d'une dixme royale* . . . (ed. Coornaërt, 1933).

110 Villars, Marie Gigault de Bellefonds, marquise de, *Lettres de Mme de Villars à Mme de Coulanges (1679–1681)* (ed. Courtois, 1868).

111 Vivonne, Louis-Victor de Rochechouart, maréchal and duc de, *Correspondance du maréchal de Vivonne relative à l'expédition de Candie (1669)* (ed. Cordey, 1910).

112 Voltaire (François-Marie Arouet), *Le siècle de Louis XIV. Supplément au Siècle de Louis XIV. Du protestantisme et de la guerre des Cévennes. Défense de Louis XIV*, in *Œuvres historiques* (ed. Pomeau, 1957).

SECONDARY SOURCES

113 André, Louis, *Louis XIV et l'Europe* (1950).

114 André, Louis, *Michel Le Tellier et Louvois* (1943).

115 Anthony, James R., *La musique en France à l'époque baroque* (1981).

116 Antoine, Michel, *Le Conseil du Roi sous le règne de Louis XV* (1970).

117 Armogathe, Abbé Jean-Robert and Joutard, Philippe, 'Bâville et la guerre des camisards', *Revue d'histoire moderne et contemporaine*, 19 (1972), pp. 45–72.

118 *L'art du XVIIe siècle dans les carmels de France* (catalogue to the exhibition in the Musée du Petit Palais of November 1982–February 1983) (1982).

119 Babelon, Jean-Pierre, *Henri IV* (1982).

120 Barbey, Jean, Bluche, Frédéric and Rials, Stéphane, *Lois fondamentales et succession de France* (1984).

121 Bardet, Jean-Pierre, *Rouen aux XVIIe et XVIIIe siècles* . . . (2 vols, 1983).

122 Benoit, Marcelle, *Les musiciens du roi de France, 1661–1733* . . . (1982).

123 Bérenger, Jean, *Les relations franco-autrichiennes. Siège de Vienne (1683)* (colloquium of 9–11 March 1983) (Coëtquidan, n.d.)

124 Bérenger, Jean, *Une décision de caractère stratégique: l'acceptation par Louis XIV du testament de Charles II d'Espagne (novembre 1700)* (unpublished manuscript, kindly lent by the author).

125 Bertrand, Louis, *Louis XIV* (1924).

126 Bezard, Yvonne, *Fonctionnaires maritimes et coloniaux sous Louis XIV. Les Bégon* (1932).

127 Bezard, Yvonne, *Les porte-arquebuse du Roi* (Versailles, 1925).

128 Blanchard, Anne, *Les ingénieurs du Roi de Louis XIV à Louis XVI* . . . (Montpellier, 1979).

129 Blet, Henri, *Histoire de la colonisation française. Naissance et déclin d'un Empire*, vol. 1: *Des origines à 1789* (1946).

130 Blet, Père Pierre, 'Louis XIV et le Saint-Siège', *XVIIe Siècle*, 31 (1979), pp. 137–54.

131 Blet, Père Pierre, 'Louis XIV et le Saint-Siège à la lumière de deux publications récentes', *Archivum historiae pontificale*, 12 (1974), pp. 309–37.

132 Bluche, François, 'A propos du *mécénat* de Louis XIV', *Anthologia di Belle Arti*, NS, nos 27–8 (1985), pp. 98–102.

133 Bluche, François, *Le despotisme éclairé*, new edn (1985).

134 Bluche, François, *Les magistrates du parlement de Paris au XVIIIe siècle*, new edn (1986).

135 Bluche, François, *La vie quotidienne au temps de Louis XIV* (1984).

136 Bluche, François, *La vie quotidienne de la noblesse française au XVIIIe siècle*, new edn (1980).

137 Bluche, François and Durye, Pierre, *L'anoblissement par charges avant 1789* (2 vols, 1962).

138 Bluche, François and Solnon, Jean-François, *La véritable hiérarchie sociale de l'ancienne France. Le tarif de la première capitation (1695)* (Geneva 1983).

139 Boissonnade, Pierre and Charlat, Pierre, *Colbert et la compagnie de commerce du Nord (1661–1689)* (1930).

140 Bonnot, Isabelle, *Hérétique ou saint? Henry Arnaud, évêque janséniste d'Angers au XVIIe siècle* (1984).

141 Bornecque, Robert, *La France de Vauban* (1984).
142 Bottineau, Yves, *L'art de cour dans l'Espagne de Philippe V* ... (Bordeaux, 1962).
143 Bottineau, Yves, 'La cour de Louis XIV à Fontainebleau', *XVIIᵉ Siècle*, no. 24 (1954), pp. 697–734.
144 Brancourt, Jean-Pierre, *Le duc de Saint-Simon et la monarchie* (1971).
145 Bremond, Abbé Henri, *Histoire littéraire du sentiment religieux en France* ... (12 vols, 1916–36).
146 Bruhier, Pierre-Jean, 'L'art naval au grand siècle', *XVIIᵉ Siècle*, nos 86–7 (1970), pp. 83–105.
147 *Bulletin de la société de l'histoire du protestantisme français* (the volumes utilized were those published during the years 1976 to 1983).
148 Burger, Pierre-François, 'Autour de deux propagandistes de Louis XIV: Vuoerden et Donneau de Visé', *XVIIᵉ Siècle*, no. 137 (1982), pp. 413–16.
149 Carré, Henri, *L'enfance et la première jeunesse de Louis XIV, 1638–1661* (1944).
150 Carretier, Christian, *Les cinq cent douze quartiers de Louis XIV* (1980).
151 Cavaillès, Henri, *La route française* ... (1946).
152 Chandernagor, Françoise, *L'allée du Roi* ... (1981).
153 Chateaubriand, Vicomte François-René-Auguste de, *Génie du christianisme* (ed. Regard, 1978).
154 Chaunu, Pierre, *La civilisation de l'Europe classique* (1970).
155 Chaunu, Pierre, *La mort à Paris, XVIᵉ, XVIIᵉ et XVIIIᵉ siècles* (1978).
156 Chérot, Père Henri, *La première jeunesse de Louis XIV (1649–1653) d'après la correspondance inédite du P. Charles Paulin, son premier confesseur* (Lille, 1894).
157 Chéruel, Adolphe, *Histoire de France pendant la minorité de Louis XIV* (4 vols, 1879–80).
158 Chevallier, Pierre, *Louis XIII, roi cornélien* (1979).
159 Clausewitz, Karl von, *De la guerre* (trans. Naville, 1955).
160 Cognet, Abbé Louis, *Claude Lancelot, solitaire de Port-Royal* (1950).
161 *Colbert, 1619–1683* (catalogue of the exhibition at the Hôtel de la Monnaie, Paris, of October–November 1983) (1983).
162 Cols, Isabelle, *La légende noire de Louis XIV* (unpublished *mémoire de maîtrise*, University of Paris-Nanterre, 1983).
163 Corvisier, André, *L'armée française de la fin du XVIIᵉ siècle au ministère de Choiseul* ... (2 vols, 1964).
164 Corvisier, André, *La France de Louis XIV, 1643–1715. Ordre intérieur et place en Europe* (1979).
165 Corvisier, André, *Louvois* (1983).
166 Corvisier, André, 'Le moral des combattants, panique et enthosiasme: Malplaquet, 11 septembre 1709', *Revue historique des armées*, no. 3 (1977), pp. 7–32.

167 Coutin, Sophie, *Les déplacements de Louis XIV, 1661–1682* (unpublished *mémoire de maîtrise*, University of Paris-Nanterre, 1985).

168 Dejean, Etienne, *Un prélat indépendant au XVIIe siècle: Nicolas Pavillon, évêque d'Alet* . . . (1909).

169 Delattre, Pierre, *Le vœu de Louis XIII* . . . (1937).

170 Dessert, Daniel, *Argent, pouvoir et société au grand siècle* (1984).

171 Dethan, Georges, *Mazarin* . . . (1981).

172 *XVIIe Siècle*. Review published by the Société d'Etudes du XVIIe Siècle (1949–84).

173 Dompnier, Bernard, 'Un aspect de la dévotion eucharistique dans la France du XVIIe siècle: les prières des quarante-heures', *Revue de l'histoire de l'Eglise de France*, 67 (1981), pp. 5–31.

174 Dornic, François, *Une ascension sociale au XVIIe siècle: Louis Berryer, agent de Mazarin et de Colbert* (Caen, 1968).

175 Duccini, Hélène, *La Littérature pamphlétaire sous la régence de Marie de Médicis* (unpublished thesis, University of Paris-Nanterre, 1944).

176 Dulong, Claude, *Anne d'Autriche* . . . (1980).

177 Dupâquier, Jacques, *La population française aux XVIIe et XVIIIe siècles* (1979).

178. Dupâquier, Jacques, and Dupâquier, Michel, *Histoire de la démographie* . . . (1985).

179. Esmonin, Edmond, *Etudes sur la France des XVIIe et XVIIIe siècles* (1964).

180 Ferrier-Caverivière, Nicole, *L'image de Louis XIV dans la littérature française de 1660 à 1715* (1981).

181 Frêche, Georges, *Toulouse et la région Midi-Pyrénées au siècle des Lumières* . . . (1974).

182 Fréville, Henri, *L'intendance de Bretagne (1689–1790)* . . . (3 vols, Rennes, 1953).

183 Frostin, Charles, 'Le chancelier de France Louis de Pontchartrain, "ses" premiers présidents et la discipline des cours souveraines (1699–1714)', *Cahiers d'histoire*, 27 (1982), pp. 9–34.

184 Frostin, Charles, 'La famille ministérielle des Phelypeaux: esquisse d'un profil Pontchartrain (XVIe–XVIIIe siècles)', *Annales de Bretagne*, 86 (1979), pp. 117–40.

185 Frostin, Charles, 'L'organisation ministérielle sous Louis XIV: cumul d'attributions et situations conflictuelles (1690–1715)', *Revue historique de droit français et étranger*, 58 (1980), pp. 201–26.

186 Frostin, Charles, 'Les Pontchartrain et la pénétration commerciale française en Amérique espagnole (1690–1715)', *Revue historique*, 498 (1971), pp. 307–36.

187 Frostin, Charles, 'Pouvoir ministériel, *voies ordinaires de la justice* et *voies de l'autorité* sous Louis XIV: Le chancelier Louis de Pontchartrain et le secrétaire d'Etat Jérôme de Pontchartrain (1699–1715)', *107ᵉ Congrès national des sociétés savantes* (3 vols, Brest, 1982), vol. 1, pp. 7–29.

188 Funck-Brentano, Frantz, *Le drame des poisons* (n.d.)

189 Furet, François and Ozouf, Jacques, *Lire et écrire. L'alphabétisation des Français de Calvin à Jules Ferry* (2 vols, 1977).

190 Gaxotte, Pierre, *Louis XIV* (1974).

191 Gaxotte, Pierre, *Molière* (1977).

192 Girard, Georges, *Racolage et milice (1701–1715)* (1922).

193 Giraud, Marcel, 'Tendances humanitaires à la fin du règne de Louis XIV', *Revue historique*, 209 (1953), pp. 217–37.

194 Goubert, Pierre, *Louis XIV and Twenty Million Frenchmen* (London, 1970; original French edition 1966).

195 Griselle, Père Eugène, *Bourdaloue. Histoire critique de sa prédication* (2 vols, Lille, 1901).

196 Guitton, Georges, 'Un conflit de direction spirituelle. Madame de Maintenon et le père de la Chaize', *XVIIᵉ Siècle*, no. 29 (1955), pp. 378–95.

197 Hatton, Ragnhild, 'Louis XIV et l'Europe: éléments d'une révision historiographique', *XVIIᵉ Siècle*, 31 (1979), pp. 109–35.

198 Hautecoeur, Louis, *Histoire de l'architecture classique en France*, vol. 2: *Le règne de Louis XIV* (2 vols, 1948).

199 Hautecoeur, Louis, *L'histoire des châteaux du Louvre et des Tuileries . . . sous le règne de S. M. le roi Louis XIV . . .* (1927).

200 Havel, Evelyne, *L'impôt du sang d'après le journal du marquis de Dangeau* (unpublished *mémoire de maîtrise*, University of Paris–Nanterre, 1975).

201 Honoré, S., *Catalogue général des livres imprimés de la Bibliothèque Nationale. Actes royaux (1610–1715)*, vols 2–4 (1938–50).

202 Hoog, Simone and Meyer, Daniel, *Versailles, musée de l'histoire de France* (1970).

203 Jammes, André, 'Louis XIV, sa bibliothèque et le *cabinet du Roi*', *The Library*, 5th series, 20 (1965), pp. 1–12.

204 Jenkins, E.-H., *Histoire de la marine française des origines à nos jours* (1977).

205 Jouan, René, *Histoire de la marine française* (1950).

206 Kopeczi, Béla, *Hongrois et Français de Louis XIV à la révolution française* (1983).

207 Labatut, Jean-Pierre, *Louis XIV, roi de gloire* (1984).

208 Labrousse, Elisabeth, *Pierre Bayle, hétérodoxie et rigorisme* (The Hague, 1964).

209 Labrousse, Elisabeth, *La révocation de l'édit de Nantes* (1985).

210 Lachiver, Marcel, 'L'hiver de 1709', *Les Dossiers de Gé-Magazine,* no. 1 (June 1984), pp. 34–40.

211 Lacour-Gayet, Georges, *Le château de Saint-Germain-en-Laye* (1935).

212 La Force, Auguste-Armand-Nompar, duc de, *Lauzun* (1919).

213 Lair, Jules, *Louise de la Vallière et la jeunesse de Louis XIV . . .* (1902).

214 Lallemand, Père Paul, *Histoire de l'éducation dans l'ancien oratoire de France* (1889).

215 Lambin, Jean-Michel, *Quand le Nord devenait français . . .* (1980).

216 Lavisse, Ernest, *Histoire de France illustrée . . .*, vol. 7 (2 parts) and vol. 8 (1st part): *Louis XIV* (3 vols, 1911).

217 Lemoine, Jean, *Madame de Montespan et la légende des poisons* (1908).

218 Léonard, Emile-G., *L'armée et ses problèmes au XVIIIe siècle* (1958).

219 Le Roy Ladurie, Emmanuel, 'La monarchie française classique', *Commentaire,* 7 (1984), pp. 418–29.

220 Le Roy Ladurie, Emmanuel, *Le territoire de l'historien* (2 vols, 1973–8).

221 Lévy-Bruhl, Lucien, *L'Allemagne depuis Leibniz . . .* (1890).

222 Ligou, Daniel, *Le protestantisme en France de 1598 à 1715* (1968).

223 Livet, Georges, *L'intendance d'Alsace sous Louis XIV (1648–1715)* (Strasbourg, 1956).

224 Lizerand, Georges, *Le duc de Beauvillier, 1648–1714* (1933).

225 Lottin, Alain, *Chavatte, ouvrier lillois, un contemporain de Louis XIV* (1979).

226 Lottin, Alain, 'La fonction d'intendant vue par Louvois . . .', in *Mélanges . . . Mongrédien* (1974), pp. 63–9.

227 Luçay, Comte Helion de, *Les secrétaires d'Etat depuis leur institution jusqu'à la mort de Louis XV* (1881).

228 Mahan, Alfred Thayer, *Influence of Naval Seapower on History,* 1st edn (London, 1905).

229 Maindron, Ernest, *L'académie des sciences . . .* (1888).

229b Malettke, Klaus, *Opposition und Konspiration unter Ludwig XIV . . .* (Göttingen, 1976).

230 Martin, Henri-Jean, *Livre, pouvoirs et société à Paris au XVIIe siècle . . .* (2 vols, 1969).

231 Maury, Alfred, *L'ancienne académie des inscriptions et belles-lettres,* 2nd edn (1864).

232 *Mélanges historiques et littéraires sur le XVIIe siècle offerts à Georges Mongrédien par ses amis* (1974).

233 Méthivier, Hubert, *La Fronde* (1984).

234 Meuvret, Jean, 'La conjoncture internationale de 1660 à 1715', *Bulletin de la société d'histoire moderne,* 63 (1964), pp. 2–5.

235 Meyer, Jean, *Les capitalismes* (1981).

236 Meyer, Jean, *Colbert* (1981).

237 Meyer, Jean, 'Louis XIV et les puissances maritimes', *XVIIe Siècle,* 31 (1979), pp. 155–72.

238 Meyer, Jean, *Le poids de l'Etat* (1983).

239 Meyer, Jean, 'La seconde guerre de cent ans, 1689–1815', in *De Guillaume le Conquérant au marché commun* (1979), pp. 153–79.

240 Meyer, Jean, *La vie quotidienne en France au temps de la Régence* (1979).

241 Michel, Père Joseph, *Claude-François Poullart des Places, fondateur de la congrégation du Saint-Esprit* (1962).

242 Moine, Marie-Christine, *Les fêtes à la cour du Roi-Soleil, 1653–1715* (1984).

243 Moisy, Pierre, 'Note sur la galerie des glaces', *XVIIᵉ Siècle*, no. 53 (1961), pp. 42–50.

244 Mongrédien, Georges (dir.), *Mazarin* (1959).

245 Morineau, Michel, 'Budgets de l'Etat et gestion des finances royales en France au dix-huitième siècle', *Revue historique*, 264 (1978), pp. 289–336.

246 Mours, S., *Essai sommaire de géographie du protestantisme réformé français au XVIIᵉ siècle* (1966).

247 Mousnier, Roland, *Peasant Uprisings* (London, 1970; French edition, 1967).

248 Mousnier, Roland, *Paris capitale au temps de Richelieu et de Mazarin* (1978).

249 Mousnier, Roland, 'Qui a été Louis XIV?', in *Mélanges . . . Mongrédien* (1974), pp. 37–61.

250 Mousnier, Roland, *Les règlements du conseil du Roi sous Louis XIII* (1949).

251 Mousnier, Roland (dir.), *Un nouveau Colbert* (conference proceedings . . .) (1985).

252 Murat, Inès, *Colbert* (1980).

253 Murray Baillie, Hugh, 'Etiquette and the Planning of the State Apartments in Baroque Palaces', *Archaeologia*, 101 (1967), pp. 169–99.

254 Neveu, Bruno, 'Paris, capitale de la république des lettres et le *De Re diplomatica* de Dom Mabillon, 1681', in *Annuaire-Bulletin de la société de l'histoire de France* 1981–2 (1983), pp. 2–12.

255 Neveux, Hugues, 'Dimension idéologique des soulèvements paysans français au XVIIᵉ siècle', *Bulletin de la société d'histoire moderne*, 82 (1983), pp. 2–12.

256 Nolhac, Pierre de, *Histoire du château de Versailles. Versailles sous Louis XIV* (2 vols, 1911).

257 Nordmann, Claude, *Grandeur et liberté de la Suède (1660–1792)* (1971).

258 *Nouvel abrégé chronologique de l'histoire de France en deux parties, contenant les événements de notre histoire depuis Clovis jusqu'à Louis XIV, les guerres, les batailles, les sièges, etc.* 3rd edn (2 vols, 1749).

259 Olivier-Martin, François, *Histoire du droit français des origines à la Révolution* (1984).

260 Olivier-Martin, François, *L'organisation corporative de la France d'ancien régime* (1938).

261 Orcibal, Jean, *Louis XIV et les protestants* (1951).

262 Picard, Raymond, *La carrière de Jean Racine*, new edn (1961).

263 Pillorget-Rouanet, Suzanne, *Louis XIV candidat au trône impérial. 1658 ...* (1967).

264 Pinoteau, Hervé, baron, *Monarchie et avenir* (1960).

265 Pouilly, Isabelle de, *Portrait de Condé* (unpublished *mémoire de maîtrise*, University of Paris-Nanterre, 1985).

266 Pris, Claude, *La manufacture royale des glaces de Saint-Gobain ...* (2 vols, Lille, 1975).

267 Putzger, F. W., *Historischer Weltatlas. Jubiläumsausgabe* (Bielefeld and Berlin, 1957).

268 Quétel, Claude, *De par le Roy. Essai sur les lettres de cachet* (Toulouse, 1981).

269 *Revue d'histoire de l'Eglise de France*, journal of the Société d'Histoire Ecclésiastique de la France (the volumes utilized were those published during the years 1935 to 1983).

270 Richard, Michel, *La vie quotidienne des protestants sous l'ancien régime* (1966).

271 Sagnac, Philippe and Saint-Léger, A. de, *Louis XIV (1661–1715)*, 2nd edn (1944).

272 Schimberg, André, *L'éducation morale dans les collèges de la compagnie de Jésus en France sous l'ancien régime ...* (1913).

272b Solnon, Jean-François, *La cour de France* (1987).

273 Taillemite, Etienne, *Colbert, secrétaire d'Etat de la marine et les réformes de 1669* (1970).

274 Taillemite, Etienne, *Dictionnaire des marins français* (1982).

275 Taillemite, Etienne, 'L'image de Colbert à la lumière du tricentenaire', *Chronique d'histoire maritime*, no. 9 (1984), pp. 7–21.

276 Taillemite, Etienne, 'Les problèmes de la marine de guerre au XVIIe siècle', *XVIIe Siècle*, nos. 86–7 (1970), pp. 21–37.

277 Taillemite, Etienne, 'Une utilisation originale des forces navales: l'expédition de Duguay-Trouin à Rio-de-Janeiro', *Annales de la société d'histoire et d'archéologie de l'arrondissement de Saint-Malo* (1973).

278 Tapié, Victor-Lucien, *Le baroque* (1961).

279 Tapié, Victor-Lucien, *Baroque et classicisme* (1972).

280 Tapié, Victor-Lucien, *Monarchies et peuples du Danube* (1969).

281 Tapié, Victor-Lucien, 'Quelques aspects généraux de la politique étrangère de Louis XIV', *XVIIe Siècle*, nos. 46–7 (1960), pp. 1–28.

282 Taveneaux, René, *Le catholicisme dans la France classique, 1610–1715* (2 vols, 1980).

283 Taveneaux, René, *Le jansénisme en Lorraine, 1640–1789* (1960).

284 Taveneaux, René, *La vie quotidienne des jansénistes aux XVIIe et XVIIIe siècles* (1973).

285 Tessier, Georges, *Diplomatique royale française* (1962).

286 Thuillier, Guy, *L'E.N.A. avant l'E.N.A.* (1983).

287 Tresch, Mathias, *Evolution de la chanson française savante et populaire*, vol. 1: *Des origines à la révolution française* (1926).

288 Tuetey, Louis, *Les officiers sous l'ancien régime. Nobles et roturiers* (1908).

289 Tyvaert, Michel, 'L'image du Roi: légitimité et moralité royale dans les histoires de France au XVIIe siècle', *Revue d'histoire moderne et contemporaine*, 21 (1974), pp. 521–47.

290 Véri, Joseph-Alphonse, abbé de, *Journal* ... (2 vols, ed. J. de Witte, 1928–30).

291 Verlet, Pierre, *Le château de Versailles* (1985).

292 *Victoires de l'armée française, 1214–1885* (1886).

293 Vigié, Marc, *Les galériens du Roi* (1985).

294 Viguerie, Jean de, *L'institution des enfants. L'éducation en France, XVIe–XVIIIe siècles* (1978).

295 Vogüé, Melchior, marquis de, *Villars d'après sa correspondance et des documents inédits* (2 vols, 1888).

296 Volkoff, Vladimir, 'Incarnation et royauté', *Commentaire*, 7 (1984), pp. 430–2.

297 Vorsanger, Michel, *Quand Louis XIV disgraciait* (unpublished *mémoire de maîtrise*, University of Paris-Nanterre, 1983).

298 Weill, Georges, *Le journal. Origines, évolution et rôle* (1934).

299 Zeller, Gaston, *Histoire des relations internationales t. III. Les temps modernes. II. De Louis XIV à 1789* (1955).

Bibliographical Note
(*Prepared by the translator of this edition*)

A LL GOOD biographers fall in love with their subject – it is part and parcel of the risks and rewards of good biographizing. When the subject in question has exercised such a perdurable fascination upon generations of a nation's historians as that exercised by Louis XIV on those of France, it is not surprising that a strong national tradition of both approach and interpretation should have become deeply established. One of the distinctive features of this biography, and one of the main reasons for its formidable success with the French reading public, is that it articulates and rationalizes that French tradition.

In Anglo-Saxon historiography, strong traditions, often of a rather different stamp, have developed. The purpose of this bibliographical note is to indicate to the reader a number of important works, mainly in English, which have appeared over the last two decades, since the publication of the last major biography of Louis XIV in English, John Wolf's *Louis XIV* (Harmondsworth, 1970). They have often sought to modify our understanding of Louis XIV's reign, and together they form a good basis for further reading and reflection upon the subject.

A series of important works have combined to suggest how much Louis XIV was the beneficiary of fundamental changes in the French polity during the years of his early life until his personal rule. R. J. Bonney, *Political Change under Richelieu and Mazarin* (Oxford, 1978), studies these changes within the framework of France's traditional institutions, whilst his study *The King's Debts: Finance and Politics in France, 1589–1661* (Oxford, 1981) reassesses the pressure for change provoked by France's royal debts. The Fronde has been a focus for further recent reinterpretations. The role of the Parlement of Paris has been re-examined by A. Lloyd Moote in *The Revolt of the Judges: The Parlement of Paris and the Fronde, 1643–1652* (Princeton, 1971), although his cautiously positive interpretation of their proposed reforms of the state has not been universally accepted – see R. J. Bonney, 'The French civil war, 1649–53', *European Studies Quarterly*, 8 (1978). A. N. Hamscher,

The Parlement of Paris after the Fronde, 1653–1673 (Pittsburgh, 1976), demonstrates how easily and uncritically historians have accepted the royal myth of a politically emasculated Parlement, whilst S. Kettering, *Judicial Politics and Urban Revolt in Seventeenth-century France: The Parlement of Aix* (Princeton, 1978), delineates the politics of faction which underlay provincial revolts during the Fronde. The noble revolts during the Fronde have recently been placed in the broader context of 'loyalist' revolts, stretching back to the middle of the sixteenth century, by Arlette Jouanna in *Le devoir de révolte* (Paris, 1989), whilst Richard Bonney's article 'Cardinal Mazarin and the Great Nobility during the Fronde', *English Historical Review*, 96 (1981), provides a clear evaluation of the cardinal's skill in comprehending, in order to defuse, the aspirations of the great nobility. The more dangerously populist elements of the Fronde have also been the subject of new investigation. Richard M. Golden studied the role of the Parisian clergy in *The Godly Rebellion: Parisian curés and the Religious Fronde (1652–62)* (Chapel Hill, 1981), whilst S. A. Westrich, *The Ormée* (Baltimore, 1972), provides the only study of an interesting populist movement in the provinces. The *Mazarinades*, pamphlets produced during the Fronde, are the subject of a considerable inquiry, directed by Hubert Carrier, whose results are not yet available. Meanwhile, however, there is C. Jouhaud, *Les Mazarinades: la Fronde des mots* (Paris, 1985), which takes publishing as a political act.

English studies of the personal rule of Louis XIV have tended increasingly to stress the discrepancy between the bolder absolutist claims of the king and the reality. The trend was already present in some of the contributions to the series of essays in R. Hatton (ed.), *Louis XIV and Absolutism* (London, 1976); but it is more clearly delineated in A. Lossky, 'The absolutism of Louis XIV: reality or myth?', *Canadian Journal of History*, 11 (1984). R. Mettam, *Power and Faction in Louis XIV's France* (Oxford, 1988), deflates the wilder pretensions of Louis XIV's defenders, and he is supported in his stress upon the continuing importance of patronage in the government of *ancien régime* France by S. Kettering, *Patrons, Brokers and Clients in Seventeenth Century France* (New York, 1986). In a subtle regional study of the southern province of Languedoc, W. Beik, *Absolutism and State Power in Seventeenth Century France* (Cambridge, 1985), offers explanations for the stability of provincial France during the personal rule other than the strategic decisions of the king. The persistence of revolt in certain localities during the personal rule has also received renewed attention. J. H. M. Salmon, 'The Audijos revolt: provincial liberties and institutional rivalries under Louis XIV', *European Studies Quarterly*, 14 (1984), investigates an important revolt in the Pyrenees. The Breton revolt of 1675 has also been re-examined, in Y. Garlan and C. Nières, *Les révoltes bretonnes de 1675: papier timbré et bonnets rouges* (Paris, 1975). The city of Paris during the reign has been the subject of a particular investigation by L. L. Bernard, *The Emerging City: Paris in the Age of Louis XIV* (Durham, North Carolina, 1970).

The self-confidence and self-advertisement of Louis XIV's regime were, nonetheless, remarkable, and they have continued to attract scholars. There is now available a partial English translation, by Paul Sonnino, of Louis XIV's *Mémoires* with a useful introduction to the text by the translator: *Memoirs for the Instruction of the Dauphin* (New York and London, 1970). This may usefully be read alongside the exposition of Louis XIV's political ideas in Jean-Louis Thireau, *Les idées politiques de Louis XIV* (Paris, 1970). Louis Marin, *Portrait of the King* (London, 1988), seeks to explain the various baroque ways in which the audience was supposed to read and react to royalist images. J. Klaits, *Printed Propaganda under Louis XIV* (Princeton, 1976), provides a balanced portrait of the Crown's objectives and mixed success in influencing the sources of opinion in France during the reign. G. Walton's *Louis XIV's Versailles* (Harmondsworth, 1986) is a thorough and up-to-date evocation of the royal palace in its first generation, whilst R. M. Isherwood's *Music in the Service of the King* (Ithaca, 1972) is an excellent evocation of musical patronage at the court of the Sun King.

The religious elements of the reign have received less even treatment from recent historians. The Revocation of the Edict of Nantes attracted a great deal of attention from historians 300 years after the event, in 1985. In addition to Elisabeth Labrousse's excellent study, referred to in the reference section above, an excellent commentary in English is to be found in the pages of Menna Prestwich (ed.), *International Calvinism (1541–1715)* (Oxford, 1985). Amongst several studies of Protestants exiled from France, that of M. Magdelaine and R. von Thadden, *Le refuge huguenot* (Paris, 1985), was the best documented, especially on the refuge of French Protestants east of the Rhine. O. Martin, *La conversion protestante à Lyon (1659–1687)* (Geneva, 1986), provided a sensitive study of the pressures on Protestants to convert, and their reactions. On the other hand, studies of Jansenism under Louis XIV, especially in English, have languished. However, Part 2 of R. Briggs, *Communities of Belief: Cultural and Social Tensions in Early Modern France* (Oxford, 1989), provides material on the background to Louis XIV's orthodoxy as well as on the inner impulses of French Jansenism.

Finally, on French foreign policy, reference should be made to Ragnhild Hatton's edited collection of articles *Louis XIV and Europe* (London, 1976), which contains both general studies of Louis XIV's strategies in foreign policy and case-studies of individual diplomatic problems. C. J. Ekburg, *The Failure of Louis XIV's Dutch War* (Chapel Hill, 1979), deals with one of the great turning-points of Louis XIV's hegemony in Europe, and P. Sonnino, *The Origins of the Dutch War* (Cambridge, 1988), provides the background to the conflict.

Appendix: European Rulers and Leading French Figures* in the Age of Louis XIV

Popes
Urban VIII (1623–44), Innocent X (1644–55), Alexander VII (1655–67), Clement IX (1667–9), Clement X (1670–6), Innocent XI (1676–89), Alexander VIII (1689–91), Innocent XII (1691–1700), Clement XI (1700–21)

Holy Roman Emperors
Ferdinand III (1637–57), Leopold I (1658–1705), Joseph I (1705–11), Charles VI (1711–40)

Sultans
Ibrahim (1640–48), Mehmed IV (1648–87), Suleiman II (1687–91), Ahmed II (1691–95), Mustafa II (1695–1703), Ahmed III (1703–30)

Monarchs of England
Charles I (1625–49), [Oliver Cromwell, Lord Protector (1653–8); Richard Cromwell, Lord Protector (1658–9)], Charles II (restored, 1660–85), James II (1685–8), William III (1689–1702), Anne (1702–14), George I (1714–27)

Electors of Bavaria
Maximilian I (1597–(1623)–1651), Ferdinand-Maria (1651–79), Maximilian-Emmanuel (1679–1726)

Electors of Brandenburg and Kings in Prussia
George-William, Elector (1619–40), Frederick-William, Elector [the

*The list of court preachers in the French edition has not been included in this translation.

Great Elector] (1640–88), Frederick III (Elector of Brandenburg in 1688, King *in* Prussia (1701–13), Frederick-William I, King (1713–40)

Kings of Denmark
Christian IV (1588–1648), Frederick III (1648–70), Christian V (1670–99), Frederick IV (1699–1730)

Kings of Spain
Philip IV (1621–65), Charles II (1665–1700), Philip V (1700–46)

Dukes of Lorraine
Charles IV (1625–75), Charles V (1675–90), Leopold I (1690–1729)

Electors Palatine
Charles-Louis (1648–80), Charles II (1680–5), Philip-William (1685–90), John-William-Joseph (1690–1716)

Kings of Poland
John II Casimir (1648–68), Michael Wisniowiecki (1669–73), John III Sobieski (1674–96), Augustus II (1697–1704, 1710–33), Stanislas I Leszczynski (1704–10, 1733)

Kings of Portugal
John IV (1641–56), Alfonso VI (1656–83), Peter II (1683–1706), John V the Magnificent (1706–50)

Tsars of Russia
Michael Feodorovich (1613–45), Alexis Michailovich (1645–76), Fedor III Alexeievich (1676–82), Ivan V Alexeievich (1682–96), Peter I [the Great] (1682–(1696)–1725)

Dukes of Savoy
Charles-Emmanuel II (1638–75), Victor-Amadeus II (1675–1730)

Monarchs of Sweden
Christina (1632–54), Charles X Gustavus (1654–60), Charles XI (1660–97), Charles XII (1697–1718)

MINISTERS AND HEADS OF DEPARTMENTS
IN FRANCE (1661–1715)

A   *Ministers of state (= members of council of state/*
conseil d'en haut/*council of ministers)*

1661	Fouquet, Lionne, Le Tellier
1661	Colbert, Lionne, Le Tellier
1671	Colbert, Lionne, Le Tellier
1672	Colbert, Arnauld de Pomponne, Le Tellier, Louvois
1678	Colbert, Arnauld de Pomponne, Le Tellier, Louvois
1679	Colbert, Croissy, Le Tellier, Louvois
1682	Colbert, Croissy, Le Tellier, Louvois
1683	Le Peletier, Croissy, Le Tellier, Louvois
1688	Le Peletier, Croissy, Louvois
1689	Le Peletier, Seignelay, Croissy, Louvois, Pontchartrain
1690	Le Peletier, Seignelay, Croissy, Louvois, Pontchartrain
1691	Le Peletier, Croissy, Louvois, Pontchartrain
1691	Monseigneur Beauvillier, Le Peletier, Arnauld de Pomponne, Croissy, Pontchartrain
1697	Monseigneur Beauvillier, Le Peletier, Arnauld de Pomponne, Pontchartrain
1698	Monseigneur Beauvillier, Arnauld de Pomponne, Pontchartrain
1699	Monseigneur Beauvillier, Arnauld de Pomponne, Pontchartrain
1700	Monseigneur Beauvillier, Torcy, Pontchartrain, Chamillart
1702	Monseigneur, the Duke of Burgundy, Beauvillier, Torcy, Pontchartrain, Chamillart
1708	Monseigneur, the Duke of Burgundy, Beauvillier, Torcy, Pontchartrain, Chamillart, Desmarets
1709	Monseigneur, the Duke of Burgundy, Beauvillier, Torcy, Pontchartrain, Desmarets, Voysin
1712	The Duke of Burgundy, Beauvillier, Torcy, Pontchartrain, Desmarets, Voysin
1713	Beauvillier, Torcy, Pontchartrain, Desmarets, Voysin
1714	Beauvillier, Torcy, Pontchartrain, Desmarets, Voysin
1715	Torcy, Desmarets, Voysin, Villeroy

B   *Chancellors of France and keepers of the seals*

1   Pierre Séguier, keeper of the seals in 1633, chancellor in 1635, †1672
2   Etienne d'Aligre, keeper of the seals in 1672, chancellor in 1674, †1677
3   Michel Le Tellier (*as above*), chancellor in 1677, †1685
4   Louis Boucherat, chancellor in 1685, †1699

5   Louis Phelypeaux, comte de Pontchartrain (*as above*), chancellor in 1699, resigned in 1714
6   Daniel-François Voysin (*as above*) chancellor in 1714, †1717

C   Heads of the royal council of finances

1   Nicholas de Neufville, duc de Villeroy, head of the royal council in 1661, †1685
2   Paul, duc de Beauvillier (*as above*), head of the royal council in 1685, †1714
3   Françoise de Neufville, duc de Villeroy (*as above*), head of the royal council in 1714 and 1715

D   Secretaries of State

First secretary (war)
1   Michel Le Tellier (*as above*), secretary of state from 1643 to 1677
2   François-Michel Le Tellier, marquis de Louvois (*as above*), next in succession to the office (*survivancier*) in 1655, an associate in 1662, secretary of state in 1677, †1691
3   Louis-François-Marie Le Tellier de Barbezieux, next in succession to the office in 1685, secretary of state in 1691, †1701
4   Michel Chamillart (*as above*), secretary of state, 1701–9
5   Daniel-François Voysin (*as above*), secretary of state, 1709–15

Second secretary (royal household, Paris, clergy, navy)
1   Henri de Guénégaud, secretary of state, 1643–69
2   Jean-Baptiste Colbert (*as above*), secretary of state in 1669, †1683
3   Jean-Baptiste Colbert, marquis de Seignelay (*as above*), next in succession to the office in 1672, secretary of state in 1683, †1690
4   Louis Phelypeaux de Pontchartrain (*as above*), secretary of state, 1690–9
5   Jérôme Phelypeaux, comte de Pontchartrain, next in succession to the office in 1693, secretary of state, 1699–1715

Third secretary (foreign affairs)
1   Henri-Auguste de Loménie de Brienne (transferred from the second secretaryship), third secretary of state in 1643, resigned the office in 1663
2   Hugues de Lionne (*as above*), minister in 1659, secretary of state in 1663, †1671
2b Interim secretaryship of the marquis de Louvois (*as above*), 1671–2
3   Simon Arnauld de Pomponne (*as above*), secretary of state in 1672, recalled in 1679

4 Charles Colbert, marquis de Croissy (*as above*), secretary of state in 1679, †1696
5 Jean-Baptiste Colbert, marquis de Torcy (*as above*), next in succession in 1689, secretary of state, 1696–1715

Fourth secretary (Protestant affairs)

1 Louis Phelypeaux de la Vrillière, secretary of state in 1629, †1681
2 Balthazar Phelypeaux, marquis de Châteauneuf, next in succession to the office in 1669, secretary of state in 1681, †1700
3 Louis Phelypeaux, marquis de Vrillière, secretary of state in 1700, †1725

E   Controllers-general of finances

1 Jean-Baptiste Colbert (*as above*), intendant of finances in 1661, controller-general in 1665, †1683
2 Claude Le Peletier (*as above*), controller-general, 1683–9
3 Louis Phelypeaux de Pontchartrain (*as above*), controller-general, 1689–99
4 Michel Chamillart (*as above*), controller-general, 1699–1708
5 Nicolas Desmarets (*as above*), controller-general, 1708–15

F   Superintendents of the king's buildings

1 Antoine de Ratabon, superintendent, 1656–64
2 Jean-Baptiste Colbert (*as above*), superintendent in 1664, †1683
3 François-Michel Le Tellier de Louvois (*as above*), superintendent in 1683, †1691
4 Edouard Colbert, marquis de Villacerf, superintendent, 1691–9
5 Jules Hardouin-Mansart, superintendent in 1699, †1708
6 Louis-Antoine de Pardaillan de Gondrin, duc d'Antin, director-general of buildings in 1708, †1736

G   Directors-general of fortifications

1 Michel Le Peletier de Souzy, director-general, 1691–1715

H   Superintendents of postal services

1 Jérôme de Nouveau de Fromont, 1639–65
2 François-Michel Le Tellier de Louvois (*as above*), having already undertaken most of the responsibilities of the office from 1655 to 1668, was created superintendent in 1668, †1691
3 Claude Le Peletier (*as above*), 1691–7

4 Simon Arnauld de Pomponne (*as above*), in 1697, †1699
5 Jean-Baptiste Colbert, marquis de Torcy (*as above*), 1699–1723

I Directors-general of finance

1 Joseph-Jean-Baptiste Fleuriau d'Armenonville, 1701–8
2 Hilaire Rouillé du Coudray, 1701–3
3 Nicolas Desmarets (*as above*), 1703–8

J Councillors to the royal council of finances

First office
1 Etienne d'Aligre (*as above*), 1661–72
2 Henri Pussort, in 1672, †1697
3 Auguste-Robert de Pomereu, in 1697, †1702
4 Michel Le Peletier de Souzy (*as above*), 1702–15

Second office
1 Alexandre de Sève, in 1661, †1679
2 Pierre Poncet, in 1679, †1681
3 Louis Boucherat (*as above*), 1681–5
4 Françoise d'Argouges, in 1685, †1695
5 Henri d'Aguesseau, 1695–1715

K Intendants of finances

1 Jacques Le Tillier, 1649–61
2 Denis Marin, 1650–78
3 Jean-Baptiste Colbert (*as above*), 1661–5
4 Vincent Hotman, from 166?–16??
5 Nicolas Desmarets (*as above*), 1678–84
6 Michel Le Peletier de Souzy (*as above*), 1684–1701
7 François-Victor Le Tonnelier de Breteuil, 1684–1701
8 Louis Phelypeaux de Pontchartrain (*as above*), 1687–9
9 Michel Chamillart (*as above*), 1690–9
10 Joseph-Jean-Baptiste Fleuriau d'Armenonville (*as above*), 1690–1701
11 Constantin Heudebert du Buisson, 1690–1714
12 Louis-Urbain Le Fèvre de Caumartin, 1690–1715
13 Armand-Roland Bignon de Blanzy, 1699–1709
14 Michel-Robert Le Peletier des Forts, 1701–15
15 François Guyet, 1704–15
16 Alexandre Le Rebours, 1704–15
17 Jacques Poulletier, in 1708, †1711

18 Charles-Henri de Malon de Bercy, 1709–15
19 Pierre Poulletier, 1711–15
20 Louis Fagon, 1714–15

L *Intendants of commerce*

1 Denis-Jean-Michel Amelot de Chaillou, 1708–15
2 Louis-François Le Fèvre de Caumartin de Boissy, 1708–15
3 César-Charles Lescalopier, 1708–15
4 Louis-Charles de Machault, 1708–15
5 Jean Rouillé de Fontaine, 1708–15
6 Noël Danycan de Landivisiau, 1711–15

M *Lieutenants of police of Paris*

1 Gabriel-Nicolas de la Reynie, 1667–97
2 Marc-René de Voyer de Paulmy d'Argenson, 1697–1718

KING'S CONFESSORS (1649–1715)

1 Charles Paulin (1593–1653), SJ, 1649–53
2 François Annat (1590–1670), SJ, 1654–70
3 Jean Ferrier (1614–74), SJ, 1670–4
4 François d'Aix de la Chaize (1624–1709), known as père La Chaize, SJ, 1675–1709
5 Michel Le Tellier [no family connection with the chancellor of France] (1643–1719), SJ, 1709–15

ARCHBISHOPS OF PARIS (1654–1729)

1 Jean-François-Paul de Gondi (1613–79), Cardinal de Retz, coadjutor of Paris and Archbishop of Corinth *in partibus* in 1643, Archbishop of Paris 1654–62
2 Pierre de Marca (1594–1662), nominated Archbishop of Paris in 1662, but died before being consecrated
3 Hardouin de Beaumont de Péréfixe (1605–70), 1662–70
4 François de Harlay de Champvallon (1625–95), 1671–95
5 Louise-Antoine, Cardinal de Noailles (1651–1729), 1695–1729

MARSHALS OF FRANCE (1643–1715)

1643 François de l'Hôpital, comte de Rosnay, seigneur du Hallier (1583–1660)
1643 Henri de la Tour, vicomte de Turenne (1611–75)
1643 Jean de Gassion (1609–47)
1645 César duc de Choiseul, comte du Plessis-Praslin (1598–1675)
1645 Josias comté de Rantzau (1609–50)
1646 Nicolas de Neufville, duc de Villeroy (1598–1685)
1651 Antoine d'Aumont, marquis de Villequier (1601–69)
1651 Jacques d'Etampes, marquis de la Ferté-Imbault (1590–1668)
1651 Charles de Monchy, marquis d'Hocquincourt (1599–1658)
1651 Henri duc de la Ferté-Senneterre (1600–81)
1651 Jacques Rouxel, comte de Grancey et de Médavy (1603–80)
1652 Armand-Nompar de Caumont, duc de la Force (c.1578–1675)
1653 Louis Foucault de Saint-Germain, comte du Daugnon, vice-admiral (c.1616–59)
1653 César-Phébus d'Albret, comte de Miossans (†1676)
1653 Philippe de Clérambault, comte de Palluau (1606–65)
1658 Jacques marquis de Castelnau (1620–58)
1658 Jean de Schulemberg, comte de Montdejeu (†1671)
1658 Abraham de Fabert, marquis d'Esternay (1599–1662)
1668 François marquis de Créqui (c.1624–87)
1668 Bernardin Gigault, marquis de Bellefonds (1630–94)
1668 Louis de Crevant, duc d'Humières (1628–94)
1675 Godefroy comte d'Estrades (1607–86)
1675 Philippe de Montaut-Bénac, duc de Navailles (1619–84)
1675 Frédéric-Armand Count of Schomberg (1619–90)
1675 Jacques-Henri de Durfort, Duke of Duras (1626–1704)
1675 Louis-Victor de Rochechouart, duc de Vivonne (1636–88)
1675 François d'Aubusson, comte de la Feuillade (1625–91)
1675 François-Henri de Montmorency, duc de Luxembourg (1628–95)
1675 Henri-Louis d'Aloigny, marquis de Rochefort (†1676)
1676 Guy-Aldonce de Durfort, duc de Lorge (1630–1702)
1681 Jean comte d'Estrées, vice-admiral (1624–1707)
1693 Claude comte de Choiseul-Francières (1632–1711)
1693 François de Neufville, duc de Villeroy (1644–1730)
1693 Jean-Armand de Joyeuse (1631–1710)
1693 Louis-François duc de Boufflers (1644–1711)
1693 Anne-Hilarion de Cotentin, comte de Tourville, vice-admiral (1642–1701)
1693 Anne-Jules duc de Noailles (1650–1708)
1693 Nicolas de Catinat, seigneur de Saint-Gratien (1637–1712)

1702 Louis-Hector duc de Villars (1653–1734)
1703 Noël Bouton, marquis de Chamilly (1636–1715)
1703 Victor-Marie, marquis de Coeuvres (later duc d'Estrées), vice-admiral (1660–1737)
1703 François-Louis Rousselet, marquis de Châteaurenault, vice-admiral (1637–1716)
1703 Sébastien Le Prestre, seigneur de Vauban (1633–1707)
1703 Conrad de Rosen, comte de Bollwiller (1628–1715)
1703 Nicolas du Blé, marquis d'Huxelles (1652–1730)
1703 René de Froulay, comte de Tessé (1651–1725)
1703 Nicolas-Auguste de la Baume, marquis de Montrevel (1645–1716)
1703 Camille d'Houston, comte de Tallard (1652–1728)
1703 Henri duc d'Harcourt (1654–1718)
1703 Ferdinand comte de Marsin and Count of the Holy Roman Empire (1656–1706)
1706 James Fitz-James Stuart, Duke of Berwick (1670–1734)
1708 Charles-Auguste de Goyon de Matignon, comte de Gacé (1647–1729)
1709 Jacques Bazin, seigneur de Bezons (†1733)
1709 Pierre de Montesquiou d'Artagnan (1645–1725)

CHIEF PHYSICIANS TO LOUIS XIV

1 Jacques Cousinot (*c.*1587–1646), chief physician to the Dauphin in 1638, and to the king in 1643
2 François Vaultier (1590–1652), chief physician to the king in 1646
3 Antoine Vallot (1594–1671), chief physician in 1652
4 Antoine d'Aquin (1620–96), chief physician 1672–93
5 Guy-Crescent Fagon (1638–1718), chief physician 1693–1715

Index